על הבּמה ועל הבּמה

WALTER ROTHSCHILD

THE HONEY AND THE STING
STUDY GUIDE [FOR CONVERSION] TO JUDAISM

FOR ALL WHO WANT TO LEARN,
AND ALL WHO WANT TO LEARN MORE

JVFG
Jewish Publisher for
Congregational Literature

Jewish Publisher for Congregational Literature
Juedischer Verlag fuer Gemeindeliteratur
JVFG
London, UK

www.jvfg.eu

published by JVFG
First Edition

Typeset in Minion
by Dr Annette M. Boeckler

Illustrations:
Cover: Details of the Wallhangings 'The Day' and 'The Night', designed by Linda Gevertz, created by members of Finchley Progressive Synagogue, London UK. ©Linda Gevertz
p. XXV: Illustrations of 'Echad Mi Yode'ah', 'Hochshule Haggadah', 1730. ©Leo Baeck College Library.
p. 289, 291 and 295: photo A.M. Boeckler

British Library Cataloguing in Publication
Data will be available

978-1-910752-15-9 paperback
978-1-910752-18-0 hardcover
978-1-910752-19-7 e-book mobi
978-1-910752-20-3 e-book EPUB

Contents

PART FOUR: THE BASIC TEXTS   245

6

PART SIX: THE JEWISH LIFE CYCLE

PART SEVEN:
SOME HISTORICAL AND OTHER THEMES   413

9

PART NINE: SOME USEFUL INFORMATION

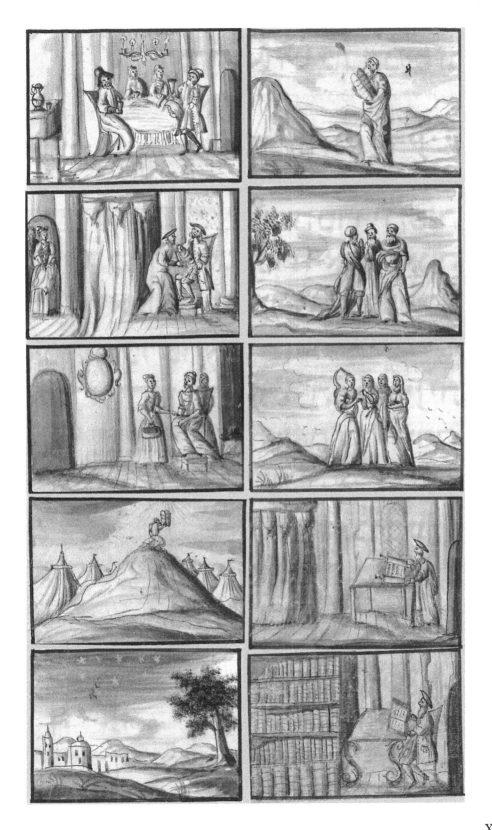

XXV

על הדבש ועל העוקץ

Al hadevash v'al haoketz	על הדבש ועל העוקץ
Al hamar vehamatok	על המר והמתוק
Al bitenu hatinoket	על בתנו התינוקת
Shmor E-li hatov.	שמור אלי הטוב
Al haesh hamevoeret	על האש המבוערת
Al hamayim hazakim	על המים הזכים
Al haish hashav habayta	על האיש השב הביתה
Min hamerchakim.	מן המרחקים
Al kol eleh, Al kol eleh	על כל אלה על כל אלה
Shmor na li, E-li hatov	שמור נא לי אלי הטוב
Al hadevash v'al haoketz	על הדבש ועל העוקץ
Al hamar vehamatok	על המר והמתוק
Al na taakor natua	אל נא תעקור נטוע
Al tishkach et hatikva	אל תשכח את התקווה
Hashiveni Ve'ashuva	השיבני ואשובה
El ha'aretz hatova.	אל הארץ הטובה
Shmor E-li al zeh habayit	שמור אלי על זה הבית
Al hagan, al hachoma	על הגן על החומה
Miyagon, mipachad peta	מיגון מפחד פתע
Umimilchama.	וממלחמה
Shmor al hame'at sheyesh li	שמור על המעט שיש לי
Al haor ve'al hataf	על האור ועל הטף
Al hapri shelo hivshil od	על הפרי שלא הבשיל עוד
Veshene'esaf.	ושנאסף
Al kol eleh …	על כל אלה
Merashresh ilan baruach	מרשרש אילן ברוח
Merachok noshar kochav	מרחוק נושר כוכב
Mishalot libi bachoshech	משאלות ליבי בחושך
Nirshamot achshav.	נרשמות עכשיו
Ana shmor li al kole eleh	אנא שמור לי על כל אלה
Ve'al ahuvey nafshi	ועל אהובי נפשי
Al hasheket al a bechi	על השקט, על הבכי
Ve'al zeh hashir.	ועל זה השיר

On the honey and the sting
on the bitter and the sweet
on our baby daughter
watch over them my good God.

On the fire which is lit
on the pure water
on the person who returns home
from afar.

    *On all these, on all these,
    please watch over them for me, my good God
    on the honey and the sting
    on the bitter and the sweet.

Please do not uproot what is planted.
Do not forget the hope.
Send me back and I shall return
to the good land.

Please, my God, keep this house,
— the garden — the wall,
from grief, from sudden fear
and from war.

Watch over the little that I have,
over the light and the children,
over the fruit not yet ripened
and that already gathered in.

    *On all these, on all these, …
    please watch over them for me, my good God
    on the honey and the sting
    on the bitter and the sweet.

A tree rustles in the wind.
From afar a star falls.
My heart's desires in the dark
are now written down.

Please watch over all these for me
and over all of those I love
over the quiet, over the tears
and over this song.

[Naomi Shemer
quoted from סדר התפלות Forms of Prayer for Jewish Worship,
vol II Prayers for the Pilgrim Festivals, London 1995, p. 151.153]

THE HONEY AND THE STING

1 . A FIRST INTRODUCTION TO THE BOOK AND ITS PURPOSE: FOR THE GENERAL READER

This book, originally written in 1994 and entitled 'Jewish by Choice' is being revised and expanded in 2015 and seeks to take into account various developments of the past two decades in British and European Jewish communities and in society as a whole — these include technological innovations such as the Internet, enabling access to large amounts of information (not all of it correct, much of it tendentious) or long-distance learning possibilities that did not exist just twenty years ago. It also incorporates the fruits of a further twenty-plus years of rabbinic life and experience. This book cannot cover all such possibilities and is almost certain to become out-dated itself in due course, but it is hoped it can give a basis at least. An outline of its background and purpose can be found also at the back. Since it aims to address both the general reader and those who are thinking of conversion the Introduction is extensive and divided into specific sections as, although there is overlap, even some repetition, there are also different needs. For some readers, what is described may seem too radical, for others too conservative. But that is the way it is.

There is no single religion known as 'Judaism'. A religion that has existed for so long and that has developed in different parts of the world is bound to have developed several successive or parallel versions. Leon of Modena in his pioneering book 'On Jewish Laws and Customs' of 1637 — which is in many respects the first attempt to do what this book does, to explain Judaism to an interested non-Jewish or not-yet-Jewish readership in the confines of a single volume — divides the issues into three: the Written *Torah* on which, he says, there is general agreement amongst all Jews of his time; The Oral *Torah*, the extension of this teaching, about which he says there is also mainly a universal acknowledgement; and then the *Minhagim*, the different Customs which have arisen in different communities, which are considered just as important by the individual communities and yet which differ widely — thus allowing for a form of pluralism.

This book can only provide an overview of many topics and does not provide all academic footnotes; anyone interested in a specific topic is urged to find further literature to consult. But it was originally compiled in Leeds in the North of England around 1990, growing out of a set of worksheets for a class of conversion candidates in a Reform synagogue. Later the author spent time serving communities in mainland Europe and then in the Caribbean, then in Germany and Austria, and in the meantime there has been expansion of communities into Eastern Europe —

especially Poland — and interest in the contents from newer communities which exist in a very different context to established suburban synagogues in Yorkshire. In consequence the attempt has been made to draw very widely upon over thirty years of congregational rabbinic experience in a variety of communities and to put together something which will not describe Everything, but which will at least give an Introduction and which may apply (when translated) to a variety of communities in a variety of countries. It is written from a very personal perspective and it attempts where possible to offer pragmatic rather than abstract explanations for what one may encounter in a journey towards and into Judaism. It attempts to cover a wide range of Jewish opinions without trying to be politically-correct or to be tied to one particular movement. Progressive Judaism tries to work as freely as possibly within the boundaries of Tradition, pushing at the boundaries where possible but not necessarily seeking to break them. It has pushed in terms of the rights of women to pray and lead prayers, the rights of same-gender couples and now the rights of transgender persons; earlier it pushed at the ideas of the language of prayer or the use of instrumental music in services, at concepts of rabbinic authority and definitions of Sabbath and the calendar. But is stays within the world of Judaism and does not seek to create a new religion, and so sometimes restraint or compromise is necessary.

To some extent all religions represent the search of Mankind for meaning in the Universe. There are many concepts in common between many if not all religions — concepts of sacrifice and offering, of prayer and meditation, of self-criticism and criticism of others; there are attempts to create social structures which encourage self-restraint and self-discipline, concern for others, family continuity and security. One can choose to emphasise what they have in common — or what separates and divides them. This book sets out to do a bit of both — to explain Judaism, at times in its context in relation to some other religions, at times in the context of modern times in Europe, at times from a purely personal perspective as a Rabbi who has worked in several communities in different countries and has encountered various problems.

Judaism has always allowed discussion and debate and so what is presented here is NOT dogma but an introduction, a 'way in' that should enable the reader to understand a little of what is going on and to join in the debate him- or herself. Critical Thinking is important. Each Jew is independent and stands alone before God, and yet at the same time each Jew seeks out others who share enough basic similarities of approach to form a Community. Each Jew should seek out at least one Teacher and continue to learn throughout their life — but we have no Popes, no Doctrinal Commissions, no Dogmas, nobody who tells us what to think. There is a living tradition of working with the texts — and sometimes even against them — of searching for loopholes and either strict or liberal interpretations, of writing new commentaries... There is always something new to learn and always the possibility of a new interpretation.

However, the 'real world' is not always so free and ideal as the tradition would allow. Modern Judaism is assailed from all sides and also from within. We have trends that lead towards extreme narrow nationalism and extreme shallow universalism; we have Zionist and Non-Zionist and Anti-Zionist positions; we have attempts to synthesise Judaism with Christianity and with Buddhism (though less so with Islam, at least, not from the Jewish side); or to extract just the social welfare and ethical concepts, dropping the religious component and creating a secular socialism. There are Jews who have no faith following what happened in the *Sho'ah*, and Jews who have faith but no knowledge, or belief but no roots. There is a concentrated (and very successful) attempt by some to turn Judaism back to some wispy 18th.-century East European nostalgia, a kind of Disney-ish religion populated with Saintly Heroes and Evil Villains.

In the end this book will therefore seek to present a personal approach to Judaism — the approach which is taken, on the whole, by Reform and Liberal Jews at the beginning of the 21st Christian century in a continent which has been devastated by religious and racial and national hatred and destruction so many times that one is always building upon ruins and memories — and yet, one cannot live only in ruins and memories. There may be elements in this book which shock or disappoint or enrage the reader — this is fine. There may be things in this book you disagree with — this is also fine. You as a reader are welcome to shout at the book and to scribble in the margin and even throw it away (so long as you have purchased it first!) But do think about what is written, and think about why it is written — and think about what is missed out, what is between the lines and behind the letters.

The book is intended to serve partially as a textbook for those seeking to adopt Judaism, to find their way into it or to find their way back into it. But it is intended for others too — for those Jews struggling with the inconsistencies and contradictions which comprise Judaism today, a mixture of ancient and modern, of exclusive and open, of limited and infinite. It is intended to teach you about Belief without forcing you to believe. It is aimed at demonstrating also what need not be believed, at confronting the superstition and neurosis and the misuse of religion which is so widespread. But it is not a 'Kol-Bo' — a book in which Everything is contained. Quite the reverse. There are many gaps and omissions, but there are also whole libraries full of alternatives.

If reading this book makes you go into a bookshop or library or online catalogue and seek out OTHER books on Judaism as well — to compare them and reflect upon them — then it will have succeeded.

Rabbi Dr. Walter Rothschild

2. WHAT IS JUDAISM?

This book provides an introduction to basic Jewish thought, belief and practice from a Reform or Liberal Jewish perspective. It is intended also for those who think that they are called to become a member of the Jewish people, who wish to convert, to 'adopt' a faith. Can one create a new identity?

Judaism is not just a Religion; It is a way of looking at the world — both this world and the next. (It assumes, for example, without being specific, that there is another world). It is not just a matter of how we approach God, but of how we approach other people, Jews and non-Jews. Judaism is often accused — by its enemies — of being 'exclusive'. This is not correct — it has always been possible to join the Jewish people if one really wanted to. But it has never been made easy. We have not gone out trying to convert people or forcing them to convert.

Why not? Here one should take note of a few ideas that are so simple, so basic, so clear, that it is truly amazing that most people do not notice them.

(A). JUDAISM DOES NOT CLAIM A MONOPOLY ON THE TRUTH

We believe in One God. This God has created the entire universe, and all the people on Earth. The majority of these people have been created as non-Jews. Therefore, it must follow logically, it must be no problem for God that there are so many non-Jews in the world. If it were so important for God that everyone be 'Jewish', then God could and should have done something about it. God should have sent an Abraham or a Moses or whoever to every people, and given each of them a copy of the *Torah*. God did not do this. God says to us 'Listen, Israel, I am your god — and You must not worship any others.' But God does not in the *Torah* prohibit other people from worshipping in other ways! (In Genesis 31:53 Jacob's uncle Laban refers to both 'the God of Abraham and the God of Nachor' — Nachor being the brother Abraham left behind when he followed God's call in Gen. 12:1.)

And later Judaism has followed this concept — influenced in some periods by the political weakness of a landless, exiled people. Judaism is very tolerant of other religions — so long as they are practised by non-Jews. It does not matter to us that Christians are Christians or Moslems are Moslems or that Hindus are Hindus. So long as these other peoples leave us alone and do not threaten us with violence or demand our submission to their versions, we can work on the basis that any good person can build a relationship with God in their own way. 'You don't have to be Jewish.'

Evidence for this assertion is that, in the State of Israel, there are full rights for Christians and Moslems of various denominations, for Baha'is and Mormons and others. It is only missionizing amongst Jews that is frowned upon. Unfortunately, other monotheistic religions have not shown the same tolerance or openness.

(B). JUDAISM IS NOT BY NATURE A 'WORLD RELIGION'

That is to say, it has never been our intention to take over the world. You will find universalistic messages in some of the Prophets — Isaiah speaks of a desire to be 'a light to the nations' (Isa. 49:6 & 51:4) and in I Kings Ch. 8 King Solomon issues a formal invitation to everyone to visit the Temple — but our interests and concerns have always been focussed on one small piece of land at the Eastern end of the Mediterranean Sea. If Jews have moved elsewhere over the centuries, it was usually for negative reasons — they were exiled and driven out, they were made unwelcome in some countries and had to flee to others... — and then some of them settled, whereas others kept moving on. If there are Jews in America, Europe, parts of Africa, parts of Asia, it is only because the tides of migration took them there — along with many other peoples. Not through conquest or a desire to spread Judaism.

Our History had two beginnings — in Genesis and in Exodus. In the first, Abraham was promised a relationship to God — but he remained a nomad. In the second, the people were led out of slavery in Egypt into the desert — but the first generation never got to the land they had been promised, they remained and died as nomads. If you look at the texts, there was never any aim to convert the Egyptians or the Canaanites or Babylonians or anyone else to 'the one truth'. The aim was always to preserve this covenant, this identity within one family, one tribe, one people. This task alone has proved to be more than enough of a challenge!

(C). DEFINITIONS OF 'WHO IS JEWISH?' AND 'WHAT IS JUDAISM?' HAVE CHANGED CONSTANTLY OVER THE CENTURIES

We have — even in Biblical and early post-Biblical times — gained and lost a Land, gained and lost a Monarchy, gained and lost a Priesthood and a Temple (twice!) and sacrificial rituals. Since the Biblical period ceased, we have lived in tension with various surrounding cultures — some of whom have even claimed to be improved versions of Judaism that make the original versions redundant! We have lived amongst peoples who believed in One God, in No God or in Many Gods. Judaism has survived only because, whilst some things have remained constant, other things have changed. Exactly what may change, at what speed, and on what authority — these are the things which lead to internal tensions within Judaism. But there is no point in anyone quoting an argument from some text that is several hundred or even several thousand years old and assuming that it automatically answers all modern questions. It is for Jews, and only for Jews, to define what our religion is, our relationship to other peoples and our relationship to a Jewish State. We have many different ideas, but we have learned to live with these internal differences and even to thrive on the constant political debate, which can be traced back to the Rabbis of the *Mishnaic* period or even earlier into the Biblical time — there were prophets who opposed corruption in the priesthood, Samuel opposed the idea of a monarchy, and so forth. For anyone else to presume to tell us what we are or what we should believe or do is — to put it mildly — *Chutzpeh*. And anyone converting to Judaism will somehow have to absorb all these differences and internal contradictions as well and will have to understand that the answers they learned last month might not always apply next month, or that another Jew who has learned different answers is not necessarily wrong!

So Jews have always been a relatively small population, usually concentrated in relatively-small areas, and often argumentative within their communities. And yet the world goes on!

3. WHY BECOME JEWISH? WHY BE JEWISH? WHY STAY JEWISH? SOME NOTES ON FAITH

What is Faith? It could be described as The Ability to Ignore the Evidence. A rational mind observes the evidence — of nature, of history, of human biology and destiny — and will draw conclusions. A faithful mind will ignore this and decide, 'Despite all the evidence, I still wish to believe.'

Judaism involves, somehow, a combination of these two contradictory approaches. We do not ignore the evidence of our sufferings. We bewail and bemoan them, we remember constantly so many low points in our past — the exile to Babylon, the destruction of both our temples and the elimination of our monarchy and independence, our homeland and security. We recall the years of slavery in Egypt, the years of wandering in a hostile desert, surrounded by potential attackers. We remember an occasion — one among many — when a monarch and his entire state apparatus were prepared to perform total genocide on their Jewish inhabitants. We remember the Crusades and the Inquisitions performed in God's name, the pogroms and the catastrophes that culminated in (but were by no means restricted to) the *Sho'ah*. We observe a current world where Jews are officially unwelcome over maybe three-quarters of the globe's surface and unofficially unwelcome in most of the rest, and have to fight constantly for their very existence in the tiny sliver of land which, against all odds, they managed to acquire for themselves after centuries of homelessness.

People who feel attracted to Judaism may be attracted for a whole host of different reasons, but sooner or later they must confront this contradiction. Quite a few — especially those who grew up within warm Christian communities — see in Judaism something wonderful, positive, filled with love, family stability, a close and loving relationship to God. From within, however, Judaism and Jewish life usually looks very different. This is another reason why a potential convert needs to take the time to see through the surface presentations (though these are not always presented by Jews themselves) and through to the reality beneath.

Judaism has always included an element of Anger with God — sometimes respectful, sometimes hidden, sometimes open, but usually there, somewhere. The very name 'Yisrael' means 'The one who argues with God' (Genesis 32:28). Abraham in Genesis 18:18-33 argues with God, that God should not over-react like an uncaring, undiscriminating tyrant, wiping out an entire city — however evil — without even bothering to check first whether everyone in the city deserves it. This implies that without Abraham's intervention God would not even have bothered to check. (The *Midrash* criticises Noah for not taking the same stand when God decides one day to wipe out almost everyone and everything and start again. See Genesis 6:13ff.) Moses will also, on several occasions, have to argue with God, calm God down, persuade God to act in a manner appropriate to the expectations people have of the divine... Almost everyone mentioned in the *Tanakh* has had some problem with God, from Adam onwards. Abraham is called by a God who tells him in Genesis Ch. 12 to leave his home without being specific as to where he should settle, who brings him to a land where he never feels at home and which he has to leave for reasons of famine and then live in fear of the host nation, who lets him spend years in mental torture about his childlessness, and then he has a home riven by factions and bitching and jealousy; a God who commands him to let one son die (Gen. 21) and then to physically slaughter the remaining one (Gen. 22); who lets his wife die before him, so that he has to grovel to local landowners to purchase a grave for her... Isaac must suffer nearly being murdered in God's name, then spends decades in a bitter, sterile marriage before fathering twins whose conflicts then ruin his old age. Jacob bargains with God and tries to manipulate God, but is forced eventually to confront his father-in-law, his brother and himself, and before he dies has to confront his own combative and competitive sons too (Gen. 49). Moses is born in a time of great fear and danger because God has somehow 'forgotten' that he brought the descendants of Jacob to Egypt several centuries earlier, and it is only when the Israelites wail about their murdered children that God 'hears and remembers'...(Exodus 2:24). He has a miserable, mixed-up childhood, always an 'outsider', he is forced to flee for his life and has to build up a new life as a refugee and he is then called away from this and his family to spend the last four decades of his life leading a people who show no sign of wanting to be led, to a place he has never seen and will, in the end, never reach.

Having promised Abraham that his descendants will be given a land which is already inhabited, God has to encourage the Israelites under Joshua to fight and conquer the country and then to distribute it, and govern it... rather than just 'presenting' it. After all, how did the Canaanites get there originally, did they find an empty territory or had they also pushed out their own predecessors? This remains into modern times a political conundrum — who has the 'right' to where? (See Deuteronomy 2:4-23 — especially v.23 which describes how Gaza was formerly populated by another tribe that had been pushed out!) The people decide after some years of administrative chaos that they would prefer a centralised monarchic and dynastic system — Samuel is not happy with this but God goes along with it, only God chooses someone who turns out to be unsuitable for the job... Eventually David takes over the crown after a life filled with intrigues and betrayals and violence, succeeds for a while in establishing a kingdom, but also suffers from a home-life plagued by further intrigue and fratricide. He loses several of his children, and is eventually persuaded, when he is weak and old, to hand over the succession to a son, Solomon, who is only later described as 'wise', perhaps because he is not warlike; In spite of his wisdom he is unable even to keep his own two sons together. So the kingdom is then split and the next generations are spent in fighting each other… until, weakened internally and subject to unsuitable foreign alliances, against which the prophets warn without success, the neighbouring superpowers overwhelm first one half, the northern kingdom of Israel (which disappears from the narrative) and then the second, the southern kingdom of Judah, which goes into exile for a generation and, on its return, has to re-establish a structure from the beginning again…

Does all this seem rather negative? Everything described is in the Bible — it is just a matter of how one looks at it. Christianity is founded on belief in a God who is prepared to condemn his own son to death by torture. Judaism <u>cannot</u> accept that, and yet it is also founded on a belief in a God who has, so many times, allowed his believers to suffer exile, bereavement or death. The prophets (we have no saints, theologians or dogmatists, just prophets who did not choose voluntarily to act as messengers, and later human rabbis who have sought over the centuries to understand all these events and to make some sense out of them) sometimes declare that certain events are God sending a warning or a punishment; sometimes they argue with God that the punishment is not deserved or is too harsh; and sometimes they have no answers at all. One just has to keep going. The world is not perfect and our task is to do what we can to make it better.

There are, of course, groups within Judaism which encourage their followers to believe unquestioningly and uncritically everything their *Rebbe* tells them, and that performance of certain rituals will somehow magically convince God to react in certain ways.

There are also groups within Judaism which tell their followers that they do not need to believe in anything, that just 'being Jewish' is enough, that one can be secular, humanist, politically or culturally active but religiously uninvolved. Their attitude could be summed up: 'Why do you need to believe? Isn't it enough to be Jewish?'

Reform or Liberal Judaism, however, demands from its followers both an enquiring and analytical mind and the ability to ignore it and switch it off (and back on!) when necessary. When reading a prayer or a psalm which includes phrases like 'God loves his people Israel' or 'God will not let those who have faith in him suffer' or 'Renew our days like they used to be' one has to switch off a part of the mind that says 'Is this actually true? Where is the evidence for this?' so that one can continue praying. When something dreadful happens to you — a loss, a bereavement, a diagnosis of dreadful illness — it is no good expecting a rabbi to be able to flick through a book and find a logical, sensible and meaningful answer to what has happened to you.

We do <u>not</u> know why, over the last several thousand years, the good have died young, why children have been murdered, why innocent people just doing their best to make a living have been dispossessed, injured and expelled from their homes. We do not know why so many otherwise-intelligent people have seemed to believe that God — the same God in whom we believe — had commanded them to do this to us. No deep heavenly voice has come to tell them to stop. Or if it has, it has never been heard. We do not know why those who deny the validity of all religions then often choose to persecute us first. We do not know why people seem to hate us because they think we are so enormously strong and powerful, but then do not seem afraid to attack us both verbally and physically, as though we were not. We do not know why people use the fact that we have been persecuted as proof that there must have been a reason to have persecuted us — thus blaming the victim for being a victim — and derive from this foolishness that it must still be a valid reason to continue doing so. We do not KNOW anything. We just have to keep Believing, despite everything, that there is a purpose to all this. This is not easy. This is FAITH.

Indeed, the situation is such that many Jewish thinkers consider that all the persecutions over the centuries have even had a positive side — they kept the Jews together — and that modern tolerance has actually led to a weakening of the communal and religious structures. They may well be right — but which would we really rather have?

The political equivalent to religious faith was Zionism. This was a reaction to the changing political structures of the western world in the 19th. century, whereby nationalism and republicanism rather than despotic monarchy defined how countries worked. The Zionists believed that forming a country where Jews could live together and stick together and work together might take the place of the 'ghetto-mentality' whereby Jews clung together mainly because no one else would have them, or would not let them into their countries, their guilds, their professions, their universities. This has only partially worked. Not all Jews have wanted to go to Israel; some have left it; many are happy to have it in the background as a possible escape-route but would like to avoid living in what is, in terms of international politics, little more than an enlarged ghetto, shunned by its neighbours, derided and spat upon by the international community. It is a tragic irony that the attempt of Jews to become 'normal' by having their own country has to a certain extent backfired. Wonderful ideals have been applied, vast amounts of effort have been expended, much care and love of the land — and much blood — have been invested. There have been wonderful discoveries and great successes. But the price has been high, very high, too high for many. And why? Why should the mere existence of Israel arouse so much visceral enmity and hostility? Why are Jews so often denied the right to have a 'Jewish nationalism' and a 'Jewish state'?

How do Jews cope with these many internal contradictions? It is impossible to say. Each Jew reacts differently, based upon their own background, upbringing, life experience, character and more. But anyone who chooses voluntarily to enter Judaism MUST realise that this is not an 'easy option', that one will not get 'closer to God' or 'understand God better' this way. They must not convert in the mistaken belief that the Jewish People have been 'chosen' and that this somehow means they are 'better' or 'wiser' or 'protected'. They must not convert in the expectation that their lives will somehow become better, safer, more fulfilling. They must above all not convert in the masochistic belief that they will then suffer for God, and that this suffering will somehow be redemptive of the sins of themselves or their ancestors or any other.

If this is what you are looking for — you might as well close this book now. Judaism — especially reflective, intellectually-demanding, honest Judaism — is not for the faint-hearted.

4. SO WHAT IS CONVERSION?

Conversion to Judaism is a combination of personal, spiritual, religious and political actions. It would be a mistake to underestimate any of these elements.

The personal and spiritual elements involve your own private journey through life. What are you going towards and what are you leaving behind? Are you fulfilling the wishes of others, or denying them, rejecting them, rebelling against them?

There might be major shocks and disappointments, as family, friends, loved ones, colleagues, even mere acquaintances, prove unable to understand or even express themselves in anti-Semitic or anti-Jewish tones.

The majority of born Jews get through a lot of theological problems by simply not thinking about them very much. They might not attend synagogue services, or if they go they might ignore the content of the prayers while concentrating on the music, the chanting, the form, the social element. A person converting is, however, forced to confront the challenges of Jewish existence — the Big Questions. Such as:
— How God can be caring, loving and omnipotent and yet still allow Jewish History to be as bloody and cruel and brutal as it has been?

Such as — What does Judaism have, that makes Jews so hated?

Such as — Why be Jewish? What does the Covenant mean?

Judaism is full of questions, many of which are never answered, and quite a few of which are never even formally asked. A good Rabbi or a good teacher will admit that we do not have answers to such questions — but will acknowledge their existence and their importance and should help a genuine enquirer come to terms with them, to absorb them. It could be that your response to these and other questions will be a decision NOT to convert — in which case, we can congratulate you on a sensible, honest and thought-through decision.

The religious element is the one many conversion candidates concentrate on. They believe that if they learn to pray aloud in Hebrew within a congregation and learn the rules for keeping festivals and running a Jewish home, then they have managed everything. Some who have been Christian see it as a form of Christianity without Jesus; others see it as a self-imposed discipline whereby life consists of obeying as many ritual rules as possible. Unfortunately, though this is all very important — it is NOT everything! This is a common error.

It also does not necessarily help if you plunge onwards and become ever more observant, ever more intolerant of yourself and those around you, to accept ever more religious duties and responsibilities and ever higher standards. This is also a common psychological phenomenon amongst those who have converted to Judaism. It is not that it is wrong to try to pray regularly several times a day, to maintain very strict levels of *Kashrut*, to wear religious clothing or similar — it is just that these actions can have an isolating rather than an integrating effect, can lead to more problems within the community, can serve to make the new 'Jew by Choice' even lonelier as he or she fails to find a suitable partner who has chosen the same way. One has to find a pragmatic, realistic 'middle way', a way that helps one feel, act and pray Jewish, while adapting to the realities of living in Europe in modern times, not in 1st -century CE Palestine or 5th.-century CE Iraq or 18th.-century CE Poland.

As regards the political factor — one seeks to become a part of '*Am Yisrael*', 'The People of Israel.' Which part, is a matter for debate. One often hears the question 'Will this conversion be recognised in Israel?' The answer depends, unfortunately, on the political make-up of the latest coalition government and has nothing to do with God and faith but everything to do with which so-called 'religious party' controls which Ministry. The Reform and Conservative movements have had some success in fighting through the Courts for the rights of converts, but have yet to convince the politicians that this is a matter they should stay out of. In essence, a Liberal convert is currently accepted as Jewish by the State of Israel, but not necessarily by the Orthodox Rabbinate of Israel.

On the other hand — does this matter? Unless one plans to go to Israel — no. The important thing is to be accepted where one is, always subject to the awareness that different communities even within Britain or the Netherlands or Poland or Germany will play the same game of 'We are more Observant than you and therefore we can deny that you are as good as us.' It is a bizarre situation, bearing in mind especially that demographers are warning that the Jewish population is shrinking rapidly and we cannot afford to alienate new members. But — learning how these political structures work and the dynamics behind them is all a part of becoming Jewish. You cannot ignore it.

It will also be assumed by most non-Jews that you, as a Jew, have a specific viewpoint on Israel. It might be that your personal political approach is the same as or differs from whichever political party is currently in power in the *Knesset* — but you will almost certainly find yourself being forced to defend things. It is important to be informed about Israel, if possible to have been there. It is vital to feel the bond that links Israeli and *Diaspora* Jews (with all their differences and conflicts), to feel truly a part of One People, '*Am Echad*'.

As a Reform or Liberal Jew you might find yourself being forced to take a stand to defend elements of traditional Judaism which are not necessarily yours — issues of Sabbath observance for colleagues who wish to take time off, issues of ritual slaughter and provision of *kosher* meals. Within the Jewish community we can have our differences and arguments — and there is certainly no desire here to impose a single voice to the outside world, for non-Jews should also learn and appreciate that not all Jews think and pray in the same way — but at a very basic level we are all linked. The enemies of Jews and Judaism make no such distinctions and when you enter the Covenant you take upon yourself also the responsibility to help and defend all other Jews, even those with whom you disagree. '*Kol Yisrael aveirim Zeh baZeh*' — 'All members of the People of Israel bear a responsibility for one another.' (*Talmud*, 'Shevuot' 39b)

The simple fact is that — without wanting to be alarmist — Jews are constantly under threat. From many different groups:

- From those who dislike our theological standpoint (because we do not accept Jesus of Nazareth as the Messiah, we do not and cannot accept that God sent a 'son' in the form of a human being who was then brutally sacrificed to save other people as yet unborn — and we must be VERY careful of those Messianic Jews who claim that you can combine these two contradictory beliefs);

- From those who despise us because we do not accept Mohammed from Medina as the Prophet of God;

- From those who dislike us because of what they feel is an historic injustice perpetrated in the Middle East. (The fact that there have been many historic injustices, including many perpetrated against the Jews rather than by them, seems often to escape these people's awareness and facts are irrelevant to them);

- From those who just dislike anything which is not what they claim 'normal' or 'English'; — Even from those who claim to love us.

Remember — No-one is asking or forcing you to become Jewish. If you feel that these threats are more than you or your children can bear — then take the appropriate action.

5. NOTES FOR THOSE WHO WISH TO USE THIS BOOK TO CONVERT TO JUDAISM

The book is designed also as a course to help the reader learn some of the realities of life as a Reform or Liberal or Progressive Jew or Jewess as they are or appear now, in Britain and in mainland Europe. (The labels vary, but the situation of being a minority within a minority is the same.) It should be supplemented by other materials but is intended to serve as a basis for discussion. Several specific topics are dealt with at the end of the book and in the Appendices. You cannot learn everything from a book, but you can learn some facts and history of the liturgy, the calendar, the life cycle and so forth. Some things one can best learn alone, reading quietly, and some things one can best learn with someone else or with a group, experiencing an event, discussing, being involved

It does not cover much History and has only a small amount on Zionism and Israel. You are encouraged to use other sources to become aware of current events in the Jewish world, some of which may have a direct impact on you and your community. No one book can cover everything!

This book cannot aim to teach you Hebrew, but it can refer you to some sources of information — in the end, learning to read is something that needs personal contact and tuition. A book 'Prayerbook Hebrew the Easy Way' (EKS Publishing; Berkeley, California, USA. 2003 ISBN 0-939144-32-8) can be especially recommended but there are various courses available.

Nothing stays still and when re-writing this book in 2015 it was clear that much had changed since the first version was prepared in 1992-94. To give just some examples:

- Technology has changed enormously and now there are social networks, internet, Skype, live-streaming, downloads and other factors which can be used either to create new forms of long-distance virtual community structure and communication and education — or to destroy the social pressures to meet actually in person. Presumably such technical developments will continue after this book is published — will there be in the future implants with apps for certain rituals? Will medical science permit even more interference in the planning and planting and development of an embryo / foetus / child? There are endless possible questions. Just a brief look back at a book written less than a century ago will reveal attitudes that seem now quite antiquated — books written before there were telephones available to everyone, or television, or near-universal mobility, or 'globalisation', or medical transplants, before the removal of certain national borders, or the creation of an independent Jewish state — and yet the people writing and buying these books considered themselves 'up to date' and progressive for their time.

- The situation of Israel and the image of Israel in the view of many peoples and countries have changed — for the worse. Israel is constantly threatened, often treated negatively in the media and there are thriving organisations devoted to boycott and defamation and delegitimisation. A few decades ago one could display an Israeli flag in public — nowadays this is associated with the risk of opprobrium or attack.— Why? A good question…

- The attitudes of both Christianity and Islam towards Judaism have changed, sometimes substantially so. Christianity has lost ground in some parts of the world, Islam has gained ground. Attitudes to religious minorities are now influenced by a fear of growing fundamentalist Islam — so that matters such as Circumcision, the ritual slaughter of animals, the role of communal legal systems such as *Sharia* within the national legal systems (for issues of personal status etc.), the inspection and control of religious schools, the wearing of religious symbols or clothing influenced by and demonstrating religious beliefs, the effect of religion on national and even foreign policy, the public celebration of non-Christian holidays (with *Chanukiot* or Moslem '*Eid*' or Hindu '*Diwali*' greetings in city centres) — these and other matters have become significant and controversial within political discourse throughout the whole of Europe.

- Attitudes towards the Holocaust have changed, partly through the simple fact that some decades have passed and there are now few survivors or eye witnesses left alive. On the one hand there are ever-more memorials, plaques and formal observances; on the other, the memory fades — and there are also those who deny the Holocaust or who try to misuse it for their own political ends. Plus, there have been (alas) other tragedies, other mass murders, other mass expulsions in the intervening time.

- Attitudes towards Gender identity and the wishes of same-gender couples or trans-gender individuals to be accepted for what they are have changed positively.

(At the same time, a word of warning: The author of this book is still waiting for the wave of same-sex divorces that can be predicted as a corollary to same-sex weddings. Progressive Judaism aims for openness and tolerance — and yet, there are several pitfalls awaiting us here, some banal, some potentially tragic, as we try to find the right balance between idealism and realism. For example: Our languages (and hence liturgies) do not yet really have words for a male wife or a female husband — we still refer to couples as 'man and wife' on official forms etc. and euphemisms such as 'partner' do not really resolve the issue. Can a child born by sperm donation or to a surrogate mother really refer to the 'legal parents' as 'Daddy and Mummy'? A small child might do so, but when the child grows into adolescence and seeks more information on their identity things can become more complex. Or — Should a couple divorce, what is the status, in terms of custody and visitation, of a child when neither of the parents is actually the biological mother or father? Some of these new problems are simply re-workings of older ones — to do with Adoption or Fostering — but it has taken decades or centuries to work out socially-acceptable solutions for some of these issues and the author has, as rabbi, encountered many cases where one parent denies another parent (or grandparent) access or when patchwork families do not function as well as is sometimes presented in romantic fiction. In a period when so many marriages end in divorce there is no reason to assume that same-sex marriages will be any different, or the consequences of division any less tragic. The decline of the nuclear family or of patriarchal structures and the relative ease and availability of divorce has not necessarily led to universal happiness, social stability, and a decline in loneliness and isolation. Potential issues of Names and Inheritance and Legitimacy and Citizenship do not disappear just because two people think they are in love. So — we must assume that developments will need to continue and that Judaism will need to play a role in this.)

CHAPTER 1

JEWISH IDENTITY & CONVERSION TO JUDAISM

1. INTRODUCTION: CAN ONE DEFINE 'JEWISH'?

Throughout the history of Judaism there have been two generally-accepted ways of becoming Jewish. The first (involuntary!) was to be born to a Jewish mother; the second was to become Jewish by conversion in later life. Marrying a Jew was not in itself enough.

There have been and still are other methods for defining a person's Jewish identity, but these tend to have been used by Anti-Semites. The Office of the Inquisition in the Catholic Church suspected 'secret Jewish tendencies' whenever a person deviated in some way from the norm they expected, for example by wearing a clean shirt or laying no fire on a Saturday. In 1930s Germany the National Socialists followed a racial theory whereby it was irrelevant what a person defined himself or herself as, what they believed or what they did — it was enough simply to have had one 'Jewish' parent or even grandparent; In the Soviet Union 'Jewish' was an ethnic description, there was even an attempt to set up a special 'Autonomous Region for the Jews' in Birobidjan and '*Evrei*' (Hebrew) was a word used on internal passports for definition; For some Islamic fundamentalists the concepts 'Westerner' and 'Jew' seem coterminous.

Within Judaism there is much debate currently as to Definitions. The concept of needing to have had a Jewish mother is called the 'matrilineal line', or if one can be classed as Jewish simply because one had a Jewish father then 'patrilineal' (or 'Unilineal' meaning 'One parent is Jewish'). Of course things are never simple. If, say, a Jewish woman has several children, even though married to a non-Jewish man, one could follow the matrilineal tradition and classify all these children as 'Jewish'; but what if a Jewish man has two children from the same non-Jewish wife, and one does want to be classed as Jewish and the other does not — what then? Or if he has children (legitimate or not) by several women? What formal action is needed to help one become a member of the community while giving the other the option to stay out? What if a male child has not formally entered the 'Covenant of Abraham' through circumcision? What about adopted children?

For some people it seems to be enough to say 'I FEEL Jewish' — but this can be not only confusing but potentially dangerous, when they have no idea about what 'being Jewish' really means or what the consequences could be. For us, Judaism is primarily a religion, a set of beliefs and actions and not just an ethnic background or a cultural phenomenon. To be Jewish means in some way coming to terms with a belief in One God — so someone who does not believe in God, or who wishes to believe in more than one deity (e.g. also a divine Son of God) should not become Jewish.

Not all Israelis are Jewish — in fact around 20% of the population of Israel is Moslem, Christian, Buddhist or totally secular. (Many of the Jewish population would also class themselves as '*Chiloni*' — 'Secular' — rather than '*Dati*' - 'Religious' or '*Charedi*' — 'Ultra-religious'.)

There are those who find this emphasis on the Mother as discriminatory; on the other hand, there are logical reasons for it. Matrilineality functions on the principle that — with a few rare and tragic exceptions — one usually knew who the Mother of a child was, but there was rarely certainty concerning the Father. Nowadays there are DNA tests but there remains the possibility for some embarrassment, should several siblings undergo the same tests and get unexpectedly different results! So, although one can understand the demand for 'consistency' by those who claim that having EITHER parent Jewish should be enough; although we are aware that not every child will even wish to remain within the faith in which they are raised; although we know that many children are raised by only one parent — usually, but not always, the biological mother — and that many fathers wish to bond with their children and others do not, and that there are patchwork families and adopted children and children born by egg or sperm donation and a myriad of other possibilities — at the end of the day we are still left with the need to decide who is 'inside' the group and who is not, but who is nevertheless welcome to take an additional formal step and come inside if they wish to. We do not want to get drawn into 'biological Judaism' — a concept which is also much misused by racists — whereby an 'egg' is 'Jewish' or a 'sperm' is 'Jewish' or 'blood' is 'Jewish'. Every person is the end result of a multitude of factors — who their parents were, how they treated their child, under what conditions they grew up (the social level, the financial options, whether in peacetime or war, in a secure home or as refugees, whether as an only child or one of several, what schooling they got, what health care, in what form of society they grew up in, etc.). The DNA alone is not enough to define someone. That would be, if anything, a form of racism.

Even the word 'Jew' is relatively late and comes first in the Book of Esther when a group of people is in exile from the defeated Kingdom of Judah and are therefore the 'Judahites'. Mordechai is described in 2:5 as an '*Ish Yehudi*'. Before this we have the term 'Ivri' - 'Hebrews' — probably meaning 'Those from Over There' as perceived by the Egyptians who first met this group when a family of pastoral nomads arrived as economic migrants from 'over there in Canaan'; and prior to this we were the 'Children of Jacob' ('B'nai Ya'akov' or 'B'nai Yisrael' — this second being the later name given to Jacob). The term indicates, incidentally, that we are descended from Jacob and not from his twin brother Esau, and in turn from Isaac and not from his half-brother Ishmael; and so although one can trace a common symbolic ancestral denominator in Abraham, the family tree diverges very early on. In Biblical times identity did indeed come from the father — but these were also times of polygamy and slave ownership and so the head of the household was *de facto* the one who applied his name and identity and observances to all under him. One belonged to a group, be it a family or a tribe or a nation, and individual identity was not so developed as nowadays in the post-Enlightenment Western culture.

Those Jewish communities which are associated with the European Union for Progressive Judaism (EUPJ) and which adhere to the general standards established and maintained by the European *Beit Din* (EBD) accept the understanding that conversion to Judaism is possible, irrespective of one's birth, and accordingly there are systems and procedures whereby a person wishing to adopt Judaism formally as his or her religion may do so.

It is important to have such widespread standards as otherwise a person who chooses to convert through one specific community — or even none, through the Internet — may not be accepted by others. One must understand at the outset that most Jewish communities in Europe are essentially small and enclosed and often feel threatened by a wave of 'outsiders' — and so it takes time before one becomes acknowledged and accepted as an 'insider'. Some also even fear being overwhelmed by 'Philo-Semites' — people who have a deep and genuine and well-meant but sometimes uncomfortable love for Judaism and Jews, as opposed to 'Anti-Semites' who have an irrational hatred for them.

2. DEFINITION OF TERMS

A convert to Judaism is known as a *'Ger'* or a *'Ger Tzedek'* (a 'righteous convert' — *'Ger'* as such means an outsider and a *'Ger Toshav'* is for example a 'resident foreigner'). The process of conversion is known as *Giyur*. The Greek word 'Proselyte' is also used frequently for a candidate for conversion and 'proselytisation' for missionary activity, the active and determined attempt to persuade and convince people to change their religion. You will note that, ironically, to become a Ger (the verb 'LeGayer') therefore means technically to become an outsider rather than an insider! But hopefully one who is accepted.

3. THEOLOGICAL BACKGROUND

Theologically there is no need within Judaism to reach out to and to convert non-Jews. Indeed, it is usually accepted as axiomatic that, in the words of Rabbi Joshua ben Chananiah in the *Talmud* (*Tosefta* to *Talmud 'Sanhedrin' 8:2*): 'The Righteous of all nations have a place in the World to Come' — which means that God can be served just as well by being a good, pious and well-behaving ethical and moral non-Jew. Jews are however understood as having accepted more burdens and responsibilities than other nations of the world — hence the term 'Chosen People' ('*Am Segulah*') — so that for a non-Jew to become Jewish involves the voluntary acceptance of additional demands. Clearly there has to be some valid reason why a person might wish to do this, some motivation. This might be a sincere search for a personal religious life-style, or it might be the strengthening and enrichment of a marriage (or planned marriage) between a Jew and a non-Jew, or it might be a search for personal roots when there are Jews in a person's ancestry. These, and others, could be seen as acceptable reasons to receive a person into the Jewish community through a formal action of conversion. On the whole, however, there is no incentive to search actively for new converts or to be 'missionaries' or 'proselytisers'.

Traditionally Abraham is seen as the one who first accepted a monotheistic view of God and he and his wife Sarah are credited with having spread this knowledge amongst those whom they encountered (Gen.12:5). There is therefore a long tradition of teaching and there have been periods in Jewish history when converts were actively sought. However, later historical developments — particularly the spread of Christianity and various decrees suppressing the practice — have led to reduced interest among many Jews in converting others to Judaism. There is, at best, an ambivalence concerning those who seek to convert, often even (alas) suspicion and hostility.

In the present, more open society, when it has become much easier to encounter people of other faiths (or none) and when many religious barriers and influences have been broken down, the Progressive Jewish movements acknowledge that the process of conversion may be an important means of strengthening the community and family life, by providing an opportunity for interested individuals and partners to learn and adopt a Jewish religious life.

Judaism understands Monotheism to mean that there is One God and that this God created Everything and Everybody. This means that God created also non-Jewish people and the implication is that one can be not Jewish and nevertheless be an integral part of the Creation and of God's Plan. There is therefore no pressure to change one's identity. Judaism does not claim a monopoly on the 'Truth'. One will not be 'damned' as a 'Non-Believer' if one remains a good Christian, Moslem, Hindu, Buddhist or whatever. Judaism demands that Jews remain Jewish, and is saddened should any decide to leave it; but it does not seek to pressurise others to become Jewish. If anything, we would rather warn interested people in advance of all the problems and negative factors, so that they have a chance to re-think their decision.

For the sake of convenience the chapters and more information on Conversion and the procedures are placed together towards the rear of this book.

CHAPTER 2

THE SYNAGOGUE COMMUNITY

1. INTRODUCTION

Since early post-Biblical times Jewish communities have been based, religiously, on the Synagogue. This word, from the Greek for 'A House of Meeting' ('*syn*' = 'together', as in 'synthesis'; '*Gogos*' refers here to a group of people, as in 'pedagogue', 'demagogue') symbolises the essential nature of the community — that it is not just a place of Prayer or other forms of worship, but a place for Meeting, Studying, acting, eating, socialising... The Temple in Jerusalem was known in Hebrew as the '*Beit Mikdash*' — the House of Holiness; the Synagogue in contrast is variously referred to as a '*Beit HaKnesset*' — House of Meeting; '*Beit Tefillah*' — House of Prayer; and '*Beit Midrash*' — House of Study. All of these names imply communal activity — remember, even Study is a communal and not just a private individual activity. It involves a pooling of resources, a coming-together for the common good. Whilst scholars may argue over the precise origins and history of the Synagogue as an institution, what is important for us now is to see the results of the development and to compare it with what we know of other forms of religious communal organisation.

2. FACILITIES AND ACTIVITIES

Clive Lawton, a Jewish educationalist, when showing groups of interested non-Jews around 'a typical synagogue' in Britain, would start with the two most important — because least expected — items: The Notice Board and the Toilets. Why?

The Notice Board showed that, in addition to services, there was a lot more happening in the community. Rotas for Security or the *Kiddush*, notices from the youth groups or announcements of classes and lectures, advertisements for fund-raising events... and so on. From the Notice Board one could get a pretty good idea of what was happening in a community (as well, perhaps, of what was lacking). Nowadays most communities have a Web-Site, and some of them even attempt to keep these up-to-date, as a 'virtual' Notice Board. But this gave a chance to explain to visitors what we often take for granted — that there is more to a 'Jewish place of worship' than just Jewish worship!

Then the Toilets ... because a building which incorporates such facilities is effectively conveying the message that these facilities will be needed, that people will be in the building for extended periods of time, that they may be consuming refresh-

ments, that they don't necessarily all live next door and so on. Few older churches had toilets! Such mundane aspects are left to the church hall, if at all; within Judaism, no distinction is made in this respect between the 'mundane' and the 'holy'.
(Just ask yourself how many railway stations and bus stops and trains and cafés have such facilities? Who do they think their customers are? People without bladders?)

For this reason a large and active synagogue will consist of a variety of facilities — including a library, classrooms, offices — that one might expect more to find in a school. But then, a _Beit Midrash_ is a school — hence also the Yiddish term '_Shul_' for the synagogue — where the members would go to read, study, argue — and worship. Whilst the ritual parts of the synagogue's architecture — the '_Bimah_', '_Aron Kodesh_' ('Ark') etc. — are important, so was the Bookcase; whilst the '_Ner Tamid_' (Eternal Light) symbolises the past, a good light to read by was just as important — and much more important that some fancy stained glass.

3. HOLY OR MUNDANE?

The question is, in fact, rather an artificial one. Few Jews in past centuries would have bothered to ask it. The synagogue, for them, was the building — or club room — where they went for the statutory prayers when they could and where they went to study. (See the discussion in the _Mishnah_, '_Megillah_' Ch. 4 and accompanying _Gemara_.) In some communities it acted also as an overnight hostel for travellers, or was the base for a small _Yeshivah_ (study academy). People would eat, drink, smoke on the premises (the latter not on _Shabbat_!) Some synagogues were small and poor — reflecting the members; some were solid, prosperous, ornate, even pompous buildings — again, reflecting the social standing of the members. Some were designed to be permanent (even if history sometimes decreed otherwise) whereas others were, from the outset, seen as fairly temporary, provisional, set up by small groups of immigrant workers, refugees or evacuees.

4. FOUNDATION AND ORGANISATION

The key thing to bear in mind when considering the organisation of synagogues is that there is no such thing. There is no 'parish' system; no geographical boundaries are set as to where a synagogue may, or may not, be established — at least, not by Jews! There have been attempts to impose such boundaries and regulations in the past, and they have all led to disaster. In the early 19[th.] century the Elders of the 'Bevis Marks Synagogue' ('Spanish & Portuguese') named after this address in the City of London attempted to prevent any other being set up — even a 'branch' community for its own members who now lived further away — within a certain distance of itself — to prevent what they saw as competition. And the result was a breakaway community and a split and eventually the foundation in 1840 of the 'West London Synagogue of BRITISH Jews'. There is nothing to stop any group of Jews from establishing its own synagogue wherever it wants to — there have been instances of several small communities sharing the one building — and throughout history Jewish leaders have vainly tried to encourage or impose some form of Unity. There are some sanctions available — such as, in England, the refusal to licence a congregation for the performance of marriages, or the refusal to grant it some rabbinical authority or membership in some umbrella organisation — but even this depends upon local laws and systems. In England there is a more centralised structure than in America; in Europe different countries allow different hierarchies or funding is controlled differently. It is quite normal to find several competing synagogues within a small area where there is a concentration of Jewish population and these may reflect ideological differences or just ethnic and social ones — *Sephardi* or *Ashkenazi*, or for Jews from Galician, Lithuanian, Polish and other geographical areas; *Chasidic* and non-*Chasidic*. Often the argument used by those defending their perceived monopoly against the establishment of a non-Orthodox synagogue is that it will 'split the community' but this is laughably wrong.

How come it is so easy? Because — since Judaism allows of no intermediaries between a Jew and God, there is no central authority that can dictate where, when and how a Jew should pray. (The Temple in Jerusalem was one such attempt to centralise and control matters — but that is why, according to one view, the Synagogue structure developed as an alternative and in opposition! The Prophets also tried to discourage Jews from making their own sacrifices outside the Temple structure and unsupervised.) If a group of Jews decides to rent a room together in which to meet, it becomes a *Beit Knesset*, a Synagogue. While there have been such things as formal 'Consecration Services' these are really artificial misnomers. The building does not become 'Holy' — it is merely 'dedicated' to a particular purpose, and this dedication is often symbolised by the ceremonial installation of a *Sefer Torah*. From now on — or for whenever the room or building is available for this purpose — it will be dedicated to the work of *Torah* — in its widest sense.

Since there are no Bishops (a 'Chief Rabbi' is something quite different and is merely a later working title) the community was historically organised on lay principles, with a committee structure. In most communities there is some form of democratic involvement of the members, or subscribers, or 'seat-holders', though this is frequently more a matter of appearance than of substance. The elected officers of a community would collect subscriptions from other Jews wishing to join the community — often, historically, in the form of 'seat rentals' on a sliding scale of expense; they would purchase or arrange the acquisition of ritual necessities and appurtenances, a cemetery, a bath-house, etc., and engage where necessary paid part-time or full-time staff to teach, preach, slaughter, clean up or do whatever was necessary. Each community functioned as an independent, self-governing, self-regulatory co-operative society; from the community's fund money would be spent to hire a teacher for the children, to pay the heating costs, provide weddings for orphan girls, funerals for the indigent, food and relief for refugees... The list goes on, but these were seen as important functions of the community, on a par with the actual religious services.

5. FINANCES

As mentioned above, the communities raised their funds from their members. Specific seats in the synagogue were rented out (the best being the most expensive). Other methods of imposing some form of taxation have been used in the past, and some still are — for example: A levy on *kosher* food; The 'selling' or 'auctioning' of certain honours within the service (a practice known in Yiddish as '*Schnoddering*' from the Hebrew '*She-Nodeh*' — 'He who offers'); Fines imposed on members who infringe communal rules; Charges imposed on gravestones; Specific levies to meet particular contingencies, and so on. Each community, as an independent entity, had its own Treasurer to collect and disburse funds.

Nowadays Membership Subscriptions and Donations are the main sources of income to independent synagogues — though in some countries there is State financial support to 'recognised' or 'Establishment' communities. Additional fees may be levied for High Holy Day tickets or for life-cycle events or for specific building and infrastructure projects. The funds are used for rental or acquisition and maintenance of community infrastructure — specifically a room or building for services and social activities but also for youth work, religious education, provision of books and a *Sefer Torah*, provision of a cemetery, publication of a newsletter and other matters. Some communities have a separate category for 'Friends' or 'Supporters' or 'Associates', intended mainly for non-Jews and others — including those in the conversion process — who wish to be on the distribution list and to enjoy specific membership discounts without being voting members. Similarly, some have 'Country Membership' for former members who now live a long way away but wish to keep in touch or retain their rights to burial in the cemetery. All contribute in some way to the support of the community.

6. NATIONAL ORGANISATIONS

Whilst synagogues are mostly fiercely independent, they have found it useful over the years to band together for certain purposes, whereby economy of scale or a spread of financial burden can be achieved — if, sometimes, at the cost of some of the independence. In Great Britain there are, for example, the 'United Synagogue' (mainly in London and the Home Counties, but whose Chief Rabbi exerts a national authority); the 'Federation of Synagogues' (mostly in North and East London); the 'Movement for Reform Judaism' (MRJ), formerly 'Reform Synagogues of Great Britain' (R.S.G.B.); 'Liberal Judaism' (formerly the 'Union of Liberal and Progressive Synagogues', U.L.P.S.); the '*Adath Yisrael*'; the '*Masorti*' (Conservative) movement, and numerous other smaller groupings or, indeed, totally-independent communities who make their own rules and employ their own ministers.

This structure makes synagogue life very flexible — it is almost a classic 'cell' pattern — but at the expense of a lack of central guiding authority or discipline. (However, experience has shown that such central authorities often become counter-productive, squashing initiatives with which a small clique is not in agreement.)

This structure also places great responsibility upon each member, whose vote, presence or activity can make a big difference in the community. One cannot always rely on 'someone else' paying the bill or doing the work. A community will often describe itself as a '*Kehilla Kedosha*' (abbreviated to '*Kuf / Kuf*') — a 'Holy Community'. What is it that makes a group of people 'holy'? It is a combination of what they try to do and how they try to do it.

7. WHO IS WHO?

Whilst no two synagogues are identical it is important to have an overview of the people involved and their roles.

(A). RABBI

A congregation should have a Rabbi. (Some need or can afford more than one). There are still a few lay leaders who have not realised this. Some cannot afford a full-time post and so employ a rabbi to come on an occasional but regular basis, some can even afford more than one rabbi. A rabbi cannot live off air and compliments but has the same financial requirements and expectations as anyone else who has trained for several years for a professional career, who has to pay health and pension insurance and may have a family to support. (This is sometimes a surprise to people who think that, because they enjoy working for their congregation voluntarily, the rabbi should do the same!) In the Reform and Liberal movements there are rabbinic associations with rules for admission and theoretically no congregation should appoint a person to a rabbinic position unless they fulfil the requirements of the appropriate organisation — which essentially involve a university degree, several years of full-time study at an accepted seminary and *Semicha* (ordination) from an acceptable source. Unfortunately there are all sorts of people around who get their *Semicha* from online institutions or who learned some Hebrew whilst working in Israel but are fully unqualified, and it is known for congregations to appoint a person who is 'cheap' — and end up getting what they pay for. The national movements also have recommended scales for salaries and expenses, weighted for seniority or location.

A Rabbi is not a Priest and one does not need to be a Rabbi to lead a synagogue service or even to perform a funeral. A Rabbi cannot 'give a blessing' — though he or she can recite one, asking God to give the blessing. The Rabbi is a Teacher and a Judge — the certificate of Ordination will often use the phrase '*Yoreh Yoreh, Yadin Yadin*' — 'He may Teach and he may Decide' — and their role is to provide the religious foundation for the community's activities, advising, encouraging, guiding, pushing, even warning as necessary. The Rabbi should decide on all matters of Jewish status and conversion, on who may marry in the synagogue, on issues of liturgy and ritual. In addition there is a pastoral role — sometimes the effectiveness of this depends upon the amount of time a part-time rabbi is employed for, or the size or geographical 'scattering' of a community — and an administrative one.

Bearing in mind that one of the major commands is not to work on the Sabbath, surprise is sometimes expressed that a Rabbi appears to be working on this day! Traditionally one got round this problem by paying the rabbi for the week and expecting him to officiate on *Shabbat* for free! Nevertheless a Rabbi is entitled also to regular time off work, to time when he or she is not 'on call', to holidays and even after a sufficient period to a sabbatical. Burn-out is a constant danger when serving a multitude of roles and members, including working in the daytimes, the evenings, weekends and responding to emergency calls at night.

(B). CANTOR (ALSO CALLED CHAZAN)

Not many Reform or Liberal communities can afford a person to sing the service (or lead a choir) but there is an important musical element in the liturgy and some communities employ a trained and qualified Cantor (a cantor is 'invested', not 'ordained') to assist in these tasks, termed *Chazanut*, thus enabling the rabbi to concentrate upon preaching. A Cantor will also then usually be expected also to perform pastoral and educational work, the preparation of *Bar-* and *Bat-Mitzvah* candidates etc. A cantorial training involves musical ability and performance rather than the depth of textual study required of a rabbi. It is important to stress this because the Cantor often has a very public role in services, whereas a large proportion of a Rabbi's work will of necessity be private and 'behind the scenes'.

(C). WARDEN / GABBAY

During services it is normal to have one or more members appointed to greet those entering, hand out (and later collect) prayer books, bibles, *Kippot, Tallitot*; to allocate various honours and *Aliyot* during the service and generally be responsible for order and the smooth running of the service.

The congregation may also employ a Musician to accompany services, an Educational Director to run the Religion School and possibly Adult Education, an Administrator or Secretary to man the building during office hours and handle the routine affairs of the community; a Youth Leader for the youth activities; a Caretaker to keep the place clean and tidy. There may be a Security consultant, there will certainly be those responsible for Catering and the *Kiddushim*. Most of these posts will be part-time or even semi-voluntary (i.e. for a symbolic pittance) or wholly voluntary.

(D). ADMINISTRATION

Congregations are run by elected Boards or Councils or 'Honorary Officers' — there is often a smaller Executive Committee as well for the routine matters — and although there are different versions of synagogue constitutions the general idea is that these tasks are voluntary and one is elected for a fixed term by the membership at an annual general meeting. (Most constitutions allow powers for co-opting members when required, subject to later ratification, and some wisely limit the number of terms an officer may hold before being compelled to stand down for a period. This ensures that the same people do not hold and dominate a position for decades.) A congregation may own substantial infrastructure and employ staff and provide facilities for members and non-members, so Finances, Insurance, Security, Maintenance, Cleaning, Personnel and Health & Safety issues need to be handled in a responsible manner — such apparently trivial matters as changing light bulbs, sweeping snow off paths, paying the bills all require commitment and effort by volunteers.

(E). MEMBERS

Congregations are voluntary associations and are formed of members who pay a regular Membership Fee and in return receive certain benefits. These could include access to services, religion school, youth club, the library, attendance at various social events, active and passive voting rights — and even burial insurance and a plot in the congregation's cemetery. The congregation's Board sets the level of fees (there may be a sliding scale to allow for reduced rates for pensioners, students, the unemployed, 'Country Members' who live further than a specified distance away, etc.) and the Treasurer is responsible for ensuring that these subscriptions are paid. Unfortunately this is often a difficult and thankless task. Some members cannot pay their assessment and need to negotiate a reduction; some can but choose not to, or to wait until the very last minute or after they have been repeatedly reminded — even though the community's outgoings have to be paid regularly. Non-members may wish to share these benefits, in which case some mutually-acceptable scheme needs to be negotiated and of course they are not entitled to any privileges or discounts. Members who consistently refuse to pay may need to be expelled from membership. Many a Treasurer can tell tales of members who roll up in an expensive new car to explain how they cannot possibly afford their subscription due to financial hardship…

The Members should play an active part in synagogue life as far as possible — attending the general meetings, volunteering their skills and services, fundraising, assisting at services or in societies and committees. Nothing happens by itself!

8. SOME ISSUES IN SYNAGOGUE LIFE

(A). THE PRAYER SPACE

In modern times it is often necessary to use an adapted room originally built for other purposes, or to meet in a private home, or to use a multi-purpose room. In such cases one must be pragmatic and flexible, one must improvise. It is not always possible to orientate the room towards Jerusalem. If there is no *Aron Kodesh* for the *Sefer Torah* then it can be laid instead on a table and covered with a cloth or a *Tallit*.

If the ark has a curtain in front of it, then this effectively separates the 'holy' part of the room from the rest, used for other activities, and no further curtain is necessary unless one wishes for security reasons to keep the scroll and other items where they are safe from disturbance.

Having described how the room is laid out, it is worthwhile to consider how it is used. Synagogues are formed of people, all of whom have their own opinions. There are often debates about issues, and these debates can become heated and can even lead to major conflicts and to splits within the community. In our experience, these splits rarely occur because of some trivial theological issue such as 'Is there a God?' and are more often concerned with burning issues of great importance such as 'Whose turn is it to open up? Why does Mrs. So-and-So always get to light the candles? Should we allow a man without a tie to go onto the *Bimah*?'

No book such as this could ever hope to resolve all these problems, but we hope that by indicating them here we can prepare the reader for what to expect and provide some context and perspective.

In general, most religions cover a 'spectrum' of meanings that range from:

(1) Everything is Forbidden, even if it is Permitted, to
(2) Everything is Forbidden, unless it is specifically Permitted, to
(3) Everything is Permitted, unless it is specifically Forbidden, to
(4) Everything is Permitted, even if it has been expressly Forbidden!

The individual Jew — and the community — will try to place themselves somewhere along this spectrum of possibilities. Reform Judaism tends to place itself somewhere near (3) but is often confused — by our opponents, or by those who haven't thought things through — with the position (4). Such people then get very, very angry when a Rabbi or community says 'No' — they have not realised or refuse to accept that the word 'No' still exists in the Reform or Liberal Jewish vocabulary.

(B). SERVICES

The first thing to note is that whilst private prayer is individual and private and can be carried out anywhere and at any time and in any form, a public act of worship is always a compromise. At some point in a congregation's development the group will decide — often influenced by only one or two people — to use a specific prayer book or a specific mixture of books — nowadays often a photocopied set of sheets — and to establish a set of times for services. The times will always be too early for some and too late for others. There will be debates about starting evening services at a time when families with children can attend — or at a time when smaller children have already been fed and put to bed. Morning services may begin early so that people can do other things once they have finished, or may start later because many worshippers have long distances to travel. Some communities are in city centres, some in suburbs, some in smaller settlements. A community may be small and only have enough volunteer leaders to be able to offer monthly or fortnightly services, or regular Sabbath evening but irregular Sabbath morning ones. There may be issues of renting premises which are not always available, especially for midweek festival services. It may be decided to hold an 'early' service once a month for families, and then there will always be some people who forget which week this is and come at the wrong time… Services may even be organised around the arrival and departure times of hourly bus or train services.

Some members will want more Hebrew, others less. Some will want prayer books with transliterations, some will find these a concession too far. Some will want a keyboard or other music, others will prefer just spoken prayers. Some will think they can sing, others will be of a different opinion. There is usually someone who insists that the service must always begin punctually, but who will then come late; who will insist on a full *Mussaf*, but will leave early for personal reasons. Members may have grown up in traditional communities or Reform ones elsewhere or in different countries or may have come to Judaism as adults but only ever experienced one congregation, one set of melodies, one style of preaching and believe that this is the only one that can ever be tolerated. This list can be extended…

Every Rabbi yearns to be his or her predecessor. After all, the predecessor was such a wonderful preacher, so good with the children, so caring for the older worshippers, had such wonderful humour, such a melodious voice and was deeply loved. The only way for the current rabbi to achieve all these positive qualities is to be succeeded by someone else, at which point they, too, become the predecessor…

So — compromise is needed. The community must agree on a specific book, on a specific translation, on a specific style of service (or a series of alternatives for different weeks) and calendar. Each community will develop its own *Minhagim* or customs. Sometimes a visiting officiant will be shown a 'marked book' with notes, the lay leader saying 'We do this bit in Hebrew, this bit in silence, we stand for this bit but not that bit…' and so on — rigid and inflexible. How sad!

(C). MINYAN

In Genesis 18:32 Abraham argues God down to ten righteous people in Sodom (and God runs away before he can argue even further down!); In Numbers 14:11 God expresses his disgust and disappointment in the ten spies who bring a negative and defeatist report back from their mission. From these sources derives the idea that Ten forms a definition of the collective and hence the idea that a 'communal prayer' requires a minimum quorum of ten (defined naturally as ten adult Jewish males…). Whilst it is important to have such definitions, it can become a problem if nine people sit around for half an hour and then cancel a service simply because a tenth has not turned up. (It could even be that several non-qualified persons, often referred to by the technical term 'Women', also wait fruitlessly for a chance to pray.) So whilst some communities retain a strict adherence to the idea that without a '*Minyan*' certain prayers or *Torah* readings may not take place, (why not? Will God not listen?) others take a more flexible view of the matter, either including this strange category 'Women' in the total or dropping the idea of a minimum number altogether.

(According to one tradition in the Land of Israel the number for a *Minyan* was seven, not ten.) This is one of those areas where one has to be careful to separate between spirituality and neurotic obsessive behaviour, the sort that makes one not walk on the cracks in the pavement, that makes one feel that a certain number of pages of text have to be mumbled regularly and ritually in order to satisfy the Creator of the Universe. Sometimes ritual is a help and comfort, sometimes it becomes either a hindrance or a cause of boredom.

(D). DRESS

What should one wear at a synagogue service? Experience shows that this can be a major issue in some congregations. The days when everyone wore 'Sunday Best' to church in the surrounding community are also largely gone.

Different communities are free to establish their own Guidelines. We live in an informal age, and many people do not even possess a suit or a formal outfit! It is no longer considered outrageous when a woman wears slacks or trousers, or a man an open shirt. Jeans and 'Trainers' are normal wear. So instead of insisting on to-tally-outdated norms we suggest simply the application within the synagogue of some common-sense and mutual respect. There are 'appropriate' and 'inappropriate' head-coverings; A cap, a *Kippah*, a hat is one thing, whereas a baseball cap emblazoned with an advertising slogan is another. We do not demand that women cover themselves from head to foot — but outfits that reveal a lot of bare skin, whether at midriff or thigh level, or enable everyone present to observe a woman's breasts without their even having to try hard, will distract. There is no point in demanding 'political correctness' and saying that this will not happen, or should not happen — it WILL happen. Individual freedoms are necessarily restricted when taking part in a communal activity. People often dress to make a point — the point here is that one has come to worship God within the community, not to shock, or to make a political message, or to attract a sexual partner. Whilst dress is often a matter of taste or fashion the fact is that a Rabbi or Cantor (whether male or female) has to be able to concentrate and it simply unfair to challenge them at a time when they already stressed. We urge people to respect the feelings of others. Respect ('*Kavod*') is a major *Mitzvah*, as much as is Modesty ('*Tzniyut*').

This is not a Gender issue — it would apply just as much to what men wear. At issue is not whether the wearer feels comfortable but whether everyone else feels comfortable with what is being worn. A synagogue is not a night club or a sports hall. A Youth Service may well have a very different atmosphere and summer is different to winter, and some rooms are easier to heat or are draughty, so common-sense rules should apply. Religious symbols from another religion are definitely NOT appropriate.

In the *Torah* (Exodus 28:42) it was laid down that the Priests had to wear long under-pants to ensure that when they climbed the steps to the altar they would not reveal anything that could distract. The same could be said nowadays for very thin blouses, low 'decolleté', miniskirts, leather jackets, chains and studs, boots and similar. Whilst soldiers can pray whilst wearing military uniform there is no need for someone who is not a soldier to do so. Outside overcoats, raincoats and mackintoshes should be taken off when entering; sports clothing or motorbike leathers or nightwear are not appropriate. The writer has seen things in his career which would not be believed if written here…

(E). SHABBAT ISSUES

It has become normal in Liberal/Reform services to light the *Shabbat* candles on or near the *Bimah* before a Friday Evening Service. Of course, since we try to apply a standard starting time, rather than varying the service times by a few minutes each week, it can be that we light the candles while it is still daylight in summer and after nightfall in winter. Essentially we agree by consensus to 'start *Shabbat*' at 19.00 or 20.00 or whenever and end it likewise, whatever the sun at our specific latitude might say.

Some people may be uncomfortable with this practice; In this case, if someone is asked to perform this ritual and declines, their wish should be respected. It is merely a relic of the time when the candles were lit to provide light to see by, not to stand in a brightly-lit room to be seen.

Security requirements mean that many synagogues now have electrically-operated doors, special lights and cameras, walkie-talkies and similar equipment. On the basis of 'saving life' ('*Pikuach Nefesch*') even traditional synagogues are coming to terms with this development.

In Liberal communities — especially in view of the distances people have to travel — we do not pretend hypocritically that everyone has walked to services. Synagogue car parks (where available) should be open. Music may be played. Doorbells may be rung. Lights may be switched on. Keys may be used. Emergency Exits should be made available, lit up, indicated, unlocked or whatever is necessary. At the end of an Evening service care should be taken to ensure that any candles which have been lit are either somewhere very safe or are if necessary extinguished. It would be mere superstition to suggest that the lights are 'holy' — it was the act of lighting them that was blessed, not the lights themselves. Once they have served their purpose and the room or building is to be left unattended there is no point in burning the place down due to misguided Piety.

It should not need mentioning that mobile phones should be switched off!

(F). USE OF THE WORSHIP SPACE FOR OTHER PURPOSES

A Synagogue is a multi-purpose building. Traditionally one met and talked and studied as well as prayed. Nowadays many communities have to set up their prayer rooms in multi-purpose rooms, or have to use the prayer room (after moving some furniture) for meetings and social functions.

There is basically no problem with this. The room itself is not holy — only the activity that takes place within it during services. The Ark is usually a closed cupboard with a curtain in front — this itself acts as a divider between the scrolls and the rest of the room — and there is no real need for yet another curtain in front of the curtain. It is, essentially, a very formal bookcase. Obviously, if the room is to be used for a youth-club disco or for ball games one needs to be sensible about protecting fixtures and books, but the room itself may be used. Rooms may also be rented out — in this case, a community may need to establish guidelines as to the sort of activities which are appropriate. Many small and new Jewish communities rent rooms from local churches and a Christian group could, for example, rent a synagogue too. Activities involving a discothèque with much alcohol, or gambling or meetings of political parties might however be considered to be inappropriate.

(G). THE PLACE OF NON-JEWS IN THE SERVICE

A synagogue service involves the worshippers sitting or standing, reading or singing. There is relatively little 'ritual', and what there is usually involves the *Sefer Torah* — holding it, carrying it, displaying it, reading from it, being called up to recite a blessing over it.

The simplest answer to the question 'What can Non-Jews Do?' is — they can take a full part in the Worship, but not in the Ritual. That is to say, they may join in singing and reading — this includes those people who are converting but who are not yet formally Jewish — but should not be called up to an '*Aliyah*' or to lead a service or to light the candles. (One can be more flexible with children, who might be allowed to help dress a scroll.) Non-Jews should not wear a *Tallit* at morning services, since this is a *Mitzvah* binding on Jews, but men (and women in many communities) should be asked to wear a head-covering, since this is a custom and shows respect. In some communities a person not yet converted may be permitted to read a psalm or something similar — but not lead a *Berachah*, something to which other congregants must respond '*Amen*', because this means he or she would be reading it on their behalves.

Another aspect of 'ritual' involves life-cycle events. If, for example, a child who is to be named or a *Bar/Bat-Mitzvah* has a Jewish mother but non-Jewish father, or a bridegroom or bride have non-Jewish family members, then different communities have different policies as to what the non-Jewish parent (or other family members) may do. The simplest answer here again is to say they can be present but should do nothing that involves actually saying or reciting something. Standing on or next to the *Bimah* or opening a curtain are relatively non-controversial means of allowing someone to feel 'included' in a *Simcha*, a festive occasion.

At a funeral anyone seriously affected is classed as a 'Mourner' and so the rules for inclusivity can be widened. But it is rare that a non-Jewish spouse or parent would wish (or be able) to say the *Kaddish*.

In Numbers Ch. 15 verses 14, 26 and 29 it is stressed repeatedly that a *Ger* — in this case a *Ger Toshav*, 'the stranger who is with you' ('*HaGer haGar betochchem*') is to be treated ritually according to exactly the same laws as a citizen. No distinction is to be made and neither will a distinction be made by God, in either positive or negative sense — only by one's actions and not by his origins should one be judged.

For many centuries this principle was not followed in many countries and there were special laws for special categories of people — meaning, usually, religious or ethnic minorities. Of course, Europe is at present confronted by a different problem — there are members of certain minorities who desire to maintain their own separate legal system, or even to impose it upon the majority amongst whom they live! This is a very new phenomenon and modern societies find themselves torn by the problem of wishing to show tolerance whilst at the same time defending their own values. Can one even make a distinction between a stranger who is in a country 'by permission' with a visa, and one who has entered (or stayed) illegally?

Within a synagogue community there is the same tension between wishing to be inclusive and friendly and at the same time maintaining exclusive boundaries regarding who may participate, or marry, or be buried. Jews who are not 'Members' and who have not paid any financial contribution to the community — for whatever reason — or who have refused to pay or who have left the community are also not always viewed in a neutral fashion when they present themselves and require or demand assistance.

(H). THE PLACE OF CHILDREN IN THE SERVICE

Experience shows that this is a complex and very emotional issue in many Reform and Liberal synagogues. In Orthodox synagogues the issue is dealt with very straightforwardly — women and most small children are simply kept away, behind a screen, or at the rear, or on a balcony. But in progressive synagogues we pride ourselves on being friendly and 'open to Families'. We lay out our synagogues and prayer rooms so that everyone is together. Men and women — and therefore fathers and mothers — may sit together, with their offspring.

This can be wonderful — but not always. What follows are merely some personal observations from a congregational rabbi — and father of three — who has seen and heard many sides to the debate. Firstly — let us assume that children who can sit quietly and concentrate are never considered a problem and in many communities they are encouraged to take part in some way, to come onto the *Bimah* for *Kiddush* or to receive a 'blessing' or to follow the scroll in procession or to assist in dressing the scroll, to learn the service for their own *Bar-* or *Bat-Mitzvah* celebrations. It is rare that there is controversy about such children. And secondly, bored teenagers who want to giggle and chatter are a separate issue and these are often better-off standing outside and communicating with their peers. But various issues are raised when smaller children, up to the age of about 8 or so, attend adult services.

What are the arguments that are often employed?

1). 'The children are our Future.' A fine statement, but is it true? Whose future are the children? There are several possibilities: (a). The future of the family or (b). the future of the congregation or (c). the future of the wider Jewish community? People are mobile these days. The chances are high that the growing adults will leave the congregation and go elsewhere for personal or professional reasons and that the congregation will acquire as adult members other people who have grown up in different cities or countries. So (a) is relevant for the family and (c) is hopefully relevant in the wider context — but (b) is a shaky argument. How many people present actually grew up in the local community? The children might be the Future, but the adults are the Present.

2). 'Everyone loves seeing children around.' Not true. Some do. Maybe most. But some people might have come to pray for children they have not yet been able to have and some might have come to pray for children they have lost. Some come whose children have at last grown up and left home and they might not want to share their pew with a sticky toddler any more — they have had enough of that! Some come for peace and a place for quiet reflection.

3). 'The children need to learn.' Yes, of course, but What should they learn? We could suggest that they learn that the Synagogue — at least during services — is a place for worship and not a Kindergarten or a playground. At other times it might indeed serve as a school or a youth club or a meeting hall, but during religious services it is a place where Grown-Ups go to think and pray and talk to God. It is not the place to show off how hard you can stamp your new shoes or to jump up onto and down from the *Bimah* or to eat lollipops. Children need to learn many things but one of the most important things they need to learn is how to behave appropriately — in a bus, in a supermarket, at a concert, with visitors, in a classroom, in a place of worship. It is remarkable how some parents consider it totally appropriate to take a noisy and disruptive, bored, tired and fretful child into a service when they would never dream of doing so at a theatre, a concert hall, or an important meeting.

4). 'What about the Parents? You cannot ban them too.' No, one does not wish to ban parents. Young families are very important to a community and we do not wish to see a situation whereby — as in some other religions — women and children are banned, or people are effectively prevented from coming to services over a period of ten or fifteen years until their youngest child is old enough to sit still! But new parents also need to learn the boundaries of acceptable behaviour and a lot can be achieved by some basic common-sense measures.
   - Ensure a small child wears slippers indoors, or socks, but not noisy boots with which he can show off on the wooden floor how hard he can jump.
   - Give it a quiet toy to play with, not a loud rattle or boxes of plastic building bricks (or a plastic toy with a hammer which makes a bell ring!! Even if this is 'his favourite toy'!)
   - Arrange to sit near the exit rather than as far away as possible from the door — which means further disruption when a child has to go in and out.
   - In some places it is possible to breast-feed discreetly (a *Tallit* makes a wonderful cover!), in others it is not — it depends on how the room is set up.

The thing is simply to realise that not everyone is automatically as much in love with your child as you are yourself. This does not make them all 'wrong, fuddy-duddy, ultra-conservative and uncaring' — the issue of Children requires sensitivity and compassion from all sides. The Rabbi or *Shaliach Tzibbur* (the leader of the service) might be totally accustomed to occasional mumbles and gurgles, but will have his or her concentration ruined by a loud chattering or screaming and constant 'Shush!' noises from within the congregation and children crawling under his feet on the *Bimah*. We are, after all, trying to establish an atmosphere of worship, a 'Ruach' or spirit in which ALL can feel at home — and that includes those who do not have children. Experience also shows that the parent often spends a large proportion of the time too tense and distracted to pray either and is constantly going 'Shush!' or providing a drinking bottle or getting up to haul a child back...

Of course there are also creative alternatives — separate or additional services for small children and their parents, a crèche or child-care or activities in an adjacent room (there is no problem for us with children using crayons on a *Shabbat*), a proper place for changing nappies. It is worth also for a community to carry appropriate insurance should an accident occur to a child — the rooms are not always 'child-safe'; there are bookshelves, lamps and other items which can fall over.

We plead here merely for some Realism. Small children are picturesque when they are well-behaved or asleep but can be very disruptive when they are either in a bad mood, tired or stressed, or have fallen over and hurt themselves. Flexibility and sensitivity from all concerned is called for.

(I). A WELCOMING IMPRESSION

A synagogue which is empty is not fulfilling its function, however interesting or picturesque or historic the architecture might be. If the acoustics are poor, leading to echoes, or making it impossible for the *Shaliach Tzibbur* to be heard; If the microphones merely squeak rather than assisting in audibility; If the room is too hot or too cold or too draughty or too stuffy or too damp; If the atmosphere is unfriendly — then people may be put off. Can your synagogue be easily found or is it hiding behind an anonymous door in an anonymous building? Is there a sign which gives at least an indication of whom one can telephone for information about the services, or when the services take place? Is the community easy to find in the telephone book, in local directories, or in the Internet? (Some congregations are listed under a Hebrew name such as under 'B' for '*Beth Shalom*', or under 'J' for 'Jewish' or 'S' for 'Synagogue' or 'I' for 'Israelite' — it is not always easy for others to find! Some are listed in directories under their name rather than under the name of the town where they are situated!)

One cannot solve all issues easily — the security issues, the nature of the neighbourhood, the parking facilities, the public transport connections, the number of steps — but experience shows that a friendly welcome, access to books and texts, and such basics as a safe Cloakroom and clean toilets are as important (or more) as the timing of the service or the liturgy used. A loop for those using hearing aids, or large-print *Siddurim* for those with poor eyesight, are also options to consider as well as step-free access when designing new buildings.

These are things which <u>every</u> member — and not just Board members — can influence.

CHAPTER 3

REFORM AND PROGRESSIVE JUDAISM IN CONTEXT: A BRIEF OVERVIEW

1. NAMES AND LABELS

At the outset let us make it clear that 'labels' are often misleading. This book was originally written for the 'Reform' movement in Great Britain but has been found useful and has since been revised to meet the needs of 'Liberal', 'Progressive' and 'Conservative' communities. This latest revision seeks also to take into account developments within Europe, where the term 'Liberal' or 'Progressive' is now often used — although care has to be taken to make a distinction with political parties which also use these terms. In Israel the term '*Mitkademet*' is often used — an adjectival use of a reflexive verbal form, 'To be moving forward' — i.e. progressing. One needs to be aware what lies behind a specific name of a community or an organisation. What is it that needs to be re-formed? The very term implies a criticism of the existing *status quo*. And in which direction is one (hopefully) 'progressing'? In addition, there is always a very human tendency to stand still and say 'We are Reformed, no longer Reforming.' There is an old joke (but it is not always a joke!) that there is nothing so conservative as a 'progressive' organisation…

2. INTRODUCTION

Progressive Judaism seeks to defend a belief system which is riddled with inconsistencies and internal contradictions, but which it accepts as a part of its belief in Pluralism, the idea that there can be more than one way of being right at any one time. In contrast Orthodox Judaism seeks to defend a belief-system which is riddled with inconsistencies and internal contradictions, but which it either denies exist or indeed claims that these are all a part of one single revelation, beyond question or challenge.

This may appear rather brutal and cynical, but it summarises the essential difference between the two worlds of what are now called 'Orthodox' and 'Progressive' Judaism.

nnot accept the idea of change, but has to perceive everything — including itself — as having already existed, only needing to be given form by 'au-cholars or writers; There was a One-off Revelation. The other is founded that everything changes — except God — and that even if one accepts s not change, then the way in which we perceive God or the way we apply God's message for us Jews as Jews can and does change. There is a Continuing Revelation.

Between these two standpoints is a gulf that goes way beyond petty squabbles over the right to drive on *Shabbat*, though this is the way the difference is usually defined or the level at which argument takes place!

3. MORE ON LABELS AND TITLES: SOME DIVISIONS OF THE PAST

It would be incorrect to state that there have never been denominational titles in Judaism before the 'Orthodox — Progressive' divide, but it is true to say that we are not always sure what other titles or labels have meant, or who gave them and for what purpose — whether as self-definition or as insults.

For example, in the centuries of the Second Temple period (which ended in 70 C.E.) groups arose known as '*Pharisees*', '*Sadducees*' and '*Essenes*'. The former, known in Hebrew as '*Perushim*' or 'Those who have Split Off', i.e. 'the Breakaway Group' are commonly assumed to have been the progenitors of Rabbinic Judaism; the latter, in Hebrew '*Tzidukim*', are understood to have been claiming descent from or owing allegiance to the descendants of Zadok, the Chief Priest in the days of David and Solomon (see I Kings 1:34, I Chron. 29:22 etc.). They seem to have represented the conservative priestly interests and to have been those concerned with maintaining the traditions of the Temple and associated rituals.

In practice after the Hasmonean period (167 - ca. 30 B.C.E.) such direct blood-links with the family of Zadok were broken and the names seem to have been used chiefly by their opponents! Indeed, what little we know of the two groups is derived only from polemical and tendentious sources and has to be treated carefully.

However, it appears that the split reflected a class as well as a theological division, and that the theological division reflected differences over belief in a Life after Death — the *Pharisees* claiming that there was such a thing, the *Sadducees* denying it. If this is true, the division reflects a fundamental difference in the way these Jews looked both at this world — and the next one.

(Note: In what Christians call the 'New Testament' the *Pharisees* are frequently roundly condemned, although at the same time it appears that Jesus had been de-bating with them as though he were himself part of the group, as though it were an internal argument about interpretations. This may represent an attempt by the later Gospel writers to distance Christianity from *Pharisaic* Judaism. Ironically, despite the condemnation of *Pharisees*, Christianity adopted many of their principles. In Matthew 22:23-33 — (cf. Mark 12:18-27) Jesus is asked by some *Sadducees* on his opinion regarding which marital partner a person will have in the next life. The question seems sarcastically phrased. He answers that this question is irrelevant be-cause in the next world the marriage contracts made in this one are invalid. This is an interesting *Pharisaic* perspective and this also explains why the Christian marriage ceremony specifically stresses 'Until we are parted by Death.' In Matthew 22:34-46 various *Pharisees* also set Jesus doctrinal questions, to which he responds in typical *Pharisaic* manner — the presentation in the text is polemical but the dialogue is clear. In Matt. 23:1-33 and Luke 11:39-53 Jesus roundly attacks 'the academics, text experts and *Pharisees*' for being very fussy about rituals and details of the laws. In John 7:45-49 *Sadducees* and *Pharisees* engage in an argument about Jesus, the latter demonstrating a degree of intellectual snobbery.

In 'Acts of the Apostles' 23:8 Paul makes a speech in the Temple courtyard which leads to argument between *Pharisees* and *Sadducees*. Although Judaism does not accept the 'New Testament' books they do provide occasional interesting near-contemporary insights into the doctrinal issues of the later Second Temple period. Our other main external source is Flavius Josephus.) The *Essenes* seem to have preferred to withdraw to all-male monasteries in the desert and live an ascetic and studious lifestyle.

After the destruction of the Temple in 70 C.E. the *Sadducees* seem to have disappeared from the scene (along with their literature — there must have been many books of rules and regulations and for the training of priests, but all will have gone up in the flames…) Rabbinic literature of the following centuries, though, reflects the division of the surviving scholars and their 'schools' into two, those based in Palestine/*Eretz Yisrael* and those based in Mesopotamia/Iraq. Eventually their deliberations were even collated separately, so that there are two *Talmud*s — the '*Yerushalmi*' or 'Jerusalem *Talmud*' and the '*Bavli*' or 'Babylonian *Talmud*'.

These did not represent a schism, just different traditions and opinions on common matters, especially as collated in the *Mishnah* which is common to them both. The *Bavli* came to be accepted as the one referred to most and therefore the more authoritative of the two.

Within both *Talmud*s the predominant style is one of debate between different opinions and 'schools' of thought over several generations — the most well-known being between those of Hillel, who tended to the lenient interpretation of any problem, and of Shammai, who tended to the stricter approach, and who are cited in the *Mishnah*. The rules of debate however meant that these differences could be 'handled' on the whole without causing further splits; a vote would be taken, and the majority view became 'authoritative'. (But — and this is VERY important — the minority view would also be recorded; just because it had been outvoted did not mean that it was 'wrong' or 'heretical'.)

In the 8th. century C.E. though a schism did occur between the followers of this rabbinic tradition of minute interpretation and re-interpretation of the details of the law and the followers of Anan ben David, a failed candidate for the position of Exilarch ('Head of the Exile') in 767 C.E., who established an anti-rabbinic sect which opposed rabbinic decisions.

The former were henceforth known as the '*Rabbanites*', the latter as the '*B'nei Mikra*' or '*Karaites*', implying a devotion to the literal word of Scripture — in Hebrew '*Mikra*'. The bitterness engendered by this schism, with accusations of heresy and corruption and with bans on inter-marriage between the two groups, continues to this day. (In 1988 a congregation of *Karaites* was 'discovered' in a Baltic state — but they wanted nothing to do with other Jews and had indeed argued successfully during the Holocaust that they were not like other Jews!) Within *Karaism* itself there were further splits and divisions.

Over the following centuries those Jews in Mediterranean lands gradually developed different customs from those in northern, western and eastern Europe. Those in the Mediterranean area became known as *Sephardi* from the Hebrew word *Sepharad* (found only in Obadiah, verse 20, where it probably refers to Sparda in Asia Minor). The name was applied to Spain and to those who were later expelled from the Iberian peninsula. Those from Germanic lands (and, by extension, the rest of Northern and Eastern Europe) became known as *Ashkenazi* (pronounced with a soft 'z', so that despite appearances it does not sound like a certain German political movement!) from the Hebrew word *Ashkenaz*, which originally referred to a people descended from Japhet (Gen. 10:3 and I. Chron. 1:6), understood by some to mean 'Asia'; from around the 10th. century however this word was applied to Slavs or Teutons. (In the *Midrash* '*Bereshit Rabbah*' 37:1 Rabbi Berechia says: '*Ashkenaz, Riphat* and *Togarmah* are *Germanikiya*' — assumed to be a reference to Germanic tribes. In the Babylonian *Talmud*, '*Yoma*' 10a and in the Jerusalem *Talmud*, '*Megillah*' 71b Gomer the father of *Ashkenaz* is translated by 'Germamia'.)

In modern times a third major group is the *Eidot Mizrach*, the name applied to Jews from Arabic-speaking countries in North Africa and the Middle East — Jews from Persia, Iraq, Egypt, Morocco, Algeria, Yemen etc.

Indeed one could argue that there are now two further significant and definable Jewish groupings — the '*Anglo-Saxim*', a modern Israeli term for Anglo-Saxons, i.e. in the broadest sense Western Europeans and all who are descended from those who left Western Europe to settle in other continents — in North America, South America, South Africa, Australasia — and the Israelis themselves, especially '*Sabras*' (the nickname for those born in *Eretz Yisrael*). A very, very rough 'rule of thumb' would be as follows: The *Sephardim* are those Jews whose culture developed in Catholic or Greek-Orthodox countries; the *Ashkenazim* those who developed in Russian-Orthodox countries; the *Eydot Mizrach* those who developed in Moslem countries; the '*Anglo-Saxim*' those who developed in Protestant countries; and the *Israelis*, those who have only known the unusual, indeed unique experience of growing up in a Jewish country.

Of course it would not take long to demolish this outline — *Sephardi* Jews were also in Turkey — but we are speaking here of cultural rather than geographical definitions. If Jews from Eastern Europe (*Ashkenazi*) moved to Western Europe or North America they found themselves in a minority and tended to cling together; *Sephardi* Jews who left to settle in the Netherlands or parts of South/Central America took their culture with them and often established their own communities. A Yemenite Jew ('*Teymani*') living in Israel may feel (religiously) more Yemenite than Israeli. Each group carries its own history, traditions, *Minhagim*, liturgies, rituals, conflicts and squabbles with it. Italian Jews were different from Spanish who were different from Turkish…Jews from Galicia and those from Lithuania had very different approaches to life…

And yet the basic premise holds true. There were always cross-influences between a Jewish minority and the non-Jewish majority amongst whom they lived. Community structures and the languages used varied. In *Ashkenazi* communities there were various forms of Yiddish (Hebrew mixed with varying elements of German, Old French, Russian, Polish, etc.); in *Sephardi* countries there was Ladino (Hebrew mixed with Italian, Spanish (old Castilian), Portuguese, Turkish, etc.); in *Eydot Mizrach* there was Judaeo-Arabic — Hebrew mixed with Arabic and of course sometimes written in Arabic script; in Israel there is *Ivrit*, the modern form of the ancient Hebrew language, and academics and religious historians speak and write in *Ivrit*. In the West — it seems that English has become the dominant language, as for historic reasons to do with emigration, flight, colonialism and assimilation most of the Jews in North and South America, Australasia, South Africa as well as Britain and Western European countries communicate in English at international conferences.

Eastern European immigrants to Britain in the late 19[th.] century brought Eastern European ideas with them, just as later Russian immigrants to Germany in the late 20[th.] century brought Russian ideas with them and North African Jewish immigrants to France brought Arabic influences with them. Nothing is static and no definition can hold true for ever. The following generations are already torn between the desire to maintain their heritage and to integrate fully into the host culture.

The 'Western' Jews can then be defined as those influenced by the very Western European phenomena of the Reformation — a Christian rebellion against centralised and corrupted Papal rule and the top-heavy rituals of the Catholic Church — and the Enlightenment, a philosophical rebellion against centralised and authoritarian religion as such and also against absolutist dynastic monarchies, an assertion of the rights and responsibilities of the Individual, as a citizen rather than a subject. (The very word 'Monarchy' means 'One Rules, alone.') So the idea that one may be free to think for oneself, speak for oneself, read or write whatever one wishes to and be free to subscribe to or to leave a religion, is very much a concept that could only flower in a cultural context where the Individual is more important than the Collective. As we know, Communism and National Socialism and Fascism were secular political attempts to assert the Collective over the Individual — the individual was deprived of any rights and was duty-bound to submit to whatever orders were handed down by 'Higher Authority', the Party taking the role of the Church.

So Reform Judaism, the first term used, grew out of the idea that one could be a 'modern' citizen in a 'modern' European state and still worship God in a Jewish way, but praying also in the vernacular, and allowing certain concepts to be modified or dropped (e.g. a belief in a personal Messiah, or a desire for a rebuilding of the ancient Temple).

While the main theological viewpoints remained similar, each group developed its own language, dialect or accent, its own musical traditions, its own liturgies and other customs, so that one could speak of Judaism as it was practised in Italy or Spain or Salonica, or the Yemen or Baghdad or Amsterdam or Poland — in other words, of one religion but many forms.

Some major works of legal interpretation or liturgy were able to gain a general acceptance, whilst others had to be interpreted or commented upon or modified in order to suit local circumstances. Thus the 'Shulchan Aruch' ('The Prepared Table'), a major legal code composed in the 16th.-century by Rabbi Yosef Karo in Safed in Palestine, had to be revised and commented on by Rabbi Moses Isserles of Krakow, Poland, before it could be wholly adopted by *Ashkenazim*.

Exactly how, when or why different customs arose is a matter for scholars to debate, but that they did — and that the different groups developed their own languages — cannot be denied. Many of the arguments in the Jewish world today centre on attempts to apply rulings made in a different era and culture, without realising the long tradition of adapting such rulings to local conditions.

(One should not forget yet further groups who do not totally fit these larger definitions — the relatively isolated Jewish communities developed their own customs also in India, in China and in Ethiopia, and when members of such communities came to settle in the State of Israel there were many obstacles to mutual understanding to be overcome. Some of these divisions are so old they pre-date much of rabbinic Judaism. Then there are the *B'nei Menashe* and other groups of 'lost Jews', some of them descendants of those who hid their identity during the time of the Catholic Inquisition — a group called '*Shavei Yisrael*' seeks out all over the world small groups of people, tribes in jungles and mountains, who all — apparently — have some claim to Jewish origins many centuries and many generations ago and whose status would need to be clarified so that they can emigrate to Israel if they so wish.)

Perhaps the only thing on which all these different groups agree is that their own tradition is the only correct one and all others are deviations from it! In fact there has always been a basic form of Jewish self-identification that goes something like this:

'**I** myself am the only real, proper and correct Jew.
To my Left — huh! — are various radicals and atheists and troublemakers and
assimilationists;
To my Right — oy! — are various extremists and naive fundamentalists;
But **I** am the only one who is right in the Middle!'

This is a near-universal perspective — each rabbi for example thought that he (it was
usually a 'he') had the right to present his own ideas on various texts, and that he
was right whereas all his predecessors were unable to see what he sees. The amazing
thing is that, on the whole, the communities still function with this individualistic
pluralism.

In the 18th. century a further division was made between those *Ashkenazim* who followed the teachings of *Chasidism*, an ecstatic, semi-mystical sect based partly on the
personality cults of certain '*Rebbes*' and '*Tzaddikim*' ('Righteous Ones'), and those
who opposed this trend — the opponents being called by the Hebrew term '*Mitnagdim*', 'Those who are Opposed'. The split was often a bitter one, with accusations of
heresy and formal excommunications a not-uncommon feature.

This schism remains a bitter one to this day, though in England and in many
countries it is often disguised by the reliance on the *Chabad-Lubavitch* movement —
a *Chasidic* and quasi-messianic sect — to provide many of the communal facilities
the rest of the (non-*Chasidic*) community has failed to prioritize.

Thus in some communities one finds Lubavitch-trained rabbis in positions leading
congregations formed of non-*Chasidic* Jews, so weak and ignorant that they frequently do not even realise that they are in fact originally of *Mitnagdic*, anti-*Chasidic*
tradition. *Lubavitch Chasidism* (in Hebrew, '*Chasidut*') — which is actually only one
group of *Chasidim* among many — therefore becomes 'normative' by default. Within Israel or North America however, not only do *Mitnagdim* still battle with *Chasidim* but the different *Chasidic* sects — each following a particular '*rebbe*' or dynasty,
usually named after the town of origin in Eastern Europe — also fight continuously
with each other. Satmarer, Gerer, Bratslaver, Belzer and other groups frequently see
each other as bitter enemies.

The purpose of this brief historical review is to demonstrate how at any point in
Jewish history there have been different groups competing with each other and how
labels have often been applied by opponents but then adopted by those being so
labelled.

The argument frequently heard even today, that 'Reform' and 'Progressive' are
somehow 'splitting the community' or 'diluting Judaism' merely demonstrates a
comfortable ignorance of how the communities have always functioned.

[See also the later Appendix 5 on the relationship to other denominations.]

4. ORIGINS OF REFORM JUDAISM

To understand the origins of Reform Judaism one needs to understand a little of the intellectual and social history of the 18th. and 19th. centuries in Europe.

The French Revolution of 1798 and its aftermath — the brief invasion of most of Western and Central Europe by Napoleon's armies — changed the entire basis of European society. Itself based on the ideas of the 'Enlightenment' — ideas such as the Equality of All Men — the revolution turned the Subjects of Absolute Kings into Citizens of Nation States, entitled to think and to decide certain matters for themselves. [N.B. The issue of Women's status took a little longer...] Established Religion — that is, the Churches — and Established procedures were overturned.

Wherever Napoleon's armies managed to stay long enough to influence matters — not in Russia or Egypt for example, but in the Netherlands, Germany and Italy — ghettoes were abolished and all citizens were granted equal rights.

It would be an exaggeration to say that Democracy ruled — women's rights, for example, remained very limited — but the State was perceived as owing its inhabitants certain rights of citizenship which they had not had before.

In a sense one can define 'Western Europe' even now as those countries which were influenced to some extent by these developments even if, like Britain, they were not actually invaded, and 'Eastern Europe' as those countries which were not. Does the State exist to serve the citizen, or does the citizen exist merely to serve the State? The political changes of December 1989 formed, maybe, a long-delayed reaction to the events in France in 1789. Much of more recent debate about what counts as 'Europe' and what count as 'European values' — the arguments about whether countries from the former Soviet bloc can be incorporated or whether a Moslem country such as Turkey can be integrated into a Continent which for the past centuries has been (theoretically) Christian, are vague reflections of this revolution.

In those countries which remained under the dominion of Emperors with absolute powers and Churches with absolute powers neither intellectual nor religious freedom flourished. For the Jewish population this meant that they remained largely in the ghettoes, cut off from secular education or political influence, living self-contained lives in self-contained communities. Their rabbis and religious courts had complete power over the members of the communities and life was lived, where possible, in isolation from the 'outside world' which was viewed (justifiably) with fear and mistrust.

(One and a half centuries later one witnessed the rise in large areas of Europe of 'counter' movements whereby an Emperor was replaced in Spain, Italy, Germany, Russia etc. by a Dictator and a Church by a Party, but the essential structures remained very similar — and their consequences. The First World War led to disenchantment with belief in a Monarch in Germany and Russia and the replacement of the Monarch by the Leader. The Second World War effectively began as the attempt by the absolute leader of one of these countries (who, ironically, had actually been elected), in alliance with others, to attack first those neighbouring countries which had remained democratic and then another major dictatorial bloc — the democratic countries ended up with a short-term necessary pragmatic compromise, supporting Russia against Germany and Italy. The end result was that Germany was defeated but Russia was not — until economic as well as political factors decades later led to a fragmentation of the Soviet Bloc. Even now there are those who are trying to restore it. This VERY brief analysis merely serves to show how the surviving Jewish communities in Bulgaria, Poland, Romania, the Soviet Union, Yugoslavia etc. retained these centralised and politically-hierarchical structures, subservient to the State.)

In contrast, in Western Europe Jews gradually gained more and more rights — to settle, to engage in occupations previously closed to them, to own property, to enter the universities and technical schools, to enter State service and political life and to become established citizens.

Of course there were problems — and anti-Semitism — but here the 'outside world' was often now seen as something attractive, which could and should be joined on its own terms. This usually meant not only the learning of German culture and literature, but also for many even conversion to Christianity to enable full integration (or assimilation).

It is worth noting, when Reform Judaism is accused by its opponents as 'leading to Christianity', that it began in part as a reaction against the trend towards conversion, as an attempt to find a 'middle path' between remaining in the ghetto of isolationism and losing one's Jewish identity totally through assimilation.

5. BEGINNINGS IN GERMANY

In 1801 Israel Jacobson, a banker in Westphalia (now North-Western Germany) opened a non-sectarian boarding school at Seesen. Jewish and Christian boys and girls studied together, religious services were held and in 1810 a small synagogue was opened. (Incidentally, the Jews in Westphalia, which was for a time ruled by Napoleon's brother Jérome, were granted citizenship in 1808 and the Jews in Prussia in 1812.) At this synagogue — effectively the 'school chapel' rather than an independent congregation — some of the prayers were recited in German as well as in Hebrew, some hymns were sung in German, the services were abbreviated and a choir and organ were introduced. In addition a sermon was delivered each week, in German.

In his Dedication Speech on 17th. July 1810 Jacobson drew a distinction between Religion — from a Universalist viewpoint — and Custom. The one required encouragement, the other could be changed or dispensed with if necessary:

'Who would dare to deny that our service is sickly because of many useless things, that in part it has degenerated into a thoughtless recitation of prayers and formulae, that it kills devotion more than encourages it, and that it limits our religious principles to that fund of knowledge which for centuries has remained in our treasure houses without increase…

On all sides, enlightenment opens up new areas for development. Why should we alone remain behind?'

In 1808 Jacobson opened a similar school in Kassel and here was held the first 'Confirmation' service for boys.

In 1815 Reform services were held in Berlin, in private homes, and in 1817 a community, the 'New Israelitisch Temple Association', was founded in Hamburg by sixty-six members. This could be said to be the first actual Reform synagogue, for its lay members produced their own prayerbook, established services for circumcisions, weddings and so forth, as well as Daily and *Shabbat* services. They produced their own constitution which declared, among other things:

> 'The undersigned [...] plan to arrange in this city, for themselves as well as others who think as they do, a dignified and well-ordered ritual according to which the worship service shall be conducted on Sabbath and holy days and on other solemn occasions, and which shall be observed in their own temple, to be erected especially for this purpose. Specifically, there shall be introduced at such services a German sermon, and choral singing to the accompaniment of an organ.
>
> ... also a religious ceremony shall be introduced in which the children of both sexes, after having received adequate schooling in the teachings of the faith, shall be accepted as confirmants of the Mosaic religion.'

We see here the desire for dignity and decorum, for solemn rituals, for sermons in the vernacular, for better music, for equality of the sexes and for the ability to introduce new rituals as well as to discard old ones. In essence, much of this remains basic to Reform Judaism today.

Further important changes were made to the translations of prayers, so that references to a 'redeemer' were replaced by 'redemption' (i.e. a better future age, rather than a personal Messiah). The prayer in the *Mussaf Amidah* for the restoration of the sacrificial cult in a rebuilt Temple was replaced by one asking that prayers be acceptable as an alternative to sacrifices. Transliterations were made in the *Sephardi* rather than the *Ashkenazi* style of Hebrew pronunciation. There have been many Reform prayer books since, but all have followed these basic principles.

There was much opposition to these changes, some of it very bitter. In 1823 the Berlin Temple was closed down by the Prussian Government, following pressure from traditionalist Jews. At the same time interest in the Scientific Study of Judaism (*die Wissenschaft des Judentums*) grew — the desire to study the origin and development of the Bible and rabbinic literature, the way that customs and liturgies had grown and been adopted, the way that each age had adapted and adopted forms of Jewish worship and practice appropriate to its needs.

In short 'Judaism' stopped being seen as a single unchangeable and monolithic fixture, to be accepted wholly and unquestioningly, but was to be seen as an evolving and living religious tradition — and one capable therefore of further evolution and development.

Throughout this period tentative changes and reforms were made to the liturgy in synagogues in Vienna, Copenhagen and various parts of Germany. (Remember, 'Germany' itself did not exist as a unified state until 1870). In a series of rabbinical conferences held in Braunschweig (Brunswick) in 1844, Frankfurt in 1845 and Breslau in 1846, Leipzig in 1869 and Augsburg in 1871, many theological issues were argued out — this was important, since many of the original impulses to reform had come from laymen rather than rabbis. Matters such as belief in the Messiah, use of the vernacular in synagogue services, use of organs or mixed choirs, the religious status of women, definitions of 'work' and observance in relation to Sabbaths and festivals, all required debate. In most cases the debate continues still — a healthy sign.

The Augsburg Conference abolished for Reform communities the status of '*Agunah*' and '*Yevamah*' — women condemned by circumstances beyond their control to remain in a half-way state between widowhood and marriage.

The 1848 revolutions in Europe and their failure led to the emigration of many liberal-thinking intellectuals, especially to America. Some Jews sought less-radical reforms and their efforts eventually coalesced into what is now called the Conservative (or '*Masorti*') movement, also very strong in the USA but also reviled by Orthodox opponents.

The 'Breslau Rabbinical Seminary' was founded (by Zacharias Frankel, the major originator of Conservative Judaism) in 1854; the 'Hochschule for die Wissenschaft des Judentums' in Berlin, 1870; the 'Hebrew Union College' in Cincinnati, USA, in 1875; the 'Jewish Institute of Religion' in New York, 1922, (HUC and JIR later merged in 1950 and established branch campuses in Los Angeles in 1954 and Jerusalem in 1963); and the 'Jewish Theological Seminary of America' (Conservative) in 1886 (with a later branch 'Neve Schechter' in Jerusalem). It trains rabbis for the Conservative (*Masorti*) Movement.

The first two of these were destroyed in the Holocaust. The latter two have expanded their campuses, and the Leo Baeck College was founded in London in 1956 by survivors of the Berlin Hochschule to provide a replacement European centre for the training of non-Orthodox rabbis.

In Hungary a 'Neolog' movement was founded in the late 1860s, strongly influenced by Zacharias Frankel and this movement still exists and maintains a rabbinic seminary in Budapest. There have been and are other training academies for rabbis.
The 'Reconstructionist' Movement (based on the teachings of Rabbi Mordechai Kaplan) was accepted into the WUPJ in the 1980s and has had since 1968 a seminary ('Reconstructionist Rabbinic College') in Philadelphia. In Argentina a Conservative 'Seminario Rabinico Latínoamericano' was established in Buenos Aires in 1962. It should be noted that a rabbi with '*Semicha*' (Ordination) from any of the

above may take a post in a congregation belonging technically to a different Movement — and that individual rabbis may place themselves on the more traditional or the more radical wings of each of these movements. There is scope for individualism and flexibility.

Unfortunately the title 'Rabbi' is not legally protected in many countries and it is possible for someone to use this title even if his or her *Semicha* is not recognised by the major international rabbinical organisations such as the CCAR ('Central Conference of American Rabbis') or RA ('The Rabbinic Assembly') or MARAM ('*Mo'et-set HaRabbanim HaMitkadmim b'Yisrael*' — the Progressive Rabbis in Israel) or the 'Assembly of Rabbis' of the MRJ ('Movement for Reform Judaism' in Great Britain). Some others — such as the 'Rabbinic Conference' of the 'Liberal Judaism' movement in Britain, or the RRA ('Reconstructionist Rabbinic Assembly') are more lenient and inclusive to what is referred to as 'Private *Semicha*' — i.e. ordination granted outside these established institutions with their rigorous academic and personal training.

One must be aware that there are also, regrettably, 'rogue' institutions which issue certificates of ordination without offering any real training at all, except by internet, fax and in return for 'tuition fees'.

The issue is that, while any Jew may teach another Jew, only those whose qualifications are fully accepted by his or her colleagues may sit on a Court and take part in a *Beit Din* as a Judge. This involves more than mere knowledge of texts. Not everyone who has studied First Aid is a Doctor! And not everyone who has a degree in Jewish Studies is a Rabbi. Not everyone who learns Latin becomes a Roman. And one cannot learn every job merely by correspondence course or Internet.

Within the world of Orthodox Judaism there are similar issues regarding the acceptance of a person's qualifications. The training of a 'Chabad'-Lubavitch *Chasidic* rabbi, for example, is shorter and would not match the requirements of a traditional European Yeshivah. Since in Germany the 'Einheitsgemeinde' are meant to be neutral and inclusive (something which not all of them have actually learned!) it can occur that a Gemeinde employs a 'Chabad' rabbi on the basis that they think he is 'Orthodox'. In other countries too 'Chabad' rabbis have been employed, often more on the basis that they look like the stereotypical expectation of what a 'Rabbi' looks like in old paintings (black hat, black suit, black beard) than because their attitudes and knowledge are of real help to their congregants.

6. BEGINNINGS OF REFORM JUDAISM IN ENGLAND

The first Reform congregation in England, the 'West London Synagogue of British Jews' began in a very individual way, not really influenced (at first) by the movements described on the Continent. Instead, as its name implies, it was established to provide a synagogue in the Western part of London (at a time when the main congregations were in the City, in the East) and to remove the distinctions between the *Ashkenazi* (still called 'German') and *Sephardi* (still called 'Spanish and Portuguese') communities. The members of the new community were now proudly 'British'!

The enormous influx of refugees from Eastern Europe still lay some four decades in the future; according to scholarly research there were about 35,000 Jews in England by 1850, of whom around 20,000 lived in London. A Sabbath census in 1851 showed that only about 3,000 attended synagogue.

It was not, therefore, a community distinguished for its piety or learning. However, as its members gained in wealth and status some of them moved from the East End of London to the new and fashionable West End. To walk to the synagogue on Sabbath now became rather difficult (though Sir Moses Montefiore continued to do so throughout his life) and eventually a group of members of 'Bevis Marks' (the *Sephardi* synagogue built near the former Beef Market in the City of London) petitioned its Council to establish a 'branch' congregation in the West End. This they declined to do and, after some further squabbles, a 'breakaway' congregation was formed instead in March 1840. This incorporated both *Sephardi* and *Ashkenazi* members from the 'Hambro' (originally 'Hamburger') synagogue — representatives of those who had, over the past decades, been complaining about the excessive length of the services at their respective synagogues, the lack of decorum, the lack of regular sermons in a language they could understand, and so on.

Some slight changes had been introduced over the years, but not enough to satisfy everyone. Also, one of the rules of the *Sephardi* synagogue had been that no other competing community should be established anywhere in London — and this rule was still rigidly applied, even though London had expanded a great deal in the period — over 200 years — since the rule had been made. (The congregation had been founded in 1657).

Although some reference had been made to the 'Reform' congregation in Hamburg and its practices in earlier correspondence, on the whole it appears that this split was due solely to internal English attitudes. The reformers' ideas were largely concerned with the services, not the theology. They wished the Sabbath service to be shortened to two-and-a-half hours (!), abolish the *Aliyot*, shorten the *Siddur* etc.; They also proposed to abolish 'Sacred days which are evidently not ordained as such in Scripture' — meaning not only the abolition of the Second Days of Festivals but also a rejection of the rabbinic authority — the Oral Law — which had introduced them.

The changes made in the liturgy however, as represented by the new prayerbook '*Forms of Prayer*', were comparatively minor. The first edition of this book was published in August 1841; the sixth in 1930; part of the introduction to the 1841 edition is reproduced on pages xiv and xv of the seventh edition of '*Forms of Prayer*' of 1977 [**and see pp.1-4 in the eighth edition of 2008**]. Other sections stress the importance of the Bible as opposed to the Oral law, and acknowledge the importance of contemporary German scholarship — the *Wissenschaft* movement — especially inasmuch as their researches had shown how the liturgy had developed in the past and was therefore not unalterable.

Reflecting the universalistic and optimistic outlook of the day and the movements towards political emancipation being made in Britain, the Introduction refers to some prayers which 'owe their origin to an age of persecution, and to a state of suffering and degradation now fast disappearing, and every trace of which will, by divine aid, speedily be effaced.'

Aramaic passages such as the *Kaddish* were translated into Hebrew and a Prayer of Thanksgiving by a mother on the birth of her child was added. There were a few other minor innovations. An English translation of the prayers was also provided — possibly for the first time in any *Siddur* — indicating that this community wanted people to understand what they were saying.

In this edition prayers for the Messiah and the restoration of the Temple were in fact retained. However, by demonstrating that prayers could be added and removed, that services could be shortened whilst retaining their meaning, that it was important to understand the prayers and that even women could have something to say — the outlines of reforms are clearly expressed. Nevertheless it should be noted that an organ was not introduced until 1859 and men and women sat separately until 1918. In other words, change and reform didn't start and stop in 1840, but continued.

In September 1841 the *Ashkenazi* and *Sephardi* authorities issued a joint ban on the new congregation, labelling as a sinner anyone who used the '*Forms of Prayer*'. After some manoeuvrings this ban was lifted in 1849. However, opposition and hostility continued. The congregation was forced to purchase its own cemetery and the 'Board of Deputies of British Jews' refused to certify the minister, Rev. D. W. Marks, as a Marriage Registrar. Eventually the West London Synagogue was authorised to perform marriages by a special Act of Parliament in 1856 — and this is still the basis of the authority of all other British Reform synagogues.

In 1870 the congregation moved to its current building in Upper Berkeley Street near Marble Arch. From 1845 to 1897 a day school existed, originally established by West London although it was independent and supported by a government grant. Boys and girls were confirmed at age 16. In 1886 the congregation was able at last to send a representative to the Board of Deputies and in 1887 to make a financial contribution to Jews' College. Earlier, in the 1860s, there had existed a fund to train ministers by sending likely candidates to institutions in Germany. In 1888 the three-yearly cycle of *Torah* readings was introduced, as was the practice of reading the *Haftarah* in English. However, in other respects the congregation remained quite conservative.

Although there was apparently a group of 'reformers' in Hull in the 1850s, the second Reform synagogue was founded at Manchester in 1856 and another was founded in Bradford in 1873 — apparently at a time when either Leeds or Halifax could also have provided an equally-viable base — and the initiative came from Jews who had immigrated from Germany. Apart from this, and a few other minor murmurings, Reform in Britain did not expand or gain strength until the 1930s when an influx of European non-Orthodox Jews fleeing Nazism led to a complete reappraisal. Having made the initial breaks, mainly on grounds connected with the synagogue rituals and without a fully-argued theological position, Reform slumbered...

It had broken the Orthodox establishment monopoly, but didn't seem to know where to go from there.

7. OTHER DEVELOPMENTS

There were other developments in the Jewish world at this period. In 1870 the 'United Synagogue' was formed by a confederation of three of the major *Ashkenazi* congregations. Ironically, in some respects it modelled itself upon the Anglican structures, the ministers were subservient to a Chief Rabbi who conducted himself like an Archbishop and many even dressed in clerical collars and robes. It wished to be Orthodox and at the same time 'English'. An 'authorised' prayer book was published. From the 1880s a vast wave of immigration from Eastern Europe led to the whole face of the Jewish community being changed, with an influx of people who were much more 'Orthodox' than the Orthodox congregations already existing — so that they set up their own little communities, clustered around the eastern suburbs of London. Most were eventually merged into a 'Federation of Synagogues'.

In the 1890s an independent group of radical-thinking Jews around Claude Montefiore coalesced into the 'Jewish Religious Union' which, after being discouraged by the West London Synagogue, went its own way and became the 'Liberal' Jewish movement (later the Union of Liberal and Progressive Synagogues 'U.L.P.S.' and now 'Liberal Judaism'). In consequence of this the Reform and Liberal movements have remained separate, though often on closely parallel lines of development, ever since, with much co-operation at some levels and at one period in the early 1990s even discussions on merger.

8. LATER DEVELOPMENTS

In 1929 Rabbi Harold Reinhart was appointed as Minister of West London Synagogue. He had been trained at Hebrew Union College at Cincinnati and brought with him some of the ideas and dynamism which characterised the strong Reform movement that had developed in the USA. In 1934 a 'Community Centre' — one of the first to be built next to any synagogue in the country — was opened.

A new prayer book was published in 1930 — the Sixth edition — which was radically different from the previous versions. References to the restoration of Jerusalem, the return to Zion and the Messiah were removed and the *Shabbat* morning service shortened so as to last about an hour-and-a-half.

New congregations were formed in Edgware and Golders Green in North London and in Glasgow and, as the 1930s progressed, several rabbis arrived as refugees from Europe and were established in communities. They brought with them the German 'Liberal' attitudes, which tended to be more traditional and at the same time more intellectual. This influx continued up to and immediately after the War.

9. POST-WAR PROGRESS AND DEVELOPMENTS

In 1942 the six then-existing congregations formed an 'Association of Synagogues of Great Britain' (the word 'Reform' being deliberately omitted). Its objects were to:
'... promote and foster a robust and virile Judaism which will contribute to the

life of the entire Jewish community, and which will play its part, together with other religions, in the spiritual and physical betterment of mankind.'

In other words, Reform was seen as an integral part of the historic Jewish continuum rather than as a 'radical fringe' and the pluralist view of the many ways in which God could legitimately be served was clearly stated.

In 1946 the 'Youth Association of the Synagogues of Great Britain' (YASGB) was formed as an umbrella organisation for the various youth clubs run by the congregations. In the 1970s it was re-named 'RSY-Netzer', the RSY standing for 'Reform Synagogue Youth' — note the dropping of the geographical label — and 'Netzer' being an acronym formed of the initials of the Hebrew 'No'ar Tzioni Reformi' or 'Reform Zionist Youth' — it is also Hebrew for 'a new young shoot'.

The Youth Department today organises a variety of educational weekend seminars and summer and winter holiday schemes in the UK, Europe and in Israel.

An 'Assembly of Ministers', later the 'Assembly of Rabbis' was formed, to enable the ministers of the various congregations to meet regularly and to standardise procedures in relation to marriages, divorces, conversions etc.

Further communities were established in Hendon, Wimbledon, Cardiff, Bournemouth, Southport and Leeds during the 1940s, in Maidenhead, Ilford, Brighton, Southgate, Harlow and Wembley in the 1950s, and expansion has continued to the present.

10. R.S.G.B. — M.R.J.; U.L.P.S. — L.J.; W.U.P.J.

In 1955 the title of the 'ASGB' was changed to 'Reform Synagogues of Great Britain' ('RSGB'). For many years the offices of RSGB remained based at West London Synagogue. After outgrowing the facilities there and after a brief period in an office at Swiss Cottage they were transferred to 'The Manor House' in 1982. This is a complex of buildings in Finchley, North London, formerly a Roman Catholic convent school and known officially as the 'Sternberg Centre for Judaism'; its official address is: 80, East End Road, London N3 2SY.

It is also the home of, amongst other organisations, the Leo Baeck College; an independent Conservative Synagogue (the 'New North London'); the youth movement 'RSY-Netzer'; of the 'Centre for Jewish Education' (CJE), an educational resource and training organisation sponsored by the Reform and Liberal movements; a Student Activities Coordinator, organising some (minimal) student chaplaincy; welfare and educational events; the MRJ *Beit Din* (to which the European *Beit Din* of the EUPJ is attached); and of the first Reform Jewish Day School in the country, the 'Akiva School'.

In 2005 the RSGB was reorganised as the 'Movement for Reform Judaism' (MRJ). This is run by a Council on which are (theoretically) representatives of each of the constituent synagogues, and an Annual General Meeting (normally held as part of a residential weekend conference) at which policy is discussed and decided.

Each synagogue is assessed for a financial contribution that it must pay to cover the central of the organisation, but each remains also fully autonomous and independent (and often rebellious!), setting its own subscription level, appointing its own minister and running its own affairs. In this respect they are much more independent that those which belong to the United Synagogue, a much more tightly-centralised body.

Other MRJ activities include the 'Israel Action' department with the services of a full-time dedicated *Shaliach* (Emissary) from Israel; a Social Action group, a Music Adviser, a Caring in the Community Committee concerned with developing welfare networks, and a Congregational Development Committee to encourage further growth; groups devoted to the improvement of communal leadership, or to social or political issues; and a Publications Committee to arrange production of pamphlets, prayer books and educational materials.

The Reform Movement, in conjunction with the parallel 'Liberal Judaism', whose headquarters are at the 'Montagu Centre' at 21 Maple Street, London W1T 4BE, is a constituent of the European Board (or 'European Union of Progressive Judaism' — E.U.P.J.) of the 'World Union for Progressive Judaism' (W.U.P.J.), an international representative and campaigning organisation whose headquarters are at 13, King David Street, 94101 Jerusalem. 'Friends of Progressive Judaism' raise funds and provide assistance for groups and congregations in Europe and Israel.

11. THE RABBINATE

In 1956 the 'Jewish Theological College' was established in London — a shoe-string operation with just two students, operating from the Cheder classrooms of West London Synagogue. It was however an attempt to fill the gap caused by the destruction of the centres of Jewish learning in Europe during the Shoah. A year later it was re-named the 'Leo Baeck College' following the death of the rabbi who had led the German Jewish community in the last years up to the war, had survived imprisonment in Theresienstadt and had then settled in London, urging the establishment of such a college.

Since then the College has produced a large number of rabbis, so that almost all those now serving English Reform, Liberal and some *Masorti* synagogues, plus some working as 'Movement Rabbi' or in other communal roles and many of those serving in Europe are graduates of the College. As such they are graduates of an institution that has been influenced by the great German centres of the 'Science of Judaism', by the atmosphere of academic freedom and individual search that imbued European universities and by the post-war realities of Jewish life in Britain and Europe.

The Assembly of Rabbis meets regularly to discuss policy or responses to events. It elects each year an Executive and Chairman but there is no 'Chief Rabbi' and no other hierarchy.

Matters of personal status are dealt with by the *Beit Din*; apart from the (part-time) Convenor and a secretary, this is formed by members of the Assembly sitting *ad hoc* as required, sometimes forming a 'Standing Committee' to adjudicate complex cases. There are no full-time judges or *dayanim* or apparatchiks.

Members of the Assembly also work on the production of new liturgy and publications. In recent decades new *Yamim Noraim* (High Holy Day — in 1985) and *Shabbat* and *Shalosh Regalim* prayer books have been produced.(In 2016 yet another new High Holy Day *Machzor* is in process of preparation.)

12. REFORM PRACTICE TODAY

With all its inherent inconsistencies Reform Judaism in Britain today reflects still the varied influences upon it — the inherent divisiveness of the Jewish community throughout the ages, the tensions between the Bible and later rabbinic interpretations, the Enlightenment and the revolutionary concepts of human rights and human equality, the academic and scientific approach to the study of religious customs, the politics of Anglo-Jewry, the relationship between the Jewish and non-Jewish worlds in Britain, Europe, the Middle East… In short, it bears the marks and scars of its development and its history.

Some of the major differences between Reform and Orthodox Judaism today are:

(a). The Oral Law (the entire corpus of *halachic* thought and literature) is seen as a human construct rather than as a part of the original Divine revelation on Mount Sinai. As such it is interesting and informative, but Reform does not feel bound by the decisions of rabbis who lived in different countries and periods and who were addressing themselves to their own contemporary situations. Where the traditional *halachic* view still appears relevant it will be applied, but where this is not feasible — or where our viewpoint has changed radically — a way needs to be found to keep our Judaism relevant.

An important principle in traditional Judaism has always been a degree of pragmatic flexibility, enshrined in the phrases '*leChatchilah*' and '*B'di'avad*' which can best be summed up as 'In theory it should be like this' and 'But in practice it is like that.' In other words, the rabbis had their ideals but they also learned to bow to the inevitable. The question comes: When is the right point not only to accept the reality of what people are doing, but to embrace it and make it into a new principle? For example: In theory, everyone should be able to read and understand Hebrew; in practice, we need to have translations, we need the vernacular; In theory, everyone should keep *Shabbat*; in practice, we have to establish service times for when we know people may be able to come; And so on. This does not mean having No standards, but having the ability to judge when a formal change can be justified and introduced. Naturally, to find agreement on such matters even between members of an association of rabbis will always be a difficult and long-drawn-out process. Which brings us back to the principle: 'Only **I** am right…'

(b). An example of this change is that men and women are considered to be completely equal. This means not only that women may sit in the synagogue with men, not only that their voices may be heard in mixed choirs, but also that they may lead services and even be ordained as rabbis to lead communities. (In 2015 there were some initial hesitant steps in some small Orthodox circles to go in the same direction.) Boys and girls are taught the same syllabus towards *Bar-Mitzvah* and *Bat-Mitzvah*. (The earlier practice of Confirmation at age 16 has largely died out, though still retained in Liberal synagogues.) Women may choose to wear *Kippah* and *Tallit*. A Bride also speaks at her wedding and is not passive.

(c). Services commence at times convenient to the congregation, rather than being tied to the hours of sunset and sunrise. (This is more practical in northern latitudes.) Since synagogue services on *Shabbat* are relatively more important in the Reform movement, *Shabbat* Evening services are longer that those in Orthodox synagogues and may include a sermon, whereas those on *Shabbat* Mornings are shorter — without a *Mussaf*. Prayers are read together, with greater stress on decorum; prayers are read in the vernacular (English) as well as in Hebrew (though the Aramaic *Kaddish* has been reinstated to replace the Hebrew one). Service times for the different congregations may be found in the Leo Baeck College Diary or online.

There is musical (and instrumental) accompaniment to the hymns, but not necessarily musical performance of the prayers by a cantor. The *Torah* reading is shorter and more educational, following the three-year rather than the one-year cycle; the *Haftarah* is read in English.

One can no longer say that a sermon in English is something distinctive, since this is a reform that has been widely adopted by Orthodox congregations too!

(d). Ancient concepts of tribal identity, especially those relating to the priesthood (*Cohanut*) are no longer considered relevant. Reform does not look forward to or pray for the restoration of the Temple, the sacrificial rites and the priesthood. In practical terms this means that we do not allow *Cohanim* extra privileges in *Aliyot*. They also have no duty to bless the congregation (the ancient blessing being read by any rabbi or layman as appropriate); they are also relieved of restrictions and may enter cemeteries and they may marry divorcées and converts.

Prayers for the restoration of the sacrificial system and study passages relating to the Temple worship, the lamps, the incense etc. are omitted from the service.

(e). Conversion to Judaism, whilst not being treated casually, is seen as a viable option for most people, especially if they are considering marriage to a Jewish person. The demands placed on a potential convert are designed to reflect those placed on congregants as a whole, rather than some intimidating ideal.

(f). Although there is a belief in the survival of the Soul after death, there is no longer belief in the Physical Resurrection of the Dead at the time a personal Messiah appears. Accordingly a Body may be cremated, a post-mortem examination may be carried out and organs may be removed for transplant to other patients, without any problems.

(g). The *Beit Din* procedures reflect a lenient view on most situations — on condition that those applying to it have displayed sincerity and commitment to the best of their ability. A *Get* can be issued to release a man or a woman from a marriage when civil proceedings have been completed, even if the other partner refuses to co-operate in the religious divorce, once other avenues have been exhausted.

(h). Personal observance is encouraged rather than enforced. Whilst the Sabbath and festivals are important, it is no longer felt that the opening of a refrigerator or the carrying of an umbrella profane the Sabbath and new approaches to the celebration of festivals have been sought to take into account the fact that few modern suburban Jews keep to the strict agricultural calendar of the Ancient Near East.

(i). Reform Judaism allows scope for <u>the informed educated individual</u> to make his or her own choices regarding personal observances. This is <u>not</u> the same as allowing complete anarchy but a way of acknowledging that the individual informed conscience is the basis of Jewish identity.

CHAPTER 4

THE LAYOUT OF THE SYNAGOGUE

1. INTRODUCTION

The word '*Synagogue*' simply means in Greek a 'Meeting Place'; A Jewish community would raise funds to rent or buy or build a room or a separate building, to have a Community Centre and here teaching and preaching and praying and socialising could take place, the exchange of news, the catering for travellers, a communal Library and Bath House and other facilities. So the terms '*Beit Knesset*' or '*Beit HaKnesset*' (a 'House of Meeting'), '*Beit HaMidrash*' ('House of Study') and '*Beit Tefillah*' (a 'House of Prayer') are used, often interchangeably. In Yiddish the term '*Shul*' ('School') is used, focussing on the educational element.

A Reform or Liberal synagogue can take a variety of forms. Some have been built specifically for a congregation; others have been converted from buildings originally constructed for another use. Some congregations meet in rented public halls and some services are held in private homes. Sometimes a different venue is used for Festival services than for *Shabbat* ones, simply for capacity reasons. There is no uniformity of design or layout. It follows that the layout of a service will vary widely, reflecting either the facilities and space available or the desire to experiment. (One can of course hold a service outside a synagogue, even in the open air, but here we wish to explore the 'normal' infrastructure.)

Some synagogues are elaborately decorated, with stained-glass windows and specially-constructed pews. Others are severely practical, with plain stacking chairs and little decoration. In some there are Memorial Plaques to the departed relatives of members, or Holocaust memorials. In some the donors of specific items are mentioned, either on the items themselves or in a special book or on a plaque listing donations. Policies vary between communities.

As a practical matter most synagogues have a shelf or table near the entrance on which are placed spare *Siddurim* (prayer books), *Chumashim* (Chumash — the five Books of Moses), *Yarmulkes* (also called *Kippot*) and *Tallitot* for the use of visitors. It is also normal to have a table at which *Kiddush* could be made, with glasses of wine or grape juice for all those who wish.

In general one can say that, where there is a proper room available and a full formal service is to be held, there will be the following:

2. CHARACTERISTICS OF A REFORM SYNAGOGUE

a). No division will be made between the seating provision for men and women but all will sit together. (In Orthodox synagogues the men and women are separated — either by a *Mechitza*, a screen which separates the genders, or a balcony (or even a separate room) to keep them apart. In nearly all of these cases the women end up with a worse view of the proceedings and more difficulty in hearing the service than do the men.)

b). The *Sefer Torah* (or, if the community has more than one, the *Sifrei Torah*) will be placed at the front, in a cupboard known as the 'Ark' (or 'Holy Ark') ('*Aron Ha-Kodesh*'). This Ark may be decorated in some way and may be covered with a curtain called the *Parochet*, itself often embroidered with various decorative symbols such as the Lion of Judah or the symbolic 'Crown of the *Torah*' ('*Keter Torah*') or the two Tablets of the Law. Modern designs often focus on images of nature, the *Torah* as a 'Tree of Life', or on flames. The cover could be of any colour but during the High Holy Days most communities would hang up a white *Parochet* and also have white covers for the *Sifrei Torah*.

c). There may be a pelmet over the *Parochet*, on which it is common to embroider in Hebrew an appropriate motto — possibly '*Da Lifnej Mi Atah Omed*' — 'Know Before Whom You Stand' or '*Ivdu et-Adonai b'Simcha*' — 'Serve the Lord with Joy'.

d). Over the Ark or in front of it will be placed a light — whether in the form of an electric or oil lamp or even a candle — known as the '*Ner Tamid*' or 'Eternal Light', a symbolic memory of the fire that was kept constantly burning in the Temple.

Sometimes other lamps symbolising the *Menorah*, the six-branched lampstand of Temple times, will be placed on the *Bimah*.

e). In the Ark will be kept one or more Scrolls ('*Sefer Torah*' or '*Sifrei Torah*' — literally 'Book(s) of the *Torah*'). Each scroll consists of sections of parchment or skin sewn together and sewn at the ends onto two wooden rollers — the '*Atzei Chayim*' (singular: '*Etz Chayim*'), 'Tree(s) of Life'. The scroll contains the full text of the five Books of Moses: Genesis, Exodus, Leviticus, Numbers and Deuteronomy; or *Bereshit*, *Shemot*, *Vayikra*, *Bemidbar* and *Devarim*. The text is hand-written by a trained Scribe (*Sofer*) without any vowels or punctuation or chapter or verse numberings.

The scroll is often bound with a knotted '*Mappa*', a length of cloth, though nowadays there are elasticated versions with clips for ease of use, and dressed in a protective cover, often decorated, and ritual decorative silverware comprising (usually) a breastplate ('*Choshen*') reminiscent of that once worn by the High Priest; a Pointer ('*Yad*'), literally 'Hand', so called because it is usually shaped like one and is used to point to where one is reading so as to avoid unnecessary finger contact with the letters, which could cause them to be stained or damaged; and either a crown ('*Keter*') or two sets of bells on bulbous covers for the tops of the *Atzei Chayim*, known as '*Rimmonim*' (literally 'Pomegranates' because of one traditional shape).

Scrolls in Oriental *Sephardi* communities are usually mounted in a wooden protective case instead, which is opened and the scroll is read from whilst it stands upright in the case rather than laid flat on the desk. There may be a crown rather than *Rimmonim* on top.

f). The service will normally be led from a Reading Desk on a slightly-raised platform known as the '*Bimah*' ('Platform') or '*Almemar*'. In many traditional synagogues the Reader, the one leading the service, stands on a central *Bimah* surrounded by the congregation and faces the Ark; in the majority of Reform synagogues the reader stands on a *Bimah* at the front, before the Ark, facing the congregation. In a sense this reflects a distinction as to whether the reader is a '*Shaliach Tzibbur*', the person representing the congregation to God, or is acting as teacher and preacher, representing God to the congregation! But it also reflects the pedagogic nature of the service and the importance of being heard, especially when preaching.

g). Improvisation. In modern times it is often necessary to use an adapted room originally built for other purposes, or to meet in a private home, or to use a multi-purpose room. In such cases one must be pragmatic and flexible. It is not always possible to orientate the room towards Jerusalem. If there is no *Aron Kodesh* for the *Sefer Torah*, then it can be laid instead on a table and covered with a cloth or a *Tallit*. If the ark has a curtain in front of it, then this effectively separates the 'holy' part of the room from the rest, used for other activities, and no further curtain is necessary, unless one wishes for security reasons to keep the scroll and other items where they are safe from disturbance.

h). Decoration. As already mentioned decoration is optional and not necessary for the good functioning of the building. Some buildings will have stained-glass windows — a common theme for such may be the twelve tribes or some Biblical quotations. Other buildings will have security windows with strengthened glass designed to protect those within from attack from without!

3. FIT FOR PURPOSE

When a room or building is improvised, one has to make the best of it. When however one is specifically designed and built, then one can only hope that the result will be one that helps those who wish to pray, to pray, and those who have come to hear, to hear. The main purpose of having a reading desk is that whoever is leading the service can be seen and heard and can in turn see and hear the congregation. There is unfortunately a tendency to build modern synagogues to impress, as 'representative' buildings or architectural masterpieces; what is often then forgotten is that one actually needs good acoustics, ventilation, lighting, heating, access to cloakrooms, wheelchair access, proper shelving for prayer books or leaflets, storage for *Tallitot*, an entrance which combines a welcoming openness with the requirements of modern security, a place for children to play, easy access from the kitchen to the *Kiddush* room, and so forth. We suspect that very few architects or those organising architectural competitions have ever tried to pray or to lead a service in a synagogue (or change a failed but inaccessible light bulb!)

(The author recalls officiating in a modern synagogue with a glass roof; when the sun shone, everyone sat in a sauna; when it began to rain, the noise from above was deafening… Also at synagogues where the sun shines right into the face of the officiant through a special window during services, or the reading desk stands in a pool of shadow whilst all around is bright; or there is just one window that can be opened for ventilation and, almost invariably, someone will come in late, walk straight to that place and close the window because they do not wish to sit in a draught…!)

PART TWO: JEWISH PRAYER

CHAPTER 5

LITURGY, PRAYER AND THE STRUCTURE OF SYNAGOGUE SERVICES

1. INTRODUCTION

We aim here to look at different parts of the *Siddur*, to help the reader to feel 'at home' with it, to understand how the services work and what the sequence of the individual services is. The aim is to give a partial overview of some of the differences between the Reform and Orthodox prayer books currently in use and, by paraphrase, to illustrate the sequence of thoughts within the services.

1 References: After some thought the translations and page references in this chapter and later in this book are taken initially from <u>both</u> current versions of '*Forms of Prayer*'; first from the 7th. edition published by RSGB London 1977 (ISBN 0 9505920 0 5) known colloquially as 'the *Siddur*' and still used in some constituent synagogues of the MRJ; those cited in **Bold** are from the **8th. Edition**, which was substantially revised and published by the Movement for Reform Judaism in 2008 and is now more widely used (ISBN 978-0-947884-13-0). The revision included a new gender-neutral translation. Citations in **Bold Italics** are from '*Siddur Lev Chadash*' used by the Liberal Movement in Great Britain — published ULPS London 1995/5775, full title '*Siddur Lev Chadash*: *Services and Prayers for Weekdays and Sabbaths, Festivals and Various Occasions*'.

(The Liberal movement in Great Britain uses for the High Holy Days '*Machzor Ruach Chadashah*' (2003) — page numbers are not included here but it is hoped anyone using these books will find their way through the following notes as well. '*Lev Chadash*' means 'a new heart' and '*Ruach Chadasha*' means 'a new Spirit'.)

2. THE SYNAGOGUE SERVICE AND PRAYER

(A). THE CREATION OF LITURGY

The *Torah*, indeed the whole *Tanakh*, hardly ever mentions prayers and never mentions synagogues. Instead the *Torah*, after describing in Genesis various offerings on altars — starting with Cain's — focusses in Exodus and Leviticus on the rituals for the mobile Tabernacle ('*Mishkan*') as used in the desert; later a fixed Temple was constructed in Jerusalem in the reign of King Solomon (the '*Beit haMikdash*' — 'House of Holiness'). Individuals such as Isaac and Rebekah (Genesis 25:21f.), Jacob (Genesis 28:20f.), Hannah the mother of Samuel (I. Samuel 1:11-14 and Ch. 2) or Manoah the father of Samson (Judges Ch.13:8) or the Psalmist(s) address God directly, sometimes in petitionary prayer, but these are exceptions. So there is no FIXED ritual, no single 'right way to pray as God told Moses to do it.'

No-one really knows when and how and by whose influence the synagogue services developed. Suffice it to say that by the 8th. century CE it seems that there were some 'standard' prayers as well as many local variations.

But whoever did develop this, whoever these unnamed geniuses were, were to some extent 'making it up as they went along'. Even in Temple times there was a need for an alternative form of worship for those Jews who could not get to Jerusalem to the Temple — often for geographic reasons, as some Jews lived well away from Jerusalem and then began to live in countries of the *Diaspora* — and since it was expressly forbidden to build any other Temples apart from this one, whatever else was created simply had to be different; It had to be a form of Jewish expression that did not involve priests and altars and sacrifices. So one could meet and sit and read from the *Torah* about what was to be done — as a substitute for actually doing it; one could sing some psalms or other quasi-liturgical Biblical excerpts; one could formulate some blessings and petitions. Then, once the Temple had been destroyed in 70 CE this informal network of 'Meeting Houses' became the successor rather than just the supplement. It became essentially the ONLY place left where Jews could still gather and worship. But how, and what should they say?

We know that several rabbis opposed the idea of 'fixing' of prayers; In discussion in *Talmud Berachot* 28b-29a Rabbi Eliezer warned 'If a man makes his prayer a fixed duty it ceases to be a true supplication' and in the *Mishnah Pirke Avot* 2:13 Rabbi Shimon bar Yohai warns 'Be meticulous with the reading of the *Shema* and with prayer. When you pray, do not make your prayers routine, but [an entreaty of] mercy and a supplication before the Almighty...' It seems it was Rabban Gamliel II (who led the surviving rabbis in Yavneh and died ca. 114 CE) who felt that the circumstances required some effort at standardisation, gathering and editing various current versions.

It may sound bizarre but one useful source for the history of Judaism in the early *Mishnaic* period is the 'New Testament' (a word applied by Christians to their scriptures — for Judaism these have no religious significance). Quite simply, the accounts here describe how several Jews of the period travelled and preached — Jesus, Paul, etc. — and how they visited synagogues or debated with others, how there were readings from the books of the prophets and occasional guest sermons and how non-Jews often came out of deep and sincere interest to sit at the back and observe. (In Luke 4:16-22 // Matthew 13:54 Jesus preaches in the synagogue in Nazareth in the Galilee and is handed the scroll of Isaiah to read aloud and to use as a basis for a '*Drasha*'; In Luke 4:31 // Mark 1:21 he performs an exorcism in the synagogue in Capernaum ('Kfar Nachum'). In 'Acts of the Apostles' there are eleven references to Paul preaching in synagogues (9:20 in Damascus; 13:5 in Salamis; 13:14 & 44 in Pisidia; 14:1 in Iconium; 17:1 in Thessalonica; 17:10 in Berea; 17:17 in Athens; 18:4 in Corinth; 18:19 and 19:8 in Ephesus; 28:17 in Rome.) This reveals a widespread network of such community centres where visitors came and, either by invitation or through mere *chutzpeh*, expressed their opinions, often starting controversial theological disputes with those who disagreed.

We do know that around the 8th century CE a community in Spain wrote a letter asking the famous Rav Amram *Ga'on* in Iraq for advice as to what they should say. (One can assume from this bald fact that the letter must have been preceded by endless committee meetings and years of bitter arguments, until somebody said 'I have an idea — let's ask a Rabbi!' Sending a letter from Spain to Iraq was also no light matter.) Rav Amram's response has been preserved (although there are differing manuscripts) — essentially he said 'I cannot really tell you what to say, but here enclosed is a copy of what we use, in case this helps.' And this is our first known intact *Siddur*!

What actually happens in a synagogue is often a cause of much concern and (heated and uninformed) debate. What prayers should be said, what MUST be said, who may say them, which ones should be said silently or aloud, together or only by the '*Shaliach Tzibbur*', which may be read in the vernacular, or which in liturgical Hebrew (which is very different to later medieval or modern Hebrew) or in Aramaic (which was the vernacular of the time)? What can be omitted and what must be repeated? Who may decide? Who may take part? Who may lead? Who may sit where? What should you do if someone makes a mistake, skips a passage, comes late?

The normal response from communal leaders, especially those who are not very secure in their knowledge, is to demand that 'Everything is equally important.' But this begs the point that not everything was written at the same time, that different prayer books include different prayers or different versions of the prayers. Are all ancient poems as important as all the Psalms? Do all the Psalms express what one wishes to express? (Psalm 94, for example, is not used used in our *Shabbat* liturgy, since it calls for God to take revenge. Traditionally it was however read on Wednesday morning services.)

One response is to turn the whole question around and instead of saying 'What one must say' ask 'What do I <u>want</u> to say? Which sections from the traditional liturgy speak to me and describe in words better than mine what I want to express, and which seem to be just meaningless?' It is not just a case of 'What must be said?' but 'What needs to be said?' We know that some people are best able to pray from a <u>closed</u> prayer book; Some find the best method is to sit in silence with their own thoughts and God's. We know that in some synagogues 90% of those present understand hardly a word of what is being said — which rather defeats the object of saying everything and repeating a lot of it — but nevertheless find some comfort just from the atmosphere, the aesthetics and the background noise, the feeling of being amongst people who are praying, or being in a place where prayers have often been said. Of course one could also point out that maybe 90% of community members rarely attend synagogue services in any case — thus indicating that the Liturgy is failing in its intended purpose of attracting worshippers and providing them with a suitable and acceptable way to pray. No-one ever seems to ask the question of what God might want to hear and whether God actually needs us to repeat the same prayers several times in each service?

We know of synagogues where, on a *Shabbat* morning, 30 minutes is required for the entire '*Pesukey DeZimra*' section, several psalms and pages rattled through at speed; where the *Torah* reading take 45 minutes with seven *Aliyot* plus *Maftir* plus '*Mi Sheberachs*' but without any indication of what is being read; when *Mussaf* adds a futher 20 minutes of chanting and muttering, most of it repeating what has (theoretically) already been said in the *Shacharit*. There is no point in discussing whether a specific blessing for Israel, the Government, the New Moon or anything else needs to be added — almost no one would notice! People are chatting, dozing... Is God even listening, if no one else is?

And yet, a *Siddur* exists to guide us in our thoughts and meditations and should hold us together as a community at prayer.

(B). PRINCIPLES OF REFORM LITURGY IN ENGLAND

For historical reasons the first *Siddur* of what became the Reform movement in Britain — that of the 'West London Synagogue of British Jews' — of 1841 incorporated both some *Ashkenazi* and some *Sephardi* elements. It is alas not unknown for some keen new convert to complain that a Reform *Siddur* is 'wrong' because some passage appears in a different form or different sequence to the 'real' *Siddur* they encountered in a different synagogue — this merely reveals their ignorance.

Every religion has its own characteristics. A standard Jewish service is full of Words, but little else — that is to say, there is very little ritual action including processions,

kneeling or bowing, dancing, use of objects, or silences. On the whole the worshipper stays in his or her place, reading words either silently or aloud, either individually or communally. Where there are exceptions to this, there is usually a specific reason — for example, to show honour to the *Sefer Torah*, or because certain prayers are traditionally said in a standing position. A service is an opportunity to say these words, but it is not a sacramental act whereby something is transformed (such as wine into blood); nothing is changed except, perhaps, the worshippers themselves.
  Liturgy has therefore developed to say what people feel needs to be said, rather than retaining for reasons of nostalgia things which no longer need to be said.

(C). TEMPLE AND SYNAGOGUE
— TWO UTTERLY DIFFERENT CONCEPTS

It is important to note that the Synagogue service, although it makes frequent reference to the Tabernacle or Temple ritual, is almost totally different to it. In the Temple there were special people — Priests ('*Cohanim*'); special places — Altars ('*Mizbe'ach*', pl. '*Mizbechot*'); and special objects ('*Korbanot*') that were sacrificed and transformed, through slaughter or burning, into forms of communication with God ('their smoke rising up to heaven'). Everything was 'holy' (*Kadosh*) and imbued with great power; if something were to have been done wrong, not in accordance with the detailed instructions as given in the *Torah*, disaster could strike — as indeed happened to two of the sons of Aharon who, for unknown reasons or inexperience, deviated from the set instructions (Leviticus 10:1-3).

  (To assist in understanding this, one could perhaps use the following simile and take a Nuclear Power Station to be in some respects a modern secular equivalent of the Temple. In this specially-constructed and very secure building complex specially-trained initiates are in touch with the elemental forces of the Universe; in consequence access for others is restricted. Through their careful actions at the Source great power can be obtained — for industry and prosperity, for healing, for the preparation of foods, for the very necessities of warmth and light. They must wear special protective clothing for their work, they must follow strict rules, take great care over the disposal of the waste matter and work on the assumption that their actions must not go wrong and that if they were to do so the consequences could last for much longer than an individual lifetime. Apart from visible catastrophes of Fire or Explosion there is also the danger of a totally-invisible but life-threatening Force (in this case Radiation) that can be released onto those who tamper with the Source. There is Power and Mystery, and the lay outsider can do no more than glimpse the occasional bits of information that are released and hope that those in charge are truly acting responsibly.)

In contrast to all this, Prayer is a 'Do-It-Yourself' way of gaining access to God; no intermediary is necessary. The Rabbis called this 'Service of the Heart' ('*Avodah sheBaLev*') — in contrast to the Service of the Sanctuary. The individual Jew may address God wherever and whenever necessary. However, it is considered that Prayer in a community is also vital — no Jew can evade responsibility by claiming that individual prayer alone is sufficient, for this leads merely to selfishness. A 'community' is defined in traditional Judaism as consisting of a minimum quorum of ten adult Jewish males and is called a '*Minyan*'. (This number is derived from two sources: In Gen. 18:31 Abraham bargains God down to accepting ten people as the minimum group for whom it is worth saving Sodom, whilst in Num. 14:27 God expresses anger at the 'wicked congregation' ('*laEydah haRa'ah haZot*') meaning the ten spies who brought back a negative report from their expedition.) Without this *Minyan* it is considered that certain prayers may not be said. Within Reform Judaism the restriction to 'men only' is dropped and we do not insist on a *Minyan* before saying prayers. Nevertheless, experience shows that it really does feel different to be worshipping with a group of others, all saying and doing the same thing, and communal prayer is to be encouraged as well as individual, private prayer.

(It is worth adding here that the attitude sometimes encountered that one is 'forbidden' to say a certain prayer such as the *Kaddish* because there are less than ten adult Jews present is a misunderstanding. One may indeed always pray alone, or in smaller groups, though it will simply not count as a *Minyan*. In the same way, one or two or more people can kick a ball about — but in order to play properly in a League match they would need a Team with eleven players; or a few people can sing privately, but to be part of a Choir they need enough members to create the desired effect. In the same way, three or four or nine Jews (with or without additional other persons present) can of course recite some prayers; the only point is that this then counts as Private and not as Communal Prayer, because the Community is numerically incomplete.)

No Jew should ever forbid a fellow Jew from praying!

There is also an issue as to whether one must always repeat exactly the same formula, constantly, or whether there can be choices of additional readings, poems, hymns, some variety to prevent the recitation becoming mechanical — as the rabbis of the *Mishnaic* period mentioned earlier feared. Here again there is debate — there are those who dismiss any suggestion of change and those who would rather experiment with new melodies, new text insertions etc. Some like the familiarity of an unchanging ritual. But — Who would go to a concert regularly if the programme was constantly the same? ('Oh no! Brahms' 4[th.] AGAIN??') Who would go to a football match if the players constantly repeated the same moves to arrive each time at the same result? There HAS to be an element of change and changeability, of excitement, of improvisation, of expecting something unexpected, of learning something new, or else the whole experience becomes sterile, a spiritless mumbling of ritual formulae without emotion or meaning and, in a word, Boring. Prayer is not entertainment — indeed the Hebrew term used, '*leHitPallel*' is reflexive and effectively means 'to work on oneself' — but a congregation that offers only boring and repetitive and incomprehensible rituals should not be surprised if worshippers fail to be inspired or supported in their own attempts to reach out to God. The regular mumbling approach is called 'Davvenning'. Sometimes people bow constantly forwards and backwards and this is called 'Shockeling'.

But why should one expect that God really wants to hear this sort of thing?

Before continuing, it is worth taking a look at what formal Worship in general meant and means. In the Temple period the assumption was that God was 'somewhere up there' (the words 'sky' and 'the heavens' are often used interchangeably) and we, down here on earth, are subject to the laws of gravity. Anything we threw up as a gift to God would come down again. So if one wished to share a ritual meal with God — a shared meal has always been a powerful communal symbol in terms of relationships — then the only way to present God with God's portion of whatever beef or lamb or poultry was being consumed was to grill it so that the solid meat was transformed into smoke and went upwards! This is really quite a simple and ingenious concept. When this option was not or no longer available, then the alternative was to create from one's own dining table a 'Mikdash Me'at', a 'Little Sanctuary' and invite God to come down to share the meal there, by involving God through blessings as the Creator of the Food and the Drink and by formally thanking God afterwards in a Grace.

In the Temple the humble worshipper could only observe from a distance and then perhaps share in a part of the roasted sacrifice; in a synagogue service however the worshippers should be participating, not just observing or forming an audience for the Cantor.

In Prayer ('Tefillah') we address an invisible Listener in the hope or belief that they are listening. Is it important whether a prayer be spoken aloud or can it be said silently and privately in one's heart? Is it important that it be in one language and not another? The history of religions, all religions, has been one of endless debates on such matters. The 'vested interests' have always been interested in maintaining their status and income and a steady flow of donations; the 'idealists' have always been more concerned with the content of what people are saying and believing than with the externalities. Within Judaism there have been many changes in the liturgy. Whilst the Torah text had to be statutorily regulated as a formal canonical universal text, no two published Siddurim are identical even if they all have a great deal in common.

In communal prayer the individuals join in reading prayers that relate to the needs of the community; the prayers are mostly composed in the 1st. Person Plural form ('We', 'Our', 'Us') rather than the 1st. Person Singular ('I', 'My', 'Me'). Traditionally prayers were recited in Hebrew — the 'Lashon Kodesh' or 'Holy Tongue' — the assumption being that everyone could understand this. However, from very early times this could no longer be assumed without question and certain prayers or affirmations were composed in the vernacular language of the time — Aramaic. In Reform synagogue services a compromise is employed, whereby some of the prayers are read or sung in Hebrew (but at a pace which allows those who need to, to follow in a decent translation) and others are read in the vernacular. The ideal is that everyone be enabled to participate in their own way, at their own level, so that prayer does not become restricted to a minority who know sufficient of the 'mysteries'. (A 'middle way' is to provide a transliteration of the Hebrew text in Latin letters, so that one can at least join in reading a text aloud, though of course without the meaning. Some find this a good idea, others less so. A language is always more than the words — it is the rhythm, tone, melody, nuances too, and someone reading a transliteration of a text in Arabic or Urdu or Cantonese will make mistakes that leave the native speaker amused or appalled.)

It is because there is no need for a 'Holy Place' that the prayers can be said almost anywhere (the Rabbis disapproved only of saying the daily prayers in an 'unclean place'), so that outside a synagogue impromptu prayer groups can also gather on trains and aeroplanes, in the homes of individuals who are sick or bereaved, at work-places or indeed almost anywhere.

Since Words form the main means of worship it is important that the words be clear and express a clear line of thought. Over the centuries various prayers have been composed, and collected in 'Orders of Service' (the word '*Siddur*' means 'Ordered').

(D). THE LANGUAGE OF PRAYER

In what language should one pray? This is not a new question. According to the *Torah* itself God only created different languages at the Tower of Babel to ensure that Mankind would not understand each other (Gen. 11:7) — but presumably God understands each. In the *Mishnah* ('*Sotah*' 7:1; see also B. *Talmud* '*Sotah*' 32a) is stated:

'The following may be recited in any language: The section concerning the woman suspected of adultery, the confession made at the presentation of the tithe, the *Shema*, the *Tefillah* (i.e. the 18 Benedictions, the '*Shemoneh Esreh*'), and the Grace After Meals.'

These were pretty basic issues — the *Shema* and *Tefillah* still form the basis of almost every service and presumably the other items were to ensure that those involved were fully informed of their rights and responsibilities. In other words, people needed to understand what was going on and be enabled to join in.

Maimonides (1135-1204) wrote ('*Hilchot Berachot*' 1:6, i.e. 'The Rules of Saying Blessings'):

'All of the *Berachot* may be said in any language, provided that one says them according to their essential character (i.e. not changing them too much)... And if one has deviated from their formula, then so long as one has mentioned the Name of God and His Kingdom, and the subject matter of the benediction, even in the vernacular, one has fulfilled one's obligation.'

So, if one has mumbled in one's own mother language something to the effect that God is Ruler of the World and loves Israel or the Sabbath or has created Food or Wine or whatever — that counts. The important thing is that one has said something to acknowledge that there is a God and that this God has done something or does something that needs to be praised and appreciated.

Unfortunately we know that there is a tendency in many religious people to prefer repetition and quantity to clarity, brevity and quality. This is manifested psychologically in all religions and is often the cause of conflict between 'extremists' with obsessive or neurotic behaviour patterns and those more moderate in their observances. It became a custom for the person leading the service to read the '*Amidah*' silently, allowing everyone else to do so, and then to repeat it 'for the sake of those who cannot read it themselves.' Is this helpful? Maimonides wrote ('*Responsum*' No. 256):

> 'Because people do not listen to the prayer leader's repetition of the Eighteen Benedictions, but talk and otherwise behave themselves in an unsuitable manner, it is sufficient if the prayer leader alone recites the Eighteen Benedictions the once, and the congregation listen to him. For two reasons: first, because the way people talk makes a bad impression on the non-Jews who sometimes visit the synagogue, and secondly, because the ignorant man, for whose benefit the prayer leader's repetition was instituted in the first place, will see how the others are not concentrating and he will himself be distracted from listening to the repetition.'

This is revealing. The impression made upon visitors to the service — not worshippers — is considered a sufficient reason to modify the service itself; but further, there were problems in maintaining concentration and pious '*Kavvanah*' and this led to disorderly conduct. Rather than just pleading for order, it was considered better and more logical to remove the cause of the boredom — an unnecessary repetition.

Similar reasoning can be found in the '*Shulchan Aruch*', '*Orach Chayyim*' 101:4. If only more 'traditional' Jews (or those who think that they are) were aware of these texts!

(E). THE IMPORTANCE OF MINHAG

It is very important to stress that no two synagogues follow exactly the same rituals, sing exactly the same melodies, or follow exactly the same customs ('*Minhagim*'). There is very rarely a single 'right way' and a 'wrong way' to do something. There are certain local traditions which are accepted here but not there, there are some things community '*Aleph*' might be willing to learn from community '*Beit*'. But do not ever fall into the trap of calling a synagogue service 'wrong' just because it is different.

Many a community has split over trivial issues of when to stand and when to sit, in which direction to bow for '*Lecha Dodi*', whether to bow first to the right and then left, or vice versa, whether one must come back from the Ark walking forwards or backwards... Enormous amounts of congregational energy are wasted in conflicts over such petty trivialities. And quite often, we observe, it is someone who has been Jewish less than five years who feels compelled to tell everyone 'what they are doing wrong'!

Some of these differences have been incorporated into the prayer books, some are just a matter of how the books are used. Some books are called *'Ashkenazi'* and some are *'Sephardi'* and some are *'Eydot Misrach'* (for Jews from Eastern, i.e. Arab countries) and there are *Chasidic* and Reform and Liberal and Reconstructionist and other prayer books. In the *Siddur 'S'fat Emet'*, produced in Switzerland for German-speaking countries, there are many, many rubrics and footnotes which advise the reader what is or is not said in communities which follow the rite established at one point in Frankfurt am Main! (This actually reflects the different sets of *Minhagim* imported by different groups of Jews from Eastern Europe.) Some Examples:

p.21. Psalmen für Schabbat v'Jom *Tov*. ('In manchen Gemeinden auch an *Hoshanah Rabba.*')

p. 36. 'In Frankfurt am Main wird nicht gesagt.' i.e. *'El Melech Ne'eman'* before *'Schema.'*

p.40. 'In Frankfurt am Main wird nicht gebetet.' (*'Go'alenu Adonai Tzewa'ot sch'mo kadosch Jisra'el.'*) in *'Tzur Jisra'el.'*

p. 42. 'In Frankfurt am Main sagt man *'Bina de'ah v'haskel'*; statt *'De'ah, binah v'haskel.'*

(Frankfurt was where Rabbi Samson Raphael Hirsch (1808-1888) introduced from 1851 his own reforms which eventually led to a reformation of Orthodox practice.)

Likewise there might be references and notes such as 'Polish Jews say this, German Jews say that.' Why? No-one really knows any more. Presumably God already knows where the worshippers come from and does not need to be reminded? In some books there are two versions of *'Modim anachnu lach'*, and usually the *Chazan* will sing one while the congregation mumbles the other. Why? Because the two versions existed and it was felt important somehow to incorporate both. In Israel a 'standard prayer book', the *'Rinat Yisrael'* with new prayers for the State of Israel, for *Yom Ha'Atzma'ut* and for IDF soldiers was published in 1970 (by *Moreshet* Publications in conjunction with the Ministry of Education). But — It comes in five different versions! (*Ashkenazi, Sephardi, Eydot Mizrach*, plus *Ashkenazi* and *Sephardi* for *'Chutz LaAretz'* — i.e. for use in the *Diaspora*.) (There are also, incidentally, sometimes different *Torah* or *Haftarah* readings for *Ashkenazim* and *Sephardim*, or different divisions within the *Sidrot*. See the Appendix on this topic.)

In England the United Synagogue attempted in 1890 to produce a 'standard' *Siddur*, the 'Authorized Daily Prayerbook of the United Hebrew Congregations of the British Empire' edited by Rev. Simeon Singer (1846-1906) for use in its constituent synagogues — the so-called 'Singer's *Siddur*' — which was 'authorised' by Chief Rabbi Nathan Marcus Adler, using Isaac Baer's '*Avodat Israel*' for the Hebrew and adding Singer's extensive translation, including a prayer for the Royal Family. This went through many editions and in 2006 was replaced by a new book, edited by Chief Rabbi Jonathan Sacks but fated to be called colloquially 'the new Singer's Book'. In America the 'Standard Prayer Book' of 1915 is basically a version of 'Singer's'. The fact that a book had to be 'authorised' tells us already how many variants were in circulation at the time and was possibly also a move against use of *Chasidic* texts.

Chasidic Siddurim may follow '*Nusach Ari*' — i.e. an order established in 1803 by Shneur Zalman of Lyadi, the founder of '*Chabad*' *Chasidism*, following the mystical teachings of the Kabbalist Rabbi Isaac Luria (died 1572) — based on the *Sephardi* rite but with different footnotes and marginal notes and meditations ('*Kavvanot*') and mystical acrostics. According to tradition Shneur Zalman compared sixty different versions of the *Siddurim* in circulation before producing his own!

Nowadays many worshippers in Orthodox services use the American 'Artscroll' series of Masora Publications, representing a form of Brooklynesque fundamentalism and using *Ashkenazi* transliterations, whereby any unaccented letter '*Taf*' is printed as 's' rather than 't' and the '*qamatz*' vowel is rendered as 'o' rather than 'a', leading to '*Shobbos*' rather than '*Shabbat*'. (In Britain most Reform synagogues decided in the 1950s to adopt the *Sephardi* pronunciation as had been adopted in the State of Israel.) It happens quite often that at a service various books are in use simultaneously, so there is little point in announcing page numbers and each worshipper must find their own way through frequent flipping of pages forwards and backwards.

The rituals are all essentially very similar, but the differences have developed and have become enshrined in local tradition. (Usually 'Tradition' has a stronger impact on people than 'Law'). Should one have a '*Hagbahah*' (elevating the scroll) before or after the *Torah* reading, or both? Should candles be lit in the synagogue at an Evening Service or not, and if so, when — at the very beginning or after an opening song — and what is one to do if the community commences evening services before nightfall in summer? Should mourners be kept outside on a *Shabbat* evening until after the 'Lecha Dodi' is sung? Should one make *Kiddush* during the service or after the service, and if during, should others, especially children, come forward as well and receive a 'blessing'? How much of the weekly *Torah* portion (*Sidra*) should be read, with how many *Aliyot* (people called up to recite the blessings) and should it be read or chanted ('*Leyned*')? If *leyned* then according to which musical tradition? — and should it be translated and, if so when, during or after the reading? Many think that a nasal oriental chanting according to '*Ta'amim*', notes which are not actually written in the *Sefer Torah* text, is more 'authentic' even though it sounds more like the Qu'ran being chanted; The *Mishnah* ('*Megillah*' Ch. 4 *Mishnah* 4) actually stresses that the reader should read and translate each verse so that those hearing can understand; with the *Haftarah* the reader should pause and translate after every three verses. Should the *Haftarah* (the reading from the Prophets) be read or sung, in Hebrew or in the Vernacular? How much Hebrew should be used, how much English or Dutch or French or German, how much Russian? Is it 'permitted' to read from a Transcription or a Photocopy? Who may 'permit' and on what basis or authority? What about music in the service, a soloist, a choir, or instrumental accompaniment? May women also sing in the choir? (In traditional Orthodoxy there is a prohibition on '*Kol Ishah*', the 'Voice of a Woman' being heard — lest it distract the male worshipper from pious thoughts.) May one walk in front of the Ark? Are children allowed in? Exactly how should you fold your *Tallit*? Should the *Bimah* face the Ark (*Aron Kodesh*) or the community? Should it be in the front or in the middle?

There are many synagogues where there is no one who can read competently from the *Sefer Torah* (the Hebrew is written without vowels) and then there are questions as to whether one 'is allowed' to read from a printed Bible instead and, if so, whether the scroll must also be laid out. In small communities — and many Jewish communities today are very small — there are issues such as what 'is allowed' when there is no *Minyan* present. (The term 'What is allowed?' reveals already the nature of the question and the questioner — they assume that someone else has the right to allow or forbid me, as a Jew, to pray in a certain way. People rarely ask 'What may I do?' but instead 'What is forbidden?' It is always very easy to forbid something, much harder to allow or to explain it.)

In a Reform or Liberal Jewish service we start from some basic principles. Once you understand these principles, many of the apparent differences become clear and logical. The service is the service, and just as in any other synagogue and in any other prayer book it consists of certain prayers, songs and readings. We use texts to help us, because it is not always easy to find the right words for ourselves. We encourage people to take part as far as possible. We read certain parts in languages other than Hebrew, to help them understand. (There is a long tradition for this — the '*Kaddish*' is read in Aramaic because that was a language people understood two thousand years ago.) In modern times this might even mean more than one language — for example, German and Russian, or German and English. We encourage men and women to take part together and not to feel excluded. We read only a section of the *Sidra* but we read it with care and with explanation, rather than reading the whole several chapters at high speed and without any explanation — which means for most non-Liberal synagogues just twenty to forty minutes of incoherent mumbling. We try to include rather than exclude. If there is no *Minyan* present we will still say the prayers. (A '*Minyan*' is understood traditionally as Ten Adult Men, but we will count Women as well.) Traditionally this saying of prayers was always allowed — it is just that it was then categorised as 'individual' rather than 'communal' prayer. (As mentioned above, a 'communal prayer service' required and requires a minimum number of participants, but one is not 'forbidden' from praying, just because only nine people have come one morning! One can still bless and praise God, still address prayers. And whilst in some synagogues the '*Shaliach Tzibbur*' will omit certain prayers — the '*Barchu*', which is a call to the community, or the '*Keduscha*' section in the *Amidah*, or the '*Kaddish*' — there is nothing to stop you saying these and other prayers for yourself.)

At the end of the day, the question is: Why are there people who are always so willing to prevent their fellow Jews from saying and doing things — especially when it is often these same people who then complain that there are so few Jews prepared to say and do these things in any case? In a small community, if people feel there is no point coming because they will in any case be 'forbidden' from saying what they want to say, one will never build up a larger group of regular worshippers. Rather than saying 'What is allowed?' or 'It is forbidden!' we should be saying 'Welcome, would you like to join in?'

(Of course, we are here considering only the participation of Jews in services. Non-Jews, and those who are converting but not yet Jewish, are always welcome to join in a service but would not take on a role in leading the prayers for others. Children before *Bar/Bat-Mitzvah* age are also technically not able to lead a prayer for adults, though in a special Children's Service all roles could be taken.)

There are some well-known stories of the ridiculous and painful situations which can ensue. In one, a new rabbi notices that his congregants always bow low at a certain point when marching around the synagogue in a procession carrying a scroll. He asks 'Why?' — but no one knows. 'It's what we have always done here, Rabbi,' they say, until eventually he learns that in the congregation's previous building there had been a low beam to which they normally came at about this verse in the processional Psalm! In another story a new rabbi sees that some congregants stand for the '*Shema*' and others stay seated, and the two groups argue loudly with each other during the recitation. Again, no one can tell him what the 'correct' local *Minhag* is until the eldest member is located in the Old Age Home, who tells him, 'Sitting? Standing? No, OUR tradition is to argue about it!'

The point is that the Prayer Book is a human construct. A Rabbi or a community has the authority to make changes or additions, or even to omit sections. This might require some discussions, some learning, there may need to be a 'Ritual Committee' for consultation and to make decisions so that conflict is avoided — issues of Authority within Liberal congregations are not always as clear-cut as in an Orthodox one, because we try to seek Consensus where possible. But — the *Torah* gives no rules about how to run a synagogue service. The *Torah* gives extensive rules as to how to worship in a Tabernacle in a tent in the desert, and later on rules were derived from this as to how to worship in a Temple in a city. But the Synagogue is never mentioned and we are free to be flexible. Let us enjoy this flexibility, whilst remaining within the basic outlines of the traditions which have developed.

(N.B. One only has to do something twice, and already it has become 'established *Minhag*'!)

3. THE ORDERS OF SERVICE

Every synagogue service (often called 'statutory services' since the Daily and *Shabbat* and Festival *Schacharit*, *Minchah* and *Ma'ariv* services were considered obligatory) consist of the same basic structure and the same basic components. The different services are then differentiated by adding specific prayers for specific needs, reflecting the different emphases on days or times of day.

The basic pattern consists of:

Bar'chu   (The Call to Prayer).

Shema   (The Oneness of God) and its accompanying blessings. (The *Shema* is however omitted in the *Minchah* Service).

Amidah   (the core service of acknowledgement, petition and thanksgiving; shortened for *Shabbat*; insertions added on Special Days);

Aleynu   (the Duty to Pray; Hope for the Future.)

Kaddish   (Glorification of God).

Everything else is peripheral, non-statutory, optional. While there are some traditional patterns — for example, specific paragraphs placed before and after the *Shema*, a hymn added at the end, various Psalms used on Sabbaths, the insertion of a '*Torah* Service' on certain occasions — the above are the essentials. If anyone were to ask how a Reform *Siddur* differed from an Orthodox one, a valid answer would be that it doesn't in any of the essentials, just in the way it handles the peripheral components, by omitting some of the medieval poems, excerpts from the *Zohar*, additional Psalms and repetitions, and by adding instead new study material and prayers, whilst retaining the basic prayers and their order.

There are of course some slight deliberate alterations in the Reform *Siddur*. For example, in the *Amidah* a personal reference to 'Slanderers' has been replaced by the more abstract 'Slander' and that paragraph recast; The names of the Matriachs are added to those of the Patriachs; in the *Aleynu* some traditional disparaging references to other people's religions have been cut out — '...for they bow down to gods of emptiness and nothingness...'; references to a coming Messiah have been toned down or omitted. These differences in liturgy and the reasoning behind them are worth further study. Nevertheless, all Liturgy is marked not just by what it says but by what it does <u>not</u> say or what it denies or rejects, as we shall see. To state emphatically that 'God is One' means that God is not 'Three-in-One'; To state that God 'loves Israel' is to reject Christian assertions that God has transferred His love from Israel to them; and so forth. By saying '*Amen*' one affirms that one agrees with what has just been said (from '*Ani ma'amin*' — 'I believe'); If one cannot agree, then one should not say '*Amen*' and one is thereby self-excluded from the group.

We can see this sequence at work by studying and comparing certain regular services. Although the Jewish day starts logically enough in the evening (when the previous day has ended!) we shall take the daily services in their sequence in the *Siddur*, using the Morning service as a basis. The sections in square brackets are extended explanatory paraphrases.

(To repeat: <u>Initial Page</u> numbers here are from the 7th. Edition; in **Bold** from the 8th. Edition; in ***Bold Italics*** from '*Lev Chadash*'. Due to the changes in translation and formulation it is sometimes necessary to mention both or all versions or to provide a paraphrase.)

Page numbers

4. THE DAILY MORNING SERVICE ('*SHACHARIT*')

4a. OUTLINE: In addition to the core structure some prayers are added that acknowledge a new (solar or working) day has started. The worshipper has survived the night with all its terrors and parallels with Death and now needs to prepare for the coming day with all its challenges.

p.213f.; **p.28**. Blessings and Meditations regarding the *Tallit* and *Tefillin*, which are traditionally worn by worshippers at the Morning Services; the *Tallit* is also worn on *Shabbat* and Festival Morning services, the *Tefillin* only on weekdays. (N.B. Do not forget that in the Jewish calendar Sunday is a 'weekday'!)

p.215. A hymn is added here; both the *Yigdal* and the *Adon Olam* are statements of belief; the former a metricated version of Maimonides' 'Thirteen Principles', the latter actually ends with the phrase '…both when I sleep and when I wake.' **p.32** (***p.29***): The '*Mah Tovu*' is an introductory sequence of verses from Num. 24:5, Psalms 5:8, 26:8, 95:6 & 69:14 expressing happiness at being able to enter the place of worship and hoping that the time is right.

p.215; **p.33**. 'My God, the soul You have given me is pure…' [i.e. I am awake again and want to thank God for that and acknowledge that God has brought me back to life after my night's sleep. Each night I 'die' in some way, but so far I have been re-born every morning by God's grace. One day, however, I will die properly and God will then take my soul and not give it back into the Body, but take it elsewhere instead. However, this prospect does not make me afraid; indeed, as long as I am still able to do so I will praise God.'] This statement of faith also denies the Christian belief in 'Original Sin' whereby one is born not with a Pure Soul but with a tainted one which needs purifying through Baptism. The Jew says that this is incorrect and unnecessary.

p.215. A sequence of seven Blessings; or in p.**33f.** the traditional series of fifteen. The '*Birchot haSchachar*' or 'Morning Blessings', omitting amongst others a traditional one that thanks God '…Who has not made me as a woman.' (On **p.33** this is replaced by a more positive one on being made in the Divine Image — which traditionally was the line said instead by women.) Incidentally, one apologia for this notorious

75

blessing, which is often rejected with great polemical dogmatism, is that the man is thanking God for having been commanded to perform so many more *Mitzvot* than a woman is commanded to do! But this explanation does not of course satisfy everyone. The woman, be it noted, thanks God for being made according to the divine will, which is also not wholly negative by any means and has therefore been adopted as standard for both (all?) genders in egalitarian versions. (See below for further discussion on Egalitarian Services.)

What is this sequence about? It could be read as relating to the physical actions one makes on waking and getting up in the morning — yawning and stretching, performing physical ablutions, rubbing one's eyes to remove the sleep from them… This is clearer in the fuller traditional version.

p.217; **p.34**. 'A Man should always be in awe of heaven…' Religious awareness should permeate one's entire life, not just public behaviour or when someone is watching.

p.217. 'Lord our God…' **p.35** 'Our Living God…' A plea for help in carrying out the above demand [i.e. Now that I am awake, I should devote my thoughts to how to use this day and to what purposes and use to best effect the good that is already in me.]

p.217. 'Master of Existence…' **p.36** 'Source of existence…' A plea for divine help in gaining a true perspective on what is and what is not important. [At this time in the morning we realise with especial force just how weak and vulnerable we are, how dependent we are on God's help to see us through the coming trials. All our achievements are really quite minor in comparison with what God can do — and everything we gain will be transitory. The only thing which will last will be the 'Pure Soul' — which will eventually have to justify its actions — a powerful warning against breaking moral and ethical laws just to gain greater worldly power or success.]

p.217; **p.37**. (*pp.30-35*): To strengthen us, we make a short time for Study, with the appropriate blessing. This is the Reform or Liberal version of the inclusion within the Orthodox service of set passages of Biblical and later rabbinic writings. Study and Prayer are considered as of equivalent importance and by including this period within the service we are enabled to fulfil the command to study each and every day.

pp.39-52; (*pp 37-48*): Songs and Psalms for use on different days. ('*Pesukei deZimra*' — lit. 'Portions of Song')

p.219; **p.52f**. 'Then David blessed…', 'The Lord does rule.' and 'Praised be Your name…' — paragraphs emphasising the sovereignty and glory of God, whose rule is eternal ('from everlasting to everlasting') and universal (including the heavens). It is our duty to thank and praise God.

p.219; **p.54**; (*p.48*): The *Bar'chu* — thus starting the formal service itself. The leader utters an imperative call and the congregation responds. [Until this point all has been merely spiritual preparation and there is much more flexibility in what can be added or omitted, but now the service itself commences.]

p.221; **p.55**; (*p.49*): 'Blessed are You...' A Morning Prayer. It is now daylight. [God forms the light — this line is based upon Isaiah 45:7, which actually stresses that God creates Death as well as light. All the animal kingdom is stirring. The creation is being renewed each morning, with parallels to the first Creation Story in Genesis Ch. 1, a poem describing the start of a new day — where first there is Light, an awareness of where it is wet and where it is dry, now the plants begin to stir, then the birds and the animals — until, last of all, human beings appear! It is only since the invention of alarm clocks that we have lost touch with the natural cycle and its daily miracle of the renewal of Light.]

p.221; **p.55**; (*p.49*): 'With deep love...' A reminder that God has chosen the People of Israel and cared for them, combined with a plea that we might be able to continue this 'special relationship', this covenant. [A new day has started — protect us in it! Help us to apply the experience of past days. 'Let our eyes see the light of your teaching', as well as the daylight.]

The prayer stresses the chosen-ness of Israel; Chosen especially 'to declare Your unity'. This leads naturally to:

p.221; **p.56**; (*p.50*): The *Shema*. Despite all the ritual excitement surrounding this passage — in some synagogues the Ark is opened, or people stand, or responses are sung chorally, etc. — this is no more nor less than a Declaration of the Unity of God, and an acknowledgement that we have a duty to keep this in mind always and to ensure that this knowledge is passed on to the next generation.

[Note that it is not a Prayer but a direct Biblical quotation from Deut. 6:4-9. It is written in the 2nd. Person Singular, each person in effect saying it to his or her neighbour. The second line is a later responsive addition, from Daniel 2:20 and is often said more quietly than the initial imperative, to distinguish it from the *Torah* text.]

There is a custom in some communities to close or cover one's eyes during the first line to emphasise that one is 'listening'.

p.223; **p.57**. The so-called 'Second and Third Paragraphs of the *Shema*'; these are also Biblical passages, quoted from Deuteronomy 11:13-21 and Numbers 15 37-41.

The Second Paragraph merely adds incentives and warnings to the basic commands of the First and is a mixture of Singular and Plural, being addressed to a group; the Third Paragraph provides a mechanism, a visual reminder for ensuring that the basic message of the Oneness of God and God's intervention in the Exodus is kept always in mind.

p.225; **p.58**. 'Your word is true…' If it were not, why would it be so important to listen to it, to keep it, to teach it? But this needs to be acknowledged, as does God's help in the past and present and the ever-present hope for God's help to rescue Israel in the future.

p.233; **p.74**; (*pp.52-61*): The *Amidah*. Originally (and still) the core of the service; known in Rabbinic times as '*Ha-Tefillah*', 'The Prayer'. The term '*Amidah*' itself is the Hebrew for 'Standing' and denotes that this position was adopted uniquely for this prayer.

Is it a prayer? It is actually a self-contained sequence of passages, some affirming God, some asking God for favours (petitionary prayer), some thanking God for providing them. It is also called the '*Shemoneh-Esreh*', Hebrew for 'Eighteen', or 'The Eighteen Benedictions' — though there are in fact nineteen! (This is a fairly typical example of the conservative tendency in some parts of traditional Judaism that makes it unable to make logical changes for the sake of consistency with reality, even down to changing the name once an extra paragraph was added!) The irony is the greater because it is accepted that these are prayers of human origin, composed within the rabbinic tradition as expressions from the heart towards God, rather than being biblical passages. On *Shabbat* there are only seven blessings, with one stressing *Shabbat* replacing the specifically petitionary prayers.

The various prayers indicate a yearning to return to some former period, some situation that has been lost — to a restoration of a justice system, a monarchy, a return of exiles — implying that it was composed in *Mishnaic* times after the catastrophes that afflicted Judaism with the loss of the Temple. There is one rabbinic source which states that Rabban Gamliel II tried to establish fixed liturgical sequences and asked Shimon haPakoli to collate various prayers into a sequence that should be said three times daily to replace the sacrifices and later asked Shimon haKatan ('Shorty') to compose an additional 19[th.] prayer against informers and heretics — this was then incorporated in what is now the 12[th.] in the sequence (M. *Berachot* 4:3); another source states that the 18 became 19 when the 15[th.] prayer was split into two separate ones, for Jerusalem and for the restoration of the Davidic throne (TJ *Berachot* 2:4). What this teaches us is that no one really knows exactly as we do not have a copy of the original '18-only' version.

To look at the component sections more closely:

p.233; **p.74**; (*p.52*): The opening line is from Psalm 51:17 and is a request to God for help and fluency in prayer. (Ironically there is a tradition in some communities of reciting the *Amidah* silently, even though this opening line asks God for help in speaking aloud! It is then often repeated aloud and at great speed 'for the sake of those who are unable to recite it themselves, so that they can at least add 'Amen' where necessary.' This turns the whole prayer experience into little more than a mumbled mantra.)

p.233; **p.74** (*p.52*): First Paragraph. Sometimes called the '*Avot*' (Fathers), it relates to God's work in History. [God's link to us is through our ancestors and specifically the Patriarchs.] (See passage 'Tradition' on p. 357 for a treatment of the ideas in the phrase 'Our God and God of our Fathers' — and p.494 for an essay on the whole service.) How would those converting to Judaism fit into this scheme? Maimonides, in his answer to a query from Ovadiah the Proselyte, specifically tells him that he should consider Abraham to be his ancestor — hence converts are traditionally given the surname or patronym '*Ben Avraham Avinu*' or '*Bat Avraham Avinu*', though in the Reform and Liberal movements we do not add the word '*Avinu*' 'our Father', as this would demonstrate publicly that someone had converted. (Though to be inconsistent we do sometimes give the surname '*Bat Avraham v'Sarah*'!)

p.233; **p.74**. Second Paragraph: Sometimes called the '*Gevurot*' ('Great Deeds'). God's power is such that it extends not only into but also beyond physical life; Death is not the end. Whereas the first paragraph has looked backwards, this one looks forwards.

(In some Progressive prayer books the phrase '*meChayeh haMeytim*' 'who brings the Dead back to life' is replaced by '*meChayeh haKol*' — 'who gives life to everything'. This shifts the entire viewpoint from the future to the present. The phrase 'those who sleep in the dust' is actually derived from an eschatalogical vision of Daniel 12:2 'And many of those that sleep in the dust of the earth shall awake, some to everlasting life ('*Chaye Olam*') and some to reproaches and everlasting abhorrence.')

p.233; **p.76**. Third Paragraph. Sometimes called the '*Kedushah*' — ('acknowledgment of Holiness'). This comes in longer or shorter forms to suit different services. It takes the form of a sequence of calls and responses, starting with Psalm 22:4 and then employing excerpts from Isaiah 6:3, Ezekiel 3:12 and Psalm 146:10.

pp.235-239; **pp.77-86**. This is a sequence of individual requests, prayers and expressions of thankfulness. The first paragraph on p. 237 (**the second on p.80**) is (so most believe — see above) the extra paragraph added later to make the total 19; it has been modified here and was originally intended as an expression of dislike of anti-Semitic (perhaps even Christian) forces. The following paragraph includes a reference to Converts — 'those who join us in righteousness.'

p.239; **p.86**: The Meditation 'My God, keep my tongue…' is not actually a part of the *Amidah* itself but a later addition composed by Mar ben Ravina and found in the *Talmud* ('*Berachot*' 17a, where several rabbis cite and compare their own compositions.) It provides in our services a chance for some silent reflection and prayer.
On Mondays and Thursdays (which were formerly market days in ancient Iraq) a brief *Torah* service may be added here. (**p.88**). This was originally for the benefit of those who came to market from outlying villages and had been unable to hear the *Torah* portion on *Shabbat* — in fact the beginning of the following *Shabbat*'s *Sidra* is read, i.e. in advance or anticipation of the main reading.

p.167; **p.310**; (*p.520*): *Aleynu*. This came originally from the liturgy for *Rosh Hashanah*. There is a tradition that it was originally composed as a Martyrs' Prayer by the Jews of Blois in France when they were being massacred. [It is our duty — not our privilege, or honour, or opportunity — to praise God. God is God of everything and everyone, but has still chosen Us in particular. Unlike others, We bow down only to the 'King <u>above</u> the King of Kings' — this title of 'King of Kings' was apparently taken by the Persian Emperor, who could not be accused of false modesty; but as far as we are concerned even he is/was only a mortal and not important enough to deserve our honour. God is portrayed as both universal and specific.] The quotation at the end of the first paragraph is from Deuteronomy 4:39.

p.169; **p.311**. 'Therefore, …' — the second paragraph of the *Aleynu*. Looking forward to a period of universal peace and universal acceptance of belief in the One God and the tasks of making the world a better place. Note — the hope is that all accept God, not that all become Jews! At the end the quotations are from Exodus 15:18 and Zechariah 14:9.

p.169; **p.316**; (*p.524*): The *Kaddish*. This is written partially in Hebrew but mostly in Aramaic — the common language of the time. It is a glorification, magnification and sanctification of God. Unfortunately this statement of faith has become associated with funerals and death, to the extent that several superstitions have arisen around it: for example, that you should not say it if your parents are still alive; or that you can say it on behalf of the Dead so as to improve their destinies; or even that you can pay other people to say it for you and to have it said for you after your own death! It probably originated as a formula to conclude lectures, became associated with the ends of sections of services, and later with the ends of funeral orations — hence the link now with Death, although *Kaddish* still exists in several different forms in the liturgy, with a shorter version ('*Chatzi Kaddish*' — 'Half a *Kaddish*') recited as a form of marker, a ritual semi-colon, to mark the end of the first part of the service before *Bar'chu* and a recitation at the end of a Morning Service before a *Mussaf* (Additional) Service, while on p.304 (**p.270**) is the longer version ('*Kaddish deRabbanan*') still used for academic occasions.

Why should the supposed link with Death have become so strong? Perhaps it is precisely when something bad has happened to you — such as the death of a relative or a loved one — that you are most likely to be angry at God, or even wish to deny God; in consequence, it is more important that you should read and say something positive. Of course, if the recitation has become something just mechanical and mechanistic, and the meaning of the words is ignored, then the use of the formula as a sort of 'mantra' or mystic incantation becomes more likely; that is precisely why it is so important for us to understand our prayers and their meanings.

p.171; **p.320**; (*p.525*): *Adon Olam*. A hymn to God's supernatural greatness and yet at the same time God's intensely personal closeness. This is the paradox underlying Judaism — belief in One God of the Universe with whom one can also have a close, intimate relationship.

p.171; **p.322**. Closing Benediction — the '*Birchat Cohanim*' from Numbers 6:24-26. In Orthodox synagogues this is read at specific times during the *Amidah* by the *Cohanim*, supposed descendants of the priestly clan, in a ceremony known as '*Duchaning*'. Within Reform it is occasionally used formally to close services.

After this fairly lengthy analysis of the 'standard' Weekday Morning Service, we can make comparison with other services to see how the same basic patterns are repeated and modified.

5. THE DAILY EVENING SERVICE ('*MA'ARIV*')

('Lev Chadash' p.13ff.)

p.227. An Introductory Reading (from Psalm 78:38) (or see **p.65**) then straight to:

p.227; **p.66**: The *Bar'chu*. The formal start of the service.

p.227; **p.67**: 'Blessed are You…' An Evening Prayer, said as the light is fading, twilight is falling, the stars are becoming visible — all at God's behest. Yet this same God also turns darkness back into light in the regular cycle of Time, so there is no need to be afraid — God is the God even of the stars (a polemic against Astrology). Several pagan religions were based on the idea of different Powers — the Sun and the Moon, for example — or a God who went to sleep at night and had to be woken by the faithful who had been left without protection during the fearful night. This is in contrast a calm affirmation of trust in the One God, who rules both day and night.

p.227; **p.67**. 'With everlasting love…' Evening can be a time of foreboding, as darkness falls; instead this affirmation confirms the feeling of security and lack of fear. [In the same way as we concentrated our minds upon Divine Teaching and Will in the morning (p.217), so we now dwell upon it '…before we sleep and when we wake' and 'both day and night', secure in God's love for the people Israel.]

p.229; **p.68**. The *Shema*. (A Rubric advises where the traditional Second and Third paragraphs may be inserted.)
p.229; **p.70**. 'All this is true…' Further emphasis on God's power and protection, even when things look dire (as at the crossing of the Red Sea) or when the mysterious enemy seems stronger than Jacob. (Possibly a reference to the encounter with his brother Esau on his return; Or the encounter with a stranger in the Yabbok at night. Genesis 32:24-30). The responses are from Exodus 15:11, Ex. 15:18 and Jeremiah

31:11. [Israel has experienced God's power in our own history; There is no need to fear.]

p.229; **p.71**. 'Cause us…' A prayer on retiring to bed, looking forward to the new day. Sleep is seen as a form of temporary Death, so that awakening is almost a return to Life. [As well as the physical covering of a blanket, cover us with peace and protection from the perils of the night. 'Guard us when we go out and come in' — i.e. When our souls go out of our bodies and return back again. This is perhaps to be understood as a wish for good dreams rather than nightmares. When we are asleep we might dream of all sorts of conflicts and adventures, encounter fearful monsters or people whom we know to be dead… and then we awake, back in our bodies again! But where were We, really, during this time?]

p.231; **p.72**. 'Blessed be the Lord by day…' or 'Blessed be God by day…' A sequence of pious thoughts on going to sleep, stressing that God is the God of both day and night, of both waking and sleeping periods, that souls are in God's care even when they have left the bodies of their previous or current 'owners'. The two quotations are from Job 12:10 and Psalm 31:6.

This is then followed by the standard *Amidah*, the *Aleynu* and *Kaddish*, concluding with *Adon Olam* with its closing verse: 'Both when I sleep and when I wake… my Lord is close, I shall not fear.'

Thus, we have the basic essential sequence, supplemented here by prayers specifically to strengthen one for the coming Night.

6. THE DAILY AFTERNOON SERVICE ('*MINCHAH*')

('Lev Chadash' p. 63ff.)

p.227. (**Or see notes on p.61 followed by Ps. 67.**) We start with a different opening reading, comprising Psalm 84:5 and 144:15. Additional Psalms may be added. *Bar'chu* is omitted. The *Shema* and its blessings are omitted, because it is traditionally recited twice a day, 'evening and morning' — i.e. at nightfall and daybreak, the Evening and Morning Services. The service then goes straight to the *Amidah* and thence follows the basic sequence.

7. THE SHABBAT EVENING SERVICE
('*KABBALAT SHABBAT*')

The weekday services reflect the weekday need to get on with things, with making a living. On *Shabbat* however there was more time, so more prayers could be added to the basic structure and readings, poems, songs… In the Temple there were additional sacrifices for the Sabbath and this is reflected in the traditional liturgy with an Additional ('*Mussaf*') Service. In line with the Reform policy of avoiding unnecessary repetition, this is not incorporated in this *Siddur*.

(In 'Lev Chadash' there are several alternative openings commencing on pages 69, 75, 79, 84 and 88.)

p.15; **p.100**. 'How good are your tents…' This sequence of introductory praises and pleas comes from Numbers 24:5, Psalms 5:8, 26:8, 95:5 and 69:14. One understanding is that these lines were to be said on actually entering the synagogue, acknowledging the glory of the place (like saying 'Isn't this place marvellous compared to my hovel / office / shop / factory!?') and hoping that one would be arriving at an appropriate time. ['Thanks to God I am in a position to come into a synagogue; I can come before the Ark in the same way as people were once able to worship in the temple; So I can now worship in this synagogue / *shtiebel* / room, full of fellow Jews; I hope that You, God, are in the right frame of mind to receive my prayers, that this is the right time to approach You with my concerns. Please respond and answer me.']

pp.15-19; **pp.96-99**. There is then a choice of modern prayers on different aspects of *Shabbat* — this choice of four options being a feature especially of this prayer book.

pp.19-23; **pp.102-110**. A choice of Sabbath songs ('*Zemirot*') (with more options available on pp. 573ff.)

pp.23-27; **pp.111-120**. there is then a choice of one of Psalms 93 to 98. These are all on the theme of singing or rejoicing, rather than specifically on *Shabbat*. [N.B. The missing Ps. 94 is an expression of anger.)

p.29; p.121; (**p.91**): *L'chah Dodi*. This is a 16th-century mystical, erotic and political hymn. The full version with nine verses can be found on pp.572-577 (pp.121f. in blue), in which can be seen the Hebrew acrostic formed from the first letters of each verse, making the name Shlomo HaLevi. (The poet was Shlomo Alkabetz of Tzfat/Safed.) At the last verse there is a custom of standing and bowing to the door, to welcome symbolically the Sabbath bride into the room. The kabbalistic image of the Sabbath as the Bride and Israel as the Groom is an intriguing one — here the Bride enters the room for the consummation of the relationship. (It is a custom in some synagogues that mourners stay outside the service until after *L'chah Dodi*, on the basis that this first part of the service emphasises Joy and might therefore grate on their nerves.)

The full text employs a large variety of biblical excerpts woven together — these include: Song of Songs 7:12; Deut. 5:12 & Ex.20:8; Zechariah 14:9; I. Chronicles 22:5; Isaiah 2:5; Amos 7:3; II Samuel 12:26; Gen. 19:29; Ps. 84:7; Isaiah 52:2; Isa. 52:1; I. Sam. 16:1; Psalm 69:19; Isa. 51:17; Isa. 60:1; Judges 5:12; Isa. 40:5; Isa. 45:17; Psalm 42:6; Isa. 14:32; Jer. 30:16; Isa. 49:19; Isa. 62:5; Isa. 54:3; Num. 26:20; Proverbs 12:4; Deut. 7:6. We see how the poet knew his Bible and pulled ideas and phrases from many places to compose a text providing comfort and reassurance. The bad times are or will soon be over, Israel should stand tall again and cease weeping.

The liturgical scholar A.Z. Idelsohn stated that he was aware of over two thousand different melodies for this piece! And that was quite a while ago…

pp.31-33; **p.124**; (**pp.89-90**): Psalm 92 (whose title specifically dedicates it for Sabbath use, although there is no reference to the Sabbath within it) and/or Psalm 93 which is a poem on God's regal power over Nature.

p.33; **p.127**; (**p.92**): *Bar'chu*.
p.33; **p.128**; (**p.93**): 'Blessed are You…' Evening Prayer (discussed above, as on p.237).
p.33; **p.129**; (**p.93**): 'With everlasting love…' (see also note re. p.239).
p.35; **p.130**; (**p.94**): The *Shema*.
p.35; **p.135**;'All this is true…' (see note on p.239)
p.37; **p.136**; (**p.96**): Evening Prayer. (see note on p.239).
p.37; **p.137**. '*V'Shamru*': Exodus 31:16-17; a reminder of the specific command to keep the Sabbath.
p.37; **p.140**; (**p.520**): The *Amidah* — in a shortened form, because it was not considered appropriate to make too many demands on God on the Sabbath. In consequence the thirteen 'petitionary blessings' are omitted, but one asking for rest is added. On p.39 the insertion of the passage from the first Creation story from Genesis 2:1-3 describing the creation of *Shabbat* is specific to this *Siddur*. The prayer 'Our God and God of our fathers…' stresses how one can serve God by resting at the appropriate time; however, we need help to clear our minds of workaday concerns so as to make the most of this marvellous opportunity.

The Meditation is added as usual to the *Amidah* itself.

Then continued with: p.41; **p310**; (**p.520**) *Aleynu*; p. 43; **p.316**; (**p.524**) *Kaddish*; p. 45; **p.318**; (**p.525** '*Adon Olam*', **p.526** '*Yigdal*') a Closing Hymn and Final Benediction.

In most synagogues there are further additions — perhaps the lighting of the *Shabbat* candles at or near the beginning, or a *Kiddush* over wine during the service rather than after it; a blessing over the children; a sermon or address or reading, possibly even a reading of the week's *Torah* portion (without the full blessings and ritual) and communal announcements — but these are all optional extras, having no bearing on the service liturgy itself.

At one period the synagogue was also used as the community's hostel for travellers, so people would eat and sleep there. This is the origin of the custom of reciting certain domestic blessings (such as those for candles or wine) in this communal environment rather than (or in addition to) at home. Nowadays those communities that retain the practice do it not for the sake of travellers but those who might not be able to say the appropriate blessings (and it is the case for many people that the community takes the role of a family.)

(There are also many misunderstandings surrounding Candles. One hears of discussions as to 'Who may light the candles?', 'May a Man light them?', claims that 'All Jewish girls should light candles!', 'May one move the candles?' and so forth. In fact what is important is Light, not how it is prepared. The idea is that on *Shabbat* one has more than the minimum single lamp, because increased light increases also a sense of joy. In ancient times a wick would be placed in a clay dish filled with olive oil. Candles are no more than an ingenious form of 'solid fuel', much easier than oil to store and not liable to spilling and incorporating the wick. Lamps — whether oil or candles — were originally provided simply to provide light to see by. Nowadays we put electric lights on and then light candles, thus defeating most of the point! The same occurs at a circumcision or a *Shivah* service — someone usually lights candles, out of a residual memory that such should be done, even though they are no longer required for their light. However, candles are alive, and flicker, and eventually use up their strength and die — just like humans. Candles can provide atmosphere on birthday tables and at romantic dinners, and in the same way they still provide a special *Shabbat* atmosphere. But the blessing for '*Ner*' (pl. '*Nerot*') is for 'a Light source', something that makes '*Or*', 'Light' — and not necessarily a tube of wax.

8. THE SABBATH MORNING SERVICE ('*SHACHARIT SHEL SHABBAT*')

The point should be clear by now; Our *Siddur* offers us a choice of various different options with different themes for the opening of the service — but all the initial sections incorporate the *Bar'chu* and the *Shema*, then all join for the *Amidah*, *Aleynu* and *Kaddish*.

9. TORAH SERVICE

The main insertion in the Sabbath Morning Service is the *Torah* Service — a self-contained sequence (pp.148-166; **pp.236-257 or 258-266**). (It can also be used, with modifications, at Daily Morning services on Mondays, Thursdays or when it is *Rosh Chodesh*, or at Festival Morning Services. The first section of the following week's *Sidra* would be read at *Shabbat Minchah* and at *Schacharit* on Mondays and Thursdays.)

The *Torah* is the basis for the entire concept of Law within Judaism (and, one could argue, subsequent religions). The idea is that God wants us to behave in a certain way and tells us what we ought to do! But the *Torah* (here defined purely as the first five Books) is much more than this, incorporating the range of cosmology, theology, the pre-history and then history of humanity in general, the story of one specific person after God has chosen to make a covenant with him and then his family through several generations; then the story of how God saved the later descendants from slavery in Egypt, led them through the wilderness of Sinai towards the land which had been promised back in Genesis Chapter 12 to Avram/Avraham, despite many setbacks and rebellions — and finally Moses' own memoirs and warnings shortly before his own death. (It is intriguing that the Book of Joshua, which largely completes the story of the Exodus by recounting how the Israelites take the land of Canaan and Joseph is finally buried at Shechem was not included to make up 'Six Books.') It was decided millennia ago (traditionally by Ezra the Scribe) that this book should be read in public on certain occasions. We see a beginning of this in Nechemiah Chapter 8 when the returning exiles had to learn from scratch what their religious duties were — because this forms the basis of Judaism and the people should hear it, even if they could not read it. In any case books were hand-written, very heavy and expensive, too much so for individuals, and it would be quite normal for a community to be able to afford only one copy.

The service comprises:

Initial readings, including from Psalm 86:8, 145:13 and 29:11, stressing God's transcendence.

A set of verses for when the *Sefer Torah* (or, if more than one, the *Sifrei Torah*) would be formally taken out of the Ark. These include: Numbers 10:35, Isaiah 2:3 and Micah 4:2. As we sing '*Ki MiTziyon teytzeh Torah…*' — 'The *Torah* will come out of Zion…' we bring it out of storage and into the synagogue. It is held during declamations (including the first line of the *Shema*, Deut. 6:4, and Psalm 34:4) and is then carried around to a processional hymn '*Lecha Adonai haGedulah…*' which itself incorporates I Chronicles 29:1, Psalm 99:5 and Ps. 99:9.

The scroll is undressed (the action is known as '*Gelilah*' and can be performed by a '*Golel*' or '*Golelet*' — this actually means 'unrolling open' or 'rolling closed') while a sequence of liturgical statements is made from *Talmud* '*Berachot*' 10a, Deut. 33:4, Proverbs 3:18, Prov. 3:17 (note the reversed order!), Psalm 29:11 and Deuteronomy 32:3. Then all would rise whilst the scroll is elevated before and/or after the reading (this is known as the *Hagbahah*, 'Lifting', carried out by the '*Magbiah*'), the chant '*VeZot haTorah…*' coming from Deut. 4:44, Deut. 33:4 and Psalm 18:30.

We now come to the actual Reading (or chanting — known as '*Leyning*'). People will be called up one by one to recite the blessings before and after the *Torah* reading and the '*Ba'al Koreh*' — the 'Master of the Reading', who has prepared — will read or chant the section.

There are complex rules as to who should be called up and how many — of course, in an Orthodox synagogue only men will be called up to an '*Aliyah*', in Reform and Liberal synagogues women may also be invited to take part in this way. Traditionally there would be first a '*Cohen*' and then a '*Levi*' and then the rest allocated to normal '*Israel*' — but a man about to be married (an '*Aufruf*') or one who has just returned from a journey or recovered from an illness (who wishes to '*bentsch Gomel*', to thank God for his safe return or healing), or one who has just become a father, or one who has just attained manhood and the age of *Bar-Mitzvah*, would be prioritised. If there was no descendant of *Cohen* or *Levi* present then someone else would be called up '*BiMkom Cohen*' — 'In the place of a *Cohen*' or likewise '*BiMkom Levi*'. Thereafter the *Aliyot* are numbered 'third', 'fourth' etc.

There would be seven *Aliyot* in a traditional synagogue on *Shabbat* morning plus a 'closing one' — the '*Maftir*'. The person called to the *Maftir* blessings is then the one who reads (or chants) the *Haftarah*. (On *Shabbat Minchah* there are only three *Aliyot*, no *Maftir* and no *Haftarah*; there are different numbers for festivals or week-days.)

One is usually called up by one's Hebrew name — as a 'regular' it may be that the *Gabbai* has a list of the names of regular congregants, in a book or a card index; as a visitor the *Gabbai* may come to you and ask if you would like an *Aliyah* and for your Hebrew name.

Once the reading from the scroll has been completed it is rolled together, there is usually another '*Hagbahah*' and it is taken to be bound up and dressed again. On Sabbath and Festivals there now come blessings for the *Haftarah*, the reading from the Prophets, read by just one person and from a printed text in a book and usually in the vernacular.

There follow additional miscellaneous petitionary prayers for the peace and wel-fare of the State or Government, for the State of Israel, for the community, for the peace of mind of various people who are in distress or mourning, and then a closing processional Hymn (often Psalm 148:13-14 or Psalm 29) following which the *Sefer Torah* is returned to its resting place to the accompaniment of '*Uv'nucho yomar…*' — from Num. 10:36, Psalm 132:8-10, Proverbs 4:1, once again Prov. 3:18 and 3:17, which refer to the *Torah* as a 'Tree of Life' — an echo of the story in Genesis Chapter 3 and explaining why the wooden rollers of the scroll are referred to as '*Atzei Chaim*', 'Trees of Life' — and Lamentations 5:32 — a plea for the past to be restored as it was. The Ark is then closed.

Incidentally the opening citation from Num. 10:35 and the closing one from Num. 10:36 relate to the wanderings of the Israelites with their portable Tabernacle which seems to have been used almost as a weapon against God's enemies!

10. FURTHER ADDITIONS

It is worth mentioning other specific 'units' of prayer, though not all are incorporated in this book.

As mentioned above, there used to be an Additional ('*Mussaf*') sacrifice on *Shabbat* and Festival days in the Temple. In Orthodox and Conservative synagogues a *Mussaf* Service will be inserted. Traditionally this described the additional animal sacrifices in the Temple and included an additional *Amidah* (but no *Barchu* or *Shema* — instead, after the *Mussaf* the *Aleynu* and *Kaddish* of the *Shacharit* were added on; alternatively, one could say that when there was a *Mussaf* these closing prayers were omitted from the *Shacharit* and said as part of the *Mussaf* to avoid duplication). In Reform synagogues a short modified *Mussaf* may be added for Festivals but normally not on *Shabbat*. (See **p.275**)

Memorial (*Yizkor*) services are added on appropriate occasions. (*p.512*)

On the Minor Festivals of *Purim* and *Chanukah*, on *Rosh Chodesh* (the beginning of the lunar month) and during the Middle Days of the festivals of *Pesach* and *Sukkot* (known as '*Chol HaMo'ed*') one adds either '*Al HaNissim*' or '*Ya'aleh veYavoh*' to the *Amidah* and after it the *Hallel* Psalms — Psalms 113 to 118 (*p.468ff.*) or a selection from them (known colloquially then as the 'Half-*Hallel*'). On *Purim* the '*Megillat Esther*' is read.

The Festival Services in general follow the basic Daily outline with specific extra prayers or observances for the festival — such as the lighting of Festival Candles, or additional *Torah* readings, the waving of the *Lulav* on *Sukkot*. The prayer '*Yehi ratzon*' is added during the *Torah* service on the Sabbath preceding a New Moon (p.162; **p.250**). As noted, the prayer '*Ya'aleh v'Yavoh*' (p.162; **p.230**; *p.59*) is added on the Sabbath that is also the New Moon (*Rosh Chodesh*) or during *Chol HaMo'ed*. On some Sabbaths there are two *Torah* readings, though incorporated into the one *Torah* Service. Guidance is offered on p.622 (**p.745**) of the *Siddur*. [See also the Appendix on the Liturgical Calendar.]

11. CONCLUSION

By now it should be clear that nothing is in the prayer book by accident. There is a logical sequence and a meaning in the order of the prayers and a significance to the presence of particular paragraphs in one service rather than another. Our Reform or Liberal services have an inner consistency and a great poetic beauty — which is lost on the one who does not bother to notice it, or who comes only for a part of the service, or who becomes bogged down instead on minutiae of what can be and must be said and when — rather than Why. If you wish to study further, beyond this brief outline, there is an extensive literature on the history of the Jewish prayers and much discussion in rabbinical literature on the importance of the right state of mind and concentration — *Kavvanah* — in which Prayer must be approached.

THREE SUPPLEMENTARY NOTES
ON MODERN LITURGICAL ISSUES

(A). A NOTE ON EGALITARIAN SERVICES

This Note is being written by a middle-aged male rabbi who is a supporter of the egalitarian principle and has himself helped to raise three children (including two daughters) but who is not a militant feminist in any way... and one who is aware of the differences that have been brought to parenthood by formula milk, disposable nappies and pushchairs — all facilities not available to parents (and especially mothers) until quite recently.

There is much misunderstanding concerning the traditional view of the role of different genders. In many forms of Christianity and Islam the same structures can be observed — and this can be briefly divided into two separate elements:

1 'Is it the Woman's role in a traditional patriarchal society to stay at home and care for the family and domestic matters?' And

2 'Does it distract the Men from their prayers if they see or hear a Woman?'

To the First — the answer is that it WAS so and in many parts of the world it still is so. Apart from a handful of known exceptions — often women who found an independent role within a religious order or through the social status of being in the aristocracy or a royal family — the fact is that, in a period before the availability of contraception and with high infant mortality, the female partner in a marriage was usually pre-occupied for a lot of the time with pregnancy, birth and the raising of children. The Bible characterises those women who had no children as being somehow lacking, as being miserable and unfulfilled. In such circumstances it was actually a benefit and not a punishment to be 'relieved' of certain time-bound duties. Women were never officially prohibited from praying, but one could not expect them to drop whatever they were doing, be it washing a child, or feeding it, or cooking, in order to be punctual for the fulfilment of a specific *Mitzvah* that had to be fulfilled at a specific time. Gradually however this Exemption came to be seen as a Prohibition — which is a clear misunderstanding.

To the Second — well, obviously the answer could be 'Yes' if a person is easily distracted by a woman, her appearance, her clothing, her voice... On the other hand, in the case of those who are not heterosexual then the same arguments could be used for others of the same gender! And there is an element of 'blaming the wrong person' — i.e. 'If I am distracted by Your presence, then You should leave' rather than 'If I am distracted by Your presence, then I must work on myself and seek ways of avoiding being so distracted.' By placing Women where they could not be seen — behind a curtain, at the back, on a balcony, wherever — and telling them that they could not stand and lead the community in prayer, the hope would be that Men could concentrate on their prayers. Anyone visiting such a synagogue will however know that this does not work!

The separation of male from female worshippers in Orthodox synagogues through a '*Mechitzah*' (a curtain or screen) or placing their seats on a different level or a balcony is actually based on an extension of just one (temporary and exceptional) measure in the Temple times. During the '*Simchat Beit HaSho'eva*', the 'Water-Drawing' ritual during the *Sukkot* festival (*Mishnah* '*Sukkah*' 5:5) the *Talmud* ('*Sukkah*' 51b — also Jerusalem *Talmud* '*Sukkah*' 5) mentions that for this event (and only for this event!) a gallery was built to separate the women from the men. This was because the celebrations lasted all night.

It would be foolish to deny that women are biologically different from men, even if one wishes to stress that they are spiritually equal, and so issues of a woman who is heavily pregnant, or menstruating, or breast-feeding, are matters that can indeed affect appearance or mood or the ability to join in (or lead) prayers at specific times. However, many Orthodox Jewish communities seem to have become little more than male clubs where the men can come to get away from their wives! Progressive Judaism sees both (or all) genders as an equal part of creation and there is no reason why a woman should not also live her spiritual life both privately and express it within the community — and this includes not only praying aloud but leading the prayers too as a '*Sh'lichat Tzibbur*'.

(B). A BRIEF NOTE ON REFERENCES TO GOD IN THIS BOOK

One of the commands in Exodus Ch. 20 (often known as 'The Ten Commandments') is in verse 7: Not to take God's Name 'in vain', usually understood to mean not to use it casually or to misuse it. This is an important concept because many people have done horrible things and committed brutal massacres 'in the name of God' — thus misusing or abusing God's name to suit their own political or racist ends.

However, it has also led to a whole range of superstitions concerning words used for God. One will find in certain books people writing 'Gd' or 'G-d' or 'L-rd' or even 'The Alm-ghty'! As a brief abbreviation when writing they will write the letter '*Heh*' with an apostrophe, signifying '*HaShem*' — 'The Name' — but then — for this is always the problem with such neuroses — one goes a step further and writes '*Daled*' plus apostrophe, so as to avoid somehow misusing the letter '*Heh*'... One may for instance find this '*Daled*' embroidered into the *Berachah* on a *Tallit*. When reading or singing in a non-worship context the word '*Adonai*' (which just means 'My Lord' or 'Sir') may be pronounced '*Adoishem*', which is a hybrid, compound and actually meaningless word. (The author has heard a cantor in a synagogue service then singing '*Adoishem*' because that is how he had studied a piece!) In fact the word 'God' is NOT God's Name — it is God's title or role, and the term for God — or for 'a god' or 'gods' — *Elohim* — which is actually a masculine plural form, is used frequently in a descriptive sense. There are other traditional euphemisms and circumlocutions, such as '*HaMakom*' ('the Place') or '*HaKadosh Baruch Hu*' ('The Holy One, Blessed be He'), or '*Ribbono shel Olam*' ('The Master of the Universe').

What IS to be defined as God's Name is the four-letter combination of Hebrew consonants '*Yud — Heh — Vav — Heh*' — known in Greek as the '*Tetragrammaton*'. No-one really knows how this is to be pronounced, because one needs vowels! Some add the vowels from **AdOnAi** to YHVH and make '*Yehovah*'; Some make '*Yahweh*'; Some try to pronounce it as though it is simply breathing, thus representing life — '*Yuhhwuh*'…Usually in the liturgy when we find this combination of four consonants in a Biblical citation we simply say '*Adonai*' — as a euphemism — and when it is used in a newer liturgical composition rather than a Biblical citation it is often abbreviated even further and printed with just two *Yuds* — and we translate it as 'God' or 'Lord' or 'The Eternal' or 'the Holy One' or 'Living God'.

The point is that one needs to have no fear of the word 'God' itself. When the *Tetragrammaton* has been used, written or printed, there is often a desire not to throw this piece of paper away but to store it (in a '*Genizah*') or place it in a box of '*Shemot*' — (Yiddish: '*Shemos*') i.e. 'Papers with the Name on them' which can eventually be buried. Thus old *Siddurim* are treated with a reverence and not just as waste paper to be burned or recycled. Now that words can be printed so easily and quickly and are not always painstakingly handwritten, there is a flood of such papers — photocopies and downloads and print-outs, usually intended to be disposable after use, and also even the possibility of calling up onto a computer screen a Biblical text, which raises the question of whether one may 'Delete' such a page! But one would much rather people concentrated on not misusing the Name in political life, rather than fussing about ink on paper.

(C). A NOTE ON GENDER IN LANGUAGE

One of the major issues facing liturgical scholars and writers in recent decades has been that of Inclusive Language or Neutral Language. A different issue to the role of either or both genders in the ritual is Equality in the Liturgy itself. Put simply, Judaism has always stressed that God is without any shape, form or gender and has forbidden pictorial representations of God; Language, however, is a more complex matter. The Hebrew language has only Masculine and Feminine genders but no Neuter. Therefore every noun (and adjective, and verb…) has to be either 'He' or 'She'. God has almost always been perceived in masculine power similes and metaphors — as 'King', 'Lord', 'Master', 'Father' — and the people as 'sons of Israel', 'sons of Jacob' and the ancestors as merely the 'Fathers', the Patriarchs Abraham, Isaac and Jacob — with no mention of the Matriarchs Sarah, Rebekah and Rachel (or, for that matter, of Hagar, Leah, Bilhah and Zilpah — and there remains the question whether should one place Rachel before Leah, because she was loved, or Leah before Rachel, because she was chronologically Jacob's first wife?)

Even words like 'You' or 'Them' must be either masculine or feminine ('*Atah*' and '*At*'…'*Hem*' and '*Hen*'). In an English translation 'You' is not problematical and one can usually modify some of these terms to make 'Sons' into 'Children' or 'King' into

'Ruler' or 'Monarch' or 'Sovereign' or to add at least some of the Matriarchs. Sometimes this works, though sometimes it destroys the fluidity of a poem, sometimes it is clumsy, and sometimes it is simply wrong. If, for example, a Biblical verse is being cited this should not be modified for the sake of political correctness. (An example is the phrase *'Bakol, mikol, kol'* in the *Birchat HaMazon*, which cites biblical verses from Gen. 24:1, 27:33 and 33:11 applied to the Patriarchs and not to the Matriarchs. So rather than adding the Matriarchs, inappropriately, one alternative is to add for them the phrase *'Heytiv, Tovat, Tov, Tov'* from Gen. 12:16, 24:16, 29:19, 30:20 — words referring to 'Good' and which in the *Torah* apply to the Matriarchs. But see the comments on this in the chapter on *Birchat HaMazon*.)

Few children address their fathers as 'Dear Parent'. There are those who consider that new prayers or new versions of old prayers should be composed and where appropriate include the Matriarchs. Some such attempts are well-intentioned, but can run the risk of disrupting a piece of poetry for ideological ends. Some Jews may have had problems with their parents and don't necessarily see the word 'Father' or 'Mother' in a positive light. In Hebrew Adjectives and Verbs may also have to be modified to agree with a changed Noun. Some modern radical versions even re-cast the blessings into the feminine form or address God as 'Yah'. Various editors of *Siddurim* have struggled to find the right balance. (*Siddur* citations here have been taken mainly from the 7th. Edition *'Forms of Prayer'* which dates from a period when this process of sensitising the reader to language issues was just starting.) For our purposes it must suffice to indicate an awareness of these issues — we cannot easily resolve them.

(As an aside — other languages also have their complications. For example: French is also divided into just two genders, as in: 'The sun rose; he was hot'; in German a Girl is officially neuter, not feminine! — as in: 'The girl came into the room; it said...')

Here for some light relief are the lyrics for a song 'The Egalitarian *Minyan*', sung (roughly) to the melody of 'Chattanooga Choo-Choo', as performed by 'The *Minyan* Boys':

THE EGALITARIAN MINYAN

'Pardon me Ma'am,
Is this the Egalitarian *Minyan*?'
'Yeah, Page 29 —
We're on the very top line.'
'I'd like to pray,
But with the members of my family;
That may be the way
To make them not stay away.'

Oh, One can render without gender all the texts of the prayers;
I like a place where girls' *Talleisim* don't attract stares.
Nothing could be fairer,
Just ignore the wearer,
Concentrate on *Mitzvot*, be a carer and a sharer!
Whether lonely or together, we can all play a part,
It's perverse to have a service where the girls are apart.
It drives me into fits,
a Shul with a *Mechitza*,
Male and Female were created both by God at the start.

In the other shul the normal rule is: 'Stay late in bed';
The folks come late, they can't relate to what's being said.
But here there is a chance
To make a great advance,
To celebrate as Jews without a great song and dance!
In the other place the ladies grace a high gallery,
The other sex must strain their necks if they want to see;
All those who want to peep'll
Become a stiff-necked people,
I weep and keep repeating that I'll end up as a cripple…

I am pained when it's explained Tradition must stay intact;
Male and female are all Israel, and that is a fact.
I find it just annoys,
To ban a woman's voice,
When there's a matter of the chatter and the clatter from the boys.
Oh, we should say and pray on every day the prayers to our God.
To separate a man and mate seems quaint and quite odd.
To be holy, on the whole
One should just think of the Soul,
So, Egalitarian *Minyan*,
Shalom, here I come !

3

PART THREE: THE JEWISH YEAR

CHAPTER 6

THE JEWISH CALENDAR

1. INTRODUCTION

All Societies have a calendar. Until you have a system for measuring time all organised life is difficult. Sports have their 'seasons', financial systems have their due dates for payments and for settling accounts, the natural world follows its own cycle and rhythms… As societies become more complex the measurements of Time need to become more exact. It was no longer enough to say 'I will see you at the next harvest time'; If you hire a labourer for a day, how long is a 'Day'? Both sides have to agree! It is not that long ago that a 12-hour working day was acceptable and expected. Birthdays were important for establishing the age of a man (for military service) or an animal (for sacrificial or taxation purposes). For many centuries the church tower with its clock or bells provided the only indication of time to a village or town and coastal places used the tides, but the introduction especially of railways in the 19th.-century led to a need for precise agreement as to when exactly a train should depart. (Arrival was often more a matter of luck! — but nevertheless important if establishing a timetable with connections.)

Any human society attempting to establish a calendar based on a regularly-repeating rhythm has to cope however with a basic problem: This planet on which we live is profoundly influenced by two celestial bodies, the Sun and the Moon — and their cycles do not coincide. This leaves several options: (a). The purely Solar Cycle; (b). The purely Lunar Cycle; Or (c). the compromise 'Luni-Solar' one — or of course (d). a complete abandonment of any attempt to make sense of the problem and the establishment instead of a totally-arbitrary system. This latter approach was adopted for example by the theorists of the French Revolution, who in 1793 developed a strict decimal system for almost everything — including time! For them, a week had ten days… a day had ten hours, an hour had 100 minutes. Their system collapsed after two years. (For the Romans a year also originally had ten months, which is why December is called 'The Tenth'; the Day was divided into 12 night and 12 daytime hours, which therefore varied in length according to the seasons. The Julian calendar was introduced in 45 BCE allowing for a normal year of 365 and a leap year of

366 days, though the regular cycle of a leap year every four years did not come until around 4CE.)

What causes this problem is that the Solar Year lasts (for the purpose of this book — we will not go to many decimal places) for 365¼ days (assuming a day of 24 hours), whereas the Lunar Cycle works on a 'New Moon — Full Moon — New Moon' sequence lasting approximately 29½ days, giving a Lunar Year of (29.5 x 12 =) 354 days. Since these numbers are not mutually divisible a certain amount of complicated 'correction' has to be applied if it is desired to maintain a regular synchronised calendar. The Moslem calendar does not make these corrections, so each year — based on the Lunar months — is slightly shorter than the solar one and a particular month will accordingly move slightly 'backwards' in relation to the Solar year. This means that a Moslem festival or the Ramadan month of fasting might fall in autumn one year, late summer the next, mid-summer the next, then early-summer, and so on.

It seems the Babylonians used a calendar based on 6 and 60 — we retain a relic of this today by dividing the hour into sixty minutes and the minute into sixty seconds. They also had the 19-year lunar cycle and counted the weeks from the new moon, every seventh day being subject to certain prohibitions, and a 12-month year with an occasional 13ᵗʰ month — clearly the Jewish calendar was influenced by this system during the period of the first Exile.

The Christian calendar, now used as the main secular calendar throughout Europe and the Americas, is essentially a Solar one but with some compromises. The months are divided into periods of days that do not correspond exactly to the lunar cycle, viz.: 31; 28*; 31: 30; 31; 30; 31; 31; 30; 31; 30; 31. (* Sometimes 29!). Because this totals 365, the extra quarter day is assimilated by adding one full day to February every fourth year — a 'Leap' year. In the intervening years the slight discrepancy of ¼, ½ or ¾ day is not great enough to cause any great inconvenience.

(It is always worth wondering whether one would be better-off being paid by the hour, the day or with a monthly salary!)

However, there are certain 'fixed points' in the Christian calendar that are fixed in relation to the Lunar cycle as well — notably the days for Easter, for which complicated tables have to be followed. There are also of course different versions nowadays of the Christian calendar (Julian and Gregorian) in the Eastern and Western churches! (The Gregorian was introduced by Pope Gregory in 1582 and involved reducing the length of a year by 10 minutes and 48 seconds — meaning an initial 'jump' of ten days to catch up). But this compromise means that there is no guarantee that the New Year, which starts bizarrely on the 1ˢᵗ of January (i.e. ten days <u>after</u> the winter solstice, which would logically have made a good solar starting point) might begin on any specific weekday. It is only Easter (which, to some extent, marks the beginning of the Christian faith) that must always span a Friday to a Monday, and therefore the festival of Whitsun, seven weeks later (like *Shavuot* following *Pesach*) bears the name 'Pentecost' (Fifty) and falls also at a weekend.

One is so used to this complexity that it barely matters any more — sometimes one has a 'long weekend' or a 'bank holiday' as secular reminders of these efforts, sometimes to general chagrin a public holiday falls on a Sunday so that there are no extra days off work…

2. THE JEWISH CALENDAR

Essentially the Jewish calendar is a Luni-Solar one; that is, the months are calculated on the Lunar cycle (allowing for occasional doubt as to the exact date of the commencement of that cycle) but it is considered important so to arrange matters that the Solar year is not deviated from too sharply. In consequence, although one sometimes speaks of a Jewish festival being 'early' or 'late' in a particular year in relation to some other secular date, it can be guaranteed that (at least in the Temperate Zone of the Northern Hemisphere!) a Spring festival will fall in Spring, or an Autumn Harvest festival in Autumn. This is achieved by inserting an additional 'Leap Month' into the year when necessary.

A further complication is the need to ensure that certain Jewish festivals which occupy fixed points in the calendar do not fall on an inconvenient day of the week — i.e. on or next to *Shabbat*. Specifically, 10th. *Tishri* (*Yom Kippur*) as a Fast Day should not fall on a Friday or Sunday (since this would interfere with practical domestic preparations) and *Hoshanah Rabba* (21st. *Tishri*) should not fall on a *Shabbat* since the pious would need to carry their willows; by extrapolation, *Rosh Hashanah* (1st. *Tishri*) should not therefore be on a Sunday, Wednesday or Friday. (Consider how it is always arranged that the moving of clocks forwards or backwards for Summer and Winter time, or the introduction of new railway timetables, is always arranged for a Saturday-to-Sunday irrespective of the actual date.)

Incidentally — Who ever decided that, from now on, THIS specific day will count as the first Monday? No-one knows. There are two books, '*Seder Olam*' ('The Order of the World' — written mid-2nd. century CE) and '*Seder Olam Zuta*' ('The Smaller book' — written later) in which the writer attempts, by counting backwards from his time through all the ages and dates given in the Bible, to arrive at the putative 'Year 0'. All cycles have to start somewhere. The only fixed points in the solar calendar are what we now call 21st. June and 21st. December — the longest and shortest periods of daylight. The Christian calendar claims to start from a 'Year Nought' when Jesus was born to the accompaniment of certain astronomical phenomena; firstly the year does NOT start on 24th. December and secondly astronomers agree that a major conjunction of planets — leading perhaps to bright lights in the night sky — occurred in 4 BCE! So no one really knows…

3. THE MONTH

One of the major units of time is the Month, known in Hebrew as *Chodesh*. This is the time between one New Moon ('*Rosh Chodesh*') and the next, a time reckoned as 29 days, 12 hours and 793 '*Minims*' (a *Minim* being 1/1080[th.] of an hour). (Note — this is just a bit more than an exact '29½ days'.)

The exact establishment of the moment of the New Moon was a matter of great sensitivity and in the Temple times was a matter for witnesses, who had to testify before the High Priest that they had seen for themselves the new crescent moon.

It is clear from the Bible that a month was normally seen as having, in round figures, 30 days; e.g. Genesis 7:11, 7:24 and 8:4 calculates five months as constituting 150 days; the Israelites mourned Moses' death for thirty days in Deut. 21:13 (hence the '*Sheloshim*' — Thirty — in current mourning practice). It is also clear from the Flood narrative in Genesis Chs. 6 — 8 (which actually appears to combine differing chronologies) that a year was composed of twelve months. However, since the Pilgrim Festivals ('*Shalosh Regalim*') were closely linked to the agricultural cycle and since they are described as falling, not when a particular crop ripens but on a specific day of a specific month, it must follow that 'corrections' were made also from early times. All of course purely on the basis of observation and calculation, without any other technical assistance.

We do not know the names of all the months as used by the Israelites before the Exile to Babylon in the 6[th.] century BCE. Exodus 12:2 refers to *Aviv* — Spring — later *Nisan*; I Kings 6:1 refers to *Ziv* — presumably *Iyyar* — as 'the second month' and 8:2 to *Etanim* as 'the seventh month'.

After the Exile the Israelites adopted the names of the months that had been in use in Babylon. These were:

Nisan
Iyyar
Sivan
Tammuz
Av
Elul
Tishri
Cheshvan (or '*Marcheshvan*')
Kislev
Tevet
Shevat
Adar.

Some of these names are used in post-Exilic Biblical books, such as Zechariah, Esther and Nechemiah. Some — *Tishri, Cheshvan, Iyyar, Tammuz* and *Av* — are not found at all in the Bible, but are used in the *Talmud* and were obviously of common useage.

4. SETTING THE NEW MONTH

As has already been mentioned, by Talmudic times the fixing of a new month depended upon a visual sighting by reliable witnesses. In the *Mishnah* ('Rosh Hashanah' 1:7) it is stated that these came before the priests; Later the *Sanhedrin* ruled on such matters. A committee of three members would assemble on the 29th. of a month and await reliable evidence. Since the lunar cycle was a little over 29½ days, and since a calendar month cannot begin in the middle of a day (but only in the middle of the night in the Christian calendar, at dusk in the Jewish one), it was necessary to decide whether the month should last 29 or 30 days — i.e. whether the extra half-day should be added to one month or deducted from it. A 30-day month was known as 'full' — '*Maleh*' — and a 29-day one as defective or 'short' — '*Chasser*'. In a year, according to the complex rules laid down in the *Talmud*, there could not be less than four nor more than eight 'full' months — so the year could be no fewer than 352 days long, nor more than 356 days. This of course led to a discrepancy with the solar year of 365¼ days, so the *Sanhedrin* had also to determine when to insert — 'intercalate' — an additional month at the end of the sequence between *Adar* and *Nisan*. This is known as 'Second *Adar*' — '*Adar Sheni*'. The lunar year is approximately 354 days, so it was hard even to correlate the length of the year, as a total of the months, with this!

Whilst local people could be informed of the New Month quite easily, the inherent difficulty of this system — that you couldn't really predict the new date until it happened — led to problems for those further afield, who could not learn of the *Sanhedrin*'s decision quickly but relied on letters or the blowing of a *Shofar* or even fire-signals from a chain of beacons. Accordingly *Diaspora* Jews developed the custom of celebrating festivals (but not *Shabbat*! And not *Yom Kippur*!) for two days, to allow for any uncertainty. The assumption was that at least one of them would be the correct one. Similar problems arose even for 'local' Jews in Jerusalem when bad weather or cloud made it impossible to see the New Moon. When a month had thirty days, the last was also celebrated as the *Rosh Chodesh* of the next month — so that certain months begin even now with two 'first days'.

Rosh Chodesh also acquired the character of a minor holiday specifically for women and some communities have a '*Rosh Chodesh* Club' for women to meet for social and educational purposes on that day.

5. THE DAY

The Day (in Hebrew '*Yom*', plural '*Yamim*' or, when combined, '*Yemei*') is the basic unit by which time is divided from the Creation story onwards. From that narrative, which describes each day as being composed of 'evening and morning' ('*Erev vaVoker*') comes the concept of starting the 'Day' at dusk and ending it at the following dusk. This is as logical as any other starting point, even though for many people a 'Day' starts when they get up and ends when they go to bed — personal and arbitrary times. Technically, in the secular calendar a 'Day' starts at a microsecond past

Midnight ('*Chatzot*') — also a fairly arbitrary point, indistinguishable from the period immediately before and after it. At least Sunset and its counterpart of Sunrise provide a clear, visually-ascertainable point in time.

Or does it? In fact the period of transition from Day to Night — known as Evening ('*Erev*') — from the Hebrew root meaning 'to mix' or 'combine' — is a gradual one, more so away from the Equator — as is the corresponding Sunrise. When it becomes important to fix the exact moment of 'Morning' — for example, when determining the time for saying morning prayers — then it becomes important to be more precise, especially when one had no clocks or watches to assist! The *Tallit* is to be worn, and the blessing for it recited, at or from the time when the colours can be distinguished and for all 'time-bound' *Mitzvot* it was of course important to be sure of the time. Whilst 'Morning' — '*Boker*' — is the general term, the actual Morning began with the 'rising of the Dawn' ('*Amud haSchachar*'). As we know, it can begin to get light long before the sun rises above the horizon. Likewise the end of Evening and the onset of Night — '*Lailah*' — was not sunset itself but the 'coming-out of the stars' — '*Tzet haKochavim*', when three stars are visible. (cf. Nechemiah 4:15, 17 — N.B. this is 4:21 in Christian Bibles.)

After midday is '*Tzoharayim*' or '*Achar Tzoharayim*' — a dual form. In most of Europe the '24-hour clock' has been adopted and so the hours are numbered from 00:00 to 23:59; in America and some other countries the 12-hour clock has been retained, and since this means that each number is duplicated one has to write '10 a.m.' or '10 p.m.' — for '*ante meridiem*' and '*post meridiem*', for before and after Midday — also known as 'Noon' (from the Latin for the 9[th.] Hour) which divides the day into 'Forenoon' and 'Afternoon'.

Sometimes a Part of a day counted as a Day — for example, a circumcision would take place at any time on 'the eighth day' following the birth, even if the child had been born almost at the end of the day. It also appears from Leviticus 7:15 that for sacrificial purposes a 'day' was calculated from morning to morning:

'The flesh of the sacrifice… shall be eaten on the day of his offering; he shall not leave any of it until the morning.'

There is even a theory that nomads in the desert often preferred to travel in the cool of the night, using the stars for guidance, and so began their journeys at Evening. Hence 'Evening and Morning'.

6. NAMES OF DAYS

This sub-heading is actually a misnomer. The Days are not named in Jewish tradition. Whilst our secular days tend to be named after ancient deities of the pagan world — e.g. Woden, Thor, Freya, Saturnus — Jewish days are just numbered 'First Day', 'Second Day', etc. — counting of course from the end of the *Shabbat*. A festival will be known as 'The Day of…' (Blowing the Horn, of Atonement, etc.) In this case the article transfers to the adjectival noun, so we have '*Yom haTeruah*', '*Yom haKippurim*', '*Yom haAtzma'ut*', etc.)

Days of the Jewish Week:

Yom Rishon, First Day
    Corresponding to Saturday night and Sunday
Yom Sheni, Second Day
    Corresponding to Sunday night and Monday.
Yom Sh'lishi, Third Day
    Corresponding to Monday night and Tuesday
Yom R'vi'i, Fourth Day
    Corresponding to Tuesday night and Wednesday
Yom Chamishi, Fifth Day
    Corresponding to Wednesday night and Thursday
Yom Shishi, Sixth Day
    Corresponding to Thursday night and Friday
Yom Sh'vi'i, Seventh Day (*Yom Shabbat*)
    Corresponding to Friday night and Saturday.

When calculating an anniversary — for example a Hebrew birthday or a *Yahrtzeit* — it is therefore necessary not only to know the secular date but also the time of day — since if someone died, say, after dusk on a Monday, that would be *Yom Sh'lishi* and not *Yom Sheni* (the third, not second day of the week) and the Hebrew date would be different.

7. THE WEEK

The Week, *Shavuah* (pl. *Shavuot*) is a further basic unit of time — running from the end of one *Shabbat* to the end of the next, i.e. seven days, not quite one quarter of a lunar cycle. It is accepted, for example, that a week's mourning is '*Shivah*' — 'Seven'.

In some documents the dating is provided by reference to the *Torah* portion read on the *Shabbat* that falls at the end of that week — thus 'On Day Four of *Shabbat Lech lecha*, the seventeenth day of the month…' There are in fact 54 different *Torah* sections, *Sidrot* or *Parshiyot*, and their name is usually applied to the *Shabbat* on which they are read and the six days leading up to it.

8. THE YEAR

The Hebrew Year, '*Shanah*' (pl. '*Shanim*') is (theoretically) counted from the date of Creation — hence the Latin term '*Anno Mundi*' — the 'Year of the World'. (According to this, the world was created in the autumn of 3760 BCE). Many and varied calculations have been made over the centuries to determine the exact point in time (or non-Time) at which this occurred, usually by calculating backwards from 'known data' — e.g. the life spans given in the Bible. This is of little practical use; it suffices to know that the the number of the Hebrew year, currently in the 58[th.] Century, is meant to represent this concept. (At the end of 1999, when many people were worried about a potential 'Y2K' catastrophe, the author of this book was asked by a journalist 'what the Jews thought about the year 2000'; I had to say that it was such a long time ago, we had totally forgotten it…) There are no 'Eras'. When referring nowadays to the secular year, it is customary to add the letters 'BCE' or 'CE' — meaning 'Before the Common Era' and 'the Common Era' — rather than 'BC' and 'AD', which reflect a Christian understanding of time whereby the birth of Jesus marked a new beginning, a year '0'.

It is clear that there were different opinions as to when the Year started and finished. In fact, there were different 'New Years' in *Mishnaic* times for Kings, Animals, Trees — and Years. This corresponds with current secular practice, whereby vehicle registrations, the ages of racehorses, tax calculations, school and college years, railway timetables and a whole host of other matters all have their own, fairly arbitrary, starting dates. The result of the differing opinions is that the first Month is *Nisan* but the Year actually starts in *Tishri* — the seventh month — i.e. in Autumn rather than Spring!

In ancient times dates were often fixed in 'the such-and-such-year of the reign of King So-and-So'. Even now the reigning monarch has an 'official birthday' which is not the same as their biological one.

One issue is that different prayers for precipitation are included in the *Amidah* — the tradition is to pray for dew ('*Tal*') during the summer while the crops are ripening and for rain ('*Geshem*') during the winter when the earth needs to be kept moist. Summer is defined as from *Pesach* to the end of *Sukkot*, i.e. *Shemini Atzeret*, inclusive, and Winter the rest.

Unlike some cultures Judaism has never named the Years but only numbered them. In the Bible dates are given only relative to some event or age — the Exodus, or the reign of a ruler — and our numbers are therefore of later calculation. Because Hebrew has no symbols for numerals, but uses letters also for numerical values, the highest being only for 400, it is difficult to write thousands; the custom is therefore to use a system known as 'the short counting' — figures are usually written abbreviated and one adds the letters '*Lamed*', '*Peh*' and '*Kuf*' — the '*LePerek Katan*' — 'Short form'.

This means simply knocking off the first digit so that the year '5776', for example, becomes just '776' and is written as '400 + 300 + 70 + 6' — In letters '*Taf*' + '*Shin*' + '*Ayin*' + '*Vav*'. Every now and then the sequence of letter-numerals creates what could be seen as a word rather than a meaningless jumble — rather as car-licence plates create words sometimes — and when this word might seem unpleasant, as for example 5744 (in 1984) which turned into what could be read as '*Tashmad*' — Destruction — the sequence is altered by pious or superstitious persons! This practice is religiously equivalent to numbering a house 12A rather than 13… or to the 'Millenarianism psychosis' whereby people think the world will end suddenly at a 'round number' such as 1,000 or 2,000…

The Jewish year can have 353, 354 or 355 days; Leap Years, which occur seven times in every nineteen year cycle, can be 383, 384 or 385 days long.

9. THE LEAP YEAR CYCLE

As already explained, corrections have to be made if the lunar and solar years are to keep roughly in step. This was done by 'intercalating' a month, the decision to do so being made by the *Sanhedrin* or a committee thereof. Around the middle of the fourth century CE the Patriarch Hillel II established the formal pattern of the calendar. The basic rule is that the lunar cycle lasts for a period of nineteen years. 19 x 354 days = 6,726, whereas 19 x 365 days, the solar equivalent = 6,935 days. This leaves a discrepancy of 209 days every 19 years, which discrepancy is 'corrected' by adding another 30-day month into the third, sixth, eighth, eleventh, fourteenth, seventeenth and nineteenth year of each such cycle. This month is called an 'additional *Adar*' so on 'Leap Years' there is no 'normal' *Adar*, normally of 29 days, but instead two months, *Adar I* ('*Adar Aleph*') and *Adar II* ('*Adar Bet*'), each of 30 days.

However — although the year ends with *Adar* and so it is logical to add the extra month there — the extra month is actually inserted BEFORE the normal *Adar*! In such years the festival of *Purim* falls on the 14th. of *Adar II* — although a 'Minor *Purim*' may be observed on the 14th. of *Adar I*. It is therefore clear that the extra month is in fact *Adar I*, which is inserted between *Shevat* and *Adar* rather than between *Adar* and *Nisan*! For most purposes, e.g. calculating the *Yahrtzeit* of someone who died during *Adar II*, the equivalent date in the only month of *Adar* in a non-leap year would be used; If someone died in an 'ordinary *Adar*' the *Yahrtzeit* would be observed in *Adar II* in a leap year.

In a 'short year' (irrespective of the Leap Year Cycle) the month of *Kislev* has only 29 and not 30 days; in a 'full year' *Cheshvan* has 30 rather than 29 days. There are thus three types of Year, plus three variants for the Leap Year (which may be 'short' but also have an extra month) making six variants in all. By these means the remaining discrepancy between the solar and lunar cycles is absorbed. Easy!

10. EQUINOX

The vernal and supernal Equinoxes (the Latin term for the points in spring and autumn when the nights are equal in length to the day — exactly 12 hours each) — are know each as '*Tekufah*'— the word signifying when the balance of the seasons changes. This Equinox date is usually noted in published diaries.

11. THE CALENDAR DIARY

The Hebrew term for such a list of dates and times is '*Luach*' — originally a tablet or board. (The two stone tablets which Moses received on Sinai are called the '*Luchot*', in plural.)

Luchot come in many forms but are considered of vital importance by observant Jews since a good one will include a large amount of information necessary for observing the 'time-bound' *Mitzvot*, as well as giving the equivalent Hebrew dates for secular ones. One can buy them each year from various publishers, usually from summer onwards.

12. THE SHEMITTAH YEAR

Technically this is only relevant to the Land of Israel but of course affects those who wish to purchase products imported from Israel that are labelled 'Free of *Shemittah*'. The seventh year in each cycle — also called the Sabbatical year — is a year in which, according to the *Torah*, the land should lie fallow and not be tilled and only what grows of itself may be harvested.

This is based on Exodus 23:10-11:

> 'You may plant your land for six years and gather its crops. But during the seventh year you must leave it alone and withdraw from it. The needy among you will then be able to eat just as you do, and whatever is left over can be eaten by wild animals. This also applies to your vineyard and your olive grove'

and Leviticus 25:1-7:

> 'God spoke to Moses at Mount Sinai, telling him to speak to the Israelites and say to them: When you come to the land that I am giving you, the land must be given a rest period, a sabbath to God. For six years you may plant your fields, prune your vineyards and harvest your crops, but the seventh year is a sabbath of sabbaths for the land. It is God's sabbath during which you may not plant your fields, nor prune your vineyards. Do not harvest crops that grow on their own and do not gather the grapes on your unpruned vines, since it is a year of rest for the land. [What grows while] the land is resting may be eaten by you, by your male and female slaves, and by the employees and resident hands who live with you. All the crops shall be eaten by the domestic and wild animals that are in your land.'

Moses in Deuteronomy 31:10-13 repeats the command and several prophets complain angrily that the system is not being followed and that the Israelites, by breaking this law, are therefore forfeiting their right to stay in the land — see Jeremiah 34:13-14 and II Chronicles 36:20.

In modern Israel there is apparently a custom now of officially 'selling' the country to a non-Jew so that the agricultural industry may continue on the basis that it is not, for this specific period of time, 'your land'!

13. THE JUBILEE

After seven cycles of *Shemittah* comes the 50th. Year, known as the *Yovel* or Jubilee, marking the end of a specific era and the return of all property to its original owners and the liberation of all slaves. Based on Leviticus 25:8-13, which states:

> 'And you shall number seven sabbaths of years unto you, seven times seven years; and the space of the seven sabbaths of years shall be unto you forty and nine years. Then you shall cause the trumpet of the Jubilee to sound on the tenth day of the seventh month, on the Day of Atonement you shall make the trumpet sound throughout all your land. And you shall hallow the fiftieth year, and proclaim liberty throughout all the land unto all the inhabitants thereof: it shall be a Jubilee unto you; and you shall return every man unto his possession, and you shall return every man unto his family. A jubilee shall that fiftieth year be unto you: you shall not sow, neither reap that which grows of itself in it, nor gather the grapes in it of your vine undressed. For it is the Jubilee; it shall be holy unto you: you shall eat the increase thereof out of the field. In the year of this jubilee you shall return every man unto his possession.'

There is much scholarly dispute as to whether this idea — wonderful in theory — was ever actually carried out in practice and whilst the *Shemittah* concept is kept alive by Orthodox authorities in Israel, the Jubilee has been quietly allowed to lapse.

12. CONCLUSION

A full understanding of all the complexities of the Jewish Calendar is properly reserved only for those with a knowledge of astronomy. The variables mentioned in the Introduction mean that seconds count and the stately motion of the spheres provides a sequential pattern that only emerges over a long period.

For the average Jew, all that is necessary is to know that the day starts in the evening, *Shabbat* on Friday evening, that festivals fall on the same date of the Hebrew months every year (whatever the weekday might be) and the knowledge of how to use a *Luach* will enable that date to be ascertained in relation to the secular date, together with some information on the start of the lunar months.

Since we are often known by the calendar we keep (e.g. whether we celebrate *Chanukah* or the period December 24th. - January 1st.) or by the days that we keep special, it is important that the rough outlines of the Calendar and the rationale behind it are known. In Britain there is a great deal of 'helpful' legislation enabling those who wish to sell on a Sunday rather than a Saturday, or to leave work early on a Friday afternoon in winter, or to take a day off for religious reasons in September, to do so without suffering any great sanction. (Remember — there were times when simply to have no fire burning on a Saturday could lead to one being burned at the stake oneself on suspicion of being a a 'secret Jew'!)

It is interesting and sad, that so few Jews nowadays take advantage of these chances to celebrate their own calendar.

CHAPTER 7

SHABBAT OBSERVANCES

Page numbers

(References to the *Siddur* are: *Seder haTefillot* — Forms of Prayer 7[th.] Edition; 8[th.] Edition in **BOLD**; '*Lev Chadash*' in ***Bold Italics***.)

1. INTRODUCTION

We start with the Weekly cycle. The Sabbath does not just happen of itself — you have to make it happen. It is not as though for 24 hours suddenly the sun stands still, or the earth stops turning, or the weather is so mild that one does not need heating, or the animals do not need feeding or milking...... In this way, one can perhaps understand the idea that God actually had to create the Sabbath, that the *Shabbat* itself is a part of Creation. One can find many parallels elsewhere in life — e.g. a Birthday is technically only a date in a calendar, but You can make it special with candles, a cake, a party, presents, greetings...

Likewise a *Shabbat* becomes a special evening, a special day, if you have candles, loaves, a drink, greetings and blessings. There is a difference between 'time off work' and 'a holiday'; to make the most of a holiday you have to plan for it, discuss ideas of how to spend it and who with (family, friends, a partner), make sure you have the right clothes... and so on. In all these cases a mundane event — a 'day off', a weekend, a family meal — becomes special <u>because You make it special</u>. Most of our *Shabbat* observances are, in effect, mechanisms for making the day special. Normal activities — eating, drinking, singing, meeting together, talking with the kids — are invested with a specialness if we approach them in the right way and say and do appropriate things. The Hebrew word '*Kadosh*', often translated as 'holy', is best understood simply as 'special.'

2. WHEN DOES *SHABBAT* BEGIN AND END?

For us, *Shabbat* begins and ends when WE begin it and when WE end it. Traditionally it was considered as starting at dusk ('*Tzet HaKochavim*') when three stars could be made out, shining in the night sky, and ending twenty-four hours later. Later the rabbis extended this to twenty-five hours to make sure that no one would, by a minor slip, be in danger of 'breaking the Sabbath'. As in so much of Judaism, there is an essential logical beauty in a custom which can sometimes be overlaid by subsequent neurotic extensions and exaggerations. When it begins to get dark, it feels like a day is over — and so by definition the next day should begin. After all, in the days before everyone had easy access to artificial light this really was the end of any time in which one could read or write or work or even travel in safety. The Night time was dangerous, full of unknown terrors — so this was a good time to stay indoors and put the lights on.

Normally a blessing is said before the action to which it refers — before breaking bread, before drinking wine, etc. — but the exception is the blessing to be said over the *Shabbat* candles because one has effectively commenced the *Shabbat* with this ritual recitation — and so the candles need to have been lit beforehand and the blessing is said afterwards! (This is one explanation for the practice of covering one's eyes whilst saying the blessing — one acts as though they have not yet been lit! But many families have other explanations, of how one gestures to bring the *Shabbat* atmosphere from around the light into the room.)

The trouble is that the *Torah* was originally given to a people living much closer to the Equator than those of us who live in Northern Europe. There are parts of the globe where the sun goes down very late in summer — up to 10pm perhaps — and very early in winter — already by 4pm. perhaps. If one goes further to beyond the Polar Circle the sun is always visible, i.e. it is never really dark, for six months at a time! The 'Midnight Sun' may be good for attracting tourists but it makes observing a calendar based on sunset very difficult! (There are also problems when one lives in the Southern hemisphere and the calendar is based on the agricultural cycle in the Northern hemisphere...) In consequence many Reform and Liberal synagogues simply establish an almost arbitrary time — there may be a difference of an hour to match the changes in Summer and Winter Time — and simply declare that, for them, *Shabbat* will begin at, say, 7pm or 8pm — regardless of whether the sun has already set or has not yet set.

The Sabbath also then needs to end at a time that matches our life-style (and possibly public transport timetables). Since one formally ends the *Shabbat* by lighting a *Havdalah* candle and reciting blessings over it (see the chapter on *Havdalah*) and since one cannot light this while it is still officially *Shabbat*, it becomes necessary to wait until it is absolutely certain that the sunlight has faded from the sky and then to fumble in the dark to light the *Havdalah* candle! By which time it could be so late that there is no chance of doing anything else on this Saturday evening — celebrating a party, visiting a concert or a cinema, etc. So we need to be practical and make priorities; It is (or should be) a priority that one celebrates a Day of Rest with worship and study and social activity and abstaining from normal work activities (see below) — but if we wish to celebrate together we need to take other factors into account, including the times that school and work may end, or the timetables that allow people to come to services and get home again.

Jewish diaries and websites will pronounce the official times for the beginning and ending of *Shabbat* in various locations down to the nearest minute, for those who wish to restrict themselves to this method. But most congregations will be forced to a more pragmatic communal compromise solution.

Yet other issues are caused by modern globalised technology. This problem has only emerged in the last century or so, thanks to the technology of near-instantaneous communications. Where I am right now might be *Shabbat*, but where my colleague is, calling me on the telephone, it may still be several hours before or already after *Shabbat*! An aeroplane might be able to take off just before *Shabbat* in one country and, depending on the direction of flight, either land just before *Shabbat* some hours later — or land where it had already become *Shabbat* before it had taken off! It is an irony that, although *Shabbat* is first mentioned in the context of the creation of an entire world, it is the re-discovery of the One-ness of our globe through communications that sometimes makes it hard to define where *Shabbat* begins or ends!

(Incidentally, after this first reference in the Creation story *Shabbat* is never mentioned again in the Book of Genesis. God never commanded anyone else in Genesis 2:1-3 to observe it regularly, did not command the animals or the birds or the fish to observe it... It seems from the texts that *Shabbat* was not marked in the Garden of Eden; that none of the Patriarchs ever celebrated *Shabbat*, the rains did not stop for *Shabbat* during the Flood, the nomads never paused with their beasts on *Shabbat*...... It is only mentioned again in the second half of the Book of Exodus, once the Israelites have been freed from slavery, when they are in the desert, when they get additional Manna on the day before so that they do not need to collect food on *Shabbat*, when they are punished for gathering fuel for fires on *Shabbat*...)

3. *NEROT* — THE *SHABBAT* CANDLES

(*Siddur* p.312; **p.417**). Light brings joy. A bright room is more cheerful than a dark, gloomy room. Spirits rise. Whilst some light is always necessary for illumination the *Shabbat* custom is to have additional light — traditionally now two candles — which some say symbolize the two separate commands to 'Remember' and to 'Keep' the Sabbath (Exodus 20:8 and Deuteronomy 5:12). However, if you look at old prints you will see that some families had multi-branched oil lamps. The key concept is simply to have <u>more than the minimum</u>. Since Light has always been expensive — remember that there used to be heavy taxes on candles! — it was a deliberate sign of celebration to light more than you had to — and never mind the expense! Nowadays we tend to put the electric light on and then light the candles — which rather detracts from the effect. Though one could replace 40 Watt with 100 Watt bulbs for the day... Dinner parties are always more romantic by candlelight — maybe we should try an occasional *Shabbat* meal the same way? We are allowed to use the light of the *Shabbat* candles — this might seem obvious, but in fact we are not allowed to use the light of *Chanukah* candles.

There is a blessing to say over the lighting of the lamps or candles — this is actually a '*Mitzvah deRabbanan*', a command created by the Rabbis, because although it states 'Blessed are You, Lord our God, who has made us holy by doing your commands and has commanded us to light the '*Ner shel Shabbat*'' — this is nowhere mentioned as one of the 613 scriptural commands of the *Torah* (a '*Mitzvah D'Oraita*'). Effectively it was composed later and given the same authority AS THOUGH it were from the *Torah*. It is customary to light the flames and then cover one's face or to wave the hands as though to stir the air and bring the light towards us, or to raise the hands towards the flames, as one recites the blessing.

'*Ner*' is singular and means 'lamp' rather than 'Candles' as such.

4. BLESSING THE CHILDREN

(*Siddur* p.314; **p.450**.) Traditionally, a Father's blessing always carried great weight. In more modern times, with split families, multi-faith families, patchwork families, rainbow families, a breakdown of the traditional 'breadwinner / housewife' division of responsibilities, this concept has become, to say the least, more complicated. There is no reason of course why the mother or both parents together may not say the relevant words.

In addition, whilst it might appear on the surface a nice idea to express the pious hope that the children might grow up to be as good as were the ancient patriarchs and matriarchs, closer inspection reveals that the traditional formulation — 'May you be like Ephraim and Menashe' for boys or 'like Sarah, Rebecca, Rachel and Leah' for girls — is ambiguous; the first two had a non-Jewish mother, were born in Egypt and formed only 'half-tribes', only one of them getting the Covenant blessing (Genesis 48:13f.); The Matriarchs lived lives of great difficulty and stress, as nomads, often having difficulty becoming pregnant… Does one really want one's children to share these problems in the future?

Nevertheless, at the end of a tiring week, during which many harsh words might have been said between parent and child, doors slammed and even (whisper it not!) bottoms spanked — it is good to be able to speak calmly and to express love and wipe out the tensions of previous days. It turns a 'meal with the family' into a 'meal together'.

5. '*SHALOM ALEICHEM*'

A traditional greeting and a traditional song for the *Shabbat* evening, which mentions the '*Malachei haSharet*', the 'Angels of Service' (*Siddur* p.29 & p.314; **p.448**). Angels play a strange rôle in Judaism; this song is based on the concept found in the *Talmud* (Tractate '*Shabbat*' 119b) that when a man returns home from the synagogue on a *Shabbat* evening he is accompanied by two angels who see what sort of home he runs and judge him accordingly. If everything is ready for the *Shabbat*, everything clean and tidy, the table laid, the food prepared, the family waiting eagerly for his arrival, then the good angel makes the wish that things should continue so in the future — and even the bad angel has to agree; Conversely, if the *Shabbat* is being ignored and nothing is prepared, the bad angel declares that this state of affairs should continue — and even the good angel has, sadly, to agree…

What lies behind this fairy-story? The firm idea that our lives are, to a large extent, what WE make of them. If we cannot put our own houses in order, cannot make the time to sit down with the family or to meditate on the past week, we are unlikely to be able to make any more fundamental changes in our lives. If we cannot switch off computers and phones for even one day, then we let the machines rule us with their demands rather than the other way around. The pattern we set, the routine we set, will eventually take us over and we will become powerless to break it.

6. THE 'ESHET CHAYIL'

Again this is a traditional greeting (sometimes set to a melody), by which the husband acknowledges how dependent he is on his wife and how grateful he is for her efforts. This passage (*Siddur* pp.316f.; **p.449**) comes from the Book of Proverbs ('*Mishlé*') Chapter 31:10-12, 20, 25-31. Although some women find this description of wifely virtues rather patronising it is worth looking at the full text to see what has been omitted from the Reform version — the fuller version includes much more about how she works to support the family financially, performs all the household chores and lets the husband take all the credit!

Further, this chapter is presented (verse 1) not as an example of male sexism but as advice which a Jewish mother gave to her son regarding her ideal future daughter-in-law! She should be a strong, valiant and competent woman. As with the blessing of the children, this passage can also be seen as a chance to heal any wounds in a 'normal' marital relationship so that no one is harbouring any hurts and grievances within the family and all are ready for the *Shabbat* atmosphere.

7. THE *KIDDUSH*

(*Siddur* p.316ff.; **p.452**; (**p.564**)) As mentioned elsewhere the Hebrew word should be understood as 'special'. By making *Kiddush* you are transforming the simple, everyday actions of eating a chunk of bread and drinking a glass of wine into a sacred act. (Very importantly — we transform both the Action and Ourselves by performing the action — we do <u>not</u> transform the Objects themselves.)

The *Kiddush* for *Erev Shabbat* (as opposed to that, say, for a Festival) consists of three blessings — for Wine, for the Day itself and for Bread. In addition we sing a passage from the first Creation story of Genesis Ch. 2 verses 1-3 and it is also customary to wash one's hands (with the appropriate blessing — p.270; **p.453**) before reciting the blessing over bread ('*haMotzi*') — i.e. before touching the food (for with the wine one touches only the cup; in some circles one remains silent from the washing until the '*haMotzi*' so as to combine these two in some way). All of these help get in the mood and remove the traces of the workaday week.

The concept of the *Shabbat* is underpinned in Jewish thought by two separate concepts: firstly, the idea that God created the Sabbath for God's own rest; secondly, the idea (revolutionary at the time) that Everyone was entitled to one day off per week — even slaves and beasts of burden — and that Jews especially, having once been slaves, should be sensitive to this requirement. The traditional way of referring to this is either 'in remembrance of the Exodus from Egypt' or 'Because you were slaves in Egypt.'

This latter idea was once the cause of a deal of anti-Semitism, in that Jews were perceived by the pagan world (who had no such day of rest) as lazy and unproductive. Christianity however adopted the idea (with detail changes and of course on a different day!) so that the idea of 'Sabbath' became commonplace in our culture. Unfortunately it usually meant mainly a series of prohibitions — on travel, recreation, trade — and the Sabbath (in puritan Christian countries) seems to mean merely a day when the pubs are closed, rather than a day to be enjoyed! Similar problems are now alas apparent in Israel too.

Of course it can be occasionally frustrating if not all facilities are available for twenty-four hours a day, seven days a week; But there are always the difficult balancing acts to be made in a society. In order for some people to be able to enjoy an excursion or to visit a museum, somebody else has to be working to drive the bus or man the doors! There are people in Europe who consider it vital to their own well-being that shops should be open on Sundays — but don't consider how many other people must then work, not only in the shops but in delivery, rubbish removal, in financial services and in security, to enable them to go shopping — all people whose entitlement to a day with their family is also put at risk by such commercial pressures. These commercial pressures are real, even if some business owners claim that workers might 'volunteer' for weekend work... It is only since artificial light and energy became available that the concept of night shifts became common — Someone has to be there on duty at 4am if you wish to report a problem or call an emergency service... Someone has to carry out overnight or weekend maintenance on machines or infrastructure...... or drive through the night... In a sense we are all dependent on each other and it is no surprise that the command to rest includes 'your servants and your beasts of burden'. The Jew is not commanded just to have a (selfish) day of rest for himself, but to ensure that all those who work for him have the same rights too.

Traditional *Halachah* draws a distinction between activities that can save a life and those which are mere routine. So the Emergency Services are usually exempted from most prohibitions, even in Israel. Nevertheless, it is one thing to expect an Emergency Admissions department at a hospital to be open every day, or trained nurses to care for patients even at night time, and another to expect, say, a regular Dermatology Clinic to be held at 4am!

A definition of a Slave is: Someone who has no control over how they spend their time. In other words a slave can be told to do anything, any time. A free person, in comparison, is one who has the ability to choose when to do something and what to do — within limits of course and dependent on previous choices and their outcomes. For example, if you choose to have a family and to eat together, then you must eat at a time that suits all.

When someone says they 'can't take the time off to do something' or 'can't make time' they are effectively admitting that they are enslaved by their work or other demands on them. If they were free, they could decide when to work and when to stop. Sadly, in our mechanised and centralised society most of us are subject to these pressures; even the Self-Employed have to work when their customers want them to. And yet… Time can usually be found for a hobby, or a night out, or for courtship… so it is possible, within limits, to exercise choice. The *Shabbat* is the opportunity granted to the Jew to say: 'There is a limit as to how far I want my work to invade my life; there is a limit to the pressures I will accept, pressures that take me from my family, my friends, my pets, my own self. For one day every week I will make time to think about something else, something less transient, less bothersome, less demanding.'

Many Jews do not take that opportunity; That is their loss — a loss they often do not appreciate until it is too late, until they are burnt-out, until their relationships have been damaged. In Britain many have found Sunday to be a suitable day to close shops and offices — but even that chance is being eroded by recent legislation and the tendency towards 'Seven-Day Opening'. The problem with taking Sunday as the Sabbath is, quite simply, that it is hard to do so in a Jewish way — because the main *Shabbat* services take place on the Saturday! However, it must also be said that were all businesses, schools, courts, banks and services to be open on a Sunday this would have a very deleterious effect on Jewish communal life as well — because it is usually on the Sundays that we can organise weddings, day conferences, movement meetings, youth events, stone-settings at the cemetery and a variety of other things, all on the assumption that MOST of our members are free of work on that day…

All of this lengthy commentary underlies the way we should understand the 'Blessing over the Day' on p.319 / **p.452** (*p.564*). We become holy by doing God's commands. We have inherited — as our own property, but also as something which we should pass on to the next generation — the idea of a Sabbath; this commemorates the order of the Creation — with *Shabbat* as the culmination of the sequence. It was the first date set aside as a special day for meeting each other in a special way — it preceded all the other festivals and anniversaries which came later in the Bible, if at all. (Hence, when a Festival falls on a *Shabbat*, the blessing for the candles is always '*Ner shel Shabbat v'Yom Tov*' — *Shabbat* comes first.) It is also a reminder that we are free, no longer slaves as we once were in Egypt. It is saying to God: 'You gave us this special gift because You, at least, think we are special and deserve it.' (By implication, if we reject it or neglect it we are rejecting our birthright as Jews, the distinctive act that makes us special.)

It is nice to drink the wine if possible from a special cup, glass or beaker — the *Yiddish* word '*Becher*' merely means 'Beaker' — and most Jewish homes have some such special silver or other cup. However, this is not vital, so if you are away from home any cup may be used. It has become a custom in some communities to drink where possible Israeli wine for the *Kiddush*. This was originally simply a symbolic act of support for the then-new Jewish wine industry in Palestine, which was beginning to export its range to Europe and America. (The trade-marked brand name 'Palwin' just means the 'Palestine Wine Company'.) Until recently all such wines were sweet

— typical Mediterranean products — and had been heat-treated to ensure their *Kashrut*. (You see on labels of such wines the words '*Yayin Mevushal*' which means it has been 'cooked' or pasteurised; the wine in such bottles remain drinkable, or at least does not turn sour too soon after the bottle has been opened.) In other communities and homes at least *kosher* wine from other countries will be used. Wine is wine — one should attempt to use *kosher* wine for such a symbolic act, but there is no need to 'suffer' if you don't like such a sweet wine or if such products are locally unobtainable. Other versions are just as acceptable.

Teetotallers, small children and others may of course drink grape juice, since the blessing refers specifically to 'the fruit of the vine' ('*Pri haGafen*') and not to wine itself or its alcoholic content.

8. THE BLESSING FOR BREAD

We can easily forget that food does not all come from the supermarket, the factory or the laboratory — some of it (still!) actually originates as a part of a natural process! 'Bread' — '*Lechem*' — is the symbolic food. According to strict Jewish tradition a meal without Bread is not really a meal, but only a Snack — and therefore one is exempt from saying the Grace After Meals! This is why one is sometimes served with sweetened rolls at a reception or in an airline meal — they are therefore classed as '*Mezonot*' (Yiddish '*Mezoynos*') — as 'cake' rather than 'bread' and somehow this means that one doesn't have to express gratitude in the same way! Nevertheless Bread and Salt remain the traditional symbols of hospitality. The blessing refers to 'Bread coming from the ground'; Of course Bread as such does not come from the ground — it is the result of a complex manufacturing process involving reaping and threshing and milling and mixing and kneading and baking — but the raw materials grow in the soil.

9. TWO *CHALLOT*

We have two *Challot* (sing. *Challah*), usually covered by a special cloth, partly as a reminder that the Manna fell in double quantity on Fridays in the desert so that there would be no need to collect (or bake) on the *Shabbat* (Exodus Ch. 16:22-29); and partly as a reminder of the 'Showbread' in the Temple (these were the loaves presented on the altar). Normally these are formed of various strands of dough twisted together, though for festivals they may be round; they can be sprinkled on the surface with poppy-seed or other seeds as decoration, but this is optional. Technically the word *Challah* itself refers not to the loaves we bake or buy, but refers to the action of taking a small part of the dough and burning it as a reminder of the fact that in Temple times bread was offered by the priests. However the word has come to mean these special loaves (in German: 'Zopf' — the same word as a braided hairstyle). Incidentally, when *Challot* are not available other forms of bread may be used; and although most *Challot* are white there is no rule preventing one from baking wholemeal or dark loaves.

One could argue that by having two loaves on the table on Friday night one is actually for the following day, but this is not the case — for lunchtime on *Shabbat* one can bring out other (pre-baked!) ones. Bread comes in many forms, depending on ingredients and methods of baking; some bread becomes hard and stale very quickly, other forms remain soft and edible for several days. This is relevant as it is good to be able to use additional *Challot* on the Saturday as well as on the Friday evening! In some parts of Europe these forms of twisted loaves are referred to as '*Zopfbrot*' or '*Barches*' — this latter name clearly derived from the term *Berachah*.

10. ZEMIROT

The Hebrew word '*Zemer*' means 'Song', and *Zemirot* is the plural. A selection of such songs can be found in the *Siddur* pp. 572-579; **p. 460.[and pp.182-195]** Once the tunes have been learned it is very pleasant to have a relaxed sing-song around the table before clearing up. The songs themselves come from different centuries and sources, some are in Hebrew and some in Aramaic, and there are many more than this selection would indicate. Booklets are available with the Grace, the Blessings and a selection of *Zemirot*.

11. GRACE AFTER MEALS

This will be looked at more fully in a separate chapter. We should note here that a specific *Shabbat* paragraph is added to the normal '*Birchat haMazon*' (pp.334f.; **pp.464-480**) and an additional blessing on pp.336f. In addition the penultimate paragraph shows a *Shabbat* Amendment from '*Magdil yeshu'ot*' to '*Migdol yeshu'ot*' — 'He increases' changes to 'He is a tower'. The former is a reference from Psalm 18:52, the latter from II Samuel 22:51. No-one knows the real reason for this change — one theory is even that someone wrote the variant in the margin of his text, with the source jotted down as '*Shin'Bet*' — an abbreviation for 'Second (book of) Samuel' — and that this was misinterpreted to mean 'On *Shabbat*'!

Slaves eat on the move — whereas free persons sit at their own tables. The *Seder* meal at *Pesach* is redolent of this distinction. On *Shabbat* one should have time to sit, digest, and thank God for the food, the day, and the freedom one enjoys.

12. WORK ON SHABBAT

How do we define 'Sabbath Rest', '*Shabbat Menuchah*'? As Abstention from all physical Effort? From Work? From Paid Work? From activities that cause others to have to work? There is scope as Reform Jews for much discussion on these points. Much of the 'normal' arguments one hears attacking Reform Judaism centre on such relative trivialities as whether one may drive on *Shabbat*, rather than the underlying principles of the definition of 'Work' as such.

But how can one really define 'Work' fully? Many workers spend up to an hour each way commuting into a major city (and some even more). Is this 'working time' or 'travel time'? One is not at home, one is not travelling for pleasure, one is under stress from deadlines and the need for punctuality — but one is not actually at the place of work. What about attendance at work-related conferences or trade fairs or business trips at some resort? What about attending an official 'function' or banquet? The outsider will see these as luxuries and 'perks' but for the one condemned to spend time away from their own home and family it is perceived as 'work' — even if one has free time in between sessions. If one takes the same journey at a weekend for leisure purposes — or to attend a synagogue — should this be classed in the same way? What about being 'on call', unable to relax even if one is not actually called out? Or 'unpaid overtime'? We get used to the idea of 'homework' when at school, or time spent privately studying when in higher education — in the same way many take work home from the office, or spend time preparing, or marking classwork, or any of a whole variety of activities which fall into that intermediate category which some employers will reward and others will simply expect to be carried out voluntarily and unpaid. There is a difference between a regular salary and a 'Zero Hours' contract which defines very strictly (and usually not very fairly) what is deemed as 'work'. What about travel time to a job in a different town? For centuries of course women have carried out a variety of domestic and family duties which were taken for granted and not classified as 'work'. Neither childcare nor care of the sick and elderly have traditionally been valued when it came to pensions insurance.

Then there are creative activities, gardening, studying, watching films, playing computer and other games, sports activities, modelling, sewing — and knitting, wine-making, the list is almost endless — which are deliberately performed so as to distract oneself from normal 'employment' and provide refreshment and recreation. Yet they would be forbidden as 'work' because the activities themselves could also be performed as work. Just ask a tax adviser what may legitimately be claimed back from tax assessments! Then one will see a modern version of this debate.

In Exodus Ch. 35 Moses commanded the people to cease their 'work' — their activities at this time being centred on the construction of the Tabernacle. From this the Rabbis derived the principle that there are 39 'categories' or 'types' of work prohibited on the *Shabbat* — the so-called '39 *Avot deMelachot*' — which are described in the *Mishnah*, Tractate '*Shabbat*', Chapter 7 *Mishnah* 2.

> 'The main labours [prohibited on the Sabbath] are forty less one: sowing, ploughing, reaping, binding sheaves, threshing, winnowing, cleansing [i.e. sifting the coarse dross by hand or by a coarse sieve], grinding, sifting [sifting with a fine sieve]; kneading, baking, shearing (the) wool and washing or beating [or combing] it, spinning, weaving two threads, separating [i.e. separating the warp from the wool or weft] two threads, tying a knot or loosening one, sewing two stitches, tearing in order to sew two stitches, hunting a deer and slaughtering it or flaying it or salting it or curing its skin or scraping it [i.e. the skin or hide] or cutting it

up, writing two letters, building, demolishing, extinguishing, kindling, striking with a hammer, carrying from one domain into another. These are the chief labours [forbidden on the Sabbath] — forty less one.'

(Translation and footnotes incorporated from 'The *Mishnah*' by Herbert Danby.O.U.P. 1933.)

Details of the exact interpretations of these fill many books. For example, does carrying a handkerchief in one's pocket count as 'carrying'? Some say 'Yes' — and tie it around a wrist instead, so that it counts as 'wearing' it — which is permitted. On the other hand, this also means tying a knot! If 'carrying from one domain into another' (i.e. from private to public, or from public to private) is prohibited, can one find a way around this restriction by classifying a whole town or a part of one as 'one domain'? Yes — if you tie a piece of string around a town (called an '*Eruv*', which technically means a Courtyard) — then you can carry within that boundary; and so on.

Many and ingenious are the additional restrictions and the additional means found to relieve them that the rabbinic minds have developed. For example, the idea of the *Eruv* is actually very simple and logical: Every time you carry a plate to a table or lift a baby from its pram you are 'carrying' but this is considered acceptable because you are doing it 'in private' and not 'in public'. In the same way a courtyard within a block of flats is private property (and usually bears a sign saying so), whereas the street outside is 'public'. There are many things one might do in private that one might not do in public — walking around half-dressed, unshaved, etc. So the act of declaring a specific area, defined by a recognised boundary (even if it be a fictive one, formed of cables, overhead wires, river banks) as 'a private courtyard' enables one to behave within this area in a more relaxed manner, to push a pram, to carry a prayer book or a *Tallit* to the synagogue, etc. (In a legal sense this is just the same as erecting a sign that declares an area of land or a complex of buildings to be 'Private' and denying unauthorised access. We see these signs on railway platforms or marking off the 'Staff' areas of department stores or the 'Service' areas of office buildings and we don't think twice about challenging the concept.)

Use of electricity is not prohibited (indeed there are even debates as to whether it should be classed as a 'stream that flows' rather than as 'fire that burns' — but switching it off and on is prohibited. So there are means of leaving an oven on low, so as to warm food up gently or keep things warm... and now there are special clocks which switch power off and on at pre-set times... and there are lifts which can be made to stop automatically at every floor so that one merely has to wait and does not have to push a button... and so forth. Ironically, although some Jews worry about the light bulb in a refrigerator coming on when the door is opened and so unscrew it before *Shabbat* begins, or worry about tearing lavatory paper and so tear this up beforehand — every time one flushes the lavatory a pump has to start working somewhere! Yet this is not prohibited, even by very pious and observant Jews...

It might be considered that Rabbis work on the *Shabbat*? Ah no! A traditional contract requires the Rabbi of a community to work during the week and to be paid as such and then to give the sermon or whatever on the *Shabbat* 'voluntarily'! Modern technology — including of course the use of electricity — has led to many complications and also new possibilities. Is a motor vehicle the same as a living animal that has to 'rest'? Is riding a bicycle 'work'? (It isn't, but repairing a puncture is and therefore it is forbidden 'just in case'!) What is the problem if one walks to or even past a door and it opens automatically because one has simply activated an infra-red detector? There are jokes in which an airline pilot announces that, due to delays, the flight will not be able to reach its destination before the onset of *Shabbat* — 'so I will have to switch off the engines and we will stay up here until *Shabbat* is past.' In reality ships must continue sailing, animals continue to need care and feeding and watering and milking… The sick and infants and the elderly still need caring for… and one needs to maintain vigilance and defence against criminals or aggressors. So one needs to be flexible and pragmatic in considering what is 'Work' and what is 'an action of loving care'. Traditional *Halachah* understood this need — unfortunately in some parts of modern Jewish life this flexibility and pragmatism has become submerged under hundreds of minutiae; Reform Judaism would seek to return to the basic ideal.

(See also the discussion in Rabbi Louis Jacobs' 'Book of Jewish Belief' pp. 96-99 and 'Book of Jewish Practice' pp.74-76.)

CHAPTER 8

HAVDALAH

1. THE SERVICE

Shabbat comes in on Friday evening and we welcome it with candles, wine, bread and song. It goes on to Saturday evening and we then bid it farewell with candles, wine, spices and song…

The ceremony at the beginning is called '*Kabbalat Shabbat*', 'Receiving the Sabbath'. At the end we make '*Havdalah*' — a Division, between the day that has just ended and the week that is to follow it. At the beginning we light a candle; at the end we douse one. The parallelism is symbolic and strong. Light was created at the beginning of the first Creation Story, *Shabbat* at the end…

The service can be found on p. 326; **pp.457-461** of the *Siddur*, (**p.567** in '*Lev Chadash*'). It consists of six introductory verses, stressing particularly the concept of Salvation. They are, in order, Isaiah 12:2; Isaiah 12:3; Psalm 3:9; Psalm 46:12; Esther 8:16 and Psalm 116:13. This is normally read whilst holding a cup filled to the brim with *Kiddush* wine (or grape juice). Then come three blessings celebrating the physical senses of taste, smell and sight and then a conclusion section stressing the distinction between Holy and Normal/Profane, between *Shabbat* and normal days (or, on occasion, a following festival) and between Israel and the other Peoples of the world.

Prior to starting the service, the following needs to be arranged:

(a). A plaited or twisted Candle. Strictly speaking all you need is an arrangement of more than one wick — because the blessing '*M'orei haEsh*' refers to 'lights of the fire' in the plural, though 'Fire' is in the singular — so two single candles held close together so that the flames merge with each other would do, but traditionally a plaited candle is used if available. Some of these have six separate strands plaited together, which some say represent the days of the week, all merging into one joint flame to represent the light of the Sabbath! The candle is lit, without any blessing, at (or after) nightfall on Saturday.

(b). A container or dish of Spices. These can be any spices and of any combination — again, as long as there is more than one sort, since the blessing '*Borei Minei Besamim*' refers to 'spices' in the plural. Any form of powdered, pleasant cooking spice can be used or even flavoured tea bags! Some people use fancy, decorated and expensive spice-holders but these are not essential. It is the sense of Smell that is to be celebrated.

(c). A cup or glass of Wine, and a plate or saucer. (It is also easier to clean if one puts a paper serviette over the plate!) Make sure you have a cheap tablecloth or similar cover where it is necessary to catch any stains or drips of wax.

Because communal *Havdalah* ceremonies are often held at youth camps or weekend conferences many people think you need a large group or at least a *Minyan*, that you need to form a circle and chant — this is not so. It is or can be a short, quiet domestic ceremony.

The cup is raised and the normal blessing over wine is recited ('*Borei P'ri haGafen*'), then the glass put down.

The spices are raised to the nose and sniffed and the blessing '*Borei Minei Besamim*' said. The spices are then passed around for all present to experience.

The candle is held up and those present hold up their hands in its direction — the idea is that, by squinting at your outstretched hand, perhaps with the fingers spread apart, you can see the distinction between light and darkness. Some people curl their fingers, so as to create a similar light/shadow effect on the palm of the hand. The blessing is '*Borei M'orei HaEsh*'.

After the closing blessing — on the distinction and division — '*haMavdil beyn Kodesh leChol, beyn Or laChoshech, beyn Yisrael ve'Amim, beyn Yom haShabbat veSheshet Yemei haMa'asei...*' — some of the wine is poured into the bowl and the candle is then extinguished in it.

The greeting is '*Shavuah Tov!*' in Hebrew — 'A gute Woch'!' in Yiddish, meaning, quite simply, 'Have a Good Week!' The *Shabbat* is now over and all we can do is look forward to the next *Shabbat* — or even the 'Great *Shabbat*' when the Messiah will come and all will be redeemed. This is the background to the various songs and chants for *Havdalah*, referring for example to the prophet Elijah ('*Eliyahu haNavi*') who will be the forerunner (according to tradition) of the Messiah.

2. CONCEPTS OF DIVISION

Much of life consists of drawing boundaries of one sort or another, setting standards, establishing the grounds of taste, time, space, quality etc. Although discrimination is increasingly viewed as 'politically incorrect', Judaism has always placed great stress on marking off particular days, animals, foods — glorifying on the distinctiveness of things and times. It is this that underlies the boundaries that we set around the *Shabbat*.

3. TRADITIONS AND LEGENDS

According to some, on the *Shabbat* we acquire an 'extra soul' ('*Neshama Yeteira*') which then leaves us again at the end of the *Shabbat* — hence we need to strengthen ourselves with sweet smells to make up for the loss! In mediaeval Germany it was thought that girls who drank the wine at *Havdalah* would grow a moustache!

At *Havdalah* all the five senses — sight, sound, smell, taste and feel — are involved.

Shavuah Tov!

CHAPTER 9

BIRCHAT HAMAZON
— THE GRACE AFTER MEALS

The basic Grace can be found in the *Siddur*, pp. 330-337; **pp.464-480**; two shorter versions can be found on pp, 338-339; **pp.481-484, & p.485,** and in addition various blessings to do with food are on pp. 270-271. (In '*Lev Chadash*' there are two versions on ***pp. 551-558.***)

1. BASIC CONCEPTS

In order to live, we need to consume Food. Our bodies need it. What is Food? It is a part of Creation. It has to be, because there is nothing else! We process it in different ways — we kill it or catch it or reap it or pluck it, we pull it from the earth or from the water — it comes from a variety of sources, but essentially it is all part of Creation. From the very beginning of Genesis we see that some parts of Creation were created to act as food for other parts of Creation — in other words a 'food chain' was established:

'And God said: Behold, I have given you every herb yielding seed, which is upon the face of all the earth, and every tree, in which is the fruit of a tree yielding seed — to you it shall be for food. And to every beast of the earth, and to every fowl of the air, and to every thing that creeps upon the earth, wherein there is a living soul, I have given every green herb for food...' (Genesis 1:29f.)

'Every moving thing that lives shall be food for you; as the green herb have I given you all.'
(Genesis 9:3 — part of the blessing to Noah after the Flood.)

(Note: The initial passage implies that Vegetarianism is the ideal state, with the later passage as a concession to more carnivorous instincts.)

This *carte blanche* to eat everything did not last long. Though the origins of *Kashrut* will be looked at separately, the basic idea was soon presented that there were certain things one could eat, and certain things one should not eat — not because they were necessarily poisonous or unhealthy, but just so — it was a taboo. So one should not (as a Jew) eat blood; or certain species; one should not eat creatures that were still alive; and so on. (As we know, there are carnivorous creatures that do indeed swallow their prey whole and still alive... Just as there are creatures which bite or beat their prey to death and those which only eat prey that is already lying dead; There are reptiles and birds that swallow insects alive; there are big fish that swallow little fish... And there are herbivorous creatures which eat only grass or leaves. But essentially everything exists in a permanent state of trying to eat without being first eaten.)

Nevertheless the basic Jewish attitude to food is that it is there for a purpose — to be eaten. There is no sense that one is somehow destroying or perverting the Universe by killing and eating an animal; on the contrary, the action (provided it is performed in the right way) is, in a sense, fulfilling part of God's plan. If we were created to need a daily regular input of proteins, vitamins, minerals, fibres, etc. then it is not a sin to use other parts of God's Creation (after all, what else is there in our world?) to satisfy those needs — provided we do it the right way, not to excess, not wastefully, not casually or destructively or brutally, and that we express our gratitude.

What is the 'right way'? It consists of taking the right food, in the right frame of mind, having it killed and/or prepared in the right way and eating it in the right manner — with blessings before and after to thank the one who made it all possible. In this way what is a mere animal action becomes, so to speak, a 'holy action'.

2. OUTLINE: WHAT COUNTS AS A MEAL

A 'Meal ' is defined as any act of eating in which Bread is involved.

The reasons for this are complex. For us nowadays Bread is often used as a snack rather than a meal, as the basis for a sandwich, but in ancient times it had to be made and eaten fresh — hence it could be understood that a meal with Bread involved sitting down and making a fire and preparing and baking something in a formal manner, rather than just taking a snack of some fruit or corn or nuts. Whatever the reason, the practice persists amongst traditionalist Jews of saying a full Grace only after consumption of Bread, i.e. only after they have begun with the *Berachah* '... *HaMotzi Lechem min-haAretz.*' (In the same way, we might wish to define a 'Meal' now as when one sits down with cutlery and crockery, rather than grabbing something from a polystyrene container or a paper bag.)

If one wants to avoid all the bother of treating anything — even a three-course blow-out — as a 'meal', one simply ensures that there is no bread included! For this reason *kosher* airline meals and similar productions contain a sweetened roll which counts as 'cake' rather than as 'bread' — known as *Mezonot* or, in Anglo-Yiddish, a '*Mezoynos*-roll' with an explanatory card, whereby the *Berachah* is '... *Borey miney Mezonot*' — 'the One who makes different forms of things to eat.'

It is doubtful whether this legalistic approach really captures the spirit of thankfulness intended by the ritual.

3. BEFORE THE MEAL

One of the first table-manners taught to a child is that one does not come to a meal with dirty hands. However, the ritual washing of hands before a meal has little to do with workaday dirt. (For a start, we use only water, no soap.)

Eating is to be a ritual act and one must learn to come to it in a state of ritual purity, rather than (or as well as) hygienic cleanliness. Hence the *Berachah* '...*al Netilat Yadayim*' which actually refers more to shaking the hands dry rather than to the act of washing them under running water — i.e. water is poured over the hands, rather than their being dipped into a bowl of still water.

The blessing before Bread (note — not 'Food' — '*Ochel*') — is then said, bread with salt is eaten and the meal can begin.

(As an aside, it is interesting that there are specific blessings to be said before certain specific types of food — for what grows on a Tree ('*Borei P'ri haEtz*'), for what grows on a Vine ('*Borei P'ri haGafen*'), for what grows in the Ground or on a low Bush ('*Borei P'ri haAdamah*'), for Bread as such ('*haMotzi Lechem min-HaAretz*') or — essentially — almost everything else ('*she'haKol niyh'eh ki'Dvaro*' — 'for everything which is created according to His word') — but there is no especial *Berachah* for Meat or Fish, which involve actually taking the life of a creature.)

4. AFTER THE MEAL

On Sabbaths and Festivals one starts with Psalm 126 (**p.464**; **p.551**) which, if you look carefully, you will see contains two themes — Thanksgiving that we have been redeemed and the prayer that those who have not yet been so will indeed be redeemed soon. Presumably this indicates that only those who have been freed and are no longer living in slavery or oppression are able to sit back and relax with a festive meal.

The 'Call to Pray' (the first five lines of p.332; **p.466**) is a formal act. The overall idea is that one person (normally but not necessarily the host or hostess) will call upon the others present formally to join with him or her in closing the meal. The minimum number is two guests (since the term '*Rabotai*' is in the plural) which means that the minimum number for a formal group, called a '*Mezuman*' ('Those who are invited') is then Three. In the *Siddur* the traditional Hebrew opening 'Gentlemen, let us say Grace' is now altered to include 'Ladies' — marking Progressive ideas of gender-equality, or else one just avoids the problem by saying '*Chaverai*', 'My Friends'. In many modern booklets published for use at formal occasions which include the *Birchat Hamazon* the Hebrew is also altered to read '*Rabotai uG'virotai nevarech*' — 'Gentlemen and Ladies, let us bless...'

The 'Caller' reads the first, third and fifth lines, the others being joint responses. The word '*Eloheynu*' is in brackets because it is considered, in some circles, that it should be added here only when a *Minyan* is present. (There is however no problem with using it when it occurs elsewhere.) In some texts the opening line reads

'*Rabotai, Mir Vollen Bentschen*' — the Yiddish equivalent of the Hebrew. The verb 'to *bentsch*', as in 'It's time to *bentsch*' is probably — and ironically — a corruption of the Latin '*benedicere*' — 'to Bless'. The name is then frequently used for the whole ritual. One speaks, for example, of '*Bentsch*-books' or '*Bentschers*', meaning the small booklets containing the Grace. It is doubtful whether many of those who gladly use this 'authentic old Yiddish word' actually realise that it comes from Catholic useage…

5. COMPOSITION OF THE GRACE

After the Introduction there are four main paragraphs, with an additional insertion for *Shabbat* and several interpolations, responses or collections of Biblical verses sung as hymns. According to Rabbinic interpretation the first three paragraphs were composed at different periods of Biblical history and the fourth added after the massacre at Bittir of the last remnants of the Jewish Revolt in 135 CE.

The first paragraph (… '*haZan et-haOlam kulo b'Tuvo…*') is a general paean of praise to God for providing food for everyone and everything; this is based partly on a quotation from Psalm 136:25. The implication is that, since God provides food for everyone through divine goodness, then any problems in food distribution must be blamed on us rather than on God. Past, present and future are combined: '… food has never failed us, may it never fail us… for he feeds…all.' This sequence is echoed elsewhere in the Grace.

The second paragraph ('*Nodeh L'cha Adonai Eloheynu…*') (p.332; **p.468**) adds references to the Exodus and to the physical reminder of the Covenant — i.e. Circumcision. Our version here stresses the concept of the Land — for without land one cannot grow food and the land was a tangible proof of God's blessing — and quotes the key verse Deuteronomy 8:10 upon which the whole idea of thanking God after a meal is based. (There is also a Progressive version which refers to the Covenant being signed upon our hearts rather than upon our flesh — '*beLibeinu*' rather than '*biV'sarenu*' — so that by avoiding specific reference to circumcision women can also say it.)

The third paragraph ('*Rachem Adonai…*') is a plea for better times — when the people will no longer be scattered and homeless, when God's bounty will be so manifest that there will be no poverty or debt. Judaism is a practical religion — hence the mention of dependence on loans as well as charity! Most of us are dependent to some extent on mortgages or credit-card firms or banks or pension funds and finance houses — and, as the prayer concludes, it is one's Self-Respect which can be the main casualty of indebtedness.

Having looked forward to a time of peace and prosperity, the paragraph for *Shabbat* is inserted — for this also looks forward to a time of peace, rest and harmony and future redemption, symbolised by the Sabbath rest and respite. The transition is made back to the rebuilding of Jerusalem as a sign of future peace.

The fourth paragraph ('*Baruch Atah Adonai…haEl Avinu, Malkenu…*') is a sequence of names, titles and characteristics of God, recited in such a manner as to encourage the further exercise of those qualities emphasised. Again, we read 'He has done good, does good and will do good…', 'He has provided, does provide and will always provide for us…'

There is an element of wishful thinking — or maybe a delicate reminder to God, since God is '… our source of power', that we are fully dependent on God. The word '*Tov*', 'Good' in various forms permeates this paragraph.

The sequence of prayers introduced by '*HaRachaman*' — 'the All-Merciful' — (p.334; **p.475**) is easily sped through without really noticing what is being said. The first three are, indeed, composed of standard 'pious' wishes — though they look forward and express the hope that there will be a future.

The fourth paragraph might seem strange: 'May he grant us an honourable livelihood.' And yet — if ever there was a prayer for the Unemployed or the Under-employed, this is it. A prayer for the intelligent Jew denied access to land or capital, to the guilds or the credit-unions, to an education suited to his talents, forced to deal in old clothes or dodgy loans, demoted from an academic post to a manual, menial job because he had applied for an exit visa… forced to start again in a new country, in exile… There is such a wealth of centuries of bitter experience in that prayer, a plea that one might be in a position to earn one's own living and so retain some self-respect, an acknowledgement that we do not live off food alone.

The line following was often set in smaller type as a compromise after a lengthy debate on the role of *Aliyah* in modern *Diaspora* Judaism. Some felt it could be omitted entirely; others demanded its retention — so it was presented 'in reduced circumstances', reflecting the ambivalence. A yoke around a neck is a physical sign of slavery — it makes it impossible to lie down in comfort, it is a burden — and life in a strange land was seen as nothing better than this.

A blessing is called down upon the place where we have eaten. Traditionally one taps the table as the word '*Shulchan*' ('table') is read, and nowadays many people join in enthusiastically in this custom since it is (sadly) the only part of the Hebrew Grace they feel able to participate in.

This is followed by a plea for the Messianic Age to come soon and a blessing on the persons present, rather than the place. (This paragraph is obviously adaptable to meet varying circumstances.) '*BaKol, miKol, Kol*' is a reference to the three Patriarchs, each of whom received a blessing of 'all' in different ways and contexts — in Genesis 24:1, 27:33 and 33:11.

(Although some versions try simply to add the four Matriarchs to this line this is not, strictly speaking, correct. Instead another method to attempt liturgical equality is to add a phrase for the four times the Matriarchs are described with the word 'Good' — '*Heytiv, tovat, tov, tov*'…… from Genesis 12:16; 24:16; 29:19; 30:20. Of course, being Biblical, these citations can also be seen as ambivalent; the first refers to Sarah being helped by God when she has been taken as a sex slave; the second to Rebekah being a 'good looker'; in the third Laban says it is good for him to give Rachel away to Jacob; only in the fourth does Leah feel blessed by God for having borne six sons to the husband who did not originally want her! These are hardly appropriate texts for positive feminist or egalitarian interpretations!)

This is followed by a plea that the Patriarchs — or our ancestors — may in some way be able to plead on our behalves.

After optional additions for specific days this section is rounded off by a final plea for the Messianic Age.

The short paragraph ('*Magdil...*') which follows shows a variant reading ('*Migdol...*') for Sabbaths etc. This is because the line exists in two versions, in Psalm 18:51 and II Samuel 22:51. There is even a theory that the change for Sabbaths is the result of a misinterpretation of a note someone made in the margin of their text, that a variant existed in '*Sh(muel) B(et)*' — misinterpreted to be an abbreviation of '*Shabbat*'. This ends with a plea for Peace.

The final paragraph in our *Siddur* — (p.336; **p.480**) 'We have eaten and been satisfied...' — was specifically composed for this book. The traditional text beginning '*Yir'u et Adonai...*' has a sequence of Biblical verses on the theme of God's care for the righteous, who shall never starve (Psalms 34:10; 118:1; 145:16; Jeremiah 17:7; Psalm 37:25; 29:11). Some, especially after the *Sho'ah*, find this difficult or impossible to say, since we have known that many good people have indeed starved to death...
(In the 8[th.] Edition **p.479** this is restored as an option, but the especially difficult verse from Ps. 37:25 is distinguished by small print.)

The Grace ends with a plea for strength and peace and the person leading it often makes a brief *Berachah* and drinks a glass of wine to round it off.

(Not included in this brief overview are 'standard' additional inserts for *Shabbat*, Festivals, *Rosh Chodesh*, *Purim*, *Chanukah* etc. found in the printed versions.)

6. MUSIC

Various melodies exist for parts or all of the Grace, but almost without exception the music does not match the rhythm of the sentences or their meaning. Many an active Jew has learned to sing through the entire sequence at various youth or student activities with great gusto but has never actually looked at the translation...
A *Sephardi* Ladino version, '*Bendigamos*' — 'Let us Bless...' — has recently gained popularity and is sung to a jolly melody.

CHAPTER 10

THE LITURGICAL CALENDAR

1. INTRODUCTION AND TERMINOLOGY

The five books of the *Torah* are divided for purposes of regular public reading into 54 sections known as *Sidrot* (sing. *Sidra*) or *Parshiyot* (sing. *Parashah*). With each is associated a reading, usually from the prophets, known as the *Haftarah*. (Incidentally, despite the coincidence in English spelling the two words are spelt quite differently in Hebrew — with different letter 'T's — and are not linked.) Each *Sidra* has a name, usually taken from the first significant or distinctive word, and this name is then given to the *Shabbat*. Thus, the Sabbath on which we read the section *Bereshit* is called *Shabbat Bereshit*.

In Orthodox synagogues the entire five books of the *Torah* are read through in one year and there is one *Haftarah* for each *Sidra*.

The Reform *Luach* (Calendrical Table) allows for a Three-Year cycle of readings. This means that we follow the standard calendar in some respects — Reform synagogues mark *Shabbat Bereshit* on the same week as do Orthodox synagogues — with a very few exceptions that will be clarified below. The *Haftarah* normally is meant to have some link with the *Sidra* in terms of the theme or subject covered, so one could have three separate *Haftarot* in each cycle to match the three different sections of the main *Sidra* that we read. Apart from the regular cycle of Festivals the Jewish calendar incorporates several *Shabbatot* which are distinguished in various ways. These can be divided into three types:

(a). Those **associated with the New Moon**; i.e. a *Shabbat* that falls either on *Rosh Chodesh* or on the day before *Rosh Chodesh*.

In the former case a second *Torah* reading is added from Genesis 1:14-19, dealing with the creation of Time, with a replacement *Haftarah* from Jeremiah 31:31-40 which speaks of the New Covenant of the future — but which includes in verse 35 mention of the fixed order of time established by the sun, moon and stars — i.e. appropriate to an anniversary.

The *Amidah* on p.240; **p.222**; (*p.383ff.*) is read and a Half-*Hallel* is added.

In the latter case the name is '*Shabbat Machar Chodesh*', meaning 'Tomorrow is the (new) Month'. There is no extra *Torah* reading but the *Haftarah* is replaced by I. Samuel 20:18-42, part of the story of Jonathan and David's relationship, which starts 'Then Jonathan said to him, 'Tomorrow is the New Moon…''

On a *Shabbat* preceding a new moon the prayer '*Ya'aleh veYavoh*' (*Siddur* p.162; p.23; (p.59) is added, inserting the appropriate month and day. This is called a '*Shabbat Mevarchin haChodesh*', 'a Sabbath on which the (coming) month is blessed.' According to custom one does not need to do this on the *Shabbat* preceding the new moon of *Tishri*, since this is *Rosh Hashanah* and one will be doing additional prayers and hoping for a good month in any case.

(b). Those incorporated **within a Festival Period**, falling into the middle of *Pesach* or *Sukkot* (these are known as '*Chol HaMo'ed*'); or the Ten Days of Penitence ('*Asseret Yemei haTeshuvah*') in which falls '*Shabbat Shuvah*' with a *Haftarah* comprising three sections to do with penitence; or *Chanukah*.

(c). Those with additional *Torah* readings and/or replacement *Haftarah* readings, but **not directly linked to a forthcoming Festival**. (Some are indirectly linked, as in the *Shabbat Zachor* before *Purim* or the 'Four *Parshiyot*' in the period leading up to *Pesach* — the *Shabbatot* referred to as '*Shekalim*', '*Parah*', '*HaChodesh*' and '*HaGadol*' which are all a form of preparation for *Pesach*.)

(d). The *Shabbatot* leading up to and down from the **9th. of the month of Av** — *Tisha B'Av* — the day of remembrance of many destructions. In the three *Shabbatot* preceding this we get texts filled with dire warnings, in the seven *Shabbatot* following it we get texts filled with consolations — in all such cases they do not 'match' the *Sidra* thematically. Since this period falls in summer these *Shabbatot* are all cases where the *Sidra* itself comes from the Book of *Devarim* (Deuteronomy).

2. THE CYCLE

Taking those in categories (b) and (c) in order from *Rosh Hashanah* the following are the special Sabbaths and their particular liturgical observances, in sequence, according to Reform custom. On most the *Haftarot* are replaced or substituted by a special one dealing with the theme of the *Shabbat* rather than the theme of the regular *Sidra* and in several cases there is an additional *Torah* reading as well. (Note: The readings in Orthodox synagogues are sometimes different.)

(A). SHABBAT SHUVAH
(THE 'SABBATH OF RETURN OR REPENTANCE')

Since *Rosh Hashanah* is on the 1st. *Tishri* and *Yom Kippur* on the 10th., the ten days of Penitence that link them (the '*Asseret Yemei Teshuvah*') must include at least one Sabbath.

The normal *Torah* reading is retained — somewhere very close to the end of Deuteronomy — but the *Haftarah* is replaced by a specific one comprising Hosea 14:2-10 and Micah 7:18-20. The first line of the Hosea passage starts 'Return, O Israel, to the Lord your God, for you have stumbled because of your iniquity...' i.e. appropriate thoughts for a time of penitence.

(B). SHABBAT CHOL HAMO'ED SUKKOT

Sukkot lasts for seven days (eight days in Orthodox synagogues in the *Diaspora*), from 15th. to 22nd. (or 23rd.) *Tishri*. Apart from the first and last days, which are marked by Festival services, the intermediate days are classed as neither wholly festive nor wholly ordinary — hence the Hebrew term '*Chol*' (meaning 'ordinary') and '*Mo'ed*' (meaning 'a special time').

On that *Shabbat* the normal cycle of *Sidrot* is disrupted and instead Deuteronomy 8:1-8 and Deut. 16:13-17 are read. (Note, this could entail using two scrolls, or one which is rolled between the readings.) The first reading looks back to the Israelites' forty years in the wilderness before they entered a fruitful land.

The *Amidah* on p.240; **p.222 with blue inserts**; (*p.391*) is read and the *Hallel* **p.663**, (*p.5468ff.*) is also added to the service.

(C). SHABBAT CHANUKAH

As another eight-day festival, there is the certainty of at least one *Shabbat* falling within the period of *Chanukah* (25th. *Kislev* — 3rd. *Tevet*). (Occasionally both first and last days could fall on *Shabbat*.)

Since this is a post-Biblical festival there is no reference to it in the *Torah* and there is therefore no special *Torah* reading, (though in some communities a small part of the description of the dedication of the Tabernacle is read — from Numbers 7 and/or Num. 28) but the *Haftarah* is from Zechariah 2:14-4:7 which describes a vision of the symbolic golden *Menorah* and is therefore a reminder of the lamps in the Temple and an indicator of the *Chanukiah*. (On those occasions then there is a second *Shabbat* in *Chanukah*, the Reform calendar adds I Maccabees 2:1-28 or Psalm 66:1-20 — i.e. a *Haftarah* that comes unusually from outside the Prophetic books.) The '*Al HaNissim*' prayer would be added (p.267; **p.374**; *[p.391]*) and a *Hallel*.

(D). SHABBAT SHEKALIM
(THE 'SABBATH OF THE SHEKELS')

This is the first in a sequence of four *Shabbatot* in the springtime leading up to *Pesach*. It is observed on the last *Shabbat* in *Shevat* that immediately precedes the beginning of the month of *Adar*; in a leap-year, when there are two such *Adar* months, it is the *Shabbat* preceding the second one, so that it is always around a month before the beginning of *Nisan*. There is an additional reading from Exodus 30:11-16 (*Sidra* '*Ki Tissa*') which deals with the command to hold a census and for everyone, rich and poor alike, to pay the Half-Shekel tax to the Temple; the substitute *Haftarah* is from II Kings 12:1-17 (some communities begin at II Kings 11:17) which relates how this payment should have been carefully collected, accounted for and used for the upkeep of the Temple infrastructure. In the *Talmud* '*Megillah*': 'Resh Lakish said: 'On the first of *Adar*, an announcement is made concerning the *Shekalim*.'

One could see this as an initial preparation — How many Jews are there who will need to celebrate the coming *Pesach*? What repairs might need to be made in advance of the festival rush? However, since it falls before *Purim*, itself a month before *Pesach*, there are those who link it also to the story of *Purim* — How many Jews were to be killed and how much money was Haman prepared to pay the King for the permission to kill them?

(E). SHABBAT ZACHOR
(THE 'SABBATH OF REMEMBRANCE')

The Sabbath immediately preceding *Purim*, therefore falling in the second quarter of *Adar* (or, when there are two months of *Adar*, in the second such month). Because *Purim* is an annual reminder of the vulnerability of the Jewish people to the whims of those who seek to destroy them there is an additional reading from Deuteronomy 25:17-19 in which Moses reminds the Israelites of the unprovoked attack by the tribe of Amalek as first recounted in Exodus 17:8-15 and the command given there never to forget how they were so assaulted. This is in a way perceived as the first 'war crime' rather than as a 'normal' act of war, for the Amalekites attacked from the rear and the weak and sick at the tail end of the column.

The special substitute *Haftarah* is from I. Samuel 15:10-35, in which Samuel finds that King Agag of the Amalekites had not been put to death by Saul as instructed and he has to do the job himself. Since the evil Haman in the Book of Esther, set much later, is described as an Agagite, the characters are perceived as being linked, representing the same anti-Jewish tendencies, so the command to remember such people and events prior to the liberation of *Purim* is observed with this link in mind.

(F). SHABBAT PARAH
(THE 'SABBATH OF THE HEIFER')

In *Adar*, after *Purim*. An additional *Torah* reading comes from Numbers 19:1-10 and describes the manner of dealing with an unexplained corpse and of purifying those rendered ritually unclean when they are involved in dealing with it. The process involved sacrificing a totally red heifer (a young cow who had not yet had a calf) together with various other items to add colour and binding, mixing the ash with water into a paste and smearing it when required — (something that seems totally bizarre until one looks into the ingredients of some modern cosmetics...) The substitute *Haftarah* is from Ezekiel 36:16-38 which also deals with a promise by God to purify the people from their sins. The idea appears to be an annual reminder to prepare what is needed in order to purify oneself in plenty of time before *Pesach*.

(G). SHABBAT HACHODESH
(THE 'SABBATH OF THE NEW/FIRST MONTH')

The Sabbath at the end of *Adar* immediately preceding the new moon of *Nisan*. The purpose is to advise the people that the month in which *Pesach* falls is about to start, so they need to concentrate on their preparations. A second *Torah* reading from Exodus 12:1-11 starts with a reminder of God telling Moses: 'This month shall be henceforth the beginning of the months' and adding instructions for the Israelites to prepare for the Exodus and the first Passover.

The substitute *Haftarah* is from Ezra 6:19 to 7:10, in which the returned exiles from Babylon celebrate their first *Pesach* back in the Land of Israel.

(H). SHABBAT HAGADOL
(THE 'GREAT SABBATH')

The Sabbath in the second quarter of *Nisan* preceding the festival of *Pesach*. There is no special *Torah* reading but the *Haftarah* is replaced by Malachi 3:3-24 (followed by a repetition of verse 23, so as to end on a positive note). There are several theories concerning the name, the two main being that the *Haftarah* refers to the 'Great day of the Lord', or that this was an important *Shabbat* on which a major sermon would be given detailing the laws of *Pesach*.

(I). SHABBAT CHOL HAMO'ED PESACH (THE 'SABBATH IN THE IN-TERMEDIATE DAYS OF PESACH')

Falling in the third quarter of *Nisan*, during the intermediate days of the festival. The *Torah* readings come from Exodus 13:3-10 in which Moses commands the Israelites to remember *Pesach* and that it is to last seven days; and Deuteronomy 8:10-18 which is a warning against becoming complacent in wealth and forgetting one's debt to God. The *Haftarah* is from the Song of Songs, a book traditionally read during *Pesach* — either the whole of Chapter 1 or the whole of Chapter 2, filled with images of springtime (e.g.2:11-13) and of love. The *Amidah* on p.240; **p.230, blue insert**; (**p.390**) is read and a Half-*Hallel* is added.

(J). SHABBAT ATZMA'UT
(THE 'SABBATH OF INDEPENDENCE')

A modern addition to the calendar, this is the Sabbath preceding Israel Independence Day ('*Yom Ha'Atzma'ut*') on the 5th. *Iyyar*. A second *Torah* reading is added, from Deuteronomy 11:8-12 which starts with a command to keep all the land. The *Haftarah* is Micah 4:1-7, a vision of future peace when everyone will come to Israel to accept the One God. (**p.372**).

(K). SHABBAT CHAZON
(THE 'SABBATH OF THE WARNING VISION')

The Sabbath preceding the Fast Day of the Ninth of *Av* ('*Tisha B'Av*'), coinciding with the reading of *Sidra Devarim*. There is no special *Torah* reading but the *Haftarah* is replaced by Isaiah 1:1-27, in which the prophet receives his first warning revelation.

This marks almost the culmination of the Three Weeks from the seventeenth of *Tammuz*, commemorating various incidents leading up to the destruction of the Temple in the year 70 CE.

(Note: If the 9th. *Av* should fall on a *Shabbat*, that *Shabbat* becomes *Shabbat* Chazon and *Tisha B'Av* is moved forward one day to the 10th. *Av*).

(L). SHABBAT NACHAMU
(THE 'SABBATH OF CONSOLATION')

The Sabbath following *Tisha B'Av*. There is no special *Torah* reading but the *Haftarah* is Isaiah 40:1-26, words of consolation after the recollection of the traumas of destruction and dispersion. (The first verse starts '*Nachamu, Nachamu, Ami…*' — 'Comfort, comfort my people…')

3. VARIATIONS BETWEEN REFORM AND ORTHODOX CALENDARS

It occasionally occurs that the Reform and Liberal and Orthodox synagogues in Britain and Europe are reading from different *Sidrot*.

The main reason for this is that Reform and Liberal synagogues follow the same calendar as do all synagogues (Orthodox and Reform) in Israel. This means that, with the exception of *Rosh Hashanah*, only One Day is observed for the festivals of: First Day *Sukkot*; Seventh Day *Sukkot* (the Eighth Day, '*Shemini Atzeret*', being combined with '*Simchat Torah*'); First Day *Pesach*; Seventh Day *Pesach*; and *Shavuot*.

(*Purim* and *Chanukah* are minor festivals and not mentioned in the *Torah* and so don't have a Second-Day observance as such even in the *Diaspora* (often referred to as '*Chutz La'Aretz*' or just '*L'chuL*'). The day known as *Shushan Purim* has a different origin; *Yom Kippur* is only marked for one day in even the most traditional community.)

The reasons for this practice date to the uncertainty in ancient times as to the exact timing of a New Moon and hence a new month and date. (Interestingly, this indicates that even communities which claim not to be sure when the 1st. of *Tishri* or the 14th. of *Tishri* fall are sure about the 10th !)

This is why Reform synagogues mark *Pesach* and *Sukkot* for Seven days rather than Eight, and hold *Simchat Torah* one day before Orthodox synagogues do; they do not duplicate the opening day of a festival. The only exception might be *Rosh Hashanah*, since this festival falls on the first day of the Hebrew month and is duplicated also in Israel. (Note, the observance of a Communal *Seder* on the second night of *Pesach* has become common but does not imply that the Second Day is treated liturgically as a repetition of the First.)

Purely technically, although one refers to a 'Second Day *Pesach*' etc. it is actually the 'Second-First-Day *Pesach*'! But by inserting this day here the festival ('*Chag*') is extended in length.

If any of the three major Pilgrim festivals ('*Shalosh Regalim*') commences on a Friday, or the Seventh Day of *Pesach* or *Sukkot* falls on a Friday, the following day would be classed as a repeat Festival Day by Orthodox calendars (and called either 'Second Day' or 'Eighth Day *Yom Tov*'), whereas it would be just a normal *Shabbat* (or *Shabbat Chol HaMoed*) in the normal cycle of *Sidra* readings for Reform synagogues. This means that the Reform and Liberal synagogues (and all synagogues in Israel) would be one week ahead of the Orthodox *Diaspora* calendar for a week or so until the chance could be taken deliberately to slow down the Reform calendar to allow the two systems to coincide once more. This is usually done by splitting a double-*Sidra* so as to make it last over two weeks.

Since there are 54 *Sidrot*, with not enough weeks for all to be read within a year, it is normal to couple some of them in pairs when necessary. These are usually (in sequence) '*Vayakhel*' and '*Pekudey*' (in Exodus); '*Tazria*' and '*Metzora*' (in Leviticus); '*Acharey Mot*' and '*Kedoshim*' (in Leviticus); '*Behar*' and '*Bechukotai*' (in Numbers); '*Matot*' and '*Masey*' (in Numbers); and '*Nitzavim*' and '*Vayelech*' (in Deuteronomy). When required by the calendar — dependent on such factors as whether festivals fall on a *Shabbat*, or whether there is an additional month of *Adar* in a particular year with four more *Shabbatot* to fill — these *Sidrot* are read either separately or combined in some way (in which case only one of the *Haftarot* would be read).

In cases where the Reform and Orthodox calendars are out of synchronicity, the first available double-*Sidra* is split to regain consistency. Otherwise a *Bar-Mitzvah* boy in a Reform and in an Orthodox synagogue might be preparing for two different *Sidrot* for the same weekend! This could also be relevant when dating *Ketubot*.

Incidentally, the final short *Sidra*, '*V'zot HaBracha*', is rarely read as a separate week's *Parashah* but as the first reading on *Simchat Torah*.

See also the Appendix on Liturgical Readings.

4. HALLEL

The *Hallel* Psalms (*Siddur* p.538; **pp.664-674**; ('*Lev Chadash*' *p.468ff.*) consist of Psalms 113, 114, 115, 116, 117 and 118.

'*Hallel*' means 'Praise' and '*Hallelu-Yah*' is a Second-Person Plural Imperative form: 'Praise God!'

Together they form a unit and are often read or recited or sung on notable days. There is a special *Berachah* recited which, though it implies a divine command to read these Psalms, reflects in fact a Rabbinic decree that they should be used to show especial praise and gratitude to God.

'*...asher kidshanu b'Mitzvotav, veTzivanu likroh et-haHallel.*'

On some occasions, i.e. *Rosh Chodesh* and *Chol HaMo'ed*, the so-called 'Half-*Hallel*' consisting of Psalms 113, 114, 115 (verses 12-18 only), 116 (verses 12 -19 only), 117 and 118 suffice. (N.B. The rubric on p. 531 implies that the whole of Psalm 116 is omitted, but this should refer to verses 1-11 only.)

The full *Hallel* is added to services on all festivals and *Chol HaMo'ed Sukkot* and *Shabbat Chanukah*, the Half-*Hallel* to services on *Chol HaMo'ed Pesach* and on *Rosh Chodesh*.

The *Hallel* Psalms are normally added at the Morning Service ('*Shacharit*') only, immediately after the *Amidah* and before the *Torah* Service. They are included also in the Passover *Haggadah* for the evening *Seder shel Pesach*.

CHAPTER 11

THE HIGH HOLY DAYS: '*YAMIM NORA'IM*'

1. INTRODUCTION

The 'high point' of the Jewish calendar is that part of the autumn season known as 'The High Holy Days'. (In Hebrew they are known as the '*Yamim Nora'im*', the 'Days of Awe' or 'Awe-ful, Awesome Days' indicating a greater degree of respect and reverence for God.) People sometimes refer to the period simply as 'the *Chagim*' — 'the Festivals' — as in 'Youth Club will recommence after the *Chagim*.'

Into this season and specifically into the month of *Tishri* are crammed the New Year ('*Rosh Hashanah*'), the Day of Atonement ('*Yom Kippur*', or '*Yom haKippurim*'), the Festival of Booths or Tabernacles ('*Sukkot*'), the Eighth Day of Solemn Assembly ('*Shemini Atzeret*', literally the 'Eighth and Closing Day'), the Rejoicing in the Law ('*Simchat Torah*') and the intervening *Shabbatot* which include the Sabbath of Repentance ('*Shabbat Shuvah*') and the intermediate Sabbath in *Sukkot* ('*Shabbat Chol HaMo'ed*'). As a prelude to the days themselves, the preceding month of *Elul* is marked with penitential prayers and '*Selichot*' (petitionary) services.

Strictly speaking, few of these have much to do with each other and it is (almost) coincidence that they come so closely grouped together. Be that as it may, the synagogue community's life is profoundly affected by this period. Arrangements have to be made for adequate seating capacity (sometimes as 'Overflow' services) since visitors, lapsed members and infrequent attenders usually wish to attend at least part of these services and the normal routine has frequently to be suspended.

The main point to be borne in mind is that, just as the Jewish Day starts in the Evening, so the Jewish Year starts in the Autumn. It starts with a period of introspection, a recollection of the previous year and a realistic assessment of the coming year. (As realistic as possible — but at least without wishful-thinking and self-deception.)

Only when one has 'tied up the loose ends' of the past can one truly face the future, with clear knowledge of one's strengths and weaknesses, one's fears and hopes. This process is known as '*Teshuvah*', literally 'Return' or 'Returning' (one is a noun, the other a gerund form of a verb — implying a continuing process). One does not so much 'return to God' as 'return to a heightened self-awareness, return to one's true self — and in so doing return to a clearer, healthier relationship with God.' The whole concept of *Teshuvah* is an exceedingly complex one, yet the bases are simple: We are meant to do our best to be Good; we are told, commanded to be Good; despite that, we often slip from the standard expected of us; in consequence we must find some way of apologising and of rebuilding the trust that such a failure often destroys. By prayer and repentance, we can do this.

Does this mean that we start again, with a 'clean slate'? Yes and No. Yes, inasmuch as the past sin can be purged and atoned for and need not drag us down further — if our repentance is truly sincere. No, inasmuch as time will have passed and opportunities will have been wasted. We can be brought back to the spiritual state we lost, but not back to the age we were when we lost it, as though it had never happened. So — a sinner can repent at any time and repentance is strongly encouraged, to the extent that some rabbis consider that a penitent sinner is, through their personal experience, even closer to God than one who has never sinned, has never known the power of temptation or the agony of guilt or the effort required to make good what can be still made good — but the sinner cannot necessarily thereby regain his or her lost youth, or lost friends, or lost business, or lost health, or lost family.

A further, important point: Atonement to God, expressions of penitence to God, are considered to be appropriate only for sins committed against God in terms of ritual or moral wrong-doing (i.e. including sins we commit against Ourselves, we who are made in God's image); Sins committed against another human being need to be apologised for and 'made good' to that human being, first.

There are many books on aspects of the High Holy Days, including anthologies of suitable readings and meditations. This chapter will refer particularly to the '*Forms of Prayer*', *Machzor*, Vol. III, 'Days of Awe', published by RSGB, 8th. Edition, 1985. (At the time of writing work is under way by the MRJ on a 9th. Edition but this has not yet been produced.)

This is the book currently used in Reform synagogues, and includes material for the period from 1st. *Elul* to *Yom Kippur*. *Sukkot* and the following notable days will be dealt with separately in a later chapter. (N.B. *Machzor*, literally 'Cycle', is the term applied to a Prayer Book for use on *Chagim*, Festivals.) (Liberal synagogues use the **Machzor 'Ruach Chadashah'**.)

2. PREPARATION: THE MONTH OF *ELUL*

The New Year does not just begin at New Year. It requires preparation. The whole of the month of *Elul*, preceding the month of *Tishri*, has therefore undertones of preparation. In synagogues which hold a Daily Morning Service the *Shofar* would be blown every day (except *Shabbat*) at the conclusion.

The RSGB *Machzor* (pp.2-18) includes private meditations and prayers for this period.

3. SELICHOT

In modern Hebrew 'S'lichah!' means 'Sorry!' *Selichot* prayers, penitential prayers, formed part of the liturgy for fast days and were recited at various sad or solemn days of the year. *Selichah* literally means 'Forgiveness' and prayers were composed asking for forgiveness or calling the individual soul to account for its actions. Some were composed as early as the 7th.-century CE and some were incorporated by Rav Amram bar Sheshna *Ga'on* (the *Ga'on* from 856 to 875) in his *Siddur*. Many were composed during the Middle Ages, times of trouble, persecution and martyrdom. The '*Akedah*', the story of the Binding (and near-murder) of Isaac, with its undertones of of the victim suffering for the sake of God but being rescued at the last minute, was a common theme.

Apparently *Selichot* prayers were initially said mainly during the Ten Days of Penitence ('*Asseret Yemei Teshuvah*'); later this was extended forwards to the week before *Rosh Hashanah*. By the 11th.-century CE the custom had spread of saying them for the whole month of *Elul*.

In more recent times the tendency has been for one particular, formal *Selichot* Service to be held on (usually) the Saturday evening prior to *Rosh Hashanah*, sometimes at midnight, sometimes with full choral treatment, sometimes quiet and meditative.

The RSGB *Machzor* (pp. 94-121) includes services for both Evening and Morning worship; these can be used as part of the self-preparation for the Penitential season. See **Machzor Ruach Chadashah pp. 9-34.**

4. ROSH HASHANAH

Literally 'The Head of the Year', this festival falls on the 1st. of *Tishri* — 'the first day of the seventh month.' One might be surprised to find the 'New Year' commencing at the half-way point through the year, but this reflects a long-running rabbinic dispute. In the *Mishnah* ('*Rosh Hashanah*' 1:1) four new years are enumerated — those for Kings (1st. *Nisan*); for Animals (1st. *Elul*); for Years (including Sabbatical Years, Jubilee Years, the tithing of trees and vegetables) (1st. *Tishri*); for Trees (15th. *Shevat*, though some say 1st. *Shevat*). In the same way modern society is based on a number and variety of 'new years' — in Britain for a long time 6th. April for taxes, 1st. August for motor car registration, 1st. September for eligibility to start school and so on. (In addition we each of us have our own new years based on birthdays, wedding anniversaries, or when certain annual subscriptions fall due.)

The name *Rosh Hashanah* is not used in the *Torah* (and, when it is used — once only — in Ezekiel 40:1 it actually refers to *Yom Kippur*!) In Leviticus 23:23-25 we read:

'God spoke to Moses, saying: 'Speak to the Israelite people thus: In the seventh month, on the first day of the month, you shall observe complete rest, a sacred occasion commemorated with loud blasts.

You shall not work at your occupations; and you shall bring an offering by fire to God.'

Here the phrase used is '*Shabbaton, Zichron Teruah*'.

In Numbers 29:1-6 we read:

'In the seventh month, on the first day of the month, you shall observe a sacred occasion; you shall not work at your occupations. You shall observe it as a day when the horn is sounded. You shall present a burnt offering of pleasing odour to the God; one bull of the herd, one ram, and seven yearling lambs, without blemish. The meal offering with them — a choice flour with oil mixed-in — shall be: three-tenths for a ram, and one-tenth for each of the seven lambs. And there shall be one goat for a sin-offering, to make expiation in your behalf... In addition to the burnt offering of the New Moon with its meal offering, and the regular burnt offering with its meal offering, each with its libation as described, offerings by fire of pleasing odour to God.'

This describes, in ritualistic terms, a three-fold observance — the daily sacrifice, the special extra sacrifice for the New Moon, and the extra special sacrifices for this specific New Moon — including one for expiation of sins.

The day is described here as a '*Yom Teruah*', normally translated as 'a big day of blowing'. The *Shofar*, the ceremonial ram's horn, was obviously used as a signal for various occasions. Psalm 81:4-5 reads:

'Blow the horn at the new moon. At the full moon for the feast-day; For it is a statute for Israel, an ordinance of the God of Jacob.'

This is really all there is about *Rosh Hashanah* in the Bible, though in the time of Ezra and Nechemiah (Nechemiah 7:73, 8:13 and Ezra 3:1-3) the first day of the seventh month was an important one inasmuch as the people were gathered together and reminded of the heritage most of them had forgotten.

Most of what we now accept as major customs for this day are much later developments.

5. THE 'SECOND DAY'

Rosh Hashanah is unique as a major festival in the Jewish calendar in falling on the First of a month. In the days before astronomy became a sophisticated science (though, to be fair, this happened very early) the exact calculation of when a new moon would appear was very difficult and procedures were instituted whereby two witnesses had to appear before the Temple authorities and swear to have seen the new crescent moon. For this reason the establishment of *Rosh Chodesh* (the New Month) was complex and the custom arose (especially in the *Diaspora*, '*Chutz LaAretz*', literally 'Outside the Land') of duplicating every major day 'just to be on the safe side'.

In Israel the festivals were not duplicated, with the exception of *Rosh Hashanah*. The Reform movement in this country now largely follows the Israeli practice, whereby we do not celebrate a Second Day of *Pesach* or *Sukkot*, but many communities do have a Second-Day service for *Rosh Hashanah*. (It should be noted that no one has ever instituted a Second-Day *Yom Kippur*! The tenth day of the month always seemed assured!)

Should the exact service be duplicated? Practice varies according to the individual synagogue. Normally we discourage repetitiveness for the sake of it and a fresh approach is often sought for the Second Day.

Traditionally the *Torah* reading for the First Day is Genesis Ch. 21 and for the Second Day Gen. Ch. 22. Since the latter is seen as more valuable and climactic a story, the RSGB calendar reverses the order (*Machzor* pp.842 and 880 — see especially the note on p.880).

6. THE *SHOFAR*

Rosh Hashanah is linked in the Jewish mind with the *Shofar*, for it is blown (some say) 100 times during the *Torah* and *Mussaf* (Additional) Services and once more at the very end of the *Yom Kippur* services (RSGB *Machzor* pp. 216-219; 228-241; 664-665; **Machzor Ruach Chadashah p. 140 and p. 143-155**). The *Shofar* is a natural horn, usually a ram's horn (tradition associates it with the ram caught by its horns in a thicket when Isaac was about to be sacrificed, *Talmud*, 'Rosh Hashanah' 16a (Genesis 22:13; *Machzor* p.853) but in fact the horns of other 'clean' animals — goats or various species of deer — are also suitable (though not cows' horns — It was felt that a cow's horn might act as a reminder of the Golden Calf! *Mishnah*: 'Rosh Hashanah' 3:2; *Talmud* 'R.H.' 26a.) There is no mouthpiece fitted.

There was also discussion as to whether a straight horn could be used (the normal type in Temple times apparently) or a curved one, the curve also signifying contrition and humility.

Strictly speaking the rabbis understood the command of the *Shofar* to mean hearing it blown, rather than blowing it. (Hence the *Berachah* is '...*lishmoʾa kol Shofar.*') This is a relief for many people, who would have difficulty coping with the mouthpiece! There is a further reason for the blowing being late in the sequence of services, during the *Mussaf*. The *Mishnah* ('R.H.' 4:7) and the *Gemara* ('R.H.' 32b) teach that it should be blown then, rather than earlier in the Morning Service, partly to avoid misunderstandings and partly because, by then, the synagogues would be full! The Jerusalem *Talmud* ('RH' 4:8) explains that children do not usually come any earlier to the services... The rules applying to how and when you may fulfil the command of 'hearing the *Shofar*' are complex, and this excerpt from the 'Jerusalem Post' (1980) reveals some of the additional political problems:

HALACHIC RULING

Many people have asked us the question: Is it permitted to participate in the High Holyday services arranged by the Movement of Masorti Judaism ('Conservative') which have been advertised in the Press. We wish to express our opinion — *halachic* ruling — (as we did in the press on the even of *Rosh Hashanah*, last year) that the Holy Tora forbids participation in these 'prayers' and that one cannot fulfil one's obligations to pray by going to a Conservative congregation, either on the High Holydays or during the year.

In the same way, one cannot fulfil one's obligation to hear the blowing of the shofar, at the 'prayer' houses of the Conservative Movement.

We therefore issue this only appeal to the public not to be tempted by the propaganda of this movement, not to participate in any of their activities and not to associate with them. Everyone can find a place at a synagogue where the form of prayers is the form used from generation to generation; there he may devote himself to the Creator of the world, and pour our his heart to Him who examines the hearts of all.

And may the Almighty bless us, hear our prayers, give us salvation, and with compassion and favour accept our prayers and grant the blessing of peace on all Israel and on Jerusalem.

May you be signed and sealed for a good year.

May it be a year of redemption for us and all the House of Israel.

Signed: Shalom Mashash and Yaacov Bezalel Zolti: Chief Rabbis of Jerusalem.'

Be that as it may, the *Shofar* is blown by a person known as the '*Ba'al Tekiah*' in response to calls from the officiant. There are several such calls known to us and many varied traditions as to how they should be sounded. Further, *Shofarot* are hard to play, they have no valves or methods of altering the tone and no two *Shofarot* have the same pitch. Accordingly it is hard to be precise about 'the correct notes'. The '*Tekiah*' is a long, sustained note; '*Tekiah Gedolah*', which ends a sequence, is sustained for as long as possible — the 'Great *Tekiah*'; '*Teruah*' is understood to be a wailing, broken cry, a triplet equivalent in length to a *Tekiah*; '*Shevarim*' is a later addition, meaning 'Broken'. It was inserted because of uncertainty over whether *Teruah* should be translated as 'Broken' as well. (*Mishnah*, 'R.H.' 4:9.)

The *Shofar* is such a strange sound to us, products of a sophisticated Western culture, that it can have a deep emotional effect. It is a raw, elemental sound, far removed from modern musical instruments and its part in the service — blown after each of the three theme-sections of the *Mussaf* service: '*Malchuyot*' (Kingship); '*Zichronot*' (Remembrance); and '*Shofarot*' (the *Shofar* blasts) — is to unify these elements and take us deep within ourselves. Like a siren, it acts as a warning sound, as well as a mere announcement of time. It should arouse feelings of fear and awe

— a bit like film music when, as in Hitchcock's 'Psycho', we are being prepared for a moment of shock or terror! When an air-raid siren goes one does not say 'What an interesting tone' but 'Oh, we are under threat!' Often in synagogues the congregation seems more concerned to congratulate the *Ba'al Tekiah* on having blown so well, than on taking in this musical message!

7. THE '*MUSSAF*' SERVICE

(See RSGB *Machzor* pp. 224-247; ***Machzor Ruach Chadasha pp. 143-154 [though not called 'Mussaf']***)

Whilst the Morning Service for *Rosh Hashanah* follows, in essence, the normal procedures for any Festival Morning Service, with some slight emendations (e.g. the addition of an extra line in the first two paragraphs of the *Amidah* p.200 and the addition of the three paragraphs beginning '*Uv'cheyn*' on pp.200 & 202 into the *Kedushah*) and the addition of the hymn '*Avinu Malkenu*', plus the *Shofar* prayer etc., the main thrust of the extra *Rosh Hashanah* liturgy falls into the Additional or *Mussaf* Service. This includes:

(A). THE 'UNETANNEH TOKEF'

(RSGB Machzor p.224; ***Machzor Ruach Chadashah p. 141***). This powerful prayer — or theological statement — is designed to shock, and it succeeds every year. According to tradition (it is not known how accurate or legendary this tradition is!) it was composed by Rabbi Amnon of Mainz in the 10th.-century CE. (This tradition is only known because a 12th-13th century writer, Isaac ben Moses of Vienna, quotes a 12th-century writer, Ephraim ben Jacob. This detail is given to illustrate the dangers of believing uncritically everything in, say, the footnotes to the 'Artscroll' *Machzor, Rosh Hashanah*, p.480, which delivers such an uncritical version!)

The gruesome legend states that the Bishop of Mainz made repeated attempts to convert Rabbi Amnon to Christianity, without success. Eventually Amnon, perhaps in desperation, asked for a three-day 'breathing space' in which to consider the matter. Troubled lest he had now given even the impression that he might break down and convert, Amnon did not appear for his appointment and had to be brought before the Bishop by force, charged with breaking his promise. At this he pleaded guilty and asked that his tongue be cut out for not having refused more categorically in the first place. The Bishop replied: 'Not your tongue, but your legs, which did not bring you at the agreed time.' At this Amnon's legs and arms were amputated bit by bit. A few days later on *Rosh Hashanah* he was carried into the synagogue and, just before the *Kedushah* prayer, asked if he could sanctify the great name of God; he thereupon recited the '*Une'tanneh Tokef*' and promptly died. Three days later he appeared in a dream to Rabbi Kalonymus ben Meshullam of Mainz and dictated the words of this '*Piyyut*' (a poetic piece of liturgy).

This is a powerful legend; it is almost a shame to spoil it by pointing out that similar texts have been found in quite ancient liturgical fragments and are probably derived from a very early Palestinian Jewish prayer.

The message of the *Piyyut* is however awe-inspiring. *Rosh Hashanah* is described as the Day of Judgement ('*Yom haDin*') on which ALL creatures pass, one by one, before their Maker, their Creator. The vulnerability of mankind is stressed and the many ways in which Death comes; God's omniscience, the existence of an exact record of all our doings, is emphasised and the way judgement is formed and a short period of grace allowed before it is fixed and sealed. And yet — there is still a way to 'avert the severe decree' — for by transforming our actions and our characters, we can also to some extent transform our destinies.

In essence this encapsulates the whole message of the High Holy Days — that we are constantly under judgement, that we need to make our own reckoning and that we need to repent and improve ourselves. There are, it is true, questions every time a 'good person' dies — for, by implication, if this prayer is totally true, they have somehow lacked or lapsed, otherwise they would have survived until the next *Rosh Hashanah*. The answer is of course not to take this so literally. It is a poem and a statement, an expression of faith and hope, and Death must come to all of us eventually, however pious, penitent or charitable we may be. Religion is not so simplistic and mechanistic — but it can transform us, if we let it.

(B). THE 'THREE THEMES'

Three themes dominate *Rosh Hashanah* — God's Power, the Remembrance of past promises (both our own broken ones and God's promises of ultimate forgiveness and salvation) and the warning sound of the *Shofar*. In the *Mussaf* service these three are each elaborated upon in separate sections, known as the '*Malchuyot*', '*Zichronot*' and '*Shofarot*' passages.

Each consists of ten quotations. In traditional Machzorim these come as follows:
Three from the *Torah*
Three from the *K'tuvim*, the Writings
Three from the *Nevi'im*, the Prophets
One more from the *Torah*.
Note that the Writings (always passages from the Psalms) precede the Prophets here.

In the Reform *Machzor* the concept of 'ten sections' is retained, but the concept of a continuing Revelation means that more modern passages are also incorporated. Thus we have:
Three from the *Tanakh* — comprising one each from *Torah*, Nev'i'm, *Ketuvim*
Three (usually) from Rabbinic writings
Three from medieval or modern authors
One more from the *Torah*.
Each quotation either incorporates the 'key word' for the section, or refers to some aspect of it.

In the 'Malchuyot' we find (p.230) the Aleynu prayer, originally composed specifically for the Rosh Hashanah Mussaf service and only later used in other services as well.

8. THE 'AKEDAH'

This is the name given to the section of Genesis Chapter 22 dealing with the 'Binding of Isaac', 'Akedat Yitzhak'. Traditionally this is read on the Second Day of *Rosh Hashanah*, with Chapter 21, the story of Hagar and Ishmael, read on the First Day (though, as mentioned above, the RSGB *Machzor* reverses this order). **Machzor Ruach Chadashah** gives boths texts as options (*pp. 123-128*).

The RSGB *Machzor* (pp. 842-862) includes many notes and commentaries. The story of the pious man obeying God even to his own apparent detriment, and of the pious youngster (assuming Isaac was still young at the time!) willingly accepting an apparently harsh destiny as divine decree, had a powerful effect on Jewish communities during periods of oppression and martyrdom.

A main message of this chapter is that there are limits to what God really demands from us, that human sacrifice is NOT God's wish — and possibly also that there are times when we should not believe uncritically everything we hear.

(N.B.: In Christianity this passage is known as 'The Sacrifice of Isaac' and is related to the later concept of Jesus being 'sacrificed' by his father, whereas in fact the whole point of the narrative is that in the end Isaac was NOT sacrificed and Jews read this as a polemic against human sacrifice! In Islam (though this is not in the Quran) it is Ishma'el / Ismail who is chosen as the potential victim.)

9. THE BOOK OF LIFE

A picturesque concept, a metaphor obviously derived from the image of the annual stocktaking and checking of the commercial account books, is that of the Heavenly Records being opened every *Rosh Hashanah* and checked for the year's spiritual balances. This is mentioned in the *Talmud* (Tractate 'Rosh Hashanah' 16b). The idea is that each person hopes that he or she may be entered or written down in the Credit rather than the Debit side — in the 'Book of Life', or just 'written down for Good' — and this thought is also expressed in the greetings for the period. In the days before *Yom Kippur* one wishes 'LeShanah Tovah Tikatyevu' — 'May you be written for a Good Year'; On *Yom Kippur* the books are closed again and sealed, so one wishes 'LeShanah Tovah T'Chateymu' — 'May you be Sealed for a Good Year!' This is reflected also in the *Yom Kippur* liturgy where 'techatem' replaces 'techatev' and a final pious greeting is 'Chatimah Tovah'.

A line is added in the first paragraph of the *Amidah*:

In the RSGB *Machzor* (p.64 and several times further until *Yom Kippur*): 'King who delights in life, recall us to life and record us in the Book of Life for your own sake, God of Life!'

In the **8**[th.] **Edition p.75** the more neutral translation: 'Sovereign who delights in life, recall us to life and record us in the Book of Life for Your own sake, God of life!'

Machzor Ruach Chadashah has: 'Remember us for life, for You, O Sovereign, delight in life; and inscribe us in the Book of Life, for Your sake, O God of life.'

There is no evidence that heaven has been computerised yet, so the Books remain in use!

10. *TASHLICH*

(*RSGB Machzor* p.791)

This is a strange custom and one that had fallen into some disuse but is being revived in some communities. It is the practice of walking on the afternoon of the First Day of *Rosh Hashanah* to a stream or other flowing water and ceremonially 'scattering one's sins' into it, so that they may be carried downstream. Some even empty symbolic breadcrumbs from their pockets into the water, representing their sins, which will be eaten by the fish and so disappear.

This custom first appeared in the fourteenth century CE; the name means 'Casting' or 'Sending'. A short prayer is read emphasising God's forgiving qualities and that God 'will cast all our sins into the depths of the sea' (This is based on Micah 7:18-20).

As an act of symbolic self-purification this rite obviously has some value. Alas, it also points to a common human fallacy that one can remove pollution from oneself or make it all disappear simply by throwing it into the water, for someone else (or natural forces) to deal with…

11. OTIIER CUSTOMS OF *ROSH HASHANAH*

The desire for a 'Sweet Year' led to the use of honey in several recipes; apple dipped in honey is eaten (representing fruitfulness as well as sweetness), *Challah* is dipped in honey rather than salt at the *Kiddush*, and sweet cakes are baked.

There is also a custom of eating a fish's head, representing the 'head of the year', or fish pies baked in the shape of a fish head. A lot of fruit is eaten and nowadays a major greetings-card industry (and the electronic equivalent) has developed around the High Holy Days.

In addition and perhaps more importantly, at this time of reflection and introspection it is common to visit family graves in the cemetery. Some communities arrange and advertise special periods when the cemetery is open.

12. THE 'TEN DAYS OF PENITENCE'

Why do we have ten days of or for Penitence? Ten is not a common number in Biblical mathematics (unlike the numbers Seven or Twelve — though one can think of Ten Plagues or Ten Commandments) but Leviticus 23:23-32, which deals with this period of the calendar, specifically states that one must mark the first and tenth days of the seventh month, the latter commencing (verse 32) 'on the ninth of the month, at the evening, from evening to evening.' Of course, if one observes two days of *Rosh Hashanah* itself the intervening period is nine not ten days, but one counts anyway from the first day.

This period is known as the '*Asseret Yemei Teshuvah*', the 'Ten days of Return' or 'of Repentance' and allows time for reflection, for work on Oneself, away from all the fuss of the 'Festivals' themselves with their complexity and intensity. Between the high drama and warning of '*Yom haDin*', 'Day of Judgement' and the tension and fasting of the '*Yom haKippurim*', 'Day of Atonement', one needs time to come to terms with oneself.

During this period distractions such as weddings are avoided; The liturgy includes additional lines in the *Amidah* and *Kaddish* for the High Holy Days. The RSGB *Machzor* includes (pp.248-258) a series of meditations for use in the daily services which can also be used for private bed-time reading and reflection. These days are not time to be wasted — if anything, some see them as a 'period of grace' when 'the gates of Heaven are opened wider' or when 'prayers are more easily heard and accepted'. This may be inconsistent with the notion that 'the gates' are always open, that prayers are always heard — but the heightened atmosphere is real nonetheless. One could say for example that shops are almost always open, but that at 'Sale' time they are even more available, or that during a 'pre-Christmas' rush they are even more popular and crowded, or that at stocktaking time you are even more likely to find what you want at a price that makes it accessible to you...

But the fact is that for most of our lives in modern society we are pressurised into consumerism and into competition with others (not so much with ourselves), into desiring always what is 'new' or what we do not really need... When can we really find the time and opportunity and incentive to stand back from this and to dwell upon our own mortality, our relationships with the generations before and following us, what do we want to be truly remembered for, and how? We may not sacrifice our children as Abraham was commanded to do, but how many family and other relationships do we sacrifice or endanger or neglect in the pursuit of profit or financial gain or status or temporary 'success'? We may not be slaves as the Israelites were in Egypt, but are we not sometimes enslaved to our need to make regular payments for accommodation or insurance or pension funds, to the extent that we feel no longer free to pursue our 'real' lives? Have we made the right priorities? Will we be able, at the end of our lives, to close our eyes with the feeling, 'Well, I have done my best, I do not fear whatever may come next'? Are we loved? Will we be missed?

These are universal human issues — of course we need to plan, to pay our bills, to fulfil our manifold responsibilities — but to have ten days set aside every year to reflect upon our priorities in life is a wonderful opportunity.

13. *SHABBAT SHUVAH*

The calendar is so arranged that, whilst one of the High Holy Days might fall on a *Shabbat*, there can never be more than one *Shabbat* in the ten-day period between the two. This *Shabbat* is known as '*Shabbat Shuvah*', the 'Sabbath of Returning', partly because of the period within which it falls, partly because the *Haftarah* is always composed of prophetic passages calling for Return. (Hosea 14:2-10; Micah 7:18-20; In Orthodox synagogues also Joel 2:15-27 which is a call to a solemn fast and a reassurance that God will care for the people.)

14. '*KAPPARAH*'

This is one of the strangest and most gruesome of the weird rituals that have entered some sections of Judaism, one which was roundly condemned as a barbarous and superstitious practice by such eminent scholars as RaMbaN ('Nachmanides') and Joseph Caro, the writer of the '*Shulchan Aruch*', who described it as 'a stupid custom' — and yet *Kapparah* is actually being revived by some groups within the Orthodox community and the service for it is even included in the 1986 'Artscroll' *Yom Kippur Machzor* (pp.2-5)!

'*Kapparah*' means 'Atonement' — from the same root as '*Kippur*' — and the custom, never referred to in Bible or *Talmud* and first known of in the 9th.-century CE consists of making a symbolic transfer of one's sins and misdeeds into an animate or inanimate object and disposing of it, though in a much more tangible form than in *Tashlich*. 'Normally' (if such a word can be used to describe this) a chicken is/was used, or some other animal of a species that could not be used for Temple sacrifice (to avoid misunderstandings with the Scapegoat when it is slaughtered); At other times plants or, more usually, money would be used, and later given to charity. (The chicken could also be given to a poor person after it was killed.) Modern refinements add that a male should use a rooster and a female should use a hen and that a pregnant female should use two hens 'in case she is carrying a female child'. The ritual, known in Yiddish as '*Schlogging Kappoyres*', consists of waving the chicken or money three times around one's head whilst reciting a version (to suit personal circumstances) of the following:

'This is my exchange, this is my substitute, this is my atonement. This chicken will go to its death (or: this money will go to charity), whilst I will enter and proceed to a good long life and to peace.'

The chicken is then slaughtered, or the money donated. Presumably the person then feels better! Psychologically, they have 'bought their way out' of whatever fate was presumably in store for them — the same psychology that lay behind the sale of Indulgences in the Catholic Church or that lies behind the sale of Life Insurance!

This ritual is normally (that word again!) carried out on the morning of the day before *Yom Kippur*, i.e. the morning before *Kol Nidrei*.

15. FASTING

In many people's eyes the greatest distinguishing feature of *Yom Kippur* is the fact that it is the only fast that is even partially observed by the majority; all the others in the calendar, even *Tisha B'Av*, have largely lapsed. In consequence it becomes an object of great terror. All Jewish festivals have some specific Food element, yet *Yom Kippur*'s distinguishing recipe is a blank menu page…

The act of Fasting is an interesting one because essentially it means doing Nothing, just abstaining for a specific period of time from either eating or drinking or both.

Why does one fast? Oddly enough the original idea was to remove distractions rather than add to them. It is true that fasting and self-denial are described in Leviticus as a form of affliction, but all work was also prohibited on the 'Sabbath of Sabbaths', a '*Shabbat Shabbaton*', so by definition cooking and food-preparation were excluded from what was allowed on that day. (However, on a normal weekly *Shabbat* one gets around this by preparing the food beforehand and indeed, since *Shabbat* is meant to be a day of joy, Fasting is normally prohibited on that day!) Some see within the *Yom Kippur* liturgy an element of symbolically Dying for the day and being reborn, purified. That would also explain the custom of wearing the '*Kittel*' or shroud on that day. On *Yom Kippur* we are 'as dead to the world'. What do the Living do? They work, eat, marry, involve themselves in worldly affairs; In contrast — What do the Dead do? They don't go to work, don't eat, don't have marital relations, but spend their time in praising God and going over their past lives. Hence on *Yom Kippur* we likewise don't eat, or wash, or apply make-up, or wear workaday clothing, and so on.

In practical terms this means not eating or drinking (or smoking!) from just before sundown to just after the next sundown, so that we can concentrate on the real character of the day. Alas, in reality this also means that many Jewish households are thrown into turmoil, with an enormous banquet prepared for before *Yom Kippur* ('to tide us over the fast') and another for afterwards ('to break the fast' — this latter often even involving such a lot of preparation that it is known for members of the household to leave the synagogue in the afternoon and miss the service in order to get it ready!) The greetings for the New Year include the anxious wish that the recipient might live 'well over the Fast' as though it is a major trauma akin to a surgical operation. One wishes '*Tzom Kal!*' — 'An easy Fast!' Details of who is invited where to 'break the fast' become a major topic of conversation.

What is the actual effect of the Fast? In reality, after a modest evening meal (recommended, since otherwise the stomach is stuffed) one does without a 'nightcap' or 'midnight snack', one then skips breakfast and one does without lunch. In these modern, stressed times, that is not such an uncommon schedule for many working people anyway! If you start the fast on a light meal with plenty of fluids — soup and salads — actual hunger pangs won't necessarily set in until well into the following afternoon. It is a mistake to 'stock up' on food beforehand — the human Body doesn't really work that way. At the end of the day one's stomach will have contracted anyway, so another light meal with fluids is much better for one than a 'blowout' and this can be something simple prepared before *Yom Kippur*, or easily warmed-up.

Whilst occasional fasting is meant to be healthy, allowing the Body to restore some of its natural balances, few would claim that it is Fun. However, there is no need for the thought of Fasting to become a greater affliction than the Fast itself!

Certain categories of people are not only exempted but actually prohibited from fasting on *Yom Kippur*. Small children (though they can be trained to extend the periods between meals); pregnant women and those breastfeeding; those on medication; even those whose unavoidable work requires concentration and a clear mind unaffected by low blood-sugar levels. (This is derived from the role of the man who led the Scapegoat into the desert in Temple times, who was permitted to eat and drink.) However, in such cases one should still take only small amounts, or multiples of small amounts, to show that this is eating for health purposes only. The technical term is '*K'Zayit*', 'the bulk of an olive', at each mouthful.

16. *YOM KIPPUR*

The Hebrew term is '*Yom haKippurim*', 'The Day of Atonements' (in the plural). It falls on the 10th of *Tishri*. Despite its popular image it is, from a theological perspective, more of a festival than is *Rosh Hashanah*, the Day of Judgement. Forgiveness is always more welcome than Warning. This is another of the reasons given for the wearing of white clothing — that it is a joyful day.

Yom Kippur is mentioned (not always by name) in the *Torah* in Leviticus 16:2-34 and 23:26-32 and in Numbers 29:7-11. In addition the Jubilee Year described in Leviticus 25:8-10 commences on the 'tenth day of the seventh month'. It is described as a sacred gathering, a day of self-denial, of abstention from work, of coming together to offer sacrifices (which are also described in detail) and as a perpetual command. Before the *Cohen Gadol*, the High Priest could perform the rituals for the expiation of the sins of the People, he had first to perform them for himself and for his fellow priests (this publicly demonstrating that he and they were no better than anyone else). It was obviously a great occasion.

A good description of the impact the Temple service had on the populace can be found in the 'Book of Ben Sirach' 50:1-24 in the non-canonical 'Apocrypha'. (This book is also known as 'Ecclesiasticus', not to be confused with 'Ecclesiastes'). This is actually a paean of praise to one particular High Priest, Shimon the son of Onias, and explains how well and thoroughly he did his job.

According to an early Rabbinic tradition *Yom Kippur* was the day when Moses received the second set of tablets with the Commandments. This was worked out from some complex but straightforward calculations:

'When the Children of Israel received the Ten Commandments on *Shavuot*, Moses ascended Mount Sinai and remained there forty days to receive the Tablets of the Law. On the seventeenth day of *Tammuz* he descended and, seeing the people worshipping a golden calf, broke the tablets. Then, for forty days, Moses placed his tent beyond the camp, and the people mourned. On the first day of *Elul* Moses again ascended the mountain to receive the second Tablets. During this period the Israelites fasted daily from sunrise to sunset. However, on the fortieth day they fasted from sunset to sunset. This day was the tenth of *Tishri*. When Moses returned in the morning, the Israelites went forth to meet him. He saw that they were weeping and he too wept as he became aware of their repentance. Then God said: 'Your repentance is acceptable to me, and this day will remain the Day of Atonement throughout all the generations.' ('*Seder Eliyahu Zutah*', 4:2).

The full Temple ritual is described also in the *Mishnah* Tractate '*Yoma*' (the Aramaic form of the Hebrew '*HaYom*', 'THE Day'). In this text we also see the worries and problems facing those in charge of the rituals when they had to deal with a *Cohen Gadol*, a High Priest who wasn't up to his job, who was unqualified and inexperienced, possibly just a political appointee.

The ritual was really frightfully important to the people at the time, for this was the system for removing punishment and catastrophe, for 'keeping God happy' (a crude way of putting it but fairly accurate). If, heaven forbid, something went wrong — if the High Priest became unclean through a nocturnal seminal emission, or he forgot the words, or one of the sacrificial animals was blemished — the results could have been terrible. For this reason the details of the ritual actions, the clothes to be worn, the procedures for removing ashes of burnt sacrifices and so on were so carefully enumerated. A good modern equivalent would be the rules governing the running of a nuclear power station; we all rely on the invisible elemental power emanating from this source (albeit electrical rather than divine power) and in consequence the safety regulations covering procedures, protective clothing, cooling mechanisms and removal of waste are matters of great concern.

The danger is that this concern might blind us to the purpose of all the ritual — the ensuring of atonement, of forgiveness and thus of personal and communal salvation. The later rabbinic literature stresses to a much greater extent the importance of repentance and forgiveness and recalls the Temple rituals more as an exercise in nostalgia. It is interesting that so much of Judaism still wishes (at least liturgically) to restore the sacrificial cult and move backwards from an ethical understanding of the duties of the individual Jew to a ritual one. The RSGB *Machzor* (pp. 462-479) recounts extracts from the ancient ritual only so as to lead up to the ethical approach (p.479) and to emphasise it.

People often refer to *Yom Kippur* as being 'a long service'. In fact this is incorrect — it is a Festival day with a sequence of services — starting with the Evening (also known as '*Kol Nidre*' or '*Kol Nidrei*'), a Morning ('*Shacharit*'), an Additional ('*Mussaf*'), followed by an Afternoon ('*Minchah*') and another leading up to the Evening (known as '*Ne'ilah*'). In addition there is a Memorial Service ('*Yizkor*') which is normally placed between *Minchah* and *Ne'ilah* but can also in some communities be placed earlier. One important feature is that the *Ne'ilah* must END at a specific time, so there is no point in rushing it and ending earlier.

Depending on the time of year and what time the daytime services are due to start and end there may be a pause in between the *Mussaf* and *Minchah*, or between the *Minchah* and *Yizkor* — in which case worshippers have an opportunity to study, or to leave for 'a breath of fresh air'. In practice it is usually a mistake to leave the synagogue and go outside, as it disrupts the atmosphere and one is confronted with the fact that 'outside' there is a whole world going about its daily, noisy, rushed business. Whilst some people may have good reasons to come and go in order to care for children, house pets, elderly relatives etc., in fact one gains the best 'impact' by simply trying to concentrate for as long as possible — otherwise one is indulging in the spiritual equivalent of popping in and out of a play and concert and thus not comprehending what is really going on. The most significant of the services is — as for any 'Special day' — the *Mussaf*, as it is here that the main themes are dealt with most deeply. Since this falls around the middle of the day (assuming that *Shacharit* was set to start around 10am or 10.30am) it is alas often the least-well attended part of the day's proceedings! And yet with some advance planning, preparation and delegation it should also be possible to deal with at least some of the urgent needs of pets and children without having to go all the way back home…

17. 'KOL NIDREI'

The Evening Service for *Yom Kippur* is known by the opening words of the opening formula (RSGB *Machzor* p.272; **Ruach Chadashah p. 174 and 436**). This is not a Prayer in the normally-accepted sense but a legal formulation for the annulment of unfulfilled vows. The origin of this formulation is lost in history. It is first referred to (and condemned) as an established practice by the Babylonian rabbis of the 8th.-century. Some scholars even think it began as a public wish that those vows made against the community, to destroy it, be wiped out and frustrated. By the 11th.-century it had become accepted, asking divine 'pardon, forgiveness and atonement' for the sin of failing to keep a solemn vow (or even for having vowed carelessly at all) 'from the last Day of Atonement to this day of Atonement'; in the 12th. -century French and German Rabbis known as the 'Tosafists' re-worded this so as to refer to future vows that might be made 'from this Day of Atonement to the next day of Atonement' — quite a difference.

According to the 'Encyclopaedia Judaica' (Vol. 10:1166) *Ashkenazi* Jews use the 12th-century version and Western *Sephardim* the 10th.-century one and other *Sephardim* both!

The rationale behind the alteration of the text from a past to a future application is based on the *Talmud* statement ('Nedarim' 23b) that:

> 'Whoever desires that none of his vows made during the year shall be valid, let him declare at the beginning of the year: May all the vows which I am likely to make in the future be annulled.'

Not surprisingly anti-Semites have, for centuries, used the *Kol Nidrei* as 'evidence' that Jews and their promises are not to be trusted. In practice however the rabbis have pointed out that *Yom Kippur* and all the prayers thereon can only apply to sins committed against God — including vows which were made and not fulfilled, thus breaking the law laid down in Deuteronomy 23:22-24:

'When you make any vow to the Lord your God, you must pay it without delay…
if you refrain from making any vow, that is no sin for you; but you must be careful to perform any promise you have made with your lips.'

The rabbis argued that any sin committed against a fellow human being can only be forgiven by the victim, not by God. Fasting and prayer on *Yom Kippur* is designed to placate God for sins committed against God (sins of both commission and omission, i.e. of doing something wrong or of failing to do something right), not to 'make up' for violence and swindling and theft and pain committed against other people.

The service commences with another solemn declaration, in which leaders of the community stand at the front of the congregation, usually holding *Sifrei Torah*; they constitute themselves into a *Beit Din* on earth, representing a heavenly Court and publicly admit sinners to the service. This was introduced in the 13th.-century by Rabbi Meir of Rothenburg. It serves to remove any lingering doubt in the sinner's mind (and we are ALL sinners) that he or she might not be welcome in the service.

The effect of both these statements is to 'clear the air', so to speak, so that the main service can start. There have been many occasions when Jews had to deny their religion in the face of forced conversion or persecution and guilt or fear about this might have inhibited them from returning. By opening the *Yom Kippur* service in this way the doors are opened to all to come and make their peace with God.

The melody dates from the 16th.-century and is anonymous. The traditional text is in Aramaic, not Hebrew. Traditionally *Kol Nidrei* should be said before nightfall, since a dispensation of vows cannot be given on a *Shabbat* or a *Chag* — a Festival — i.e. technically it forms a prologue to the Evening Service, not a part of the service itself.

18. *YOM KIPPUR* SERVICES

As already mentioned above, although the day may seem at times to be one long service it is in fact a sequence following the 'normal' regular pattern of services for festivals — it is just that each of the services is extended and so it can be that, depending on the schedule, they are all joined up together to form one continuous sequence through the daylight hours, without significant pauses between them.

They are (with page numbers from the RSGB *Machzor* and **Machzor Ruach Chadashah**):
 (a). Evening Service. *Kol Nidrei* (p.272) (*p. 171*)
 (b). Morning Service. *Shacharit* (p.346) (*p. 213*)
 (c). Additional Service. *Mussaf* (p.454) (*p. 283*;
     some congregations use a separate booklet)
 (d). Afternoon Service. *Minchah* (p.536) (*p. 352*)
 (e). Memorial Service. *Yizkor* (p.600) (*p. 385*)
 (f). Concluding Service. *Ne'ilah* (p.632) (*p. 405*)

The addition of a *Yizkor* is normal at certain festival services and really only the Conclusion in the later afternoon / early evening is a specific 'Extra', though it corresponds in some respects to the service at the Conclusion of a *Shabbat* and one can add *Havdalah*. (In some communities a short 'Daily Evening Service' is then added!)

Both *Shacharit* and *Minchah* services incorporate *Torah* readings and *Haftarot*. (The *Haftarah* for the *Minchah* is the Book of Jonah.) The core of the *Mussaf* service is the 'Avodah' — the recollection of the old Temple ritual. If this is seen as the centre of the day, the services assume a symmetrical pattern: One works inwards and downwards from our daily world to the mysteries of the ancient past and its secrets; then upwards and outwards, cleansed and purified, back to our daily reality. This makes the *Mussaf* and the *Avodah* the high-point of the liturgy rather than the bit to miss out on by taking a walk or a lunch-break!

19. THE 'AVODAH' SERVICE

(RSGB *Machzor* pp.463-477; **See: 'From Creation to Redemption' in Ruach Chadashah p 289-314.**)

We have already discussed briefly the importance of the High Priest, who was to carry out the purification rites for the whole people, being in a state of purity himself. This is the content of the first part of the service. Then, however, he came to a key section: Two goats, unblemished and identical, were brought; Lots were cast over them, and one became a sacrifice there and then, while the other was symbolically loaded with all the sins of the people (becoming the 'scape-goat') and led by an attendant into the desert on the way to Jericho where, in a secret place, it would be thrown off a cliff so that it broke its neck (i.e. it was killed, but not by an act of ritual slaughter).

It was said that, when the goat died, a scarlet thread tied to the outside of the city gate would miraculously turn white — and that, after this embarrassingly failed to happen on one occasion, the thread was thereafter tied inside the gate, where only the priests could see it, so that they could call out the transformation, but it couldn't be checked!

The goat led into the wilderness was described as being 'for *Azazel*', in accordance with the instructions in Leviticus 16:8-10:

> 'And Aharon shall cast lots upon the two goats, one lot for the Lord and the other lot for *Azazel*. And Aharon shall present the goat upon which the lot fell for the Lord, and offer him for a sin-offering; But the goat on which the lot fell for *Azazel* shall be set alive before God, to make atonement for him, to send him away for *Azazel* into the wilderness.'

The trouble is, no one really knows what this means. Surely '*Azazel*' cannot refer to some other, primitive desert deity? Another name for the Devil? The rabbis tried to interpret the name as meaning 'Rugged', 'Strong', referring to the cliff down which this goat — the scapegoat — was pushed. (Incidentally, Leviticus does not actually say it should be killed, but there were obvious problems if the bearer of the nation's sins were to wander back, like a strayed dog, following its attendant back to civilisation! On the other hand — have you ever tried to throw a struggling goat off a cliff?)

Behind all this mumbo-jumbo and scholarly interpretation lies however a real problem. How do you cleanse an entire people of its guilt? This is still a major contemporary issue in terms of, for example, war guilt. One needs a ritual, however strange — some would say the stranger the better — to 'act out' the feelings of people and lay them to rest. We no longer use goats to carry our burdens, but we still 'scapegoat' others to carry our guilt for us and this psychological mechanism seems almost universal.

20. THE 'NE'ILAH' SERVICE

(RSGB *Machzor* p.632, plus Introduction p. 630; **Ruach Chadashah p. 406**)

Every day in the Temple the gates were closed at the end of the day and this was known as 'Ne'ilat She'arim' or 'Neilat Sha'arei Heichal' — the Closing of the Temple Gates, one hour before sunset. On the Day of Atonement this began at twilight and ended with nightfall, signifying the end both of the day and of the service.

In the 'Jerusalem *Talmud*' ('Ta'anit' 7c) the action was interpreted as a symbolic parallel of the closing of the heavenly gates and the *Ne'ilah* service was developed as a separate entity, incorporating an *Amidah*, various confessions and supplicatory prayers and hymns, building up to a climax as the service ends on, literally, a high-note — a *Tekiah Gedolah* on the *Shofar*.

21. CONFESSION

In Hebrew: '*Vidui*' — 'Making known'

There is no real emphasis in Judaism, as in Christianity, on ritual confession by individuals — except, perhaps, on a death-bed. However, on the High Holy Days the whole congregation recite together several formulae of confession of sins. These are phrased in the first-person plural: 'We have sinned.' Two of these formulae are the '*Al Chet sheChatanu*' and the '*Ashamnu*' (versions of the former can be found in the RSGB *Machzor* pp.304/305, 306/307, 320/321, 324/325, and 406-509; and of the '*Ashamnu*' on pp.302 and 404; **in Machzor Ruach Chadashah pp. 198-201, 259-262, 377-380, and the** *Ashamnu* **on p. 256**).

These are known as the 'Great' and 'Short' confessions and original versions are known from the 8th.-century CE. The *Talmud* ('Yoma' 87b), declares that such confessions of sins is required in every service of *Yom Kippur* (except *Ne'ilah*).

Various interpretations have developed over the years. The rabbis have stated that we all list all the sins that might theoretically have been committed by somebody, so that no one will be embarrassed by being the only person saying a particular bit; also, that we are all responsible one for another, so that if one of us should sin, we are all to some extent bound up in it.

The 'Al Chet' lists sins by categories of commission; the 'Ashamnu' is an alphabetical list (22 lines long in some versions, 44 in others). One interpretation is that we list our sins in this artificial, poetic way because, while there is no end to our sins, there is at least an end to the alphabet!

22. 'MOTZA'I YOM KIPPUR'

The end of *Yom Kippur*, when the day 'goes out', was a time of great joy in ancient times. Rather than collapsing in an exhausted heap it was a time for parties, when the girls would dress in (borrowed) white dresses and go out hunting men. After all, the greatest burden of guilt for the year had just been removed, and a lightness of spirit is to be expected.

Since *Sukkot* is also so close it was also a custom — and still is in many households — to start the erection of a *Sukkah* immediately the service is over.

So, a lengthy period of introspection and worry is over — it is time to prepare for harvest festivities!

CHAPTER 12

SUKKOT AND SIMCHAT TORAH

1. THE FESTIVALS OF *SUKKOT*

The Festivals of *Sukkot*, *Shemini Atzeret* and *Simchat Torah* are commonly considered as a part of the High Holy Days, since that is the period in which they fall. Strictly speaking, however, they have almost nothing to do with the *Yamim Nora'im* of *Rosh Hashanah* and *Yom Kippur*. They mark instead different cycles of the agricultural year and the liturgical rhythm, external rather than internal change and development. It is only the coincidence of timing that throws them together,

2. *SUKKOT*

Sukkot itself is one of the Harvest Festivals, the third (if one starts from Springtime) of the '*Shalosh Regalim*' or Three Pilgrim Festivals, so called because all Jewish males were supposed to make the pilgrimage to the Temple in Biblical times on those occasions. It is described in different ways in different part of the *Torah*:

In Exodus 23:14-17 in a context concerned with social justice and regular rest for the land, (the Sabbatical Year) and the workers and the beasts (the Sabbath), together with an avoidance of idolatry:

> 'Three times a year you shall hold a festival for Me: you shall observe the Feast of Unleavened Bread — eating unleavened bread for seven days as I have commanded you — at the set time in the month of Aviv, for in it you went forth from Egypt; and none shall appear before Me empty-handed; And the Feast of the Harvest; of the first-fruits of your work, of what you sow in the field; And the Feast of Ingathering at the end of the year, when you gather in the results of your work from the field. Three times a year all your males shall appear before the Sovereign, the Lord.'

Here we see that the exact dates of *Pesach*, *Shavuot* and *Sukkot* are not given, but that *Shavuot* marks the beginning of the summer harvest period when the first results appear and *Sukkot* marks the end, or at least the climax of the harvest in the autumn. 'At the end of the year' actually means two weeks into the New Year, but this refers obviously to the agricultural year which starts with the preparation of the ground and ends with the gathering of the produce. From this the name Feast of Ingathering, '*Chag He'Assef*', is taken.

Elsewhere the festival is referred to by its better-known name, the Feast of Booths (or Tabernacles) — or *Sukkot*, a '*Sukkah*' being understood as a type of temporary shack erected in the fields at harvest time to provide shelter for the harvesters or those guarding over the crops. This is taken from Leviticus:

> 'The Lord spoke to Moses saying: 'Say to the Israelite people: On the fifteenth day of this seventh month there shall be the Feast of Booths to the Lord, (to last) seven days. The first day shall be a sacred occasion: you shall not work at your occupations; seven days you shall bring offerings by fire to the Lord. On the eighth day you shall observe a sacred occasion and bring an offering by fire to the Lord; it is a solemn gathering; you shall not work at your occupations...
>
> Mark, on the fifteenth day of the seventh month, when you have gathered in the yield of your land, you shall observe the festival of the Lord (to last) seven days; a complete rest on the first day, and a complete rest on the eighth day. On the first day you shall take the product of the Hadar tree, branches of palm trees, boughs of leafy trees, and willows of the brook, and you shall rejoice before the Lord your God seven days. You shall observe it as a festival of the Lord for seven days in the year; you shall observe it in the seventh month as a law for all time, throughout the generations. You shall live in booths seven days; all citizens in Israel shall live in booths, in order that future generations may know that I made the Israelite people live in booths when I brought them out of the land of Egypt, I am the Lord your God.'
>
> (Leviticus 23:33-36 and 39-44 [JPSA translation])

We see here a variety of elements. The passage (whose context in Lev. 23 is the ritual instruction concerning the observance of *Pesach, Shavuot, Rosh Hashanah* and on *Yom Kippur*) describes first the sacrificial rules, the date and duration of the festival. Naturally there is an ambiguity in the text — instructions of what to do on the eighth day of a seven day festival! — and this ambiguity is maintained down to the present day, as we shall see later.

There is a command to live in Booths but not actually to build them! These booths are, further, linked historically to the experience of the Exodus from Egypt rather than to any association with the harvest — even stranger, in that God did NOT necessarily make the Israelites live in booths; In the desert they lived in tents, as we see from Balaam's exclamation in Numbers 24:5: 'How fair are your tents, O Jacob, your dwellings, O Israel!' ('*Mah tovu Ohalecha, Ya'akov; Mishkenotecha, Yisra'el* — though '*Mishkan*' means a dwelling place and could theoretically be a shack.) The word '*Sukkah*' appears in Genesis 33:17 meaning the cow-shed that Jacob built, but otherwise appears in the *Torah* only in Leviticus Ch. 23 and Deuteronomy Chs. 16 and 31, referring to the festival.

Further, although the Israelites are commanded to take 'four species' for the celebration, these are not species connected with the harvest! Rather than taking, say, apples and grapes and figs and dates, they take willow-branches and myrtle-branches, palm fronds rather than the fruit themselves (dates)... It all seems rather a strange way of celebrating a harvest festival, especially when compared with the more specific offerings of new grain or new lambs at the other two in the calendar. If anything, it appears that the *Torah* is discouraging a 'normal' form of celebrating the harvest as practised by other, pagan peoples, complete with over-indulgence and debauchery. Instead it establishes a very different principle, of living in primitive conditions, abstaining from work and a ritual sublimation into something quite harmless — the waving of branches and an inedible sort of lemon!

And yet the Deuteronomy passage appears much freer in tone:

> 'After the ingathering from your threshing floor and your vat, you shall hold the Feast of Booths for seven days. You shall rejoice in your festival, with your son and daughter, your male and female slave, the Levite, the stranger, the fatherless, and the widow in your communities. You shall hold festival for the Lord your God for seven days, in the place that the Lord will choose; for the Lord your God will bless all your crops and all your undertakings, and you shall have nothing but joy. Three times a year — on the feast of Unleavened Bread, on the Feast of Weeks and on the feast of Booths — all your males shall appear before the Lord your God in the place that he will choose. They shall not appear before the Lord empty-handed, but each with his own gift, according to the blessing that the Lord your God has bestowed upon you.' (Deuteronomy 16:13-17)

The festivities are to embrace all classes of society and the men at least are to bring thanksgiving sacrifices.

Sukkot was also a time for national re-dedication to the *Torah*, though no reason is given for the choice of this date other than that it was a convenient one when the people were gathered together and when, it being a Sabbatical or '*Shemittah*' Year, there would be no urgent need for them to return home to start work in the coming months of preparation of the soil. Hence:

> 'Moses wrote down this Teaching and gave it to the priests... and Moses instructed them as follows: 'Every seventh year, the year set for remission, at the Feast of Booths, when all Israel comes to appear before the Lord your God, in the place which He will choose, you shall read this Teaching aloud in the presence of all Israel. Gather the people — men, women, children, and the strangers in your communities — that they may hear and so learn to revere the Lord your God and to observe faithfully every word of this teaching. Their children, too, who have not had the experience, shall hear and learn to revere the Lord your God...'(Deuteronomy 31:9-13)

Sukkot was therefore, during the 'blank' agricultural years, a time for religious instruction and for study. For us nowadays, who are not bound to the agricultural life-style, this idea should perhaps take greater prominence.

3. *SUKKOT* IN OTHER BIBLICAL
AND POST-BIBLICAL WRITINGS

In the Bible, in I Kings 8:1-5 we read that Solomon dedicated his new Temple 'at the Feast in the month *Ethanim*, which is the seventh month.' The parallel passage in II Chronicles 7:8-10 is more specific:

'So Solomon held the feast at that time seven days, and all Israel with him, a very great congregation… And on the eighth day they held a solemn assembly; for they kept the dedication of the altar seven days, and the feast seven days. And on the three-and-twentieth day of the seventh month he sent the people away unto their tents, joyful and glad of heart…'

Partly as a consequence of this dedication, which was symbolically celebrated on behalf of all nations of the world so that the temple would be seen as somehow 'belonging' to the whole world, *Sukkot* is still frequently perceived as a 'universalist' festival, one which Christians in Israel often observe with pilgrimages to Jerusalem! (See also Zechariah 14:16-19 which stresses this universality.)

When the Israelites returned from the Exile in Babylon in 458 BCE they had largely forgotten the majority of their religious traditions; in the Books of Ezra and Nechemiah we see the painful re-adjustments they had to make. In Ezra 3:1-5 we read that they offered burnt offerings on a makeshift, temporary altar (they had not yet rebuilt the Temple) including those for 'the festival of Tabernacles' — but not that they built *Sukkot*. In Nechemiah 8:14-19 we read how the 'Book of the Law' was read in public on the 1st Tishri (of probably the year 445 BCE); the next day the heads of the community came together, more privately, to study it more carefully:

'And they found written in the Law, that the Lord had commanded by Moses that the children of Israel should dwell in booths in the feast of the seventh month; and that they should publish and proclaim in all the cities, and in Jerusalem, saying: 'Go forth unto the mount, and fetch olive branches, and branches of wild olive, and myrtle branches, and palm branches, and branches of thick trees, to make booths, as it is written.'

So the people went forth and brought them and made themselves booths, every one upon the roof of his house, and in their courts, and in the courts of the house of God, and in the broad place of the water gate, and in the broad place of the gate of Ephraim. And all the congregation of them that were come back out of the captivity made booths, and dwelt in the booths; for since the days of Joshua the son of Nun unto that day the children of Israel had not done so. And there was very great gladness. Also day by day, from the first day unto the last, he read in the book of the Law of God. And they kept the feast seven days; and on the eighth day was a solemn assembly, according to the ordinance.'

In this passage it is clear that the laws of *Sukkot* were really a new discovery for the people. It is significant that we are told that the Israelites had let the whole practice drop almost as soon as Moses had died, thus proving the point Moses was making towards the end of Deuteronomy! (See especially Deut. 31:29).

We also see that they built booths in public places — the broad squares near the gates — as well as in their private domains. The greenery is associated with the construction of booths and there is no mention of the *Etrog* and *Lulav*.

In later post-Biblical writings we see that the celebration of *Chanukah* was modelled by the Maccabees on the *Sukkot* festival they had been forced to miss whilst hiding in the mountains (II Maccabees 10:6-8). In the non-canonical Book of Jubilees, a sectarian work much concerned with proving the antiquity of various religious practices and imposing a rigid calendrical pattern on Israelite history, the unsubstantiated claim is made that the patriarch Jacob added the eighth day to the festival, which he called 'Addition', now known as '*Shemini Atzeret*'.

4. *SUKKOT* IN RABBINIC WRITINGS

There are many references to *Sukkot* — both the festival and the booths themselves — in rabbinic literature. One whole section of the *Mishnah* (and its accompanying *Gemara*) is entitled '*Sukkah*' and deals with definitions of how one may or may not build a *Sukkah*, when, where, how big, how sturdy, with what materials and supports (Chaps. 1 & 2); rules for eating and sleeping in the *Sukkah* (Chap. 2); definitions of the state and legitimacy of the *Lulav* and *Etrog* (Chap. 3); rules for the waving of the *Lulav* and *Etrog* (Chaps. 4 & 5); the manner in which the festival was observed in Temple times, including the Water-Libation, the Psalms that were sung and the sacrifices (Chaps. 4 & 5.)

The *Sukkah* should be made specifically for the festival (i.e. it must not be more than 30 days old, otherwise it counts as an 'old' one); it should be between ten handbreadths and twenty cubits high; it shouldn't be indoors or under a tree; it should be able to withstand normal breezes. There are accounts of rabbinic arguments over whether a *Mezuzah* is required or not ('*Yoma*' 10b — the answer is that one is not required, because it is only a temporary construction); whether you may leave it and shelter elsewhere if it rains heavily; and so on.

5. THE WATER-DRAWING CEREMONY

The previous notes referred in passing to the 'Water Libation'. It appears that in Temple times *Sukkot* was marked also by a ceremony in which water was poured into a basin at the side of the altar during each of the seven days, during the morning service (i.e. at dawn). In the *Mishnah* ('*Sukkah*' 4:9) we are told that the Levites went in procession down to the 'Women's Court', which had been re-arranged for the occasion ('*Sukkah*' 5:2). (One could, of course, argue that since re-arrangement was only made for the week of *Sukkot* that there would be no need for this separation for the rest of the year...) A golden flask was filled with three '*log*' (about 4½ pints or 2 litres) of water from the Pool of Siloam, carried up to the Temple via the Water Gate, greeted there by *Shofar*-calls and great rejoicing, ceremonially carried to the basin at the side of the altar and poured out there. Care had to be taken lest any were spilt and it is said that one rather lax High Priest (Alexander Jannaeus, 103-76 BCE; he was also the king and presumably thought he could get away with anything) was pelted with *Etrogim* by angry worshippers when he spilt the water all over his feet!

There is no Biblical basis for this custom, though this did not stop at least one rabbi (Rabbi Nehunya) claiming that it was a law given by God to Moses, which Moses had not written down! It is, in all likelihood, an echo of the pagan custom of pouring out water as a form of 'sympathetic magic' to encourage the autumn rains to fall. In fact the only relic of this whole custom — and the reason for mentioning it here — is that the re-arrangement of the Women's Court involved building a gallery for the women, while the men stood on the floor below — and this is the sole *halachic* basis for the later custom of '*Mechitza*', the separation of men and women in synagogues during prayer! The term 'Women's Court' does not mean it was exclusively for women but that women could come this far into the concentric layout of the Temple precincts — it was in fact 'mixed'. One could of course argue that since re-arrangement was only made for *Sukkot* there would have been no need for separation of the sexes during other services — e.g. on *Yom Kippur* only a few days earlier...

A further slight relic is that a brief prayer for Rain is added to the *Amidah* from *Shemini Atzeret* through till *Pesach* (after which, for the summer period, one prays for dew instead). 'You make the wind blow and the rain fall' and 'You cause the dew to fall.'

6. THE *SUKKAH*

The word '*Sukkah*' in Biblical Hebrew means a 'thicket' or 'booth' and is derived from the root '*S'chach*' which means 'to weave together'. As 'booth', 'shack', 'bothy', 'shed' or 'hut' it could be used to mean any temporary construction slung together in the field by soldiers (II. Samuel 11:11; I Kings 20:12), to shelter cattle (Gen. 33:17), by an individual desiring shade (Jonah 4:5), etc. However, its main meaning has come to be the booths (known in quaint English as 'Tabernacles' from the Latin for little taverns, places where one can sit and eat) constructed specifically for this autumn harvest festival (e.g. Lev. 23:42 and Deut. 16:13).

Whilst originally made presumably from boughs and twigs, they may be made from all sorts of planks or other materials but should still be recognisable as huts — i.e. the ratio of openings to sides must not exceed a certain amount, it shouldn't be a tent, or too high, or too permanent...

The covering (known as the '*S'chach*', from the word shown above) should be of natural materials, of things that have grown from the soil. However one European custom is to build a hinged roof or lid that can be used to keep the thatched, interleaved vegetation dry! This is considered obligatory in Ganzfried's '*Kitzur Shulchan Aruch*' and obviously reflects bitter experience of Central European autumnal weather. Prints of this sort of *Sukkah* exist, also showing *Sukkot* of various improvised types built on the rooftops, somehow — especially an issue in crowded medieval towns. Once again we see the problems of transferring concepts from a Middle Eastern culture and climate to different circumstances in other countries and latitudes.

One should be able to look through the roofing vegetation and see the stars. This is why it is difficult to build a *Sukkah* on a balcony of a flat, if there are other balconies on the floors above. Nowadays many 'synagogue' *Sukkot* are semi-permanent, or even built indoors because of the dangers of vandalism, with only an opening skylight as a symbolic relic of the Great Outdoors.

It is a tradition to start building the *Sukkah* immediately after *Yom Kippur* has ended. A *Sukkah* may be plain, it may be decorated with fruits, pictures and ornaments. One should be able (technically) to eat in the *Sukkah*, and the pious even sleep in it during the period of the festival. Construction can involve the whole family and there is little reason why most households these days with some private yard, balcony or garden space should not have some semblance of a rickety lean-to shack for the duration. Garden Centres and Do-It-Yourself stores have a variety of netting, planks, bolts etc. Alternatively groups of neighbours or members of a community may share one — since the *Mitzvah* is simply to be in one, not to build one's own.

7. THE '*ARBA MINIM*'

The other major symbol of the festival is the *Lulav*, consisting of three items bound together (and hence treated as one unit) and the *Etrog* — together comprising the '*Arba Minim*' or 'Four Species'.

The Biblical basis for this custom lies in Lev. 23:40 (see above) but the underlying reasoning is harder to find. As mentioned, the species are not representative of crops grown for consumption — quite the reverse. One theory is that the rattling of the twigs is an echo of a pagan custom, designed to simulate — and hence stimulate — the patter of rainfall.

The *Lulav* consists of a young Palm branch, cut before the leaves begin to spread, so that it is still stiff and firm. Because it is the most conspicuous item, towering above the others, this palm — *Lulav* — gives it name to the whole assemblage.

To it are tied — usually these days in a little 'cupped' holder woven from palm straw — twigs of Myrtle ('*Hadass*') and of Willow ('*Aravah*') — specifically, willow that grows near a brook or stream. These three components are tied together with something that is of the same species as themselves — usually three loops of palm fibre — since otherwise there would be five species!

The *Etrog* is something of a mystery. It is not referred to by name in the Biblical text, which speaks only of '*P'ri Etz Hadar*' — the 'fruit of a good or attractive Tree' — but this has traditionally been taken to mean the *Etrog*, which is a yellow citrus fruit looking a little like a lemon but without the same flavour. Indeed it is said to have an unpleasant flavour, it is not grown for any other than ritual purposes and it is not eaten after the festival! It is important to use a 'valid' *Etrog* for the waving and this is defined as one that has no undue discolouration, is at least the size of an egg, and retains its '*Pitom*', the stem from which it hung on the tree.

For many years a main source of supply of *Etrogim* was Corfu and they were distri-buted (somehow) throughout Europe for *Sukkot*. They can grow to an enormous size and the very pious pay enormous sums for 'perfect' specimens. Nowadays there is a number of specialist importers, who advertise for orders before the High Holy Days, make up sets (though often without the Willow, which simply dries out too quickly) and despatch such sets, boxed, by mail order throughout the country.

According to Maimonides ('*Sefer Mo'ed*' 6:7), a *Lulav* should consist of one Palm branch, two Willow twigs and at least three Myrtle twigs.

8. SYMBOLIC MEANINGS

Since there is no obvious physical or historical reason for this *Mitzvah* the rabbis have attempted to find other, homiletical ones. The Four Species are said to represent four types of character — each has a different combination of aroma and edibility or edible fruit, representing human types who have different combinations of know-ledge and good deeds ('*Pesikta Rabbati*' 51:2). They are also taken to represent dif-ferent parts of the human Body — the Palm is the spine, the Myrtle the eyes (as the leaves are shaped so), the Willow-leaves look like lips and the rounded *Etrog* is the heart. The fact that all are bound together, or at least held together, is taken to show that we are all inter-dependent, that only when all four species are together does one have a viable Whole.

9. USE OF THE *ARBA MINIM*

Strictly speaking the *Arba Minim* are not used for anything; some find a use for the *Etrog* afterwards by making jam from it, or sticking cloves into it and using it as spices for *Havdalah*, but the rest is just thrown away once the festival is over and the leaves have dried out. (It is noticeable that the willow leaves, coming from trees that need to grow near plentiful water supplies, dry out much quicker than the rest and may even need replacing during the week.)

However, they are used ritually during the week of *Sukkot*. The *Mitzvah* is to wave them — hence the *Berachah* '...al Netilat Lulav') — rather than to observe someone else waving them. (Compare this with the *Mitzvah* of Hearing rather than personally Blowing the *Shofar*.)

In Temple times the people would process around the altar each day of *Sukkot* and chant from the *Hallel*, Psalm 118:25 ('*Anah Adonai, Hoshia-Na...*') — 'O Lord, we beesech Thee, save us, O Lord, we beseech Thee, grant us well-being.' Nowadays in synagogues there is either a procession around the *Bimah* — which was originally placed in the centre of the synagogue to enable such processions — or the *Lulav* is waved from the *Bimah* at the beginning and at verse 25 of this Psalm. The *Berachah* is:

'*Baruch Atah Adonai, Eloheynu, Melech ha'Olam, Asher Kidshahnu b'Mitzvotav, veTzivanu al-Netilat Lulav.*'

The *Berachah* is said facing East; the *Etrog* is held in the left hand, with the stem or *Pitom* pointing downwards during the blessing; it is then reversed to face upwards during the actual waving. The *Lulav* is held in the right hand, the two being held close together, and with the *Lulav* held in such a way that the willow is to one's left, the species are given a shake in the following order: towards the East, South, West, North, Upwards, Downwards — symbolising God's presence throughout the heavens and the earth.

10. *HOSHANAH RABBAH*

On the seventh day of *Sukkot*, the 21st. of *Tishri*, in the Temple period the people used to go to cut more willow branches (presumably the original ones were by now quite dessicated), decorate the altar with them then process around the altar as before, but this time seven times. As a consequence of this the day was known as 'The Great *Hosha-Na*'— the day when the verse 'Lord, save us' — '*Hosha-Na!*' — was said a lot. Hence the name in Hebrew '*Hoshana Rabbah*'.

It was also a custom to beat bunches of willow twigs on the ground.

In synagogues it is the custom to make processions around the *Bimah* seven times carrying the scrolls and singing short prayers with the refrain '*Hosha-Na*' — hence again the name, which can also mean 'The Day of Many *Hoshanot*'.

According to one tradition the willow symbolised rain and the following day — *Shemini Atzeret* — was the day on which the amount of rain for the coming month was decided up in Heaven! Maybe the rattling noise made by the twigs was intended to sound like rainfall and 'remind' the rain to come...

11. *CHOL HA-MO'ED*

The period forming the 'intermediate days' of the festivals of *Pesach* and *Sukkot* is known as '*Chol*' — meaning 'normal', secular', 'ordinary' — '*Mo'ed*' — meaning 'season', 'festivity', 'important period'. Thus these days are 'neither one thing nor the other'. They are not days of especial festivities — as are the first and eighth, laid down in the *Torah*, and the seventh, as noted above — but neither are they completely normal. (Think, if you wish, of the period December 26th to 30th in the secular calendar. These have no religious significance and yet people are in holiday mood.) So one still uses the *Sukkah*, for example, and the *Lulav* and *Etrog* would be used during morning services.

On the *Shabbat* during *Chol HaMo'ed* the Book of Ecclesiastes ('*Kohelet*') was traditionally read. In the RSGB / MRJ cycle this book is used for the *Haftarah*. The *Torah* readings do not follow the regular cycle but come from Deuteronomy 8:1-18 and 16:13-17.

12. *USHPIZIN*

In the '*Zohar*' (103b) the idea is presented that, on each of the seven days of *Sukkot* a pious person who sits in his *Sukkah* is visited by 'holy guests' — the '*Ushpizin*'. These are Abraham, Isaac, Jacob, Joseph, Moses, Aaron and David. Formulae were composed whereby these invisible guests were welcomed and invited to partake of refreshment.

They were also seen as reminders of the need to provide hospitality to the poor — the pious person's *Sukkah* should always be full of guests.

It is considered that Isaac Luria (1534-1572) originated this custom of inviting and welcoming the *Ushpizin*.

13. *SHEMINI ATZERET*

The *Torah* commands a seven-day festival, to be marked on the first and eighth days. The eighth day is the 'Closing' day — hence the name '*Shemini Atzeret*', the 'Eighth Day of Closing'. (The Hebrew word '*Atzar*' is also used to mean 'closing the skies' to prevent rain — i.e. a very physical 'shutting up'.)

As a relic of the agricultural origins of the festival and of the annual seasonal cycle of the Middle East this day is still associated with prayers for rain. The rainy season would normally begin about this time. Indeed one rabbinic tradition has it that the *Atzeret*, the end of *Sukkot*, should come fifty days after the beginning in the same way that *Shavuot*, the *Atzeret* of *Pesach*, is; however, this would mean all the pilgrims getting wet on their ways home, so the *Atzeret* is placed as soon as possible after *Sukkot* itself!

Since it marked the end of *Sukkot*, with a major gathering, it is often called the 'Eighth Day of Solemn Assembly' — rather a misnomer in current conditions. However a *Yizkor* (Memorial) Service is also incorporated in the liturgy.

14. *SIMCHAT TORAH*

Simchat Torah is a post-Biblical festival. The end of *Sukkot* was marked by great rejoicing and festivities. In Israel the day of *Shemini Atzeret* was therefore marked also by rejoicing with the *Torah* — specifically the *Sifrei Torah* — and the name '*Simchat Torah*' came to be applied, though this is first found in the '*Zohar*' (*Pinchas* 256b). Possibly it originated in Babylonia around the 9th century, when the regular annual cycle of *Torah* readings was developed and *Sukkot* became the starting-point for each cycle. In Palestine, where a three-year cycle of reading the *Torah* developed, a festival meal to mark the end was held only once every three years!

In the *Diaspora*, which already had the custom of celebrating the first day of *Sukkot* twice (because of doubts concerning the exact date) *Simchat Torah* came to be celebrated on the 'ninth day' — i.e. the effective repetition of *Shemini Atzeret*.

On this day the last section of the *Torah* was read, amid great joy. Then it was thought by some that there could be a misunderstanding; It might perhaps be thought that the Jews were happy because they had finished the *Torah* at last! In consequence the custom was introduced of reading the first part of the next cycle straight away, so that it would be clear that the merriment was because the Jews were re-starting — rather than finishing — the *Torah*!

Various customs have evolved. The Scrolls — *Sifrei Torah* — are removed from the Ark and carried in processions — *Hakkafot* (sing. *Hakkafah*) — around the synagogue; Children join in the processions and are rewarded with sweets. The congregation honours two people by calling them up to these first — i.e. Last ('*V'zot haBracha*') — and second — i.e. First! ('*Bereshit*') — readings from the *Torah*; they were traditionally called the '*Chatan Torah*' and the '*Chatan Bereshit*' respectively — the 'Bridegroom of the *Torah*' and the 'Bridegroom of the 'In the Beginning' section' — and were escorted to their positions with all the ceremony and jollity of real bridegrooms at a wedding.

The custom of processions is known from around the 16th. century and the scrolls were so carried during both Evening and Morning services.

15. MODERN REFORM CUSTOMS.

There are several ways in which current Reform practice differs from current Orthodox practice, though it should be noted that much of the latter is itself of recent development. The first, most obvious difference is that Reform follows the older custom, now maintained in Israel, of not duplicating the first day of festivals. We therefore celebrate seven days of *Sukkot* plus a combined *Shemini Atzeret* & *Simchat Torah*, finishing this sequence of notable days a day before the Orthodox community celebrates its own *Simchat Torah*. Hoshanah *Rabbah* has fallen into disuse. To symbolise the equality of the sexes within modern progressive Judaism one of the persons called up on *Simchat Torah* might be a woman — known therefore as the 'Bride' rather than the 'Bridegroom', the *Kallat Torah* or *Kallat Bereshit*. The emphasis on praying for rain, or inserting such a line into the *Amidah* at certain times of the year, has been reduced. Nevertheless we still have a busy week of services and observances in the *Sukkah*, with *Lulav* and *Etrog*, guests, special *Torah* readings and reminders of our traditions.

CHAPTER 13

CHANUKAH

1. INTRODUCTION

First, some general points about the festival of *Chanukah*:

(a). There are many ways of writing this Hebrew word in English! We find '*Hanukah*', '*Hannukkah*', '*Chanuka*' and other forms of transcription. Don't panic! The word is Hebrew and means 'Dedication'.

(b). This is a Minor Festival — post-Biblical, not tied to the agricultural year — and the special observances and rituals are therefore all of later origin.

(c). To complicate matters — the historical, religious, national and spiritual significance of this festival is different for different groups of Jews. For example, some see it as a symbol for national liberation, some of the need for rampant militarism, others see a festival of religious freedom and yet others a victory of intolerance over assimilationism, and so forth.

To avoid such problems most Jews unfortunately nowadays tend to see it purely as a festival for children and stress the paganistic or sentimental aspects over the stories of heroism, martyrdom and bigotry given in the sources. This is very ironic.

2. A PAGAN BACKGROUND? SOME IDEAS

Although Jews celebrate *Chanukah* in their own way and for their own reasons, it is possible to see many parallels and links with other religions. The complex background to this festival includes the following:

(a). Season: It is a Winter festival — moreover, falling almost in mid-winter, nearly (but not quite) at the Solstice (which is December 21$^{st.}$ in the secular calendar.)

(b). Date: It falls on the 25$^{th.}$ of a lunar month — compare with the Roman 'Saturnalia' (the birthday of the sun on December 25$^{th.}$, celebrated with candles and lights) or 'Christmas Day' on 25$^{th.}$ December. Most other Jewish festivals are characterised by being at a certain point in the lunar cycle — usually at Full Moon (the 14th/15$^{th.}$ of a lunar month).

(c). Light: At the depth of winter darkness many cultures have or have had a custom of kindling lights, to 'remind the gods to come back' or to remind themselves that a time of light would return after the grimness of winter. Nowadays we dress our city centres up likewise, to improve morale and attract shoppers and improve their mood so that they buy more!

(d). A problem with the sources is that there seems to have been a tradition about kindling the lights quite separate from the tradition about the victory of the Maccabees and the two were only merged later. This would point to a much earlier (yet non-Biblical) practice — i.e. one absorbed from pagan neighbours.

3. THE DATE AND DURATION: 25th KISLEV.
WHY DOES THE FESTIVAL LAST FOR EIGHT DAYS?

(a). There is a well-known tradition that a small cruse (a sealed bottle) of pure oil with the High Priest's seal was able to burn for eight days rather than one. (This incidentally means that the 'miracle' is technically only of the seven extra days, unless one prefers to argue that on each of the eight days only a small amount was consumed.) This is taken from the *Talmud 'Shabbat'* 21b and NOT from the accounts in the Book of the Maccabees. It is nowhere stated exactly what made this oil 'pure' or why it took eight days to prepare a new supply. Would more olives have needed to be plucked and pressed, in midwinter, well after the normal harvest?

Stories of Heroism or Miracles are dramatic and romantic and often avoid the need to look deeper into a history. There are many songs and stories for children involving the miracle of the oil, but no evidence that this was even an original story. Adults are not compelled to believe fairy stories.

(b). II Maccabees 10:5-8 links the new festival with *Sukkot*:

> 'It happened on the same day on which the sanctuary had been profaned by the foreigners, that is, on the twenty-fifth day of the same month, which was *Kislev*. And they celebrated it for eight days with rejoicing, in the manner of the feast of booths, remembering how not long before, during the feast of booths, they had been wandering in the mountains and caves like wild animals. Therefore bearing ivy-wreaths, wands and beautiful branches and also fronds of palm, they offered hymns of thanksgiving to Him who had given success to the purifying of His own holy place. They decreed by public ordinance and vote that the whole nation of the Jews should observe these days every year.'

> (It is interesting that II Maccabees here refers to an eight-day rather than seven-day festival of *Sukkot* in the Land of Israel rather than the *Diaspora* — normally the eighth day is classed as separate. See under '*Sukkot*'.)

(c). Note that Christianity counted the 'Octave' of Christmas from the 25th December to 1st January (New Year, or the 'Feast of the Circumcision') — this is also eight days.

4. STATUS

Because *Chanukah* does not appear in the Bible (despite attempts to link certain prophecies from Daniel Chap. 11) and indeed hardly appears in the Rabbinic writings, Judaism had to find a way to 'absorb' the practice and make it consistent with Judaism. The (quasi-)historical texts of the books I and II Maccabees were preserved only in the Apocrypha — ironically a Christian term for those books which the Church wanted to keep, but did not want to ascribe Divine Inspiration to — and were written in Greek!

Several legends were collated and preserved in a so-called 'Scroll of Antiochus' ('*Megillat Antiochus*') or 'Scroll of the Hasmoneans', probably written in Aramaic before the tenth century and presumably intended to be read on *Chanukah* in the same way as the Scroll of Esther ('*Megillat Esther*') was read at *Purim*.

The Rabbis instituted the custom of reciting a blessing over the *Chanukah* candles. Despite this the blessing includes the words 'Blessed are You, Lord our God, who has commanded us...' — even though, strictly interpreted, God has not commanded us this in any of the books of the *Torah*. (The same rabbinic rule applies to the command to read the *Megillah* on *Purim*, to recite the *Hallel* Psalms, to light *Shabbat* candles, and other examples.) [See Maimonides: '*Mishneh Torah*': '*Hilchot Megillah v'Chanukah*', 3:2-5.] In consequence of all the above the status of *Chanukah* is rather confused; there is no especial *Torah* reading available which refers to it (though there is a custom of reading from Numbers Chap. 7 since this includes the dedication of the original Tabernacle); most of the customs are for domestic rather than synagogue use; some additions are made to the regular synagogue service and the *Hallel* Psalms are recited, but there is no 'Festival' Service' as such.

5. OBSERVANCES

(See *Siddur* pp.266-269, and pp.590-593; 8[th.] **Ed. p.374** for Blessings, Prayers and Songs. ('*Lev Chadasch' p.391 & p.393*)

The key observances are those relating to the Lights and those which refer to the 'historical' and 'miraculous' aspects. There are other customs, such as eating oily food (in remembrance of the oil used to light the lamps) or to play games with a top (Yiddish: *Dreidl* — something you '*dreh*' — spin; Hebrew '*Sevivon*') — and these have assumed an importance they do not really deserve... It is likely that some of these 'traditional games' reflect merely amusements that were developed to fill up long winter evenings when one would stay up longer than usual to watch the special lamps. It is hard to believe that a form of gambling or a game of chance involving a spinning-top can truly be considered to be of religious significance.

6. THE LIGHTS OF *CHANUKAH*

The special holder for the lamps or candles (either may be used — remember that oil-lamps with wicks were the norm until quite recently) is called the '*Chanukiyah*'.

It will have eight holders or lamps, plus an additional one for the 'servant candle' or '*Shamash*' which is used to light the others.

The main candles or lights should be in an even row and sufficiently separated so that the flames do not merge into one (it is, after all, important that you can count them). The *Shamash* can or should be to one side, or lower, or differentiated in some way so that it is not confused with one of the 'Day' lamps.

Because it is always considered a good thing to perform a commandment 'with style', i.e. to do it as well as possible, it is customary to use a nice silver candelabrum as a *Chanukiyah*; however, this is not vital and *Chanukiyot* come in various shapes and sizes. You could even use individual lamps or candle-holders arranged in a row. Although there was a debate about this in Talmudic times, the custom is to start with one light for the first evening and then progress upwards, two for the second evening and so forth, till the eighth night when all eight — plus the '*Shamash*' — are lit. The *Shamash* is lit first every night and used to light the other(s) and then burns for as long as do the other lights. The idea is that the *Chanukah* lights are for display purposes only and are not to be used as illumination — therefore it is the light of the *Shamash* that is theoretically being used if, for example, you read the blessings afterwards using light from the candles!

The first candle is placed on the far right of the *Chanukiyah*; the second is placed to the left of that, the third to the left of that, and so on; however, they are then lit from the left — i.e. using the *Shamash*, which is lit for this purpose, you light the most recent addition; the one representing the current number of the day of *Chanukah* is lit first, then you continue lighting towards the right, 'downwards' in number, and then return the *Shamash* to its place.

Since the purpose of lighting the candles is '*Pirsum haNes*' — 'to advertise the Miracle' — they should be lit in public if possible and placed where the public can see them — on a window-ledge for example. Originally, in the days of enclosed courtyards, the lights would be placed outside the gates. This also means that when we refer to 'left' and 'right' we could mean as seen from outside! This might be the reverse of the way you are standing in your home. So we have possible confusion over the question of which is left and which is right — from your perspective behind the window, or the view of those outside the window!

One of the few references in the *Talmud* in '*Shabbat*' 21b to the festival practice concerns the legal issue of damages and who is responsible if a passing pack animal comes in contact with open flames placed for this purpose outside the house — i.e is it in the householder's domain and therefore legitimate or is it in the street and has he put a major cause of danger into the public domain, whilst arguing that he is fulfilling his religious duty?

7. THE MIRACLES

Traditionally the prayer '*Al HaNissim*' is read, inserted into the *Amidah* or separately, at the kindling of the lights (*Siddur* p.267; **p.374 (p.393)**). This relates to the historical and spiritual significance of a victory of the few against the many, the weak against the strong — and thus the need never to despair, always to retain faith in God and in a better future, even in times of darkness…

Although the Maccabees won a victory over their enemies, the fact is that they took the initiative themselves, they fought, they did NOT just sit back and rely on miracles!

8. HISTORICAL BACKGROUND AND SOURCES

(a). From **I Maccabees** — originally written in Hebrew but preserved for many centuries only in other languages; probably composed in the 1st.-century CE. (If so, then over one and a half centuries after the events described.)

In 16 chapters the author writes of the history of the period over a period of some forty years in a sober factual style — though obviously from the point of view of one for whom the Maccabees are the heroes. Dates are carefully given and various official documents — letters, treaties etc. — are quoted extensively. Starting with the decline and death of Alexander the Great he traces the course of the break-up of the Empire (323 BCE) into two main areas — the Ptolemaic (based on Egypt) and the Seleucid (based on Babylon).

This was the result of a testosterone rivalry (i.e. not one based on any major theological or ideological grounds) between the two generals Ptolemy and Seleucus and took effect in 312 BCE. The situation of Syria and the Middle-East, between these two super-powers, was complex.

Syria became part of the Seleucid domain but Israel — lying geographically between these two blocs — was fought over continuously. In 175 BCE Antiochus Epiphanes (actually Antiochus IV, but he took the title 'Theos Epiphanes' meaning 'God made Manifest') gained power over the Seleucid throne. His reign lasted until 164 BCE and was marked by the usual campaigns against the Ptolemies in Egypt. (In some books he is referred to as 'Antigonos'.) In 168 BCE an attack on Egypt was thwarted by Roman intervention but on his return, frustrated, he attacked and punished Jerusalem for a supposed rebellion. One of the further counter-measures to prevent further trouble, as he saw it, was a decree enforcing a 'standard' form of worship — i.e. of Himself — on the inhabitants, a sort of loyalty oath.

Although the Jewish community was already divided into those who were prepared to compromise and accommodate themselves to Greek or 'Hellenistic' culture and those who were more traditionalist, this decree caused an outright rebellion by the latter party. The rebellion began at Modi'in and was headed by a priest Mattityahu (Mattathias) and his five sons John, Judas, Simon, Eleazar and Jonathan. Judas' nickname was 'HaMaccabee' — in Hebrew 'The Hammer', indicating his physical strength. From 167 to 164 BCE various bloody campaigns were fought — sometimes against the armed forces sent by Antiochus, sometimes against fellow Jews — for this was to some extent a civil war between two sections of the population.

After various guerrilla campaigns Jerusalem was 'recaptured' by the Maccabean rebels and the Temple was cleansed and rededicated 'on the twenty-fifth day of the ninth month, which is the month of *Kislev*' of the year 164 BCE (I Maccabees 4:52). The rest of the book is occupied with an account of the campaigns waged by the Maccabees against Syrian counter-attacks, attacks on troublesome neighbours (who were mostly despatched with great violence or otherwise subdued) and various unpleasant (but alas, still typical) political deals and double-crosses and Maccabean victories.

(b). **II Maccabees** — originally written in Greek sometime in the years 150 - 0 BCE, a compilation and digest of a (lost) five-volume work by Jason of Cyrene and composed (with a great deal of sweat and toil — see the author's own comments in II Maccabees 2:19-32!) with a view to arousing the reader's sympathy for the heroic characters described in the narrative.

The book includes a fair amount of non-historical material and some of the history is in a different sequence to that given in I. Maccabees. Again, certain letters and documents are quoted. There are several atrocity stories of horrific martyrdoms and massacres.

(Note: There are two further so-called 'Books of Maccabees' in the Apocrypha, but they have nothing to do with this history.)

(c). **Flavius Josephus: 'Jewish Antiquities'** (Book XII, esp. from Ch. 5 - 7) — a Jewish author writing in Greek for a Roman readership towards the end of the 1st. century CE. He puts the story into an historical context and explains amongst other things that the Hellenized Jews had wished to adopt Greek customs such as sporting activities while naked and wished to reverse or hide their circumcisions.

In Ch. 6 he describes the outbreak of the rebellion:

'Now at this time there was one whose name was Mattathias, who dwelt at Modin, the son of John, the son of Simeon, the son of Asamoneus, a priest of the order of Joarib, and a citizen of Jerusalem. He had five sons: John, who was called Gaddis, and Simon, who was called Matthias, and Judas, who was called Maccabeus, and Eleazar, who was called Auran, and Jonathan, who was called Apphus. Now this Mattathias lamented to his children the sad state of their affairs, and the ravage made in the city, and the plundering of the temple, and the calamities the multitude were under; and he told them that it was better for them to die for the laws of their country, than to live so ingloriously as they then did. But when those who were appointed by the king were come to Modin, that they might compel the Jews to do what they were commanded, and to enjoin those who were there to offer sacrifice, as the king had commanded, they desired that Mattathias, a person of the greatest character among them, both on other accounts, and particularly on account of such a numerous and so deserving a family of children, would begin the sacrifice because his fellow citizens would follow his example, and because such a procedure would make him honoured by the king. But Mattathias said he would not do it; and that if all the other nations would obey the commands of Antiochus, either out of fear, or to please him, yet would not he nor his sons leave the religious worship of their country. But as soon as he had ended his speech, there came one of the Jews into the midst of them, and sacrificed, as Antiochus had commanded. At which Mattathias had great indignation, and ran upon him violently, with his sons, who had swords with them, and slew both the man himself who sacrificed, and Apelles the king's general, who compelled them to sacrifice, with a few of his soldiers. He also overthrew the idol altar, and cried out, 'If,' said he, 'anyone be zealous for the laws of his country, and for the worship of God, let him follow me.' And when he had said this, he made haste into the desert with his sons, and left all his substance in the village. Many others did the same also, and fled with their children and wives into the desert, and dwelt in caves...'

In Ch. 7 he describes the climax:

'When therefore, the generals of Antiochus' armies had been beaten so often, Judas assembled the people together, and told them, that after these many victories which God had given them, they ought to go up to Jerusalem, and purify the temple, and offer the appointed sacrifices. But as soon as he, with the whole multitude, was come to Jerusalem, and found the temple deserted, and its gates burnt down, and plants growing in the temple of their own accord, on account of its desertion, he and those who were with him began to lament, and were quite confounded at the sight of the temple; so he chose out some of his soldiers, and gave them order to fight against those guards that were in the citadel, until he should have purified the temple. When, therefore, he had carefully purged it, and had brought in new vessels, the lampstand, the table [of showbread], and the altar [of incense], which were made of gold, he hung up the veils at the gates, and added doors to them. He also took down the altar [of burnt offering], and built a new one of stones that he gathered together, and not of such as were hewn with iron tools.

So on the five and twentieth day of the month of Chislev, which the Macedonians call Apellaios, they lit the lamps that were on the lampstand, and offered incense upon the altar [of incense], and laid the loaves upon the table [of showbread], and offered burnt offerings upon the new altar [of burnt offering]. Now it so happened, that these things were done on the very same day on which their divine worship had stopped, and was reduced to a profane and common use, after three years' time; for so it was, that the temple was made desolate by Antiochus, and so continued for three years. This desolation happened to the temple in the hundred forty and fifth year, on the twenty-fifth day of the month of Apellaios, and on the hundred fifty and third Olympiad: (167 B.C.E.) but it was dedicated anew, on the same day, the twenty-fifth of the month of Apellaios, on the hundred and forty-eighth year, and on the hundred and fifty-fourth Olympiad. (164 B.C.E) And this desolation came to pass according to the prophecy of Daniel, which was given four hundred and eight years before; (575 B.C.E.) for he declared that the Macedonians would stop that worship [for some time].

Now Judas celebrated the festival of the restoration of the sacrifices of the temple for eight days; and omitted no sort of pleasures thereon: but he feasted them upon very rich and splendid sacrifices; and he honoured God, and delighted them by hymns and psalms. Nay, they were so very glad at the revival of their customs, when, after a long time of intermission, they unexpectedly had regained the freedom of their worship, that they made it a law for their posterity that they should keep a festival, on account of the restoration of their temple worship, for eight days. And from that time to this we celebrate this festival, and call it Lights.

I suppose the reason was, because this liberty beyond our hopes appeared to us; and that hence was the name given to that festival. Judas also rebuilt the walls around the city, and reared towers of great height against the incursions of enemies, and set guards therein…'

[Translation by R.B. Vincent: from 'Josephusabridged.htm']

The reference to 'Asamonaeus' would be an explanation of the Hebrew term '*Chashmonaim*', 'Hasmonaeans'. The reference to Daniel is to Dan. 12:8-13, the end of the book, where the prophet explains how he has failed to understand a series of mysterious eschatalogical symbols and is told 'Many shall purify themselves and make themselves white; but the wicked shall do wickedly; and none of the wicked shall understand; but they that are wise shall understand. From the time that the continual burnt-offering shall be taken away, and the detestable thing that appals shall be set up, there shall be a thousand two hundred and ninety days. Happy is he who waits, and comes to the thousand, three hundred and thirty-five days…' — i.e. A restoration of the sacrificial ritual after a break of a little over three years.

(d). *Talmud* — **Tractate '*Shabbat*' page 21b** — one of the few references to *Chanukah* in the Rabbinic writings — mentions almost in passing the supposed miracle of a jar of oil sufficient for one day, which actually burned for eight days, filling the gap until fresh oil could be prepared for Temple use. (Note: This story does not appear in any of the books mentioned above! It may even have been a deliberate attempt by the rabbis to deflect attention from the Maccabees and their Hasmonean successors.) Other brief references in the Babylonian *Talmud* include: '*Shabbat*' 23a, '*Sukkah*' 46a; in the 'Minor Tractate' '*Sofrim*' 20:3-9; further: '*Pesikta Rabbati*' 2:1, 4:1, 8:1.

e). *Megillat Antiochos* (Also known as *'Megillat haChashmona'im'*) — this is preserved in both Aramaic and Hebrew versions — the Hebrew being a literal translation of the Aramaic original, composed probably in the 7th. Century CE, though we do not know exactly when, where, by whom or why. The answer to the latter question is probably to provide a liturgical roll of some sort to read at *Chanukah*, there being no obvious *Torah* readings available. Sa'adiah *Ga'on* attributed its authorship to the Five Sons of Mattathias — though this is strange, since both Judah's and Eleazar's deaths are mentioned in it!

The structure is chronological without a chronology, sequential with some parts of the sequence being afforded considerable detail and others — major campaigns and conquests — being glossed over in a single sentence. There are no 'Chapters' but 76 'Verses'.

As stated above, the aim was clearly to create a parallel text that could be used liturgically during *Chanukah*, similarly to the *Megillat Esther* at *Purim*. There are stylistic parallels, starting with 'In the days of King...', including the King sending letters to all his provinces (v.47), issues of how a man may be publicly honoured (v.19) and ending with the establishment of a festival for all time, on a specific date (v.76). There are many differences with the other sources known to us — it appears the author had access to a store of legends but not to the 1st. and 2nd. Books of Maccabees. As a further parallel to the *Purim* story the conflict is portrayed as involving purely external threats and enemies, not internal divisions between hellenised and traditionalist Jews; (This externalising is also expressed in the way the enemies of the Jews come and go by sea, or from the coast, rather than marching on land from Syria to Egypt and back.) There is a jumble of events and a minor defeat in Judea is portrayed as leading to the total downfall of the Greek (not Syrian or Seleucid) Empire.

Important for us is that this was apparently the only version of the story available and accessible to most Jews for centuries throughout the Middle Ages and into modern times, since the Books of the Maccabees were unknown to them. And yet there are so many divergencies from the texts of I and II Maccabees and from the legends normally recounted! Therefore questions are raised — here Yochanan is more important than Judah and yet our songs glorify Judah.

(cf. also Handel's oratorio 'Judas Maccabeus' which is based on the Apocrypha accounts. *Chanukah* is mentioned incidentally once in the 'New Testament' in John 10:22 where Jesus is described as going to the Temple at the time of this festival and gets involved in a religious argument, since he had earlier criticised the Temple and its authorities during *Sukkot* in John Ch.7.)

9. 'MA'OZ TZUR'

This has become 'The *Chanukah* song', associated with the festival in the minds of most Jews; and yet only two of the verses, at most, connect directly with *Chanukah*. Is this a song or a collection of notes? It is very abrupt and concise, using one word or phrase to refer to a whole period of history. To a large extent this is forced upon the author by the need to keep to a tight rhyme and rhythm scheme so that a single word or phrase has to convey a whole group of associated meanings. This is a Poem, not a History.

We know from the acrostic word-play with the initial letters of the five traditional verses that a certain 'Mordechai' wrote it — but precisely Where, When and Why remains a mystery. At some point a sixth verse, wishing revenge on our enemies, has been added in certain Orthodox *Siddurim*; at some point the fourth verse, with its relishing of the hanging of Haman and his sons, has been quietly dropped from some Reform *Siddurim* (e.g. 'Forms of Prayer').

A boy once described the whole history of Judaism and Jewish festivals as 'They tried to kill us; We won; Let's eat.' Not a bad definition of certain Jewish festivals. Not those associated with the Calendar, such as *Shabbat* or *Rosh Chodesh*; nor those associated (originally) with Harvest, such as the '*Shalosh Regalim*' of *Pesach*, *Shavuot* and *Sukkot*; nor those associated with inner renewal, such as *Rosh Hashanah* and *Yom Kippur*. But there are other 'notable days' associated with historical or quasi-historical events in our national consciousness. This song actually focuses, in its five verses, on four such 'notable days' — in each case a day or an event when destruction of the Jewish people was threatened, but was averted due to divine intervention. And strangely, two of those days are NOT marked with any specific celebration.

The first verse is a general introduction to the idea of God rebuilding and restoring the ancient centre of our worship so that we can, once more, worship there with offerings. (Interestingly this verse is retained in Reform liturgies since — presumably — the first words are vital as introduction to the rest.)

The second verse encapsulates in the first phrases a lengthy period of Jewish history — as slaves in Egypt (described as 'the land of the Calf', presumably as the Israelites later built a calf to remind them of the Egyptian gods they had known). And then came freedom. This would normally be associated with *Pesach*. But then — the final line stresses not the spiritual liberation from slavery but the physical liberation from massacre by Pharaoh's army. This is an allusion to the crossing of the Red Sea (Exodus Ch. 14 & 15) when the Israelites crossed through safely and dry, but the pursuing army was engulfed and drowned. An event traditionally associated not with the *Seder* evening but with the 7th. Day of *Pesach*.

They tried to kill first our sons and then all of us; then they threw us out, but changed their minds and tried to massacre us; but we won. So — Let's eat!

The third verse jumps to a much later period — that of the First Exile. Interestingly we mark the beginning of the First Exile — on *Tisha B'Av* — but we have no celebration to mark the Return from the Exile. (In Nechemiah Ch. 8 we read that the Law was read to the newly-returned exiles on the 1st. day of the 7th. month — i.e. *Rosh Hashanah* — but this date is never referred to in this context, only as the '*Harat Ha'Olam*', the 'Birthday of the World', or in some spiritual context of '*Yemei Teshuvah*' — 'Days of Penitence' or 'of blowing the *Shofar*'.) In the same way we mark the beginning of the Second Exile also with *Tisha B'Av*, by semi-historical association — but now we can mark its formal end with '*Yom Ha'Atzma'ut*'.

However this verse speaks of Exile — an exile that we had deserved, for (depending on the translation!) either we had served wine-offerings to strange gods, or strange wine of madness had been prepared for us. But there is an indication of religious lapses leading to our punishment. And yet, at the end of seventy years, even the Empire of Babylon collapsed and one of its high officials, Zerubbabel, arranged for us to be sent home. (Zerubbabel was appointed Governor of the province of Judea and began the rebuilding of the Temple after the return from Exile; he is referred to in Haggai 2:23 and four times in Zechariah Ch. 4.)

They had tried to wipe us out — with invasion and exile and the disappearance of ten of the twelve tribes; But we survived, some of us returned and re-established ourselves. We won. So let's eat!

The fourth verse changes the scene to the Persian Court — also a part of Exile; the names are those of 'Hammadatha' and 'the Agagite' — i.e. Haman. We know from *Megillat Esther* what Haman tried to do; Not content with eliminating his political opponent Mordechai he wanted to destroy by genocide the entire people, scattered across 127 provinces. But he lost and ended up — with his sons — on the very gallows he had built for Mordechai. A fitting end. (For him — we may have some ethical reservations about the fate of his family!)

So — thanks to Esther — we won. Let's go eat!

The fifth verse — at last — brings us to *Chanukah*. Here the enemies are '*Yavanim*' 'the Greeks' — which may be a tactful euphemism for 'Greek-influenced Jews' or may be a direct reference to Antiochus Epiphanes as a foreigner. It all depends whether you see *Chanukah* as an heroic resistance against an outside oppressing force or an internal civil war between two groups of Jews. Both interpretations are possible from the limited and polemical data available to us. Was the threat to Judaism or to Jews, of spiritual or physical destruction? But — whatever happened — the song sings of the miracle of the oil and the result was that the 'Sons of Understanding', '*B'nei Veena*', established from the following year a commemorative ritual. Which is why we are still singing '*Ma'oz Tzur*' and lighting the candles. And eating!

So — we have covered 7[th.] Day *Pesach*, the Return from Babylon, *Purim* and *Chanukah*. Other 'notable days' remain forgotten — such as the day the Israelites entered the Promised Land under Joshua. But the common link between these four notable days is the survival of a threat to our physical national (not individual) existence.

10. FOOD

Since there is so much emphasis on the miracle of the oil it is customary to eat oily foods — potato pancakes ('*Latkes*') deep-fried in oil (this cannot be such an ancient custom since potatoes were only introduced to Europe a few centuries ago) or oily doughnuts ('*Sufganiot*'), often filled with jam. Whilst many people nowadays are overweight if not actually obese, in former times to add a bit of oil and fat to one's body in the cold midwinter time was not a bad idea at all.

11. THE MEANING OF *CHANUKAH* — A REFORM VIEW

The above accounts describe a variety of meanings for *Chanukah*. As Reform Jews we may prefer not to dwell on accounts of violence or legendary supernatural miracles, but more on the idea that religious freedom is a valuable, vital part of life — one worth fighting for indeed, when necessary — and that one should not lose faith, even in dark and difficult times.

CHANUKAH CANDLE LIGHTING INSTRUCTIONS

1. The *Chanukah* candles should be lit at evening on each of the eight nights of the festival.

2. Either wax candles or oil lamps can be used for the lights. (In public places electric bulbs are often used but these are not really tasteful for private use; however, they are valid.)

3. The Process of Lighting:
    (a). Although there is a Talmudic dispute regarding this, the now-accepted custom is to increase the candles from one to eight as the festival progresses. (Obviously the other alternative was to decrease from eight to one. However, since we should be constantly increasing joy and light in the world, rather than diminishing it, the former opinion is superior.)
    (b). The candles should be placed in the *Chanukiyah* begining from the right side and extending to the left with each day.
    (c). Light the *Shamash* (an additional 'servant' candle used to light the others) and recite the two blessings on p.266; p.373; (p.393)
    (d). On the first night recite also the '*Shehecheyanu*' blessing, p. 266; p.373 (p.393)
    (e). Light the candles with the *Shamash* from left to right — so that the candle for the new evening is lit first.
    (f). Place the *Shamash* in its special holder on the *Chanukiyah*.
    (g). It is customary to say/sing '*Hanerot hallalu*', 'We kindle these lights…' and '*Maoz Tzur*', 'Rock of Ages' following the lighting.

4. According to some authorities each person in a household should light his or her own candles. Traditionally, women as well as men are obligated to light *Chanukah* candles. This is not strictly necessary, but it is nice when children can also make or light their own.

5. It was customary to light the candles in the doorway, and look at them from outside, but now they are commonly lit in a window facing the street. This should if possible be on the side of the doorway away from the *Mezuzah*. Lighting by a window or in the doorway is based both on a common custom of mid-winter fire

festivals and on the principle of 'Pirsum HaNes' — 'Making Known the Miracle'. In either case it is important that people passing-by should be able to see the lights and know by their number which night it is! (Presumably the initiated would always be able to deduct one and think 'Oh, that's the Shamash'.) Of course, from outside the beautiful decoration of a Chanukiyah or the colour of the candles is irrelevant — one sees only the flickering flames.

6. The candles should if possible be lit soon after sunset; if necessary one can light them anytime during the night. (These days in Europe in winter many people return from work only hours after darkness has fallen.)

7. They should burn for at least half an hour.

8. The light of the Chanukah candles should not be used for any purpose. (See above: 'We kindle these lights…'). The idea here is that they are to be seen, not to be seen by — think of the difference between street lighting and illuminated advertisements; or the difference between a car's headlights — used for the driver to see where he or she is going — and the rear and brake lights — used to enable the car to be seen by those behind.

9. On Friday night the Chanukah candles are kindled before the Shabbat candles. On Saturday night they can theoretically be kindled before Havdalah in the synagogue, because people will be going home straight after Havdalah and so would not get to enjoy the lights, but at home Havdalah is said first.

10. Forty-four candles are needed for the festival — on the basis of 1 + 1, 1 + 2, 1 + 3, etc. till 1 +8. Candles can be bought in boxes or packets from Jewish shops or through a local synagogue, or they can be made quite easily. In fact any candle will do, including the flat stable ones ('tea lights') sold in houseware stores. Important is that the candles are stable, and that they are well away from any curtains or other items that could catch alight! Many Chanukiyot require specific candles due to the size of the 'cups'.

(Taken and adapted from 'First Jewish Catalogue',
Ed. Siegel / Strassfeld. JPS 1973 pp. 44-45.)

CHAPTER 14

PURIM

1. BACKGROUND

Purim is a strange festival — and also one of the most festive. Although its theoretic basis — the Book of Esther (actually the 'Scroll of Esther') is in the Bible, it is in the Writings ('*Ketuvim*') section and not in the *Torah* and the festival cannot therefore claim the authority of *Rosh Hashanah* or *Shavuot*. It has nothing to do with the agricultural cycle of rains or harvests, nor with some 'theological' concept of inner self-examination or repentance. In many ways its status in the Jewish calendar is similar to that of *Chanukah* — (albeit *Chanukah*'s basis lies in extra-Biblical books).

We say a blessing over the reading of Esther, we recite *Hallel* Psalms and we add '*Al HaNissim*' (p.264; p.384; p.406), treating it liturgically as a Notable Day even though we are never actually commanded in the *Torah* to do so.

2. THE *MEGILLAH*

The core of *Purim* lies in the '*Megillah*' or '*Megillat Esther*' — known in English as the 'Book of Esther' because it is a book in the Bible but actually the term means a Scroll, something that is rolled up. And so it is still traditional if possible to read from a scroll.

This *Megillah* tells in 9½ chapters (Chapter 10 is only three verses long!) a weird story of Eastern intrigue, sex and violence, set in the court of King *Achashverosh* (Ahasuerus) of Persia in the city of *Shushan* — the capital of the vast Empire, stretching from India to Ethiopia, amongst magnificent feasts in opulent surroundings. After the king has disposed of his wife Vashti (because she apparently disobeyed in public his order to dance naked before his guests, thus setting an example of disobedience that other wives might have been tempted to follow) he decides on an enormous beauty contest in order to find a replacement.

After much searching and much preparation (it takes a year just to get the girls to smell nice — see Esther 2:12) and a great deal of experimentation lasting several years (but alas, it is impossible to calculate exactly 1001 nights out of the dates given) the King (a *Nebbich*) falls for a nice Jewish orphan girl called Esther (or Hadassah) — the Heroine — an orphan who has been brought up by her uncle Mordechai (the Hero). Mordechai is an exile from Judah.

179

In the meantime the Villain Haman is elevated to a high position within the Court and gets angry with Mordechai who refuses to grovel to him like everyone else. Rather than just arranging for this impudent person to 'disappear' he decides to wipe out ALL the Jews, in revenge for Mordechai's actions — a fairly typical response from a despotic psychopathic tyrant not ruled by any form of reason and with almost absolute power. To pick the best date for this fiendish act — for which he gets King Achaschverosh's permission with frightening ease — he and his friends cast lots — known in Persian as *Pur*, plural *Purim*. Eventually they do this for almost a year, without giving up, until the dice tell him the time is right. This indicates an obsessive and superstitious personality. By royal decree the 13th. of *Adar* is chosen (Esther 3:13) and an order to this effect is circulated throughout the entire Persian domain — allowing eleven months for its distribution and preparation for genocide…

Not unnaturally Mordechai is upset by this turn of events and tries to get a message through to Esther — not an easy task, since the Royal Harem was well protected. He then has to convince Esther that even she, despite her privileged position at Court, is threatened by this decree and she then needs to find a way to gain access to the King without losing her own head — remembering that Vashti's fate was a warning to wives who 'got in the way'.

Eventually Esther succeeds in inviting the King — and Haman — to dinner. Haman is very pleased with this honour and, not knowing that Mordechai is the Queen's uncle, decides to have him hanged the next day to celebrate his good fortune. Now the plot thickens… That very night the King has an attack of insomnia and calls to have his Cabinet Minutes read aloud to him… rather a revealing insight into the nature of such records throughout the ages! It is discovered that Mordechai had saved the King's life some while back by foiling an assassination plot but (such being the vagaries of government) has not been rewarded for this. When Haman appears the next morning to ask permission to hang Mordechai, he is forestalled by being asked for advice as to the best way to honour someone. Thinking, naturally, that he is the intended recipient of the honour, he is rather upset to be told that he has now to arrange a civic reception (a sort of ticker-tape parade) for — of all people — Mordechai! This is a bad omen for his plans — see Esther 5:13.

However… he has been invited to a second banquet with the King and Queen and here his downfall is complete. The Queen pleads with the King for her life. He is rather astonished, not understanding how she is threatened and by whom. When he asks for clarification, Esther points to Haman and accuses him! The King is furious and stalks out into the garden to clear his head (he has been drinking too much). Haman falls upon Esther to plead for mercy — slips — the King returns, suspects attempted rape as well as murder — and Haman ends up on the gallows he had prepared for Mordechai! A combination of theatrical farce and tit-for-tat.

The tables are now turned and Mordechai is raised to Haman's position and Esther begs the King to reverse his former decree.

They now hit a snag so bizarre as to be almost comic; the Persian legal system and bureaucracy being what they are, there is no way a royal decree can be annulled!

Not even by the King himself! The only solution is to issue a counter-decree! This is accordingly done and the Jews of the Empire are commanded to kill their enemies instead, on the very day that their enemies were supposed to be killing them.

So on this day, 13th. *Adar*, they commit great slaughter on their enemies, with local governmental help and assistance, but it is stressed that they don't take any plunder. (The implication is also that they would not have had to do this had the Persian system been more flexible — so this is not their fault.) Esther then asks the King's permission to have another day of slaughter as well in *Shushan*. This is granted (Esther 9:14) and eventually — totalling the sums given, it appears that 75,810 anti-Semites bite the dust…

So on the next day (14th. *Adar* in the provinces but the 15th. in *Shushan*, where they'd had Extra Time) the Jews celebrated their deliverance from certain extermination.

Mordechai instituted this, by letter, as a permanent feast for the Jews (Esther 9:20f.) and they all, well, sort-of lived happily ever after… (albeit they stayed in exile, scattered over 127 provinces… and only the majority of the Jews supported Mordechai, not all of them!)

3. THE MEANING OF THE *MEGILLAH*

It is a jolly story — but what does it mean, if anything? There are many possible answer but first, some points that need making:

(a). Nowhere in the whole story does God appear, either by name or deed. This caused great trouble to the rabbis, who debated for some time whether the book even deserved a place in the Bible or not. Eventually they came to a consensus that the story showed such evidence of divine intervention that God MUST have been somehow involved — in secret, behind the scenes. At some time someone went to the trouble of re-writing the whole story, but adding God in! Prayers by Esther were composed and inserted and similar bits and pieces, which now exist in the Apocrypha as 'The Additions to Esther' and are not accepted as part of the original book.

(b). The characters are impossible to 'pin down' historically. Some scholars have felt that the name 'Ahasuerus', in Hebrew 'Achashverosh', referred to Artaxerxes — but this is a guess. The name 'Mordechai' looks suspiciously like that of the Persian deity *Marduk* and 'Esther' like that of *Astarte* or *Ishtar* — so the whole story could be, or be based upon, a pagan romance in which one goddess is deposed by another.

(c). Perhaps because of the above the story includes many elements aimed at stressing the Jewish identity of Mordechai and Esther; see 2:5-7 for Mordechai's family tree and 2:15 and 9:29 for Esther's patronym. More significantly, Mordechai is introduced and referred to not as an Israelite or Hebrew but as an '*Ish Yehudi*' — a man from Judah, or 'a Jew'. This is the first usage of this term, which we nowadays take for granted.

Because of the use of *Yehudi* the story of Esther has come to be a paradigm for all instances of irrational anti-Semitism — where a prejudice based on some narrow experience leads to suffering on a wider scale. It has come to be seen as a paradigm for the eternal conflicts that Jews seem to suffer, whatever they do. Haman is called the Agagite (3:1, 8:3, 8:5, 9:24) and from this the rabbis deduced that he was descended from King Agag of the Amalekites, whom Saul was commanded to kill in I Samuel Ch. 15 though in the end Samuel himself had to do the job (I Samuel 15:34). In this way Haman becomes but one in a long line of Amalekites — archetypal enemies of the Jews since Exodus Ch. 17 when they attacked the Israelites shortly after they had entered Sinai and Deuteronomy 25:17-19 where this unprovoked attack is recalled.

Even if the story of Esther should turn out to be factually untrue and unhistorical — and all the signs are that this is the case — it would therefore have a significance and a validity on a different level, as representing the sort of thing that <u>has</u> happened and <u>does</u> happen (though without the happy ending) to so many Jews in so many countries in so many centuries under despotic rule. It only takes the rise of one irrational psychopath, or a change in government, and entire communities can be placed at risk for no real reason whatsoever.

The book becomes especial only in that, according to this story at least, the worm turned, the underdog arose and the righteous survived. (However, at the end they are all still in exile, in 127 provinces but without their own country, still vulnerable to the next potential psychopath.)

4. SHABBAT ZACHOR

Partly as a consequence of the link made, via Agag, with Amalek, the *Shabbat* preceding *Purim* is named 'Shabbat Zachor', the 'Sabbath of Remembrance'. An additional reading from the *Torah* — Deuteronomy 25:17-19 (which starts '*Zachor et-asher assah lecha Amalek…*' — Moses reminding the Israelites of their eternal enemies) — and a special *Haftarah* (from I Samuel Ch.15 — see above, relating to the death of Agag) — are included in the service. Significantly, although there are many references to warfare in the Bible the attack by the tribe of Amalek in Exodus Ch.17 is singled out as something especially horrible because they are described as attacking from the rear, massacring the old and the weak, rather than making a frontal attack against the warriors — this is therefore perceived as a War Crime than an Act of War. How do we nowadays distinguish — or try to distinguish — between 'legitimate' military or strategic targets and 'collateral damage' and 'attacks on civilians' and 'ignoring human rights' and unjustified casualties amongst civilians and prisoners during armed conflicts?

There is an ironic inner contradiction inasmuch as the Israelites are commanded to remember constantly to wipe out the memory of Amalek! And to remember to forget but not to forget to remember to forget…

In recent times the custom was at one point being encouraged to devote some thought to the plight of Jews still living in the general region of the empire of King *Achashverosh* — specifically in Syria — living under the sway of modern Hamans and their ilk. In fact there are now hardly any Jews living in Arab or Moslem countries any more — many ancient communities have dissolved themselves through emigration when they could. In November 2015 the last remaining Jews were brought out of Syria… There are less than 8,000 Jews in Iran. The Jewish community of Iraq, attacked by pogroms in June 1941, shrank from 100,000 in 1947 to some 5,000 after many fled to Israel in 'Operation Ezra and Nehemiah', was down to 2,000 by 1968, and by 2014 to 500, being permitted to live only in Baghdad and Basra. (Source: *Beth HaTfutsot* website).

5. SOME CUSTOMS AND CELEBRATIONS

Purim has absorbed and acquired various customs over the ages — remember, there is no specific instruction in the Bible as to what to do, as there is for other festivals, but only a general decree to 'be merry'. What follows is a selection:

(a) Alcohol. Normally drunkenness is frowned upon in Judaism; Although wine itself is considered a 'good thing', it is to be taken in moderation.

Not on *Purim*, though!

In the 4[th.] century Rava in the *Talmud* (*Megillah* 7b) declared that one should drink so much on *Purim* that one would no longer be able to tell the difference ('*Ad lo yada!*') between the phrases 'Cursed be Haman' and 'Blessed be Mordechai'! Apart from the obvious meaning, other interpretations of this saying include that of Maimonides who (as a doctor) toned this down a little, suggesting that it really meant that one should only drink until one fell asleep, and that of the '*Maharil*' (the complimentary name for Rabbi Jacob ben Moses, 1365-1421, Germany) who thought it meant that one should be so befuddled that one could no longer cope with the mental games of *Gematria*. (Incidentally *Gematria*, the technique of giving each Hebrew letter a numeric equivalent and then calculating similarities or coincidence, reveals that the numerical equivalents of the Hebrew words '*Baruch Mordechai*' and '*Arur Haman*' — 'Blessed be Mordechai' and 'Cursed be Haman' — are both the same — 502! You can work this out for yourself — *Bet + Resh + Vav + Chaf / Mem + Resh + Daled + Chaf + Yud* = 2 + 200 + 6 + 20 / 40 + 200 + 4 + 20 + 10); and then compare with *Aleph + Resh + Vav + Resh / Heh + Mem + Nun*; = 1 + 200 + 6 + 200 / 5 + 40 + 50).

Many are the stories of *Purim* drunkenness; In one, also in *Megillah* 7b concerning Rava and Rabbi Zeira, a rabbi who had miraculously been brought back to life after being killed in a drunken brawl with a colleague declined a further invitation to sup with him the following year on the grounds that 'one should not rely on miracles'!

(b). Costumes. A bit like 'Carnival' (with which it has a lot of common) *Purim* became a time for dressing up in weird or outrageous costumes.

'Drag' i.e dressing up as in the other gender, which is normally strictly forbidden, was permitted and humorous plays ('*Purim-Shpiele*') were put on, usually based in the *Megillah* story. People would make fun of those in authority, dressing-up as rabbis or local bigwigs, holding processions through the streets, and so on. Much of this merriment was of course fuelled by alcohol…

(c). Parodies. As part of the general 'letting the hair down' parodies were composed and sung. The more learned, of course, prepared more learned parodies, even complete fake Tractates of the *Talmud* (such as '*Massechet Bakbuk*', the 'Chapter on the Bottle') devoted to such topics as the best way to get drunk.

Even now Jewish newspapers often run fake stories and 'take-offs' of regular features, the best being of course those that look so plausible at first sight. (As on April 1st. in British media). Every year, too, there are people who get taken in by the jokes or who don't understand the humour…

(d). Hamantaschen. This delicacy originated in Europe; The name is, strictly speaking, derived from the German/Yiddish word for poppy-seeds (*Mohn*) and pockets (*Taschen*) but the sound has been 'bent' so that the word sounds like 'Haman's pockets'; these triangular seed-filled pastries are also known in some places as '*Osnei Haman*' — 'Haman's Ears' — again, presumably, because they look like big ears.

Originally filled with poppy-seeds, there are also versions with jam and other fillings.

(e). Noise. The worst curse that a Jew can utter against a person is that someone's name should be blotted out. '*Yimach Sh'mo!*' We all know that we have to die sometime but at least we hope that there will be remain some memory of us, somewhere, that we will not be totally forgotten as though we had never been.

Since Haman represents the worst enemy of the Jewish people the custom is to 'blot out' his name when it is read out in the synagogue. With boos and shouts, thumps on the floor, blowing of whistles, waving of rattles ('*Raashanim*' — things which make a noise; also known from the Polish/Yiddish as '*Greggers*') and so on. The result is pandemonium!

(f). Reading the *Megillah*. An essential part of *Purim* is to hear the old, old story being read again — complete. (There is even a learned argument over whether you can be deemed to have heard it all if the noise blotted out Haman's name!)

Accordingly it is read both evening and morning in the synagogues. The *Megillah*, although often printed in book form, is still retained for ritual purposes as a scroll — though, as it is a little less 'holy' than a *Sefer Torah*, it may be handled with a little less reverence and is often decorated or illustrated or printed with translations.

6. THE MEANING OF *PURIM*

Traditionally this was the one occasion of the year when Jews could laugh at themselves and the world around them. Although some modern Jews find this festival a little embarrassing or the biblical story rather distasteful being, after all, merely a rehearsal of the joys of revenge and blood-lust — or they even have difficulties coping with a story that probably never happened — we can see from modern events that life is often as confusing and irrational — and violent — as in the *Megillah*.

The Gulf Wars, the recent events in Iran and Iraq and Syria and all over the Middle East, the massacres, the random viciousness of tyrants everywhere — all are sadly evidence that, even if the *Megillah* isn't true in a historical sense, it still has a lot of universal truth in it.

In a way the point of *Purim* is to be so different from the rest of the year. Normally Judaism places great stress on making distinctions — between right and wrong, between blessing and curse, between what one may eat and what not, when one may work and when one should not, between the sexes and their roles, between the learned and the unlearned and so forth. On this day we are commanded to reach a stage of inebriation where none of these differences matter any more — that is, in a way, we become for a day just like our enemies, who clearly are also not concerned with behaving according to the correct standards!

Haman is an *Agagi*, Mordecai a *Yehudi* — neither are actually Persians in this large multi-cultural Empire.

7. FURTHER CUSTOMS

(a). *Al HaNissim*. 'For the Miracles…' This prayer is added to the service (during the *Amidah*) and the Grace After Meals — similar to the (different) *Al HaNissim* prayer said on *Chanukah*. (See RSGB *Siddur* p.264f. **p.384**; (*Lev Chadash p.406*)

(b). *Mishlo'ach Manot*. 'The Sending of Portions'. Because one indulges in feasting and merrymaking the custom is to spread the joy by sending gifts of food to one's friends and acquaintances — defined as 'at least two portions of something (hence the plural) — to at least one person.' Also, one should give charity to the poor — defined as 'at least one present (of food or money) to at least two poor people.'

(c). '*Ta'anit Esther*' — the 'Fast of Esther'. Of fairly late origin (at least 8[th.] century) and not frequently observed these days is the custom of fasting on the 13[th.] of *Adar*, the day before *Purim*, in commemoration of Esther's decision (in 4:16) to fast for three days before attempting to see the King to avert the catastrophe.

(d). '*Shushan Purim*'. Since the Jews in *Shushan* had an additional day of slaughter they celebrated *Purim* a day later than everyone else; therefore in 'walled cities' *Purim* is still celebrated in the 15[th.] *Adar*, not the 14[th.] (In modern practical terms this means in Jerusalem only.)

(e). '*Purim Katan*'. A 'Little *Purim*' — this would be the name assigned to a local celebration of some deliverance from trouble and commemorated for years later.

CHAPTER 15

PESACH

1. INTRODUCTION

This chapter is in no way intended to duplicate all the many books and articles and resources available on the subject of *Pesach*, but only to supplement them with a few matters relevant to this festival in a Reform or Liberal context. Go and Learn!

2. WHY DO WE CELEBRATE *PESACH*?

Scholarly accounts stress the agricultural origins of the festival. It is seen in early pre-history as a Springtime Nature festival — the new lambs are being born, the new grain is growing. To mark the former, one of the lambs is ceremonially sacrificed and eaten; to mark the latter, the new grain is baked into new bread and all the stale stuff that has been stored and used during the winter is cleared out and destroyed.

Obviously the Lamb festival would have been appropriate to a nomadic pastoral society and the Crop festival to a more settled, agricultural community. It may be significant that both are combined from an early date.

However rabbinic Judaism is not, as such, a Nature-based religion. Rather it has taken the significant dates in an agricultural calendar and transformed them into something significantly different, with a deeper religious context. So with *Pesach* we have a festival devoted not only to Springtime but also to the concept of Freedom in all its manifestations — Current freedom as contrasted with the slavery our ancestors endured, Future freedom as contrasted with our current unredeemed pre-Messianic Era state.

In our observance, in the '*Haggadah*', we combine a modified version of the Biblical account of the Exodus from Egypt with prayers, songs and symbols which look forward as well as back and which speak of the need for and importance of Freedom in all times, not just Biblical ones. It may be hard for each of us to think of ourselves as participating in a process of rejoicing over new lambs — but we can and should 'think ourselves' into the more abstract state of enjoying and valuing Freedom.

3. THE BIBLICAL ACCOUNT

In Genesis Chapters 37-50, by a long and complex process involving attempted fratricide, famine, injustice, political climbing etc. the family of Jacob is changed from a nomadic tribe in Canaan into a settled people in the area of Lower Egypt known as Goshen.

They start (Gen. 46:26-27) as a total of seventy persons. Before his death Joseph, son of Jacob, experiences the growth of the people over several generations and prophesies (Gen. 50:24) that God will, in the future, lead the people back to the land (Canaan) which he had originally promised to give them. In other words this stay in Egypt is seen as a temporary provisional sojourn, not the people's ultimate permanent destiny (even though Abraham had been warned in Gen. 15:13 that his descendants would one day have to serve another people for four hundred years).

In Exodus Chap. 1 the atmosphere changes as political upheavals lead to a new regime, which distrusts the Hebrews because they are 'different' and strange. Accordingly their privileges and civil rights are removed and the people are enslaved and put to forced labour on behalf of the State. This does not however stop them growing in numbers, so the Pharaoh attempts to wipe them out gradually by eliminating all male new-born children. Two Hebrew midwives, Shifra and Puah, attempt resistance by refusing to obey their orders.

In Exodus 2:1-10 one Hebrew family tries to avoid this fate for their son by floating him in a small crate on the Nile. By luck, miracle or (more likely) design (it seems they stuck the box in a safe place where they knew the princess came regularly to bathe) the boy is rescued by Pharaoh's daughter and named by her '*M's's*' or (Hebrew) *Moshe*. (It seems he was never named by his father Amram, but is referred to in some later hymns such as '*Mipi El*' as '*Ben Amram*'.) This does not actually mean 'I picked him out of the River' as often supposed but 'I don't know what else to call him, since I picked him out of the River.' (cf. 'Ramses' is the son of Ra; 'Tutmoses' is the son of Tut. Effectively with '*M's's*' she is saying 'I don't know who his father is.')

We read in Exodus 2:1-22 how Moshe grows up nominally as an Egyptian courtier, but feels himself an outsider, becomes aware of social injustice, reacts to it, kills a brutal Egyptian overseer in the heat of the moment and, threatened then with betrayal by one of the very people he has helped, has to flee for his life into the desert, where he settles in Midian, becomes a shepherd, marries Zipporah the daughter of a Midianite priest Yitro and has a son of his own.

Exodus 2:23-25 is a 'flashback' to Egypt, where the Israelites are still suffering; God hears their cry and decides on action.

In Exodus Chap. 3 God calls to Moshe (Moses) from a burning bush in the desert and commissions him (much against his will) to go back to Egypt and lead the Israelites out. (This implies that God was already fully aware of where Moses was and how to contact him.)

In Exodus Chap. 4 God finally convinces Moses (by getting angry at his prevarications) and sends him back to Egypt, to perform miracles and to threaten Pharaoh.

(Note: Verses 22ff. are a prophetic threat to kill Pharaoh's first-born son and a warning that God will harden Pharaoh's heart.)

Aharon / Aaron, Moses' elder brother, is sent by God to meet up with Moses, a brother he actually never knew, and together they work to transform the morale of the Israelites.

In Exodus Chaps. 5 and 6 initial problems are encountered and setbacks suffered. Their initial demand is met by Pharaoh making the work still harder, so that the slaves have to make their own bricks without reducing their current work-quotas. The Israelites turn against their supposed liberators, and Moses in turn appeals to God for help. In a parenthetical section the family background of Moses is explained in only four generations: Levi — Kohath — Amram — Moshe. By this time Moses is 80, and his brother Aaron is 83.

In Exodus 7:1-13 the confrontation with Pharaoh continues, neither side being willing to concede defeat:

7:14-24:	The First Plague	— The Nile is turned to blood, together with all other water supplies. All the fish die.
8:1-15:	The Second Plague	— of Frogs.
8:16-19:	The Third Plague	— of Lice.
8:20-31:	The Fourth Plague	— of Flies.
9:1-7:	The Fifth Plague	— of Cattle Disease. The beasts die.
9:8-12:	The Sixth Plague	— of Boils.
9:13-35:	The Seventh Plague	— of Hailstorms. The crops are damaged.
10:1-20:	The Eight Plague	— of Locusts. All the remaining plants are devoured.
10:21-29:	The Ninth Plague	— of Darkness.

In Exodus 11:1-10 God warns of the final and most terrible plague — the Killing of the First-Born — and advises that the climax is near. In consequence 12:1-29 are occupied with instructions for the short-term and long-term futures. In the short term the Israelites, counting from that particular moment, have to wait ten days then take a lamb or kid, slaughter it on the 14th. day, eat it all, roasted, that night, but beforehand smear some of its blood over the door-lintels as a sign that the house is an Israelite one. In the longer term they are to observe a seven-day festival of eating *Matzah* at this time every year.

In 12:29-30 this final Tenth Plague does take place. In consequence Pharaoh not only allows the people to go, he actually expels them in great haste (though not before they have plundered their terrified neighbours, as prophesied in 3:21ff.).

600,000 Israelite (men) leave, plus their families, plus a 'mixed multitude' (an '*Eruv rav*') of non-Israelite hangers-on who take the opportunity to leave as well. The date is given as exactly 430 years to the day since they had originally entered Egypt (This date was however not given in Genesis). In the rush they have to take unleavened bread, *Matzah*, since there is no time to let their dough bake slowly.

In Exodus Chap. 13 Moses reinforces the experience by ordering two symbolic observances in future years to commemorate what the people have just gone through. Firstly he repeats the instruction to hold a seven-day *Matzah* festival, specifically now as a reminder of the Exodus (the '*Yetzi'at Mitzrayim*') and as a means of educating the next generation; Secondly all the First-Born (who were saved, whereas the Egyptian First-Born were killed) have to be dedicated to God. This means that if they are animals they are to be sacrificed, if they are humans they are to be formally redeemed from the obligation.

In Exodus Chap. 14 the Egyptians, having second thoughts, chase after the fleeing Israelites to bring them back, but the Israelites are enabled through a miracle to walk through the 'Red' or 'Reed Sea' ('*Yam Suf*') whilst the pursuing Egyptian Army is then drowned in it.

This marks the end of that particular threat and the people move on into the desert — since the sea has closed again behind them they cannot return.

5. SOME NOTES ON THE BIBLICAL ACCOUNT

(a). Five times Pharaoh responds to the Plague, but each time refuses to grant Moses' request in full, and the confrontation gets deeper. These are: after the Frogs (8:8-15); after the Flies (8:25-32); after the Hail (9:27-35) and again after some discussion with his advisers and Moses and Aaron (10:7-11); after the Locusts (19:16-20); and after the Darkness (19:24-29).

The Plagues have always been a source of concern amongst commentators, partly because the innocent inhabitants suffer along with Pharaoh, partly because Pharaoh seems at times to be being manipulated by God. We note here only the following points:

(i). They are part of a theological conflict in which the Egyptian deities are attacked, defeated and humiliated in sequence. The Nile, source of Life — becomes Blood, a symbol of Death; Ra, the mighty Sun-God, is switched off for three days; Deities of Fertility must watch powerless as hail and locusts destroy the crops; Holy creatures die of disease, holy insects become a pest.

(ii). With the exception of some slaves who are left outside despite warnings before the Hail, (9:19-23) none of the first nine plagues is specifically or directly fatal to humans. They cause discomfort and distress, but not death.

(iii). The 10th. Plague singles out the First-Born, who were probably the Priesthood or dedicated in some way to the temple and cultic rituals.

By the end of these Plagues the economy of Egypt, its agriculture in fields and orchards, its fishing and its religion have all been ruined. All that is left is the Military — which will also be destroyed in due course…

(b). If you look carefully at Chapter 12 it looks almost as though Moses has misinterpreted God's command. Verses 2 to 13 deal with God's instruction about the lamb to be killed this month; verses 14 to 20 refer to the act of removing leaven (*Chametz*) and eating *Matzah* as a continuing reminder of this period. Yet Moses on instructing the people (verses 21 to 27) omits the reference to *Matzah* (as not being relevant yet), but describes the Lamb sacrifice as a continuing requirement.

(c). Because of this omission the Exodus itself comes as a surprise to the Israelites, who end up eating *Matzah* not for ritual reasons, or as part of some annual festival, but only because they have not prepared themselves for the event and have no time left to bake anything more elaborate. (12:34: 'So the people took their dough before it was leavened, their kneading bowls being bound up in their mantles on their shoulders', and 12:39 — 'And they baked unleavened cakes of the dough which they had brought out of Egypt, for it was not leavened, because they were thrust out of Egypt and could not tarry, neither had they prepared for themselves any provisions.' See also Deut. 16:3.)

Only in 13:3-10 does Moses hand on the message about eating *Matzah* as an annual memorial of the Exodus.

(d). In the *Haggadah* the fourth Plague is described as '*Erov*', being attacks by wild beasts. Several Biblical translations also translate the word '*Erov*' this way. The dictionary understands this word as meaning a 'swarm', from the same root as the word for 'Mixture' (and indeed '*Erev*', Evening, which is a mixture between day and night). Obviously there is room for different interpretations of the Hebrew.

(e). The actual month of the Exodus is not named — though in 12:2 God specifically instructs Moses that a new Calendar is to commence, as with most revolutions — but the name *Nisan* is only used in post-Exilic books of the Bible (in Nechemiah 2:1 and Esther 3:7). In the Book of Exodus reference is made to the 'Spring' month, the month in which the ears of corn develop, known as '*Aviv*' (Ex.13:4, 23:15, 34:18). In Deuteronomy 16:1 when the laws of *Pesach* are repeated the 'month of Aviv' is again referred to.

(f). In 13:8 the Israelites are told that each should say to his son, in future times, 'This is because of what God did for me when I came out of Egypt.' This is obviously seen as a positive statement. In the *Haggadah* however it is presented as a confrontational reply to the '*Rasha*', the 'Wicked Son', the stress being placed on the word 'Me'.

6. PASSOVER IN THE MISHNAH
AND LATER RABBINIC WRITINGS

From an early time it became apparent that there were two distinct levels of observance of this festival — the public one, performed in Temple times as a sacrificial service and the private one, performed as a domestic service around a festive meal — the *Seder*. In addition the search for and removal of all leaven from the household was ritualised into '*Bedikat Chametz*'. Much of what we now practice in terms of

Pesach observance can be seen to be based on Rabbinic interpretations of the Second Temple period (i.e. till the end of the 1st.-century CE) and the immediately-following centuries. Only the Samaritans, still a small sect in Israel today, observe the ancient 'Paschal sacrifices' — nowadays on Mount Gerizim near Nablus.

The main rules are found in Tractate *'Pesachim'* of the *Mishnah* — elaborated later in the *Gemara* and elsewhere. It is in the *Mishnah* that we get the first outlines of what we now know as the *Seder* meal — though with some significant and interesting differences.

6A. AN OVERVIEW OF MISHNAH 'PESACHIM'

- Chapter 1 deals with the search for *Chametz*.
- Chapter 2 deals with the use of *Chametz* during *Pesach* for commercial transactions and certain miscellaneous rules.
- Chapter 3 deals with definitions of *Chametz*, when to remove it and what to do if for some reason you forgot to.
- Chapter 4 discusses whether or not one may work on the 14th. *Nisan*, the day before *Pesach*.
- Chapter 5 deals with the details of the Passover sacrifice as it was performed in the Temple.
- Chapter 6 discusses what problems arise when *Pesach* falls on a Sabbath, in terms of the sacrifices.
- Chapter 7 deals with the details of the cooking of the Passover sacrifice; how it must be handled, what to do if something goes wrong and how to dispose of the remains.
- Chapter 8 deals with different categories of people or relationships — mourners, master-slave, father-son, etc., and rules for who may share a *Pesach* sacrifice and who should perform their own.
- Chapter 9 deals with problems that may arise — that a person may be away from home, or be ritually unclean on *Pesach*; He should therefore observe *'Pesach Sheni'* (a 'Second *Pesach*') instead, a month later (14th. *Iyyar*). Alternatively, a mistake could be made with the sacrificial animal, or two offerings confused with each other.
- Chapter 10, the final chapter, deals with details of the *Seder* meal and is reproduced here in full (adapted from 'The *Mishnah*', Herbert Danby, O.U.P. 1933, pages 150ff.)

Mishnah 'Pesachim' Chapter 10:

1. 'On the Eve of Passover, from about the time of the Evening Offering (1), a man must eat naught until nightfall. Even the poorest in Israel must not eat unless he sits down to table, and they must not give them less than four cups of wine to drink, even if it is from the [Pauper's] Dish. (2)

2. After they have mixed him his first cup, the School of Shammai say: He says the Benediction first over the day and then the Benediction over the wine. And the School of Hillel say: He says the Benediction first over the wine and then the Benediction over the day. (3)

3. When [food] (4) is brought before him he eats it seasoned with lettuce, until he is come to the breaking of bread; (5) They bring before him unleavened bread and lettuce and the *Charoset* (6), although *Charoset* is not a religious obligation. R. Eliezer b. R. Zadok says: 'It is a religious obligation.' (7) And in the Holy City (8) they used to bring before him the body of the Passover-offering.

4. They then mix him the second cup. And here the son asks his father (and if the son has not enough understanding his father instructs him [how to ask]), 'Why is this night different from other nights? For on other nights we eat seasoned food once, but this night twice; on other nights we eat leavened or unleavened bread, but this night all is unleavened; (9) On other nights we eat flesh roast, stewed, or cooked, but this night all is roast.' (10) And according to the understanding of the son his father instructs him. He begins with the disgrace and ends with the glory; and he expounds from '*A wandering Aramean was my father...*' until he finishes the whole section. (11)

5. Rabban Gamliel used to say: 'Whoever has not said [the verses (12) concerning] these three things at Passover has not fulfilled his obligation. And these are they: Passover, unleavened bread, and bitter herbs. 'Passover' — because God passed over the houses of our fathers in Egypt; 'unleavened bread' — because our fathers were redeemed from Egypt. In every generation a man must so regard himself as if he came forth himself out of Egypt, for it is written: And thou shalt tell thy son in that day, saying, It is because of that which the Lord did for me when I came out of Egypt.' (13) Therefore are we bound to give thanks, to praise, to glorify, to honour, to exalt, to extol and to bless him who wrought all these wonders for our fathers and for us. He brought us out from bondage to freedom, from sorrow to gladness, and from mourning to a festival day, and from darkness to great light, and from servitude to redemption; so let us say before him the *Hallelujah*.' (14)

6. How far do they recite [the *Hallel*]? The School of Shammai say: To 'a joyful mother of children.' (15) And the School of Hillel says: To 'a flint-stone into a springing well.' (16) And this is concluded (17) with the '*Ge'ullah*'. (18) R. Tarfon says, 'He that redeemed us and redeemed our fathers from Egypt and brought us to this night to eat thereon unleavened bread and bitter herbs.'

But there is no concluding Benediction. (19) R. Akiba adds: 'Therefore, O Lord our God and God of our fathers, bring us in peace to other set feasts and festivals which are coming to meet us, while we rejoice in the building-up of thy city and are joyful in thy worship; and may we eat there of the sacrifices and of the Passover-offerings whose blood has reached with acceptance the wall of thy Altar, and let us praise thee (20) for our redemption and for the ransoming of our soul. Blessed art thou, O Lord, who has redeemed Israel!'

7. After they have mixed for him the third cup he says the Benediction over his meal. [Over] a fourth [cup] he completes the *Hallel* and says after it the Benediction over song. If he is minded to drink [more] between these cups he may drink; only between the third and fourth cups he may not drink.

8. After the Passover meal they should not disperse to join in revelry. (21) If some fell asleep [during the meal] they may eat [again]; but if all fell asleep they may not eat [again]. R. Jose says: 'If they but dozed they may eat [again]; but if they fell into deep sleep they may not eat [again].'

9. After midnight the Passover-offering renders the hands unclean. (22) The Refuse (23) and Remnant (24) makes the hands unclean. If a man has said the Benediction over the Passover-offering it renders needless a Benediction over [any other] animal-offering (25) [that he eats]; but if he said the Benediction over [any other] animal-offering, it does not render needless the Benediction over the Passover-offering. So R. Ishmael. R. Akiba says, 'Neither of them renders the other needless.'

Notes to the above:

(1). See Num. 28:8. In the *Mishnah* 5.1 'The Daily Whole-Offering was slaughtered at a half after the eighth hour, and offered up at a half after the ninth hour; [but] on the eve of Passover it was slaughtered at a half after the seventh hour and offered up at a half after the eighth hour, whether it was a weekday or the Sabbath. If the eve of Passover fell on the eve of a Sabbath, it was slaughtered at a half after the sixth hour and offered up at a half after the seventh hour. And, after this, the Passover-offering was slaughtered.' [i.e. The rituals were brought forward by one or two hours to suit the conditions.]
(2). Compare with the definitions for charity in *Mishnah 'Pe'ah'* 7:7: 'A poor man who is journeying from place to place should be given not less than one loaf worth a '*podion*' [from wheat costing] one *sela* for four *se'ahs*. If he spends the night [in such a place] he should be given what is needful to support him for the night. If he stays over the Sabbath he should be given food enough for three meals. If a man has food enough for two meals he may not take aught from the [Pauper's] Dish, and if enough for fourteen meals he may not take aught from the [Poor-] Fund. The [Poor-]Fund is collected by two and distributed by three.' [i.e. welfare meals are for those who do not have enough for a day, social security for those who do not have enough for a week.]

(3). See *Mishnah* '*Berachot*' 8:1 'These are the things wherein the School of Shammai and the School of Hillel differ in what concerns a meal. The School of Shammai say: '[On a Sabbath or a Festival-day] they say the Benediction first over the day and then over the wine.' And the School of Hillel say: 'They say the Benediction first over the wine and then over the day.'

(4). Some texts add: 'Vegetables and lettuce.'

(5). In the variant of Ovadia of Bertinoro, who wrote a 'standard' commentary on the *Mishnah* published in Venice 1598-99, is 'the bread condiment' (*parperet*, as in '*Berachot*' 6:5 & '*Avot*' 3:19.) i.e. The bitter herbs.

(6). Made of nuts and fruit pounded together and mixed with vinegar. The bitter herbs were dipped into this to mitigate their bitterness. Some texts add 'and two cooked dishes.'

(7). To recall, by its appearance, the mortar out of which the Israelites made bricks in Egypt.

(8). Lit. Temple. See *Mishnah* '*Shekalim*' 1:5.

(9). Some texts add, 'on other nights we eat all other manner of vegetables, but this night bitter herbs.'

(10). Some texts add: 'on other nights we dip but once, but this night twice.'

(11). Deut. 26:5ff.

(12). Ex. 12:27, 12:39 and 1:4.

(13). Ex. 13:8. This whole sentence is omitted by older sources.

(14). Usually referred to as the '*Hallel*' — Psalms 113-118.

(15). End of Psalm 113.

(16). End of Psalm 114, 'When Israel came out of Egypt...'

(17). Lit. 'sealed' — cf. '*Berachot*' 1:4.

(18). Lit. 'redemption' — i.e. a Benediction recounting God's redemption of his people out of the hands of the Egyptians.

(19). As in the following version by R. Akiba.

(20). Some texts add: 'with a new song.'

(21). Heb. '*Epikoman*'. Cf. Isaiah 30:29. The joy of the Passover meal with its solemn symbolism must not degenerate into an ordinary convivial gathering. The traditional interpretation however is: 'they may not finish with 'dessert''.

(22). It could be eaten only until midnight: See '*Zevachim*' 5:8. Ex. 12:10 only forbids it to remain 'until the morning'. cf. '*Berachot*' 1:1 for a definition of 'morning'.

'*Zevachim*' 5:8 reads: 'The Firstling, the Tithe [of Cattle] and the Passover-offering are of the Lesser Holy Things; they were slaughtered anywhere in the Temple Court and their blood required to be sprinkled with but one act of sprinkling, provided that it was sprinkled against the [Altar-]base. There is a difference in their manner of eating: the Firstling was eaten only by the priests, and the Tithe [of Cattle] by any man; they could be eaten anywhere in the City, and cooked for food after any fashion, during two days and a night; but the Passover-offering could be eaten only during that night and only until midnight, and it could be eaten only by the number that were assigned to it, and it could only be eaten roast.'

(23). Lit. 'abomination'. Lev. 7:18; Lev. 19:7. cf. '*Zevachim*' 2:2-3, 3:4 and '*Menachot*' 1:3.

(24). Lev. 7:15; Lev. 19:6.

(25). The freewill festival-offering spoken of above in Ch. 6:3-4.

(26). We can see from these texts firstly that there was already scope for a great deal of disagreement and different interpretation; secondly, that the basic outline is already the same as that which we observe today — though the Four Questions are slightly different. A scholarly apparatus also reveals the danger of quoting simply 'The *Mishnah* says...' without being more specific about which text and which variant and which edition is being referred to!

6B. THE 'TOSEFTA'

These are the 'Additions' to the *Mishnah* containing much early, contemporaneous material:

> 'A person is obligated to occupy himself with the laws of *Pesach* [i.e. to relate the story of the Exodus] throughout the night, together with his son or even alone or with his pupil. It once happened that Rabban Gamliel and the elders were reclining (at the *Seder*) in the home of Boethus bar Zonin in Lod, and were occupied with the laws of *Pesach* all night until the rooster crowed (and the morning star appeared). They thereupon arose and arranged to go to the House of Study.' ('*Pesachim*' 10:7)

There are echoes here of the story in the *Haggadah* of the five Rabbis who spent the whole night at B'nei Barak. One scholarly interpretation of the latter story, as portrayed in the *Haggadah*, is that the five Rabbis were in reality discussing whether the time was ripe to start the 'Bar-Kochba Rebellion' in the year 135 CE and that their students' summons in the morning is in fact a coded call that 'morning has come — it is time to start the revolt.'

In the *Mishnah* ('*Pesachim*' 9:5) we see a reflection of the differences between the first *Pesach* — that of the Exodus — and later ones:

> 'Wherein does the Passover of Egypt differ from the Passover of the generations that followed after? At the Passover of Egypt the lamb was got on the 10th. of *Nisan*, sprinkling of the blood with a bunch of hyssop was required on the lintel and on the two side-posts and it was eaten in haste and during one night; whereas the Passover of the generations that followed after continued throughout seven days.'

In this short paragraph we see that attention was already being given to the discrepancies between what the Bible commanded in the specific situation facing Moses and the Israelites and what the Jews were accustomed to observe in later times. This process of development has continued, particularly with regard to argument over what is considered *Chametz* and what is considered '*Kosher le'Pesach*'.

Much rabbinic thought was devoted over the centuries to clarifying, extending and systematising the laws of *Pesach* for *Diaspora* communities in post-Temple times — and there are many sources of these laws elsewhere than in this brief guide — but the modern equivalent is the obsession with '*Kosher le'Pesach*' tea, sugar, detergents, milk, etc.

7. SEARCHING FOR *CHAMETZ*

7A. DEFINITIONS

The term '*Chametz*' applies to anything that is, or could become, leavened — i.e. it could rise or ferment, given sufficient time and moisture. Specifically there are references to 'the five grains' — wheat, barley, oats, spelt and rye. A separate category of non-grain products — pulses — that could, under certain defined circumstances, either ferment or be thought to do so are called '*Kitniyot*'. (These include rice, peas, beans, chickpeas, sesame and sunflower seeds, maize, lentils, possibly also soy beans and peanuts, etc.) *Ashkenazi* authorities took this potential 'problem' seriously and forbade the use of *Kitniyot* during *Pesach* 'in case it confused people'; *Sephardi* authorities took a more relaxed view. Liberal Judaism has decided, together with Conservative Judaism and other authorities, that the concept of '*Kitniyot*' has outlived whatever usefulness it ever had.

The underlying idea of the search for *Chametz* is the removal of anything that could be called 'last year's food', the foodstuffs stored during the winter, which can now be cleared out (together with any pests that may have accrued) and replaced with fresh produce now that Spring has arrived. Modern food technology complicates matters to some extent, in that it is now much more normal to have food kept in storage — in tins, packets, jars, in the freezer — and to keep it there for months on end or even longer. This might mean that some compromises need to be made — in terms of where to keep the stuff, not on whether it may be eaten during *Pesach*!

In terms of alcohol, whiskey and beers are made from grains and are therefore classed as *Chametz* and prohibited, as is vodka made from grain rather than from potatoes. Gin is from juniper berries and acceptable and of course wine is from grapes.

7B. BEDIKAT CHAMETZ

The procedure for '*Bedikat Chametz*', the 'Searching for *Chametz*', can be found in the front of most *Haggadot*. It is based on the *Mishnah* '*Pesachim*' Chap. 1. Some excerpts follow:

> 'On the night of the 14[th.] *Nisan* the *Chametz* must be searched for by the light of a lamp. Any place into which *Chametz* is never brought needs no searching.

They need not fear that a weasel may have dragged *Chametz* from house to house, or from place to place; for if so, it may likewise have dragged it from courtyard to courtyard, or from town to town; there is no end to the matter.'

Note the common-sense reasonableness of this approach! In 3:1 we find the following list which also indicates the extent of international trade at the time:

'These must be removed at Passover: Babylonian porridge, Median beer, Roman vinegar and Egyptian barley-beer; also dyer's pulp, cooks' starch-flour, and writers' paste. Rabbi Eliezer says: Also women's cosmetics. This is the general rule: Whatsoever is made from any kind of grain must be removed at Passover. These are included in the prohibition, yet punishment by excommunication is not thereby incurred (by neglecting to observe the rule).'

In modern times it is amazing how many products have flour as an additional ingredient for bulking or stiffening — one finds flour in ketchup, mustard, soups, etc. Coeliac sufferers have learned to beware of such. Some very pious Jews go through every book in their library searching through every page in case a stray crumb has survived... More realistic is for one member of a household to wrap a few pieces in foil or similar and another goes searching for it with the aid of a candle and a dustpan. Do not forget where you have hidden the last piece!

7C. 'MECHIRAT CHAMETZ'

The concept of '*Mechirat Chametz*', the 'Selling of *Chametz*', is a complex one. Strictly speaking the prohibition in the Bible is against having any *Chametz* in your property, within your boundaries. It isn't just on on eating it but on <u>owning</u> it. Since it was often inconvenient (or financially ruinous) to get rid of everything at *Pesach* (although the Ethiopian Jews used to do this by burning down their grass huts and building new ones, a rather drastic but probably effective way of keeping down the mite population) the method devised was simply to 'sell' symbolically and temporarily (for just over one week!) whatever you couldn't dispose of, usually to a Gentile neighbour. That way it was no longer yours! A proper '*Shtarr*' or document of sale would have to be drawn up and the transaction properly witnessed; after that the *Chametz* could stay safely stowed away in whatever cupboard or room was designated in the Bill of Sale and you could get through *Pesach* with a clear conscience, safe in the knowledge that it wasn't really 'yours' and that at the end of the festival you could regain your goods!

Several Jewish newspapers or websites publish advertisements before *Pesach* from rabbis and *Batei Din* offering this facility; there is no 'Reform attitude' as such but the whole process is considered to be little more than a legal fiction and a sham. Although Maimonides stresses that one should not just 'hide it away', this is in fact a reasonable alternative to 'selling'; in other words put all *Chametz* articles in secure storage, in an attic or garage or locked box room or specifically-sealed and labelled cupboards, so that there is no chance of using it by accident during the days of *Pesach*.

7D. 'BIYUR CHAMETZ': THE BURNING OF CHAMETZ

After clearing away or using up most of your *Chametz* and retaining a little bit for breakfast on the day before *Pesach*, the portions that have been deliberately 'hidden' and then 'found' should be burned.

Bitter experience teaches that you will not get far trying to set fire to a piece of stale bread with a match! Instead, it is suggested that you wrap the *Chametz* to be burned in old newspaper, place it in a small cardboard box to hold it together and set fire to that — in the garden, on the patio, or balcony or wherever, but somewhere safe and where you can later clear away the ash!

8. THE LENGTH OF *PESACH*

Whilst the command to slaughter the *Pesach* sacrifice applies only to the first night and the command to 'tell your son', the origin of the *Seder*, the Bible commands us that we should eat *Matzah* and keep our property clear of leaven for 'seven days' (e.g. Ex. 12:14.20; 13:4-10):

12:14. 'This day shall be for you a memorial day, and you shall keep it as a feast to the Lord; throughout your generations you shall observe it as an ordinance for ever. Seven days you shall eat unleavened bread;

15. On the first day you shall put away leaven out of your houses, for if any one eats what is leavened, from the first day until the seventh day, that person shall be cut off from Israel

16. On the first day you shall hold a holy assembly, and on the seventh day a holy assembly; no work shall be done on those days; but what every one must eat, that only may be prepared by you.

17. And you shall observe the feast of unleavened bread, for on this very day I brought your hosts out of the land of Egypt; therefore you shall observe this day, throughout your generations, as an ordinance for ever.

18. In the first month, on the fourteenth day of the month at evening, you shall eat unleavened bread, and so until the twenty-first day of the month at evening.

19. For seven days no leaven shall be found in your houses; for if anyone eats what is leavened, that person shall be cut off from the congregation of Israel, whether he is a sojourner or a native of the land.

20. You shall eat nothing leavened; in all your dwellings you shall eat unleavened bread.'

13:4. 'This day you are to go forth, in the month of Aviv.

5. And when the Lord brings you into the land of the Canaanites, the Hittites, the Amorites, the Hivites, and the Jebusites, which he swore to your fathers to give you, a land flowing with milk and honey, you shall keep this service in this month.

6. Seven days you shall eat unleavened bread, and on the seventh day there shall be a feast to the Lord.

7. Unleavened bread shall be eaten for seven days; no leavened bread shall be seen with you, and no leaven shall be seen with you in all your territory.

8. And you shall tell your son on that day, 'It is because of what the Lord did for me when I came out of Egypt.'

9. And it shall be to you as a sign on your hand and as a memorial between your eyes, that the law of the Lord may be in your mouth; for with a strong hand the Lord has brought you out of Egypt.

10. You shall therefore keep this ordinance at its appointed time from year to year.'

Despite this, the custom in a large proportion of the Jewish world is to observe eight days of *Pesach*. The reasons for this go back to early uncertainties about the calendar when, to be certain of getting the day right, communities in the *Diaspora*, distant from Jerusalem (which was the place where the official New Moon was discerned and proclaimed) decided to observe the first day twice — to be on the safe side. One of them at least should then be the correct day! This then became the norm for all major festivals with the exception of *Yom Kippur*. In Israel only one day of each festival was observed, with the exception of *Rosh Hashanah* — because this festival, falling on the first of the month, could be subject to some uncertainty concerning the exact point at which the month began.

In consequence, in Israel now only one day is observed as 'First Day *Pesach*' and the Reform movement follows this approach. (However, in some communities a *Communal Seder* will be held on the Second Evening, as an option mainly for those who were unable for whatever reason to celebrate with a family on the First Night.)

Orthodox communities in the *Diaspora* ('*Chutz LaAretz*') observe not so much two days at the beginning of *Pesach* as the First Day twice, the only difference being the *Torah* and *Haftarah* readings. But by counting seven days from each of these 'First Days' one ends up with a repetition too of the 'Seventh Day', which in theory marks the end of *Pesach*.

Orthodox and Reform variant Readings are:

Orthodox First Day: Exodus 12:21-51; Numbers 28:16-25.
   Haftarah: Joshua 5:2 to 6:1, plus 6:7.
Orthodox Second First Day: Leviticus 22:26 to 23:44; Numbers 28:16-25.(i.e.
   same as 1st. Day);
   Haftarah: II Kings 23:1-9, 21-25.
Reform First Day: Exodus 12:37-51; Deuteronomy 8:10-18.
   Haftarah: Isaiah 11:1-16.

Orthodox Seventh Day: Exodus 13:17 to 15:26; Numbers 28:19-25.
   Haftarah: II Samuel 22:1-51.
Orthodox Eighth Day (Second Seventh Day): Deuteronomy 15:19 to 16:17;
   Numbers 28:19-25. (i.e. same as 7th. Day);
   Haftarah: Isaiah 19:1-12:6.
Reform Seventh Day: Exodus 14:30 to 15:18; Deuteronomy 4:32-39.
   Haftarah: Ezekiel 37:1-14.

It can be seen that the Reform readings fall within the Orthodox ones in terms of the first *Torah* reading; differ in that they avoid the lists of sacrifices and substitute instead Deuteronomic references to the Exodus for the second reading; and there are different *Haftarot* (though the Reform 1st. Day *Haftarah* fits into the Orthodox 8th. Day one) — a section of Isaiah that includes in 11:15 a curse on Egypt.

The complications that ensue from this differing length of observance are not just in rituals or the length of time one eats *Matzah* or when one can start purchasing or baking or using leavened foods again. If *Pesach* starts on a *Shabbat* we find that the following *Shabbat* counts as 'Eighth Day' for the Orthodox communities and festival services with their *Torah* readings are held, whereas in the Reform/Liberal communities this is merely the 'normal' *Shabbat* that follows the end of *Pesach*.

In consequence, for a few weeks (until the Calendar can be jiggled) Reform synagogues are reading the same *Sidra* as communities in Israel but are one week ahead of and not in synchronicity with those read by their Orthodox neighbours!

9. 'CHOL HA-MOED'

The Intermediate days of a 7- (or 8-)Day Festival (the other example is *Sukkot*) are called '*Chol HaMo'ed*'; '*Mo'ed*' is Hebrew for a special time or season, and hence refers to a particular time or festival season; '*Chol*' is the term for 'normal, non-holy, ordinary' days. We can see that these days form an intermediate period, not quite one thing, not quite the other, on which some of the rules apply but others don't. For instance, the command to talk about the Exodus (in modern terms, to hold a *Seder*) only applies to the initial day.

The *Shabbat* that falls during this week is therefore known as '*Shabbat Chol HaMo'ed Pesach*' with the 'special' *Amidah* (p.240; p. 230 in the RSGB *Siddur*), a 'half-*Hallel*' added in the Morning service (p. 663 — Psalms 113, 114, 115, 116, 117, 118) and especial *Torah* readings.

10. FAST OF THE FIRST BORN ('*TA'ANIT BECHOROT*')

It is traditional that a first-born child should fast on the day preceding the *Seder* (i.e from the morning, not the previous evening). This is largely as a sign of gratitude that the Israelite first-born, unlike those of the Egyptians, were spared.

In some Orthodox communities a '*Siyyum*' is deliberately organised — i.e a feast to mark the completion of the study of a section of the *Talmud* or some such event. By this means (actually an excuse!) the positive command to feast and celebrate is deemed to overrule the command to fast, and whilst the womenfolk are frantically preparing the house, the menfolk are having a party in the synagogue!

11. THE *HAGGADAH*

The origins of the *Haggadah* itself are lost in the mists of time. The name itself means 'Narrative' or 'Narration' and applies to the book or booklet filled with prayers, readings and songs used at the *Seder* Evening. The versions we have today are the result of a long period of development.

Nevertheless, although modern versions are still being continually produced, with variants or additional prayers (for example, some had prayers for '*Refusniks*' — the term in the 1970s and 1980s used for Jews held back from emigration from the Soviet Union, whose applications to leave Russia were refused; or for Jews still oppressed in Arab lands) one can speak of a 'normative' basic *Haggadah* text. The illustrations vary considerably as each generation has added their own ideas and interpretations, some bound by inhibitions against portraying human faces, some running riot with the benefits of modern printing techniques. In one *Haggadah* the 'Wise Son' is portrayed as a '*Yeshivah Bochur*' and the 'Wicked Son' as a Jesuit priest — an apostate! In another the 'Wicked Son' is portrayed in Nazi uniform, as a Collaborator.

The roots of the *Haggadah* go back not only to the instruction to 'tell your son' (Ex. 13:8) but to the fact that, unless one were in Jerusalem, there would be no sacrifice visible or feasible and therefore no other really distinct form of worship. Once the Temple was destroyed (in 70 CE) no one had a Paschal sacrifice any more and all that was left was to talk about it. (Other instructions to tell of the Exodus are found in Ex. 12:26, Ex. 13:14 and Deut. 6:20).

So — what should one tell? At this point it should be made clear that there were many times in Jewish history when it could be dangerous to be too specific about hopes for liberation and much of the *Haggadah* is actually in a form of polemical code, saying one thing but meaning another; some scholars find references to anti-Roman revolts; one thinks that the 'three things' which Rabban Gamliel demands be mentioned are an attack on those who wished to transform the *Seder* into a form of 'Last Supper'. How could one hint at the expectation of a Messiah without giving ammunition to those who claimed he had already come? In consequence, there is always something going on between the lines of the *Haggadah*.

There is a stress on the number Four. Why? No-one really knows. There are the four references mentioned above, to the command to tell the story; the four Cups, four Questions, four Sons…

Significantly there is no mention of Moses in the entire *Haggadah*! The liberation from Egypt is described solely in terms of Divine action and intervention. 'God, and not an angel…' No credit is given to any human being. This must be deliberate.

12. THE *HAGGADAH* — TEXTUAL DEVELOPMENT

The following précis on the textual development of the *Haggadah* is based largely on Philip Goodman's work, 'Passover Anthology'. (JPSA, Philadephia, 1973)

The oldest portions of the *Haggadah* are probably Psalms 113 and 114 — the latter being very specifically a 'Passover Psalm' referring to the Exodus from Egypt. Substantial portions may have originated in the pre-Maccabean period; the first introductory statement 'We were Pharaoh's slaves in Egypt' is believed to have been composed in the 3rd. century BCE, reflecting the reaction in Palestine to the Egyptian sovereignty that prevailed at that time. The second, or alternative opening 'In the beginning, our ancestors were idolators', which stresses the antiquity of Israel and its origin in Mesopotamia before even the discovery of Monotheism, is attributed to the High Priest Jason around 175-172 BCE. It is also claimed by one scholar that he composed the '*Dayenu*'.

The excerpt from Deuteronomy 26:5-8 'A wandering Aramean was my Father,' also translateable as 'An Aramean tried to kill my Father' (note the problems of translating Hebrew!) is subjected to a lengthy homiletical *Midrash* — 'Come and hear…!' — which, from its theological stress on the visible appearance of God and the denial of angels having taken part, appears to be pre-*Pharisaic* and therefore also very early.

By the time the *Mishnah* was compiled (around the second century CE), as we have seen from the excerpts from '*Pesachim*' Chapter 10 the basic outline of the ritual was clear. However, there are only three Questions mentioned, one of which is not the same as we have today. The 'pivotal passage' — 'Every person in every generation must regard him- or herself as having been personally freed from Egypt' and the *Kiddush* and the Four Cups are already fixed.

Neither of the opening statements is referred to specifically — the likelihood is that they circulated independently, but were both included when the *Haggadah* was redacted.

The rabbis of the *Gaonic* period (6th.-11th.-centuries CE) added further *Midrash*ic interpretations. One of these is the four types of Son, which is found in the Jerusalem *Talmud* ('*Pesachim*' 34b) and in the '*Mekhilta de-Rabbi Ishmael*' (I.166-7) though different questions are asked!

The four Questions are rooted in the Biblical text: the Wise Son ('*Hacham*') asks Deut. 6:20; the Wicked Son ('*Rasha*') Ex. 12:26; the Simple son ('*Tam*') Ex. 13:14 whilst the one who cannot ask ('*she'lo yode'a lish'ol*') is addressed in terms of Ex. 13:8.

Strangely, the story of the five Rabbis of the second-century CE who spent the whole night at B'nei Berak talking about the Exodus is not found anywhere else in rabbinic literature.

A number of other selections were added to the *Haggadah* later. '*Sh'foch Chamatcha...*' — 'Pour out thy wrath!' — composed of the verses Psalm 79:6-7, Psalm 69:25 and Lamentations 3:66, protesting against cruel outrages and invoking divine retribution on heathens, was inserted during the Middle Ages when the Jews were frequently subjected to false accusations and libels. The custom of opening the door at this point is probably a formal sign to Christian neighbours that there is nothing to hide — no Christian blood in the wine-glasses, no punctured body under the table.

Most of the above passages were incorporated in the *Haggadah* included by Rav Amram *Ga'on* in his *Siddur* of ca. 850 CE. The *Siddur* of Rav Sa'adia *Ga'on* of the 10th.-century incorporates the earliest complete text of the *Haggadah*, though with a different beginning than the current one.

The version of the '*Machzor Vitry*' (11th.-century) is close to today's. That in the '*Mishneh Torah*' of Maimonides (RaMba'M 1135-1204) is essentially the same as today's. However, many poems and songs were later added. The poem 'The *Seder* is ended' is by Joseph Tov Elam of the 11th.-century. The song '*Adir Hu*' appears in the 14th.-century; the songs '*Echad — Mi Yode'ah*?' and '*Chad Gadya*' first appear in print in a *Haggadah* published in Prague in 1590.

The first printed *Haggadah* was produced in Guadalajara, Spain about 1482 — ten years before the Expulsion; the second in Soncino, Italy about 1486. Since then at least 3,000 different editions have appeared, in many languages, and this creativity continues.

Many appear with translations into the vernacular; Moses Isserles (1520-1572) in his commentary on the '*Shulchan Aruch*' ('*Orach Chayyim*', *Rama* 473) advocated the practice of making the *Haggadah* available in the vernacular, so that woman and children could also understand it (!) and mentioned that this had already been done in England!

13. *KOSHER LE-PESACH*

Kashrut is a subject in itself and is dealt with in a different chapter. But there are specific additional regulations for *Pesach* — as mentioned above, to do with any foodstuffs which might contain ingredients that could be classed as liable to ferment, to contain flour or yeast... and nowadays it is amazing where one finds flour added to sauces, jams, soups, condiments, etc. Accordingly many families purchase items which bear the special distinctive '*Kosher for Pesach*' label and of course for many owners of *kosher* delicatessens this is one of the busiest periods of the year and an opportunity to earn enough to tide them through leaner months. Every now and then a scandal breaks out when a shopkeeper is found sticking 'Kosher for Passover' labels on quite normal products whose price is then effectively doubled… Whilst it is important to help fellow Jews make a living and to support such local communal facilities as a supplier of *kosher* foods, one does not have to become wholly hysterical about this. Many basics — tea, coffee, sugar, butter, milk — are already quite OK for *Pesach* use. Beer and whisky (and some brands of vodka) are of course fermented grain products and therefore forbidden.

Many families maintain one (or two) separate sets of dishes and cutlery and kitchen utensils for *Pesach* and bring them out of the cupboards for this week only. (Since this is a week where one might have many *Seder* guests there need to be many sets and settings.) Work-surfaces in the kitchen are scrubbed and maybe covered in aluminium foil… This is all wonderful — if it is possible. At the same time a pragmatic bit of advice is that — especially for communal meals or those with limited storage space and resources — disposable cutlery and crockery are also perfectly acceptable. Anyone who has tried to butter a piece of hard, stiff, flat *Matzah* in a typical dished plate will know how hard this is to do — but to use a piece of paper kitchen towel or a paper serviette is much simpler, if less elegant! Afterwards one simply folds it up and the crumbs are easily removed.

14. A REFORM VIEW

When leading a *Seder* in a Reform context — whether in a family or in a synagogue or other communal setting — it would be appropriate to acknowledge the equality of the sexes by referring to 'The Four Children' rather than the 'Four Sons'; the 'Fast of the First-born' could become an obligation which first-born daughters might also wish to observe.

Some *Haggadot* bear rubrics which refer to 'The Head of the Household says…' but there is no reason why those present could not take turns, join in and share the act of leading the *Seder*.

Some Reform and Liberal Jews dislike the sentiments behind '*Shefoch Chamat'cha*' and would rather either omit it or replace it with something more positive — 'Pour out your love upon those who DO respect and love you…' This certainly adds to a 'feelgood' factor but omits the cathartic effect of the original which is, after all, composed of Biblical verses which indicate that it is legitimate to express anger, hurt and rage even if this is currently 'politically incorrect'.

15. THE '*OMER*'

From *Pesach* onwards one starts counting the *Omer*, the period of 49 days culminating on the 50th. day (6th. *Sivan*) with the festival of *Shavuot*. (See later chapters on this topic.) The question was: From when should one start counting?

16. CONCLUSIONS

Despite its length this chapter has only tackled a few aspects of this festival and even that superficially — but hopefully enough to show that there is a great deal hidden beneath the surface of household cleansing, food-preparation and family feasting that tends to dominate thoughts at this time.

We are free to celebrate our freedom — something one should never take for granted.

CHAPTER 16

A BRIEF GUIDE TO THE PESACH SEDER

1. A GUIDE TO THE *SEDER*

The *Seder* is the part of *Pesach* that most Jews recall best from childhood, or observe themselves, for it is a home ritual, a family ritual and becomes laden with personal, private meanings and memories. This is good and as it should be… But — the *Seder* works at a variety of levels, from the scholarly to the simple. The description of the 'Four Sons' illustrates a part of this variety. Some Jews can ask learned questions and cope with learned answers; some feel quite alienated from the whole process, perhaps find the *Seder* a bore to be endured rather than enjoyed and by their behaviour threaten to spoil it for others — and therefore need to be sharply brought to heel; some can only cope with a childish level of question and answer; and finally, some cannot even formulate an intelligent question — they may be too young, or disturbed, or handicapped, or shy, or nervous…

The trouble is that many of us have learned the *Seder*, if at all, as children and learned only the childish versions of the interpretations and procedures. If we do not go on to deepen our knowledge, as questioning adults, we will only be able to pass on the childish answers to our own children and we could find ourselves giving both the three-year-old and the sixteen-year-old the same answers — answers that we ourselves might find unsatisfying — whereas we are specifically told in the *Haggadah* that each level of questioning deserves its own answer. (To employ an example from another religion: There is more to the Christian festival of 'Christmas' (a Mass said for the '*Christos*' — the 'anointed one') — than just Santa Claus, reindeer, snow and presents — yet many parents are unable to help their children learn more of their religion because that is all they ever learned themselves! Yet, when the child stops believing in Santa Claus all religious belief is vulnerable, for there is no clue to the child that there is something more to learn… about a theology based on messianic hopes and yearnings for salvation.)

In the same way there is much more to the *Seder* than pulling a face at the *Maror* or watching for Elijah to drink his wine; Much, much more. This brief guide can do no more than hint at some of the subtleties and mysteries in the *Haggadah*.

A problem is that the *Haggadah* is written partially in a form of Code and we no longer have the key. It was designed to convey a certain message — and this message is one of Hope for the Future, but based on a story from the Past — yet at the same time it is a hope based NOT on any individual human person, but instead on God and God alone. It can be seen as a polemical work, opposing any dependence on human Messiahs — whether Shimon Bar-Kochba, or Jesus, or any other such charismatic figure in history. It would have been so much easier simply to institute the reading of the first 15 chapters of the Book of Exodus; instead a composite work with *Midrashim*, songs, questions and — very significantly — with major gaps has been created. By eliminating Moses from the story entirely the *Haggadah* is saying that it is not the messenger but the One who <u>sends</u> the messenger who is important.

There is great significance to sitting together with other Jews for the *Seder*. It is truly a time to invite others or to be invited, rather than to be on one's own on *Seder* night. Since not everyone has a family to be with on this night, many communities also organise such a *Seder* for either the First or Second night — as well as *Sedarim* arranged by youth groups, old age homes, student fellowships, refugee clubs, etc. After all, one of the most important sentences in the *Seder* is the invitation for all who need to and who wish to, to come and eat. An expensive catered meal is not necessary; simple foods or shared contributions will do just as well.

The *Seder* celebration is a defining moment in the Jewish calendar, an affirmation of our identity — a reminder of our liberation from slavery and also of the responsibilities that come with this. In one evening we taste bitterness and sweetness, we recall the dry, unsatisfying bread of slaves and we eat a filling meal; we sing songs that celebrate how we have survived so many problems and terrors. The ritual itself is filled with hints at past catastrophes and salvations, the 'hidden code' being found as much in what is <u>not</u> included as in what is. For example we do not simply read from the first chapters of the Book of Exodus ('*Shemot*'); we do not make Moses into a hero figure (quite the reverse! He is written out of the story entirely); we stress that God alone can save us, no delegates, whether human or angelic or messianic — and this is possibly a polemic against those who believed in those messiahs, whether self-proclaimed as such or not, who failed to 'save' us — such as Shimon Bar-Kochba or a carpenter's son from Nazareth. We focus instead on how God saved us from our troubles in the past and the unspoken assumption is that God can therefore save us from our troubles in the future. We take part in a chain of tradition that has held Jewish families and communities together over centuries.

2. THE *SEDER*

The *Seder* should be fun; it is not an overly-solemn ritual. One is after all recounting a marvellous story of redemption and freedom, not just ploughing dutifully through a lengthy prayer book. The wine is there to be drunk, not sipped at daintily or played with. It is true that there are contradictions in the way we observe the *Pesach*; for example, a lot of the foods we eat are not mentioned in the Biblical text and what is indeed mentioned in the Bible — animal sacrifice — is now reduced to a symbolic bone and egg. On *Pesach* we commemorate a hurried midnight flight — an expulsion of our ancestors, who were oppressed slaves. We do this by means of deliberate contrast — by taking our time over a lengthy meal, sitting back to relax, singing songs until late into the night...

The word 'Seder' means, of course, 'Order' or 'Sequence' and refers, strictly speaking, to the 'Order of Service' rather than just the meal. The meal is itself merely a part of that order (No. 10) so when you 'invite someone to the Seder' you are in fact inviting them to the whole ritual and should not skimp or skip bits. Alas, the author has noticed that there is often a tendency to 'cut out' sections so as to get quickly to the meal, and then after the meal there is little desire to complete all the text! This is more than a pity... Why rush?

It is important to understand that many of the sections of the Haggadah are in fact wholly routine or normal for almost any meal and have little to do with a specific 'Pesach' theme; lighting candles for light, blessing the wine or bread one is to consume, or washing one's hands, or reciting a Grace after eating, are all 'routine' matters even if some slight alterations are made for the festive day. Even the Hallel Psalms are normal for a festival. However, for most Jews it is only on such a formal occasion as a Pesach evening that these will be observed in such detail.

Candles are lit at the beginning — mainly so that one has light to read and eat by! The Berachah over these is the standard one for a festival — '...lehadlik ner shel Yom Tov.'

After reciting or singing the Order, the first section is:

3. 'KADESH'

The Kiddush — the standard Berachah — blessing over wine, coupled with the festival version of the 'Blessing of the Day' and the relevant additions for Shabbat or Havdalah for when Pesach falls on the appropriate Friday (Erev Shabbat) or Saturday evening (Motza'ei Shabbat). One then drinks the First Cup of wine and can pour the Second. The Four Cups are drunk at the beginning and the end of the first section of the Seder, i.e. before the meal; and at the beginning and end of the second section, i.e. after the meal and its accompanying Grace. (One may drink more glasses of wine during the meal, but this is just for pleasure, not for the symbolic blessings.) Of course Grape-Juice is also acceptable for those who are either too young or sick, or who are pregnant, or who are recovering from addiction, or who need to drive home afterwards... The Berachah '...Borei P'ri HaGafen' refers merely to 'Fruit of the Vine'.

Why do we lean to the left when drinking? In Graeco-Roman times the polite etiquette at a formal mealtime or banquet (a 'Symposion') was to recline on couches when eating, leaning on your left arm and elbow, picking up food with your right hand. (In many societies the right hand is reserved for 'clean' actions and the left for 'unclean' ones. It is unclear how people coped when they were left-handed!) At the

Seder the Jews of the *Mishnaic* period (i.e. Roman times) modelled their behaviour on that of their non-Jewish aristocratic neighbours and so adopted this method of demonstration that, on *Seder* night, they were as free and relaxed as anyone else. (Alas, this was not necessarily so for the rest of the year!)

4. 'UR'CHATZ'

Literally: 'And Wash' — from the Hebrew '*Rachatz*'. Judaism incorporated the idea, revolutionary for centuries, that it was a good idea to wash your hands before using them to pick up something you would put into your mouth; and also to bathe regularly in flowing, not stagnant water (in a '*Mikveh*'). In hindsight it is amazing how long it took for this idea to percolate through to some other sections of European society — or even for surgeons to start to wash their hands before operating rather than afterwards. We can have no idea how many people have died needlessly due to such ignorance of basic hygiene. (Of Queen Elizabeth I of England it was written with approval that 'she took a bath every year, whether she needed it or not!') Often it was because Jews employed such basic hygienic rituals that their rate of death during frequent outbreaks of typhoid or bubonic plagues was lower — and then they would often be blamed instead for having started the plagues, of having poisoned wells, and they were made the scapegoats. It is not just a matter of lack of clean flowing water in medieval towns — of course most developments of modern plumbing and sewerage are just that, modern! — but even a symbolic cleansing could have an effect and is commanded in the *Torah*. Most non-Jews (or non-Moslems, for Islam also has its intensive cleansing rituals) must have stunk terribly and would have been infested with a variety of lice. Travel in closely-confined spaces with such people was a nightmare, which is why even now specific quantities of tobacco, alcohol and perfumes are freed from Customs duties for travellers — they were not 'luxuries' but basic necessities to cover the stench.

In this case the hands are washed before taking some Herbs and so no *Berachah* is said — this is reserved for the second occasion, the '*Rachtza*', when Bread will be taken.

5. THE 'KARPAS'

This strange word occurs only three or four times in Jewish writings, in the Jerusalem *Talmud*. It is usually understood to mean 'parsley' or 'celery'; in the '*Shulchan Aruch*' radishes are recommended. One could also use leek, or spring onions. Be that as it may, the *Karpas* refers to a green herb or vegetable that one dips into a tart sauce — vinegar or salt water (maybe also to remove any insects?) — as an aperient. It certainly takes away the taste of the wine! Theoretically one can thereafter keep taking bits to crunch or chew during the following narration. A modern equivalent would be crudités — sliced or whole raw vegetables served as an appetiser.

The blessing is the standard one over any vegetable — '*Baruch Atah Adonai, Eloheynu, Melech HaOlam; Borei P'ri haAdamah*' — we bless God as being the one who creates the 'Fruit of the Soil'. There is no particular tradition that the *Karpas* represents anything symbolic at all and it is probably just a relic of ancient eating customs, to commence with a 'starter' that got the taste-buds tingling. This could be equivalent to laying out crisps or salted nuts or pretzels or olives or similar items for one's guests at a modern dinner party for them to nibble during conversation before the formal meal itself starts. This has nothing to do with *Pesach* as such and theoretically there is no reason why those present should not continue to nibble a bit during the narration — that is, once the initial blessing has been said, the *Karpas* can be eaten continually to allay hunger.

6. 'YACHATZ'

Three flat, dry *Matzot* have been placed especially at the head of the table — the 'ritual *Matzot*' as opposed to the others that people will eat during the evening and the rest of the week. These are the ones that form a part of the symbolic actions. Why are there three? One traditional answer is that they represent the three divisions of the Jewish people — 'Cohen', 'Levi' and 'Israel'. This is picturesque, but unlikely to be any more than an attempt to find some link with another number Three. Why, after all, should it be the 'Levi' *Matzah* that gets broken in two? It is more likely that Three is simply the minimum number required to have a 'middle one'. For now, all that happens is that the person presiding over the *Seder* (called in some households the 'Father' or 'Master of the House'! — though there is no reason why a woman should not lead the *Seder* and families come in different forms) ceremonially breaks the middle *Matzah* in two; one half will be used for the *Afikoman* and hidden at some point during the proceedings, to be searched for (often by the children present) after the meal. It will then be eaten by those present before the *Birchat HaMazon*, the Grace after Meals is said.

It is perhaps significant that there is no formula or blessing or prayer to say to accompany this action. Its true significance remains a mystery. The word 'Afikoman' is not Hebrew but is probably derived from the Greek 'Epikomenos' and refers to one who is hidden or who has not yet come... Some translate it merely as 'Dessert' which is also what comes at the end, after the main course of the meal and for which one must wait.

7. THE 'MAGGEED'

The word 'Maggeed' just means 'Narration' — telling the Story — from the same Hebrew root as the verb 'leHagid' and the noun 'Haggadah'. The narration now lasts until the symbolic hors d'oeuvres that precede the meal. The *Matzah*, the symbolic 'poor bread' or 'bread of poverty' (Deut. 16:3) is the reminder that we were once poor and afflicted; it serves therefore as the stimulus to what follows. The statement 'Ha Lachma Anya' is in Aramaic, not Hebrew, and encompasses past, present and future — poverty and hospitality, slavery and freedom — in four short sentences.

8. THE SECOND CUP

The Second Cup will be raised and lowered symbolically three times before being raised for drinking at the fourth time (we see the number four again and again). It is also the cup that will be used to illustrate our feelings about the Plagues. (See below)

Traditionally red wine is used at the *Seder* — but there were periods in Jewish history when this could be a risky thing to do, inasmuch as suspicious neighbours might think that it contained blood! Accordingly some Rabbis authorised, or encouraged, the use of white wine in times of high risk.

9. THE FOUR QUESTIONS

Really these should be the minimum number of questions and those present (especially the children) should be encouraged to ask whatever other questions they wish. The questions themselves reflect a different reality to that which we experience today — for example, few of us eat *Matzah* regularly with our meals (even though it is freely available during the year) or lean on cushions at a normal dinner. The idea is that something is noticed which is out-of-the-ordinary — so a lot depends on what is 'ordinary'. Indeed, one could argue that these questions come 'too early' in the evening's sequence, since at the time they are asked we have not yet dipped a second time, nor eaten the bitter herbs......Still, if no questions were to be asked, there would be no 'cue' to answer.

In fact, as already mentioned, a great deal of what appears in the *Haggadah* is not really 'special' at all. Although for many people today almost all of the ritual would seem strange, a large proportion of it was 'normal' in ancient times. The washing of hands, the basic blessings over wine, over bread or vegetables, the Grace After Meals should belong to <u>every</u> meal, not just the *Seder*; the *Hallel* Psalms belong to every festival. In the Four Questions we see that interest is aroused by the fact that there are special factors, but significantly what interests the questioner is not that we have *Matzah* on the table — we can eat '*Chametz* or *Matzah*' on any occasion — but that the Bread is missing!

The questions are partly based on those asked in the *Mishnah* tractate '*Pesachim*' Chapter 10. In the *Talmud* '*Pesachim*' 109a the importance of ensuring that children do not fall asleep partway through the ceremonial is stressed!

10. THE ANSWER

The Answer commences with a very fundamental but logical statement: If History had been different, the Present would also not be the same as it is! In all our lives we can think of things that happened or didn't happen, of the strange chances and events that brought our parents together, and before them our grandparents... or how we found our partners or discovered the beauties and challenges of Judaism... Rather than getting smug about our own knowledge and achievements, it behoves us to keep in mind just how lucky we are to be here, in a position to talk so freely about our past and our hopes for the future.

The story of the Five Rabbis at B'nei Berak is a mysterious one, not found elsewhere in rabbinic literature (though in *Tosefta 'Pesachim'* 10:12 is a story of Rabban Gamliel staying up all night at Lydda). These were all senior and influential figures. Eliezer ben Hyrcanus was a disciple of Rabbi Yochanan ben Zakkai and is cited in *'Pirkei Avot'* 2:11-15 as saying 'Do not be easily provoked to anger'; Rabbi Joshua ben Chananyah was also a noted student of Yochanan ben Zakkai and in *'Avot'* 2:11-13 is cited as believing that friendliness is the best quality a man should have; Akiva ben Yosef only began studying at the age of forty, taught many disciples and is quoted in *'Avot'* 3:18f. stressing that the People of Israel are God's children but that all are granted free will, the right and ability to make their own choices between good and evil; Rabbi Tarfon (a former priest) was renowned for his modesty and is quoted in *Avot* 2:20f. as explaining that, even though one cannot finish a project, one is not free not to start it... and Elazar ben Azaryah is cited in *'Avot'* 3:22 as warning that moral actions are more important than intellectual debate.

As they lived at the time of the Bar Kochba rebellion against the Romans in 135 CE it has been postulated that the story refers actually to a planning meeting for that revolt; the Exodus (the *'Yetzi'at Mitzrayim'*, the 'Coming-Out of Egypt') was in fact a coded term (should any spies be listening) for the political liberation from the Romans instead that was being plotted.

Hence, the following anecdote of Rabbi Elazar ben Azariah might be a cryptic reference to a philosophy that one should recall the miraculous powers of God not only during good times — 'the days' — but also the hard and bitter times — 'the nights'. It seems that the other four however overruled him, considering that the term 'all the days' includes 'the Messianic times' — and we know that Bar Kochba was perceived by many, including Rabbi Akiva, as the Messiah who would rise to save the people from occupation, his revolt marking the beginning of the messianic Kingdom. What we can also deduce is that the argument was long and deep — it lasted all night — because the outcome was not clear and the participants represented different viewpoints and in the end it was the students who came, young, impatient men, eager to see the new dawn, who overruled their teachers by saying 'It is time for the morning *Shema*, time to declare the Oneness of God!' And — an especial irony, or perhaps an important hint that we should in future always be extra careful not to get drawn into such political speculations — in the *Talmud* ('Berachot' 61b) is recounted the story of Rabbi Akiva ben Yosef and his students who, once the revolt had been defeated with massive casualties, were arrested by the Romans and tortured to death in the Circus, skinned alive — 'at the time of the Morning *Shema*'. Akiva makes from this a final moral lesson for his students, that now at last through being martyred he is in a position to fulfil the command to worship God with ALL his strength and he expires while doing so, stressing the word 'Echad'. The tradition (in *Talmud 'Yevamot'* 62b) that many thousands of Akiva's students died in the weeks following *Pesach* — a tradition maintained in the 'Omer' observance

— 'because they did not respect each other' — is probably also linked to these disastrous historical developments which led to the utter end of any hopes for Jewish self-determination or the restoration of Jerusalem.

11. THE FOUR SONS

Perhaps it is significant that it is at this point that we have, again in ritualised form, references to the different ways of understanding and interpreting events. What to some might have been a political struggle, to others would have been a messianic one — and still others would have wanted to distance themselves from it. We see echoes of this debate today in terms of the different attitudes Jews still have to the rebirth of the State of Israel in 1948 and developments since then.

- The *Hacham*, the Wise Son, wants to know everything and can safely be told everything about the ritual, even down to mystic, esoteric details about the (true?) meaning of the *Afikoman*.

(The '*Afikoman*' is a bit of a mystery. The Aramaic word itself is derived from a Greek word, '*Epikomonos*'. In the rabbinic literature it is understood as a reference to the after-dinner entertainment — and when used in *Mishnah* '*Pesachim*' 10:8 or *Jerusalem Talmud* '*Pesachim*' 37 the implication is that one should not break off after the *Pesach* meal to indulge in normal activities — the eating of dessert, of fruits, nuts, dates and sweets. The answer to the Wise Son was based on this *Mishnah* reference — and perhaps means 'Stay on afterwards — there is yet more to talk about.'

On the other hand — it could also be a messianic reference, based upon an understanding of the Greek term, that the culmination, the climax, comes after a period of waiting, the dessert is kept hidden until the right time and is only then revealed...... There must be some reason why it is only the Wise Son who gets initiated into the specialness of the *Afikoman* and it cannot just be a straightforward suggestion that the Dessert be served!)

- The *Rasha*, the Wicked Son (note — not the 'Stupid' one) wishes to distance himself from the proceedings and is spoken to sharply on the lines of 'That kind of attitude wouldn't have helped you in the past, and won't help you now!' There has always been the phenomenon of what is often referred to dismissively as the 'Self-hating Jew', the one who is embarrassed about his Jewishness or wishes desperately to be accepted by the non-Jewish world and is possibly even prepared to betray others or to support anti-Jewish movements as a part of this psychological need, or even to join another religion — thus excluding himself.

(The irony is that the *Rasha* is actually citing the question as given in the *Torah*. Could it be that he is criticised for not having moved onward from the *Torah* text — he has remained a fundamentalist — or maybe even that he is being criticised for employing and misusing the *Torah* text in a sarcastic manner?)

- The *Tam* — the Simple Son — is the one who cannot cope with anything too complex or abstract or intellectual, but still has a healthy curiosity that needs to be satisfied if he is to feel a part of what is going on. There are for example many people who are fascinated by weapons and forms of warfare, but are not interested in the political backgrounds of conflicts or in conflict resolution — for such a person, to be told that 'God helped us, as though with a mighty military power!' is enough, all they can cope with intellectually.

- What about the one *'sh'lo yodea li'Shol'* — who does not know how to ask? Why can he not ask? Traditionally this son is often portrayed in illustrated *Haggadot* as simply being too young — but he may instead be handicapped, or mute, or unable to understand what is going on and therefore feel too shy to ask anything… He may be autistic or suffer from some syndrome that hampers him in social discussion… He may even simply be bored, or gullible, he has never learned to distance himself from whoever is speaking and to formulate critical questions. Nevertheless he needs to be addressed and to be incorporated into the gathering. How many thousands of people have stood at political rallies and never queried the rubbish that is being spouted so dramatically at them?

One should note that, in a Reform or Liberal context, the term 'Sons' can be interpreted as 'Children' and involve both genders.

12. THE TIMING OF THE *SEDER*

This paragraph merely illustrates the sort of rabbinic reasoning and deductive logic that is always applied to such matters, working from minor details of the written text. But the underlying issue is that almost all other rituals are performed in the daytime and daylight and this is therefore an exception.

13. 'OUR ANCESTORS WERE IDOL WORSHIPPERS'

Not a nice thing to admit — yet that is why it is stressed here. In order to understand how we as a People came Out of Egypt we have to review quickly the history of how we as a Family got there in the first place. This is the context. The whole of the Patriarchal period is encapsulated in a few brief sentences, then attention is focussed on the details of the oppression suffered in Egypt, seen as but one example of a problem that has existed in every generation. The passage *'VeHi she'Amdah'* stresses that not a generation has gone by without some experience of anti-Semitic threat — including the present one.

The verses of Deuteronomy 26:5-8 are then teased out phrase by phrase with explanations and a reference to the direct intervention of God himself, rather than a deputy, based on Exodus 12:12.

14. THE TEN PLAGUES

(In Hebrew these are called the '*Makkot*', the 'Blows against Egypt'. A 'Plague' would be a '*Magefah*' and would imply illness or sickness rather than 'natural phenomena'.)

These have always been a moral problem for many people; It doesn't seem right that we should recount, with glee, the sufferings imposed upon others. Further, since Pharaoh ruled Egypt as an absolute autocrat, why did the rest of the population have to suffer for something they could not influence or prevent?

There are several possible responses to this problem. The first is to note that we do not in fact rejoice fully at the Plagues. They are regarded as historical fact in terms of the story of the Exodus, an unfortunate necessity (as is any form of casualty in war); but for this reason we deliberately spill a drop of wine as each Plague is mentioned — so that our own 'cup of joy' is not full.

Secondly, if you look at the Biblical text carefully Pharaoh seems to have had a great deal of popular support in his repressive measures against the Israelites (See Ex. 1:8-14, 3:7, 5:10-14, etc.) Of course this cannot 'explain' the sufferings caused to animals and children.

A third approach is to note that the first nine Plagues caused inconvenience and annoyance and disruption, but were not in themselves directly life-threatening. (The only exception was the Hail, but even in this case there was a warning to stay indoors — so that only those who didn't heed the warning or their slaves actually suffered. See Ex. 9:18-21, 25.)

A fourth answer is to see the Plagues as part of a theological war, in which God selectively deposes or destroys the Egyptian deities, one after the other, as though to say, 'Don't bother trusting in the Nile-God — I can turn the river that brings life-giving water into blood, a symbol of Death rather than Life; Don't bother worshipping Scarab Beetles — I can make insects into a cause of irritation rather than comfort; Don't bother worshipping fertility gods — I can destroy everything that grows in the fields; Don't bother worshipping Ra, the Sun God — I can plunge the whole land into Darkness, and he cannot do a thing to prevent it!' — and so on. One by one the Egyptian religions are ridiculed by God, until at the end the First-born are wiped out. The First-born are not necessarily 'innocent' or random victims: the First-born would have been dedicated to the various temples, either as priests or as sacrifices; thus God shows that God can destroy the whole pagan system if God so chooses.

None of this is meant as an 'apologetic' but merely an attempt to show that there are different possibilities to be taken into consideration. At the end of the day the fact is that our history tells us that many people suffered in different ways as part of the process of our liberation. So as we recount each 'Blow' we take a little wine out of our cups and spill it on the table.

(Another method is to see how each of the 'blows' damages or destroys a part of the Egyptian economy — the fishing, the pastoral and agricultural work, then the priesthood — and finally, although it is not counted as one of the Ten Plagues, the destruction of the Egyptian Army in the Reed Sea eliminates the military infrastructure as well, leaving the once-proud and mighty country impoverished and defence-less — all thanks to one autocratic ruler who refused to compromise or negotiate. Sounds familiar? However, by this time the Israelites are on the eastern side of the sea and there is no way back for them.

In the *Talmud 'Megillah'* 10b God is described as also agonizing over the need to destroy some of His creation in the sea, in order to save others; and in Proverbs 24:17-18 we are admonished: 'Do not rejoice when your enemy falls, do not exult when he is overthrown...')

Rabbi Judah's additional abbreviation of the initial letters of the Plagues as a mean-ingless mnemonic *'Detzach Adash Be'Achav'* is seen by some as a code. One medieval priest declared polemically it stood for the Hebrew for 'We have all required blood as we were told to do in temple times in Jerusalem' — and the Rabbis in response told him that it stood for 'The words of our oppressors are slanderous; the accusations over blood are false; the children of Abraham are innocent!'

— *'Dam Tzerichim Kulanu; Al Derech She'assu; B'Oto Ish Hachamim BeYerusha-layim'* — or as reaction:
'Divrei Tzerorenu Katzav; Alilot Dam Shaker; B'nei Avraham Halila B'Zot!'

It isn't always so easy to 'turn' a Blood Libel!

Despite the ethical doubts expressed above we now move on to a section that applies rabbinic reasoning to expand the number of plagues yet further, in a form that is almost a parody, extrapolating from a 'finger' to a 'hand'; but then move on to a sequence that stresses that this isn't really necessary, since even one small part of God's redemption would have been 'enough'.

15. 'DAYENU'

This song is ascribed to the High Priest Jason in the second century BCE. The mes-sage is simple: 'We would have been grateful enough for but a small part of the help we have received; how much more grateful should we be that we have received it all!' The sequence starts with the Exodus and moves on to the establishment of the Temple.

Intriguingly the content of the song is also a move to distance ourselves from any moral responsibility for what happened — inasmuch as we say 'We would have been quite satisfied with much, much less.' The song says in effect — 'Don't blame us for all that happened — since we would have been quite content with only a fraction of all these signs of divine help. We were just passive recipients.' So we all join in the rhythmic refrain!

16. RABBAN GAMLIEL'S COMMENT

What are the basic component parts of the *Seder*? If we pare it to the (lamb) bone, what can we classify as the absolute minimum observances? Gamliel provides an answer: Everything else is an optional extra, but these three symbols are the core — the Lamb, the *Matzah*, the *Maror* — and they need to be explained — as they are indeed in the paragraphs that follow. The Passach lamb will represent the blood smeared on the doorposts, the *Matzah* represents the bread of affliction, the *Maror* the bitterness of that time; Or they represent what was eaten formerly in the Temple rite. Even if the sacrifice can no longer be brought, one can still talk about it and what it once meant.

17. THE '*HALLEL*' PSALMS

In fact the *Hallel* section of the *Seder* is divided into two; before the meal we read or sing just the first two Psalms — Nos. 113 and 114, the latter being especially relevant to the Exodus.

18. '*RACHZAH*' — THE SECOND WASHING OF HANDS

Since one is now going to handle food the normal blessing over this action of washing one's hands — actually, of shaking the water off them — is said. '...*al Netilat Yadayim*.'

19. '*MOTZI, MATZAH*': THE SPECIAL BREAD

The normal blessing over Bread of any form is '...*haMotzi Lechem min-HaAretz*'; since *Matzah* is essentially a form of Bread, that is what we say. Since however we are also specifically told to eat *Matzah* (e.g. in Ex. 12:15) we add the more specific blessing for this command as well.

20. '*MAROR*': THE BITTER HERBS

The bitter taste represents the bitterness of slavery and suffering. In some families the custom is to eat a small flake of horse-radish root by itself, or something equally sharp; in others, where horse-radish sauce ('*Chreyn*') is used it is harder to 'dip' this into the *Charoset*, so a piece of *Matzah* has to be used as a backing.

21. '*KORECH*' — THE SANDWICH

From the Aramaic word '*Karach*' meaning 'to enwrap or surround'. This course is symbolic of a rather literalistic interpretation of the command in Ex. 12:8 — 'Since it says we should eat 'a' with 'b' and 'c', then obviously we should eat it all together.' Hillel therefore goes down in history as inventor of the club sandwich. Note however that, since we no longer have the paschal sacrifice, only two of the three ingredients are nowadays used! Though some add *Charoset* to the mix.

This is however a good moment to point out that the portable dish of roasted lamb meat, wrapped in floppy unleavened bread and served with chopped, crispy, bitter vegetables such as raw cabbage or onion and thus eaten together, is still quite common in many Middle Eastern countries. Except — that it is called a Döner or Dürüm Kebab or a Shawarma… and it is still the food of the poor and the workers, those who have to eat while on the move, unable to sit down with a plate and cutlery to eat their meal. What we now call *Matzah* may originally have been much more moist and floppy, bread made from flour and water and baked quickly, but not hard and cracker-like as it is today. Over the centuries our concept of 'unleavened bread' has developed from a simple mix of flour and water baked over a hot plate before it has time to rise, into something much more complex and vacuum-packed.

(Please note: This comment is NOT an encouragement to eat Kebab with Pittah during *Pesach*!)

22. THE *SEDER* PLATE

Before moving on to the meal, now is a good time to note what else is laid out symbolically on the *Seder* Plate:

- The *'Zeroah'* — a Lamb Bone (some people use a chicken bone, some vegetarians even use a carrot!) represents of course the sacrificial lamb of *Pesach*, both the original one in Exodus and the one brought later each year in the temple.

- The *'Betzah'*, a roast or burned or scorched egg represents the regular Festival sacrifice brought at the Temple — the *'Chagigah'*. There is no formal representation of the Daily sacrifice — the *'Tamid'* — since that is now substituted by the service itself to a large extent.

- *Charoset*, the sweet mixture of apples, wine, honey, nuts and so forth (there are many recipes) is mentioned nowhere in the Bible but is well-known by the time of the *Mishnah*.

- The Salt Water is likewise not a part of the 'statutory' memorial, though it is an old custom to dip vegetables into some such liquid, maybe to wash them. Some explain it as representing the tears of the slaves.

- Finally, some *Seder* Plates have a space for *Hazeret* — understood as Lettuce or some other broad-leaved green vegetable. This is not used at all, but reflects early confusion about the *Karpas*.

23. 'SHULCHAN ORECH': THE TABLE IS SET!

The set Table, the meal, is not additional to the *Seder* service but an integral part of it. In Temple times it was considered very important to share as a group in the eating of a roasted animal that had been offered to God. In this way God was a part of the group — the smoke of the roasted or burned meat going up into the heavens, while we humans took part in our section of the joint meal down here on earth. With the loss of the Temple the concept was reversed — we eat a meal and, by saying bless-ings, invite God 'down' to join us.

Several customs exist as to the content of the meal and all groups of Jews have their favourite recipes. It is common to start with hard-boiled eggs in salt water — the egg representing life and fertility, the accompaniment bitterness and perhaps the fluid-ity of life. Some families eat lamb, in commemoration of the sacrifice; others avoid lamb, for the same reason!

24. 'BARECH'

This is really the standard 'Grace After Meals' but incorporates the 'Ya'aleh ve Yavoh' paragraph normally inserted on special days — in this case, in the form of wording for *Pesach*. However, before we commence the piece of *Matzah* that was hidden from the '*Yachatz*' — the symbolic '*Afikoman*' — has to be found (this is often made into a game for children, with a reward for the finder) and this is ceremonially divided and eaten. It is not as though this will be the last thing consumed on this evening — there is still wine to come — but it is the last to be eaten. In this respect it really is the dessert.

25. THE THIRD CUP

At the end of the Grace the Third ritual cup is drunk and the Fourth poured out in readiness. At this point the door is opened and '*Sh'foch Chamat'cha*' is read. This is a compilation of Psalm 79, verses 6 & 7, Psalm 69 verse 25 and Lamentations Chap. 3 verse 66. It expresses bitterness and anger at the behaviour of the peoples amongst whom the Jews have had to live — and the act of opening the door is probably not 'to let the Prophet Elijah in', as is often told to children, but a relic of the need to check outside for any lurking enemies, or even a 'planted' corpse placed near the door to act as an excuse for a pogrom. We live still in an unredeemed state.

The so-called 'Elijah's Cup' ('*Kos Eliyahu*') is likewise not actually a cup for Elijah to drink, but the relic of an ancient rabbinic argument as to whether one should drink four or five ritual cups on *Seder* night — it depends on how one reads a specif-ic verse and how many verbs are included — the eventual compromise was to make four of them mandatory and leave the fifth as a question for Elijah to solve when he eventually comes (as a precursor of the Messiah — to clear up any uncertainties; Eli-jah is viewed as one who went up to heaven — in a fiery chariot — and never actually 'died' in the normal way).

26. 'HALLEL' (THE REST)

The second half of the *Hallel* Psalms continues with Psalms 115, 116, 117 (very short — only two verses!) and 118. This is followed by Psalm 136, called in the *Talmud* ('*Pesachim*' 118a) the '*Hallel Hagadol*', the 'Great *Hallel*' to distinguish it from the sequence Psalms 113-118, known collectively as 'the Egyptian *Hallel*'. This has the regular refrain '*Ki le'Olam Chasdo*' — 'God's Mercy endures forever.'

27. '*NISHMAT*' PRAYER

A small section of a normal Evening Service is now incorporated. The '*Nishmat kol-Chai*' prayer is very old (part of it is quoted in the *Talmud* '*Berachot*' 59b and '*Ta'anit*' 6b) — as part of the prayer for rain. (The raindrops are seen as the 'countless favours' God bestows.) In '*Pesachim*' 118a a 'blessing of song' is recommended to close the *Haggadah* and this is considered to be the '*Nishmat*'.

28. SONGS

Various songs are now incorporated in the *Haggadah*, of differing origins; They include the 'Who knows One, Two, Three...?', 'It came to pass at Midnight', 'A little Kid my Father bought' ('*Chad Gadya*' — in Aramaic) and the idea is that all present participate! Some come before and some after the:

29. FOURTH CUP AND '*NIRTZAH*'

The blessing after the Fourth Cup looks forward to future redemption. The poem 'Ended now is the *Seder*' written by Joseph Tov Elam was added to the *Haggadah* in the 11th. century.

The *Seder* is now formally over — though one can continue singing, talking, drinking until sleep comes!

30. CONCLUSION

This Guide to the *Seder* has not gone too deeply into the mystic symbolism behind the *Afikoman*, or a host of other matters, but hopefully it will help you understand the *Seder* better and help to make 'this night different from all other nights.'

Chag Same'ach!

CHAPTER 17

MATZAH

1. WHAT IS *MATZAH*?

Matzah (plural: *Matzot*) is primitive, simple bread. The discovery of the process of leavening, whereby the yeast works on the flour and water, making Bread dough rise and become more filling and more palatable and increasing the mass, is very old. There are yeasts in the air. However, poor people could not necessarily afford to wait for the process to work and in consequence *Matzah* came to be called '*Lechem Oni*' ('The Bread of the Poor': Deuteronomy 16:3). The Aramaic translation of this phrase as used in the *Haggadah* is '*Lachma Anya*'.

The distinctive feature of *Matzah* is that is is made from water and (usually but not always) wheat flour, without any yeast or chemical substance and it is prepared quickly, so as to ensure that the dough has no chance to start the process of spontaneous fermentation that would turn it into *Chametz*. No salt is used, as a precaution against fermentation, even though it is accepted that salt does not aid this process! ('*Shulchan Aruch*', '*Orach Hayyim*' 455:5) *Matzah* can also be made with eggs or with fruit juices or honey added, since it is considered these will not aid fermentation. This is called 'rich *Matzah*', '*Matzah Ashir*' and is, strictly speaking, not appropriate for the *Seder* night though it is *kosher* for the rest of *Pesach*. (*Talmud* '*Pesachim*' 36a)

Since it has not risen it does not satisfy hunger so well as 'normal' bread and there can be a tendency to eat several slices of *Matzah* and regret it later...

2. HOW IS *MATZAH* BAKED?

Traditionally *Matzah* was baked by hand. About 1855 *Matzah*-baking machinery was invented in England and was soon introduced into America. However, many rabbis objected to machine-made *Matzah*, claiming that the process of rounding-off the *Matzot* took extra time and increased the risk of fermentation: in consequence, the machine-made *Matzot* were made squared-off with corners! (The only exception to this is the '*Hollandia*' brand made in Enschede, The Netherlands.) Commercial *Matzot* are therefore mostly sold wrapped against moisture, inside oblong boxes.

In theory *Matzah* could be made from any of the 'Five Species of Grain' — wheat, barley, spelt, rye and oats. However in practice wheat is normally used, even though the beginning of the wheat harvest was associated more with *Shavuot*, not *Pesach*. (There are also gluten-free variants available for those suffering from a coeliac condition.) The flour has to be carefully handled to ensure that it is kept totally dry, since any moisture could start off the fermentation process. 'Shemurah Matzah', 'Guarded', comes from flour which has been watched and guarded from the time the wheat is harvested and is more expensive; 'normal' Matzah would come from flour which had been guarded or supervised from the time it had been milled.

The water used should be pure and cold. In the *Talmud* ('*Pesachim*' 94b) Rabbi Judah stated that *Matzah* should be kneaded with water that has lodged overnight in a tank or cistern ('*Mayim she'Lanu*') and has been exposed to the cold night air, since it was believed that during the night the sun was under the earth and warming up the wells and underground streams, so making the water tepid! Be that as it may, warm water will hasten the process of fermentation and cold water will slow it down, so it should be as cold as possible. ('*Shulchan Aruch*' O.H. 455:2)

The preparation of the dough and the kneading, rolling and baking should all be done in the time it takes to walk a Roman mile ('*Pesachim*' 46a). This is defined as between 18 and 24 minutes so, to be on the safe side, the shorter, stricter time-limit is used. The *Matzah* is rolled flat and perforated — nowadays by machine but in earlier times by hand with various fork-like spiked implements and in all sorts of decorative patterns. This perforation also helps the dough to dry out quicker, reduces the chance of warm air bubbles forming and prevents the *Matzah* turning into a sort of pittah-bread while baking. (In fact simple *pittot* or poppadoms are essentially very similar — flour and water mixed and baked flat rather than in a mould, on a hot plate rather than in an oven — and represent the sort of bread made in a hurry by other Eastern peoples.)

Of course great precautions must be taken within the bakery to prevent water-droplets hitting the flour, or flour-dust floating in the air onto the surface of the water. The machinery needs to be scrupulously cleaned of any bits of dough sticking to it from a previous batch.

It is considered that, once it has been baked, *Matzah* cannot ferment again. In consequence '*Matzah*-Meal' is also produced — either specially, or from the crushed fragments of *Matzot* broken during the packing process. This can be used in cooking and baking.

Matzah can be eaten throughout the year — it was, after all, traditionally used in the daily sacrifices or when food had to be prepared in a hurry for unexpected guests (e.g. Genesis 18:6 & 19:3). Its eating is only obligatory on *Seder* night.

CHAPTER 18

THE OMER

1. INTRODUCTION

The *Omer* is the name for the period between *Pesach* and *Shavuot*. The word literally means 'Sheaf' and referred to the barley sheaves which were brought to the Temple on *Shavuot*. The period is marked traditionally by a ceremonialised Counting of the Days, in Hebrew '*Sefirat HaOmer*'.

2. THE COUNTDOWN IN THE BIBLE

Why do we count the days?

Because the date of the festival called *Shavuot* is not given directly in the *Torah*! Rather than saying 'On such-and-such a day in the such-and-such month' as usual, we are told instead to take *Pesach* as a marker and then to count for seven weeks — hence the name of the festival ('*Shavuah*' is the Hebrew for 'Week' and '*Shavuot*' the plural). This makes a total of forty-nine days and the fiftieth day is then the festival itself (hence the Greek name '*Pentecost*', meaning 'Fifty').

'And the Lord said to Moses:

'Say to the people of Israel: When you come into the land which I give you and reap its harvest, you shall bring the sheaf of the first-fruits of your harvest to the priest;

And he shall wave the sheaf before the Lord, that you may find acceptance; on the morrow after the Sabbath the priest shall wave it…

And you shall count from the morrow after the Sabbath, from the day that you brought the sheaf of the wave-offering, seven full weeks shall they be, counting fifty days to the morrow after the seventh Sabbath; then you shall present a cereal offering of new grain to the Lord…'

(Leviticus Chap. 23 verses 9-11, 15-16.)

'For six days you shall eat unleavened bread; and on the seventh day there shall be a solemn assembly to the Lord your God; you shall do no work on it.

You shall count seven weeks; begin to count the seven weeks from the time you first put the sickle to the standing grain.

Then you shall keep the feast of weeks to the Lord your God...'

(Deuteronomy Chap. 16 verses 8-10.)

From these two passages we see already that there is scope for argument: Does one start counting from the First Day of *Pesach*, or from the Seventh Day, or from the Sabbath during *Chol HaMo'ed*, or from the Sabbath after *Pesach*?

If you always start counting from 'the day after the Sabbath' ('*miMochorat haShabbat*') then *Shavuot* will always end up on a Sunday (and preceding Saturday evening); If not, it becomes a 'moveable feast'.

There was a great deal of argument in ancient times due to this irritating unclarity; suffice it to say that the rabbis eventually established the custom of counting the *Omer* from the 2nd. Day of *Pesach* (which means beginning on the evening after the First Day) — the 16th. of *Nisan* — and this means that *Shavuot* will always fall on the 6th. *Sivan*. This was significant for it provided a 'date-link' with the story of the giving of the *Torah* on Mount Sinai, which the Rabbis decided also occurred on 6th. *Sivan*, so giving *Shavuot* itself an additional dimension beyond the purely agricultural one. The festival is now linked to the Revelation and not just the Harvest.

The *Omer* is therefore a 'count-down', starting originally with the the offering of a sheaf at the end of *Pesach* in Spring, ending with the Harvest festival of *Shavuot* almost two months later in Summer. The Rabbinic name for *Shavuot* is indeed '*Atzeret*' meaning 'The End, the Closing of the period.' (cf. The closing day of *Sukkot* in the autumn, known as '*Shemini Atzeret*').

3. THE *OMER* PERIOD IN LATER HISTORY

Aside from all the debate and argument over the exact definition of the customs of Temple times — how big the sheaf should be, who should cut it, whether *Omer* meant just a measure of weight and so on — the *Omer* period later came to be seen as a period of semi-mourning when restrictions were placed on certain activities. The exact reasons for this mourning are lost in the mists of time; there are allusions in the *Talmud* ('*Yevamot*' 62b) to a plague striking down thousands of Rabbi Akiva's students during the time between *Pesach* and *Shavuot*, but little specific information. However it was deemed that this mysterious plague subsided by the 33rd. Day of the *Omer* period and this day became in consequence a sort of 'mini-festival', known as '*LaG BaOmer*' from the Hebrew letters *Lamed* and *Gimmel* which stand numerically for 'Thirty plus Three'.

During the first part of the *Omer*, until the 33rd. (and in some communities even beyond that) it is the custom not to celebrate marriages and to avoid loud music and festivities; some people refrain from having their hair cut, also as an external sign of mourning. In consequence, since this period falls in Springtime which is a popular period for weddings, it can happen that synagogue weddings are postponed for just over a month from *Pesach* and will be held on *Lag BaOmer*. In Israel this day is also marked by bonfires and celebrations in memory of Rabbi Shimon Bar-Yohai, assumed to be the author of the *Zohar*, who had hidden himself in a cave at Meron in the Galilee and came out again on this day. Many Jews make a pilgrimage to this spot on this day and often young boys aged three are ceremonially given their first hair-cut at this time.

In view of what little we do know it seems very probable that this period of semi-mourning is a relic of the deep trauma caused by the defeat of the Bar-Kokhba revolt against the Romans in 135 CE — a period in which, quite clearly, many of the followers of Bar-Kokhba were killed (and Rabbi Akiva had acknowledged Shimon Bar-Kochba as the potential saviour of the people from the Roman oppression). We are reminded of the mysterious account in the *Haggadah* of the five rabbis at B'nei Berak (Akiva was amongst them) debating the topic of liberation from oppression and the students coming at dawn to tell them the time had come; in which case the revolt would have started at *Pesach*, the festival of liberation, when messianic expectations were high. Possibly after 32 days the string of military defeats of these 'students' against well-armed and well-trained legionaries reached a pause. This is all, however, speculation — there are no specific surviving texts confirming the full course of events.

Following the defeat Akiva himself was captured and martyred by the Romans, dying 'at the time of the Morning *Shema*' — which may be an echo of the statement in the *Pesach Haggadah* that 'the students' came to the Rabbis at B'nei Barak and said 'It is time for the Morning *Shema*' — which would mean not just daylight, not just time for the morning service, but a political cry, that it was time to declare the Oneness of God. Instead of which, having been perhaps rushed by his students into a hasty decision, Akiva paid with his life, being tortured and skinned alive whilst reciting the Morning *Shema*… ('*Berachot*' 61b; See also the theologically-disturbing reference in '*Menachot*' 39b to Akiva's martyrdom being fore-ordained.)

4. *SEFIRAT HA'OMER*

Since it is a command to count the *Omer* period there is a blessing recited each evening and then the number of days, which are then when appropriate divided into full Weeks and the remaining Days. Calendars are available, rather like desk calendars with moveable cards, to assist the memories. These days are marked as such in Jewish diaries. (See **p.308**; '**Lev Chadash' p.578**.)

The *Berachah* reads:

> 'I am ready and prepared to perform the positive command concerning the counting of the *Omer*, as it is written in the *Torah*: 'You shall count from the day following the day of rest, from the day you brought the sheaf of the wave-offering, seven full weeks shall be counted; you shall count fifty days; to the day

following the seventh week you shall count fifty days.'

Blessed art thou, Lord our God, King of the universe, who hast sanctified us with thy commandments, and commanded us concerning the counting of the *Omer*.' ('... *veTzivanu al-Sefirat-ha-Omer*.')

There follows the sequence:

- *Hayom Yom Echad LaOmer.*	This is Day One of the *Omer*.
- *Hayom Sh'nei Yamim LaOmer.*	These are Two Days of the *Omer*.
- *Hayom Sheloshah Yamim LaOmer.*	These are Three Days of the *Omer*.
- *Hayom Arba'ah Yamim LaOmer.*	These are Four Days of the *Omer*.
- *Hayom Chamisha Yamim LaOmer.*	These are Five Days of the *Omer*.
- *Hayom Shishah Yamim LaOmer.*	These are Six days of the *Omer*.
- *Hayom Shivah Yamim,*	These are Seven Days;
sheHem Shavuah Echad LaOmer.	that makes One Week of the *Omer*.
- *Hayom Sh'monah Yamim,*	These are Eight Days,
sheHem Shavuah Echad	that makes One Week
veYom Echad LaOmer...	and One Day of the *Omer*...'

and so forth...

Nowadays the counting of the *Omer* is one of those customs that has fallen largely into disuse; particularly since the date of *Shavuot* is in any case now fixed and known well ahead, it seems less necessary. However the custom does provide a useful reminder of the historic links between the festivals of *Pesach* and *Shavuot*.

CHAPTER 19

SHAVUOT

1. INTRODUCTION

Shavuot is classed as the second of the 'Three Pilgrim Festivals' ('*Shalosh Regalim*') (counting from Springtime, not from *Rosh Hashanah*!) and falls in late-Spring or early Summer. It marks in ancient Palestinian agriculture the ripening of the wheat harvest.

The *Torah* refers to *Shavuot* in several ways, but never gives an exact date. Instead it tells us to count forty-nine days from '*miMochorat haShabbat*' — 'the day after the Sabbath' (later interpreted to mean from the day after the beginning of *Pesach*) and to celebrate on the fiftieth day (Leviticus 23:9-22). (From the Greek word for 'Fifty' the festival is sometimes known as '*Pentecost*'. Christianity believes that a 'new Revelation' was received on this day, when the disciples of Jesus suddenly began speaking in strange languages in a state of transcendental ecstasy ('Acts of the Apostles' 2:1-14) and the 'Pentecostalist' movement within Christianity stresses this sort of religious fervour, sometimes to the embarrassment of other Christians!)

What has any of this to do with *Shavuot*? The so-called 'New Testament' is, in many places, modelled closely on the Hebrew Bible and *Shavuot* was accepted traditionally as the date on which the original revelation on Mount Sinai was given by God to Moses. Hence, as well as '*Shavuot*' (which means simply 'Weeks' in Hebrew) or the '*Chag HaKatzir*' ('Feast of the Harvest' — the name used in Exodus 23:16) or even '*Chag HaBikkurim*' ('Feast of the First-Fruits' — as used in Numbers 28:26), the names given in the *Torah*, this festival is also known as '*Z'man Mattan Toratenu*' — 'The Time of the Giving of Our *Torah*'. This last name is a later one — not found in the Bible itself — but it reveals a side of the festival that has gained greater prominence over the centuries as Jews were cut off from their agricultural roots and cycle; It reflects the rabbinic understanding that the Israelites came to the Wilderness of Sinai in 'the third month' (Exodus 19:1) — counting *Nisan* as the first month, based on Exodus 12:2. It may even be significant that the term '<u>Our</u> *Torah*' and not simply 'The *Torah*' or 'God's *Torah*' is used, to distinguish it from other claimants.

Shavuot has become in essence a Revelation festival, a time for recounting the story of the giving of the *Torah* on Mount Sinai, of studying (perhaps all night) and of glorifying the Tradition.

2. SYMBOLS OF *SHAVUOT*

The plain fact is that there are no real obvious symbols for *Shavuot* as an agricultural festival. There is no *Matzah* as at *Pesach* and no hut to build as at *Sukkot*. There is a tradition in some communities to decorate the synagogue with greenery. There is no firm evidence for the origin of this custom. The '*Shulchan Aruch*' states: 'It is the custom on *Shavuot* to spread grass in the synagogues and houses in remembrance of the joy of the giving of the *Torah*' (The '*Rama*' on '*Orach Hayyim*': 494 — i.e. writing for *Ashkenazim*). According to the *Talmud* ('*Rosh Hashanah*' 16a) the 6[th.] *Sivan* is the New Year for Fruit Trees. The mediaeval '*Sefer Maharil*' states: 'It is customary to scatter spices and roses on the synagogue floor for the enjoyment of the festival.' The baskets of first-fruits brought to the Temple and the horns of the ox that was brought as a Peace-offering were decorated with greenery.

As with any case where there are several reasons brought to justify something, the chances are that none of them is the sole 'true', correct one. It probably reflects merely the act of harvesting, thus being akin to any pagan harvest festival. Indeed Rabbi Elijah 'the *Gaon* of Vilna' (1720-1797) tried to prohibit this custom, on the grounds that non-Jews used trees as part of their festivals.

3. FOOD FOR *SHAVUOT*

It is a tradition that one eats Dairy produce on *Shavuot*. Again there is no one obvious reason for this.

Some say that, as the *Torah* is likened to 'milk and honey', one should eat sweet dairy food.

Others say that the Israelites realised to their horror on *Shavuot*, with the revelation of the laws of *Kashrut*, that they had been eating non-*kosher* meat all the time until now, so they had to kasher their pots and pans — but had to wait until after the festival to do so and in consequence ate only '*milchig*' in the meantime!

Some take the first letters of four words in Numbers 28:26 ('*Minchah Chadascha La'Adonai B'Shavuotchem*' to read '*MeChalav*' (i.e. 'from Milk'). Mystics read significance into the *Gematria* of the Hebrew word for Milk, '*Chalav*' (*Chet* + *Lamed* + *Vet*), i.e. giving each letter a numerical value, which amounts to $8 + 30 + 2 = 40$, the number of days Moses was on the mountain… and so on.

Be all that as it may, it is now customary to indulge in cheesecakes, *blintzes* and suchlike delicacies in response to no command but only to custom itself, and to show that this anniversary is really a joyful day.

4. THE '*TIKKUN LEYL SHAVUOT*'

The 'Service of the night of *Shavuot*' is a tradition, probably from early-mediaeval times, whereby the pious used to stay awake the whole night and involve themselves in *Torah* study. The Israelites at Sinai were trembling with expectation, so the *Kabbalists* used to ensure that the night did not pass in mere sleep!

One custom was to read the first and last verse of every chapter in the *Torah*, other books in the Hebrew Bible, the beginnings and ends of tractates in the *Mishnah* and so on — in effect, 'speed-reading' through the entire body of Jewish literature. Alternatively, one could study the 613 Commandments of the *Torah*, the '*Taryag Mitzvot*'.

The custom is being revived in modern times with the night — or a portion of it — being spent in communal study of either one or a miscellany of topics, possibly continuing (if endurance allows) till a very early Morning Service as the dawn rises…

5. THE DATE OF *SHAVUOT*

As already stated, it is now customary to start counting the '*Omer*' from the day after *Pesach* begins. This means that *Shavuot* falls on the 6th. *Sivan*. (Orthodox congregations observe the 7th. *Sivan* as well as a 'Second or Duplicate Day of the festival'.) One tradition has it that it was on 6th. *Sivan* in the year 2448 AM (i.e. '*Anno Mundi*' — 'in the Year of the World since Creation' — equivalent to, say, 1308 BCE!) that the *Torah* was given to Moses. Three days prior to this the people were told to get themselves ready (Exodus 19:11-12) and to 'set bounds' around the mountain, to prevent anyone or anything from getting too close; these last three days of the *Omer* before *Shavuot* are therefore known as the '*Sheloshet Yemey Hagbalah*', the 'Three Days of Setting Boundaries'.

It is important to stress that the *Torah* itself does not specify an exact date apart from the reference to the third month as given above. If anything it refers to Moses receiving the revelation over a lengthy period of forty days and then having to repeat the process after the Golden Calf interruption! The Rabbis calculated this from various hints and allusions in the Exodus story. In Temple times *Shavuot* was primarily, perhaps solely a Harvest festival and the whole emphasis on *Torah* and Revelation ('*Mattan Torah*') came later.

6. MODERN MEANINGS

What does *Shavuot* mean to us nowadays? Obviously the Harvest element is not really relevant to urban and suburban dwellers (though it has gained a revival on Israeli *Kibbutzim*). The *Torah* remains the basis of all Judaism, even if our interpretations of it differ, and the *Torah* readings for the day emphasise the universalism of its message — through Time — and stress the ethical basis of Society represented in the Ten Commandments (the '*Asseret haDibrot*').

The *Torah* has become a sort of weekly 'part-work' read in synagogues. At the least, *Shavuot* represents the time when we renew our subscription! It is a time to remind ourselves that there are eternal values, there are important traditions that give value and perspective to our lives. It is not a dramatic festival — no horns are blown or cupboards cleared out or special candlesticks lit — but in a way this is a part of its charm. *Torah* does not have to come always from fiery mountain-tops amidst thunder and lightning; it is an ongoing source of spiritual and ethical nourishment.

It is well worth while once a year, without a great deal of hullabaloo but with some prayer and study, to remind ourselves of that.

Do note: Reform and Progressive Judaism believes strongly in a continuing revelation — a Progressive Revelation — i.e. not one confined to a one-off incident at Sinai over three thousand years ago. We believe that God speaks anew to each generation. In some respects the stress on the Sinaitic event clashes uneasily with the idea that every generation receives its own continuing (and relevant) revelation of God's will.

Shavuot is often taken as the occasion for a 'Confirmation' service in some Liberal synagogues — the young people commit themselves voluntarily to *Torah*.

7. THE BOOK OF RUTH

Each of the five *Megillot* (scrolls) is read at some commemorative day of the year — 'Megillat Esther' at *Purim*, 'Eycha' ('Lamentations') on *Tisha B'Av*, *Shir HaShirim* ('Song of Songs') on the *Shabbat* in *Pesach* and 'Kohelet' (Ecclesiastes) on the *Shabbat* in *Sukkot*.

On *Shavuot* by ancient tradition the 'Megillat Ruth' is read — a short (only four chapters) novelette describing the way in which Ruth, a girl from the land of Moab (and hence shunned by the Israelites) first marries an Israelite, is widowed, moves to Bethlehem with her mother-in-law Naomi, scrabbles for a frugal living and eventually 'marries the boss' Boaz and settles down to become in due course the great-grandmother of King David! (Ruth 4.17).

Why is this book read? Some say because the action in Bethlehem takes place at the barley-harvest (1:22), though this could in fact make the book have more relevance to *Pesach*; others, that Ruth becomes the prototype, not only of the convert to Judaism, but of anyone who voluntarily accepts the *Torah* — and hence, acts as a reminder of the Israelites at Sinai.

Indeed the message of the readings for *Shavuot*, both the Ten Commandments and the Book of Ruth, is that the *Torah* is something that has to be voluntarily accepted and acknowledged, even by those born into Judaism. In this respect the person choosing to become Jewish of their own volition is seen as in no way inferior to the one born into it — for all the Israelites at Sinai had voluntarily to accept the *Torah* (even though they had been descended from Abraham, Isaac and Jacob) — they had to say 'Na'asseh veNishmah' — 'We will do it, we will listen/learn it' — and all their descendants theoretically do so again when they are reminding themselves of this event.

Ruth, the Moabite girl, is not only absorbed into Bethlehem society but becomes the ancestress of the famous King David and, for those who seek a Messiah of the Davidic line, becomes indeed an ancestress of the Messiah as well! It would be hard to think of a more powerful message for the full integration of the willing convert into any society.

A further significant aspect of the Book of Ruth is that the main characters are all women — the men play a comparatively minor role and are in most cases mere ciphers. Ruth builds up a bond with Naomi, not with Boaz. In her famous declaration (1:16) she continues in the next verse to declare that the bond and her commitment will continue even after death. It is significant that this additional verse is so rarely quoted! A person converting to Judaism is also — in the longer term — opting to have a Jewish funeral… Often overlooked is also the sequence of statement — 'Your people will become my people, and your God my God' — i.e. integration into the community comes first!

CHAPTER 20

TISHA B'AV

1. INTRODUCTION

The name of this Notable Day (it might be inappropriate to refer to it as a *Chag*, a festival) is simply the date. *Av* is the fifth month (counting from *Nisan*: *Iyyar*; *Sivan*; *Tammuz*: *Av*); The Hebrew word for 'Nine' is '*Teysha*', hence the '*Tisha B'Av*', the 'ninth day of the month of *Av*'.

It is a post-Biblical commemorative date, mentioned first actually in the *Mishnah*, section '*Ta'anit*' ('Fast Days') Chapter 4 *Mishnah* 6:

> 'Five calamities befell our ancestors on the seventeenth of *Tammuz* and five on the ninth of *Av*.
>
> On the seventeenth of *Tammuz* the Tablets [of the Law] were broken [Ex. 32:19]; The *Tamid* daily burnt offering ceased [owing to the scarcity of animals during the siege of Jerusalem by Aristobulus]; the walls of the city were breached; and Apostomos [possibly an officer of Antiochus Epiphanes] burned the Scroll of the Law and set up an idol in the Sanctuary. [This first incident is not mentioned elsewhere and is possibly a part of the *Chanukah* story, 167 BCE; however the second could be referred to in Daniel 12:11.]
>
> On the ninth of *Av* it was decreed against our forefathers that they should not enter the Land [Num. 14:29ff.] and the Temple was destroyed the first time [by Nebuchadnezzar in 586 BCE] and the second time [70 CE] and Bettar was taken and the City was ploughed up [by Titus].
>
> With the advent of *Av* we should limit rejoicing.'
>
> (Adapted from Philip Blackman's edition of 'The *Mishnah*'.)

From this *Mishnah* we see already several things: that the 9th. *Av* was seen as a culmination of a period of approximately three weeks from the 17th. of *Tammuz* (also observed as a fast day by some traditionalist Jews today); that the date was seen as significant in relation to past Biblical events and that it had great significance for then-recent political events. Interestingly the references to 17th. *Tammuz* are not wholly in biblical and post-biblical chronological order and of course these dates are mostly of symbolical rather than historic importance — for the exact dates on which Moses in his rage at the Golden Calf cast down the first two stone tablets, or on which the Israelites bewailed the negative message of ten of the twelve spies, are not given in the *Torah* text. (However, traditional mathematicians have calculated that Moses ascended Mount Sinai in response to God's command 'on the seventh day' (Ex. 24:6) on 6th. or 7th. *Sivan*, when the Commandments were given; since in this year *Sivan* had 30 days, Moses, who spent forty days there, would have been on the mountain for 24 days of *Sivan* and 16 of *Tammuz* and therefore encountered the people's betrayal on the 17th.).

The reference to Bettar (also Bethar or Bittir, now an Arab village west of Jerusalem) is to the final catastrophic defeat of the Bar-Kochba rebellion against the Romans in 135 CE.

2. THE DESTRUCTION OF THE JERUSALEM TEMPLE

In the year 70 CE Jerusalem was captured by the Roman legions following the revolt against Roman rule that had begun some four years earlier and Titus set the Temple alight. (There is actually a theory that he wanted to capture it intact and that the fire was an accident of the conflict.) For a fuller account of this terrible period it is well worth reading 'The Jewish Wars' by Flavius Josephus, a contemporary Jewish fighter and commander who later wrote this history for a Roman audience. It is available in several translations. The brutal Roman reaction with three Legions had commenced in 67 CE under Vespasian, who in summer 69 CE returned to Rome following the suicide of of Nero and the deaths of two of his successors to take over the Imperial throne and fill the power vacuum, ruling as Caesar from 69 to 79. In the meantime he handed over command of the campaign in Judea to his son Titus. This catastrophe had been preceded by a lengthy and frightful siege, during which many of the inhabitants of Jerusalem starved to death and others fell victim to violent internal conflicts. The commemorative and triumphant 'Arch of Titus' was built in the Forum at Rome to celebrate the suppression of the Jewish Revolt.

Some sixty years later Shimon (known as 'Bar-Kochba' — 'The Son of a Star') led a further revolt against the Romans from 132 to 135 CE and this time the Roman General Hadrian led so vicious and thorough a campaign that Jerusalem was demolished almost stone by stone, a Roman shrine and city (Aelia Capitolina) was built in its place and the majority of the Jews in the country were massacred or deported as slaves. Bettar marked the 'last stand' of this last attempt (for centuries) at Jewish self-determination.

A major problem for Jews of the time was that it was not permitted by the *Torah* for any other Temple ('*Beit Mikdash*') to be built anywhere else and so no obvious substitute was feasible, even had circumstances permitted it. So the Temple worship, the sacrifices, the libations, the priestly castes, the dynasties, all ended on that catastrophic day. What survived was a Judaism influenced by scholars, centred on communal worship (the '*Beit Knesset*') and on the home — which became the '*Mikdash Me'at*' — the small substitute sanctuary. This 'Rabbinic Judaism' is what has continued, even though there have always been optimistic or nostalgic prayers for 'rebuilding the Temple' in the liturgy.

These events were still comparatively recent history at the time the *Mishnah* was compiled. Many famous figures — Rabbi Akiva, for example — had lost their lives and much of Jewish life had been decimated or destroyed. The destruction of the Temple marked the end of the sacrificial cult, of the priesthood, of the accepted manner of divine worship, even of the system for establishing the calendar — of almost everything that distinguished the Jewish nation.

How could this be understood? How could the omnipotent God have caused the destruction of God's own shrine? It is easy to understand that some could posit that there is no God, or that God is not omnipotent — it is truly difficult to believe that God not only allowed such horrible things to happen but even to some extent arranged them. Whilst it is relatively easy to create a theology whereby humans have free will and are therefore free to choose to commit evil crimes, this does not provide any comfort to the victims, who may not actually wish to choose to be the victims for the sake of proving a theological theory or theodicy but are usually given no choice!

In response to these and other questions the date of the event was turned into a solemn day of fasting and lamentation. The Rabbis declared that those who did not share in the mourning for Jerusalem would not see the joy of its restoration either (based on Isaiah 66:5f.). The destruction was interpreted as a punishment by God for Jewish arrogance and corruption. This theological response had a two-fold effect: On the one hand it gave meaning and purpose to the tragedy; on the other it implied that, just as God had brought this destruction so God could — when God so wished — restore the glory of what had once been — IF the Jews deserved it. After all, the Temple had been destroyed already once before, and yet had been later restored.

There are still Jewish authorities who (misguidedly in the opinion of this author) maintain that the *Shoah* was also a 'punishment' directed at assimilated Jews. The futility of this argument is easily revealed by the manner in which observant Jewish communities were also destroyed, not to mention innocent children. Almost all such attempts at 'answers' are doomed to collapse into their own inner contradictions. Sometimes a horrified silence is the best or only response. Self-criticism is a valid and important part of Jewish thinking, but criticising others is too easy a get-out and should not be encouraged.

3. CALENDRICAL CONTEXT

As mentioned above the period of national depression starts with the 17th. of *Tammuz*, a fast day which is seen as marking 'the beginning of the end'. There follow 'The Three Weeks'. The three *Haftarot* for the Schabbatot preceding *Tisha B'Av* are composed of severe warnings from Jeremiah 1:1 - 2:3; Jeremiah 2:4 - 4:2; and Isaiah 1:1-27. These are called the 'Three *Haftarot* of Rebuke'. The Isaiah passage begins with the words '*Chazon Yeshayahu*' — 'a Vision of Isaiah' — and thus gives its name to '*Shabbat Chazon*'.

To balance these the month of *Av* was often renamed '*Menachem Av*' — 'The Comforting' month, reflecting the concept that the Messiah was born when the Temple was destroyed. The seven *Haftarot* which follow *Tisha B'Av* are called the 'Seven *Haftarot* of Consolation', being selected from Isaiah. The first of these, taking a reading from Isaiah 40:1 which begins '*Nachamu, nachamu, Ami!*' — 'Comfort, O comfort my people!' — gives its name to '*Shabbat Nachamu*'.

These *Haftarot* are:

(1) Isaiah 40:1-26;
(2) Isaiah 49:14-51:3;
(3) Isaiah 54:11-55:5;
(4) Isaiah 51:12-52:12;
(5) Isaiah 54:1-10;
(6) Isaiah 60:1-22; and
(7) Isaiah 61:10-63:9.

(In addition the *Haftarah* for *Shabbat Vayelech* on those years when the two *Parashiyot* '*Nitzavim*' and '*Vayelech*' are split and read separately is Isaiah 55:6-56:8 in the *Ashkenazi* rite; whereas *Sephardim* read Hosea 14:1-10 and Micha 7:18-20 — for '*Shabbat Shuvah*'.)

Should either 17th. *Tammuz* or 9th. *Av* happen to fall on a *Shabbat* the commemorations are moved to the following day, since it is forbidden to combine a *Shabbat* with a fast day.

4. LAMENTATIONS

The prophet Jeremiah was present at the destruction of the First Temple by Nebu-chadnezzar in 586 BCE and the Book of Lamentations ('*Eichah*' in Hebrew, from its opening words of woe) is ascribed to him. It is one of the five Scrolls or *Megillot*. It is customary to sit on the ground or on low chairs, as if in mourning, and read this book on *Tisha B'Av*.

The book consists of five separate elegiac poems, written in accordance with strict rules for Hebrew verse (though the rhythm is unusual, a 'limping' effect which powerfully evokes a feeling of sadness). The first, second and fourth chapters consist each of 22 verses, each starting with a Hebrew letter in alphabetical order; the third has 66 verses, three for each letter of the alphabet; the fifth is not alphabetical, but also contains 22 verses.

Since the last verse (5:22) is a thoroughly depressing one it is always followed by a repetition of 5:21, which looks forward more hopefully.

Also read at the services — which are otherwise simply daily Evening and Morning services, without any special *Torah* or other readings — are '*Kinot*' — sad poems written in different periods but all bewailing loss and tragedy.

The loss of each Temple is referred to as a '*Churban*' — a waste, a desolation — and it became a custom to leave a part of a house unfinished or some other visual symbol '*zichur leChurban*' — as a reminder of what we had lost.

5. OTHER ASSOCIATED DAYS

As we have seen, once the day became associated with sadness a variety of earlier and later tragedies became associated with it too. It was assumed that the First Temple had been destroyed on the same date as the Second; but it was also said that King Edward I signed the royal edict expelling the Jews from England on *Tisha B'Av* in 1290; that King Ferdinand and Queen Isabella of Spain expelled the Jews from there on *Tisha B'Av* 1492. There are those who try to find more modern 'coincidences' linking the date to events in the World Wars or the *Sho'ah* (the Holocaust).

6. REFORM AND LIBERAL ATTITUDES

Although frequently referred to as being equally important as the *Yom Kippur* fast day in the 7[th.] month, *Tishri*, in practice this day is not observed so intensely in most communities.

Tisha B'Av is a time to contemplate communal sins and their consequences, *Yom Kippur* more for personal failings and their consequences.

On this day we consider also several major theological problems at once — problems so enormous that we have no real full answer, but only partial answers available — and yet, to maintain faith, we must at least be honest about these problems.

For example — In the *Talmud* ('*Ta'anit*' 29a) Rabbi Jonathan states that the Israelites in the desert, the '*Dor HaMidbar*' refused to obey the divine command on what became the 9th. *Av* and God's response was that, since they had cried on this day for no reason, they and their descendants would be given good reasons to cry on this day in the future. This is suspiciously close to a concept of 'inheriting the sins of a previous generation' — like 'Original Sin' — something which, in principle, Judaism denies. (The statements that the sins of the fathers will pass onto the children of the third and fourth generations can be understood to mean not that the <u>blame</u> will be carried forward, but that the <u>consequences</u> will be felt into the future.) Self-criticism and the outspoken wish to learn from errors and not to repeat them is a very important (and very rare) political dynamic, but it can be carried to excess. When a Victim blames him- or herself for things for which they were NOT responsible this can become a self-destructive neurosis.

The destruction of the First Temple in 586 BCE followed an 11-year reign by Jehoiakim, who was NOT the King the people had chosen for themselves after the untimely death in battle of Josiah, but instead the elder brother who was imposed upon them by Pharaoh Neco of Egypt who had defeated Josiah (see II Kings 23:29 and II Chronicles 35:20-24). If this is the case — and Josiah himself had been classed as a 'good King' who had reformed the Jewish cultic religion — then one could ask what the People had done that was so bad as to deserve their invasion, destruction and exile so soon afterwards? On *Tisha B'Av* we consider a concept of Collective Punishment which is hard to reconcile with the rabbinic stress on Individual Autonomy and Responsibility.

Liberal Judaism derives from the lessons of the Enlightenment the concept that the individual person matters, that what he or she thinks, believes and does should or could affect their destinies. And yet often the Individual in the world in which we live appears totally powerless when confronting forces of Evil. Many enemies of modern civilisation express their enmity in their hatred for the Individual; they stress instead collective concepts such as 'the Race' or 'the Nation' or 'the Party' or 'the Believers' of a particular religion; they apply stereotypes whereby 'All Jews' are responsible for something — even if they live thousands of miles and hundreds of years away from whatever it is that is annoying this enemy.

We stress these issues here because we are confronted with similar problems in later generations too. Throughout history innocent people have suffered terribly due to the political and military ambitions of tyrants and mobs. It is NOT always legitimate, theologically or in any other way, to blame the victims for what has befallen them. (We could not accept an accusation of assimilation or faithlessness as justifying the fate of the victims of the *Sho'ah*, though some have tried this approach.) So those of us who believe in a God are left with the mystery of Why this God allows these things to happen and what the nature and origin and even purpose of Evil is in the world. Sometimes just to sit and cry is the most therapeutic way we have to cope with the enormity of human experience.

Tisha B'Av is therefore a sort of ritualised communal Depression. Perhaps this is why it has lost much meaning in recent years, in contrast to the whole day of ritual and confession which mark *Yom Kippur*, when even irregular worshippers usually make an effort to attend at least some of the services. And perhaps this is why the original efforts to concentrate all modern mourning days into this one Day failed and instead *Yom HaShoah* for the victims of the Holocaust and *Yom HaZikaron* for the victims of conflict in Israel were eventually established as separate dates.

Since Reform Judaism does not look forward to the restoration of a Third Temple and indeed sees Judaism as having progressed since the days of the sacrificial cult, the loss of the Temple is not felt as keenly and references to a yearning for its rebuilding have been largely removed from our liturgy. Furthermore, now that Jerusalem the city is regained and rebuilt (though not yet, alas, fully a City of Peace) some of the sorrow and mourning seems redundant. When one considers what controversies are aroused at the remaining fragments of wall (the '*Kotel haMaʾaravi*' or 'Western Wall') when different non-Orthodox groups wish to pray according to their own wishes, one can imagine what a horror and catastrophe a single monopolistic Temple in the hands of one specific fundamentalist party would be! Not to mention the fights for control over it — thus repeating the corruptions and abuses that several prophets protested against — and that is not to mention the problems connected with its physical location, which is currently contested with another religion...

Some synagogues and rabbis do not therefore commemorate *Tisha B'Av* fully any more whilst some others treat it as a day of mourning for a variety of tragedies rather than specifically the destruction of the Temple. Unfortunately, Jewish history provides many possible examples.

See the *Siddur*, **8ᵗʰ· ed. p.402f.** (*'Lev Chadash' p.377*) for special readings.

CHAPTER 21

OTHER NOTABLE DAYS

1. INTRODUCTION

The Jewish calendar is filled with days of varying importance. Some commemorate events that were considered very important in their time but have now been largely forgotten; Thus there are several 'Minor Fasts' Days that are nowadays usually ignored.

Conversely there are new days that have acquired prominence in recent times and have become important in the *Diaspora* in the Communal Calendar if not necessarily in the Ritual Calendar. In other words, there may not necessarily be special formal synagogue services, but a local community may arrange some form of commemoration or celebration in a secular manner, with a few prayers attached. The RSGB *Siddur* p.623 has details on suggested modes of observance.

2. YOM HAZIKARON

'Remembrance Day'. In memory of all those who have fallen for the creation and defence of the State of Israel, and including victims of terrorism. It is observed on 4th. *Iyyar* — the day immediately prior to Independence Day, *Yom Ha'Atzma'ut*. In Israel it is a time of solemn gatherings in military cemeteries and at war memorials.

The RSGB *Siddur* has a memorial prayer on p.263 (**p.394**). In the *Diaspora* any commemoration is normally linked directly to *Yom Ha'Atzma'ut*, rather than a separate full day being dedicated to this sad subject, because we are less likely to have lost close family, friends, neighbours or colleagues to such violent deaths.

3. YOM HA'ATZMA'UT

This is Israel Independence Day and is celebrated on 5th. *Iyyar*. Following much debate the United Nations passed a resolution (No. 181) on 29th. November 1947 approving the proposal to divide the area of Palestine, then and since 1920 under the League of Nations 'Mandate' of Great Britain, into three areas — two independent states, one for the Jews and one for the Arabs, and a third neutral international sector around Jerusalem and Bethlehem. There had been much fighting between Jewish and Arab Palestinians before this date and much more followed. The British Government declared that they would evacuate their forces unilaterally from the country by 14th. May 1948 and from the Haifa area (where they had many bases and ammunition stores to evacuate by sea) by 31ˢᵗ· July (the so-called 'Haifa Enclave') rather than arrange an orderly handover to a new Administration. The State of Israel was officially proclaimed in a ceremony at Tel Aviv on 15ᵗʰ· May 1947, but the War of Independence, in which the new State had to resist determined attacks from all sides simultaneously, did not end until various armistice agreements were signed — with Egypt on 24ᵗʰ· February 1949, with Lebanon on 23rd. March 1949, with Transjordan on 3rd. April 1949 and with Syria on 20ᵗʰ· July 1949 (i.e. over a year later).

The Hebrew date equivalent to 14ᵗʰ· May 1948 was the 5ᵗʰ· *Iyyar* 5708 and this was declared the anniversary, marked in Israel by festive parades. The *Siddur* pp.259-263; **p.394-400**; (**'Lev Chadash p.372**') has appropriate prayers and study passages.

(It is worth noting here that, until this point, the Jews living in the Mandate territory of 'Palestine', which was not an actual State but governed from London through a local Administration, had ALSO been 'Palestinians'. Following this war — which was in many respects a civil war between different ethnic and political groups — the neighbouring countries of Egypt, Jordan and Syria occupied militarily and administratively much of the land which had been officially allocated either to UN supervision or to the Arab population in November 1947 — but they did NOT establish an equivalent State for the Moslem and Christian Palestinians. Embittered, many descendants of the Moslem and Christian populations still declare themselves to be 'refugees' — even several generations later — and refer to these events as the '*Naqba*' or 'Catastrophe'. It was indeed a catastrophe for many, but it is ironic that they direct their rage purely at those Jewish Palestinians who fought mainly for the right to keep those areas allocated to them by the United Nations — and for their lives — and not against those who were more directly responsible for the new political landscape.)

4. YOM HASHO'AH

27ᵗʰ· *Nisan*. 'Holocaust Memorial Day'. The word '*Holocaust*' is from the Greek and means an Offering consumed by Fire. Because of these pagan ritual overtones many Jewish scholars prefer the Hebrew word '*Sho'ah*' meaning 'Utter Destruction' when referring to the events that led to the brutal elimination, dispossession, exile or orphaning of several million Jews in the years 1933-1945. (Although exact statistics will never be possible, partly because sometimes entire villages were wiped out or many records were burned in air raids, it is normally stated that six million Jews were killed for being Jews; others died in conflict, in air raids, while fleeing… and many millions of other people were also displaced, murdered and traumatised. In addition different definitions of 'Jew' were used — many suffered even though they neither considered themselves Jewish (having perhaps been baptised) or would not be considered Jewish by other Jews. There is however little point in quibbling about exact numbers or definitions of victims; We are all mortal, but these people either had the natural course of their lives destroyed or their very lives were brutally and prematurely ended.) Some refer to this as 'the third *Churban*' — referring to the previous two destructions of the Temple. (The word 'Sho'ah', written either *Shin / Aleph / Heh* or *Shin / Vav / Aleph / Heh*) appears in Isaiah 10:3, Isa. 47:11, Zephaniah 1:15 — which actually refers to a '*Yom Shoah uM'Shoah*' — , Job 30:14, Psalm 35:8, Psalm 63:10, etc.)

In April 1951 the Israeli *Knesset* declared the 27th. *Nisan* as a Holocaust and Ghetto Uprising Memorial Day ('*Yom haShoah uG'vurah*' — commemorating also the heroism of those who resisted, and thus stressing that not all were utterly helpless victims) and in Israel places of entertainment are closed on this solemn day. In the *Diaspora* it became common to mark 19th. April, the day in the civil calendar on which the Warsaw Ghetto Uprising began in 1943. (In this last-ditch uprising the Ghetto was utterly wiped out by the militarily-superior German forces, but the mere act of resistance in such hopeless circumstances was an act of great moral courage.)

The Israeli Rabbinate has declared the 10th. *Tevet* as a day on which those who do not know exactly when their relatives died in the Shoah can mark the *Yahrtzeit*. (Sometimes this problem is a cause for additional emotional distress; on occasion it is also of legal significance because the sequence of an inheritance may depend on the sequence in which members of a family were killed. Some countries adopt a definition of 'so many days following the known date of the departure of a deportation train' to fill this gap in the statistics for this purpose and so provide a legal date of death.)

27th. January, the date of the liberation of the camps at Auschwitz-Birkenau in 1945 by the Red Army, is also often marked as a civil anniversary for commemoration of these events. (See p.405).

The *Siddur*, pp.256-258, (**p.388-393**) ('***Lev Chadash*** *p.367*') has some prayers and readings for this day and the martyrs of the *Sho'ah* are also recalled on *Yom Kippur* (*Machzor* p.618).

5. *YOM YERUSHALAYIM*

28th. *Iyyar*, 'Jerusalem Day'. This commemorates the re-unification of the city of Jerusalem during the Six Day War of June 1967. In 1948 the Jewish inhabitants were forced out of the Jewish Quarter of the Old City of Jerusalem by Jordanian and other forces following a spirited defence and from 28th. May 1948 to June 1967 the city was divided into the Jewish section (the 'New City' that had developed from the mid-19th. century onwards) in the West and the 'Old City' within the Walls and the surrounding Arab suburban areas to the North, East and South. (The conquerors showed no interest in creating or maintaining a 'neutral' area under international supervision in accordance with the UN Resolution No. 181.)

Between the two sections of the city was a No-Man's Land, made dangerous for Jews by sniper fire. The only official crossing-point, used only by foreigners and diplomats, was the 'Mandelbaum Gate' to the north. A wall and barbed wire divided the two parts of the city. The Hebrew University on Mount Scopus, founded in 1920, and the adjoining Hadassah Hospital formed a tiny enclave in Jordanian-held territory, closed to students but manned on a treaty basis by 'shifts' of Israeli troops. Jews were forbidden access to the Old City and the significant religious sites there — including, of course, the '*Kotel HaMa'aravi*' or 'Western Wall' of the former Temple complex, and the cemeteries on the Mount of Olives.

In what became known later as the 'Six Day War' in 5-10[th.] June 1967 Israeli forces reacted to threats from the surrounding Arab countries, which had culminated in the closure to Israeli shipping of the sea approaches to Eilat, the country's southern port in the Gulf of Eilat, a part of the Red Sea. Pre-emptive air strikes on Egyptian and Syrian forces neutralised a part of the threat, especially in terms of air superiority; requests and warnings were issued to Jordan not to join in the attacks on Israel but on 5[th.] June Jordanian forces opened fire. In reaction Israeli forces, including paratroops and armoured columns, managed to break into the walled city and conquer it on the 7[th.] June.

Yom Yerushalayim commemorates this event. Politically the capture of sections of the highlands of Judea and Samaria — the original heartland of Israelite settlement in Biblical times — brought a reaction from other countries that led to the exacerbation of the refugee problem, exploited by many nations for their own or dubious ends. This matter has not yet been settled and presumably will never be settled until both sides really want to and are prepared to show the necessary desire for and ability to compromise — and until everyone else lets those most concerned, who have the most to gain and the most to lose, simply get on with it without interfering. From a purely Jewish point of view however it meant that Jews were once more able at last to visit their holy places. The Day is commemorated on 28[th.] *Iyyar*, equivalent to 7[th.] June 1967.

It is worth noting here that Moshe Dayan formally allowed the Moslem authorities, the 'Waqf', to retain control over the Temple Mount on which various Moslem shrines and institutions were based and any visitor to Jerusalem now will see Christians of many denominations and Moslems, as well as Jews, all free to pursue their religious needs. This is in stark contrast to the '*Al-Quds* Day', called into being by Iranian politicians in August 1979 for the last Friday of the Moslem fasting month of Ramadan, on which demonstrations are held denying Jews and Israelis any right to the city at all ('*Al Quds*' is Arabic for 'The Holy City').

6. *TU B'AV*

The 15[th.] of *Av* — '*Tu*' is from the Hebrew letters *Tet* and *Vav*, equivalent numerically to 'Nine plus Six = Fifteen'. (The more rational sequence of the letters *Yod* and *Hey*, equivalent to Ten plus Five, is not used because it looks like one of the Divine names.) This was in ancient times a day of jollity, referred to in the *Mishnah* ('*Ta'anit*' Chapter 4 *Mishnah* 8) as one of the two days (the other was the end of *Yom Kippur*) when the young girls would dance out in the orchards, dressed in white dresses, and take the initiative in approaching the young men — a sort of equivalent to Valentine's Day. The Day is no longer commemorated but may appear in some Jewish diaries.

7. TU B'SH'VAT

The 15th. of *Shevat* — the word '*Tu*' derived as above. It is also of course Full Moon. In the *Mishnah*, '*Rosh Hashanah*' Chapter 1, four New Years are described — for Kings, Animals, Trees and for the Years themselves. The 15th. of *Shevat*, falling in early Springtime, is the New Year for Trees. This was important for judging the age of a tree (important for assessing whether its fruit could be used for offerings) without having to cut it down to count the rings! Not a religious event as such and not observed for many years, it has regained importance as the Land of Israel was re-settled and the planting of trees became an important part of the 'Redemption of the Land'. Tree-planting ceremonies are held. See *Siddur*, p.594, **p.380-383 (*p.402*)** for a text or song by a modern Hebrew writer.

It is perhaps unfortunate that, as a jolly day with picturesque observances, falling around midway through the Spring Term, many Religion Schools place more emphasis on *Tu B'Sh'vat* than on the more important festivals!

8. LAG BA'OMER

The 33rd. Day of the *Omer* period (from the Hebrew letters *Lammed* and *Gimmel* — equivalent numerically to Thirty plus Three). A minor festival day, often used for weddings. See the chapter on '*Omer*'.

9. MINOR FAST DAYS.

There are four Public Fasts in the traditional calendar, including *Tisha B'Av* (see separate Chapter). The other three are:

(a). 3rd. *Tishri.* 'Tzom Gedaliah' or the 'Fast of Gedaliah'. This commemorates the murder of Gedaliah, the Jewish governor appointed by King Nebuchadnezzar after the destruction of the First Temple in 586 BCE. His assassination by political extremists led to the last remnant of the Jews in the Land being exiled or executed.

(b). 10th. *Tevet* marks the day when Nebuchadnezzar, King of Babylon, commenced the siege of Jerusalem that led ultimately to the city's downfall on 9th. Av (*Tisha B'Av*).

(c). 17th. *Tammuz* has a variety of disasters associated with it including the breach of the city wall of the besieged Jerusalem, the abolition of the daily Temple sacrifices due to the shortage of animals during the siege, the desecration of the Temple through the placing of an idol and even the breaking of the first stone tablets of the commandments.

From 17[th.] *Tammuz* to 9[th.] *Av* are three weeks of mourning, during which weddings are not celebrated; from 1[st.] to 9[th.] *Av* the restrictions are increased.

These days are not marked by the majority of Jews at the present time, though they appear in diaries and cause occasional embarrassment when it is discovered that some public function has been scheduled for a day when the few who are observing such a fast cannot attend!

In modern times the anniversaries of such events as the assassination of Prime Minister Yitzhak Rabin on 4[th.] November 1995 are also considered significant and are commemorated in the media.

4

PART FOUR: THE BASIC TEXTS

CHAPTER 22

THE BIBLE

1. INTRODUCTION TO THE (FIRST) PROBLEM

One of the major problems facing any believing person of whatever religion is: 'What to Believe?' There are two major sources for Faith and/or Belief (the two are not, of course, necessarily the same thing): one is personal experience, in one's own life, of some form of transcendence, some divine action or intervention; the other is the accumulated tradition of divine action in the lives of previous generations — a tradition which can be conveyed verbally by a teacher or, if written down, can become 'Scripture'. (This is from the Latin and, strictly speaking, simply means 'Something Written' — but is usually understood to mean a text of religious significance.)

The difference between these two sources is well-illustrated in this excerpt from the teaching of the *'Baal Shem Tov'* (the founder of *Chasidism*):

'Why do we say 'Our God and the God of our Fathers'? There are two sorts of persons who believe in God. The one believes because his faith has been handed down to him by his fathers; and his faith is strong. The other has arrived at faith by dint of searching thought. And this is the difference between the two: The first has the advantage that his faith cannot be shaken, no matter how many objections are raised to it, for his faith is firm because he has taken it over from his fathers. But there is a flaw in it: It is a commandment given by man, and it has been learned without thought or reasoning. The advantage of the second man is that he has reached faith through his own power, through much searching and thinking. But his faith too has a flaw: It is easy to shake it by offering contrary evidence. But he who combines both kinds of faith is invulnerable. That is why we say: 'Our God', because of our searching, and 'the God of our fathers', because of our tradition.'

(in RSGB *Siddur* p.357)

There can indeed be a conflict between one's own experiences and the ancient tales of different cultures which make up so much of any established religious scripture

— including the 'New Testament' for Christians, the Koran (or Qur'an) for Moslems and so on. Few of us really live in 1st.-century Palestine or in the deserts of the Arabian Peninsula, and tales of miraculous incidents involving camels or strolls across the Sea of Galilee do not necessarily match our own everyday lives! The following extract from J. B. Priestley's 'An English Journey' of 1933, describing a visit to a Nonconformist Chapel in Birmingham that year, is a clear exposition of the conflict:

'... Returning after a long absence, I saw how odd it was that these mild Midland folk, spectacled ironmongers, little dressmakers, clerks, young women from stationers' shops, should come every Sunday morning through the quiet grey streets and assemble here to wallow in wild oriental imagery. They stood up in rows, meek-eyed and pink-cheeked, to sing modestly about the Blood of the Lamb. After a few little coughs, they announced that certain sacred names and symbols induced in them fits of incredible ecstasies. They sat with bent heads listening to accounts of ancient and terribly savage tribal warfare, of the lust and pride of hook-nosed and raven-bearded chieftains, of sacrifice and butchery on the glaring deserts of the Near East. They chanted in unison their hope of an immortality to be spent in cities built of blazing jewels, with fountains of milk and cascades of honey, where kings played harps while maidens clashed the cymbals; and one could not help wondering what these people would do if they really did find themselves billeted for ever in this world of the Eastern religious poets. What, in short, had these sober Northern islanders to do with all this Oriental stuff? What did it, what could it really mean to them? Could anything be less aptly shaped and coloured to match their own lives? If this was the time when their thoughts turned to the creator of this universe, when they were asked to consider the deep truths of life, to face their consciences and search their hearts, why should they be dragged into this far-away world of goats and vines and deserts and smoking sacrifices and tribal kings?... Must God, I asked myself, remain for ever in Asia? Are these people always to assume that He is still brooding over Babylon? What if He is now brooding over Birmingham?'

What indeed? For many people the Bible is a 'turn-off', a large compendium of close, cramped print, of old-fashioned language and difficult, alien imagery. How is this to be transformed into a basis of religious belief?

2. THE SECOND PROBLEM: WHAT IS TRUE?

Assuming we have a large black bound book called 'The Bible' or 'The Holy Scriptures' — how do we know whether what it says is true? Who wrote it? When? Why? Where? For whom? In what language? Is the translation accurate? What, in fact, was the original language? Why are there different versions of some accounts? Does any of it matter? Is it even allowed to ask such questions?

Depending on your responses to these questions, you may be a Fundamentalist (believing that every word, every letter, is inspired by God and cannot be challenged, neither by you nor by anyone else...); or you may be a Christian — if you accept certain later books as having Biblical authority — or a Jew — if you reject these books. You may be confused, or certain, or indifferent… Yet, it is responses to questions like these, and the interpretations of the answers, that have led to many of the religious wars and arguments throughout history and which now (as this book is being revised in 2015) have led to a fear of a worldwide spread of fundamentalist and primitive belief in certain *Qur'an* texts or the manner in which certain preachers have taught them. Much conflict — in but not restricted to the Middle East — is based on concepts taken from biblical texts and the interpretation of ancient blessings and borders. 'Apartheid', the policy of 'Separateness' in South Africa was justified for many years on the basis of the curse on Noah's son Ham (Gen. 9:22-26); Slavery, or the subjugation of women, or the prohibition of certain sexual practices; or the 'divine right of Kings' — there are many other examples — were often defended using Biblical texts. These matters cannot be simply ignored.

Christians read the Hebrew Bible differently, partly because (with very few exceptions) they use translations which are themselves based upon translations (such as the Greek 'Septuagint' or the Latin 'Vulgata'). This can lead to widespread but actually incorrect myths — for example, Eva never offered Adam an 'apple' in the Garden of Eden! Firstly, she did not get the name 'Eva' (from Adam) until AFTER they had left the garden and secondly the text refers only to a 'fruit'! But more significantly, many people still believe the Bible says you 'Should not Kill' and some even extend this to include the killing of animals — whereas in fact the Hebrew text in Exodus 20:13 clearly says you 'Should not Murder' — ('*Lo Tirzach*') — something very different indeed and requiring complex moral discussion to define the boundaries between what might be classed as legitimate killing — e.g. animals for food, or in self-defence, or as capital punishment, or in military service — and what is not — murder for personal reasons of lust or greed or brutality. Where does 'mercy killing' come into this spectrum? Or Abortion — the prevention of a person's life before it even starts? Of course there is much room for debate but the simple mistranslation here leads many astray into extreme views. (One can even be an extreme Pacifist!)

It may be significant that one of the so-called 'Ten Commandments' is not to misuse God's Name for other ends. And it is also sadly significant that the texts are always used by those who wish to say, 'See! It says here that I am better than you and you must do everything I say!' — never the other way around.

3. THE FUNDAMENTALIST APPROACH

For the Fundamentalist everything is simple. God wrote the whole Bible and delivered it (usually) in the form of a small black bound book written in King James English or some suitably-antiquated version of some other local vernacular language. Such a person is (normally) not a scholar, not bothered with details of dates or language or manuscripts. Whether Jewish or Christian (differing only in their attitudes to the 'New Testament') they are convinced that the Bible came down from heaven not as a stream of inspiration but in its current form. This sort of attitude allows great stress to be placed on every word, every letter, in the firm belief that it was destined to be there and must, in consequence, be significant. 'It is written...' — or in Yiddish 'es steht geschrieben'.

Fundamentalists see everything in black and white. Since they are (by definition) right, then everyone else must be wrong. This is a psychological phenomenon one sees in all religions. Because they believe they already have The Answer it follows that they stop asking Questions and will not tolerate anyone else who either still asks Questions or who has come to a Different Answer (which must be, by definition, Wrong). If the world is lucky, the fundamentalists withdraw from it into their own small enclosed worlds; If the world is unlucky, the fundamentalists determine to take it over and eliminate all other opinions (and the people who hold them, who might hold them, who might have held them, who might conceivably in the future know someone who has held them, plus all their relatives. They will do this in the name of The Truth, their own Truth, whether this be God, a Prophet, or a Party).

Fundamentalists tend on the whole to be rather humourless and just do not, indeed cannot understand that there are also jokes in the Biblical texts, word games, sarcasm, irony, deliberate ambiguities, etc. With such people there is little chance for any useful dialogue, discussion or mutual respect.

4. THE FORM-CRITICAL APPROACH

There are many scholarly versions and methods of analysing the Bible text. For our purposes the main one is the view that the Bible, as we now have it, was at some point in history put together by human hands — under Divine inspiration, perhaps, but nevertheless as a human product.

The glimmerings of this approach can be detected in the mediaeval Jewish scholar Abraham Ibn Ezra (1092-1167) who cited Daniel 12:10 ('They that are wise will understand') to hint at deeper and more challenging interpretations. But many people have asked themselves some obvious questions, such as: 'How does anyone know what Eve said to Adam?' or: 'How could Moses write about his own death and burial at the end of Deuteronomy?' (Indeed, it is hard for those who believe that the ENTIRE five books were dictated by God to Moses on Sinai, half-way through the Book of Exodus, to explain how everything that happens after this point nevertheless appears to come as a surprise for both God and Moses!)

In addition there are several places where the Biblical text seems to repeat or even contradict itself — leaving the serious believer with a problem to resolve.

A German non-Jewish scholar Julius Wellhausen (1844-1918) started a furore by dividing the *Torah* — the first five books of the Bible — into four sections, written by four different sources and edited together later — edited so clumsily that, in many places, the joins showed. He named these sources the 'J' (for '*Jahwist*', pronounced '*Yahwist*'), 'E' (for '*Elohist*'), 'P' (for '*Priestly*') and 'D' (for '*Deuteronomist*') — hence the shorthand term 'JEPD' to represent this theory. The *Jahwist*, according to him, used the Tetragrammaton (the technical term for the four consonants '*YHWH*') for God's name (which we normally pronounce just as '*Adonai*', 'My Lord', but which he pronounced as '*Yahweh*' — others try adding the vowels of *AdOnAI* to these consonants to make '*Yehovah*' or '*Jehovah*'); the *Elohist* used instead the word '*Elohim*' for God; the Priestly source was obsessed with ritual detail and was responsible for a lot of the sacrificial sections in Leviticus or details on the tabernacle in Exodus, and the Deuteronomist wrote Deuteronomy!

All was (as one might expect from a German theologian) logical and rational and detailed and organised — the only problem being that it didn't quite work, for sometimes the *YHVH* and *Elohim* names are used in the same verse... This theory as such has been largely discredited — scholars have even resorted to computers to 'prove' that the linguistic style is unified in various other ways or that certain verbs appear only in certain books — but the general approach is an interesting one and was a bit of a breakthrough. Was the Bible really given 'whole' — or did it gradually get 'put together'? (Incidentally, at the same period the 'New Testament' was also being subjected to similar scrutiny — e.g. which Gospel came first, which borrowed from which other one or from some other source?)

5. THE CANON

The 'Bible' is not a Book but a collection of Books. (The word itself comes from the Greek '*Biblos*' for 'Book'.) The Books that 'belong' in the Bible are called the Canon or Canonical Books. Other books of great age that were excluded from the Canon (sometimes after much argument among the scholars and religious leaders of the time) are termed 'extra-Canonical' and were either lost (mention is occasionally made of books that no longer exist) or were preserved elsewhere — usually by non-Jews in collections known as the '*Apocrypha*' and '*Pseudepigrapha*' — Greek terms for books whose authenticity could not be guaranteed, or which claimed to be have been written by people who had not done so. (It was at one time common practice to claim that Abraham or Moses or someone similar had written your book — this made it seem older, more likely to be accepted.)

Do not forget that at this time each book was painstakingly written out or copied out by hand and it remains a fascinating topic to wonder who wrote them, whether or how they were paid for their work or perhaps did it simply out of personal conviction — there was no copyright, no check against occasional scribal errors, no distribution network, no book trade and yet travellers clearly took manuscripts with them on their journeys and books spread across the ancient world.

It is of course vital, if one wishes to ascribe divine authority to a piece of writing, that one can have complete faith in it and so the Rabbis (and later, for the Christian church, their own early bishops) had the task of deciding which of many texts in circulation — or which of several versions — could be classed as 'authentic' by their standards (and what to do with others). The Rabbis used the technical term for such a book as 'making the hands unclean' which may seem a little contradictory but indicates that after touching such a holy object, with such awe and respect, one should not just use one's hands for mundane matters without first washing! But this has led to some interesting decisions. The Book of Joshua was not incorporated into the *Torah* although it forms the continuation and conclusion of the narrative that starts with Exodus. (Should one argue that this is because Moses plays no part in it, then the same could be said of Genesis!) The Book of Esther is accepted into the Canon but not the 'Additions to Esther'. The Books of Ezra and Nechemiah are accepted but not what are later termed the 'Third and Fourth Books of Ezra'. The Books of the Maccabees, although concerned with heroic deeds by Jews to rescue their Temple from desecration, were not included but were kept by Christianity in the '*Apocrypha*' instead (whereby there are Four 'Books of the Maccabees' but only the first two are concerned with this narrative). It follows that some of these ancient writings are, ironically, only to be found in non-Jewish publications, often printed in combined volumes as a third section between the 'Old' and 'New' Testament. (Early Christian authorities also had to decide which of several contradictory quasi-biographical 'Gospels' were acceptable, and which of many Letters circulating. We know they rejected several.)

The Jewish Canon — the Hebrew Bible, which Christians call the 'Old Testament' although we Jews had it when it was still new! — is divided into three main sections:
   The *Torah* (The Five Books): *Taf / Vav / Resh / Heh*
   The *Nevi'im* (The Prophets) : *Nun / Vet / Yud / Aleph / Yud / Mem Soffit*
   The *Ketuvim* (The Writings): *Kaf / Taf / Vav / Vet / Yud / Mem Soffit* (Sometimes called 'the *Hagiographa*' in Greek)

From the initial letters in the Hebrew *Taf / Nun / Kaf* or *Chaf* — we get the abbreviation or acronym '*Tanach*' or '*Tanakh*' — which is simply used to mean 'The Hebrew Bible'. (We do not use the term 'Old Testament' as this might give legitimation to the idea of there being also a 'New' one.)
   It appears that these sections reflect three separate stages in the canonisation of the Scriptures — i.e. The '*Torah*' was 'fixed' first, and so on.

6. THE *TORAH*

The name, applied later to the entire corpus of Jewish teaching, also refers purely to the first five books of the Bible — known as the 'Five Books of Moses' or the '*Pentateuch*' (from the Greek word for a 'Five-fold book'.) For synagogue use these are often printed together with the relevant *Haftarot* sections from the *Nevi'im*, to be read during the services, sometimes even with explanatory notes and commentaries, and are then referred to as a '*Chumash*' — also from the Hebrew word for 'Five'.

(Incidentally, as mentioned above Moses himself does not appear in the first one and because the story of the Israelites' journey through the desert to the Promised Land does not end with his death but continues through the following Book of Joshua, there are occasional discussions as to why we do not have a '*Hexateuch*' — Six Books — which would at least bring the story of the People's Journey, rather than the life of Moses himself, to a logical conclusion.)

The *Torah* comprises:

Genesis	*Bereshit*	'The Beginnings'. — Cosmic pre-history, then (from Ch. 12) the history of the relationship between God and one family — that of Avram (later Avraham), his son Yitzhak, his son Ya'akov, his son Yosef.
Exodus	*Shemot*	'The Names'. — The first section up to Ch. 15 describes the situation of the Israelites as slaves in Egypt, their rescue in the Exodus; then follow chapters on the early part of their journey through the Sinai Desert, the revelation on Mount Sinai (repeated) and the description and construction of a special mobile shrine to enable God and Moses to be in close contact.
Leviticus	*Vayikra*	'And He Called' — largely ritual regulations for the Tabernacle and the various forms of sacrifice and purification. Also issues of the priesthood and also some important ethical commands.
Numbers	*Bemidbar*	'In the Desert' — the people continue their journey but lose faith, rebel, anger God and must eventually wait until the next generation can continue the military campaigns necessary to reach the Promised Land.
Deuteronomy	*Devarim*	'The Words' — The Repetition. Moses' farewell speeches and warnings, ending with his own death.

7. THE *NEVI'IM*

A Prophet in Hebrew is a '*Nav'i*', plural '*Nevi'im*'. The Prophets in the Hebrew Bible are listed in a different order to how they may be found in the Christian Bible; also, several books are included in this category which may at first seem to have little to do with specific named Prophets.

The 'Twelve Minor Prophets' are so named because their books are all short, not because they are less important. In general these cover the period up to and including the First Exile.

A Prophet is someone chosen (he never volunteers!) to pass a message on, usually orally — so their books and words have survived almost by accident.

The **Prophets** comprise:

Joshua	*Yehoshua*
Judges	*Shoftim*
I Samuel	*Shmuel Aleph*
II Samuel	*Shmuel Bet*
I Kings	*Melachim Aleph*
II Kings	*Melachim Bet*
Isaiah	*Yeshayahu*
Jeremiah	*Yirmiyahu*
Ezekiel	*Yechezkel*

The 'Twelve Minor Prophets':

Hosea	*Hoshea*
Joel	*Yo'el*
Amos	*Ammoz*
Obadiah	*Ovadyah*
Jonah	*Yonah*
Micah	*Meekah*
Nachum	*Nachum*
Habbakuk	*Havakkuk*
Zephaniah	*Tzephanyah*
Haggai	*Chaggaiy*
Zechariah	*Zecharyah*
Malachi	*Malachee*

It is considered by the Rabbis that Malachi was the last Prophet... that this form of direct communication by God ended with him. Any later person claiming to be a Prophet would not be accepted.

8. THE *KETUVIM*

'The Writings' have the appearance of a miscellaneous collection — 'the rest' — after the other two categories were fixed. They comprise poetic and wisdom works, the 'Five *Megillot*' and some historical accounts.

The Psalms are (mostly) ascribed to David and the Proverbs to his son Solomon — and the Books of Chronicles parallel in many respects the accounts given in Samuel and Kings. Daniel is set in the Exile, Ezra and Nechemiah describe the return from Exile, so it is hard to categorise this section in any obvious way.

The **Writings** comprise:

Psalms	*Tehillim*	— 150 liturgical poems.
Proverbs	*Mishley*	— 31 chapters filled with wise short sayings.
Job	*Iyyov*	— The story of a man tested VERY severely by God to see if his faith will hold.

The 'Five Scrolls / *Megillot*'

Song of Songs	*Shir HaShirim*	— A series of erotic love poems.
Ruth	*Root*	— The story of a woman who chooses to move from Moab to Israel.
Lamentations	*Eycha*	— Mourning poems over the destruction of Jerusalem.
Ecclesiastes	*Kohelet*	— Philosophical reflections.
Esther	*Esther*	— The story of an attempted genocide against all the Jews.

Daniel	*Daniel*	— Set in Babylonian Exile.
Ezra	*Ezra*	— The return from the Exile.
Nechemiah	*Nechemyah*	— The return from the exile.
IChronicles	*Divrey HaYamim Aleph* —	Dynastic histories.
II Chronicles	*Divrey HaYamim Bet* —	Dynastic histories.

9. THE RABBINIC BIBLE

Traditionally one did not just accept the Biblical text as it was — despite accepting its divine origin — but one sought to understand it, to explain it, to interpret it and where appropriate to apply it. In this way layers of commentary were added to the basic text, some of which were considered so important and helpful that they were later incorporated — not into the text but into the books which held the text, in the form of explanatory footnotes, marginal notes or even parallel translations and paraphrases.

In this way the basic text becomes gradually surrounded with the work of scholars over several generations, often quoting, agreeing or disagreeing with each other, each keen to probe and analyse from their own perspective in an attempt to get to what is really being said.

Although these comments are not read as part of the synagogue service (in the way that the *Torah* and *Haftarah* are read) they are retained for use in private or public study and some have become so 'hallowed' in use that they are almost accepted as authoritative too. (One hears for example the phrase '*Chumash-with-Rashi*' pronounced almost as one word, as though *Chumash* without *Rashi*'s commentary would be somehow defective!)

A modern equivalent could be a Website page which includes many links — these links are not actually a part of the text on the website page, but they provide further information, confirmation, observations which enrich the reading of the basic text.

Such a 'Rabbinical Bible' (known in Hebrew as a '*Mikraot Gedolot*' or 'A Large Anthology of Readings') is illustrated here. What do we have? As just one small example, a selection of interpretations based on the first verse of the Book of Exodus.

Let us explore how it works.

(I). THE TEXT

'And these are the names of the children of Israel, who came to Egypt with Jacob; (Each) man and his house(hold) came in.'

(II). TARGUM ONKELOS (ARAMAIC TRANSLATION)

'And these are the names of the children of Israel who came into Egypt with Jacob; (each) man with the men of his house(hold) came in.'

(III). RASHI'S COMMENTARY

'Now these are the Names.'

[Note: The words *Rashi* comments on, as with the others, are printed in ordinary 'block' Hebrew letters to help them stand out from the comments themselves which are printed in a different cursive script known as '*Rashi* script', developed by the early Hebrew printers. This is equivalent to using Italics so as to differentiate in a Roman typeface. One is amazed at the skills of these printers and their proofreaders! Not to mention their eyesight.]

'Although (Scripture) has already enumerated them by name whilst they were living (*Note Aleph*), it again enumerates them when it tells of their death, to show that they are compared to the stars, which (God) causes to come out and to enter in by their holy names, as it says (Isaiah 40) (v.26): 'He brings out their host by number, he calls them all by name.' '

['Sh.R.' is '*Shemot Rabbah*' — *Rashi* has derived this comment from the *Midrash* on Exodus of that name. It is often a tough intellectual exercise to derive from the brief, terse notes given by *Rashi* the actual question or problem he had seen and was trying to clarify!]

The '*Note Aleph*' refers to the bottom of the page, to the '*Ikkar Siftei Hachamim*' which provides the source-reference to the earlier enumeration:

'See in the commentary on (*Sidra*) 'Vayigash' (Genesis) 46:8.'

(*Rashi* is concerned here with the word 'Names' — Why are these names so important? Because, he says, they are an indication of God's love and an individual relationship to each of those named — and he draws as an illustration a totally different parallel out of a *Midrash*ic text.)

(I) THE *TORAH* TEXT

The basic text of the *Torah* with added punctuation, vocalisation (vowels) and musical notation.

This particular page deals with the Book of Exodus, Chapter 1 verses 1-9 (*Aleph* to *Tet*) hence the heading *Shemot Aleph*.

The letter *Peh* פ at the end of verse 7, (short for 'Patuach' or 'open') signifies a paragraph break in the text. (Also used is *Samech* ס , short for 'S'tumah' or 'closed'.)

The vowels and punctuations were provided by the Masoretes, who worked mainly in Tiberias between the 6th- and 10th centuries.

(II) Targum Onkelos

An Aramaic translation and paraphrase of the Hebrew text. Onkelos lived in the 2nd-century and converted to Judaism in the time of the Emperor Hadrian — a very dangerous act. He made his translation under rabbinic guidance.

The *Masora* — 7th- - 10th- centuries. Comments on the text, punctuation, spellings, etc.

(VIII) T'A = Toldot Aharon, which cross-references to the Talmud.

< *Torah* text ends here

(III) *Rashi's* commentary. *Rashi* (Rabbi Shlomo ben Yitzak) lived in Troyes, France, 1040-1105. He studied in Worms and Mainz. He wrote in a terse, concise style, to bring out the literal meanings.

(V) Rabbi Abraham Ibn Ezra,
Spain, 1089-1167

A grammarian, poet, philosopher, astronomer and biblical commentator.

Born in Tudela. Left Spain in 1140 (possibly due to his son's conversion to Islam).

Spent the rest of his life as a wandering eccentric and poverty-stricken scholar living and writing in Rome, various parts of Italy, southern and nothern France, London (1158), then back to France and possibly to *Eretz Israel.*

(IV) Ramban. (Nachmanides)

Rabbi Moshe ben Nachman. Spain, 1194-1270.

Commentary on text based on *Rashi's* commentary, yet disagreeing with it frequently. Often disagreed likewise with *Ibn Ezra.*

In 1263 took part in a public disputation with the monk Pablo Christiani (a Jew who converted to Christianity) in Barcelona. Won, but in 1267 had to flee and went to *Eretz Israel*, re-establishing the Jewish community there, founding a *Yeshivah* and synagogue. Had lived in Gerona, establishing a famous *Yeshivah* there, too.

Perush al Ibn Ezra

A super-commentary on Ibn Ezra, by Rabbi Shlomo Zalman Netter, who tries to clarify difficult matters in Ibn Ezra.

(VI) Sforno. Ovadiah ben Yakov Sforno, ca 1470-1550. Born Cesna, Italy. Studied medicine in Rome; settled in Bologna. Aimed at a literal exegesis of the text, though with a scientific, universal outlook.

(VII) Perush Rashbam.
Rabbi Shmuel ben Meir. A grandson of Rashi, ca 1080-1174.

שמות א

אונקלוס

א וְאִלֵּין שְׁמָהָת בְּנֵי יִשְׂרָאֵל דְּעַלּוּ לְמִצְרַיִם עִם יַעֲקֹב גְּבַר וְאֱנַשׁ בֵּיתֵהּ עַלּוּ: ב רְאוּבֵן שִׁמְעוֹן לֵוִי וִיהוּדָה: ג יִשָּׂשכָר זְבוּלֻן וּבִנְיָמִן: ד דָּן וְנַפְתָּלִי גָּד וְאָשֵׁר: ה וַהֲוָה כָּל נַפְשָׁתָא נָפְקֵי יַרְכָּא דְיַעֲקֹב שִׁבְעִין נַפְשָׁתָא וְיוֹסֵף דַּהֲוָה בְמִצְרָיִם: ו וּמִית יוֹסֵף וְכָל אֲחוֹהִי וְכֹל דָּרָא הַהוּא: ז וּבְנֵי יִשְׂרָאֵל נְפִישׁוּ וְאִתְיְלִידוּ וּסְגִיאוּ וּתְקִיפוּ לַחֲדָא לַחֲדָא וְאִתְמְלִיאַת אַרְעָא מִנְּהוֹן: ח וְקָם מַלְכָּא חַדְתָּא עַל מִצְרָיִם דְּלָא מְקַיֵּם גְּזֵרַת יוֹסֵף: ט וַאֲמַר לְעַמֵּהּ הָא עַמָּא בְּנֵי יִשְׂרָאֵל סַגִּי וְתַקִּיף מִנָּנָא:

המימין (main text)

א וְאֵ֗לֶּה שְׁמוֹת֙ בְּנֵ֣י יִשְׂרָאֵ֔ל הַבָּאִ֖ים מִצְרָ֑יְמָה אֵ֣ת יַעֲקֹ֔ב אִ֥ישׁ וּבֵית֖וֹ בָּֽאוּ: ב רְאוּבֵ֣ן שִׁמְע֔וֹן לֵוִ֖י וִֽיהוּדָֽה: ג יִשָּׂשכָ֥ר זְבוּלֻ֖ן וּבְנְיָמִֽן: ד דָּ֥ן וְנַפְתָּלִ֖י גָּ֥ד וְאָשֵֽׁר: ה וַֽיְהִ֗י כָּל־נֶ֛פֶשׁ יֹצְאֵ֥י יֶֽרֶךְ־יַעֲקֹ֖ב שִׁבְעִ֣ים נָ֑פֶשׁ וְיוֹסֵ֖ף הָיָ֥ה בְמִצְרָֽיִם: ו וַיָּ֤מָת יוֹסֵף֙ וְכָל־אֶחָ֔יו וְכֹ֖ל הַדּ֥וֹר הַהֽוּא: ז וּבְנֵ֣י יִשְׂרָאֵ֗ל פָּר֧וּ וַֽיִּשְׁרְצ֛וּ וַיִּרְבּ֥וּ וַיַּֽעַצְמ֖וּ בִּמְאֹ֣ד מְאֹ֑ד וַתִּמָּלֵ֥א הָאָ֖רֶץ אֹתָֽם: פ ח וַיָּ֥קָם מֶֽלֶךְ־חָדָ֖שׁ עַל־מִצְרָ֑יִם אֲשֶׁ֥ר לֹֽא־יָדַ֖ע אֶת־יוֹסֵֽף: ט וַיֹּ֖אמֶר אֶל־עַמּ֑וֹ הִנֵּ֗ה עַ֚ם בְּנֵ֣י יִשְׂרָאֵ֔ל רַ֥ב וְעָצ֖וּם מִמֶּֽנּוּ:

[Masorah, Rashi, Ibn Ezra, Ramban, and Rashbam commentaries in surrounding columns — dense rabbinic Hebrew text]

The beginning of the 2nd book of the Torah, 'Shemot', in an edition of a Rabbinic Bible.

ב   ירושלמי   יונתן בן עוזיאל

ואלה שמות ואלין שמהת בני ישראל דעלו למצרים עם יעקב גבר עם אנש ביתיה עלו: (ב) ראובן שמעון לוי ויהודה: (ג) יששכר זבולן ובנימין: (ד) דן ונפתלי גד ואשר: (ה) והוה סכום כל נפשתא נפקי ירכא דיעקב שובעין נפשתא עם יוסף ובנוי דהוו במצרים: (ו) ומית יוסף ובתרוהי מיתו כל אחוהי וכל דרא ההוא: (ז) ובני דישראל נפישו ואיתילידו

בעל הטורים

(א) ואלה שמות ב"ה הכפים ל"ח בגים. שאם כתביו ואלה שמות ג"י לא שימו ...

אבן עזרא

ואלה. ולם וי"ו יאמרו שורק מחת מיק כאלו סוי"ו נקריאת אל"ף כמו ...

יונתן

(ו) ומית יוסף ובתריהי וכו' ...

פירוש על אבן עזרא

שטוש בית אביו. שא זבול ונקרא אלף בנוסג. וכו' ...

פירוש רשב"ם

(ז) פרו. בהריון. וישרצו לידה. שלא יכלו ברחם. שבכל מקום קטנים קדוים שרין על הארץ. וירבו. גדלו. וגעשו הקטנים גדולים ולא שתו בקטנותם

Targum Yerushalmi.
The Palestinian translation into Aramaic of the Pentateuch.
From 14th-century, often erroneously ascribed …

'Targum Jonathan'.	**'Baal HaTurim'.**
Super-commentary on 'Targum Jonathan', also known als 'Pseudo-Jonathan' since he didn't in fact write it.	Rabbi Jacob ben Asher, ca 1270-1340. Moved in 1303 from Germany to Toledo. Wrote collection of straightforward explanations culled from others.

< *'Baal HaTurim'* ends here.

(V) ibn Ezra.
Further commentary from Ibn Ezra.

Ibn Ezra's exegetical writings began in 1140.

'In his introduction he enumerates various types of commentators: those who interweave their expositions with discussions unrelated to the text; the anti-traditionalists who believe that they can dispense with the explanations of the rabbis and feel free to interpret them according to their own reasoning; those who believe that the Bible is wholly allegory and mysteries; and those who follow the Midrashim without regard to the plain meaning of the text. Ibn Ezra rejects all four tendencies and states his intention of establishing independently the literal meaning of the text, but following the explanation of the Talmudic sages in interpreting the legislative part of the Pentateuch.' (Encyclopaedia Judaica 8:1166).

Interested in etymological and grammatical explanations.

Often disagrees with predecessors with scorn and satire. Attacks Karaites and literalists.

Alludes (very subtly) to the possibility that Moses did NOT write all the Pentateuch, but is careful not to be too specific on this.

Comments are sometimes based on personal experiences during his travels. A terse, concise, enigmatic and witty style.

Perush al Ibn Ezra (continued)

(VII) **Perush Rashbam** (continued)

(IV). *RAMBAN'S COMMENTARY*

'The meaning of 'And these are the names' is that the text wishes to count concerning the matter of the Exile from the time when they went down to Egypt, for then they were exiled 'at the head of the exiles' (Amos 6:7), as I have explained. Therefore it returns to the beginning of the matter, which is the verse 'And all his seed he brought down to Egypt' (Gen. 46:7). And there it is written, after it: 'And these are the names of the children of Israel, who came to Egypt...' etc. and this is the same verse which he returns to and repeats here; for even though they are two books, the story speaks of matters following one after another (i.e. of a continuing narrative) and when it recalled/mentioned 'the children of Jacob' it did so concisely concerning his children's children and all his seed and mentioned them (not individually but) all together, as he said there: (Gen. 46:27) 'All the souls of the house of Jacob, who came to Egypt, were seventy.' And like this it is recounted (i.e. and a similar example may be found) in The Book of Chronicles and the Book of Ezra; for the Book of Chronicles finishes with 'And in the first year of Koresh King of Persia, that there might be accomplished the word of the Lord by the mouth of Jeremiah, the Lord stirred the spirit of Koresh,' etc... and the same two verses with their very same language he repeats at the beginning of the Book of Ezra, to connect the narrative. (II Chron. 36:22-23 and Ezra 1:1-2) But since they were two books, he finished the first with what came before the building of the House (i.e. Sanctuary) and the second book (dealt with) what happened after the building, And this, likewise is the case of the two books *Bereshit* and *V'eileh Shemot.'*

Ramban's commentary, continued (from middle of line 13):

'And Rabbi Abraham (Ibn Ezra) says that because it recounts at the end of the first book that 'Joseph saw of his son children of the third (generation) (Gen.50:23) it therefore recounts that his brothers, on their going down, were few, and multiplied exceedingly. But this is not correct! And *Rashi* wrote, 'Although Scripture had already enumerated them...(Here Ramban quotes *Rashi's* entire comment)... by name,' these are words of *Aggadah* (i.e. homiletic interpretation) and they are words of truth in the matter of the love which the Holy One, blessed be He, loves them and repeats their names; but the connection of the verses, and the significance of the letter *Vav*, they are as I have explained.'

(i.e. 'I respect Ibn Ezra and *Rashi*, but actually **I** am right!' He is concerned at the apparently needless duplication of these verses at the end of one book and the beginning of another and therefore draws upon other examples elsewhere in *Tanakh* where the same verses are employed as a link in this way. He is also concerned that the first word in the new book begins with 'And', implying continuity with the previous Book. Since later it will be stated that the Israelites were exactly four hundred and thirty years in Egypt (Ex.12:40 — cf. Genesis 15:13f.) he wishes to date the beginning of this period to the moment they arrived rather than to the time they were enslaved.)

(VI). SFORNO'S COMMENTARY

'These'. 'Those recalled here were those worthy to be known by name, for each one of them was worthy to be considered, each one by his name, which teaches (something) concerning the stature and character (of them). And these, all the days of their lives were as shining lights, and that generation did not decline into an evil state. However, after their deaths, the righteous one amongst their children were not all that important in the eyes of God and man.'

(i.e. He is concerned to discuss how it is that we start off with a small specific defined group, named (in fact they are not all named here but are defined as a family group) whereas the history continues to show how this grows into a large but anonymous collective group, the individuals being relatively then less important. He focusses on the word 'These' to imply that ONLY these were worth mentioning, not the rest, not their descendants.)

(VII). COMMENTARY OF 'RASHBAM

'And these are the names.' Because he wishes to explain and say 'And the children of Israel were fruitful and multiplied exceedingly' (Ex.1:7), etc. It is accordingly necessary to denigrate, and to stress that on their coming into Egypt they were no more that seventy (Ex.1:5). And after the death of this generation, they were fruitful and multiplied.'

So Rashbam is stressing the deliberate contrast between the small group at the outset and the larger group into which they grew.

(VIII). TOLDOT AHARON

Makes no comment here at all, since there is no reference to Exodus 1:1 in the *Talmud*; the first note concerns verse 7 and refers to '*Berachot*' 7a and '*Chullin*' 92a.

[Note: All the English translations here are fairly literal. Very good scholarly translations into English are available — by Silberman (*Rashi*), Chavel (*Ramban*), Pelcovitz (*Sforno*) and Schacter (*Ibn Ezra*) — Portions only.]

What do we learn from all the above? That for a thinking, educated Jew the word 'Bible' does not mean something in English only that can be thumped to make one point only, but a reservoir of meanings which can be extracted and interpreted in different ways. It is quite legitimate to disagree with someone who has gone before you, if you can do it clearly and logically and explain why; It is quite in order to print an edition of the Bible in which learned scholars from a wide variety of countries and centuries argue with one another! Disagreement does not mean Heresy. Just because one answer is right does not mean that all others are wrong — there could be several correct interpretations, depending on what is required. Different readers will see different things in the text, pick up different nuances, focus on different words or phrases and ask it different questions. One scholar's argument might not suit another's. The Bible becomes a living thing, responding to the insights of each new generation.

You can approach the Bible as one committed to modern scientific knowledge — in terms of medicine, or astronomy; you can come to it with knowledge of different manuscript traditions, different versions of different but comparable cultures — and still there will be something of value in it for you, and your approach might be classed as 'different' but not (necessarily!) 'wrong'.

10. METHODS OF INTERPRETATION

How does one interpret a particular Bible passage? According to traditional Jewish scholarship there were (at least) four levels to every *Torah* text, known as

P'shat
Remez
Drash and
Sod

and collectively known from their initials as the acronym '*PaRDeS*', the Hebrew for 'Orchard' or 'Garden'. (The same word is the root for the word 'Paradise' and so, by immersing oneself in *Torah*, one is in a way re-entering Paradise; Perhaps this is the origin of the idea in Proverbs 3:7 that the *Torah* is like an '*Etz Chayim*', a 'Tree of Life' — that this is the replacement for what God was so concerned to prevent the first people in the '*Gan Eden*' (Garden of Eden) from consuming, that the *Torah* is eternal and so we get a 'taste of eternity'...)

- The *P'shat* represents the plain, obvious surface (and maybe even superficial) meaning;
- The *Remez* is that meaning which can be hinted at, derived from clues, contexts, parallels...
- The *Drash* is the homiletic way of interpreting a text in order to draw out some moral lesson or insight;
- The *Sod* is the secret, mystical meaning, that only the initiated can understand.

How does this system work? Let us take an easy, non-Biblical example: The classic Question-and-Answer Riddle:

'Why did the Chicken cross the Road?'
'To get to the Other Side!'

The *Pshat* is straightforward. 'This text deals with a feathered creature that walked across a road with a purpose in mind, and ultimately achieved that purpose.'

What is the *Remez*? 'What is being hinted at? The Chicken maybe had a purpose in crossing that road. But — What was this purpose? Could it be, perhaps, to lay an egg? Or to meet another Chicken? (Or a Cockerel??) Was it really necessary to get to the other side for this purpose? What was wrong with the side on which it already stood? Was there perhaps a pressing need to escape from something on that side? Was it alone, or with a flock, or breaking away from the flock? Would the same story apply equally well to a Turkey or a Duck?' And so on, almost ad infinitum.

As a *Drash*, a sermon, one could make up all sorts of scenarios and turn them into moralistic or even admonitory sermons, thus: 'We all have Roads to cross — and sometimes indeed dangerous ones — if we are to achieve our purposes in Life. Yet nothing must be allowed to prevent us making the crossing. This is like the story of a hedgehog who once wanted to cross a stream...' (and so on). Or: 'How did the Chicken know it was safe to cross the Road? She couldn't — but she had faith in her Maker. In just such a way, we too should...' (and so on). Or: 'When the lorry driver saw the Chicken starting to cross the Road, the Evil One attempted to persuade him to accelerate and to flatten the bird. But the Holy One, Blessed be He, sent an angel who caught the Chicken by the wing and...' (and so on). Really, the possibilities here are also endless — and this is why this sort of interpretation, known as '*Midrash*', is so popular. It seizes upon gaps in the story and supplies possible fillers.

And the *Sod*? Here we can go both deep and wide: 'Who is this Chicken? It represents the Soul, which must cross the Road on the way to its destiny. Every Road has two sides — as does the human soul — which, when it reaches The Other Side, will...' and so forth. You get the idea?

In addition to all these one can have the modern scientifically-scholarly approach, which will compare the word 'Chicken' with another place where this appears in the literature — (say, a Jewish recipe book) and note that this animal is normally called a 'Hen' — and could discuss at great length whether the road crossed were the A61 from Leeds to Harrogate or, as some German scholars theorise, the Jaffa to Lydda camel route. In addition someone, somewhere, will have found an ancient variant text in which the Chicken 'criss-crossed' the road, and there will be a Talmudic scholar who can throw light on a further text in which the word 'crossed' is omitted as being an indirect reference to Christianity, or perhaps cut by the mediaeval censor, being replaced with 'walked over'. Maybe there will be learned footnotes trying to reconstruct a former, maybe lost 'Ur-Text' and whether the Hebrew word '*Rechov*' or '*Derech*' or even '*Kvish*' had been used for 'Road' and whether '*Tarnogol*' should be translated as 'Chicken' or just more generally 'Fowl'. An archaeologist will have found some old chicken bones and a few dried feathers in an excavation and may claim that these must be from the Chicken in question...

This example is, of course, totally fictional and deliberately whimsical. But now take this alternative text which, we could say, had been found on a fragment of old paper:

'H. and M. Smith, Station Road 11a, 20351'

Such a text fragment could be found anywhere. Is it current or old, out-of-date?

- The *Pshat* is relatively straightforward: Two people live or lived (it depends how old the text fragment is) at a house or flat with a specific address, and the number following — well, it could be a telephone number, in some countries it could be a post-code, but it could also be a membership number or a subscription number or the number in any other form of list.

- The *Remez*: Who does it refer to? What are the actual names of 'H. and M' Smith? Harry and Mary? Horst and Margarethe? Horace and Miriam? Even Henry and Michael, or Hilary and Maud?

Assuming we have established the forenames, how old are they? How long have they been together? Do they have children? Have they been trying to have children? Have they perhaps had children but lost them? When and where and how did they meet? Was it love at first sight? Did 'M' marry 'H' because she was already pregnant? Did 'H' find 'M' attractive because she had a rich father who owned a business? Have either or both of them been married before? Are there step-children? Foster children? Adopted children? 'Patchwork' children?

Is 11A a flat or a house? If so, why '11A' — is it because it is located above '11', perhaps a flat above a shop, or behind '11', a bungalow built behind the main house? Or is it a way of avoiding the number '13' for superstitious reasons? Is it rented or their own property or a flat linked to a specific profession — owned by the firm? Is H. Smith an employee of the railway, hence he lives near the station? Or a commuter who finds it convenient to live close to the station for his daily journeys to the City? Is there still even a station in Station Road or was it closed down decades ago? Do they have a car? What do they do? Do they even work from home?

Are they actually both still alive? Could it be that 'H. Smith' died over a year ago but his widow still keeps getting mail addressed to him, or to them both? — a twist in the heart each time, of course.

Is this address a 'good' one or a 'poor' one in terms of insurance premiums and crime rate and car thefts and vandalism?

Assuming this number is a telephone number (albeit without a prefix or code) — (it is clearly a land-line) — is it just a phone or is there also a fax attached and an answerphone? Can one call at any time or is it kept in a room (say, an office) where there is no one to answer in the evenings? Can one leave a message to be called back later? Is the phone on a bedside table so that late-night calls may disturb?

A scientific approach:

Where was this scrap of text found? As a bookmark? In an archive? In a recycling bin? Does the paper look new or faded? Is the text hand-written, indicating that someone made a note so they could visit, or is it printed? Does it look like a scrap of envelope (as used in the post) or a page torn from an address book?

- Now to the *Drash*. What can we learn from this? That these people, whoever they are (or were) were not afraid to appear in public, in a list; that they were stable people who had a place to live and a bank account (otherwise they would not have been able to get a land-line telephone number!) not refugees or temporary residents. Are we also prepared to appear in public lists or are we afraid of who might find our data? Do we hide behind 'Ex-Directory' numbers?

- And the *Sod*? The mystic approach? Well, let us assume that when they wish to speak to each other they use either their real names or nicknames, affectionate names, that they do not communicate through this phone number but more directly and more intimately…

One might think that most of these questions do not matter and indeed in many circumstances they do not — Unless, perhaps, you are trying to contact someone named Smith but cannot recall the address and you are unsure which of the seventy entries for Smiths in the telephone book is the right one… or you are 'cold-calling' a number to attempt to sell them double glazing or a new kitchen… or car insurance — without knowing anything much apart from the name and address…

Or: you are researching your own family history and are searching for traces of former family members, using their last known address… or a bit of an old post-card… This could even be from a list of members of an organisation or community, or it could be from a list of deportees with their last known address…

Or: if you wish to communicate with God — are you limited by not knowing God's name, or whether God can be reached at all times and places or only at specific times and in specific places?

Or: if you are reading and trying to understand a Biblical story — say, the story of Lot and Sodom in Genesis 18:17-33 — and you want to know how big the city is, what the population of Sodom is, whether 50 'good' inhabitants is proportionally many or few? What actually was the sin which had made God so concerned? How many victims had there been, 'crying out'? How long had it been going on for before this drastic action was taken? How would the story have been different if God had let Abraham bargain him down further below ten in verse 33? How old was Lot, how long he had been living there? How many daughters did he have? (The answer is — at least four, since as well as the two who left with him he visited at least two sons-in-law beforehand); What were their names? What was his wife's name? (Presumably she was herself from the city and so was losing all her own family, whereas Lot was just a foreigner moving on… This might explain why she looked back whilst he in panic rushed ahead…)

But the same questioning techniques, hunting through the text for hints, for strange grammatical endings, for parallel texts somewhere else that shed more light — can be applied almost everywhere. The Biblical text often expands over half a chapter for one conversation and then suddenly skips over several years; some characters are named and others are not; sometimes we are told how much time has elapsed and sometimes not.

Whenever someone says 'The Bible says...' or — even worse — 'The *Midrash* says...' (implying that there is only one *Midrash*, or that it is authoritative) they are guilty of drastic over-simplification — usually for dubious theological goals.

The *Torah* belongs to us all and we are all permitted to approach it, with due reverence, our own way. We are entitled to disagree with someone else's way, but not to deny them the right to have their own way. This is the basis of the 'pluralist' understanding of religion which lies at the root of Progressive Judaism.

11. THE ROLE OF THE BIBLE IN MODERN JUDAISM. PROGRESSIVE REVELATION

Very, very simply, Liberal Judaism is based on a theological understanding of God as constantly present and constantly providing new revelations. This is in contrast with what has become known as 'Orthodox Judaism' (the term '*Orthodox*' is actually Greek, is derived from Christianity and means 'the only correct belief.' It has only been used in connection with Judaism for around 200 years, mainly to distinguish it from Liberal Judaism!)

According to this 'Orthodoxy' God spoke with Mankind just once — at the encounter with Moses on Mount Sinai when the Israelites had just left Egypt. Everything, both the entire Written *Torah* and the entire Oral Tradition which accompanies it, was given then and everything written by 'authoritative' writers since, including those who composed the *Midrash*ic collections and the accepted commentators, is somehow tapping into this original Revelation. It follows that the further away we are in time from this significant moment, the further we are from the Truth. It is forbidden to change anything we have received because, by definition, the generation before us, and the generation before that, and the one before that, were closer to the source and so knew more than we do!

In contrast Progressive Judaism (there are various names which have been used — 'Reform', 'Liberal', 'Progressive', 'Neolog') bases itself on the belief that God did not reveal divine wisdom once only, for all time, but reveals it on a constantly-renewing basis, that each generation is therefore receiving Revelation and that therefore each generation can know MORE than the one before it! Change is in consequence permitted if it seems to bring us — as Jews, as human beings — forward, if it makes us more aware of the natural world around us and of the spiritual world within us, if it broadens us and our limits whilst not cutting us off from our roots.

Of course this also raises spiritual or theological problems. For example, why does it take so long in human history for us to learn of certain medicines or simple procedures which can save millions of lives? If we now have access to the formerly-lost knowledge of ancient civilisations and their alphabets, literatures, religions and cultures, and if this helps us to understand the Bible text differently — why was this knowledge withheld from major thinkers who lived five hundred or a thousand years ago? We know now the Earth is a ball and not a disc, that it orbits the sun and not the other way around, that there are more planets than are visible even to the trained naked eye — this makes it logically impossible for us to accept uncritically all the 'learning' of the past, which was based on different knowledge. Of course the implication is also that those who come after us should receive more wisdom than we have now — and we do not know everything!

There is still a lot to be done before the world is truly perfect, before no one needs to die unnecessarily from a trivial disease or lack of clean water or a basic medicine or nourishment, before the population growth matches the materials available and not exceeds it, before every human can relax in peace. We are therefore required to retain some humility and not assume arrogantly that we have already attained the limits of human knowledge. There is still a lot that God can teach us and our descendants — if only we are willing to learn.

But at least in Progressive Judaism we declare ourselves willing to try to learn and not to forbid any change, any progress, merely on the basis that it is 'new' !!

Opponents of Progressive Judaism often describe it as a form of religious 'laziness', 'Judaism-Light' inasmuch as many ancient rules are no longer observed. On the other hand. Progressive Jews do have a duty to learn, to understand what they are praying and what the ancient biblical and liturgical texts tell us — rather than to sit without understanding as these texts are mumbled in an ancient and incomprehensible language (often accompanied in synagogues by an incomprehensible manner of reading and poor acoustics and with the women placed where the vision and the acoustics are even worse!)

In the end there is no resolution of this conflict and in fact there are important and positive elements in both — and the extremes at both ends can be dangerous. There will always be some Jews who tend to the conservative approach, who want to keep things as they are, and others who tend to the more radical approach, who want to make changes — and not always grounded in sufficient thought and study of the consequences. But Judaism now is not what it was in the Middle Ages, before the Enlightenment, before the re-establishment of a Jewish State, before the political developments of the Western world (the introduction of Republics, of Parliamentary Democracies and freedom of thought and observance, of multi-cultural societies where there is no religious coercion). Judaism now does not exist in the same social structures as before. Rules regarding slavery, polygamy, sexuality and ritual require adaptation to the contemporary situation. (Note — this does not mean that there are not still slaves, nor that there are not still men with more than one partner, nor that every sexual taste is to be permitted and encouraged, nor that the concept of Giving is irrelevant — it means merely that we need to think the issues through. Slaughtering a bullock or stoning a sinner are not the modern ways of dealing with issues. At least, they shouldn't be!)

Judaism changed drastically during and since the Biblical period, with the Exodus from Egypt, the revelation on Sinai, the conquest of an own country, the development of the 'Judges' system, then the introduction of a monarchy (against the advice of the prophet Samuel), the political changes and disasters that led to the division of the tribes, the loss of ten of them, the Exile to Babylon (where a new alphabet, a new universalist vision and new religious vocabulary were absorbed), the return and rebuilding, later the influence of Hellenism (resisted by the Maccabees), the influence of the Romans, the destruction of the second Temple and the renewed Exile... (which involved the simultaneous loss of the Temple and Priesthood, the entire sacrificial ritual, the political independence), the development of the Synagogue and rabbinic leadership, new prayers and rituals, adaptation to life in countries where the main religion was also monotheistic but not Jewish (or hostile to Judaism, claiming even to be a better and updated version!) — we cannot really believe that all this was 'revealed to Moses at Sinai'.

So — *Torah* plays a major role in our religious life; it provides, still, the foundation for what comes later and remains a reference point. The Prophets, who often spoke against a too-close observance of the *Torah*'s ritual laws and a neglect of wider ethical issues, also play a major role. The Rabbis who discussed over centuries what the *Torah* texts mean, who created both the '*Halachah*' and the '*Aggadah*' — How we should walk, How we should explain — and how they could be applied in the daily life of their times show us that this discussion, this challenge is allowed and is a part of our task as Jews — we are not obliged to be Fundamentalist and simply quote a text without trying to analyse it first, to place it in its context and understand it. Different rabbis came up with different answers — and yet all are legitimate. There is more than merely One Version of the Truth.

It is with this understanding that we should approach and learn Bible and later Jewish texts — with respect, with reverence, but not with blind gullibility.

CHAPTER 23

THE ORAL LAW

---

1. INTRODUCTION

The term normally applied to Jewish law, legal thought and jurisprudence is 'Halachah'. This is derived from the verb 'lalechet', 3rd. person 'halach', meaning 'to walk'. Accordingly its strict meaning is actually 'A Way of Walking' rather than 'A Way of Standing Still' and it should properly be understood not as a fixed 'Law' but as a 'Process of Legal Reasoning'.

Unfortunately many of the divisions within the Jewish community reflect not only divergent opinions as to the interpretation of certain laws but deep disagreements over the very process whereby these laws are promulgated and imposed.

Put very simply, the disagreement is over whether every new interpretation must always depend on a fixed precedent or whether there is room for creative innovation and a selective 'weeding-out' of outdated regulations, in response to new conditions.

One view argues that the Oral Law is firm and unchanging and that each new generation, being that much further from the original revelation at Sinai, is even less qualified to institute changes than the ones before.

The other argues that Judaism, Jewish thought, custom and even belief is a dynamic rather than a static entity and each generation may make modifications to the system, within the system itself, so long as certain basic fundamentals remain unchanged — effectively, belief in the One God and in the importance of Ethical Behaviour to one's fellow human beings. They argue that differences in climate, forms of government, geography, diet, surrounding culture, means of communication and technology have all been reflected in Jewish law in the past and there is no valid reason why they should not continue to be so reflected in the present.

Of course, between these two extremes is much scope for intermediate views. There is a strong contemporary movement to adapt traditional *Halachah* where possible to modern technology, especially with reference to *Shabbat* observance or advances in medical science — but always by quoting some precedent from earlier sources, to maintain the 'continuity of tradition'.

There are also those who abandon the whole concept of Jewish legal reasoning and wish to establish new systems with no link whatsoever with the past.

Modern Reform or Liberal Judaism is based on the idea that change — responsible change — is possible and that, where no precedent for a particular change can be found, one is still justified in instituting change for valid reasons — for example to relieve human suffering or discomfort or injustice, however defined. One example of this would be the slight changes made in the divorce laws, enabling a woman to be freed from a marriage even if the husband refuses to be co-operative. This is a change that the Orthodox groupings have felt themselves unable to make, despite the fact that they accept the problem exists and express sympathy for those who are victims of it.

In recent years Reform Judaism has moved gradually in the direction of restoring certain traditions that had fallen into disuse, whilst at the same time moving to 're-form' (which is a verb!) other issues of status or gender definition. So the process of continuous re-evaluation can and does work both ways simultaneously.

2. THE CONCEPT OF THE ORAL LAW

How does the concept of 'Oral Law' work? The *Torah* itself, the 'Written Law' ('*Torah sheBichtav*') is very brief and concise. It gives instructions and commands, but rarely gives reasons for them or details of how to observe them apart from some general statements on the lines that this is to act as a 'Reminder of the Exodus' or as an 'aid to being holy' or 'no work should be done'. That is why the Oral Law, the '*Torah sheBe'al-Peh*' (literally '*Torah* which is on the Lip') developed, to flesh out these bare bones, explain what is meant, add the details and modify the basic rule to suit the circumstances of the time.

Here is a fictitious example, simply to demonstrate the problem and some of the process:

'And you shall take this Pen, and write down these words that I command you.'

On the surface this is a simple command. But now ask — as the Rabbis would have done — some basic questions of Definition: Which pen? What sort of pen? A quill? If so, with which sort of feather and from which bird? Does it have to be your own pen, or will any pen do, even one borrowed? What does 'This pen' mean? Does it have to be in ink, or will a ball-point do? What about a felt-tip pen? Would a pencil do, or a stylus with which one can write on clay? Does it have to be a permanent sort of pen, or would chalk do — even though it is a transient writing material? On what should one write — on paper, parchment, skins, plaster, wood, leaves, stones? What colour should it be — would any colour do, or should it be in Blue-Black, made according to a certain recipe or specification? Is a typewriter or some modern technological form of creating a script even without the physical act of writing — by typing on a keyboard and getting a printer to produce the finished version — included as valid? Must it then be an inkjet printer or are other forms acceptable?

(Note — When completing many official forms today the instructions specify the sort of writing — e.g. 'Complete in Block Capitals...', 'Signature' — and the colour of ink!)

Then ask some questions of Purpose. Why should this be written? Does it have to be You who writes this, or could anyone else do it for you? Can you pay someone to do it for you? Does it matter who reads it? Do you have to read it as well and if so alone, or aloud? Does it matter if you wrote down 'these words' but in a translation? Are translations even allowed, or would they distract attention from the original 'These words'? What about shorthand symbols or abbreviations? Is the text valid if you make a spelling mistake? What happens if you lose the text you have written — are you allowed to re-write it? May one copy the text? Print it? Duplicate it?

Behind these technical issues could be the philosophical argument — Which is the more important, the act of writing or the content of the words themselves?

One could go on — but these are the sort of questions that evolved for example around the commands to write down the *Torah*, or to write a '*Get*' (divorce document), or to define the colours of *Tzitzit*. They are the kind of questions that still concern people worried about writing the 'Tetragrammaton' — the four-letter 'Name of God'. If this Name is to be treated with respect and reverence, one should not delete or deface it; so bearing in mind that the command was originally given in the age before printing, so that every mention of a word had to be carefully and laboriously written by hand, avoiding casual misuse — what should you do if the Name now appears on a photograph of a text, appearing in a newspaper? How should you treat it if it is printed several hundred or thousand times in a book — does each copy become equally 'holy' or 'precious'? What should you do if you bring the Biblical text up on a computer screen — are you allowed then to 'Delete' it?

Is a printed book the same as a *Sefer Torah*? If so — can you read from it at a synagogue service and does it count? Do you need to bury it in the same way when it becomes unusable? What arrangements can you legitimately make if there is no one who can still write it in a certain way or read it properly in the original script and layout? Can you simply buy a copy or should 'You' write personally each one you possess?

When the Temple, the '*Beit Mikdash*' was destroyed the surviving Rabbis of that period chose not to create a new one elsewhere. They could — theoretically — have said that the act of bringing sacrifices, as commanded in the *Torah*, was more important than the specific location of the altar as commanded — Jerusalem — and the specific priesthood — descendants of the House of Aaron. They could have said that, in the changed circumstances of the time, Sacrifices ('*Korbanot*') should now be brought in another place — in Yavneh or Tiberias or Damascus or Baghdad or anywhere — and that another family could be appointed or nominated as successors to act as hereditary priests. (After all, when a specific King or Dynasty is ended, the importance of maintaining the institution of Monarchy is more important than any specific family dynasty.)

Instead however they decided that the destruction of altar and priesthood in Jerusalem marked the end, at least for the time being, of ALL sacrificial worship and henceforth Prayer would have to suffice — for this was an action that could be performed anywhere and led by anyone; so that is how Judaism developed historically. Technically though, under the principles of the Oral Law, they could equally have justified a different decision. Sometimes you have to draw up a series of priorities and decide, when circumstances have changed, which elements of a command you wish to maintain and which you are prepared to alter or even discard.

All (sensible) legal systems work in this manner. Let us take another British example:

'Thou shalt observe the Speed Limit.'

How to define the term 'Speed Limit'? Who sets the Limit? Parliament? A local Council? With what legal authority? What speed should it be? Should there be different Limits for different places — residential areas, trunk roads, Motorways, near a school? Should there be different limits for different types of vehicle — cars, Heavy Goods Vehicles, caravans and trailers? Should there be minimum as well as maximum limits on certain roads designed for speed? Should the limits vary for different classes of traffic or different times of day? How should the limits be advertised — how big should the boards be, what colours, where should they be placed, should the signs indicate Miles per Hour or Kilometres per Hour or just a number and does this matter? Should signs be repeated on every lamp-post? What rules should apply to the Motorists, to ensure that they have a means (regularly checked and certified) in their cars to know what speed they are travelling? What happens if you break a Limit — and is there a distinction to be made between a 'minor' and a 'major' infraction, between going at 40 in a 30 Zone or going at 100 in a 40 Zone? Should the Limit still apply in conditions of fog or frost? Or heavy rain? And so on... Can we learn from how other countries manage this issue? Or from how other forms of transport are regulated — e.g. railways? We could even go back to the traditional, original speed limit of 7 miles per hour and insist that a man walks in front of each vehicle with a red flag — a sort of 'back to the good old days' approach to the law... Should it even be allowed to build or sell vehicles which can so easily go so much faster than is ever legally permitted?

When an accident then occurs, which is often because at least one vehicle or its driver was unable to stop in time, it is usually the task of the lawyers representing each party to prove that their client was not responsible or that the other party was, because of whatever conditions applied at the time — the weather, the sun shining at a certain angle, warning signs not properly visible, mechanical failure, road conditions, other road users or whatever; Or police authorities have to prove that this rule was being infringed. There is debate about how fast is 'too fast'. (In fact the 30mph limit in built-up areas was introduced in 1930 due to 'excessive casualties', the 70mph limit on motorways in 1965 due to crashes in fog, buses should be limited to 65mph, there are differential limits for goods vehicles under and over 7.5 tons or whether articulated and so forth. Do not forget that life and death are at stake here, also that if two vehicles crash they do so at a <u>combined</u> speed...)

In short, the *Torah* often states a simple Legal Principle but the actual application of it is a matter for discussion and legal interpretation taking into account different aspects of history, geography, technology and social circumstances. For example, how is one to observe 'sundown' or 'sunrise', which are relevant to the timing of the

Morning Service or the onset of *Shabbat*, when living north of the Polar Circle where each day and each night lasts effectively for six months? This process of *Halachah* continues into the present — and the arguments within the Jewish community often reflect the different answers given to the same questions, or even a denial of the validity of the decision-making process.

The 'Written Law' without an 'Oral Law' to modify it and clarify it is a fundamentalist burden rather than a help. (One only has to see as a comparison how strict literal interpretations of ancient Sharia Law, applied mercilessly in the present, seem so out-dated.)

However, as long as you are involved in thinking about the process you are a part of it. Ironically, when one declares that the Oral Law is of Divine Origin it limits one's ability to become involved so that the more seriously one takes the Origin, the less one can think about, analyse or change the Law — one has merely to accept it unquestioningly.

A system of Laws — any system — realistically works only if:
- (a) People want the system to work, or
- (b) The Authorities can enforce the system.

For centuries the Jewish community was without any formal temporal powers and could not therefore impose or enforce the civil laws upon its own members; those who observed them did so because they personally valued them. Ritual laws could be enforced (within certain limits and with some interruptions under specific anti-Jewish rules) so that the Jewish community could make regulations concerning, for example, who might be honoured in the synagogue or the supervision of *kosher* meat.

We are now seeing, firstly, attempts in the State of Israel to impose religious laws in the civil domain — so that marriages and divorces, contracts and Sabbath observances must all follow rabbinic regulations — and also a broadening of the interface between religious and civil laws so that civil courts might be called in to affirm or deny a *Kashrut* certificate or to enforce the provision of a *Get*.

The Codes of Jewish law have gone through a continuous cycle of first broadening, with more detail, and then summarising, with less. Just as the many and varied laws on motoring are sometimes encapsulated into one small volume ('The Highway Code' — what you need to know as a driver) and are then expanded into thick tomes on the laws of motor insurance, road-worthiness, etc., so we see throughout history that some rabbis have become famous for writing full treatments of specific laws whereas others have become famous for preparing 'digests'.

(In a sense this entire book — 'The Honey and the Sting' — is merely an attempt to reduce and summarise the results of several hundreds of years of religious development and to give a brief overview within one volume!)

The best and most succint explanation of the traditional understanding of the development of the oral tradition can be found in the Introduction written by Rabbi

Moshe ben Maimon (also known as '*Maimonides*' or '*Rambam*') to his '*Mishneh Torah*', 'The Repetition of the *Torah*' published in 1180 CE.

Briefly, it was accepted that two 'revelations' were made simultaneously on Mount Sinai — the Written *Torah*, '*Torah SheBichtav*' and the Oral *Torah*, '*Torah sheBe'al Peh*'. One was written down by Moses, the other was not written down properly until centuries later and then only in summary form, so that the work of recreating this unwritten but legitimate interpretation of the written text continues to this day.

Here is Philip Birnbaum's condensed translation of the relevant parts of this Introduction, which Maimonides composed partly to explain why he, too, felt the need to re-state and re-formulate the laws, since the changing times had rendered the texts difficult and inaccessible. (See also the footnotes.)

'All the precepts that were given to Moses at Sinai were given with their interpretation, as it is written (1) 'I will give you the stone tablets with the teaching and the commandment.' (Exodus 24:12). 'Teaching' implies the 'written *Torah*' and 'Commandment' — its interpretation. He has commanded us to practise what the *Torah* teaches in accordance with the *Mitzvah*, which is referred to as the Oral *Torah*. Moses wrote the entire *Torah* himself before he died, and presented a copy to each tribe. He placed one copy in the Ark, as a witness, as it is written: 'Take this book of the *Torah* and place it beside the Ark of the Covenant of the Lord your God...' (Deuteronomy 31:26). He did not write down the *Mitzvah*, which is the interpretation of the *Torah*, but bequeathed it to the elders, to Joshua and to all the people of Israel, as it is written, 'Be careful to observe everything that I am commanding you...' (Deuteronomy 13:1). For this reason, it is called Oral *Torah*.

Although the Oral *Torah* was not committed to writing (2), Moses taught the whole of it to the seventy elders who were included in his court. Elazar, Phineas and Joshua, the three of them, received it from Moses. He handed down the Oral *Torah* to Joshua, the disciple of our teacher Moses, and charged him concerning it. Joshua, too, taught it orally throughout his life. Many elders received the oral tradition from Joshua; Eli received it from the elders and from Phineas; Samuel received it from Eli and his court; and David received it from Samuel and his court...

Our saintly Rabbi Judah (3) compiled the '*Mishnah*'. From the days of Moses to the time of our saintly Rabbi Judah they had composed no work to be taught in public on subjects of the Oral *Torah*; but in each generation the head of the supreme court, or a prophet who lived in that period, would note down for himself a memorandum of the traditions which he apprehended from his teachers, transmitting them to the public orally. So too, everyone would note down for his own use as much as he could of the traditional interpretation of the *Torah* and the rules of conduct that were based on it, as he perceived them...

This used to be the regular procedure until the appearance of our saintly Rabbi Judah. He compiled all the traditions, laws, comments and interpretations, which had been transmitted by our teacher Moses and by the courts of the preceding generations, with regard to the entire *Torah*. He employed all this material, of which he composed the work of the *Mishnah*. Then he taught it diligently to the students in public, so that it became well known to all the people of Israel, who made copies of it and taught it everywhere, so that the Oral *Torah* might not be forgotten among the Jewish people.

Now, why did our saintly Rabbi Judah do what he did and did not leave things as they were?

Because he realised that the number of students kept decreasing, while ever new troubles kept coming; a wicked government was spreading out in the world and rising in power; the Jewish people were wandering about, migrating to distant localities. So he composed a work, designed as a handbook for everybody, in order that they might study from it speedily and that it should not be forgotten. He spent all his life teaching the *Mishnah* in public together with his colleagues, members of his court...

(4) (5) (8) Rav compiled the '*Sifra*' and the '*Sifre*' to explain and to impart the principles of the *Mishnah*. Rabbi Hiyya (6) compiled the '*Tosefta*' to explain the subject matter of the *Mishnah*.

Similarly, Rabbi Hoshaya and Bar Kappara compiled '*Baraithot*' to interpret the wording of the *Mishnah*. Rabbi Yohanan (7) compiled the Jerusalem *Talmud*, in *Eretz Yisrael*, about three centuries after the destruction of the Temple...

(9) (10) Ravina and Rav Ashi were the last sages of the *Talmud*. Rav Ashi compiled the Babylonian *Talmud*, in Babylonia, about one century after Rabbi Yohanan's compilation of the Jerusalem *Talmud*...

It follows therefore that Ravina and Rav Ashi, together with their colleagues, were the last great sages who transmitted the Oral *Torah*...

The scholars who rose shortly after the compilation of the *Talmud* and studied it deeply became famous for their wisdom. They are called *Geonim*. The *Geonim* who rose in *Eretz Yisrael* and Babylonia, Spain and France, studied the method of the *Talmud*, elucidated its obscure passages, and explained its subject matter; for indeed, the way of the *Talmud* is exceedingly deep... The inhabitants of every town addressed many questions to each contemporary *Gaon* and asked for explanations of difficult passages in the *Talmud*. The *Geonim* would answer the questions to the best of their knowledge. Those who composed the questions compiled the responsa into books for purposes of study.

The *Geonim* of successive generations also wrote commentaries on the *Talmud*. Some of them interpreted specific laws, while others explained particular chapters that were found difficult in their time. Still others expounded complete tractates and entire orders of the *Talmud*. They also made compilations of established rules concerning what is forbidden or permissible, what is or is not punishable, in matters of immediate concern, so as to make them intelligible to anyone who cannot penetrate the depths of the *Talmud*. All the *Geonim* of Israel were engaged in this work of the Lord ever since the *Talmud* was compiled until this date, which is the eighth year of the eleventh century after the destruction of the Temple, corresponding to the year four thousand nine hundred thirty-seven since the creation of the world. (= 1177 CE).

At the present time, when severe disasters keep following one another and the needs of the moment brush aside all things, our wise men lose their wits, and the understanding of our clever people is hidden. Hence, the commentaries, the codes of law and the responses, which were written by the *Geonim* who regarded them as easily intelligible, have presented difficulties in our days, so that a mere few are capable of understanding their subject matter properly. Needless to say that this applies particularly to the *Talmud* itself, the Babylonian as well as the Palestinian, the Sifra, the Sifre and the Tosefta, works that require wide knowledge, a learned mind, and ample time…

I bestirred myself therefore, I, Moshe ben Maimun the Sefardi, and relied upon the Creator, Blessed be He, and made a thorough study of all these books, and decided to put down in writing the results obtained from all these works as to what is prohibited or permitted, unclean or clean, and the other laws of the *Torah* all in plain language and concisely, so that the entire Oral *Torah* might become familiar to all systematically, without arguments and counter-arguments, one man saying so and another something else; but rather clear, convincing statements, governed by the logic derived from all these compilations and commentaries that have appeared since the time of Moses until now. So that all the laws be open to old and young alike, whether they belong to the precepts of the written *Torah* or to the enactments and ordinances introduced by sages and prophets.

(11) In brief, in order that no one should be in need of any other work dealing with the laws of Israel this work is to include the entire oral *Torah* along with the ordinances, customs and decrees instituted from the time of Moses till the compilation of the *Talmud*, and in accord with what the *Geonim* explained to us in all their works composed after the *Talmud*.

(12) I have named this work '*Mishneh Torah*' because the person who first reads the Written *Torah* and then this *Mishneh Torah* will know from it the entire Oral *Torah* without having to read any other book between then…

The number of precepts of the *Torah* that are observed through all generations is six hundred thirteen. Two hundred forty-eight of these, corresponding to the number of bones in the human Body, are affirmative; three hundred sixty-five precepts, corresponding to the number of days in the solar year, are negative.'

The Notes on Maimonides' work:
(1) '*V'etnah L'chah et-Luchot haEven, v'HaTorah v'haMitzvah*.' What is at issue here

is the possible difference between '*Torah*' and '*Mitzvah*' — are these two separate and parallel systems?

(2) Compare with *Mishnah* '*Pirke Avot*' (Sayings of the Fathers) 1:1: 'Moses received *Torah* on Sinai, and handed it on to Joshua, and Joshua to the elders, and the elders to the prophets, and the prophets handed it on to the men of the Great Assembly...'

In this version the Priests, the *Cohanim*, are totally excluded from having any part to play in the transmission of what in other religions would be called the 'Holy Mysteries'. In Maimonides' version however Elazar (a son of Araon), Pinchas (a grandson of Aaron — cf. Numbers 25:11) and Eli (the priest of his day — cf. I. Samuel 1:9) are included.

(3). Rabbi Yehudah *HaNasi* — Judah the Prince — who compiled the *Mishnah* in around 200 CE.

(4). '*Sifra*' — 'The Book' (the Aramaic for the Hebrew '*HaSefer*'). An *halachic Midrash* — i.e. a legal commentary — on the Book of Leviticus, frequently quoted in the *Talmud*. According to Malbim (19[th.] century) and later scholars it was actually compiled by Rabbi Hiyya.

(5). '*Sifrei*' ('The Books') — an *halachic Midrash* on the Books of Numbers and Deuteronomy; from the Amoraic period — i.e. ca. 3[rd.]-century CE onwards. The section dealing with Numbers has many parallels with the '*Mechilta*'; that dealing with Deuteronomy has a different character and may derive in part from the 'school' of Rabbi Akiva — i.e. his students and followers.

The first printed editions of both the above were published in Venice in 1545. It is known that manuscript texts varied quite a bit.

(6). Rabbi Hiyya bar Abba — an early teacher ('*Tanna*') of the 2nd. century; born in Babylon but moved to Palestine. He and his pupil *Hoshaya* collected *Baraitot* — teachings omitted from the text of the *Mishnah*. From the time of Sherira *Ga'on* in the 10[th.] century he was considered to have compiled the '*Tosefta*' ('Addition' or 'Supplement') — which is modelled on the *Mishnah* and adds details to its teachings — but this is probably not the case.

(7). Rabbi Yohanan ben Nappaha. Born in Sepphoris, died in Tiberias 279 CE. He established an academy in Tiberias and became a famous and respected and much-quoted teacher. The Palestinian *Talmud* (also called the 'Jerusalem *Talmud*' or '*Talmud Yerushalmi*') is ascribed to him but, although he must have influenced it greatly, he died at least a century before it was completed.

(8). Rav — the title by which Rav Abba Arika ('The Tall One') was known. He founded an academy in Nehardea in Babylon in 219 CE, later moved to Sura. There he established the basic methodology of the *Talmud* — taking as a base the *Mishnah* text of Rabbi Judah the Prince, adding other early, '*tannaitic*' teachings and deriving from the whole body of tradition the theoretical explanations and practical applications of the teaching. Died at Sura 247.

(9). Ravina I — a Babylonian '*Amora*' ('Later Teacher'), he died ca. 420 CE.

(10). Rav Ashi. 352-427. Re-established and rebuilt Rav's academy at Sura and led it for at least 52 years (some say 60). Instigated the compilation of all the teachings produced there and, with the help of colleagues, produced the Babylonian *Talmud* ('*Talmud Bavli*').

(11). Literally 'Repetition of the *Torah*' — from the Hebrew *Shanah*, 'to repeat', which is also the basis of the title *Mishnah*, reflecting the days when books were memorised and repeated for pupils to hear and learn.

(12). In the Babylonian *Talmud* ('*Makkot*' 23b) it is stated that the 248 positive commandments correspond to the number of organs or joints in the human Body and this was later interpreted to mean that every part of the Body had some part to play in the performance of *Mitzvot*; also that the 365 negative commands correspond to the days of the solar year. The total is 613 written in Hebrew letters as *Taf* + *Resh* + *Yud* + *Gimmel* (corresponding numerically to 400 + 200 + 10 + 3 = 613). From this they are frequently alluded to as the '*TaRYaG Mitzvot*' — an acronym based on the Hebrew numerals.

There was (perhaps not unsurprisingly) much violent opposition by other rabbis to his rather immodest claim that his book alone could supplement all other works! What he did was to codify all the laws on a particular topic and place them in order, omitting all the discussions and alternative responses.

Various attempts have been made to find exactly what these 613 commands in the Written *Torah* are and Maimonides himself produced a list in his '*Sefer Ha-Mitzvot*' — the 'Book of the Commandments'. In fact, the 13th.-century writer of the '*Sefer HaChinuch*' states that, after all the redundant laws to do with sacrifices, the Temple and ritual purity are discounted, only 270 laws of any relevance remain — 48 positive and 222 negative. Yet fundamentalists continue to place great stress on 'the fulfilment of the *Taryag Mitzvot*'.

Certain terms in these brief notes will themselves require explanation, but we can already see that Maimonides quotes very concisely the history of the textual transmission as he understood it, whilst later scholars disagree with some of these beliefs.

Scholars also expend great effort in trying to reconstruct 'original' texts for some of these works, since often we have only later, incomplete versions of them. It is not infrequent that a quotation from one work appears in another — but not in the text of the work itself that we have! Since we are dealing with complex traditions, often involving disagreements between teachers of different centuries and in different countries, sometimes with very similar names (there were several Rabbis called Yochanan or Hiyya... and of course transliteration issues mean that a 'J' or 'Y', a 'H' or a 'Ch' may be used) and then with a period of further centuries in which manuscripts were copied and re-copied by hand, it is not surprising that these discrepancies appear.

We must bear this in mind, however, every time someone says 'The *Gemara* says...' or 'It says in *Sifrei*...' Any good scholar will also quote the edition he is using and point out any variant versions known to him.

3. 'HALACHAH' AND 'AGGADAH'

These two important words need a (brief) explanation. The former has already been explained as 'the process of legal reasoning' and is generally used to mean any passage within the corpus of tradition that prescribes what one should or should not do in a certain circumstance. '*Aggadah*' is, in effect, everything else — homiletic interpretations of a text rather than a legal interpretation, anecdotes, tales, moral lessons derived from a text, and so on.

The Hebrew root *Nun - Gimmel - Daled*, 'N-G-D' (and the verb form '*leHagid*') means 'to tell a tale or story', so '*Aggadah*' means 'Recounting of Stories' and a '*Maggid*' is a storyteller — hence the similar title '*Haggadah*' given to the annual recitation of the Exodus story.

We find a process of specialisation takes place within the tradition in that the *Mishnah* tends to give fairly bare summaries of brief discussions, some of which lead to no real conclusion, whilst others lead to a statement of 'the *Halachah*' — the conclusion accepted by the majority. The minority opinions are preserved, but more as a form of background context and some of the arguments brought forward are more '*Aggadic*' in the *Gemara* (i.e. the commentary on the *Mishnah*, the two between them forming the *Talmud*). This process is expanded quite extensively, with contemporary science and geography being quoted to support a particular argument and much insight being given into the cosmology, mathematics, superstitions and even recipes of the times, leading to a vast 'ocean' of comment in which the actual *Halachah* is easily lost amongst the side-issues.

From this fairly chaotic mass of material (one sometimes finds the same story in different places, perhaps with variations or ascribed to different characters) later compilers extracted just the final legal conclusions, creating 'Codes of Law' which comprised just the *Halachic* elements and omitting the rest. Similarly collections of *Midrash* were compiled over the centuries, which concentrated on stressing homiletical messages and extracting them from various sources within the textual traditions and by various means.

The upshot is that we find modern published versions of the 'Jewish Laws' that present just one side of a discussion and provide no context for the decision presented — whereas the Rabbis of the Talmudic period would frequently preserve the minority opinion so that it could be referred to later, or came to their decision on grounds that may no longer apply — such as an understanding of the natural world that has since been superseded, or a political situation that has since changed.

This perhaps explains why, for so many Jews, the word *Halachah* has come to mean something static, restrictive and inexplicable. Many modern simplistic guides also omit to give any explanation of the reasoning behind the instructions they give and this is not very satisfactory for a thinking person. But alas! — not every believer is also a thinking person…

5. THE KARAITES

It should be noted that the Rabbinic tradition of interpretation of the Scriptures to derive laws for the community met with opposition and from the 8th. century one particular group formed a distinct sect, known originally as the Ananites after their founder Anan ben David (ca. 715 — ca. 795 CE)

After his death the movement grew but also split into many smaller sects, around Palestine, Persia and what became Turkey, the Ukraine and Russia. What they had in common was that they declared that only study of the *Torah* itself — the scriptures or '*Mikra*' — could validly produce the rules for Jewish life. From this stress on 'The Written Word' they became known as '*Karaites*'.

As far as the '*Rabbanites*' were concerned — those who accepted the Rabbinic system of thought and interpretation — this group was merely an heretical group of outsiders and the two groups fought each other fiercely.

One can see echoes of this argument in, of all things, the Christian Reformation, with its leaders' repeated calls to return to the original texts for guidance rather than to rely on a top-heavy and clumsy network of additional and later laws; there are also (very slight) parallels with the later Reform Jewish attempt to clear away some of the centuries of accumulated rabbinic thought and law in the desire to reveal once more some of the original simplicity and universal relevance of earlier forms of Judaism — particularly that of the Prophets.

In 1970 it was estimated that there were still 7,000 *Karaites* living in Israel — i.e. Jews who rejected the whole rabbinic apparatus. Since then contact has of course also been resumed with the Jews of Ethiopia, who had also had absolutely no knowledge of or influence from 'Rabbinic Judaism', having been isolated many centuries ago! This should at least serve as a warning against the mistaken belief that 'all Jews' accept or reject the same things.

6. THE '*MISHNAH*'

The Hebrew word '*Shanah*' means 'to repeat or do again' (hence the noun '*Shanah*' means 'Year' — something regularly repeated in seasonal cycles). The noun '*Mishnah*' is used in the Bible to mean something repeated, such as Pharaoh's dream in Genesis Ch. 41; something doubled — such as the amount of money that needed repaying by Jacob's sons in Genesis Ch. 43:15; something copied, such as the Book of the Law that the king must write out for himself, in Deuteronomy 17:18.

In the days before printed books (let alone e-Books!) much teaching was done by repeating a passage until the listeners had learned it by heart, when they would be able to pass it on the same way. This is, really, what is meant by an 'oral tradition'. (Think also of the 1953 novel 'Fahrenheit 451' by Ray Bradbury, filmed in 1966, of a future in which books have been banned but a group of rebels memorises as many as they can to 'keep them alive'.)

'*Mishnah*' therefore came to mean the whole of traditional law from the Babylonian Exile to the end of the 2nd. century CE (a period of around 800 years); it can also be used to refer to the 'teachings' of a particular Rabbi. 'A *Mishnah*' is an item, a unit — a statement or a paragraph — from this period, whereas '<u>The *Mishnah*</u>' refers to the work of that name compiled by Rabbi Judah, often called '*Ha-Nasi*' — 'The Prince', or 'The Patriach'. He is also often referred to simply as 'Rabbi' — everyone knew to whom reference was being made!

According to one tradition (in '*Midrash Bereshit Rabbah*' 58:2) Judah was born in 135 CE on the very day that Rabbi Akiva was martyred. He was descended (in the sixth generation) from Hillel the Elder, and followed his father Rabbi Shimon ben Gamliel II as Patriach, around 165 CE.

He lived in the Galilee where his teachers included Rabbis Judah ben Ilai and Shimon ben Yohai who, along with Rabbi Meir, had been disciples of Akiva. It is therefore clear that he could be said to have belonged to 'the school' of Akiva; when he compiled his '*Mishnah*' he used, according to a report in the *Talmud* ('*Nedarim*' 41a) thirteen different prior collections of teachings from different masters.

The *Mishnah* itself refers (in '*Sanhedrin*' 3:4) to 'The *Mishnah* of Rabbi Akiva, and the First *Mishnah*…' — this latter being obviously a still earlier version. Several sections that deal with the Temple and its ritual seem to be derived from eye-witness accounts — yet the Temple had ceased functioning in 70 CE. In the *Talmud* ('*Menachot*' 18a) mention is made of a *Mishnah* of Rabbi Eliezer ben Hyrcanus, and in '*Yevamot*' 49b to a *Mishnah* of Rabbi Eliezer ben Jacob. Both of these teachers lived in the generation <u>before</u> Akivah.

Rabbi Judah's achievement was therefore not to compose a set of laws, but to edit a series of different collections into one fairly-coherent whole. As Herbert Danby wrote in the Introduction to his translation of the entire *Mishnah* (p.xxii):

> 'It was Rabbi's task to bring together this mass of *Halachot*, the work of many generations, handed down in the form of miscellaneous collections of oral teachings, stored in many memories, and growing ever more complicated and unwieldy by reason of controversy between rival teachers and contradictory traditions; to reassemble this material and to present it as a single coherent whole, arranging it systematically, abbreviating arguments, summarising discussions, rejecting what seemed superfluous, sometimes in disputed cases giving his own ruling, or adding arguments if these seemed called for.

> He did not reproduce his material in a rigidly uniform pattern, reducing it to a single standard of literary style; so far as possible he adhered to the principle of repeating a tradition in the very words in which it had been handed down. Nor did he omit a tradition because it had later been held to be wrong, or suppress the ruling of an individual Sage because it had been repudiated by the Sages as a whole. Thus, Rabbi did not aim at promulgating the *Mishnah* as an authoritative, definitive legal code, a final summary of Jewish law… It was, simply, a compilation of the Oral law as it was taught in the many rabbinical schools of his time; it sought to contain all that was worthy of preservation in older or more recent

collections, preserving even divergences of opinion, both such as had originated among earlier generations, such as in the Schools of Hillel and Shammai, and such as were due to more recent disputes among the contemporaries and disciples of Rabbi Akiva. Many of these opposing views he leaves without attempting to decide between them.'

We have therefore almost a miscellany of traditions, roughly systematised. There is no Introduction or Index (at least, not until modern scholars set to work!) and nowhere is it even stated that Judah (often referred to as above as just 'Rabbi') was responsible for the work, though this is taken for granted by all later sages. For centuries argument has raged as to whether Judah actually wrote down the *Mishnah* or merely taught it orally. It appears that written texts were available from early times, but the rabbis of the later generations whose work eventually culminated in the *Talmud* normally used '*Tannaim*', professional memory-men (the word is from the Aramaic equivalent of '*Shanah*' — a 'repeater') who knew the entire texts and would recite passages of text on demand.

According to one of Judah's younger contemporaries Rabbi Jochanan ben Napaha, 'all anonymous rulings in the *Mishnah* are those of Rabbi Meir' (who taught around the year 160) 'and all are according to the teaching of Rabbi Akiva.' It may be assumed that Judah used as a basis for his collection a list of Meir's teachings, which were themselves based on his own teacher's. Judah also quotes with great frequency his own teacher Rabbi Judah ben Ilai.

Judah spent the last seventeen years of his life in Sepphoris — some think interned there by the Roman authorities — and probably compiled the *Mishnah* there. He died around the year 220 CE. At this difficult period in history the times were indeed bad for the assured maintenance of an oral tradition. After the destruction of Jerusalem in 70 CE and the crushing of the Bar-Kochba revolt in 135 things must have looked rather bleak for the future of the whole of Jewish law and lore. It is clear that some of the sections had no relevance even at the time they were compiled — in the absence of the Temple, the Priesthood, the sacrificial Ritual, the Tithing system, etc. — and were therefore included largely to keep the memory of past times alive.

(A personal observation: The Leo Baeck College was originally established in London in 1956 to provide an opportunity for surviving teachers from the Berlin 'Hochschule für die Wissenschaft des Judentums' to convey their personal knowledge and perspectives and memories to a new generation of rabbinic students in what was for them Exile, in a new language; these students in turn matured to become future teachers at the same College… and so a 'school' of Central European thought was transplanted and then grew in its own way in a different country, language and decade, but still rooted in this European culture. We can see many parallels to the earlier attempts to salvage some continuity from the catastrophe.)

7. THE ORDER OF THE '*MISHNAH*'

The *Mishnah* was divided by Judah into six main sections — '*Sedarim*', 'Orders' — which are in turn divided into a total of sixty-three sub-sections called '*Massechtot*' (singular '*Massechet*', 'Tractate'). These are:

A. *ZERA'IM* (*'SEEDS'*)

— Matters involving Agriculture and its Products

1. *Berachot*   ('Benedictions') — Blessings and when to say them.
2. *Pe'ah*   ('Gleanings') — The Corners of the Fields, etc. — for the Poor.
3. *Demai*   ('Produce which might have been Tithed, but there is No Certainty') — the Tithe was the one-tenth tax payable to the Temple.
4. *Kila'im*   ('Mixtures of Different Kinds')
5. *Shevi'it*   ('The Seventh, or Sabbatical Years')
6. *Terumot*   ('Heave Offerings')
7. *Ma'aserot.*   ('Tithes' — 'the Tenths' — the portion allocated to the Priests)
8. *Ma'aser Sheni* ('Second Tithes' — the further proportion taken from the already-tithed produce)
9. *Challah*   ('The Dough-Offering')
10. *Orlah*   ('The Status of Fruit from Young ('uncircumcised') Trees)
11. *Bikkurim*   ('First-Fruits') — Rituals of Thanksgiving.

B. *MO'ED* (*'SET FEASTS'*)

— Matters involving Sabbaths and Special or Festival Days

1. *Shabbat*   ('The Sabbath') — Rules thereon, and its observances.
2. *Eruvin*   ('Mergings') — the combining of Sabbath limits to enable activities within the Sabbath framework.
3. *Pesachim*   ('*Pesach*') — Passover and its observances.
4. *Shekalim*   ('Shekel Taxes') — for the upkeep of the Temple and Ritual.
5. *Yoma*   ('The Day') — i.e. The Day of Atonement, *Yom Kippur* and its observances.
6. *Sukkah*   ('Tabernacle') — *Sukkot* and its observances.
7. *Betzah*   (or *Yom Tov*) ('Egg') — Matters relating to Festival Days and produce thereon.
8. *Rosh Hashanah* ('The New Year')
9. *Ta'anit*   ('The Fast Days')
10. *Megillah*   ('The Scroll of Esther') — *Purim* and its observances.
11. *Mo'ed Katan* ('Minor Special Days') — the middle days of Festivals; Mourning Periods.
12. *Chagigah*   ('The Festival Offering') — Festival rituals.

C. *NASHIM* *('WOMEN')*

— Matters dealing specifically with Women, or the Man-Woman relationship.

1. *Yevamot* ('Sisters-in-Law') — rules concerning remarriage 'within a family' for various reasons.
2. *Ketubot* ('Marriage Contracts')
3. *Nedarim* ('Vows') — Rules for making, witnessing and revoking Vows.
4. *Nazir* ('The Nazirite Vow')
5. *Sotah* ('The Suspected Adulteress' — and testing thereof)
6. *Gittin* ('Divorce Documents') — production, witnessing and delivery.
7. *Kiddushin* ('Betrothals') — rules of Engagement and Marriage.

D. *NEZIKIN* *('DAMAGES', 'TORTS')*

1. *Baba Kamma* ('The First Gate')
2. *Baba Metzia* ('The Middle Gate')
3. *Baba Batra* ('The Last Gate')

('These three tractates are divisions of what was originally one tractate entitled '*Nezikin*', dealing with various problems arising out of property. The 'First Gate' treats of injuries by man or beast and the questions of responsibility and restitution; the 'Middle Gate' treats of lost property, guardianship, usury and the hire of labourers; and 'The Last Gate' treats of ownership of immoveable property and problems relating to it.' [Danby p.332n.])

4. *Sanhedrin* ('The *Sanhedrin*') — Courts.
5. *Makkot* ('Stripes') — Punishments.
6. *Shevuoth* ('Oaths') — Legal, as opposed to religious Vows.
7. *Eduyot* ('Testimonies') — Witnesses.
8. *Avodah Zarah* ('Strange Service') — i.e. Idolatry — definition and punishment.
9. *Avot (or Pirkei Avot)* ('Fathers' or 'Sayings of the Fathers') — an anthology of aphorisms and apothegms of the Sages.
10. *Horayot* ('Instructions')

E. *KODASHIM* *('HALLOWED' OR 'HOLY THINGS')*

1. *Zevachim* ('Animal-Offerings')
2. *Menachot* ('Flour-Offerings')
3. *Chullin* ('Animals killed for Food') — what makes them acceptable for food.
4. *Bechorot* ('First-Born Animals')
5. *Arachin* ('Values') — Vows of a particular valuation.

6. *Temurah*   ('Substitution of Offerings')
7. *Keritot*   ('Cutting-Out') — i.e. Sins which are punishable by Excommunica-
                   tion and how to atone for them.
8. *Me'ilah*   ('Bad Faith', 'Sacrilege') — Misuse of Holy Things.
9. *Tamid*   ('The Continuous', 'Daily') — i.e. The Daily Burnt Offering.
10. *Middot*   ('Measurements') — the Dimensions and Routine of the Temple.
11. *Kinnim*   ('Nests', 'Pairs of Birds') — the Bird-Offerings.

F. *TOHOROT* ('CLEAN THINGS, 'CLEANLINESS')

1. *Kelim*   ('Vessels', 'Utensils')
2. *Oholot*   ('Tents', 'Living Quarters')
3. *Nega'im*   ('Signs of Leprosy')
4. *Parah*   ('The Red Heifer') — Rules for cleansing.
5. *Tohorot*   ('Cleannesses') — Levitical Uncleanness.
6. *Mikva'ot*   ('Ritual Baths')
7. *Niddah*   ('The Menstruant', 'Menstruation')
8. *Machshirin*   ('Things that make something Unclean')
9. *Zavim*   ('Persons suffering a Discharge')
10. *Tevul Yom*   ('Someone who had Immersed that Day') — Whether they are
                   clean.
11. *Yadayim*   ('Hands') — How they can be rendered Clean.
12. *Uktzin*   ('Stalks', 'Shells', 'Rinds') — of fruit and vegetables.

A total of 63 Tractates.

At first sight this seems a marvellous system for dealing with almost any matter of
religious and civil concern. At a second look there are some apparent anomalies,
often due to the ambiguous nature of the material; for example the laws of Menstruation, '*Niddah*', are classified under 'Ritual Cleanness' rather than under 'Matters
relating to Women'. It appears that Judah himself adopted no set sequence of Tractates within the Orders — in most cases, allowing for presumed alterations such as
the splitting of '*Nezikin*' into 'Three Gates' (the Gate of a city being the area used for
Courts) the Tractates are arranged mainly in order of decreasing length.

It is clear that a lot of the subject-matter is of little direct relevance nowadays —
or even at the time of compilation — though it should be noted that the contents of
the Tractates often include a variety of subjects. For example, one of the four chapters of '*Bikkurim*' ('First-Fruits') actually deals with androgynous people — people
both male and female at the same time — and the problems of classifying them!

When referring to or quoting from the *Mishnah* the general rule is to ignore the 'Order' and cite the Tractate Name together with 'Chapter' and '*Mishnah*' — i.e. Sub-unit. Thus '*Parah* 3:2' or '*Bikkurim* 4:3' or 'Chapter Four, *Mishnah* Three'.

8. THE 'MINOR TRACTATES'.

Additional to the above list is a miscellaneous collection of fifteen other Tractates that were not, for whatever reason, incorporated into the *Mishnah* — being prepared later, in the *Tannaitic* period — but which are often printed towards the end of *Nezikin* and known as the '*Messechtot Katanot*' or 'Minor Tractates'; a citation from one of these would be referred to as a '*Baraita*' rather than a '*Mishnah*'.

These comprise:

'*Avot deRabbi Natan*' — an expansion of the ethical comments in '*Pirke Avot*'. (There are two known versions, with 41 and 48 chapters.)

'*Sofrim*'   — the laws of writing sacred books and reading the *Torah* in public.

'*Evel*'   — laws of Funerals and Mourning. It is sometimes called in contrast '*Semachot*' — 'Celebrations'.

'*Kallah*'   — 'The Bride' — laws on Engagement, Marriage and Sexual matters.

'*Kallah Rabbati*' or sexual, marital matters. (Only on '*Kallah*' is there rabbinic discussion — this version being therefore expanded as '*Kallah Rabbati*'.)

'*Derech Eretz Rabbati*' — a larger compendium of rules on behaviour and ethical relationships.

'*Derech Eretz Zuta*' — a smaller compendium of moral lessons for students and scholars.

'*Perek HaShalom*' — statements on Peace.

'*Sefer Torah*'   — laws for writing a *Torah* scroll.

'*Mezuzah*'   — laws for the *Mezuzah*.

'*Tefillin*'   — laws for *Tefillin*.

'*Tzitzit*'   — laws for *Tzitzit*.

'*Avadim*'   — lit. Slaves — the laws for indentured service and employer-employee relations.

'*Gerim*'   — the Conversion process and how Converts are to be treated.

'*Kutim*'   — relations with Samaritans, who were to be treated in some respect as Jews and in others not.

Reference is also made to a 'lost' Tractate '*Eretz Yisrael*' dealing with laws that applied to the land.

It is not clear why these tractates which, as can be seen, mostly deal with everyday matters, were not included more formally into the Canon.

9. THE *TALMUD*

The word *Talmud* means 'Learning' (from the Hebrew verb '*Lamad*', 'learn') but is usually used to mean specifically the collection of rabbinic debates and decisions on the *Mishnah*; this collection is called the *Gemara*, or 'Completion' (from the Hebrew word '*Gamar*' — 'to finish', 'complete') and the *Mishnah* and *Gemara* together are called 'The *Talmud*'. From the term '*Shishah Sidrei*' (Six Orders [i.e. of the *Mishnah*] it is sometimes also called 'The *Shas*'.

However, there are two *Talmud*s! These are (a) the *Jerusalem Talmud* (also called the *Palestinian Talmud*) and (b) the *Babylonian Talmud*.

(a). One produced by the Rabbis in *Eretz Yisrael* (usually called the '*Talmud Yerushalmi*' '*Jerusalem Talmud*' though it was in fact compiled not in Jerusalem but in Tiberias and Sepphoris in the Galilee, around the middle of the 4th. century). It was probably compiled by the school of Rabbi Jochanan.

(b). One produced by the Rabbis in Babylonia (modern-day Iraq), known as the '*Talmud Bavli*', '*Babylonian Talmud*', over the period from the mid-3rd. century CE to the end of the 5th. century CE in the academies of Sura, Pumbeditha and Nehardea.

Although these two *Talmud*s are largely similar in outline they do display substantial differences. They are based in places on different texts of the *Mishnah*. The '*Jerusalem Talmud*' for example has no section '*Kodashim*' and only a very minor concern with section '*Tohorot*'.

For a variety of historical reasons it is the Babylonian version which is usually referred to as 'The *Talmud*' whereas the '*Jerusalem Talmud*' is referred to mainly by specialist scholars. It is useful to know about its existence though, as it demonstrates the way in which the process of *halachic* debate was carried on in different places over the same general period. Each represents the work of several generations of teachers known as '*Amora'im*', whereas the teachers quoted from the *Mishnah* are known as '*Tanna'im*'.

The Babylonian *Talmud* follows the sequence of the *Mishnah*, as outlined above. There are however some sections of the *Mishnah* which have no *Gemara*. The '*Bavli*' is nowadays printed in a standard format, often referred to from the location of the original edition as 'the *Vilna Shas*'. This dates from Vilnius in Lithuania and comprises 37 volumes with a total of 2,711 double-sided pages or Folios; It is a breathtaking triumph of early layout, typesetting and printing, using different typefaces and font sizes to indicate in a straightforward black-and-white where the enormous amount of information is placed. *Rashi*'s commentary is printed on the inner margin and the Tosafists on the outer one. It is in turn based upon the first printed version produced by Daniel Bomberg (a Christian from Antwerp!) in Venice between 1516 and 1539 and who first numbered the folios.

First, in a centre column, the section from the *Mishnah* which is to be discussed is printed; it is then followed, for the rest of that centre column and sometimes for several other pages, by the *Gemara* for that section. (Where the *Gemara* starts is indicated by a large '**Gimmel / Mem**'). Around the central column are then gathered some major commentaries and 'super-commentaries' (i.e. Commentaries on commentaries), footnotes, references to other locations in the *Talmud* or the *Tanakh*, etc. The *Talmud* is formed of Folios, pages of paper which of course have two sides — so each Folio is numbered 'a' and 'b' — front and back — which are bound together. So — When referring to or citing the Babylonian *Talmud* now the general rule is to write 'TB' (for '*Talmud Bavli*'), then the Tractate, then the Folio, front or back — thus 'TB *Yevamot* 14b' or 'TB *Gittin* 20a'. When a volume lies open the left-hand page will be an 'a' side and the right-hand page the previous 'b' side.

The full study of *Talmud* can be a life-long task and no attempt is made here to summarise it all. Briefly, the rabbis debated issues raised from the *Mishnah* text, sometimes with their contemporaries and sometimes with their predecessors, in a way which can make it very hard for the uninitiated to know exactly what is going on.

Sometimes there are questions raised and several answers provided, usually based on some scriptural reference though this might have been ripped from its context or only partially quoted. Although only one of the answers given is in the end considered the 'authoritative' one it is important that the other arguments are preserved, so that the student can discern the reasoning process and the answers that were discarded at the time. It is a VERY important principle that, just because one answer is classed as 'Correct', this does NOT make all the other answers 'Wrong'. This is the basis for all Jewish debate — one's opponent (or 'debating partner') may have a different correct answer and in the end one may have to compromise in order to be able to agree on one common answer for now... Just because he or she has a different answer to you does not (necessarily) make him or her a fool, an idiot, a heretic, a blasphemer... It is considered always better to learn not alone but with a companion, a *Chevruta*, reading a passage and discussing it together, brainstorming.

Often specialised abbreviations or 'coded terms' are used, or nicknames for the rabbis. The end result is a massive series of volumes covering the six major Orders and the 63 Books or Tractates in which a variety of topics are discussed, often in no particularly logical order, with one topic sparking off debate on another because of some Biblical reference or some other vague link; If one did not know the whole lot it would be impossible to find a specific debate in a specific topic — and this is where the value of such encyclopaedic knowledge was best appreciated. Nowadays there are English and other translations of the *Talmud* (or major sections of it) and an Index, thus making it much easier to find specific items. There are now of course computer programmes and CD-Roms or USB Sticks and internet downloads which can call up all references to a particular topic throughout the entire body of rabbinic literature almost instantaneously. However, before these modern aids became available the only practical manner for most educated Jews who did not have access to the entire knowledge of the *Talmud* (or to someone else who had such knowledge) to learn the law on a particular topic was to turn to one of the Codes or compilations of Jewish Law, systematically laid out by Subject. Here is one small example:

The first page of an edition of the *Mishnah* (printed Hamburg, 1841).

(The text of the *Mishnah* is in the middle. On the right is the commentary on the *Mishnah* by Rabbi Obadiah of Bertinoro [1450-1510], on the left the commentary by Rabbi Yom-Tov Lippmann Heller ['*Tosefot Yom Tov*', 1579-1654]. At the outer margin are further commentaries and crossreferences.)

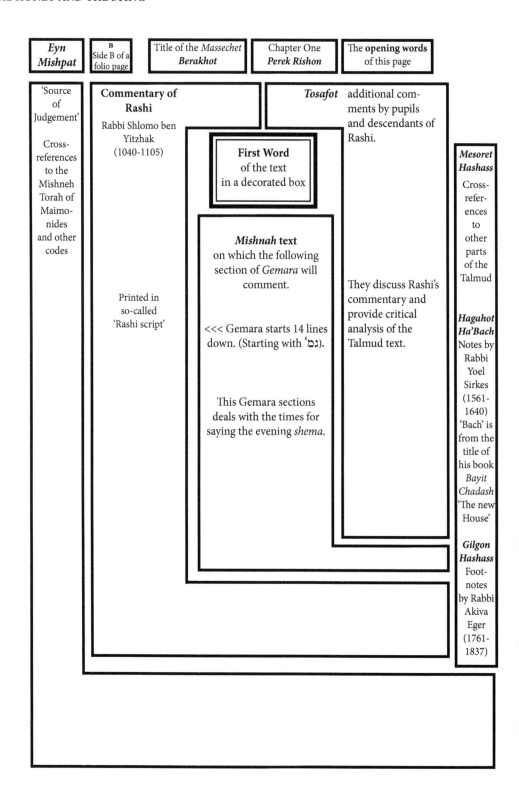

| Eyn Mishpat | **B** Side B of a folio page | Title of the *Massechet* *Berakhot* | Chapter One *Perek Rishon* | The **opening words** of this page |

'Source of Judgement'

Cross-references to the Mishneh Torah of Maimonides and other codes

Commentary of Rashi

Rabbi Shlomo ben Yitzhak (1040-1105)

Printed in so-called 'Rashi script'

First Word of the text in a decorated box

Mishnah text on which the following section of *Gemara* will comment.

<<< Gemara starts 14 lines down. (Starting with 'גמ').

This Gemara sections deals with the times for saying the evening *shema*.

Tosafot additional comments by pupils and descendants of Rashi.

They discuss Rashi's commentary and provide critical analysis of the Talmud text.

Mesoret Hashass Cross-references to other parts of the Talmud

Hagahot Ha'Bach Notes by Rabbi Yoel Sirkes (1561-1640) 'Bach' is from the title of his book *Bayit Chadash* 'The new House'

Gilgon Hashass Footnotes by Rabbi Akiva Eger (1761-1837)

עין משפט ‎ ב ‎ ברכות ‎ פרק ראשון ‎ מאימתי

מאימתי

The first page of the Talmud.

10. THE CODES

Both the *Mishnah* and the *Gemara* are Codifications of the *Halachah* to some extent, but here we refer to the post-*Talmud* attempts to encapsulate all the essential laws in a manner which was easier to refer to than searching the entire *Talmud*. It must be noted that these efforts were designed not to make the whole of the earlier work redundant (apart from Maimonides' claim!) but merely to make access easier for those who could not attain to the fuller knowledge. There were also problems where the *Talmud* had left a particular matter unresolved.

11. MAIMONIDES — THE *RAMBAM*

Although writers of the *Geonic* period (8th-9th centuries CE) and later Isaac ben Jacob Alfasi (of the mid-11th century) compiled books of *Halachot*, laws on specific tractates, the first major effort to break the system of the 63 *Massechtot* (Tractates) down into more manageable Books and Chapters was the 'Mishneh Torah' of Rabbi Moses ben Maimon (known from the initials of his names by the acronym 'R[abbi] M[oshe] B[en] M[aimon] as 'The Rambam', but often referred to in the Greek form 'Maimonides'.

Maimonides compiled a list of the 613 *Mitzvot* or Commandments derived from the Written *Torah* (there are in fact divergent lists of these basic commands) and the *Mishneh Torah* ('Repetition of the *Torah*', the word '*Mishneh*' coming from the same Hebrew root as the *Mishnah* itself).

This work, published in 1180, was compiled in fourteen Books (whence it derives its Hebrew nickname as the '*Yad*', literally 'Hand', from the Hebrew letters *Yud* and *Daled* which together make up the numeral 'Fourteen'). It is then divided into 83 *Hilchot* or Sections, themselves divided into a total of 1,000 Chapters which comprise a total of some 15,000 Paragraphs (each called a '*halachah*').

Into this systematic format Maimonides claimed to have distilled the results of all the *halachic* debates, so that anyone wanting to know more about the rules for a *Mezuzah*, or Fasting, or a specific festival, or warfare, etc. would not have to leaf through the various tractates of the *Talmud* but could turn simply to the relevant Book where all the appropriate answers were listed clearly by heading, sub-heading and paragraph number.

A magnificent work (one could call it the Wikipedia of its time!) it nevertheless attracted a great deal of hostility from those who felt keenly the lack of the cut and thrust of debate, the puns, humour, asides on historical or scientific matters and alternatives provided by the full *Talmud* text. Maimonides also omitted to give his references and these had to be supplied later by commentators. Two major critics were the '*Rabad*' (Rabbi Avraham ben David of Posquières in Provence, ca. 1125—1198) who lived during Maimonides' own lifetime) and Rabbi Asher ben Jechiel ('the *Rosh*') (1250-1327) who lived a century later.

The result was the growth of a series of explanatory commentaries (such as the '*Kessef Mishneh*' of Rabbi Joseph Caro) which had the effect of turning Maimonides' unified and simplified Code back into an extensive and complex work again.

12. THE '*BA'AL HATURIM*' (THE MASTER OF THE '*TURS*')

To this problem was added the large amount of 'Responsa' literature (i.e. Responses to Questions) and legal decisions across the scattered Jewish world. Eventually Jacob ben Asher (a son of the '*Rosh*') who was a *Dayan* (Judge) in Toledo, Spain in the first half of the 14[th.] century compiled a Code entitled the '*Tur*' or '*Turim*' ('Rows' or 'Columns').

In this he divided the relevant Jewish laws as practised in his time (i.e. omitting many that applied only to the Land of Israel or to the Temple ritual, though Maimonides had included these in his own Code) into four main Divisions ('*Turim*') combining the Talmudic decisions where appropriate with later legal rulings or '*P'sakim*'.

These four Divisions are:

1. ***Orach Chayyim*** — relating all the rules of daily conduct, including prayers and blessings, and *Shabbat* and Festival observances.
2. ***Yoreh De'ah*** — relating the ritual laws of purity, circumcision, dietary rules, visiting the sick, mourning — and laws relating to lending on interest, seen here as a religious rather than purely commercial matter.
3. ***Even HaEzer*** — matters of family law, such as marriage and divorce.
4. ***Choshen Mishpat*** — matters of civil law and criminal law, including courts, evidence, loans, property, partnerships, theft and robbery.

This book appeared in print in 1475 — the second Hebrew book ever to be printed — and it was soon adopted by the Western communities (e.g. in Germany, Italy, Poland) as the authoritative Code — although the Eastern communities remained largely faithful to Maimonides' '*Mishneh Torah*'. Of course, there soon appeared many other commentaries and explanatory additions to the '*Tur*' as well!

13. JOSEPH CARO

Caro was born in Spain in 1488 and was expelled with his family at a young age, eventually settling in Safed (Tzfat) in Israel.

The previous two centuries had seen major upheavals of Jewish life following the Black Death (1348-50) and the persecutions of German, Spanish and Portuguese Jews. The legal systems in use reflected this fragmentation.

Caro set to work to compile a major Code that would include both the substantive legal text of the *Tur* and the decisions of up to thirty-two other scholars, analysing their different answers to various questions and stating the laws in accordance with certain principles of precedence or majority opinion between them.

This massive work was entitled '*Beit Yosef*' ('The House of Joseph' — after his fore-name) but was so vast that he decided to write a shorter, simplified version for non-scholars and this was called the '*Shulchan Aruch*' ('The Laid Table' — i.e. the Table was already laid, prepared, all the reader had to do was to partake of the nourishment of the prepared legal sustenance).

The basic divisions into the four Divisions of the *Turim* was followed, though the sub-divisions were more concentrated and given numbers and headings and the '*Shulchan Aruch*' became a popular and widely-used compendium. It deliberately omitted anything that wasn't strictly relevant to the legal rulings — such as ethical and moral statements, scriptural references or arguments. The '*Shulchan Aruch*' was completed in 1563 and printed in Rome in 1565.

(Such a bare statement almost beggars belief. How was the lengthy manuscript written, how was it safely transported from the Galilee to Rome, how was a printer found (and paid) to perform the enormous amount of careful work required to set it out and typeset it, how was such a book later advertised, distributed and sold? All within two years?)

Naturally anything as simple and straightforward as this, designed for the layman (or even the housewife!) was almost bound to stimulate reactions from opponents who soon added their own commentaries and disagreements and so the composite work grew in size yet again in later editions. One of these commentators was:

14. MOSHE ISSERLES

Rabbi Moshe Isserles (known by his acronym as the '*RaMA*') was a leading scholar in Poland (especially Krakow) during the 16[th.] century. He disputed Caro's choice of rabbinic authorities, especially as Caro had used the teachings of *Sephardi* authorities and had omitted much of the legal debate of *Ashkenazi* ones.

He wrote (amongst other things) a commentary or series of 'glosses' on the *Shulchan Aruch* which he defined as a sort of 'Tablecloth to the Prepared Table' in which he presented counter-arguments or different practices and decisions based upon *Ashkenazi* teachings.

His main aim was of course to ensure that readers would have a choice where appropriate between two different schools of thought and he thus undermined the concept of a standardised and uniform Code for the entire Jewish people with which no one would be able to argue.

His comments are usually printed on the lower half of each page of the *Shulchan Aruch*.

References to the *Shulchan Aruch* are usually given by the name of the Division, then the number of a Topic chapter, then the paragraph — e.g. '*Orach Chayim* 103:3' — and if necessary 'The *Rama* to...'

15. LATER CODES

The process of codifying and expanding has continued without pause though the *Shulchan Aruch* (with the glosses of Isserles) has remained the 'standard work'.

Many subsequent Rabbis have published collections of their 'Responsa' — i.e. Responses to questions sent to them — known in Hebrew as '*Sh'aylot*' ('Questions') and '*Teshuvot*' ('Answers').

One well-known work is the '*Kitzur Shulchan Aruch*' ('Condensed *Shulchan Aruch*') published in 1864 by Soloman Ganzfried (Hungary 1804 — 1886) which could well be defined as a 'Reader's Digest Guide to *Halachah*' incorporating almost everything that an ordinary person would need to know to live an ordinary Jewish life (i.e. omitting matters relevant only to specific positions). This became a standard handbook for many *Ashkenazi* Jews and is still on sale (and often confused because of its title with the 'real' *Shulchan Aruch* with which it has little in common!)

There is also a large amount of *halachic* literature produced especially in contemporary Israel and America whereby Laws on specific subjects such as *Shabbat* Observance, Business Ethics, Medical Ethics or Modesty are published in a variety of handbooks designed either for laymen or specialists. Not to mention a vast number of websites from various organisations.

The process of Oral Law, of adapting and refining the basic principles to suit changing political, social or technological realities, continues...

The first page of an edition of the *Shulchan Aruch*.

PART FIVE:
HOME, COMMUNAL AND PERSONAL OBSERVANCES

CHAPTER 24

KASHRUT

1. INTRODUCTION AND DEFINITION

The Hebrew word '*Kasher*' — *Kaf / Shin / Resh* — means 'to be proper, suitable, succeed'. It is used in the *Tanakh* only in Esther 8:5 and Ecclesiastes 10:10 and 11:6 and is thus a very rare, late word.

In Rabbinic Hebrew it is more common, again meaning 'to be proper, fit, right; turn out well, to succeed' and, deriving from this, 'to be ritually permitted, legal, fit-for-use.'

It is important to note that Fitness, '*Kashrut*' (the noun from the adjective '*Kasher*') applied not only to food and animals but also to actions and to people and their status, e.g. whether someone was 'fit' or 'suitable' to marry a priest, whether the act of digging a hole makes someone the 'proper' person to take responsibility for damage caused when someone else falls into it (*Mishnah*: '*Kiddushin*' 4:6; '*Baba Kamma*' 1:2). (In terms of clothing the correct term would be '*Sha'atnez*', confirming that a piece of clothing is not made from both wool and linen, i.e. from animal and vegetable products. See Lev. 19:19 and Deut. 22:9-11.)

When we describe food or a *Sefer Torah* or a *Mezuzah* as '*Kasher*' (in Yiddish: '*Kosher*') we do not therefore necessarily mean that it is fit to eat! — but that it is in its correct state, complete, whole, intact, in good condition, as it should be — and that it is therefore fit for use in its intended function or capacity and not either '*Possul*' ('unfit') or '*Treife*' — ('torn rather than properly cut meat, and therefore forbidden for consumption').

In practice however the term in its Yiddish pronunciation '*Kosher*' is used mainly with reference to food products by the average Jew in daily life.

2. ASPECTS OF *KASHRUT* OF FOOD

The details of *Kashrut* have filled many books and will no doubt fill many more and legal arguments about the exact definitions show no sign of abating — indeed, the reverse seems to be true, as issues of animal welfare rights or modern food technology are added to the mix. This chapter will not try to duplicate all these arguments or even summarise all the results, but give an outline only.

Taking Animal products first, we have three main categories of concern before meat may be eaten:

(a). It must be the right sort of animal;

(b). It must be killed in the right way;

(c). It must be prepared, cooked and served in the right way.

Let us now expand each of these categories.

2(A). THE RIGHT SORT OF ANIMAL

Jews are meant to eat only certain species of animal — effectively vegetarian, herbivorous, non-hunting mammals defined by their physiological characteristics:

'You shall not eat anything abhorrent. These are the animals you may eat: The Ox, the Sheep and the Goat; the Deer, the Gazelle, the Roebuck, the Wild Goat, the Ibex, the Antelope, the Mountain Sheep and any other animal that has true hoofs which are cleft in two and brings up the cud — such you may eat.' (Deut. 14:3-6) (JPSA Translation).

Note: The JPSA also has the honesty to point out that 'a number of these creatures cannot be identified with certainty.' Many older English translations speak of 'Coneys' and 'Rock Badgers' since some of the Hebrew terms are simply untranslatable. However, an Israelite finding an animal would at least have been able to find out whether he was allowed to eat it. This is emphasised by the continuation of the passage:

'Hence, of those that bring up the cud or have true hoofs which are cleft through, you may not eat: The Camel, the Hare, and the Daman, for although they bring up the cud, they have no true hoofs; they are unclean for you. Also the Swine, for although it has true hoofs, it does not bring up the cud; it is unclean for you. You shall not eat of their flesh or touch their carcasses.' (Deut. 14:7-8)

The definitions are therefore clear: an animal has to conform to BOTH of these required characteristics, otherwise it doesn't count. Much thought has been given to Why they are so important, but no conclusive answer has emerged and *Kashrut* remains a '*Choq*', an unexplained and inexplicable category of laws.

Some have theorised that the animals listed are unhealthy or that the pig, for example, is biologically so close to *Homo Sapiens* that certain infections or organisms are more readily caught from it. The fact remains however that other peoples eat pork or camel or horse — and they haven't died out yet!

Similar theories — which are no more than theories — have been propounded that the Israelites were commanded to eat only gentle, non-carnivorous animals almost as a counter to the widespread superstitious belief that one gained strength through eating wild beasts and their blood, that their ferocious spirits were somehow thereby absorbed into one's own. Instead the Israelites were fixed in their roles of shepherds, keepers of domesticated animals, rather than as hunters of tigers... The whole canine and feline families — which have paws rather than hoofs — were excluded. The Israelites were meant to become gentle people, domesticated themselves, continually chewing over the cud of their traditions... All species with toes — such as mice and rats — are also excluded. Few find this to be a problem.

Similar rules applied to fowl, fish and other creatures:

'These you may eat of all that live in water; you may eat anything that has fins and scales. But you may not eat anything that has no fins and scales; it is unclean for you.

You may eat any clean bird. The following you may not eat: the Eagle, the Vulture and the Black Vulture; the Kite, the Falcon and the Buzzard of any variety; every variety of Raven; the Ostrich, the Nighthawk, the Sea Gull and the Hawk of any variety; the Little Owl, the Great Owl and the White Owl; the Pelican, the Bustard and the Cormorant; the Stork, any variety of Heron, the Hooper and the Bat.' (Deuteronomy 14:9-18)

Not everything that lives in water, whether salt or fresh, is a Fish; not everything that flies is a Bird! The 'Fish' are therefore categorised into those that are true 'Fish', and other things that just happen to live in the sea but of which some — Dolphins and Whales, Seals etc. — are mammals and some are flesh eaters rather than other-fish-eaters, such as Sharks — and some are just weird and in a different biological category entirely, such as Eels or Manta-rays or Octopi and Squid, and some are crustaceans — Lobsters and Crabs and Prawns — and there are also other creatures such as Mussels, Oysters which are also in shells, and tiny Krill. (Incidentally, in 1987 it was claimed that scientists had discovered that Eels were after all covered in microscopic scales and therefore were theoretically *kosher* after all! Several thousands years of tradition were suddenly at risk... The Sturgeon is also classed as being without scales.)

Birds are likewise defined and categorised. (N.B. The translations of the names of the birds are — like those of the animals — sometimes uncertain.) There are those which eat carrion (dead and decaying meat), or those which are birds of prey (killing their victims before or while they eat them), taking either flesh or fish; and there are those which are acceptable because they eat only fruit, berries, grains or insects. (Insects and Worms somehow do not count as 'prey' in this respect.) Flying mammals are also excluded.

How about Insects? (Remember — Locusts are a delicacy in many parts of the world):

> 'All winged swarming things are unclean for you; they may not be eaten. You may only eat clean winged creatures.' (Deuteronomy 14:19-20)

So — having defined that the animal, fish or bird is acceptable, that its own characteristics are the sort we might wish to emulate, that it is not violent or vicious and does not prey on its own kind or eat carrion — How is it to be killed?

2(B). THE RIGHT SORT OF SLAUGHTER

Jews are meant to eat only the flesh of animals and birds that have been killed in the approved manner. This means that:

(i). Animals that have died of natural causes are forbidden to Jews — (though they need not be wholly wasted). This is called 'Nevelah' — the word means 'corpse' or 'carcase'.

> 'You may not eat anything that has died a natural death — give it to the stranger in your community to eat, or you may sell it to a foreigner — for you are a people consecrated to the Lord your God.' (Deut. 14:21)

(ii). Animals that are killed by violence in a hunt, or by another animal, are forbidden. This is known as 'Terefah' — 'torn' or 'ripped' — the origin of the Yiddish term 'Treife' now used generally to mean 'Non-Kosher'. Obviously Hunting was a custom in Biblical times, so the prohibition is later. Until recently Venison, for example, was almost impossible to use as *kosher* meat, since before deer were 'farmed' they were only 'taken' in hunts.

(iii). Animals are to be slaughtered in accordance with strict tradition, in a ritual manner and by qualified, supervised professionals.
The act of ritual slaughter is called 'Shechitah', the verb in Yiddish 'Shechting' and the slaughterer is a 'Shochet'. Very, very basically the process involves the extremely-swift cutting of the windpipe and major carotid artery at the same time, so that there is almost immediate loss of blood pressure to the brain, the animal loses consciousness almost instantaneously and hence feels little or no pain. The knife used must be razor-sharp and checked each time it is used so that the flesh is not torn or 'nicked' in any way. If it were, the entire animal would become 'Terefah' at a substantial financial loss to the butcher. The slaughterer should be a pious person, he is to be aware that he is taking a Life and he must treat the animal with some respect as a part of God's creation.
The term 'Ritual Slaughter' has evoked a lot of emotive reactions from a variety of sources — animal welfare groups, vegetarian activists and also anti-Semites — and every few years debate is raised as to whether or not it should be allowed to continue.

(The same applies to '*Halal*' meat for consumption by Moslems, which follows similar but not identical procedures.)

The Jewish response is that *Shechitah* is actually MORE humane that the alternative methods of slaughter normally employed in other abattoirs — which may involve repeated shooting through the skull with a metal bolt, for example — and that one swift cut through the jugular vein, arteries, nerves and windpipe is in fact the most humane method known. Scientists have attempted to determine the exact number of milliseconds in which electrical activity in the brain can still be detected, in an endeavour to measure relative amounts of pain — conscious or unconscious. The debate rages still, but it can be said with certainty that the methods used in *Shechitah* (when properly carried out) are a great advance on almost every other method used in industrialised slaughtering with which they should be compared, free of any emotional trappings. There is debate also on whether the animal to be slaughtered should be standing upright or, strapped into a cage, turned onto its back to extend the neck.

Related problems are increasingly seen as relevant in the Jewish community, though not necessarily by the rather conservative authorities in charge of licensing *Shechitah*! For example the growth of Factory-Farming is a recent but significant development. If the rules within the Jewish tradition are so strict that an animal should Die without pain, then what about its Life? How can we tolerate it living its whole life in distress in a 'battery' or under cover, away from fresh air and sunlight and natural feeding?

What should our attitude be towards hormone treatment of animal feeds? Towards 'forced-feeding' of animals and birds to produce enlarged livers (considered by some a delicacy)? Or towards the conditions of transport to the abattoir and the conditions for the live animals there? Should animals awaiting slaughter be able to see other animals being slaughtered? Should a 'casting pen' be used, a metal frame onto which the animal is strapped to keep its head and limbs at the right angle and prevent it from damaging itself in its death throes and if so, what kind of pen? Every now and then scandals emerge into the media whereby animals with broken limbs are transported long distances across Europe in agony... It is also noticeable that many of those who protest at the way animals are slaughtered for food do not protest as much when other human beings are slaughtered for ideological reasons — and this can make one rather cynical about their motives. It is sadly ironic that Jews, who have been the first people to consider the welfare of the animals they slaughter, have not always been themselves treated with the same consideration...

From the Biblical account it seems as though the antediluvian ideal was for humans to live off fruit (although some fruits were forbidden!) whereas after the Flood in Genesis Ch. 9:3-5 Noach is permitted to eat animals. Of course some Jews are vegetarians (or even vegans) by choice and there is a Jewish Vegetarian Society (with its own website for details). It is however important to clear up one common misunderstanding: In Exodus Ch. 20:13 there is NO command, as is often misquoted from translations, not to Kill. The command is '*Lo Tirzach*' which means it is forbidden to Murder and this is defined as killing another human being for no good reason. Indeed the very same chapter, a few verses on (20:21) instructs the Israelites as to how to slaughter certain animals for sacrifices! There may be other religions which prohibit the taking of any life at all — even of a beetle or a mosquito — but Judaism is not one of these.

Jews are therefore allowed to eat meat — but the questions of the animal's life as well as its death are surely important? In Biblical times half of these problems just did not exist.

'When the Lord enlarges your territory, as He has promised you, and you say, 'I want to eat meat', for you have the urge to eat meat, you may eat meat whenever you wish. If the place where the Lord has chosen to establish His name is too far from you, you may slaughter any of the cattle or sheep that the Lord gives you, as I have instructed you; and you may eat to your heart's content in your settlements.' (Deuteronomy 12:20-21)

Maimonides takes the verse '... as I have instructed you' to refer to the laws of *Shechitah* (Positive Commandment No. 146 in his '*Sefer Mitzvot*') and the Tractate '*Chullin*' in the *Talmud* deals in detail with the instructions, which include checking the animal beforehand for any signs of disease or injury and checking the carcase afterwards, especially the lungs and gullet, for any nodules or other signs of something being amiss.

Certain conditions do not affect the *Kashrut* of slaughtered animals, but others do. Nowadays many animals that are found to be 'not quite *kosher*', plus sections of *kosher* animals that are not permitted to Jews, are sold to Moslem butchers, as it is usually acceptable to the standards of *halal* meat.

Some check the interior of the lungs to ensure they are quite smooth (German: '*Glatt*') and free of indications of disease and from this comes the term '*Glatt Kosher*' meaning, if this is possible, 'extremely *Kosher*'.

2(C). THE RIGHT WAY TO PREPARE AN ANIMAL

This is not a cookery book, nor an instruction manual for new Jewish housewives! Such detailed instructions do exist elsewhere if required. But here are some basic principles.

(i). There must be No Blood

Blood plays a major part in magic and rituals; in the sacrificial cult it was daubed over the altar or sprinkled around it. Many superstitious people link the eating of blood to the acquisition of strength or wisdom. Jews are forbidden it, totally.

'Make sure that you do not partake of blood; for the blood is the life, and you must not consume the life with the flesh. You must not partake of it; you must pour it out on the ground like water; you must not partake of it, in order that it may go well with you and with your descendants to come, for you will be doing what is right in the sight of the Lord.'

(Deuteronomy 12:23-35)

Blood is therefore drained from the carcases and the meat is soaked in water or salted to remove any last vestiges. Certain sections of the animal are difficult to cleanse in this way because of the large number of fine blood-vessels, or because the organ (e.g. the liver) is saturated in blood. Liver, for example, has to have its glossy surface cut across several times, then be sprinkled with salt and roasted or grilled on an open fire to draw all the blood out. The practice of drawing out veins and membranes which could still contain blood or which could be constituted of forbidden fat (known as '*Chelev*') is called '*Porging*'.

Nowadays most households that still eat *kosher* meat buy it ready-prepared from the butcher or delicatessen and few still employ the soaking-bowl (in which the meat was soaked for half an hour) or the salting-board (on which the meat was laid for an hour after soaking, salted so as to draw out any remaining blood and let it drain away) and the domestic skills involved have lapsed into widespread disuse. How many people in this country still pluck their own chickens?

(ii) The Animal must have been Healthy

Whilst an animal is being prepared it should be checked for any signs of ill-health, injury or infection. If a chicken turns out to have a broken wing, for example, or to have swallowed a rusty nail which is embedded in the gullet, complex rules apply. (Most *Kashrut* guides or Jewish cookbooks will advise 'Consult a Rabbi'!)

We have already learned that *Nevelah*, animals that have died naturally, are forbidden — but it always possible that an animal was correctly slaughtered whilst actually in the process of dying and becoming *Nevelah*! And this cannot be checked until later. While some of the rules for checking might appear abstruse, they date from a period before microscopes, blood tests and the sort of analyses that can now check for BSE or various traces of hormones or bacteria. The Shochet had to use his eyes and his judgement to make decisions. The *Kashrut* regulations were developed (or revealed!) before people were much concerned with BSE, Listeria or various modern diseases caused as much by the way we treat and feed livestock as by anything else. Nevertheless the people were sensible enough to know that eating a sick or dying animal was unlikely to make them healthy, so they used the methods available to them to ensure the best possible outcome. A trained '*Schochet*' also has considerable veterinary knowledge.

3. MILK AND MEAT

Few areas of *Kashrut* cause as much concern and confusion as this.

First, the terms used. In Hebrew, Meat and meat products are called '*Bassar*' or (as an adjective) '*Bassari*'. Milk and milk products are '*Chalav*' (or '*Halav*') or (as an adjective) '*Chalavi*'. Food which is considered to be neither one nor the other is '*Pareve*' or '*Parve*', which is from the Russian/Yiddish and is considered to be Neutral. In Yiddish, Meat is '*Fleischig*' and Milk '*Milchig*' and these are the adjectives normally used by *Ashkenazim* in conversation or to describe utensils or parts of the kitchen. (Note: As far as Vegetarians and certainly Vegans are concerned, many items labelled '*Parve*' are still of course animal products!)

Fish (i.e. *Kosher* fish species with fins and scales) are *Parve* — even though they have to be killed before being eaten (Apparently some Eastern *Sephardim* will also avoid eating fish with milk); Eggs are *Parve* (despite coming from chickens). All fruits and vegetables and grains are *Parve*. So whilst a cheeseburger — combining meat and cheese — is forbidden, fish in cream or a cheese omelette are fine.

The source of the law or custom of separating meat and milk products is found in the *Torah*, where we are told three times (Exodus 23:19; Exodus 34:26 and Deut. 14:21):

> 'You shall not boil a Kid in its mother's milk.'

The first and second time this is mentioned, the context is of festivals and sacrifices; The third time in the context of forbidden animals and food.

Maimonides takes this prohibition of 'cooking meat in milk' and that of 'eating meat cooked in milk' as Negative Commandments Nos. 186 and 187 in his '*Sefer Mitzvot*', pointing out that in the *Talmud* (Tractates '*Chullin*' and '*Makkot*') any transgression is punished by Whipping! However, no reason for this law is given and in his 'Guide to the Perplexed' (III.48) he writes:

> 'Meat boiled in milk is undoubtedly gross food and makes overfull; but I think that most probably it is also prohibited because it is somehow connected with idolatry, perhaps forming part of the service, or being used on some festival of the heathen.'

We see from this that the actual reason for the prohibition remains unclear and that even Maimonides sought an explanation in terms of magic and pagan practices.

Anthropologists have explained that the use of such a dish would be considered a very potent symbol — the young being boiled in the very liquid that would normally be giving it life and sustenance — and that this is why the text specifically (and repeatedly) refers to 'a kid in its (own) mother's milk' rather than to 'mixing all meat and all milk.'

Nevertheless 'Mixing' is how it was interpreted and a vast array of laws concerning the storage, cooking, serving and washing-up of food and utensils has developed. These are mostly very distant in concept from the idea of combining 'Life' and 'Death' (both Milk, which suckles young mammals and can be obtained without killing the provider, and Meat, which is the flesh of an animal that has had to die so that it can be eaten) in the same meal.

Strictly speaking indeed, and rather strangely, it is theoretically permitted to eat Meat AFTER Milk, but not the other way around (although few would dare to serve them at the same time). This concept is derived from the story of Abraham's hospitality to the strangers in Genesis 18:6-8:

> 'Abraham hastened into the tent of Sarah and said, 'Quick, make three measures of choice flour! Knead and make cakes!' Then Abraham ran to the herd, took a calf, tender and choice, and gave it to a servant boy, who hastened to prepare it. He took curds and milk and the calf that had been prepared, and set these before them, and he waited on them… as they ate.'

Since, the fundamentalist logic goes, our saintly Father Abraham could not possibly have done something wrong, obviously he was permitted to serve the milk and curds before the calf! (This was also, of course, before the *Torah* was given in Exodus.)

This is also further rationalised on the lines that pieces of meat might stick between one's teeth, whereas milk and cheese will be immediately swallowed — so that by eating meat first there is the risk of milk coming into contact with meat still in one's mouth, but not the other way around… (You are meant to rinse your mouth first!)

In practical terms a strictly-observant household will now employ two complete sets of utensils — crockery, cutlery and pans — and frequently two sets of washing-up bowls, brushes, tea-towels etc. to ensure that there is no way that even a fragment of one 'sort' of food might come into contact with another.

Tablecloths, salt-cellars, even (in some cases) the loaf of bread with which one ate a meat or a milk meal will be kept separate and distinct. In communal and private kitchens *milchig* items may be marked in blue and *fleischig* items red — a simple colour code to avoid mistakes. Arguments rage over Glassware — which can in theory be so smooth that it can be thoroughly cleaned with no remaining particle adhering afterwards and so be used for both milk and meat; and over 'Pyrex' brand ovenware, which some maintain can acquire minute surface scratches and so retain traces of its previous contents.

There are rules for how to cope with an accidental mixing, when a small lump of cheese may fall into a pan of meat or a drop of meat gravy into a bowl of milky soup… In these cases the proportions of the items concerned are of importance; If the contaminant is equivalent to $1/61^{st}$ of the volume that it touches (i.e. 1:60) or less, then it is considered to be negligible and unimportant (this is known as '*Bittul b'Shishim'* — 'cancelled by a factor of 60'); otherwise, the whole lot may need to be thrown out...

As in other aspects of life there is a spectrum between pious interest in ancient regulations and neuroticism. On the other hand, how would one feel if one heard that the cook had had a slight nosebleed into a pan of food or that 'only one cockroach fell into the stew so it must be all right'?

In modern prepared and processed foods it is important to check carefully the labels listing the ingredients. Many apparently-innocuous items — such as biscuits — may contain unspecified 'animal fats' or dried mashed potato may include 'milk solids'. Not everything is as it looks! This brings us to:

4. APPEARANCES: FOOD SHOULD LOOK KOSHER

The technical term for something which looks like something else and which could therefore deceive or mislead an innocent person is *'Mar'it ha-Ayin'* — it 'confuses the Eye'.

It is part of the Jewish ethical rather than ritual law that one should not place anyone in a situation where they might be encouraged to make a mistake. (Based on Leviticus 19:14, not 'putting a stumbling-block before someone who cannot see it.') The *'Shulchan Aruch'* describes the practice of collecting the blood of fish in a bowl as one such. It is technically permitted to eat fish blood, since Fish is *parve*, but if one saw a bowl of blood and were insufficiently educated one might perhaps think that blood itself (i.e. animal blood) was permitted; likewise diluted ground almonds look like milk and may confuse someone...

In modern times a veritable industry has developed whereby foodstuffs are prepared so as to look like something else. It is a moot point whether these transgress the rules against *Mar'it ha-Ayin* — e.g. pressed beef designed to look like bacon, or vegetarian sausages and cutlets designed to look like meat products — even 'kosher spare ribs'. etc. Modern food technology permits flavourings to be added at will, so that one can buy something called 'Smoky Bacon Crisps' which actually contains no meat at all — but the packet <u>looks</u> as though it contains pork!

It is terribly hard to draw a line once one gets into this sort of area. To some extent a person watching should have enough sense to know what is and what isn't a vegetarian 'alternative' food. How can you tell the difference between a lump of cheese which was 'cured' with rennet — an animal product — and a lump of vegetarian cheese? Does bread from a non-*Kosher* bakery (which might have been baked with some animal fat) look so different from similar bread from a *Kosher* one?

The result is that one has to make a personal choice as to what to accept and observe and what not. Some play safe and eat (or use as washing materials) only items which bear a special label, a *'Hechsher'* (from the same Hebrew word as *'Kasher'*) which specifies that the foods are prepared under rabbinical supervision. Others buy vegetarian alternatives (which are often certified and marked as such), or prepared foods which may not be 'supervised' but which at least contain no animal products.

A further development is the neurosis — there is no better word for it — that drives some people to purchase daily and normal items such as butter and sugar only with a '*Hechsher*' — and moreover to become involved in deep theological debates as to the competence and piety of a specific rabbi who has given a specific *Hechsher*. One might in a *kosher* Delicatessen overhear conversations on the lines of 'Is this Antwerp Seal better than that Strasbourg Seal? Does Rabbi A's authority extend to these matters, or should I trust only Rabbi B'? There is '*Chabad*' *Shechita* and — especially if one is ordering a *kosher* meal on an airline — a variety of *kosher*, more-*kosher* and super-*kosher* variants ('*Kedassia*' and '*Adass Yisroel*' and others) and there are *Batei Din* from *Ashkenazi* and *Sephardi* and *Haredi* rabbis and exported articles from Israel with labels filled with minute Hebrew script, and from America items bearing a 'U' symbol. All of which tends to drive a person mad rather than to make them into a better and more caring person.

A fairly recent development is the reintroduction of '*Kosher* Milk' ('*Cholov Yisroel*') — which, technically, used to mean merely that it was purely cow or goat milk and was not mixed with donkey milk (donkeys not being *kosher* animals). Now it is an excuse to use different packaging and add to the price. One finds bizarre new rules introduced from time to time, often by new rabbis eager to demonstrate how strict they are. May one break an even number of eggs into a bowl? When catering at a non-Jewish hotel, must one set fire to the entire hotel to make it '*kosher*', or is it enough just to install a brand-new kitchen, new cutlery, crockery, pans, ovens, plumbing etc.? Must one spread aluminium foil over every surface in sight, using only disposable paper plates and plastic cutlery? There is no end to the demands placed by insecure persons and there can be no end, and this is why it is important sometimes to say 'Enough!'

Most Jewish institutions that care (there are some that do not care at all) have now given up on the whole business and serve purely vegetarian food — most synagogues have purely '*Milchig/Pareve*' kitchens, and it is rare that meat will be served at official functions. This demonstrates that the amount of fuss and bother is not considered worth the privilege of fulfilling the *Mitzvah* of eating *kosher* meat. And many observant Jewish households have also decided to go vegetarian, not because they truly believe it is wrong to slaughter animals for food, but because the trouble and the expense is unbearable.

There is also a concept of '*Eco-Kashrut*' whereby certain Jews will decide on moral grounds to avoid factory-farmed animals and eat only 'free-range' or 'Bio' foods — this is not in strict accordance with the letter of the *Kashrut* regulations but is, they feel, in harmony with the spirit of these rules. The same applies to boycotts of *Kosher* food manufacturers who use un*kosher* methods with their workforces.

5. KOSHER WINE

Very briefly, this is a comparatively modern concept but one which has caught on in some communities. Jews were forbidden to drink wine that had been used for pagan and heathen practices — '*Yayin Nesech*' — ('Wine which is poured out') — this would have been part of some sacrificial ritual to a pagan deity, thus making its consumption a horror! To avoid this possibility it became the practice to buy wine only from Jewish sources and vintners and even to drink wine poured only by Jews (as a non-Jewish waiter might deliberately spill a bit, without your noticing, to placate his god!)

The same problem did not apply to beer and spirits.

In later times the practice was rationalised as preventing young Jewish people from drinking with and therefore mixing socially with (or being immoral with) non-Jews.

The growth of the wine industry in Palestine in the late 19th. and early 20th. centuries and the desire to support the settlers economically led also to the recommendation by many rabbis that one should endeavour to purchase this '*kosher*' wine for *Kiddush* purposes. (Few people realise that the brand-name 'Palwin' stood for the 'Palestine Wine Company'.) Nowadays several rabbis in France and Germany, in California and South Africa and elsewhere also supervise local vineyards and the crushing and fermentation processes; *halachically* however the practice is still riddled with inconsistencies.

What are the supervisors actually guarding against? One of the treaders dropping his sandwich into the grape-tub? In practice, a lot of the supervision probably boils down to guarding against work being done on the Sabbath, or various agricultural laws to do with the mixing of species.

A separate category is '*Yayin Mevushal*', wine which has been 'cooked' (i.e. Pasteurised) to between 74° and 90°C. *Kiddush* wine is usually so treated, becomes very sweet but is then in a state where a bottle can be kept open for a lengthy period since all bacteria that could cause it to go sour and turn to vinegar have been eliminated. There is also a new method of 'flash heating'.

6. PESACH

The laws of what is and is not '*Kosher* for Passover' use are, of course, much more complex and stringent (since the *Torah* applies the threat of being 'cut off' to those who do not observe the prohibition on *Chametz*), but essentially additional to what has already been described above. Since one does not actually eat the '*Zero'ah*', the symbolic lamb bone on the *Seder* plate (assuming one has not replaced it with a carrot or parsnip) one can still have a *milchig* or pareve meal. Many households endeavour to have another complete set (or sets) of crockery etc. for use during the *Pesach* week.

The rules are more concerned with matters of possible fermentation, of the presence of grains or yeasts, and again most people simply look for the appropriate labels. (N.B.: The production of the '*Kasher lePesach*' labels is often more profitable for retailers than the production of food...)

7. HYGIENE

One hears frequently that 'Hygiene has nothing to do with *Kashrut*' and vice versa. Strictly speaking, from a legalistic point of view this might be correct — but in fact it is wrong, and dangerously wrong. The presence of dirt or insects would not be allowed in a fully-*kosher* kitchen. In Leviticus Ch. 19:7-8 it is made clear that anyone who eats sacrificial meat that is no longer fresh takes upon themselves the responsibility for what happens. Meat should not be left out for long periods, liquids would be covered, utensils cleaned thoroughly.

8. CONCLUSION

This chapter should not be taken as a definitive guide to *Kashrut*, but it does explore some of the underlying concepts and some of the details. There are many pitfalls for the unwary and many different customs. For example:

Is Fowl, Poultry to be considered Meat? Birds are not mammals, they do not produce milk, and so there is no way one can boil a chicken in its mother's milk (though one can eat an egg and a chicken at the same time!) An Egg, although produced by a fowl, is classed as '*Pareve*' and so can be mixed with milk (in an omelette). Apparently one Jewish community, that of Rome, decided (quite logically) that fowl (Hebrew '*Off*') could therefore be eaten with milk products. (Of course, one still has to slaughter the chicken properly before eating it!)

Fish also has to be killed before being eaten. Strict Vegetarians therefore abstain from these also — and Vegans also from Eggs — yet according to the laws of *Kashrut* they are to be treated also as *Pareve* (so long as there is no blood spot in the egg, indicating that it had been fertilised).

How long should one wait after eating meat, before being free once more to eat milk? Some say six hours (including Maimonides and the '*Kitzur Shulchan Aruch*'). Others say three hours, yet others say one hour. Is the main principle that of making a clear distinction, or of ensuring that even one's intestines and bowel are clear?

One can go much further. Certain food additives, known by the 'E' numbers, are considered *kosher* and others not — yet at least one well-known (in Britain) brand of *kosher*, supervised margarine contained an ingredient with a 'forbidden' E-number. On investigation the firm responded that there are in fact different types of E-such-and-such and that the type they use is in fact all right…

In the end one has to say that there is a lot of truth in the statement that 'You Are What You Eat' — Indeed, the way you eat and who you eat with are also ways of characterising a person. Does one make-do continually with 'junk food', eaten in the street or at work? Does one scoff large quantities of greasy muck in an insalubrious establishment? Does one care at all about what is in the food served?

The laws of *Kashrut*, in essence, boil down to a concern about what one eats — the sort of animal or fish, the way the creature lived and died, the way the food was prepared, and so on.

Keeping *Kosher* does not have to entail becoming neurotic, or bankrupt, and most Jews end up with some form of legitimate compromise.

It is food eaten in a spirit of distrust or dislike which causes physical — and spiritual — indigestion!

CHAPTER 25

MEZUZAH

1. INTRODUCTION

The Hebrew word '*Mezuzah*' means literally 'door-post' or 'gate-post'. As such it appears several times in the Bible: referring to a normal house in Exodus 12:7, Ex. 12:22, Ex. 12.23, Ex. 21:6, Deuteronomy 6:9, Deut. 11:20, Isaiah 57:8; to the Temple gate in I. Samuel 1:9, I Kings 6:33, Ezekiel 41:21, Ezek. 43:8, etc.; to a city gate in Judges 16:3.

Twice, in Deut. 6:9 and 11:20 the *Torah* states: '*U'Chtavtam al-Mezuzot Beytecha u'vi'Sha'arecha*' — 'You shall write them (i.e. the words of God) upon the *Mezuzot* of your house and on your gates.' In consequence the word *Mezuzah* has come to mean not the doorpost itself, but what is written upon or attached to it. It is in this sense that it is now commonly used.

2. THE '*MEZUZAH*'

The *Mezuzah* itself consists nowadays of a piece of parchment made from the skin of a clean animal. This is known as a '*Klaf*. It is normally rolled up tight and placed inside a case, which is then nailed (or otherwise attached) to the doorpost in a prominent position. The case can be of wood, metal, plastic, even glass or ceramic material (though be careful with the hammer!) and can be of varied size and degree of ornamentation. However the important part is not the case but the text itself enclosed inside it!

Over the centuries different customs have developed — *Karaites*, for example, used blank tablets without any writing at all — but the 'standard' rabbinic *Mezuzah* consists of the two sections of Deuteronomy mentioned above — Deuteronomy 6:4-9 and 11:13-21 (known as the 'First and Second Paragraphs of the *Shema*') written in square ('Assyrian') Hebrew script in 22 lines. Traditionally it must be properly hand-written by a certified scribe (a '*Sofer*') though many currently on the market consist of photographed or photocopied texts which are not considered '*Kosher*' (because the text says 'You shall write…' and not 'You shall affix.').

The *Klaf* has the text on one side and, on the reverse, some other markings. The text is written in a standard scribal form with each of the paragraphs ending in an 'open' manner. On the reverse is the word '*Shaddai*' and, upside down and near the top of the *Klaf*, the mysterious nonsense-formula '*Kozo B'mochs'z Kozo*'. The *Klaf* may be sold in a packet which might be printed with an assurance that the *Klaf* has been prepared '*Al-Yedei Va'ad leKashrut Stam, BePhikuach Harav...*' — meaning 'prepared through the auspices of the Council for the *Kashrut* of *Sifrei Torah*, *Tefillin* and *Mezuzot*' (hence the acronym 'S-T-M') under the supervision of Rabbi So-and-So.'

3. THE REVERSE SIDE

The wording on the Reverse side is of interest. The word '*Shaddai*' is one of the mysterious terms used for God and for Divine Power and is often translated as 'The Almighty', i.e. 'The One of Limitless Power'. According to one interpretation it comprises also the initial letters of the phrase '*Shomer D'latot Yisrael*' — 'Guardian of the Doors of Israel'.

Maimonides (1135-1204) in his '*Mishneh Torah*', '*Hilchot Mezuzah*' 5:4 writes:

'There is a widespread custom to write down the word *Shaddai* on the outer side of the *Mezuzah*, opposite the blank space between the two sections. Since it is written on the outside, there is no harm done. On the other hand, those who write inside the *Mezuzah* names of angels or names of saintly men, some biblical verse or some charms, are included among the individuals who have no share in the world to come. Those fools not only fail to fulfil the commandment but they treat an important precept, which conveys God's Oneness as well as the love and worship of Him, as if it were an amulet to benefit themselves, since they foolishly suppose that the *Mezuzah* is something advantageous for the vain pleasures of this world.'

This revealing comment not only shows that unauthorised additions were being made to the text, but also that the purpose of the *Mezuzah* was being misunderstood as a protective amulet against evil spirits or suchlike. This is perhaps hardly surprising; In the story of the Exodus from Egypt the Israelites were told to smear lamb's blood on their doorposts and this protected their houses from visitations from the 'Angel of Death'.

In Talmudic times the concept of the *Mezuzah* as a guard against evil was known and understood. The difference between God and a human King is described in Tractate '*Avodah Zarah*' 11a thus: 'A human king sits in his house, and his subjects stand outside to guard him; [In contrast] God's subjects stay in their houses, and He keeps guard over them.'

Throughout Jewish history there have been tendencies towards superstition, belief in demons and dybbuks and efforts to ward them off — and these tendencies have been fought continuously, as we see from Maimonides' attack and his grudging acceptance of one such 'custom', on the grounds that at least it does not affect the text itself.

The other line is in fact a code, a cryptogram formed by moving the alphabet forward by one letter, so that *Yud* becomes *Kaf*, *Hey* becomes *Vav*, *Vav* becomes *Zayin* and so on. If one moves the letters back again one place the text reads 'The Lord, Our God, the Lord' — '*YHVH Aleph/Lamed/Hey/Yud/Nun/Vav YHVH*' — '*Adonai Eloheynu Adonai*'.

This practice was known to the 13[th.]-century commentator Asher ben Yechiel. Why the text is written so is unknown, nor why it is written upside down — though the two facts may be connected inasmuch as, once it was established that it should be written upside-down, then it would not be considered respectful to write the Name of God in its normal form. There is even a theory that it was just a 'warming-up' and a testing exercise of his pen by the *Sofer*, before he turned over and wrote the 'proper text'!

The rules for writing a *Mezuzah*, the length of lines, the style of script and layout, how it should be rolled, and so on can be found in the *Talmud*, Tractate '*Menachot*' 31b-41b.

4. FORMAT

The parchment is rolled up tightly. According to Maimonides this is done from the bottom to the top, so that anyone opening it would be able to read the first line easily. This would also accord with the interpretation that the *Mezuzah* is to be fixed horizontally. However, they are nowadays rolled from right to left, i.e. from the beginnings of the lines, so that when rolled the word '*Shaddai*' on the reverse is visible.

Because most protective cases are not transparent the letter *Shin* is usually carved, engraved, painted or moulded on them, or even the whole word '*Shaddai*.'

5. WHERE SHOULD THE *MEZUZAH* BE FIXED?

The basic rules are simple though there has been (of course!) much scope for argument.

Firstly: The command is 'on the Doorpost'; But where? Which side, how high, which direction, how big? The accepted tradition is that the rolled parchment is placed at approximate shoulder-height on the right-hand side of the door as one goes in to a house or flat or room. The right side has nothing to do with whether one is right-handed or not; Right is traditionally, in many cultures, the 'good side'. In case of doubt the priority is always to an outer door, which is passed by more people, than an inner one, which is used by fewer or only by one specific individual.

Secondly, the command is 'of your houses'; this is interpreted to mean dwelling-places where one lives for a period of time — not offices, shops, factories, tents, temporary (e.g. hotel) rooms, a *Sukkah* and so on. In the *Diaspora* one has thirty days after moving in to new accommodation before it becomes mandatory to affix a *Mezuzah*.

However it has become the custom in relatively recent times to fix a *Mezuzah* even to non-dwellings, to public buildings and even synagogues, though this is not mandatory and is effectively just a form of dedication of a particular building. There is even a custom that one does not need a *Mezuzah* on a room in which there is a copy of the *Torah* (because, after all, the aim is to 'remind you' of these teachings and the presence of a copy implies that one is already aware of them; so a synagogue or a Yeshivah classroom would not need one. Nevertheless, one is often affixed).

Thirdly, the understanding has been that a *Mezuzah* should be fixed to every room in which one 'lives' — i.e. every room apart from bathrooms, lavatories, storerooms, stables and garages and suchlike. Modern homes are sometimes much more complex than their Biblical or Talmudic counterparts, with more porches, halls, balconies, foyers, 'winter gardens', walk-in cupboards, open-plan areas, walk-in-cupboards and the like, so the exact definition of a 'room' is not always an easy one!

Fourthly, it should be placed at an angle, slanting at roughly 45° inwards towards the top. This position is itself a deliberate compromise. According to *Rashi* (1040-1105), based presumably on earlier traditions he had received, the *Mezuzah* should be placed vertically; according to his grandson Jacob ben Meir Tam, a rabbi in France known affectionately as '*Rabbenu Tam*' (1100-1171), who was also a famous commentator and who frequently disagreed with his grandfather's opinions, it should be placed horizontally! So to be fair to both and to indicate perhaps to everyone who enters the house how important the art of Compromise can be it is now usually slanted at approximately 45° (depending on how wide the doorpost itself is — if it is a narrow doorpost the degree of slope will have to be less, but this does not really matter).

The Deuteronomy passage continues with 'on your gates' (in the plural). The *Talmud* (Tractate '*Yoma*' 11a) interprets this to include the gates of courtyards, gates of cities and gates of provinces (i.e. border posts). In other words, in the same way as in modern life one erects signs welcoming 'Careful Drivers', announcing with which foreign city one is 'twinned', perhaps indicating when church services are held or even warning against smuggling, the idea was that any traveller would immediately, on entering an Israelite area, be made aware that this was a place where Monotheists lived — a statement of principle as well as information, perhaps akin to the custom of erecting signs 'Nuclear-Free Zone'! (Once upon a time certain towns had signs at the entrance reading 'Jews not Wanted Here'...)

Nowadays the word 'Gate' for most urban or suburban dwellers means their garden gate. In the Middle East however houses were built with surrounding courtyards in which the livestock and the servants dwelt, so the gate into the courtyard was actually the main entrance to the property. In the towns the Gate was the open area where public meetings and law-courts might be held.

6. WHAT DOES ONE SAY?

The brief service of Dedication of a Building or '*Chanukat haBayit*', with the appropriate blessings for affixing a *Mezuzah*, can be found in the *Siddur* pp.308-309;

pp.436-437, (*'Lev Chadash' p.601-603*). Essentially they comprise the *Berachot* '*Shehecheyanu*' and '*…al likbo'ah haMezuzah*', plus the '*Shema*' passage itself.

Anyone can perform this ritual — it does after all refer to 'YOU shall do it on YOUR house.' Of course it can be combined with a house-warming or a dedication party.

It is not vital to nail the *Mezuzah* case to the doorpost — modern houses may have doorposts of metal and so a glue is quite adequate. The commandment is to 'fix the *Mezuzah*', not to break it with a hammer while trying to fix it.

7. WHAT ABOUT WHEN ONE MOVES AWAY?

The *Mezuzah* is your property, yet it becomes an integral part of the house when you fix it. If you sell your house to a Jew you are meant to leave any *Mezuzot* in situ and include them in the sale; If you sell to a non-Jew you may remove them, but should make it clear to the purchaser that you will be doing so and why and maybe leaving marks on the doorposts.

8. WHAT ABOUT CHECKING?

Every now and then the Jewish press contains fervent pleas that householders should have their *Mezuzot* checked — some of the more extreme fundamentalists have even claimed that those who didn't have theirs checked were more liable to suffer a disaster, a rather strange idea akin to the concept of the 'magic' only working under certain circumstances. Occasionally one reads bizarre statements that the victim of some tragedy was somehow themselves to blame because their *Mezuzah* text, when checked afterwards, has a letter faded or missing…

Of course hand-written texts do fade and deteriorate in time and scribes have a living to make in checking and re-touching the letters and, according to one opinion, they should be checked twice in every seven years — (in the same way as, say, a Smoke Detector or electrical wiring or heaters should be checked that they are still functioning correctly).

However a tightly-rolled, protected parchment should not really fade or become damp, especially if affixed indoors and it is more likely to be damaged by removing it for checking.

Here, from an item in the 'Jewish Chronicle' 17[th.] Jan. 1986:

> 'The London Beth Din has made arrangements for *kosher mezuzot*, specially produced under supervised auspices in Israel, to be sold here. Large numbers of invalid *mezuzot* have been arriving in this country from Israel. In a statement… this week, *Dayan* Chanoch Ehrentreu, head of the London Beth Din, explained: 'Mezuza-writing, unfortunately, is frequently done in private homes, without any proper form of control or supervision. Apart from deliberate forgeries, paper photocopies and suchlike, many are written without due care and attention to all the *halachic* requirements, resulting in a mezuzah which is posul (invalid) and

virtually worthless.

Sometimes, in order to boost production and increase earnings, irresponsible individuals, or even children, are employed.

An extremely high proportion of random samples checked by the Chief Rabbinate of Israel, and independently, were recently found to be completely posul. These abuses have compelled the rabbinate in Israel to withdraw its sanction from all *mezuzot*.' ·

As a result, *Dayan* Ehrentreu added, special societies for the training and supervision of scribes have been set up in Israel and America to ensure that proper standards are maintained. The London Beth Din was arranging for *mezuzot* produced by them to be sold here…They are slightly larger than those used in the average household but… they were certainly reasonably priced.'

This is an interesting example of how what starts out as a simple rule — for each individual to write some words on their doorpost — can lead to cottage industries and abuses!

Never forget — the *Mezuzah* is not a magic charm that will protect your house from burglars (unless they are VERY superstitious, ignorant and stupid!!) or from fire, flood, earthquake or rot, but it IS there to remind you that God should always be present in your life, at home and not just occasionally in the Synagogue.

CHAPTER 26

TEFILLIN

1. INTRODUCTION

The wearing of 'Tefillin' (also known by their Greek-derived name 'Phylacteries') is one of the stranger and more complex customs of Judaism. It has been said that

> 'There are more laws — ascribed to oral delivery by God to Moses — clustering about the institution of Tefillin than about any other institution of Judaism.' ('Jewish Encyclopaedia' Vol. X. 21f.)

As so often, the basic idea is quite simple. The traditional custom is that, during the Daily Morning service (i.e. not on *Shabbatot* and on *Chagim* (Festivals) and there is dispute concerning *Chol HaMo'ed*) adult male Jews wear certain scriptural verses, which are symbolically tied over the upper left arm and forehead, so as to come close to the heart when the arm is held against the chest and on the forehead so as to be close to the brain or mind. These verses are written on parchments, which are placed for protection (against sweat etc.) inside secure leather boxes and tied on with flexible leather straps. Presumably the original purpose was to assist one in preparing for and concentrating on one's prayers — the word *Tefillin* (which is first used in the *Mishnah*) is an Aramaic plural form of the Hebrew word 'Tefillah' meaning 'Prayer'. It is possible that they were at one point worn all day but, during the times of Roman persecution, restricted to use during prayers only. (N.B. The word 'Phylactery' is derived from a Greek word meaning 'Protection' — as in the word 'Prophylactic' — and perhaps reflects a superstitious belief in *Tefillin* as a form of protective amulet to ward off evil.)

The Rabbis derived from this basic concept a complex and detailed set of regulations concerning the exact size and shape of the boxes in which the texts are held, the manner in which the texts are written and inserted and the manner in which they are worn. It is claimed that all these rules came 'MiMoshe miSinai' — 'From Moses on Mount Sinai' — but it is hard to believe this in any rational way. However early *Tefillin* have been found amongst the relics discovered near the Dead Sea and it is clear that the basic traditions had become concrete and accepted by *Mishnaic* times.

The reason for not wearing *Tefillin* on *Shabbat* and *Chagim* was that they are classified as an 'Ot HaBrit', a 'Sign of the Covenant' with God. Other 'Ottiyot' include *Milah* (Circumcision — which is certainly not removed on certain days!

Gen. 17:11), and the '*Keshet*' (Rainbow — Genesis 9:12, 13, 17) which is not under human control. *Shabbat* itself is an '*Ot*' (Ex. 31:13, 17) and therefore additional duplication is considered unnecessary.

2. WHAT ARE *TEFILLIN*?

Tefillin come in pairs; they consist of two square boxes, each made of a single piece of leather and painted black and each affixed to a base. One, known as the '*Tefillah shel Yad*', that 'of the Hand', is attached to a long leather strap which passes through a small knotted loop, allowing adjustments to be made. This is worn on the upper portion of the left arm, the strap is drawn through the loop to hold it tightly against the inner arm so that the box faces the left side of the chest. The strap is then wound round the arm (some say seven times) and then over the palm of the left hand (three times, so that it makes a pattern, like the Hebrew letter '*Shin*') and the remainder wound round the middle finger, to hold it tight and prevent the whole strap unwinding. (Some say that in this way it represents also the Hebrew letter '*Yud*').

The other is the '*Tefillah shel Rosh*', that 'of the Head'. This is attached to a lengthy strap in such a way that a large loop, permanently knotted, is formed with the two loose ends (of some length) springing from the knot. The loop is worn over the crown of the head like a form of headdress with the box high over the forehead (some say that this is where the hidden 'third eye' is situated) and the loose ends just dangling down without any function.

The two *Tefillin* are therefore easily distinguishable, being specifically designed for the different parts of the Body on which they are worn. Nothing should come between the *Tefillin* and the skin, so wrist-watches, shirt-sleeves etc. have to be removed. (This is of course not wholly logical because the leather, and not the parchment itself, is then in contact with the skin!)

The leather boxes themselves are called '*Battim*' (Houses); that for the hand ('*shel Yad*') is smooth on all sides; that for the Head ('*shel Rosh*') is scribed with vertical lines to signify the four compartments inside it and bears on the two vertical sides (i.e. not the front and back) a letter '*Shin*' but written unusually with four vertical strokes rather than three. The exact reason for this strange letter is not known — but see below.

They are usually kept in a small velvet bag when not in use.

3. WHAT'S INSIDE THE *TEFILLIN*?

Each of the two boxes contains exactly the same text, consisting of four passages from the *Torah*:

Exodus 13:1-10
Exodus 13:11-16
Deuteronomy 6:4-9
Deuteronomy 11:13-21.

The first two deal with the duty of Jews always to remember their liberation from Slavery and their duty to teach their children of these matters; the latter two are what are now known as the First and Second Paragraphs of the *Shema* (as in a *Mezuzah*). Originally the Ten Commandments formed a fifth passage, but this was omitted from the *Tefillin* once Christians began claiming that these were the only important commandments, as a direct reaction to their claim. Some say that the four strokes of the *Shin* reflect the emphasis on there now being only four and not five passages.

For the 'Hand-*Tefillin*' — '*Tefillah shel Yad*' — these passages are written together on one small scroll of parchment and inserted into the hollow compartment formed by the box; for the Head-*Tefillin* ('*Tefillah shel Rosh*') they are written on four separate small scrolls and inserted in order into four compartments formed inside the box by thin partitions.

According to *Rashi* (1040-1105) the passages should be in the order in which they appear in the *Torah* — i.e. the order as given above. His grandson *Rabbenu Tam* however (1100-1171) decided that the latter two should be reversed, so that the first paragraph of the *Shema* (Deut. 6:4-9) would come last. Why the difference? A good question. But the consequence is that whilst nearly all modern *Tefillin* follow *Rashi*'s pattern some Jews (just to be on the safe side!) change their *Tefillin* part-way through the service and put on a set arranged according to *Rabbenu Tam* as well. What good this is supposed to do to themselves, their souls or the world is not clear.

4. WHY ARE *TEFILLIN* IMPORTANT?

For some reason a large proportion of Jews sees the mere physical act of wearing *Tefillin* as frightfully important. Male tourists in Israel are often accosted by members of a certain fundamentalist sect asking them to put on a pair and say the appropriate blessing, and a set is often given to a Bar-*Mitzvah* boy. The regular wearing of *Tefillin* is frequently used as a gauge by which to measure a person's piety.

Yet — the original Biblical passages exhorted the Jew to keep certain <u>words</u> and divine concepts always in mind, to 'bind them as a sign upon your hand and as a frontlet between your eyes'. The word '*Totafot*', translated as 'frontlets', only occurs in Exodus 13:9, 13:16 and Deut. 6:8 and 11:18 — and could just as well mean 'encircling bands' — and indeed one could understand the verse to read 'You shall have these words 'AS *Totafot*' or even 'INSTEAD OF *Totafot*' — meaning that the words, the content, the meaning is more important than whatever else people wore on their headbands at the time. There is the question of how literally one should take this command and whether by tying the words invisibly inside boxes with black leather straps one is in danger of getting so involved with the minutiae of the ritual observance that the essential point is missed. The 'Jerusalem *Talmud*' ('*Sotah*' 3:4) points to this danger:

'Who is the pious fool? He who sees a child struggling in the water and says: 'When I have taken off my *Tefillin* I will go and save him,' and while he does so the child drowns.'

And yet… religion must never remain something totally abstract, but should involve observance and a continuing quest for meaning. Sometimes a particular ritual might have meaning, sometimes not — but it is dangerous to deny all validity to a particular observance. Franz Rosenzweig, on being asked whether he wore *Tefillin*, answered 'Not yet', leaving his options open…

The Reform attitude is that *Tefillin* are an optional part of the traditional morning observance, whether in private or as part of public worship. The appropriate blessing may be found in the RSGB *Siddur* pp.212-215; **pp. 30f.**

Traditionally it was, of course, also an exclusively male observance. It was because their wearing was considered to be a command (*Mitzvah*) observed only on specific occasions — i.e. a 'time-bound *Mitzvah*' — that rabbinic authorities exempted women from wearing *Tefillin*. This exemption evolved in later traditional Judaism into a prohibition (as with other such *Mitzvot* such as the wearing of *Tallit*) but Reform Judaism would permit women to wear *Tefillin* if they so chose.

It is now a matter of personal choice whether *Tefillin* are worn on a weekday morning. If the act of putting them on and wearing them helps one to concentrate upon the devotions, their purpose has been fulfilled — but they should never be seen as a substitute for religious thought or religious (and ethical) action. The fact that they are often so seen by other members of the Jewish community, who display an almost superstitious regard for them, merely reveals the weaknesses of human nature.

CHAPTER 27

HEAD-COVERINGS

1. INTRODUCTION

It is now an accepted matter of public knowledge that 'Jews cover their heads'. Such was not always the case and the exact manner, the occasion and style of head-covering and even the question of whether to cover the head at all have become matters of heated debate within the Jewish community. As one of the more obvious 'outward signs' of piety or supposed piety, the use or non-use of a head-covering and the type of covering used are frequently cited in terms of a person's character or depth of religious observance.

In fact the custom, widespread though it is, appears to be the result of a combination of influences, among them the interpretation of, and imitation of, certain Biblical passages; anti-Semitic decrees; a desire to 'be different'; a desire for modesty; common sense in countries that are either extremely hot or extremely cold; and fashion.

2. HEAD-COVERING IN THE BIBLE

Nowhere in the *Torah* is a head-covering made obligatory for the average Jew. In Exodus Chap. 28, in which the clothing of the the High Priests is described, verses 4 and 37 refer to a '*Mitznefet*', normally translated as a 'Mitre'; verse 40 refers to '*Migba'ot*', translated as 'Caps' or 'Turbans'.

It is sometimes stated that Jews wear a head-cover in imitation of the priests; however, the priestly robes were quite complex and included such unusual (for the time) garments as under-drawers (Ex. 28:42). We are even told in the *Mishnah* ('*Sukkah*' 5:3) that in the time of the Second Temple they made wicks from the worn-out underwear of the priests, so these were considered significant garments. However, no one has so far suggested that Jews wear underwear in memory of the priests, so this argument in favour of head-covering seems weak.

To cover one's head and face was a sign of mourning — as in 2 Sam. 15:30: 'David went up the ascent of the Mount of Olives, weeping as he went, barefoot, and with his head covered; and all the people who were with him covered their heads…'

In 2 Sam. 19:5 (19:4 in Christian Bibles) David mourns his son Avshalom and is accused by Joab, because 'the King covered his face and the king cried with a loud voice…'

The mere fact that this is described as happening indicates that these are exceptions and that people's heads were not normally covered. The prophet Jeremiah describes a period of drought, when the people afflicted themselves and went into a form of semi-mourning: (14:3f.)

> 'Her nobles send their servant for water:
> They come to the cisterns,
> They find no water,
> They return with their vessels empty;
> They are ashamed and confounded and cover their heads,
> Because of the ground which is dismayed,
> since there is no rain on the land.
> The farmers are ashamed,
> they cover their heads.
> ('Revised Standard Version' translation)

Apart from a similar reference in Esther 6:12 when Haman returns to his wife 'mourning, and with his head covered' after being discomfited, this is all there is in the *Tanakh* — and it would appear that, by the very nature of these references, something unusual is being described.

3. HEAD-COVERING IN THE TALMUD

As is normal, one can find contradictory references in rabbinic literature. '*Mo'ed Katan*' 15a states that mourners, lepers and those placed under a '*Cherem*' ('Exclusion', 'Excommunication') should cover their heads — an obvious indication that they would therefore stand out from the rest of the population. '*Ta'anit*' 14b declares that those fasting during a drought should (as in Jeremiah Ch. 14) cover their heads — so those not fasting, or at more fruitful times, would clearly not do so.

On the other hand to cover one's head was also seen as a sign of status as a scholar, or as an indication of awe and reverence, in the Divine Presence, during prayer or deep, mystical studies

However it does not follow that this necessarily means a head-covering as such — more of a wrapping-around with one's *Tallit*, around and over the head. Thus in '*Rosh Hashanah*' 17b, interpreting a passage from Ex. 34:6, Rabbi Yochanan says: 'This verse teaches us that the Holy One, blessed be He, drew His robe round Him like the *Shaliach Tzibbur* (the leader or reader) of a congregation and showed Moses the order of prayer.'

In '*Ta'anit*' 20a the tale is told of Nakimon ben Gurion who owed a non-Jew a large amount of water in a time of drought. He entered the Temple, depressed, and wrapped himself in his cloak and prayed for rain. Afterwards he did the same to stop the rain falling.

In '*Chagigah*' 14b Rabbi Eleazar ben Arak asks Rabbi Yochanan ben Zakkai to teach him some of the mystic knowledge termed '*Ma'asei Merkavah*' — 'The Works of the Chariot' — in reference to Ezekiel Chap. 1 where the prophet flies up to heaven in a flaming chariot. Before starting Yochanan dismounted from his ass and wrapped himself up — in what Israel Abrahams designates, in the notes to the Soncino edition, as his *Tallit*: 'By wrapping himself in his *Tallit*, R. Yochanan ben Zakkai showed his sense of the holiness of the occasion.'

Perhaps as a derivative of this idea developed the concept that one showed awe of heaven by keeping one's head covered. In '*Shabbat*' 118a, in the context of various rabbis describing how well they have behaved in terms of their modesty and humility, Rabbi Chuna ben Rabbi Yoshua said: 'May I be rewarded for never walking four cubits bare-headed.' In '*Kiddushin*' 31a in a parallel passage we find 'Rabbi Yoshua ben Levi said: 'One may not walk four cubits with haughty mien, for it is said (Isaiah 6:3): 'the whole earth is full of His glory'.' Since Rabbi Chuna is mentioned specifically as having kept his head covered, one can deduce that others did not.

Elsewhere a head-covering known as a '*Sudarium*' is referred to as the head-covering worn by a married man (Rabbi Kahana in '*Kiddushin*' 8a; Rabbi Hammuna in '*Kiddushin*' 29b). Indeed, the latter passage relates a slight argument when Hammuna, having been praised as a great scholar, appears for an interview without his *Sudarium*. When asked why he has no head-dress, he replies that he is not married and he is told to go away and get married straight away! Jastrow's Dictionary defines a *Sudarium* as a form of scarf or turban, something wound around the head or neck and even used (on occasion) for strangling people!

It is possible that a superstitious belief in the power of wearing a head-covering developed as a consequence. There is a tale in '*Shabbat*' 156b, often quoted as a source for the custom, which is actually designed to combat astrology and superstition: 'Rabbi Nachman ben Isaac's mother was told by astrologers, 'Your son will be a thief.' So she did not let him go bare-headed, saying to him, 'Cover your head so that the fear of heaven may be upon you, and pray.' Now, he did not know why she spoke that to him. One day he was sitting and studying under a palm tree; the evil inclination overcame him, he climbed up it and bit off a cluster (of dates) with his teeth.'

The idea is that the doom pronounced by astrologers can be averted by pious actions. However we are not told if Nachman was wearing a head-covering at the time he climbed the tree! Did it fall off? The mother's pedagogic methods are also suspect, not explaining the reasons for her instructions!

Finally, in '*Nedarim*' 30b a person who makes a vow not to benefit from people with black hair is allowed to benefit from women and children — 'because men sometimes cover their heads and sometimes not; but women's hair is always covered, and children are always bare-headed.'

This brings us to the point that all the above, till now, have referred to men only; however, in *Mishnaic* times it was the norm for women's hair to be covered and violation of this practice was sufficient grounds for a divorce without payment of the *Ketubah* sum ('*Ketubot*' 7:6).

It is worth noting that illustrations from around this period — on Egyptian or Babylonian tablets, or in mosaics in synagogues — normally showed Israelites (or Jews) without any head-covering.

4. IN LATER RABBINIC WRITINGS

The dispersed Jewish people were exposed to a variety of influences. Greeks offered sacrifices with uncovered heads whereas Roman priests sacrificed with covered heads — evidence of the danger of quoting *'Chukkat HaGoy!'* — 'The customs of the non-Jews!' — polemically as a reason for Jews to cover or not!

Paul, a contemporary Jew, in his first 'Epistle to the Corinthians' (1 Cor. 11:4-7) told the early Christians:

> 'Any man who prays or prophesies with his head covers dishonours his head, but any woman who prays or prophesies with her head unveiled dishonours her head — it is the same as if her head were shaven. For if a women will not veil herself, then she should cut off her hair; but if it is disgraceful for a woman to be shorn or shaven, let her wear a veil. For a man ought not to cover his head, since he is the image and glory of God, but woman is the glory of man.'

In verses 9 and 10, Paul (clearly a misogynist) attempts to justify this discrimination by reference to Genesis 1:26 and 2:21-23, then in verses 11 and 12 he undermines his position by stating that nowadays things have changed since the time of the Creation. He therefore returns, belligerently, to the defence of his original prejudice in verses 13-16, rhetorically asking:

> 'Judge for yourselves; is it proper for a woman to pray to God with her head uncovered? Does not nature itself teach you that for a man to wear long hair is degrading to him, but if a woman has long hair, it is her pride? For her hair is given to her for a covering. If anyone is disposed to be contentious — we recognise no other practice, nor do the churches of God.'

So there! Though not, strictly speaking, a Rabbinic writer, Paul is clearly laying down rules for a religious community of believers in early *Mishnaic* times — albeit a group which became a 'breakaway'. This passage is quoted at length to demonstrate that one could legitimately argue, if one wished, that the practice of male Jews covering their heads in prayer could be equally well understood as a deliberate move to distinguish themselves from Christians — whereas the practice of women covering their heads could be understood as 'Chukkat HaGoy'!

In the *Midrash* ('Shemot Rabbah' 3) the behaviour of Moses in covering his face in awe of God in Ex. 3:6 is contrasted with the behaviour of his nephews Nadav and Avihu in Ex. 24:9f. (though it is not there stated in the text) in gazing upon God bare-headed and hence less-reverentially — in consequence of which they were killed later in Lev. 10:2.

In Islamic countries it was universal for men to cover their heads in prayer, or when receiving guests, and one might even swear by the turban as an important object.

By the Middle Ages the various Codes and the commentaries upon them reveal a mixture of attitudes. Maimonides in his '*Mishneh Torah*' ('*Hilchot* De'ot' 5:6) considered the covering of the head to be a sign of awe and respect; this is especially important during prayer ('*Tefillah*' 5:5).

However, the 13th. century Isaac of Vienna wrote that the rabbis of France said the Prayer (presumably the '*Amidah*') with uncovered heads and that on *Simchat Torah* the boys were called to the reading bare-headed. Abraham ben Nathan of Lunel, a 13th.-century French rabbi, noted that he found during his travels in Spain that the people covered their heads during prayer — obviously something he was not used to at home and hence worth remarking upon. Whilst the '*Zohar*' ('*Nasso*' 122b) forbids any man to walk four cubits with an uncovered head (obviously basing itself upon Rabbi Chuna's teachings) Rabbi Joseph Solomon Del Medigo (1591 — 1655), a much-travelled Rabbi who grew up in Candia in Spain, then moved to Cairo, Amsterdam, Frankfurt and eventually Prague, commented on this: 'It is, however, customary in all parts of Italy, in Crete, and in many countries under the dominion of the Emperor [of Germany] and other Christian rulers.'

Isaac Luria in the 16th. century attacked his contemporaries for paying more attention to 'the mere custom' of not walking bareheaded than the more important Talmudic rule against walking four cubits 'insolently'.

David Halevi of Ostrog in the 17th. century denounced bare-headedness as 'Imitation of the Christians' ('Chukkat HaGoy') but Elijah, the Vilna *Gaon*, also considered a head-covering to be merely a matter of custom or propriety.

5. TYPES OF HEADCOVERING

It is clear that in most of the above references, what is meant (apart from priestly turbans) is a form of 'normal' headgear of the oriental type, similar to the modern Keffir, or at least to the types of headgear worn in the locality. In one of the early Reform communities, in Berlin in 1845, worshippers were obliged to remove their hats, but to wear skull-caps instead — obviously a form of compromise, to replace 'outdoor' with 'ritual' coverings.

Nowadays there are several specific types of headgear, mostly of differing cultural origins. Thus sects which maintain an Eastern-European attitude retain also the round fur hats once worn by noblemen who wished to keep their heads warm and their ears from being frostbitten during cold Russian nights — even though the wearer may now live in Jerusalem during the heat of the summer! This form of fur hat is called a 'Streimel'.

Many European Jews have adopted the forms of hat — top hats, bowlers, homburgs — once commonly worn by non-Jews as well. Just look at photographs of the early-to-mid-20th. century to see how 'normal' this once was, yet now the hat-wearers form the exception. Hats are a matter of fashion and it is now rare for a non-Jew to wear such head-coverings. Working-class Jews, especially in Eastern Europe, often wore a form of peaked cap.

The rounded 'Skullcap' has now come to signify, for most people, the 'traditional' Jewish headgear — for men only, of course! — though it is uncertain when this was first introduced as such. It is after all not that dissimilar from the caps worn by devout Moslems, or even the 'smoking caps', on an oriental model, once popular in Western Europe.

These caps are known sometimes as '*Yarmulkes*' — apparently a Russian or Polish diminutive word for 'little cap' though some argue that the name derives from the Aramaic '*Yareh Malkah*' — 'Awe of the King' — referring to the idea that a head-covering will indicate religious respect and feelings! In Yiddish it is called a '*Kappel*' — 'A little Cap' — and in modern Hebrew a '*Kippah*', 'a Cap' or 'Covering'.

As in many 'ethnic' groups it is possible to determine to some extent the allegiance and status of an individual by the variant of the basic theme that he wears. Dark hats come in differing widths of brim; *Kippot* come in silk or cotton or crocheted versions, in different sizes — from a large skull-cap to a flat egg-cosy, little more than a beer-mat — and different colours. In the contemporary Israeli political scene these differences are (or can be) of significance and one hears talk of the 'Knitted-*Kippah* brigade' ('*Kippah S'ruga*') — indicative of a certain political viewpoint.

The smaller the skull-cap, the more impractical it is to wear — especially as one's hair thins — and elaborate arrangements have to be made with different types of clip. One recent invention is a form of 'Velcro' (TM) that keeps the cap on one's head even when one bends down! Various forms of hair grip may be employed. It is clear that a small *Kippah* provides little or no protection from sun, rain, wind or cold.

6. WOMEN AND HEAD-COVERING

As mentioned above women are often considered in some extreme circles as almost a different species and horror is aroused if a woman appears wearing a *Kippah*, which is now seen as a 'masculine garment' — hence subject to the laws against transvestism.

The history of Women's head-covering and whether it varied between the married and unmarried state is as complex as that of Men's, but of much less concern because there is much less fuss made about it nowadays in most Jewish communities — albeit we see the same arguments raging in Moslem ones. The general principle was that Women covered their hair, when they did so, out of modesty rather than religious feeling — to prevent onlookers being roused to sexual lust by its beauty. Hence punishments for bad behaviour might involve disarranging the hair (Numbers 5:18 — the suspected adulteress) and captive women had their hair shaved (Jeremiah 7:29). In the *Midrash*, '*Bemidbar Rabbah*' 18:20 (on 'Numbers') On Ben Pelet's life is saved by his wife making him drunk and then sitting down outside the tent with her daughter, both having their hair uncovered. When his conspirator friends come to collect him they are shocked at the sight and so turn away. The *Talmud* ('*Baba Kamma*' 90a) sets a fine of 400 drachmas on any man who pulls off a woman's headgear in the street, thus shaming her in public. In '*Pirkei d'Rabbi Eliezer*' 14 women are described as being like mourners, hence covering their hair, because of Eve's sin — an astonishing statement and one very close to Christian doctrines of 'Original Sin'... However in many countries it came to be accepted that married women kept their hair covered and this became in effect a sign of being married. One's beautiful, lust-arousing hair became a sight reserved only for one's own husband, in private.

Some pious women prefer to shave their heads and then cover them. One contemporary custom is for women to use a headscarf for this purpose, known in Yiddish as a *'Tichl'* — 'a little Tuch' — 'Tuch' being merely the German/Yiddish word for a small cloth. (A 'Taschentuch' is a handkerchief in German). Others wear a 'Snood', a form of bag or hairnet which contains and covers the hair and can be very decorative.

Yet another custom is the wearing of a wig, known in Yiddish as a *'Sheitel'*. This custom dates from the 16th. century, and was opposed by several prominent rabbis of the period, including Moses Isserles in his comment in the *'Shulchan Aruch'* (*'Orach Chayyim'* 75:2). Sometimes the wig nowadays is more beautiful than the wearer's own hair — thus rather defeating the object of not attracting men's attention! Sometimes women will even wear a scarf over the wig! (To be fair, one occasionally sees fundamentalist men wearing a plastic bag over their hat to protect it from the elements!)

7. THE 'JEWISH HAT'

A further reason for the wearing of hats was an involuntary one. In many places in Christian countries during the Middle Ages Jews were forced to wear a distinguishing mark or badge on their clothing — a custom that was made a general order for all Christendom in 1215 at the Fourth Lateran Council under Pope Innocent III and was of course revived later by the Nazis. Even in Moslem countries, since the time of Omar in 640 Jews had been ordered to wear a yellow seam on their upper garments — compare this with the Jewish command to wear a blue thread in the clothing — and in the 11th. century Jews (and Saracens) in Egypt were compelled to wear yellow turbans. Pope Paul IV in 1555 decreed that all Jews should wear yellow hats. (It is interesting that this colour yellow should be so extensively used, though many 'badges' were also white or red or a combination of colours.) From the 13th. century pictures of Jews show them wearing pointed or conical hats — the enforced headgear known as the 'Judenhut'. Whilst distinguishing badges varied from country to country, it appears that in Austria and Poland at least the hat was the main form of distinction. Of course, to be caught not wearing such a hat meant a heavy fine, at least.

It is possible that Jews became so used to having to wear hats that, even when the regulations relaxed and there were no longer rules as to the ridiculous shape or colour, the idea of wearing a hat — almost to spite the makers of these laws — was retained.

8. THE REFORM VIEW

As we have seen, the wearing of head-coverings (by men) is simply that — a tradition rather than a specific law (except, under certain circumstances, in response to anti-Semitic laws). However, Custom (*'Minhag'*) has always played a major part in Jewish life and it is now generally accepted by the world at large that Jews wear hats. Non-Jews who attend a service or a funeral are usually concerned to 'do the right thing' and wear some form of headgear.

In the days prior to the Reform movement and in the early 19th. century in Germany there were isolated instances of preachers who did not wear a head-cover: It is noted of both Ludwig Philippson and Abraham Geiger, two early leaders of the new movement, that they did not cover their heads when preaching in the Berlin Reformgemeinde. In America however the practice of praying bare-headed was introduced in several Reform communities (starting in Baltimore and New York) and became the prevalent custom; the Conservative movement always retained head-coverings.

In Great Britain all Reform congregations and almost all Liberal congregations maintain the tradition of covering the head during prayer; however, less insistence is placed (as in Anglo-Jewry generally) on covering the head at other times. It is commonplace at functions and receptions of most denominations for the Chairman to request 'Gentlemen to cover their heads whilst Grace is said' — implying that heads are bare during the actual meal.

Now that the wearing of hats has become much less common in general, the term 'head-covering' has come to mean, almost exclusively, the purely-ritual skullcap, *Yarmulke*, *Kappel* or *Kippah*.

The wearing of hats remains a strong custom amongst women, yet many people are still shocked to see a woman wearing a *Kippah* — though Reform Judaism, with its stress in the equality of the sexes, could have no formal theological objection to this.

It has already been noted that there are many contradictions in the history of this tradition, and much scope for misunderstanding or even tragi-comedy. There are few sadder sights in the modern Jewish world than that of men at a communal function embarrassedly wearing handkerchiefs or folded serviettes on their heads, for lack of anything more dignified. To paraphrase Luria, we should place at least as much stress on what is inside the head as on what rests on top of it!

CHAPTER 28

TALLIT AND TZITZIT

1. INTRODUCTION

Often confused, the title of this chapter refers to two separate aspects of the same commandment — to wear Fringes on a Four-Cornered Garment. It is worth stressing that this commandment accomplishes nothing in itself; it is intended purely to remind us of other commandments. A sad feature of contemporary Jewish life is that some sections of the community place so much emphasis on the details of the mechanisms for reminding us constantly of the Oneness of God and the duties to our fellows which this means — the *Mezuzah*, *Tefillin* and *Tzitzit* — that the actual message of which they are reminding us tends often to get overlooked!

2. 'TZITZIT'

The Hebrew word '*Tzitzit*' (plural '*Tzitziyot*') means 'Fringe' or 'Tassel' or 'Lock' (in Ezekiel 8:3 it is used to mean a lock of hair on the forehead). Apart from this reference, its sole use in the Bible is in Numbers Ch. 15 where, in the context of a ghastly incident in which an Israelite broke the Sabbath laws and in consequence had to be put to death, God issues a command to institute precautions, reminders, to prevent this sort of incident recurring:

'The Lord spoke to Moses, saying:

'Speak to the Israelite people and instruct them to make for themselves fringes on the corners of their garments throughout their generations; let them attach a cord of blue to the fringe of each corner. That shall be your fringe: Look at it and recall all the commandments of the Lord and observe them, so that you do not follow your heart and eyes in your lustful urge. Thus you shall be reminded to observe all my commandments and to be holy to your God.' '

(Numbers 15:37-40. J.P.S.A. Translation.)

In Deuteronomy 22:12, in a sequence of miscellaneous laws we find:

'You shall make tassles on the four corners of the garment with which you cover yourself.'

Here however the Hebrew word used is '*G'dilim*', 'twisted threads', a word used only here and in I. Kings 7:17 where it refers to material festooned around columns.

From these passages it is clear that the Israelites were commanded to wear something distinctive, something that would strike the attention and remind them of what they were meant to be doing — and not be doing. That the garments had corners was not, it seems, particularly special at this time; like many peoples, a large square of cloth wound round the Body in some way was a normal item of clothing, presumably for both sexes. Attaching fringes however WAS special, and using a thread of a different and unusual colour — blue — that was very expensive and rare in ancient times would certainly stand out.

There are those who argue that the addition of fringes would actually distinguish male from female clothing. Others see them as a sign of group-identity (much as distinctive clothing has always acted; people are often judged by whether they wear ties, or top hats, or Lederhosen, or kilts, or denim — or whether they wear scarves of a specific colour denoting support for a specific football team). Some even see the wearing of fringes almost superstitiously, as a form of protective amulet. In the *Talmud* ('*Menachot*' 44a) the tale is told of a pious man who determined to visit a famous and rather expensive (400 gold Dinars!) prostitute; as he approached her, his four fringes slapped him across the face; he realised what he was doing, and stopped. The girl, hurt and insulted at this seeming rejection of her charms, wanted to know what had made this client lose interest so suddenly and, on having the miracle explained to her, gave up her profession and converted to Judaism!

In this section of the *Talmud* — '*Menachot*' 37b - 44a — are collected many of the traditions and explanations dealing with *Tzitzit*. They are only obligatory on a four-cornered garment (if one reads the text so literally), so that if one corner is cut off it is not necessary to add fringes. (This does not apply however if the corner is merely folded up and sewn down.) There is much discussion about the use of wool and linen, the colour of various threads, the method of tying and knotting the fringes, etc.

It is clear from the discussions recorded that there was much scope for argument over the details and the interpretations of this rather basic commandment.

There is also a 'Minor Tractate' of the *Talmud*, '*Massechet Tzitzit*', which deals exclusively with the rules regarding which garments and which persons are liable to the command, the relative importance of the white and blue, and the use as a shroud of a garment from which *Tzitziyot* have been removed, etc.

The extensive discussion in the *Talmud* is based on just two short references in the *Mishnah* — '*Menachot*' 3:7 and 4:1 — in which the discussion hinges upon the validity of a garment which might be missing one of the four corners and the validity of a fringe which is lacking the blue thread. The conclusion is that the four corners are vital but the blue thread can be dispensed with if necessary without breaking the command. This shows that the availability of the blue dye was already a major problem and that a compromise had to be reached; however, fringes composed purely of blue thread were also acceptable!

Other *Mishnaic* references are not really relevant; in '*Mo'ed Katan*' 3:4 a Mourner may spin thread for his *Tzitzit*; in '*Eduyot*' 4:10 the schools of Hillel and Shammai argue whether a linen cloak with woollen ornamental fringes — thus transgressing the rules of '*Sha'atnez*' — requires fringes of blue thread as well. For the record, *Beit* Shammai say it doesn't, *Beit* Hillel insist it does, if it is to be worn during the day (when the colours are presumably visible); In '*Kelim*' 16:4 and 29:1 and '*Nega'im*' 11:10 other types of fringes are meant. In '*Berachot*' 1:5 the *Shema* may be said in the morning only when the light is sufficient to distinguish blue from white (presumably in one's *Tzitzit*) and the reason for reciting the passage concerning *Tzitzit* in the Evening *Shema* (when *Tzitzit* as such are not worn) is explained as being that passage's reference to the Exodus from Egypt (which took place at night).

3. HOW THE '*TZITZIT*' IS MADE

Three thumb-breadths from the corner of a garment a hole should be made and properly sewn to prevent tearing. Through this the threads (nowadays only white) — are passed, one long and three short, and folded so as to make eight threads. The long one is wound round the others, after a double knot has been made, seven times — then tied with a further double knot; it is then wound round eight times — and a further double-knot; then eleven times — and a further double knot; then thirteen times — and a double knot. According to one interpretation, the Hebrew numerical equivalent of *Tzitzit* is 600 (*Tzadi* + *Yud* + *Tzadi* + *Yud* + *Taf* = 90 + 10 + 90 + 10 + 400) which together with eight threads and five double knots equals 613, the total number of *Mitzvot*! (Since there are in fact Four doubled threads and five doubled knots on each, i.e. at each corner, it is clear that this calculation could have arrived at a different answer had this been required; further, one of the Yods could easily have been dropped from the Hebrew spelling.)

Another tradition is that the 39 windings of the threads equal the numerical value of the words '*Adonai* Echad' — 'The Lord is One.'

The minimum length of the *Tzitzit* threads should be four thumb-lengths. A silk or cotton *Tallit* should have *Tzitziyot* of the same material, but *Tzitziyot* of wool or linen are acceptable for a *Tallit* of any material — since the fringe is not actually a part of the *Tallit* but merely affixed to it. (See the earlier reference to the *Mishnah*.)

4. THE '*TALLIT KATAN*' — THE 'LITTLE TALLIT'

Strictly speaking the rules of *Tzitzit* apply only to garments with four or more actual corners. Since Jews soon began to adopt other modes of dress, to match the peoples among whom they lived, the problem soon arose that none of their clothes had corners. Accordingly the custom arose amongst the pious of wearing a special four-cornered garment, for no other purpose than to enable them to fulfil this *Mitzvah*. The '*Tallit Katan*' is an oblong piece of cloth with a hole in the middle for the head, draped over front and back, with fringes on the corners and worn underneath the outer clothing. Opinions vary as to whether the fringes should stick out — to remind you of the *Mitzvot* but also serving to show others how pious you are — or be kept decently and modestly tucked inside.

Since Numbers 15:39 specifically mentions the purpose as being 'so that you may look upon it' this is understood to mean that *Tallit* should be worn only during daylight hours, when such looking was feasible. (This then relates to the discussion in *Mishnah 'Berachot'* 1:1 as to whether one can say there is sufficient light.) The *Tallit Katan* is therefore not worn at night. Indeed, it is only this reference to the *Mitzvah* being 'bound by time' that led to the idea that women should be exempted from the command and therefore, by later extrapolation, prohibited from it. Which leads to the question:

5. WHO MAY WEAR A '*TALLIT*'?

In the Reform movement some stir was caused initially by the desire amongst certain women to challenge this tacit prohibition. The then-RSGB published in 1987 a booklet 'Women and *Tallit*' with brief essays discussing this theme when it was still a new and hot topic. One response by non-Liberal opponents has been to declare that the *Tallit* and *Tallit Katan* have become (by custom) male garments and that for a woman to wear one is tantamount to transvestism! (See '*Menachot*' 43a) The Orthodox authority Rabbi Moshe Feinstein ruled that women could wear a *Tallit* if they did so for reasons of personal spirituality but not if it were only for reasons of political provocation — an interesting compromise in some respects, because motivation is not such a vital issue for obedience to other *Mitzvot* — but then rather spoiled matters by deciding that women's desire to do so is always political... In most Liberal synagogues it remains a minority of women who choose to wear a *Tallit* but the important thing is that they can CHOOSE.

There is also a variety of new designs of *Tallit* available, of many colours or different forms of colouring and decoration, including one produced by and for the 'Women of the Wall' group in Jerusalem.

In private anyone can choose to wear a *Tallit* during prayer, but in public worship it is advisable that those who are not or not-yet Jewish should not, simply because it could cause confusion in those communities which need to count how many Jews are present for a *Minyan* or to decide who is eligible to be given an honour during the service. In such cases, if one enters a synagogue during a morning service and a *Gabbay* offers you — as a male! — a *Tallit* a simple murmured 'No thanks' is normally enough and hopefully nobody is insulted. (And see below.)

6. THE BLUE THREAD: '*TECHEYLET*'

As has been noted, even by *Mishnaic* times the supply of blue-dyed thread was a major problem and all-white Tzitziyyot were of necessity declared acceptable.

The blue dye '*Techeylet*' was a special, sacred colour used in the hangings of the Tabernacle and in the High Priest's robes (Exodus Ch. 25-28, etc.) or for covering the sacred utensils (Numbers 4:6-12). Colour is important for many reasons; certain brands of cigarette or chocolate or petrol or public services or firms are identified by the colour used. Supporters of sports teams identify themselves with coloured scarves (and the players with coloured clothing); supporters of political parties use a colour code. In Islam green is a 'special colour'.

In the *Talmud* ('*Menachot*' 43b) Rabbi Meir explained the reason for using blue for this particular commandment:

'Blue resembles the colour of the sea, and the sea resembles the colour of the sky, and the sky resembles the colour of [a sapphire, and a sapphire resembles the colour of] the Throne of Glory, as it is said: 'And there was under his feet as it were a paved work of sapphire stone'. (Exodus 24:10). And it is also written: 'The likeness of a throne as the appearance of a sapphire stone.' (Ezekiel 1:26).' [Bracketed section found in one text.]

It was because the blue threads were harder to obtain than the white ones that Rabbi Meir went on to declare that the non-observance of the use of the latter was a more serious offence than the omission of the former.

Why was the blue colour so difficult to obtain? Until the invention of aniline dyes (extracted first from indigo plants and then from coal tar) in the 19th century Blue was the most difficult colour to synthesise. According to Rabbinic tradition the *Techeylet* was derived from a species of snail or mollusc called the '*Hillazon*' which 'resembles the sea in its essence (i.e. Blood) and in shape resembles a fish; it appears (comes up from the sea bed) once in seventy years, and with its blood one dyes the blue thread; and therefore it is so expensive.' ('*Menachot*' 44a)

In consequence one had to make sure that the dye used to colour thread was the genuine article; in '*Menachot*' 42b Rabbi Samuel described his method of testing a dye whilst it was being manufactured, but the Rabbis eventually conclude: 'There is no manner of testing the blue thread; it should therefore be bought only from an expert' — to ensure that no vegetable dye had been used instead. Despite this, various strange tests were devised by individual rabbis, whereby thread would be soaked overnight in a noisome compound or baked to see if the colour deteriorated.

In most sources the '*Hillazon*' is understood as being found only, or mainly, in Haifa Bay and along the coastline northwards up to the border with Phoenicia. At the end of the 19th century one Italian Rabbi caused consternation by declaring that the *Hillazon* — a blue-blooded fish-snail — could be found there too, and advocating that the practice of wearing a blue thread in the fringes be reintroduced. This move did not succeed. However it has been the practice to dye stripes of dark blue (or even black) into the *Tallit*, not as an actual fulfilment of the command (since only the special *Techeylet* dye would be valid for that) but as a reminder of the Blue Thread — i.e. as a visual reminder of the visual reminder!

7. THE 'TALLIT'

As mentioned above, as the style of everyday clothing changed so the chance to observe the commandment of wearing fringes became a matter of deliberate choice. It was understood (and explained by Maimonides in his 'Laws of *Tzitzit*' in the '*Mishneh Torah*' 3:1) that:

> 'The garment that one is biblically obliged to provide with fringes is a four-cornered garment or one that has more than four corners. Its size should be large enough to cover the head and greater part of the Body of a child big enough to walk by himself in the street without anyone requiring to watch and accompany him.'(Birnbaum translation)

Since few wore this sort of garment any more on a daily basis, it became the custom to wear a special cloak matching this specification during prayer. The word '*Tallit*' originally meant just a gown or a cloak, but is nowadays used to refer specifically to what has come to be known as a 'Prayer Shawl'.

This consists of a rectangular sheet, usually white with strips of black or blue (some modern ones include stripes of several colours, or Batik illustrations of Jerusalem, or other patterns) usually decorated with subsidiary fringes in addition to the obligatory *Tzitzit* at the corners, and with a special piece of cloth sewn in around the section worn at the neck, to mark the upper side. This is called the '*Atarah*' ('Diadem') and is often sewn with silver threads or embroidered, sometimes with the blessing to be said on putting on the *Tallit*.

It has become the custom amongst the pious to prefer the coarse off-white lambswool *Tallitot* of the pattern originally made in Turkey or Russia, but cotton or silk ones are also acceptable.

When not being worn the *Tallit* is normally kept folded in a small bag, usually referred to (in the Yiddish pronunciation) as a '*Tallis*-Bag'. This is often of velvet and embroidered with the word '*Tallit*' ('*Tet*' / '*Lamed*' / '*Yud*' / '*Taf*') — or perhaps the owner's initials. Some worshippers leave the *Tallit* in the synagogue during the week, some bring and take it each time, and a synagogue normally has a few spare *Tallitot* (the Yiddish plural is '*Talleysim*') available for visitors.

The *Tallit* is worn during Morning prayers (except on the morning of *Tisha B'Av*) and throughout *Yom Kippur* from Evening ('*Kol Nidrei*') to Evening ('*Ne'ilah*'). In many communities it is the custom for the *Chazan* or '*Shaliach Tzibbur*' (i.e. the person leading the service) or for anyone else reading from the pulpit to don a *Tallit* as well, even during an Evening service — this is more out of 'Respect for the Congregation' — ('*Kibbud HaTzibbur*') — since when wearing a *Tallit* it is not so important whether one is wearing a smart suit or not beneath it.

In the *Talmud* there are references to scholars enveloping themselves in the *Tallit* so as to cut out all extraneous distractions during prayers; normally however the

Tallit is draped over the shoulders. From the 18[th.] or 19[th.] centuries the *Tallit* was also worn in some communities folded, like a scarf more than a shawl.

In *Ashkenazi* communities even children wear small *Tallitot*; in *Sephardic* communities it was once the custom that only married men would wear a *Tallit*. The *Tallit* can even be spread over a couple to form a *Chuppah*. In some communities a *Chatan* (bridegroom) wears a *Tallit* under the *Chuppah*. Jews are usually buried in their *Tallit*, but in this case one of the fringes is cut off to make the garment ritually invalid ('*Possul*').

A father may wear a *Tallit* when saying the blessings for the circumcision of his son.

A *Tallit* is not normally worn when on a Cemetery.

In the *Talmud* ('*Menachot*' 43a) it is stated that one should not sell a garment with fringes to a non-Jew, since this might confuse a Jew into thinking that he was with a fellow-Jew whereas he could actually be in the company of a disguised robber! From this we see that the *Tzitzit* were seen very much as a type of distinguishing uniform. In consequence, when a non-Jew visits a synagogue it is the custom to ask that he cover his head — out of respect, though this is a later custom — but not that he wear a *Tallit*, since this is a command only upon Jews.

8. THE BLESSING

Since the *Tzitzit* (albeit not the *Tallit* itself) is a Biblical commandment, there is a *Berachah* to be said. This can be found in the *Siddur* p. 212; **p.28**) preceded by a brief meditation. It may be noted that this traditional meditation refers to to *Tzitzit* in the singular. The command is translated as 'to wrap ourselves in the *Tallit*' whereas the Hebrew refers to the *Tzitzit*.

9. CURRENT REFORM AND LIBERAL PRACTICE

As with *Tefillin*, we see in the history of the Fringes a development from a period when they were worn continuously to a period when only pious scholars maintained the custom in a distinctive manner, then to a time when it is generally accepted that men wear a prayer-shawl during certain ritual occasions — particularly in the synagogue. Varieties of *Tallit* now exist, of different materials and colours (so much so that many *Tallitot* made in Israel now come with a certification of *Kashrut* from the Rabbinate there) and there is also a growing tendency for women to wish to fulfil this *Mitzvah* as well. A *Tallit* remains a very common gift for a boy on his Bar-*Mitzvah*, but is not yet given so frequently to girls on their Bat-*Mitzvah*. This may yet change.

Many synagogues now encourage the wearing of *Tallit* by both sexes after Bar/Bat-Mitzvah as an outward sign of being a Son or Daughter of the Commandment. A *Tallit* is also a very appropriate gift for someone entering Judaism in adult life.

6

PART SIX: THE JEWISH LIFE CYCLE

CHAPTER 28

BIRTH; BRIT MILAH; PIDYON HA-BEN

1. INTRODUCTION

The 'Life-Cycle' is the shorthand technical term used by clergy and others to describe the important life-events that are fairly standard in almost all human existence — Birth, Marriage and Death customs — often supplemented by Puberty rituals and, in some cases, divorce. Frequently known by the shorthand term 'Hatch, Match and Despatch', the growth of divorce in recent years has led to 'Detach' being added.

This book can give only brief outlines of the relevant Jewish customs and traditions.

2. BIRTH

Who is affected by a Birth?

Obviously the Child, but also Parents, Grandparents, older Siblings (or Half-Siblings), etc.

(A). BIBLICAL RITUAL ISSUES

There is much discussion on various aspects of childbirth in the *Tanakh* and *Talmud*. The command to have children is the first in the *Torah* — in Genesis 1:28; the pains of childbirth are referred to in Gen. 3:16, Jeremiah 6:24, 22:23, 49:24 etc. The possibility of death during childbirth was a very real one — we learn of the deaths of Rachel (Genesis 35:18), Eli's daughter-in-law (I Samuel 4:20) and according to the *Talmud* Michal (cf. II Samuel 6:23) — hence of course the relief, gratitude and thanksgiving on a safe delivery.

In Biblical times it appears that the major effects from a ritual point of view were on the Mother — who became 'ritually unclean' ('*Tameh*' — i.e. Exempt) for a period of days (more for a girl than for a boy! — See Leviticus Ch. 12:1-8 which lays down 40 days for a male child, 80 for a female and a Sin-Offering to be brought at the end of the period.) Why of all things a Sin offering? The *Talmud* ('*Niddah*' 31b) suggests that during the pains of labour the mother may have decided that she doesn't want to go through all this again — and would then have to break this vow in order to have more children! (She also brings a Thanksgiving Burnt Offering.)

There is much discussion in modern times, especially amongst those eager to impose total equality at all costs, about the apparent discrepancy. Why should the period of 'impurity' (a negative-sounding word) be doubled for a girl child? (Leviticus 12:2 — and cf. *Talmud* '*Niddah*' 31a/b) There is no definitive answer, but we suggest the following be borne in mind:

- 'Impurity' is not a Punishment. It is a chance for the new mother to be left alone and be allowed to recover from the birth, before renewed sexual contact takes place. If anything it means that she is less likely to be pestered by a husband eager to try again for a male child.

- the laws of 'Purity' and 'Impurity' are complex but the principle is simple — there are some people who at some periods should keep away or be kept away from certain actions, until they are ready to resume 'normal life'. It could be classed as 'Time-Out'. To be '*Tameh*' is therefore not a punishment; Those who have been in contact for any reason with elemental aspects of life — Blood, Semen or a Corpse — are included in this category; We might say they had been traumatised and need a pause, a 'leave of absence'. Women become 'unclean' when they have issued blood — in menstruation or during childbirth — and by producing a female child a woman has given birth to a person who will in turn menstruate, perhaps thus 'doubling' the period.

- The *Talmud* ('*Niddah*' 31b) includes a discussion on this very topic, suggesting that everyone will be happy when a son is born but less happy when a daughter is born and the new mother will be influenced by the general mood! But we are not bound by these comments.

- As is often the case, one could perceive the period for a girl as being double that for a boy — or the period for a boy as being only half that for a girl. Is the cup half full or half empty?

- Incidentally, it is unclear what to do in the case of multiple births, whether or not all the children are the same gender!

(B). VIABILITY, STILLBIRTH AND INFANT MORTALITY

When is an Embryo viable? In theory from six months and one day, though even an eight-month foetus could be considered non-viable. In any case where the mother's life could be considered to be at risk from some embryo-related condition her life was considered to take precedence and the foetus could be aborted if necessary. This priority only ceased once the head or the major part of the child had been born (*Mishnah*: '*Oholot*' 7:6). Once born, a child is not considered fully viable until 30 days old — in other words, if it were not in a fit state to survive thirty days, no murder is committed by letting it die. (And see below).

(C). THE 'BACHUR'

Special ceremonies and responsibilities attended a first-born child, one who 'opened the womb' ('*Petter Rechem*' — Exodus 13:2). [This is in many respects the equivalent and culmination of the loss of virginity... The 'first time' of both involves 'opening up' and possibly the tearing of membranes.] However a late miscarriage or Caesarian section meant that the womb was not fully opened in the 'normal' way and subsequent children might not be classed as 'first-born' in this respect either.

(D). LIFE AND NEW LIFE

The above commentary is but a fraction of the debate and the doctrine, but it does show that many questions that are still of burning importance were matters of discussion — or indeed, of life and death — two millennia ago. The Rabbis of two thousand years ago did not have the modern technology, the X-rays and Ultrasounds and measuring and analysing techniques, but they had eyes and they had life experience and they could use their intelligence to make intelligent deductions about the human condition. The debate within Jewish legal circles still continues since medical technology is constantly developing and matters such as Artificial Insemination, Sperm Donation, Embryo-viability, treatment of Genetic Defects and babies born with them, Sterilization, Cloning and so on cannot necessarily be said to have a 'definitive' Jewish answer even yet.

All of Life is a Mystery. How people are conceived and born, how and why they 'fall in love', what happens when we die — all peoples have developed rituals to help give some shape or form to these mysteries.

We begin with Birth. What does it mean? A new Person comes into the world. Yes — but where from? A tiny living body comes out of a woman's body — remarkable in itself, since at most only a small amount of fluid ever went in. But now from nowhere it has bones, nerves, organs, a brain, a digestive system, a voice... an identity. What does the new person represent? What elements of the parents does it carry within it? (Our traditions date from a period when genetic research as we know it did not exist, but good observation and intelligence showed that some facial and other characteristics could be identified. There is also a discussion in the *Talmud* '*Niddah*' 31a where it is stated that the white parts of a person — the bones, teeth, the whites of the eyes — come from the father, whereas the red components — flesh and blood — from the mother, a primitive but brilliant way of describing the need for two parents to start a conception, one of whom produces white fluid and the other red fluid...).

'Our Rabbis taught: There are three partners in man, the Holy One, blessed be He, his father and his mother. His father supplies the semen of the white substance out of which are formed the child's bones, sinews, nails, the brain in his head and the white in his eye; his mother supplies the semen of the red substance

> out of which is formed his skin, flesh, hair, blood and the black of his eye; and the Holy One, blessed be He, gives him the spirit and the breath, beauty of features, eyesight, the power of hearing and the ability to speak and to walk, understanding and discernment. When his time to depart from the world approaches the Holy One, blessed be He, takes away his share and leaves the shares of his father and his mother with them.' ('*Niddah*' 31a)

Apart from the Body — flesh and bone and blood — where does the rest of the Person come from, the bit that makes it move and cry? Experience showed that on occasion a fully-formed baby could be born — that did not have these qualities, that was dead before it had been alive. In addition, although Giving Birth is such an obvious and important function for the female of the species, it is coupled with pain and with danger — many new mothers dying during or shortly after childbirth. (Jacob had to cope with this bitter-sweet element of becoming a father while losing his wife in Genesis 35:16-20.) Also many women — or maybe their husbands — seem physically incapable of ever fulfilling this biological function — How can this be, how is it to be understood? Is it a punishment? In the Bible this is so, God is even described as 'closing the wombs' of women at certain times — e.g. the wives of Avimelech at Gerar (Gen. 20:18). Both Sarah (Gen. 16:1 and till 21:1) and Rachel (Gen. 30:1) and later Rivkah (Gen. 25:21) all spend long periods childless. Some women become pregnant after they or their husbands have prayed extensively — e.g. Rivkah (Gen. 25:21-23), Samson's mother (Judges 13:3), Hannah (I Samuel 1:5-17). There is even the issue of Multiple Births — as in Genesis 25:22-26, and 38:3 — though an agricultural nation was already aware that this occurred in certain animal species, not in others.

Where does the Soul originate? Is it new every time or is it 'recycled' from previous people who once lived? Is there a 'store' somehow somewhere, with a finite number of souls waiting to be born, or does God generate new ones as and when needed? How is it that all human beings are now known to be biologically 99.9% identical (cf. the Human Genome Project of 1990-2003) — i.e. we all have almost identical nervous and circulation and skeletal and digestive and reproductive systems, our eyes and ears and hearts and livers and spleens and kidneys all work in the same way — and yet no two people are exactly alike? Who is responsible if a child is born with a defect or handicap? How does Gender work, and who or what decided which chromosomes a child will receive?

> 'R. Isaac citing R. Ammi stated: If the woman emits her semen first she bears a male child; if the man emits his semen first she bears a female child; for it is said, 'If a woman emits semen and bear a man-child' (Lev.12:2).

> 'Our Rabbis taught: At first it used to be said that 'if the woman emits her semen first she will bear a male, and if the man emits his semen first she will bear a female', but the Sages did not explain the reason, until R. Zadok came and explained it: 'These are the sons of Leah, whom she bore unto Jacob in Paddan-

aram, with his daughter Dinah' (Genesis 46:15). Scripture thus ascribes the males to the females and the females to the males.'

(From the Talmud 'Niddah' 31b)

We do not provide definitive answers here, nor do we wish to adopt uncritically the answers of the Rabbis who lived in a pre-technological age — we merely wish to show that these and other topics were being discussed by the Rabbis in the *Talmud* almost 2,000 years ago. The passage cited above seems to indicate that it is in the interests of a man who wants a son to ensure that his wife should reach orgasm before he does!

Defining when a Person 'begins' is as important as defining when he or she 'ends'. Is it at Conception, or at a certain stage in foetal development, at birth, or with the first breath, or the first cry, or when a child is 'viable' and breathing without assistance? (cf. *'Yevamot'* 69b for a discussion on the stages of foetal development.) These are moral and theological as well as biological questions.

(E). MISCARRIAGE OR STILLBIRTH

Very briefly — in Judaism a Person is defined as someone who has legal Rights — and these rights begin with Birth, not before. Hence Stem-Cell research, or Abortion (under specific conditions) are not forbidden. When there are problems during a birth the doctor or midwife has the duty first and foremost to save the Mother, not the not-yet-born Child. The mother is legally a 'Person' whereas the child is (only) a 'Potential Person'. Once the child has been delivered, or at least once the head has emerged and it can breathe and cry, only then does it have the same rights as the mother.

In the *Torah* the accidental killing of a foetus in a fight in which a pregnant woman is injured and caused to miscarry is classed as a civil rather than as a murder case (Exodus 21:22). The child had not been born and did not therefore exist as a legal entity ('*Shelo ba BaOlam*' — 'It did not come into the World'). The unborn child is Potential Life, not Life itself.

This is, of course, a different opinion to that of certain other religions and philosophies. But it is a logical manner of coping, amongst other things, with the fact that not all the children which are conceived are born alive or stay. Some will be born too early, some will die 'in utero', some will be apparently alive at birth but will be born with some major handicap or a missing organ and be incapable of living long outside the womb. These are tragic incidents for the families concerned, but indicate that one has to draw up a pragmatic boundary for defining when 'Life' — independent life — begins.

Traditionally no great fuss was made about a Miscarriage or Stillbirth — it was sad, but the assumption until not that many decades ago was that a woman would have many pregnancies and that a large proportion of these would not end successfully, or that many children would die in the first year or so of life. So there were no fixed mourning rituals, no name was given to the 'Non-Child', there was no *Shivah* and no *Yahrtzeit*, and such small pitiful items were often buried without ceremony at the edge of the cemetery. Nowadays our view is different; we know that parents expect fewer but more successful pregnancies, that they can bond much more to their un-born child, seeing it on a screen, moving, that they make plans for what they will need when the baby is born — and that the feelings of loss and grief, not just for the mother and father but also for grandparents and other family members — can be deep. Circumstances vary — sometimes there is something to bury, sometimes there was never much at all, from a physical point of view; sometimes a hospital has 'disposed of' a small splodge; sometimes there is a premature but formed, or a full-size baby.

Whilst Reform Judaism would still counsel against a full-scale funeral or using a name for the unborn child (keep it for the next opportunity? That always sounds so heartless, but is not so...) or any expense, where there are remains to bury a small ceremony is provided — though not necessarily using a full, expensive grave plot. Even where there are no remains to bury there are support groups and sometimes formal commemorative joint Mourning Services are organised to which the families of 'lost children' can come and where they can express their feelings of grief.

Miscarriage remains for many couples a 'taboo' subject — until it happens, and then one is grateful for support groups and one learns that many others, neighbours and relatives and friends, have also experienced this — but had never mentioned it.

(F). ABORTION

One corollary of this is that Abortion — the deliberate termination of a pregnancy — is not classed as Murder and is therefore not totally forbidden. It is not recom-mended as a form of casual contraception, nor as a cure for carelessness, but in cases where the mother's health is severely threatened — and we would include in this her mental health, if she has for example been made pregnant through rape or incest or is aware that the child will be severely and incurably handicapped — if there is evi-dence of severe foetal abnormality — then the unborn child is classed as a 'Rodef', one who is 'hunting' the mother and threatening her life and well-being (cf. *Mishnah* '*Oholot*' 7:6). In such cases the threat may be, even has to be removed... The grow-ing foetus within her body is not yet a separate legal 'person' but has, effectively or legally, the same status as a tumour.

(G). FOETAL MATERIAL

Another corollary of this is that there is no moral prohibition on using elements of a foetus for research or medicinal purposes. Indeed in the *Talmud* '*Niddah*' 21b, if a shapeless foetus is discharged the Rabbis insisted it be inspected and checked, cut open to see if there is blood inside.

(H). CONTRACEPTION

Yet a further corollary is that Contraception is not forbidden. By preventing an egg from being fertilized or a sperm from reaching its goal one is not 'murdering' a living being but merely ensuring that the process of Life does not start. The first *Mitzvah* in the *Torah* is '*p'ru ur'vu*' (Genesis 1:28), to 'be fruitful and multiply' and the rabbis discussed at some length how this was exactly to be defined. The argument boiled down to whether two Children or two Sons provided the 'minimum' whereby a man could say he had 'fulfilled his reproductive duty.' But either way, once this duty was fulfilled there was no obligation on him to go on to have more children than his financial or social situation or his wife's health allowed. This is discussed in the *Talmud* '*Yevamot*' 61b.

(I). ADOPTION

In cases where it proves impossible for whatever reason to conceive a child of their own — (and sometimes for other motives, for example to help a child from the Third World or when a member of the family has been orphaned) — many couples turn to the idea of Adoption — defined simply as offering an Ersatz, substitute parenthood, by providing an already-existing child with new parents. In such a situation there is of course no direct genetic link between the adoptive parents and 'their' child. (There are a very limited number of exceptions, when for example an uncle adopts the child of his deceased brother or sister — as Abraham did with Lot, Gen. 12:5 — or when an illegitimate child is formally absorbed into the family.)

There are many problems and pitfalls involved — this is not the place to go into them — and usually the couple are confronted with many bureaucratic hurdles and expenses. It is very rare that Jewish children are available through the Social Services. If children are adopted from abroad — and it is usually 'Third-World countries' which tolerate this 'export' of youngsters — then there are many unknown factors of health and potential handicap and usually limited choice when it comes to the parents' 'wishes'. But if the desire is great enough, ways are usually — not always — found.

From a Jewish point of view, when a family adopts a child the community is faced with the fact that the child is undeniably not born to the Jewish mother and then needs to be formally 'converted' into the Jewish religion and brought into the covenant — and for boys this involves of course circumcision. Here there are sometimes problems if the adoption authorities class this as an unnecessary medical intervention, or maybe even express opposition to a child being converted to another religion. The *Beit Din* can give further advice in specific cases but usually the new 'parents' will have to appear before a *Beit Din* and give formal guarantees concerning the way the child will be raised, there will be '*Tevilah*' and the Court can then issue a document confirming the child's new religious identity.

Sometimes an adopted person, on reaching adulthood, wishes to learn their original identity and return to their true cultural roots.

(J). SURROGACY

The issue of 'Surrogate' pregnancy is an intriguing one. On a purely moral basis most rabbis would strongly discourage the idea that a woman should deliberately get pregnant just to provide another woman with a child — especially when this is done in return for financial reward. On the other hand the Bible (Deuteronomy 25:5-6) allows for precisely this when it means providing another man with a child — for when a man dies childless, it became a duty on his brother to impregnate his widowed sister-in-law so that she could bear a child in his deceased brother's name! ('*Yibum*' or so-called 'Levirate Marriage'). Onan was even punished for failing to perform this duty! (Genesis 38:8-10). (This idea is no longer practised in this form and the Rabbis in '*Niddah*' 32a placed several restrictions on the practice also. Instead, the ceremony of '*Chalitza*' allows both parties to withdraw from this biblical duty; the brother-in-law declares before a *Beit Din* that he does not wish to do this, the widow removes his shoe and throws it on the floor and spits — it all seems a bit bizarre to modern eyes but it means that they are not forced into something neither of them want.)

(K). OTHER RELATED ISSUES

There are many other very modern variants where modern Society finds itself coping with a range of challenges. Artificial Insemination with the sperm of an anonymous donor, not the marriage partner, raises the risk, from traditional Jewish perspectives, that one will never know who the 'biological father' is and therefore there is a risk in the next generation of unwitting Incest — the same donor could be the originator of several boys and girls who will never know that they are in fact half-brothers and half-sisters. How do we, as Liberal Jews, treat situations where a lesbian couple decide to have a child through Artificial or In Vitro Insemination, whether through a known Donor or an anonymous one? Or when a widow decides to have a child using the frozen sperm of her late husband? Or when a homosexual couple seek to adopt a child? In such debates one tends to hear a lot about the 'rights' of the prospective parents and relatively little about the rights of the potential child — including its right to grow up in a caring, balanced and adequate environment. Both sides to the debate are important.

There is of course never a guarantee that any family will remain healthy and stable, but at the same time it would be wrong to deny that there are certain factors — the age of the parents, their social situation, whether they are already addicted to drugs or are alcoholics, or heavy smokers, or infected with AIDS, or are known to be carrying a genetic problem such as Tay-Sachs Disease or Riley-Day Syndrome/ Familial Dysautonomia, conditions which occur mainly amongst *Ashkenazi* Jews — which could make stability even less likely. There are as yet no 'authoritative' Jewish answers to all these questions — but they are issues which many congregations, rabbis, teachers and families face. And we have not even begun to tackle other modern issues of genetic manipulation and cloning... though the following excerpt from the Babylonian *Talmud* 'Bechoroth' 45b shows that observant people were already aware of the roles played by two partners contributing to the genes of their offspring:

> 'Said Resh Lakish: An abnormally tall man should not marry an abnormally tall woman, lest their offspring be like a mast. A male dwarf should not marry a female dwarf, lest their offspring be a dwarf of the smallest size. A man abnormally white-complexioned should not marry an equally white-complexioned woman, lest their offspring be excessively white-complexioned. A very dark-complexioned man should not marry an equally very dark-complexioned woman, lest their offspring may be pitch black.'

As we see — it is sometimes hard to avoid extremes!

(L). THE NEXT GENERATION

Incidentally — some people decide to have children mainly because they want Heirs, people who will take over the family firm or the throne. However — Dynasties rarely work. The reason is fairly simple: There is no guarantee that genes will transmit not only physical but also mental characteristics. The person who establishes a company needs a particular personality — but the one who inherits it and needs to run it needs a different one. Just being born into a royal family does not make you an interested or competent ruler or a military genius.

This situation is reflected many times in the *Tanakh*. Noah was classed as 'good in his time' — but at least one of his sons ended up cursed for being the opposite. Abraham's sons were not the type to carry on the Brit, though Isaac inherited it; Jacob obtained his position by deception. The first example of such a problem within a monarchic system comes with King Saul who, himself appointed by prophetic choice, sought to make his son Jonathan his heir — but Jonathan had other interests. It is noticeable that, despite the messianic fuss over 'the House of David' none of our major leaders — Moses, or the judges or the prophets — ever passed on their role to their sons and David, too, faced major problems in finding an appropriate successor.

Some recent research into the genetic make-up of *Cohanim* — or those who claim to be descended from the priestly family — does indeed show that by marrying within their own community the gene pool has been kept restricted and certain characteristics are maintained beyond statistical norms; but this would be no guarantee that they would all have been good and pious priests!

Therefore, if you are fortunate enough to have children, it is so that they can be Themselves, not smaller, younger versions of You. This is a hard lesson for all parents to learn…

So the Baby is born. Then what?

In Biblical times the Weaning was a major event marked often by a feast (see Genesis 21:8). This custom seems to have fallen into disuse, not helped by the vast array of semi-solid baby foods currently available or the rise of bottle-feeding. Obviously it marked the time when the child was no longer dependent on the mother for all its nourishment.

At various times in Jewish history superstitions were adopted from surrounding cultures and mothers would be surrounded with magic amulets to keep evil spirits away from them and their children. This practice was almost always frowned upon by the rabbinic authorities of the time.

3. A NAME

What's in a Name? According to Jewish tradition your whole personality, your destiny, your history... A brief look at how babies were named (or adults re-named) in the Bible shows the significance attached to the name.

Traditionally, a boy was named at his *Brit Milah* (circumcision) and a girl at some later time, perhaps in the synagogue when the mother was well enough to attend. This would usually be on the *Shabbat* after the 30th day when the father would be given an *Aliyah* and a '*Mi SheBerach*' blessing. *Ashkenazi* Jews often avoid naming a child after a living relative, whilst *Sephardi* Jews consider that this is a good thing to do!

The current Reform attitude seems to be non-committal — any suitable name will do, perhaps commemorating a deceased relative, perhaps not. The birth announcements in the Jewish newspapers reveal distinct trends in 'fashionable' names. Many parents choose Biblical (and not necessarily Jewish!) names, or several names of which one is specifically Jewish and another more 'everyday'. Of course, names with direct links to Christianity are best avoided — 'Christopher', 'Christine', 'Luke' and so on, though many 'New Testament' names also occur in the Hebrew Bible and are therefore 'safer' in this respect.

At birth a child has no say in its name — so the naming decision mainly involves the parents. Later, maybe when he or she can form opinions, the child may adopt some nickname or abbreviation in preference, or use only one name if there is more than one.

HEBREW NAMES

Since (on the whole) modern British Jews have euphonious English-sounding names the question of a Hebrew name has assumed prominence. This is the name used in a synagogue or ritual context — when one is called up to the *Torah* reading, or written into a *Ketubah* during marriage, or written on a *Matzevah* (gravestone)... Of course, in the 'old days' when communities did not intermingle so much the Hebrew name was the only or main one. Some Jews may have had a Latin or German name in addition to their own, or a form thereof, for the purposes of business when non-Jews were involved. Many a 'Baruch' for example became 'Benedict' in mediaeval court rolls.

Again rules vary, but it is safe to say that should a child have a name already associated with Hebrew — e.g. 'Benjamin', 'Daniel', 'Sarah', 'Miriam', etc. it would be silly not to use this as a Hebrew name too. In other circumstances it might be an idea to pick a Hebrew name that at least starts with the same initial letter or phonetic sound, or even choose a name or names for personal reasons — that of a relative or a favourite character, or having a personal meaning of significance to the parents.

Naturally one may have several forenames.

4. CIRCUMCISION ('*BRIT MILAH*')

It shouldn't need stating, but perhaps better had be, that Judaism does NOT practise or recommend Female Circumcision…

The term '*Brit Milah*' is a composite one. '*Brit*' (in Yiddish: '*Briss*') is the Hebrew for 'Covenant' and a covenant, an important treaty or contract between two partners, was marked not only by solemn affirmations but by the ritual spilling of a small amount of blood. '*Milah*' is the noun from the verb '*laMul*' — 'to circumcise' — which word itself is from the Latin 'to cut round'.

It is therefore possible to have a circumcision for medical or other reasons which have nothing to do with the Covenant. Conversely, Jewish males enter the Covenant by means of this cut in the flesh. Anthropologists get very excited by all this and others, for various reasons, like to interpret this as an assault on a child's human rights (though accepting without protest all other interventions in a child, from cutting the umbilical cord to a variety of injections and blood tests).

The initial command concerning circumcision of infants is in Genesis 17:10-12 (though the passage goes on to deal with adults):

> 'This is my covenant which you shall keep, between me and you and your descendants after you. Every male among you shall be circumcised. You shall be circumcised in the flesh of your foreskins, and it shall be a sign of the covenant between me and you. He that is eight days old among you shall be circumcised…'

The rite therefore consists of the symbolic cutting-off of a part of the foreskin from the penis, accompanied by a ritual and prayers that signify that this is a covenantal act as opposed to merely a surgical operation. Despite widespread trembles at the thought of what this entails, mainly based on fears and taboos concerning where on the Body it is carried out, it is fact a very minor operation (involving no bones, muscles or major arteries) and can normally be carried out at home by a specialist — known in Hebrew as the '*Mohel*'. No real anaesthetic is needed; Where appropriate, sweet *Kosher* wine is given to the infant to dull its responses. Modern medical science suggests that a clotting factor in the blood reaches a peak on the eighth day after birth and that Jewish women are less likely than others to contract cervical cancer (the assumption being that they have only ever had intercourse with circumcised males!) but while these may be interesting side-issues and relevant in polemical debates the basic purpose is still to mark, publicly and indelibly, the entry of another male member of the Jewish people into the Abrahamic covenant with God. Until now no one has complained that cutting a child's fingernails or having a tooth extracted or having swollen tonsils extracted are grave assaults on its human rights or that its written agreement as an adult is required for such operations.

The prayers said on the occasion stress the hope that the infant will grow up to become a fully Jewish adult, will study Judaism, marry Jewishly and act according to Jewish ethical principles. This is his birthright.

The service may be found in the RSGB *Siddur* pp.310-313; **pp.438f.** It can be adapted to suit circumstances — if, for example, the father is not Jewish, or is not present, the mother or another male relative could also take over this role.

Another male is appointed to be *Sandek* — usually translated as 'Godfather' though this is not understood in the same way as it is in Christianity. This Hebrew word is probably derived from the Greek '*Sandekos*' ('Patron') or '*Suntekos*'— ('Companion of the Father'). The function of the *Sandak* or *Sandek* probably arose from the necessity of having someone assist the *Mohel* by holding the child firmly during the circumcision operation. To act as *Sandek* is considered a great honour, also as a meritorious religious act.

> 'Where a grandfather of a child is still alive, it is customary to bestow the honour of *Sandek* upon him. The woman who brings the child to the circumcision and hands it over to the *Sandek* is called 'Sandeket'. Some Jews of European origin also use the name '*Kvater*' (the woman, '*Kvaterin*'), which is corrupted form of the German '*Gevatter*' ('Godfather').'
>
> (Source: 'Encyclopaedia Judaica' Vol. 14 cols. 826f.)

The prophet Elijah ('*Eliyahu haNavi*') is traditionally assumed to be present at every circumcision ceremony, so a chair ('*Kisseh shel Eliyahu*') is put aside for him and the child formally presented to him before commencement. The ceremony can usually be carried out in the home.

If the eighth day following birth falls on a *Shabbat* or a festival — even *Yom Kippur* — the *Brit Milah* still takes place, often in the synagogue. (In such case the *Mohel* would take his equipment there the day before, to avoid carrying on the *Shabbat*.) If however for health or other reasons the circumcision has had to be postponed, it can then be re-arranged to a suitable convenient day, but avoiding Sabbaths, etc.

If a baby boy has been born to a mother before she has finally converted to Judaism a *Mohel* from the 'Association of Reform and Liberal Mohalim' will perform a surgical circumcision identical in all respects to the physical operation of a *Brit Milah*; This is in the circumstances not (yet) a religious operation, since the child does not formally enter the Covenant at this stage, so there is no need for prayers or the bestowing of a Hebrew name. If a child has already reached the age of several months or years then a proper anaesthetic is required and surgical facilities. Once the family has appeared before the *Beit Din* no further operation is required. Similarly, if an adult has already been circumcised before conversion no additional operation is normally required. (In Orthodox and Conservative and some Reform circles a symbolic re-circumcision, effectively no more than the drawing-off of a small droplet of blood known as '*Tippat Dam Brit*' or 'Drop of Covenantal Blood' would be required.)

Adult circumcision is performed under anaesthetic, local or general depending on the *Mohel* and the patient's wishes and usually in a doctor's surgery or a hospital. Again, the actual entry into the Covenant follows the *Beit Din* interview and *Tevilah* in a *Mikveh*, so this is treated as a minor but necessary preparatory surgical procedure rather than as a religious ceremony.

5. THE BIRTH OF DAUGHTERS

In some Reform circles new alternative ceremonies are being developed to create a '*Brit Bat*' (plural: '*Brit Banot*') — a 'Covenant of the Daughter' — as an equivalent domestic celebration of the new life. In Genesis 17:15ff. 'Sarai' is re-named 'Sarah' at the same time as 'Avram' is renamed 'Avraham' — i.e. she is included in the new covenantal relationship and given a blessing. (The actual term Covenant —'*Brit*' — is admittedly restricted in 17:4 to Avraham and in 17:19 to Yitzhak, but in Reform Judaism the birth of a daughter who is capable of taking upon herself the obligations of an educated Jewish life and continuing the Jewish people is considered as joyful an occasion as the birth of a son.) See p.440 for a '*Zeved Ha-Bat*' ceremony.

'*Zeved*' means 'a precious gift' — this is derived from Leah's comments in Gen. 30:20 when she bears Jacob her sixth son whom she names Zevulun, saying 'God has endowed me with a precious gift' — '*Zavadni Elohim oti Zeved Tov*' — ironically and sadly, when her daughter Dinah is born in the very next verse she makes no such comment!

6. BIRTHDAYS

An important part of the modern secular life-cycle, oddly enough the Birthday is completely neglected in Judaism as a festive occasion. (It was of course important for legal reasons, for establishing a person's age for Bar-*Mitzvah*, military service, marriage and so on.) Indeed, the only time a Birthday is celebrated in the Bible is when Pharaoh throws a party in Genesis 40:20!

7. 'PIDYON HA-BEN' —
REDEMPTION OF THE FIRST-BORN SON

This is a ceremony — and concept — which has been virtually dropped by Reform Judaism. The underlying concept is clear — the First-Born (the 'Bachur') is somehow special and this special status has to be marked. It appears that in early times the first-born males became dedicated to the priesthood, though later in the *Torah* Moses specifically appoints the tribe of *Levi* to the Priesthood and thereby 'deposes' the first-born from this role. Thus Exodus 13:1-2 reads:

'God said to Moses: 'Sanctify every first-born who opens the womb among the Israelites, both man and beast. It is Mine.'

And Exodus 13:13 reads:

'You must redeem every first-born son.'

However, Numbers 3:11-13 reads:

'God said to Moses, 'I separated the Levites from their brethren so that they may take the place of all the first-born who open the womb among the Israelites. All first-born are Mine since the day I smote the Egyptian first-born. I sanctified the Israelite first-born, both man and beast shall be Mine.' '

Obviously the beasts didn't become priests — but the idea of the first-born, just as the first-fruits of the harvest, being subject to special forms of demonstrating gratitude is clear. The beasts would be offered as sacrifices, the humans dedicated somehow to the service of God.

In the ceremony a *Cohen* (i.e. a male descendant of the priestly line) ceremonially asks the parents whether they would like to 'relieve the child of its sanctity' by paying, instead, a donation of five Shekels.

This ceremony takes place on the 31st. day — a child which died before that age would not need to be redeemed — and it would not need to take place at all if the child were born by Caesarian section, or if either of the parents were themselves descended from a *Cohen* or a *Levi*, or the mother had previously had a miscarriage after the fortieth day of gestation. (The rabbis considered that an Embryo became a recognisable Foetus at that time.)

Because *Pidyon HaBen* amounts to a commercial transaction it would normally be postponed should the thirty-first day fall on a *Shabbat*.

The direct origins for this ceremony lie in Numbers 3:39 which states that there were 22,000 Levites and Numbers 3:43 which states that there were 22,273 first-born sons. Obviously there was an excess of 273 men who could not be exchanged on a one-to-one basis by the Levites, so they had to be 'redeemed' from their obligation. So God told Moses to take five Shekels apiece and give these to Aharon and his sons in lieu (Numbers 3:44-51).

Since Reform Judaism no longer lays any stress on the separate privileges and duties of a priesthood and no longer distinguishes between a *Cohen* and a *Levi* or any other Israelite the ceremony has lost its purpose for us.

8. SERVICE OF THANKSGIVING

A new ceremony introduced by the Reform movement has been the formal public Thanksgiving service in the synagogue. (This is derived from earlier Naming ceremonies for girls in Orthodox synagogues and of course Thanksgiving Offerings would have been made in Temple times.) This usually takes place during a service, but may also be held quietly with just family members present. The service can be found in the *Siddur* pp. 284-286; p.360 (in 8[th.] Edition p. 440 is also a ceremony *'Zeved Ha-Bat'* — 'Thanksgiving for the precious gift of a Daughter' — as an equivalent to a circumcision celebration). In most congregations both parents come before the Ark with the new child when it is a few months old and all are healthy and strong.

The initial reading by the father is from Psalm 116 verses 1, 2, 5, 7, 12, 14, 17 and 19b. It is sometimes necessary to make some adaptations — for example if the father is not Jewish, or not present (in which case the mother or another relative could take his place). The Mother's Prayer already has some possible variations, though it may also need adaptation if, for example, there are twins or if the father is not actually a husband! The Rabbi — or whoever else is leading the service — then formally names the child and recites the Priestly Benediction ('*Birkat Cohanim*') from Numbers 6:24-26 — hence this ceremony is often colloquially referred to as a 'Baby-Blessing' though strictly speaking it is a Naming and Thanksgiving Service.

CHAPTER 29

'BAR-MITZVAH', 'BAT-MITZVAH'

1. INTRODUCTION

The phrase 'Bar- and Bat-*Mitzvah*' is a clumsy one but reflects the reality that, in our synagogues, men and women, boys and girls are treated equally, have the same rights and privileges but also the same responsibilities.

Accordingly throughout this Chapter the term Bar-*Mitzvah* will include Bat-*Mitzvah* and the hope is that, if one has both sons and daughters, they will all go through the same experience of learning and express the same commitment at this important stage of their lives.

2. WHAT DOES THE TERM MEAN?

Literally the term is Aramaic for a 'Son (or 'Daughter') of the Commandment'. In former times the phrase used to mean attainment of religious authority and autonomy. Until this point the child was not considered fully responsible for its actions, should it break a religious or moral law; after this time the Child would become an Adult, responsible for his or her own actions in terms of prayer, or fasting, or moral behaviour.

Nowadays the term has come to be used more and more to mean the occasion of the ceremony itself, rather than the fact that the person's status is being changed.

(Who is an Adult? The concept of a 'teenager' or of an 'adolescent' — one who is in the process of becoming an adult — is relatively new. Just for some historical context: In 1833 a Royal Commission into Child Labour recommended that children between eleven and eighteen should work no more than twelve hours a day in the mills and mines; Children between nine and eleven should work eight hours a day, and those under nine ought not to work at all. Until this time twelve-hour days were common even for children as young as five, who could be hit by leather straps if they were considered lazy or careless by the overseer... In 1833 followed a Factory Act which regulated working hours — nine-to-thirteen-year-olds were not to work more than eight hours a day and those under eighteen were not to work at night. In 1844 it was legislated that older children could work a maximum of twelve hours and must be given an hour and a half for meals. The 1847 Factory Act reduced the working day to ten hours or fifty-eight hours a week. In 1850 this was extended to ten and a half hours but in 1874 the ten-hour day was reintroduced. Theoretically after the 1833 Factory Act mill owners had to prove that they provided workers under 13 with two hours of schooling a day for six days of the week. From 1874 children between ten and fourteen were allowed to work part-time in order to make time for education. In 1880 education was made compulsory for five- to ten-year-olds. Compulsory education was extended to children up to 14 in 1918. Just something to think about next time someone grumbles about the amount of homework they have…… And of course such conditions remain sadly the norm in many countries today where cheap clothing is produced for western teenagers. In such an historical context the drive within Judaism to ensure that every thirteen-year old could read the *Torah* and explain it has to be admired.

3. THE OCCASION

Having said the above, how does one mark the occasion? What should one do? After a circumcision a boy remains circumcised; after a wedding a couple is married (for a good long time, one hopes); after a funeral a person, alas, tends to stay dead and buried… But what does a Bar-*Mitzvah* service actually do? Can it make a Child into an Adult? Can it fill a person with wisdom, knowledge, and commitment? Can it make a person into a Good Jew? Obviously not — so we must look at the background and make preparations accordingly. And this means more than preparations for a large and expensive party!

In modern times the Bar-*Mitzvah* is usually called up during a *Shabbat* morning service as '*Maftir*' (i.e. to the last *Torah* reading) — to which he would normally recite the *Torah* blessings and chant the last three or four verses — and then the *Haftarah*, which unfortunately in many synagogues is chanted in Hebrew in a meaningless manner. In Reform and Liberal synagogues both Bar- and Bat-*Mitzvah* may be called to a fuller reading from the *Torah*, with blessings, and will also read the *Haftarah* — which can be done in the vernacular. He or she should deliver a speech about the readings, demonstrating that they have read and understood the content and have some personal insights to offer — a '*Dvar Torah*' or a '*Drascha*'. In our *Siddur* (pp.566/567; p.350) there is a special Prayer for the Bar- or Bat-*Mitzvah* in which the parents, teachers and community are thanked. The family should ideally take part in the Evening Service as well and at the Morning Service sponsor a *Kiddush* at which the Bar-*Mitzvah* might recite the *Kiddush* or the Grace After Meals.

Since *Torah* is also read on Monday and Thursday mornings it is also common, for example when celebrating in Israel or when it is desired to travel and take photographs and video, to hold the Bar-*Mitzvah* service on the weekday when *Shabbat* restrictions do not apply.

Several other customs have attached themselves more recently to the celebration — such as presenting the new young adult with a *Tallit* before the beginning of the service (or even an older *Tallit* inherited from a relative). In some synagogues the congregation will shower the Bar- or Bat-*Mitzvah* with sweets — a pleasant idea but something which can get dangerously out-of-hand if hard boiled wrapped sweets are deliberately thrown hard! — or, at a reception a number of candles are lit to symbolise specific individuals.

As indicated above it has also recently become a custom for a Bar-*Mitzvah* to be celebrated in Israel — often on a Monday or Thursday morning at Masada or at the Western Wall ('*Kotel HaMa'aravi*'). Without wishing to undermine the Israeli tourist industry, this rather misses the point of celebrating within the community where one lives. A family trip to Israel is a wonderful way — for those who can afford it — to mark that a Bar-*Mitzvah* has been celebrated, but it need not be the place where it is celebrated. Another custom slowly gaining currency is for a family to choose to celebrate such an event in a community in Europe to rebuild former links.

4. EARLY BACKGROUND

What does the Bible say about Bar-*Mitzvah*? Nothing at all. The references to Maturity — for eligibility for military service, or liability for tax — cite 20 years old as being the relevant age (Exodus 30:14; Leviticus 27:3-5; Numbers 1:3, 1:20).

By the time of the *Mishnah* (around the end of the second century CE) the ages of 13 for boys and 12 for girls were recognised as the times when a full observance of religious commandments and rituals became obligatory, when vows were binding and so on. A father was considered responsible for his child's actions only until the age of 13.

In '*Pirkei Avot*' ('Sayings of the Fathers') 5:24 Rabbi Judah ben Temach declares:

'At 5 one is ready to study the *Torah*; at 10 to study the *Mishnah*; at 13 to fulfil the *Mitzvot* (commandments); at 15 to study the *Talmud*; at 18 to be married...'

Strictly speaking there had to be evidence of physical maturity as well — the secondary sexual characteristics such as pubic hairs — before one could reach full maturity, for one could not be legitimately committed to not breaking the laws if one were physically incapable of breaking them in the first place! Puberty for boys means production of semen, for girls means production of eggs and menstrual blood... and whole new areas of personal responsibility in terms of self-discipline and potential disasters.

Since Bar-*Mitzvah* meant the age at which one became liable for one's actions the *Talmud* ('*Keritot*' 50a) declares that at this age a person also becomes liable to the death penalty!

The 'Rambam' (Maimonides) states:

'A girl at 12 and a boy at 13 cease to be called Minors and are called Adults.'

It is important to realise that there was no ceremony involved at this time. One didn't 'have a Bar-*Mitzvah*', one became Bar-*Mitzvah*. In modern terms one's status as an adult, voter, motorist, drinker etc., your right to sign contracts or to run your own financial affairs, changes on one's 18th. birthday whether or not one chooses to mark the occasion with a party.

5. LATER HISTORICAL DEVELOPMENT

In Europe from the 13th. century onward the Bar-*Mitzvah* became more of a communal occasion. Boys of 13 were called to the *Torah* in the synagogue and by the end of the 18th. century a variety of customs were established — perhaps just saying the blessings, or reading the *Maftir*, or the *Maftir* and *Haftarah* etc. From the 13th. century on a formula was recited by the Father, denying all further responsibility for his son ('*Baruch asher Patarani meOnsho shel Zeh...*' — 'Blessed be the One who has freed me from any further responsibility for the sins that this one here might commit'— based on the *Midrash* 'Genesis *Rabbah*' 63:10). The boy — now man! — might give a short '*Drasha*' or exposition; there was a festive meal; the boy — now man! — formally donned *Tefillin* for the first time as an adult. Sometimes the Bar-*Mitzvah* was marked on the Monday or Thursday immediately following the 13th. Birthday (since the *Torah* was read on those days), sometimes on the following *Shabbat*.

6. *BAT-MITZVAH* FOR GIRLS

'Bat-*Mitzvah*' was introduced first in France and Italy in the late 19th.-century. Around 1810 the early Reformers in Germany replaced Bar-*Mitzvah* at age 13 with Confirmation at age 15, 16 or 17, an age when the candidates were considered more capable of understanding the significance of the ceremony. This was for both boys and girls.

This practice is retained in most Liberal synagogues in America and Britain, often with a joint Confirmation service for a class of candidates at *Shavuot*, a time symbolically linked with the 'acceptance of the *Torah*'. In many respects a later age is really to be preferred, since we now know much more about how children and teenagers develop intellectually and personally in these few adolescent-but-not-yet-adult years.

Partly in response to the growing popularity of this ceremony some Orthodox communities have introduced a female equivalent of Bar-*Mitzvah* in their synagogues too — usually known as 'Bat-Chayil' — 'A Daughter of Worth' or 'Daughter of Strength' (the name derived from Proverbs Ch. 31, the 'Eshet Chayil' passage) since it is not considered that females have the same relationship to *Mitzvot* as do males. The course of instruction is based mainly on domestic skills for the Jewish housewife and the girls are not called up to the reading of the scroll or allowed to lead a synagogue service. Customs vary in different communities but the Bat-Chayil girls are usually treated as a group or class, rather than as individuals.

However, times are changing and even in Orthodox communities there is pressure for more involvement by women.

7. BALANCE

Nowadays it often appears that the catered banquet and the presents have become the main purpose of a Bar-*Mitzvah* or Bat-*Mitzvah* celebration, to the extent that it has been known for parents to avoid any public celebration at all on the grounds that the 'necessary expense' would be too great for them — and certainly there is a tendency to make a 'Bat-*Mitzvah*' 'optional' for a daughter, to save money, but 'Bar-*Mitzvah*' compulsory for a son.

From the Rabbi's or Synagogue's viewpoint this is a sad mistake and misunderstanding. No expenditure on catering is strictly necessary; what is required is honesty and commitment.

What, these days, should be the point of the celebration?

Our answer would be to do all possible to ensure that a Jewish child, at this delicate stage in their personal development, passing through puberty and entering adolescence, acquires a sense of the history and continuity of Judaism and the part he or she can play in furthering that continuity. This can be achieved by making sure that the child gets a chance to learn something of the religion, its customs and history; learns to become a part of the community, making friendships within the synagogue to match those of school and elsewhere; becomes confident in participating in the services and so be less likely to stay away in the future due to embarrassment; and in general, begins to think and act like an adult Jew.

If this is the result, the process has worked. If it is not, the process has to some extent failed, with possible dire future consequences — and no elaborate celebration will hide that sad fact.

8. WHAT DOES *BAR-* OR *BAT-MITZVAH* MEAN IN A REFORM OR LIBERAL SYNAGOGUE?

In terms of the synagogue service customs vary but at the very least the Bar- or Bat-*Mitzvah* would be called up to read from the *Sefer Torah* for one *Aliyah* section, with the appropriate *Berachot* before and after (in some synagogues the *Torah* section is chanted, in others read or read and translated); Then to read the *Haftarah* (in some communities in Hebrew, in others in the vernacular) also with the appropriate *Berachot*; to give a short explanatory sermon / *Drasha* explaining both the content and their own feelings and ideas about these verses; and maybe to lead the blessings at the *Kiddush* following. Theoretically they could also lead sections of the service, sharing this responsibility with the Rabbi / Cantor / *Shaliach Tzibbur*.

In some communities a '*Mitzvah* Project' is also recommended and the young person is encouraged to take part in and to encourage others to take part in some social project, or fund-raising or awareness-raising of injustices elsewhere. This can include 'twinning' a service with a child in another country who cannot celebrate because of restrictions on their religious freedom, or even recalling another child, who maybe had a similar name or birthday, who perished in the *Sho'ah* (the Holocaust).

The problem underlying this ceremony is that it marks a traditional age of maturity that modern Western society no longer recognises. In former times one was either a child or an adult and in many parts of the world, unfortunately, children are still exploited as 'cheap adults', as soldiers or workers; in the Western countries the concept of a 'teenager' as 'a transition stage between childhood and adulthood' has developed, a person who is still being educated or trained, who is not yet able to sign contracts or bear arms or drive vehicles or liable to pay taxes and yet is no longer an infant. At age 13 this process of 'adolescence', of 'becoming adult' is just starting. Synagogues may call up a Bar-*Mitzvah* boy or a Bat-*Mitzvah* girl in the service but then treat them still as just that — as a boy or girl — rather than as a young man or a woman. This is inconsistent! In this respect a formal ceremony at age 16 would actually make more sense — we know how much young people develop physically and emotionally in these years. (There are even cases where parents say 'Let's get it over with before he/she enters puberty and starts thinking differently' — revealing a sad view of adolescent psychology. The ceremony is then seen as an end to childhood rather than as a beginning of adulthood and the two are very different.)

As well as becoming eligible for religious 'privileges' such as *Aliyot* and liable to religious obligations such as Fasting it would be helpful to treat these teenagers as adults in a more formal way — perhaps by granting them some form of 'Young Adult' membership at a nominal fee, or allocating them their own newsletters or High Holy Day tickets, and representation for the 13-18 age group on the synagogue's Council! Too often the ceremony is seen in isolation and as a part of childhood rather than as a transition to adulthood. It is forced upon the child rather than chosen voluntarily and in too many cases marks an end rather than a beginning of religious education.

CHAPTER 30

KIDDUSHIN, MARRIAGE

1. INTRODUCTION

When one starts to consider this topic most people think immediately of the Wedding. However, this is only a tiny part of the overall subject, even though it is the part which seems to attract the most planning, the most emotion and (often) the most expense.

Marriage customs vary with the centuries and the particular Jewish community. There are some basic 'standard' outlines however, which this chapter sets out. (A warning: Beware of professional 'Wedding Planners' and others who will encourage you to great complexity and expense on the grounds that 'Everyone is doing this these days'!! And if you want a rabbi to officiate, make sure to ask and confirm the date with the Rabbi BEFORE booking the venue, caterer, photographer, band, hairdresser, honeymoon flights... It is amazing how often a couple decide to marry on a Saturday or a Jewish festival and are then surprised when no Rabbi is available! Make the 'holiness' the main part of what you are the doing and the rest just detail!)

What is Marriage actually all about? There are many misunderstandings, with some couples even avoiding it 'due to the expense' — meaning the costs of the Wedding ceremony, not of the Marriage itself. Here is the Ideal, which underlies the Jewish concepts:

Within a society Marriage represents Continuity and Security. The (ideal) theory is that Four people, part of God's creation, have formed two Couples; each has produced offspring, these offspring are now old enough to be united so that in due course they can produce their own offspring and the cycle will continue through another generation. From children should come in due course grandchildren... The parents of the bride and groom have fulfilled a major social and familial responsibility placed upon them — and only they know, probably, how many difficulties were encountered and had to be overcome along the way, only they know the risks that were taken, the efforts, the savings, the arguments, the errors... But they have raised and educated their child, supported and guided it, prepared it as far as possible, set it examples in their own lives... and now they entrust their child into the care of another person who is someone else's child and who has also been raised to be a responsible and caring adult, and they can only hope that the new young couple, with their ideals intact and their love for each other, will be able to replicate the process and overcome any difficulties they will themselves encounter — and these could be health, financial, professional, political, personal, relational and intimate difficulties. It is a 'bitter-sweet' occasion for the child now leaves home for good, to establish their own home.

In other cases people may come 'burnt' and hurt from previous painful experience or loss, but willing to make another attempt to build up a life together with a new and different loving partner.

Within a society Marriage also assures Clarity. Children are born — but if they are born to a recognised, distinct family unit one knows (hopefully!) who the father is, one can trace the blood line back (look at the long lists in Genesis, where A marries B and produces C, C in turn marries D and produces E and so on), one knows who is a legitimate heir and who not. No-one lives alone, we live in relationship to each other, even if some of these relationships may appear damaged or broken. Everyone who was ever born once had a mother and once had a father and the fortunate ones are those who know who each of these are and who grow up with them both. It means you will have the chance to know your grandparents, your aunts and uncles and cousins, your siblings. You will inherit a set of cultural and religious values which you will share with your partner and which you will jointly pass on to your own offspring.

All this is not always possible, but it is nevertheless presented as the Ideal.

Of course the Ideal is not often attained, but it is important to have this basic concept in mind. The Wedding ceremony is just a brief event — causing great stress and expense but over in a few minutes — whereas the Marriage should last somewhat longer!

And where the Ideal is unattainable, one seeks compromise. Compromise means seeking an arrangement which is not ideal and not perfect but which, it is hoped, will be 'good enough' for all concerned — and of course definitions for this vary enormously. This is where one needs rules and traditions and guidance to aid in making the compromise decisions. These rules and traditions are usually based on bitter experience, distilled and conveyed in terms which may seem negative but which are intended to assure that at least some of the more obvious mistakes can be avoided. One cannot predict all of the future, but one can at least predict that certain circumstances are more likely to lead to conflict or disappointment than others. In all human societies structures developed whereby people married within a particular culture or class or religion or caste, on the basis that these formed at least a basis for common interests and expectations. In contrast, romantic attraction or physical attraction are phenomena which can come — and go.

Of course we are free to move beyond these boundaries — but it helps to be aware of some of the additional risks one is thereby taking! Love can conquer much — but not all — and it often blinds those who are 'in love'. Love should not be an excuse for Naivety. How much literature (Romeo and Juliet? Pelléas and Mélisande?) is filled with tragic tales of couples whose love was forbidden and it did NOT save them from certain consequences?

The principle is that two people form a bond which they mark in public through religious or civil rituals and through a contract. This means that they become for administrative purposes one 'unit' or household, able to control jointly their financial affairs and assets and to take joint responsibility for children or for their own insurance and pensions. Two people who choose to live together without making these formal moves do not have the same status — although modern society has developed some quasi-alternatives as compromises.

Whereas the ideal is to find one person with whom can find complete trust and security for the rest of one's life, experience shows that people can grow apart as well as growing together and an equitable solution then needs to be found to end the marriage — a later Chapter will deal with this.

The desire to find a partner for life (or even for a part of one's life) is built into our natural instincts (See Genesis 2:24). (Incidentally, whilst some people find the concept of a marriage being ended by Death rather 'unromantic', this is theologically and practically very important. It means, for example, that a widowed person is totally free to remarry. In Christianity the marriage vows specifically state 'Until death breaks the marriage contract' whereas in Hinduism it does not!) Finding the right partner(s) can however be very difficult. This is especially so if one adds specific factors to the list of what is desired — for example, not just fertility or health, but also a particular ethnic or cultural or religious identity. And yet, with a very few tragic exceptions there really does seem to be, somewhere, a right partner for everybody. It is just that this partner is so often very hard to find… even in the days of internet social networks.

The Rabbis spoke of marriages being 'arranged in Heaven'. Abraham was very concerned that his son marry a girl from his own home country (Genesis 24:2-4). More prosaically there are organisations and agencies here on Earth which try to assist in narrowing down the choices — but even they cannot work miracles. The fact is that the smaller the possible pool of choices, the 'critical mass', then the lower are the chances of finding someone who matches all the desired factors — and there are now so few Jews left in the world that the chances of finding the appropriate JEWISH partner are alarmingly small. (You may be reading this because you have decided to share your life with someone Jewish and become Jewish yourself; but if you are reading this because you wish to become Jewish and THEN look for a suitable Jewish partner — be warned! At present the rate of Intermarriage — Jews marrying non-Jews — is alarmingly high in many countries and even within Orthodox circles (which sometimes claim smugly to be free of this issue) it is often only strong social pressure and strict imposition of parental control that provides the stability — experience shows that many people brought up in a strong Orthodox Jewish environment are only too keen to escape it if given the chance to make choices for themselves.)

Total reliance on first or superficial impressions is usually dangerous. The whole issue of finding the 'right partner' is extraordinarily difficult — though not impossible. (There are some people who give up and decide never to marry, which is more than a pity.) So often it appears that one's ideal partner is not interested, or is already married to someone else, or is from a totally different culture. People make the most remarkable mistakes and some require several attempts, hopefully (but not always) learning from their experiences. In former times — and this is still the case in some societies — the respective families played a major role in deciding who would be suitable, but this approach is rejected in modern times by those who like to feel totally independent and in control of their own lives. People who would always get professional advice before buying a car or a house, or investing their money, seem capable of deciding to invest themselves and their lives without taking any advice whatsoever (or rejecting it when offered) and tying themselves into unhappy and expensive relationships — the result often being that they have less rather than more self-respect when it comes to trying again. One is looking not just for a disco or holiday partner, not just for attractive outward appearance, but for someone with whom one can hopefully bring up children together, someone who will care for you and someone whom you may need to care for when illness or old age take their toll.

A successful pairing is called a '*Shidduch*' and the one who arranges it, by introducing the partners to each other, a '*Shadchan*'. Once this meant a person who went from village to village, making a note of an unmarried girl here, an unmarried boy there, and then discussing first with the families and then with the individuals a possible introduction based on whatever qualities were available or desired. Nowadays there are several commercial agencies which work with modern computer technology to try to 'match' their clients to each other. Some focus on matching Jewish partners.

It is impossible to analyse the concept or the phenomenon of 'Romantic Love' fully, which is why there are so many books, songs, poems, plays, films and more concerned with this complex combination of emotions. (The term 'Love' is also of course used for the emotional bonds to parents, children, places, all mankind, God etc., and not just for the romantic or erotic pairing of two individuals. In Greek there are different words for these, but in Hebrew '*Ahavah*' tends to be used for all.) But there is a psychological force — possibly assisted by hormonal or chemical factors — which sometimes acts upon two people to the extent that they lose interest in anyone else and form a close bonded pair. Sexual attraction is often but not always a part of this. Many works of literature speak of the 'eyes across a crowded room' phenomenon, the special 'spark' or quasi-magnetic attraction that singles one person out of a crowd. It is also the case that it is often hard or impossible for the friends and acquaintances of someone to understand exactly what he or she sees in their partner, and vice versa! But it is so…

On the other hand, experience throughout human history shows that this strong feeling can weaken over time, or can be challenged by the appearance of other potential partners — and then the bonds linking a pair can be severely weakened or even end altogether. It is also a widespread phenomenon that one person might feel this attraction and the other not!

2. CONDITIONS FOR MARRIAGE

In Jewish law and tradition a Marriage may take place between a Man and a Woman who are not prohibited from contracting such a relationship for other reasons (e.g. age, family closeness, being already married…).

In Biblical times (and until the end of the 11[th.] century CE for *Ashkenazi* Jews, till modern times for *Sephardim*) this meant that a man could already be married, whilst a woman could not. Nowadays Polygamy (having more than one wife) is forbidden, just as Polyandry (having more than one husband) always was, so neither party may have any prior 'attachment' — e.g. a previous marriage that was not fully and clearly dissolved. The couple must also not be related in any of the ways that would cause such a marriage to be classed as incestuous. Seventeen such categories are given in Leviticus 18:6-18 and a further twenty-six in the *Talmud 'Yevamot'* 21a. These are:

BIBLICAL PROHIBITIONS	TALMUDIC EXTENSIONS
1. Mother	Grandmother, paternal as well as maternal
2. Father's Wife (stepmother)	Father's or Mother's Stepmother. Some authorities forbid Father-in-law's Wife; and some also add the Wife of the Father's Mother's Father.
3. Sister	
4. Half-Sister, on Father's or Mother's side	
5. Daughter (inferred by the Rabbis from Grand-daughter)	
6. Son's Daughter	Daughter of Son's Daughter Daughter of Son's Son
7. Daughter's Daughter	Daughter of Daughter's Daughter Daughter of Daughter's Son
8. Father's Sister	Grandfather's Sister, whether maternal or paternal
9. Mother's Sister	Sister of Mother's Mother

BIBLICAL PROHIBITIONS	TALMUDIC EXTENSIONS
10. Father's Brother's Wife	Wife of Father's Brother of one Mother Wife of Mother's Brother; Maternal as well as paternal Wife of Grandfather's Brother of one Father

11. Son's Wife,
  even if only betrothed by means of
  Kiddushin
	Son's daughter-in-law
	Daughter's Daughter-in-law
	Some authorities add:
	Wife of former Son-in-law

12. Brother's Wife,
  except the case of Levirate
  (See below)	

13. Wife's Mother	Wife's Grandmother, on her father's or mother's side
14. Wife's Daughter	
15. Wife's Son's Daughter	Daughter of Wife's Son's Son
16. Wife's Daughter's Daughter	Daughter of Wife's Daughter's Daughter
17. Wife's Sister (i.e. One may not marry two Sisters, and one is not permitted to marry the Sister of his divorced Wife during the lifetime of the latter)	

Notes:

(i). Of course by 'Wife' in (2) is meant 'Former Wife' or 'Widow'.

(ii). 'Son of One Mother' means a Full- and not a Half-Brother; one's Father may have had more than one Wife.

(iii). When there was Polygamy and people had children when they were still very young the possibility of such cross-generational complications was of course much larger; the age-gap may not have been so great as one imagines.

(iv). In English law circumstance No. 12 is permitted, but as in No. 16 it also forbids Uncle/Niece marriage.

(v). Jacob, in marrying both Rebekah and Rachel, broke Rule 17! But this was in Genesis 29:16-30, before the *Torah* was revealed (and one could argue it was not his initial intention). Reuven broke Rule 2 (Genesis 35:22) when he had sex with Bilhah, his father's concubine and the mother of two of his half-brothers.

(vi). There are occasional complex and often tragic cases and scandals in the media, whereby for example half-brothers and half-sisters in a 'patchwork' family fall in love, people who have become 'Half-Siblings' through their respective parents' second marriage; Or two siblings who were split soon after birth and find each other as adults wish to marry, despite the prohibitions. Much is made by some commentators of the 'human right' to marry (or have sex with) almost whomever one wishes, but in fact there are good social and biological / genetic reasons for many of the above regulations which help to ensure that people know who is with whom and, just as importantly, who is NOT with whom. Especially in the days before DNA testing one wanted to be as sure as possible who was the father of any child and where they fitted into the family structure — and frankly, despite different social mores, the same basic questions of identity are still just as important, also in terms of Inheritance — e.g. issues of the rights of illegitimate children as heirs.

(vii). Omitted here are issues of Adoption — i.e. an adopted son may be legally classed as someone's son but is not biologically so. Their parents may be known if one adopts an orphaned child from within a family, as Abraham did with Lot (Gen. 12:5), or within a circle of friends or a community; or they may be unknown, and even from a different continent. What relationship does an adopted child have to a sibling who is the biological child of their parents?

(viii). The issue of Same-Sex Marriage will be dealt with (briefly) below, but it is already interesting (and vital) to start wondering whether similar rules are not also needed — a prohibition on a man marrying his former Husband's Brother, for instance, or his Uncle or his Half-Brother or his former-Wife's Husband... or on a woman marrying her former Sister-in-law...

And what is the status of someone born to a woman through a sperm donation? What rights may a biological Father have even if the mother of his child is married to another woman? What is the relationship of two children born to the same mother by two different sperm donors? (This is not necessarily the same as the classic case of a woman having children by two fathers, because in this case she might also be legally married to another woman who has the 'husband' role and acts in a parental fashion.) Orthodox authorities are usually opposed to conception by anonymous sperm donation because there is the danger that the same donor may have provided sperm for several children, who are therefore related through having the same biological Father but would have no means of finding this out.

One can see plenty of scope for work (and income) for Family Lawyers in the future. These issues are not dealt with in traditional Jewish sources but are becoming relevant to modern Jewish communities and require careful consideration, using as far as possible the ethical and legal guidelines laid down (in other contexts) in earlier texts. Marriage is NOT just about the couple, who may have met at a party, at work, on holiday or through the Internet, but about all the family members surrounding them, preceding them and descending from them. In an 'arranged marriage' this concept is clear — it is two Families that marry and rather than the couple hoping that their in-laws will get on with each other, it is the families which negotiate and make all the arrangements and then hope that the couple will get on with each other!

Let us not deny that the fact that this system lasted so long and lasts still in some parts of the world indicates that the idea is not wholly without merit!

Do note that Polygamy was not forbidden in the *Torah* or *Halachah* (which technically allowed a man to have up to four wives on condition he could keep them all equally provided for and satisfied!). Rabbenu Gershom (960-1040 CE, born and died in Metz but worked in Mainz) instituted several '*Takkanot*', religious rulings based essentially on his own authority though supported by later rabbinic synods. One of these was that it was forbidden for a man to marry more than one woman — or better formulated, to be married to more than one woman at a time. Another was that he could only obtain a divorce with his wife's consent. Initially these rulings were valid in the communities under his jurisdiction in the Rhineland (Speyer, Worms and Mainz, known by an acronym based on the first letters of their Hebrew names as the '*Sh'U'M*' communities — this is also Hebrew for Garlic and so this symbol is sometimes used) but they spread through the *Ashkenazi* world, many *Ashkenazi* communities being in any case situated in Christian countries where Monogamy was the rule. *Sephardi* communities, many based in Moslem countries where Polygamy was the rule, retained Polygamy until the founding of the State of Israel in 1948 made the institution of 'Western European' legal norms necessary even on new immigrants and refugees from Arab lands. (The pragmatic compromise solution was to accept as a 'legal wife' any woman who arrived in the new state with that status, but not to permit any further polygamous marriages once a family was settled in Israel.)

There is now some rabbinic debate as to whether a *Takkanah* is valid for 'only' one thousand years — in which case, technically, Rabbenu Gershom's has expired!

Since other communities including the Mormons practised polygamy (officially the Mormon church ceased teaching this in 1890, thus enabling Utah to become a U.S. State — but there was a doctrinal split and certain breakaway fundamentalist groups still practise it) and Islam permits a man to have up to four wives, we see that 'Polygyny' — the Greek for 'to have more than one female partner' — is technically feasible and in some places socially acceptable and is even justified by reference to ancient religious texts!

Divorce is possible in Judaism and it would often help couples to know more about the process and what is expected of each of them before it is too late. In the 1950s American Conservative rabbis under Saul Lieberman instituted an additional clause in the *Ketubah* to make this clearer — the so-called 'Lieberman *Get* Clause' by which both parties commit themselves, should the marriage fail, to appear before a Conservative *Beit Din* and to abide by its rulings and give/accept a *Get*. There is dispute between Orthodox and other authorities as to whether this is wholly valid as it restricts the freedom of both parties — but that was exactly the point, there had been too many cases of recalcitrant husbands abusing that freedom and creating difficulties for their wives.

3. REASONS FOR MARRIAGE

In terms of the traditional viewpoint it would be hard to better the description given by Rabbi John Rayner z'l' in his booklet 'Guide to Jewish Marriage' (U.L.P.S. 1975) p.1.

> 'Judaism regards marriage as ordained by God for man's good. The good is three-fold.
>
> Firstly, the propagation of the human species, so that the world may remain inhabited (cf. Isaiah 45:18) and God's purposes for it fulfilled. Therefore the first commandment addressed to man in the Bible is: 'Be fruitful and multiply' (Genesis 1:18).
>
> Secondly, companionship. 'It is not good for man to be alone... Therefore shall man leave his father and his mother, and cleave to his wife and they shall be one flesh' (Genesis 2:18, 24). The joining of two lives in marriage is the best remedy for loneliness and the best recipe for happiness. As the rabbis hyperbolically put it, 'A man without a wife lives without blessing, life, joy, help, good and peace.'
>
> Thirdly, the establishment of the family as the basic social unit. The one-family home provides the ideal setting in which children can enjoy their childhood and grow up to maturity under parental protection and guidance. When the Temple was destroyed, its place was taken by the home, as well as the synagogue. The Jewish home, ideally, is 'a little sanctuary' (Ezekiel 11:16), in which the father is like a priest, the mother like a priestess, and the dining-room table like an altar. In it, religion is experienced and practised, and transmitted from generation to generation. Its sanctified atmosphere helps to keep family relationships on a high ethical plane of mutual courtesy, respect, consideration and affection.
>
> Such a lofty conception of marriage obviously implies the ideal of permanence. That marriage was so viewed already in Bible times can be seen from the Prophets' frequent use of the husband-wife metaphor for the Covenant between God and Israel, especially when they wished to stress its abiding nature and the unfailing fidelity which it demanded.
>
> But though marriage is ideally a life-long union, it is not indissoluble. Human nature being what it is, it can break down, sometimes irretrievably. Then it would be unrealistic, and even harmful both to the individuals concerned and to the marriage ideal itself, to maintain the empty shell of its outward legality. In such cases, therefore, when all attempts at reconciliation have failed, Judaism regretfully allows divorce.'

4. SOME OTHER POSSIBLE PROBLEMS

There are many other possible, potential problems in ascertaining whether a marriage is fully acceptable according to Jewish Law and this chapter will not attempt to be fully comprehensive or authoritative. However, here are some examples:

(a). A Widow must be able to prove that she is really a Widow. If her husband is classed after a war or a maritime disaster as only 'Missing — presumed Dead' she is not free to re-marry because there is always the vague possibility that he might return — even after years of being a prisoner or a castaway. If he has simply left her, she is an '*Agunah*' — there is no formal 'closure' of the marriage possible and therefore it remains in effect, albeit in a highly unsatisfactory state for all concerned. She is 'chained' to her previous marriage.

The same applies if the husband is alive and his location is known but he refuses to co-operate in a '*Get*', provision of a divorce document that would dissolve the marriage formally.

(b). If a person is married to a person who is in a coma they are not 'free' even though marital life as commonly understood has ended.

(c). There are issues of providing 'permission' when two persons who are mentally handicapped wish to marry. Are they considered capable of taking such a formal, legal decision? Who may speak or sign for them?

(d). Both parties must be Jewish — yet definitions of what that means vary between different groups within Judaism and even from community to community. In most, still, the basic definition is that both parties have a Jewish mother, or have formally converted; In some, having or having had a Jewish father is enough — but what happens when someone comes from a community where 'Patrilineality' is accepted but wishes to marry in a synagogue where it is not? Or when their conversion certificate is not accepted by the rabbi of the community in which the couple wish to marry? See the passage below.

(e). A *Cohen* (a descendant of the ancient priestly caste) is not allowed, within Orthodox Judaism, to marry a divorcée or a proselyte (a woman who has converted to Judaism). In Reform Judaism this desire to maintain pure Jewish blood-lines for the Priesthood is not considered relevant.

(f). There are no other 'Caste' divisions within Judaism, but historically there were major problems for anyone classed as a '*Mamzer*' (female '*Mamzeret*'), people who 'should never have been born' because they were conceived in an adulterous or incestuous relationship — who, according to tradition, are only allowed to marry another '*Mamzeret*' or '*Mamzer*' for several generations. Although this is in no way

their own fault, they are stigmatised. Reform Judaism has discarded this concept.
(g). A divorced person must allow time to pass before re-marrying — three festivals
for a man, at least ninety days or until a child she is carrying is born and weaned,
for a woman.

(h). A man or woman was forbidden to marry a co-respondent — a person who,
through a sexual or other relationship, was directly involved in the breakdown of a
previous marriage.

(i). Traditionally a major purpose of marriage was to ensure the birth of more children. If a woman had shown symptoms of infertility (assuming it was not the husband's problem!) her husband could divorce her; such a woman was then in a difficult position, since she would be unlikely to find another partner except one who
already had a family or did not want one. Of course there are also cases where an
elderly couple, a widow and a widower marry and no children are expected to come
from the new union.

j). Levirate Marriage: Another complex matter is that of 'Yibum' and 'Chalitza' —
which Reform Judaism has dispensed with. The idea is (or was) that if a man died
without leaving an heir it is the duty of his family to 'continue his line' by making his
widow pregnant with a child who will then be classed as the child of the deceased
rather than of the brother who is the biological father. This may sound ridiculous
and traumatising to us nowadays — the idea of a widow being effectively compelled
to have sex with the brother of her deceased husband — but reflects a perspective
where the Family, the Community, is more important than the feelings of any individual (a pre-Enlightenment concept but still common in many parts of Eastern and
Southern Europe). In a positive way this also kept the widow 'in the family' — she
would be the mother of a grandchild to her former parents-in-law — and thus gave
her a status and material support. Otherwise she would be 'just' a vulnerable widow
on her own, maybe a long way now from her own former home and family, and with
no evidence that she was able to bear children — thus having poor chances in the
marriage market.

This concept, known as 'Levirate Marriage', was based on Genesis 38:8 where
Onan is told by his father Judah to father a child for his deceased brother Er; By
Deuteronomy 25:5-10 it was the duty of only one brother of the deceased to perform
this duty of marrying his former sister-in-law and, if he did not wish to do so, a
ceremony known as 'Chalitza' was developed whereby, before witnesses, the widow
would remove the shoe of her former brother-in-law, spit on the ground and recite a
formula complaining that he was unwilling to perform this duty. Both parties were
then formally freed from any further obligations towards each other. It did not take
long (see 'Yevamot' 39a) for 'Chalitza' to be vastly preferred over 'Yibum' and this
became the rule rather than the exception — becoming in effect little more than a
brief Beit Din ceremony that freed a widow from any dependency from or commitment to her former husband's family and vice versa …

Civil legislation also has to cope with these and other issues. What should the minimum age for consent to marriage be? What should one do when those marrying are physically handicapped in some way — and cannot read the document or hear what is being said? Who may act as their representatives, be trusted with power of attorney to sign documents? What could or should be done if one suspects that one partner is marrying simply to get a visa or a residence permit? Or if a Minor is sent back by her family to 'the homeland' for an arranged marriage under the local prevailing legal system? Many European legal systems struggle with these aspects of family law, where different cultures conflict in a multi-cultural environment — issues of 'child brides' or the 'family honour' that prevents a girl from choosing her own male friends (and permits her punishment or even murder for infringing the rule), or proxy marriage to some person back in a 'homeland' in the Near East or Asia — these are real and difficult issues.

Jewish law is merely one system amongst others — but it should be considered relevant for Jews! Nevertheless, the rule is always that civil law takes priority over Jewish law for civil matters; for example, although Jewish law would allow marriage after the age of Bat-*Mitzvah*, civil law prescribes a higher age and this is what is followed. We do not seek to impose our own legal system onto the existing one.

In many areas the attitude of Reform Judaism has been to facilitate marriage wherever possible, by removing some (but not all!!) of the restrictions that have developed and by re-interpreting 'case law' so that a lenient judgement can be reached. However these actions occasionally lead to accusations that 'invalid marriages' are being performed and the issue is one of great strife and confusion.

Civil society is also having to struggle with legal definitions of what is just a passing sexual encounter, what is a serious 'relationship', what is a mutually-binding 'partnership', where may two people jointly sign a contract for a mortgage or run a joint bank account or inherit from each other…? Even what family surname is someone entitled to register? Technically the institution of Marriage was the clear formal solution to these questions — either one was married or one was not, one was born into a family or not — but nowadays many couples 'choose not to marry' but to live together as couples and expect to be treated as couples, with the same rights as though they were married. Conversely, many a married couple who have retained their original surnames has encountered surprise and rejection when registering at hotels in other countries… In some European countries a widow's pension will only be paid to the surviving partner if they had been officially married for at least 12 months, thus ruling out 'deathbed ceremonies'.

Of course we are still just scratching the surface of possible issues! For example, there is a wide spectrum of personal sexual identification — the *Mishnah* ('*Bikkurim*' Ch. 4) is also aware of androgynous persons, those who have both male and female characteristics, as well as those who had neither. Then there are Transgender issues.

What is the situation if you yourself wish to adopt a different gender than the one on your birth-certificate, or if your Uncle becomes your Aunt, or your Half-sister your Half-brother? Essentially no two people are alike and yet the rules have to be made on the basis of what the statistical and historical norm is. When and how rules are changed, and with what authority and based upon what consultative process — that is the issue.

And what would happen if someone had illegally committed Bigamy — what would be the status of the members of the 'second' family?

Technically you do not need a Rabbi to officiate at a Jewish wedding — a Cantor can do it, provided there are two *kosher* witnesses — but you do need a Rabbi to act as the '*Mesader Kiddushin*' ('The One who Arranges the Ceremony') i.e. someone qualified to check beforehand that the people concerned may actually marry according to Jewish law and rites.

5. MIXED MARRIAGES.

The term 'Interfaith Marriages' implies a link bridging two people of two faiths, whereas 'Mixed Marriage' is more vague and could include any form of mixture — e.g. between a religious and a secular person, both Jewish! In modern open societies the chances of a Jew meeting and falling in love with a non-Jew are of course very high. Without descending into vitriolic condemnation and intolerance, or withdrawing into self-built restrictive ghettoes, what is the best way forward, respecting ALL those involved? Which pressures are legitimate and which are not? History and literature are full of tales of doomed love affairs and tragedies due to prohibited relationships so we need to be more constructive, open and welcoming. In this book we seek not to cover every eventuality but merely to point out some of the issues from a Jewish perspective. There are some rabbis who are prepared to officiate at a wedding ceremony where both partners are not Jewish, but many who are not. Why not?

From empirical experience and observations there are several different categories and demands upon a rabbi to officiate — e.g. (for now assuming two different genders):

Between a Jew and a non-Jewess;

A Jewess and a non-Jew (i.e. Will the kids be automatically Jewish? — what if there are boys to be circumcised?);

A Jew and a Christian;

A Jew and a secular agnostic with no religious identity;

A secular ignorant not-very-Jewish Jew and someone of another faith or none;

A case where the ceremony should be co-officiated with a Christian minister

* or in a church

* or the request for this even in a synagogue

* or in a neutral location, e.g. a hotel, beach, home, etc.

Many Christian ministers are prepared to officiate at some form of joint nuptial ceremony (for Protestants it is not a sacrament, for Catholics it is, but so long as they get a promise for the children to be raised Catholic they can work on the assumption that they have the next generation… This of course denies any validity to claims that the couple will also 'raise the children Jewishly').

There are different sets of problems that may arise. Often it is not the couple but the parents of the Jewish partner who make the approach to a rabbi. Often they have already heard that 'Reform never say 'No' to anything' and are shocked and disappointed and angry at a rejection. Sometimes a local Orthodox rabbi has given them the number of the Reform rabbi and told them that 'there will be no problem'… Often a couple set a wedding date (usually on a Saturday or a major festival!), book the caterer, the flowers, the hairdresser, the cars and THEN start to look for a Rabbi who will officiate…

Marriage as a whole has lost a lot of its power, social status, symbolic and legal importance… So many marriages end in divorce anyway, and yet there is an increasing emphasis (maybe as a consequence?) on the Wedding ceremony itself. For many secular or ignorant Jews this comprises mainly (a). *Chuppah*, (b). a 'Blessing from the Rabbi' and (c). Breaking the glass — anything else, any moral or social or legal commitments is beyond their conception. Offering an alternative to full *Kiddushin / Nisuin*, e.g. a '*Brit Ahavah*' is not necessarily a solution — the officiant might be clear in their mind that what they are doing is NOT a formal *Kiddushin* but for the families, the bride and groom, the wedding guests and the photographer all that will count was that 'the rabbi was there and said something' and merely by his or her presence therefore gave their confirmation and blessing to the event and the union.

The entire issue of a 'Mixed-Faith Marriage' is complex and contentious. Usually a couple who have fallen in love are blinded to most possible consequences — such as the status of their children. (If the husband is Jewish but the wife is not, then the children would not be classed automatically as Jewish in many communities and would need to be converted; Conversely, if the wife is Jewish and the husband not, the husband may find himself later being confronted by strong pressure from his in-laws to have his Jewish son circumcised!) One can often find a Catholic Priest or a Protestant minister prepared to 'co-officiate' at a form of wedding ceremony but whereas for Christianity (especially in Catholic and Orthodox Christianity) Marriage is technically a Sacrament, for Judaism it is a contract 'according to the law of Moses and Israel' ('*K'Dat Moshe veYisra'el*'), a contract which both parties sign in that they accept these laws and promise to build up 'a household in Israel' (meaning the People, not the State).

In former times in Europe this issue was much less common, for marriage was a purely religious rather than a civil matter and so only religious authorities were involved. This remained the case in the Ottoman Empire and the State of Israel has inherited this legal system, whereby marriage is only licensed by respective religious authorities, be these Jewish, Armenian, Russian or Greek Orthodox, Coptic, Moslem, etc. Anyone whose relationship does not fit the requirements laid down by their religious community has to leave and marry abroad in a country where a purely civil secular ceremony is permitted and is classed as legally valid.

Although many people complain about how 'old-fashioned and restrictive' this attitude is, one has only to look at some of the other horrors which occur — for cultural or quasi-religious reasons — to be thankful for some initial clarity. It occurs quite frequently for example that a European girl marries a Moslem man who — it turns out — then has a totally different view of the role of husband and wife than the one she herself grew up with… or who is enabled to take 'his' (not 'their') children away to his home country where there is a different legal system… or she has in-laws who demand that their granddaughters be circumcised or be married-off at a young age… It really does pay to work out in advance under which legal system one is marrying. Would Divorce be permitted? If so, how? What rights and responsibilities would either party have? Look at the long-term and not at the wedding day! It is not just Judaism which has such restrictions. Many communities contain a proportion of single mothers (and bereft fathers) bearing the emotional and financial scars of lengthy conflicts over access to, custody of, maintenance of, education of and religious upbringing of their children — this is a reality which Rabbis and other community professionals see. Marriages should not exist merely to provide income for lawyers when they break down…

Incidentally, the author knows also of cases where a European girl marries a *Sephardi* Israeli whose culture — perhaps influenced by a Moslem background in North Africa or Iran or Yemen — is also very different from her own and which can also lead to problems and a breakdown of the marriage. Definitions of 'mixed' can be much more complex than one initially thinks! The author also likes to point out, mildly, that his father was a man and his mother a woman, and one cannot get much more mixed than that!

6. SEVERAL STAGES OF MARRIAGE

No-one should rush into a marriage! Originally the process of marrying was one of three stages (just as we nowadays in secular society have the Proposal, then the purchase and giving of an engagement Ring — and then the Wedding ceremony).

The first stage was the Engagement (known as '*Tena'im*') — a written (or oral) agreement between the parties or their representatives that, at some future date, they would be married.
Whilst having no legal effect it was nevertheless seen as 'Breach of Promise' if this agreement were broken.

Then came the Betrothal (known as '*Erusin*' or '*Kiddushin*'). The Bridegroom ('*Chatan*'), in the presence of two acceptable witnesses ('*Eydim*'), would give the Bride ('*Kallah*') an object of a certain clear minimum value, while saying to her, 'You are betrothed to me, according to the law of Moses and Israel' or similar words: '*Harey At mekudeshet Li, k'Dat Moshe ve Yisrael*.' Note that the word '*Kadosh*' means 'holy' or 'sanctified' and through this formula the bride becomes exclusively the partner of the groom. In Reform ceremonies the bride makes a similar declaration to the groom ('*Harey At mekudash Li, k'Dat Moshe ve Yisrael*') and gives him a ring too, so assuring mutuality. It is actually a sacred act as well as a commercial one.

At the same time a document, the '*Ketubah*' would be drawn up — a written contract attesting to the transaction — and signed and witnessed.

Once betrothed, a couple were not necessarily yet able to live together but were nevertheless considered 'married'. Should the arrangement be terminated, a proper Divorce would be required to dissolve the agreements that had been made.

The final act was the '*Nissuin*' — the Wedding itself, consisting in essence of the physical Consummation. The *Chuppah* (originally the tent acting as what would now be called the 'Honeymoon suite' — see Psalm 19:5) became ritualised over time into a simple square or oblong canopy held over the couple while the Betrothal vows were being exchanged.

It follows that until the relationship has been consummated the marriage is not yet valid!

7. SOME CONTEMPORARY CUSTOMS

The '*Aufruf*'

Not a part of the wedding ceremony itself, it is a custom for a bridegroom (and in Reform and Liberal synagogues, also the bride) to be given an *Aliyah* and called to the *Torah* reading on the *Shabbat* before their wedding. The word '*Aufruf*' is simply German/Yiddish for 'A Call-Up'. There is no specific additional blessing to say apart from the usual ones (maybe a reference in the '*Mi Sheberach*' to the forthcoming celebration) but it provides an opportunity, for example, to involve the congregation in a *Kiddush* or to involve friends and family in one community if the wedding ceremony will be held in another.

The Marriage Service may be found in the RSGB *Siddur* pp.276-283; 8[th.] ed. pp.356-359 plus Psalms on pp. 40 and 52; (*Lev Chadash* pp.596-600). The key components are the same as for all Jewish wedding ceremonies, viz. a *Chuppah*, vows, a *Ketubah*, a ring (or two rings), two cups of wine and two witnesses.

Before going further it is perhaps useful to stress once again what you do NOT need at a wedding, despite many friends and others who may pressure you into having them. There is actually no need for a Rabbi, as any competent layman can also lead the service. There is no need for flowers, organ, choir, cameras, even a synagogue — for a *Chuppah* can be held almost anywhere. (Note: This does not necessarily apply to a civil marriage ceremony, which has its own constraints.) There is no need for bridesmaids, page boys or chauffeur-driven limousines. All these can distract from the true point of what is happening.

All you really need are the two people who wish to marry, two acceptable witnesses (i.e. Jewish but not too closely related to either party), an object of value (normally a plain gold ring) and a *Ketubah*. (A plain ring was preferred because it was easier to assess its value, based on weight, and harder to fake than a jewelled one.)

A marriage ceremony may take place on almost any day but not on a *Shabbat* or a Festival, nor on a Fast day observed by the community (Reform Judaism no longer observes the Fasts on 3rd. *Tishri* or 10th. *Tevet*, for example) and on certain other days which vary from community to community. A strict Orthodox view is to prohibit a wedding also during *Chol HaMo'ed*; the *Omer* period between *Pesach* and *Shavuot* or parts thereof, with the exception perhaps of the 33rd. Day (*LaG Ba'Omer*), or *Rosh Chodesh*; or the Ten Days of Penitence ('*Asseret Yemei Teshuvah*') between *Rosh Hashanah* and *Yom Kippur*. Put simply, these are times when it is seen as wrong to mix a happy occasion either with another happy occasion, or with a sad or contemplative one, or a day when commercial transactions are forbidden.

In the Reform and Liberal liturgy both Bride and Groom make the vows of Betrothal, being asked by the officiant and agreeing, and rather than the Groom 'purchasing' the Bride they exchange rings and speak similar albeit not identical formulae. (The Ring represents the 'object of value' and must be the absolute property of the person handing it over, not only part-paid or borrowed. This effectively acted as payment of the 'bride price' whereby the partner is 'acquired' — the process is called '*Kinyan*', 'Acquisition' — hence our stress on the mutuality of the agreement.) In some *Sephardi* communities the ring would earlier be worn in the nose, or ear, or as a bracelet, and not on a finger.

Both then sign the *Ketubah* before witnesses and then both enter a short period of seclusion (the '*Yichud*' or 'One-ness', 'Togetherness') representing the consummation (based on Gen. 2:24 where they become 'one flesh').

8. ORIGINS OF SOME OF THE CUSTOMS

As in almost everything else in Judaism the origins of many of the things we say or do are lost in antiquity, or may be found in a variety of other customs. Much of the traditional liturgy reflects an ancient patriarchal society in which daughters were kept securely locked away, only being let out — under supervision — to get married. Hence the period of *Yichud* would be the first time that bride and groom were alone together without a chaperone being present.

- The *Chuppah* represents not only the 'shared roof' that will be theirs — but is also a vague echo of the special tent or room in which the consummation took place —

often, in olden times, with eager witnesses waiting for visible proof of the Bride's virginity (see Psalm 19:5). After all, the traditional *Ketubah* distinguishes between a Virgin ('*Betulah*') and a Non-Virgin — perhaps a Widow ('*Almanah*') or Divorcée ('*G'rusha*') — and one might require proof that the higher price of 200 *Zuzim* was justified!

- The use of a Ring itself is probably a Roman or a Christian custom. Some see it as symbolizing eternity as it has no end.

- The glass which is broken at the end of the ceremony is a reminder of the destruction of the Temple and has come to symbolise in addition all the destructions which have been wrought on Jewish households through the ages — a poignant reminder that things can, and do, go wrong — even in happy marriages. Many a happy, optimistic couple has been torn apart later by violence, war or persecution.

9. THE *KETUBAH*

The Hebrew word means simply 'Something written', 'Document'. Traditionally introduced by Rabbi Shimon ben Shetach in the 1st. century BCE this document acts as the formal recognition of the contract between the bride and groom, detailing the price paid, the conditions to be fulfilled and the responsibilities binding on the parties.

There were standard sums laid down for different categories of bride — whether she was a virgin or previously married, for example. The document was signed by the husband before witnesses, but became the wife's property since it detailed the claim she would have on her husband's estate should she be widowed or should he divorce her. In this way 'casual divorce' was discouraged and maintenance of the wife assured.

(Do not forget, in previous times it was possible for a man to have more than one wife and in addition 'concubines' — sometimes translated as 'co-wife', who did not have the same rights as a 'Wife' — not to mention any number of slave girls. In such circumstances a document giving the female partner in a marriage specific rights was a major breakthrough. In Genesis 29:20-30 Jacob had to work for seven years to 'pay' for Leah and then another seven for Rachel, but there is no mention of any form of ceremony when he just absorbed into his household the maids of each of his wives, Bilhah and Zilpah, who also became the mothers of four of his sons…)

The original *Ketubah*, written in Aramaic, was in consequence a predominantly financial document even though the 'Abstract' frequently printed on the reverse of English Orthodox versions omits this to stress the 'love' and 'devotion' of the bride and groom.

Here is a slightly-edited translation of the traditional text, taken from '*HaMadrich*' (Hebrew Publishing Co. New York, 1956 pp.17-22). Those present and signing confirm:

'On the (…) day of the week, the … day of the month… in the year five thousand, seven hundred and … since the creation of the world, [corresponding to … in] the era according to which we are accustomed to reckon here in the city of [name of city, state and country] how [name of bridegroom] son [name of father] surnamed [family name] said to this virgin [or Widow or Divorcee, as the case may be] [name of bride] daughter of [name of father] surnamed [family name]:

'Be thou my wife according to the law of Moses and Israel, and I will cherish, honour, support and maintain thee in accordance with the custom of Jewish husbands who cherish, honour, support and maintain their wives in truth. And I herewith make for thee the settlement of virgins, two hundred silver *zuzim*, according to the law of Moses and Israel [in the case of a widow or divorcee, insert 'settlement of widows (divorcees), one hundred silver *zuzim*, which belongs to thee according to the ordinance of the Rabbis']. And I will also give thee thy food, clothing and necessaries, and live with thee as husband and wife according to universal custom.'

And Miss [name of bride], this virgin [or widow or divorcee] consented and became his wife.

The wedding outfit that she brought from her father's house [in case of a widow, divorcee or orphan, insert instead 'from her family's house'] in silver, gold, valuables, wearing apparel, house furniture, and bedclothes, all this [name of bridegroom], the said bridegroom, accepted in the sum of one hundred silver pieces [in the case of a widow or divorcee: fifty silver pieces] and [name of bridegroom] consented to increase this amount from his own property with the sum of one hundred silver pieces [or 'fifty silver pieces'] making in all two hundred silver pieces [or 'one hundred silver pieces'].

And thus said the [name of bridegroom] the bridegroom: 'The responsibility of this marriage contract, of this wedding outfit, and of this additional sum, I take upon myself and my heirs after me, so that they shall be paid from the best part of my property and possession that I have beneath the whole heaven, that which I now possess or may hereafter acquire. All my property, real or personal, even the mantle on my shoulders, shall be mortgaged to secure the payment of this marriage contract, of the wedding outfit, and of the addition made thereto, during my lifetime and after my death, from the present day and forever.'

[Name of bridegroom], the bridegroom, has taken upon himself the responsibility of this marriage contract, of the wedding outfit and the addition made thereto, according to the restrictive usages of all marriage contracts and the additions thereto made for the daughters of Israel, in accordance with the institutions of our sages of blessed memory. It is not to be regarded as mere forfeiture without consideration or as mere formula of a document.

We have followed the legal formality of a symbolic delivery (*kinyan*) between [name of bridegroom], the son of …, the bridegroom, and [name of bride], the daughter of… this virgin [or etc.] and we have used a garment legally fit for the purpose, to strengthen all that is stated above.

AND EVERYTHING IS VALID AND CONFIRMED.

Attested to………(Witness)

Attested to………(Witness)'

As one can see, this amounts in many respects to what would nowadays be termed a 'pre-nuptial agreement'. Should the husband die, or go bankrupt, or divorce her, the woman (if this is her first marriage) is entitled to a substantial capital sum of 200 *Zuzim* before any other claims can be made upon the estate. The reference to a garment is a reminder that one could hand over a cloth or item of clothing in the absence of a ring. (In colonial times there was a concept known as 'Marrying the Glove', whereby a man working on some distant plantation or mine would send a glove or similar back to his home country where his fiancée would, in the presence of a civil servant, formally marry this glove as representing him. She was then classed as his wife — and this was important in terms of the Company paying her fares out to the Colony, or classing her later as a widow.)

In most cases neither party nowadays has a clue as to what they are signing. Here is a copy of a typical 'Abstract', taken from a printed *Ketubah* issued by the *Beth HaMidrash Hagadol* synagogue in Leeds in the 1970s:

'On the […] day of the week, the […] day of the month […] in the year [57…] A.M., corresponding to the […] of [19…], the Holy Covenant of Marriage was entered into, in Leeds, between the Bridegroom: [………], and his Bride: [………]

The said Bridegroom made the following declaration to his bride:

'Be thou my wife according to the law of Moses and of Israel. I faithfully promise that I will be a true husband unto thee; I will work for thee; I will protect and support thee; and will provide all that is necessary for thy sustenance, even as it beseemeth a Jewish husband to do so. I also take upon myself all such further obligations for thy maintenance, during thy lifetime, as are prescribed by our religious statute.'

And the said Bride has plighted her troth unto him with affection and sincerity, and has thus taken upon herself the fulfilment of all the duties incumbent upon a Jewish wife.

> This Covenant of Marriage was duly solemnized and witnessed this day, according to the usage of Israel.'

Note the use of antiquated language to make the message 'seem' more traditional and legal.

And here is the translation of the Reform Movement *Ketubah* as used at the same time:

> 'On [...] the [...] day of the month of [...] in the year [57...] corresponding to the [...] here in [...] the bridegroom [.........] said to the bride [.........]

> 'Be my wife according to the law of Moses and Israel and I will cherish, respect and support you in the faithful manner in which sons in Israel cherish, respect and support their wives.'

> And the bride [.........] said to the bridegroom [.........]

> 'Be my husband according to the law of Moses and Israel and I will cherish, respect and support you in the faithful manner in which daughters in Israel cherish, respect and support their husbands.'

> And the bride [.........] agreed to the proposal of the bridegroom.

> And the bridegroom [.........] agreed to the proposal of the bride.

> Accordingly they both entered into this covenant of love and companionship, of peace and friendship, to create a Jewish home to the glory of the Holy One, blessed be He, who makes His people holy through the holy covenant of marriage.

> This has taken place in our presence and is all valid and binding.'

Here the language between the two equal partners is fully mutual (albeit the reference to God is not gender-neutral!)

There is some discussion as to when the *Ketubah* should be signed: whether before or during or even after the ceremony. Firstly, in most European countries a *Ketubah* serves only as a religious wedding document and the parties should already have a civil wedding certificate. In some communities in Britain this can be done at the same time, but even so the couple should technically sign the civil register before the *Ketubah*; In other countries a visit to the Register Office should precede the synagogue wedding.

Then we have the issue of whether it makes much sense to ask the bride and groom whether they wish to marry each other, if they have already signed the document stating this! It rather makes more sense to ask them verbally and, once they have verbally agreed before the witnesses, to ask them then to sign the confirmatory document. (This also, incidentally, gives more guests an opportunity for photographs.)

10. 'BEDECKEN'

This is a quaint custom, known by its German-Yiddish name, whereby before the wedding ceremony the bridegroom in front of witnesses lifts the bride's veil to check that it is the right girl!

Traditionally this goes back to the unfortunate experience of Jacob, who woke up after his wedding night to discover himself married to Leah rather than Rachel (Genesis 30:25). (No-one ever asks what Leah thought about this.) There is no formal blessing to say, though there is a custom for the blessing of Rebekah in Genesis 24:60 to be said: 'O Sister! May you grow into thousands of myriads!'

Strictly speaking the term 'Bedecken die *Kallah*' means to cover rather than uncover the bride and reflects the ceremonial veiling of the girl by her attendants prior to her being escorted to the *Chuppah*.

Sephardim do not practise this custom.

In a Reform wedding ceremony, with full equality for both partners, it may be appropriate for both to acknowledge before the witnesses that they truly intend to marry each other.

11. ESCORTING THE BRIDE

'*Hachnasat Kallah*', the act of 'Leading the Bride' to her wedding, is considered to be a major honour and a *Mitzvah*. In ancient times it meant taking her from her own home to her future home and of course an attractive young woman laden with worldly goods would need to be protected along the way — the escort had a real protective function! Nowadays the task is mainly to ensure that both parties arrive, reasonably upright, at the right time in the place where the ceremony is to be held.

Modern customs vary; traditionally (where possible) the groom's father and the bride's father escorted the groom to the *Chuppah*, the groom's mother and the bride's mother the bride. This also symbolised the extent to which both families were supporting the marriage. Other variations include the bride entering between both her parents or on her father's arm. However the number of attendants may include bridesmaids, 'Best Man', page-boys and all the paraphernalia of modern wedding etiquette, mostly borrowed from the surrounding culture. There is nothing wrong with any of this, but it is all dispensable if necessary. There is no 'Jewish law' about it and it should not be allowed to distract from the main point of the ceremony, which is to bring bride and groom together to start their new lives together. Details of the flowers, arguments about matching dresses and shoes etc. can get really out of hand…

When a bride was an orphan it was especially important for the community to ensure that she was safely married (or married-off). In the absence of parents she would be led by an '*Unterführer*' (Yiddish for 'one who leads you under'). This practice is often used nowadays when the parents of either bride or groom are non-Jewish, but it is not compulsory — in most Reform communities non-Jewish family members are encouraged of course to be present for the ceremony and to take part in it as far as possible or as far as they wish.

It should be noted that *Chuppot* come in various sizes but the aim is to escort the couple TO the *Chuppah*, not UNDER it. Occasionally one hears major discussions as to who should stand where 'under the *Chuppah*' and the simple answer is that just the Groom and Bride (and possibly the officiant) actually stand under the *Chuppah* — it is, after all, meant to represent their space — and everyone else stands around, but not under the canopy.

12. BREAKING THE GLASS

At the end of the wedding ceremony, after all the formulae and blessings, the groom ceremonially breaks a wine glass (usually wrapped in something to prevent the fragments scattering). Since this marks the end of the ceremony it is often greeted by cries of '*Mazal Tov!*' by those attending, but in fact it is a sad, solemn reminder of destruction. In the *Talmud* ('*Berachot*' 31a) according to mediaeval commentators the custom was introduced by two rabbis who deliberately smashed expensive glassware to reduce the general hilarity of the wedding guests, which was getting out of hand!

Later it was seen as a reminder of the destruction of the Temple and nowadays it is seen as a reminder of the all-too-frequent instances which destroy and have destroyed Jewish families. It would really be more appropriate to count to ten and stand in silence and only THEN begin the congratulations.

In some places an old light bulb is used. This is cheating! A wine glass provides important symbolism of its own.

13. THE '*SHEVAH BERACHOT*'

(RSGB *Siddur* p.282; p.358.) The 'Seven Blessings' are quite ancient but do not all follow 'standard' formulae for blessings. The first is made over wine — as this is a festive occasion. The others are understood to refer firstly to general humanity, then secondly to the specific couple being married. The context is of the tragedies of the past (the destruction of Jerusalem) and the hopes for a better and happier future.

At the wedding feast the *Shevah Berachot* are added to the '*Birkat HaMazon*' (Grace After Meals). These blessings would then be said at every meal in the week following the ceremony (though the order is changed slightly, that over Wine is then said at the end, not the beginning).

They are not included here in the '*Forms of Prayer*' 7[th.] Edition pp.331-337, but the additional opening formulae for Wedding banquets are included in the 8[th.] Edition on **pp.487f.** In addition small booklets are often printed for such festive occasions and these include the additional lines for wedding meals.

The text (here from the 8[th.] Edition **p.358**) reads:

'Blessed are You, our Living God, Sovereign of the universe, who creates the fruit of the vine.

Blessed are you, our Living God, Sovereign of the universe, who created everything for the divine glory.

Blessed are you, our Living God, Sovereign of the universe, who forms human beings.

Blessed are you, our Living God, Sovereign of the universe, who formed human beings in the divine image, to be like God, to imitate and to resemble God and prepared from human beings and for human beings a constant sharing and renewal. Blessed are you God, who forms human beings.

Let Zion, deprived of her young, rise up again and cry out for joy as her children are gathered around her in happiness. Blessed are You, God, who gives joy to Zion through her children.

Give these companions in love great happiness, the happiness of Your creatures in Eden long ago. May Your children be worthy to create a Jewish home that honours You and honours them. Blessed are You God, who rejoices the bridegroom and the bride.

Blessed are you, our Living God, Sovereign of the universe, who created joy and happiness, bride and bridegroom, mirth, celebration, pleasure and delight, love and companionship, peace and friendship. Soon, our Living God, may the sound of happiness and rejoicing be heard in the towns of Judah and in the streets of Jerusalem, the voice of the bridegroom and the voice of the bride. Blessed are You, God, who causes the bridegroom to rejoice with the bride.'

One popular idea is to ask a particular honoured guest or several different guests to share in reciting the seven blessings after the meal.

14. SAME-GENDER MARRIAGES

For obvious historical reasons these are a relatively new phenomenon in both civil and religious spheres and the situation regarding them is not yet fully clear, nor are they fully accepted by all Progressive rabbis or communities. This paragraph can therefore only be a brief (and unsatisfactory) and personal preliminary overview of the current situation. It has become fashionable to accuse anyone showing any hesitancy or criticism of 'Homophobia' but in fact there are good reasons for rabbinical Judaism to take a certain distance and to analyse this situation carefully — more carefully than is sometimes done under this sudden social pressure to 'make everyone happy'.

People are different and there is a whole spectrum of sexual identities — all can be seen as being a part of Creation. This is not the issue. The concern is whether an emphasis on the 'rights' of people to marry or to found families is always going to be beneficial to everyone in the longer term. The topics discussed above have shown that even within heterosexual relationships there can be many pitfalls and problems and one needs structures (or sometimes one needs to modify structures) to ensure that society as a whole survives. Medical science has changed drastically in recent decades and it is now possible for someone who feels they are 'in the wrong body' to take treatment to change — or even to change back. It is now possible for a man to use his sperm to fertilise an egg taken from a donor living in a different country which is then implanted in a surrogate mother living in a third country and so become a 'parent' — but what of the feelings of the child when he or she becomes old enough to understand the circumstances surrounding their conception and birth? Such matters need at least thinking about. Questions of sexuality and sexual identity are hardly new. *Halachah* does concern itself with persons of neither of both sexual identities (see *Mishnah* 'Bikkurim' Ch. 4 — referring to the 'Androgynos' — one who has both gender characteristics — and the 'Tumtum' — one who may be either/or but it is uncertain which) and, as we have seen, with 'appropriate' and 'inappropriate' relationships. The feelings between two adults may and should be respected for what they are; but complications arise when they wish to start a family through one of several means.

Should a gay couple adopt two children of different backgrounds — are they then full siblings or not? Should both partners in a lesbian couple produce through sperm donation (the donor either known or anonymous) each a child — to what extent are these children related to each other? The simile 'patchwork family' is interesting because it is much easier to rip a patchwork apart along the seams than a single sheet of cloth. Adding these extra dimensions to 'patchwork' can lead in the future to major issues. The potential problems are never noticed so long as everyone is happy — but the problems can and do arise when one or more persons in the complex non-nuclear families of modern times stop being happy — when there are divisions or when there is a death. Who is or may be the legitimate heir of whom? How may an inheritance be divided? Who may have custody over which child? To what extent are the children permitted or forbidden sexually to each other when they grow up?

In the *Torah* there are enough problems when Abraham has first two sons from two wives, and then (in Gen. Ch. 25:1-6) six more sons from a third wife — to whom he is careful to give capital sums and then dismiss, thus excluding them from inheritance issues. Isaac has twins — and there is conflict over inheritance. Jacob has sons through four wives of different legal and emotional status and there is intense jealousy amongst the (half-)siblings, not to mention a relationship between one son and one wife. These stories provide a realistic context to the sort of issues that can arise in families.

In Progressive Judaism a 'Brit Ahavah' (a 'Covenant of Love') has been created to provide an alternative form of ceremony. Whilst many same-sex couples are eager to have a 'traditional *Chuppah* ceremony' (and some rabbis are prepared to officiate) the simple fact is that this is a contradiction in terms. It is not 'K'dat Moshe veYisrael' — according to Mosaic Law. To put it at its simplest, we still do not really have the right and universally accepted vocabulary in either English or Hebrew for a male

Wife or a female Husband (and in Hebrew the gender is grammatically significant for nouns, adjectives and verbs). Of course there are modern possibilities in some places and States for two men to adopt a child or two women to have a child conceived and born through sperm donation, so it is not as though the creation of a family is *a priori* impossible despite biological hindrances, but it is still too soon to work out how this will all develop in the future. We are still in the first generation or generations creating these new structures.

The time will surely come when people can describe what it is like to have two fathers-in-law just as they have a brother and brother-in-law, and the time will come when there is sufficient sociological data to be able to form a better picture of what this will mean to children and grandchildren — but not yet. Where there is a substantive difference between biological and social/familial roles, this can also cause confusion: For example, should two men adopt a child, and then later split, then neither is biologically the 'mother'. How are custody and visitation rights and support responsibilities to be divided and allocated (and enforced)?

It is good when two people wish to be happy with each other and to form a serious and hopefully permanent bond with each other and to seal this with some form of religious ceremony, and it is good to seek ways to make this public affirmation — but to expect Jewish tradition to offer helpful answers 'out of the box' is to expect too much. It is ironic that many gay and lesbian couples yearn so deeply for a 'traditional' wedding, or at least a ceremony with many 'traditional' components and seek to establish a 'traditional' nuclear family; consistency would of course require that they then, if and when necessary, co-operate in a traditional divorce procedure and 'Get' — or at least, with such traditional components as are feasible.

Possibly in twenty years or so one will look back and wonder what all the fuss was about; but for now it is important not to be rushed by fashion or political pressures into overlooking the issues that Family Law and *Halachah* have taken centuries to consider (and have in many cases still not satisfactorily resolved).

15. OTHER WEDDING CUSTOMS

There are many other wedding customs and variations on the ceremony, involving costumes, veils, melodies, where and when one marches in or out, whether the bride walks solemnly seven times round the groom (or each take turns to walk so round each other), whether and when the bride's attendant or mother raises her veil, on which finger the ring is placed (it doesn't matter!) and so on, but those described above will hopefully give the main outline and the rest is open to negotiation. Often the bride — or both bride and groom, but separately! — will immerse in a *Mikveh* the day before. One is, after all, preparing oneself for an act of holiness. The modern custom of 'stag' or 'hen' parties with both partners getting inebriated and making fools of themselves has nothing to do with such mental and spiritual preparation. Some of the symbolism is actually related to Death. In some communities the groom wears a '*Kittel*' (shroud) and the couple fast on the day of the wedding being, so to speak, 'dead to the world', dying in their old single identities and then being re-born into their new identity as part of a Couple.

It is quite common that at the celebration after the ceremony the bride and groom are placed on chairs and lifted up as the guests dance, sometimes holding together the ends of a cloth.

16. ANNIVERSARIES

There is little fuss about wedding anniversaries in Judaism and of course one faces — as with other issues such as birthdays or *Yahrtzeits* — the question of whether the Jewish or the secular date is the one to be marked. Of course it is good to mark and celebrate a happy occasion and in '*Lev Chadash*' p. 604 is a prayer for a Wedding Anniversary.

In some families the wedding anniversary is even marked after one of the spouses has died. Which brings us to:

17. WIDOWHOOD

There is not a great deal to write about this and not a lot written — it is one of those 'taboo' subjects — and yet, if one thinks about it, it is a condition which will statistically afflict around 50% of those who marry and stay married, since it is comparatively rare that both partners will die simultaneously. It is rare that people think about it in advance and plan for it, except — at most — in terms of insurance and pensions and providing in some way for the material well-being of the surviving partner.

The rules for Mourning apply to the initial period following a bereavement and are described in a later chapter. The rabbis describe the loss of one's first spouse ('the spouse of one's youth' — '*Sotah*' 2a, see also Proverbs 5:18 or Isaiah 54:6) as an incomparable tragedy. Rabbi Yochanan said that a man whose wife dies is as despondent as one who has seen the Temple destroyed. Rabbi Shmuel ben Nachman said 'Everything can be replaced, except the wife of one's youth' ('*Sanhedrin*' 22a). The widow — '*Almanah*' — is one of the categories of those who by definition need help and support in society (see Deuteronomy 10:18, 14:29, 16:11, 16:14, 24:19-21, 26:12f., 27:19, Isaiah 1:17, Jeremiah 7:6, Jeremiah 22:3, Ezekiel 22:7, Zechariah 7:10; Malachi 3:5, Psalm 94:6, Psalm 146:9); A Priest was forbidden to marry a widow, amongst other categories — (Leviticus 21:14, Ezekiel 44:21); Elijah helped a poor widow in I Kings 17:10; A widow (and a divorcée) is permitted to make vows (Numbers 30:10). Normally a younger widow would return to her father's house to be protected until she could be found another partner — in Ruth 1:8 Naomi tells her widowed daughters-in-law to return to their mothers' houses, implying that their mothers are also widows.

On the other hand the hope is that, if circumstances allow, a widow or widower will remarry in due course and rebuild their lives. In which case — depending on the age at which one was widowed and whether there are children and what age they have reached — one may need to confront other questions. What if the new partner also has children, and how will they relate? Should one try for children from the second marriage also? How does one show respect and love for the new partner whilst still maintaining certain mourning rituals, e.g. *Yahrtzeit* and *Yizkor* for the former one? What inheritance issues — involving, say, children from the first marriage — must be very carefully considered so that no one fears lest someone is marrying a wealthy widow or widower purely from financial greed?

There is no extensive *Halachah* about these issues — apart from the advice to wait a sufficient period of time to ensure that the paternity of any new child is clear. Widows and Widowers who remarry will of necessity be stepping part-way into their new partner's life as well. There might be questions concerning reserved grave plots — should one choose to lie next to the first or second spouse? How can one relate second-time around? What are the new characteristics one is seeking in a partner this time around? Does one even wish to change one's official status (important when it comes to issues of pensions and inheritance)? In which case, be aware that no synagogue can perform a *Chuppah* unless the civil wedding has taken place first.

CHAPTER 31

DIVORCE

1. INTRODUCTION

Divorce is not encouraged in Judaism, but it is seen as a 'necessary evil' and it is allowed.

In all matters involving human relationships it is possible for these relationships to sour and become destructive rather than constructive. In such a situation Jewish law and tradition takes the position that it is better for all concerned that the relationship be dissolved — but dissolved properly, openly and in writing.

The rate of divorce has gone up steeply in Europe and so it is important to be at least informed about it. One interesting (and for many people surprising) statistic is that, of all those who divorce in a given year, 100% had been married! This implies that they had thought they had found a suitable partner and so the disappointment and the loss of self-respect ('How could I have made such a mistake? How can I ever trust anyone again?') can be great. One often seeks to apply blame for the breakdown of the relationship and it is usually impossible to counsel both partners in a failing or failed marriage together. Destructive arguments over possessions, furnishings, pension funds and savings, the children and who is the 'better' parent — can poison the atmosphere.

2. IN THE BIBLE

There are several 'passing references' to divorce in the Bible, showing that it was not something unusual. For example:

'(The priests)…shall not marry a woman divorced from her husband' (Lev. 21:7)

'If a priest's daughter is a widow or divorced, and has no child, and returns to her father's house…' (Lev. 22:13)

'Any vow of a widow or a divorced woman… shall stand…' (Num. 30:10)

A man was not allowed to divorce his wife if he had slandered her by falsely accusing her of pre-marital 'infidelity' (Deut. 22:13-19), nor if he had raped a non-betrothed virgin, was caught and was compelled to marry her (Deut. 22:28-29). In these latter cases the aim is clearly to provide some protection for a woman who would be unlikely to find another marriage partner if she were divorced.

The key passage is Deuteronomy 24:1-4 which deals with the possibility of a man wishing to re-marry the wife he had divorced after she had — in the meantime — been married again, and divorced or been widowed. This is prohibited. However the wording of these verses has had profound influence on Jewish divorce procedures:

> 'When a man takes a wife and marries her, if then she finds no favour in his eyes because he finds something obnoxious about her, and he writes her a bill of divorce, and puts it in her hand, and sends her out of his house...' (Deut. 24:1).

The exact wording of this 'bill of divorce' or '*Get*' is not known, though in Hosea 2:4 we find the prophet makes a declaration 'She is not my wife, and I am not her husband.' The definition of the 'obnoxiousness' is also not clear and the rabbis of the *Talmud* discuss at length what constitutes this '*Ervat Davar*' — whether it means any unpleasant mannerisms, something sexual, or general incompatibility. Divorce may have been threatened by barrenness, or jealousy — especially when there was more than one wife, as in the case of Sarah and Hagar, albeit wives of different status.

It is important to bear in mind always that in Biblical law we are dealing with a very different kind of society (though there are still many quite like it around in the world today). There is no mention of the necessity for love and romance in marriage, so the loss of romance would in itself constitute no ground for ending it. Women are vulnerable creatures in a brutal male-dominated society, whether nomadic, agricultural or urbanised. They are captured as slaves, taken as concubines or (like Dinah) just raped on the streets. They have no resources or careers of their own. Within this context the Jewish marriage and divorce laws have a strong internal coherence, even if they may sometimes seem strange, primitive and one-sided to us today. They provide some modicum of security. A woman may not be taken in marriage without her consent, with written proof and witnesses; Neither may she be discarded lightly, but must have accepted a document from her husband and the transaction must follow strict rules. The husband also has marital duties laid down for him and may not, for example, take a new job that involves further absences from home or working with stinking materials without her consent.

3. IN THE TALMUD

Many of these rules were developed during the Talmudic period. In essence they follow the procedure described in Deuteronomy, viz. the document has to be specifically written and handed by the husband to the wife. One of the major problems facing the traditionalist Jewish community today is that, on a strict interpretation of that verse, there is no basis for a revised procedure whereby the wife herself may initiate divorce proceedings, or whereby a divorce document may be issued when the husband is insane or unwilling.

It is worth noting that the divorce is not actually issued by a Court, as in English law. The *Get* is witnessed by the Court (and nowadays usually prepared by it) but divorce itself remains an act between the two parties to the marriage. Mutual consent, without specific causes or blame or 'guilty parties' and so on, is sufficient cause.

4. IN LATER JEWISH LAW

The rabbis always tried to discourage divorce by attempting to effect a reconciliation between the parties concerned. Under certain circumstances a wife has the right to demand a divorce — if the husband's behaviour is really intolerable for instance, or if he has certain repulsive physical defects of which she was unaware when contracting the marriage. (If she had been aware, or has condoned them at all since marriage, these can not be brought later as reasonable grounds for divorce.)

Likewise a husband has the right to demand a divorce for similar reasons as above, plus conditions that could interfere with marital life such as epilepsy or barrenness. (According to the 'Shulchan Aruch' 'Even HaEzer' 154:1 etc. a husband may demand divorce if his wife has failed to bear children within a period of ten years, if he can convince the Court that he has no other children and sincerely desires some.) However the concept of 'compulsory divorce' is a complex one, since it contradicts the earlier stress on free-will delivery and acceptance.

It should be noted that, however distressing a divorce may have been to a wife, one of the alternatives — being deserted by her husband — would have led to even worse problems since she would have become an 'Agunah', a 'chained woman', forbidden to re-marry.

5. THE *GET*

In order to prevent casual use of pre-printed forms the provision of a *Get* must follow stringent rules. It must be written by a scribe (*Sofer*) upon the husband's specific instructions to write it 'for him, for her, and for the purpose of divorce.' The scribe formally presents the writing materials to the husband as a gift, so that they might be 'his property'. The text itself is largely standardised and normally written in Aramaic. Here is a slightly condensed form of the traditional Aramaic wording of an *Ashkenazi* Get:

'On the [...] day of the week, the [...] of the month of [...] in the year [...], from the creation of the world according to the calendar reckoning we are accustomed to count here, in the city of [...], I [...] (also known as [...] the son of [...] (also known as) [...], who today am present in the city [...], do willingly consent to release, to set free, and put aside thee, my wife [...], in order that thou may have permission and the authority over thyself to go and marry any man thou may desire. No person may hinder thee from this day onward, and thou art permitted to every man. This shall be from me a bill of dismissal, a letter of release and a document of freedom, in accordance with the law of Moses and Israel.

Witnessed [.........]Witnessed [.........]'

By this means a married woman, by definition forbidden to everyone except her husband, becomes an unmarried woman again, free to form new relationships. If she does not do so, she may re-marry her former husband. If, however, she had had a further relationship, she may not then re-marry her former husband. The change of status is clear and unequivocal.

6. PROCEDURES

The act of marriage is a public one, performed in front of witnesses; The act of ending a marriage is also public, performed in front of witnesses. During the act of marriage the bride is given the '*Ketubah*'; at a formal ceremony of divorce this is formally torn and she is given instead a '*Get*'.

The main problem with the procedures today is that, by definition, a couple who marry are keen to see each other, whereas a couple whose marriage has broken down are not. This means that tactful handling of the situation is necessary. Many people who have gone through traditional procedures have complained afterwards that they felt 'humiliated'. This is a shame. Handled correctly, the meeting of husband and wife at a ceremony to dissolve formally the ties between them could theoretically be a healthy, cathartic act. Not necessarily a pleasurable one of course, but akin to funeral rites (a marriage has died, after all) which are painful at the time but which leave healthier memories of a release from tension and of a formal leave-taking. Often rabbinic courts do not seem to realise when the time for mediation and reconciliation is past and the time for a good, clean break has come. (One of the issues for Jewish feminists, Orthodox as well as Reform, is the lack of a women's perspective in many such courts and the need to change this and give a broader and more balanced viewpoint.)

Because of this desire to avoid a personal meeting — even a short one, in which the husband may drop or throw the document into the wife's hand (so avoiding physical contact) the possibility exists for agents ('*Sh'lichim*') to be appointed by either party. They would have power-of-attorney to hand the *Get* to the wife and the wife can also appoint an 'agent of receipt' to accept the *Get* on her behalf. Members of the Court will act as witnesses. This is a procedure followed largely by the Reform *Beit Din*, which enables it to act on behalf of cases involving people in different parts of the country or even in other countries if they have signed (and had witnessed) an 'Agency form'. This procedure is similar to the one whereby houses are 'conveyed' from one owner to another through third-parties — solicitors — without the owners actually being present.

7. CIVIL DIVORCE

A major complication nowadays is that matters of personal status — marriage and divorce, for example — now come under the civil law of the land as well as under religious law where desired.

In practical terms this means that a couple can be civilly divorced (and therefore free to re-marry in a civil ceremony at a Register Office) before their religious marriage is dissolved as well. Since a wedding is usually organised with a great deal of ceremony, involving families and friends, whereas a divorce is usually a frighteningly-lonely process fraught with bitterness and feelings of guilt and failure, there is a tendency to ignore religious divorce entirely as an irrelevance, an additional bother and expense. The task of the rabbi has often changed from witnessing the *Get* to pleading with the couple (or former couple) to arrange one or agree to one! Part of the problem stems from ignorance.

At their wedding many Jews have little idea what they are signing in the *Ketubah*, or that they are in effect marrying twice over at the same time — both civilly and religiously — in accord with both civil and religious laws — and are therefore bound by 'the law of Moses and Israel' to dissolve BOTH marriage ties.

In Israel, where civil marriage and divorce do not exist at present, the Rabbinical Courts are in full control over status matters. This means that if a husband deserts his wife she may go to the Rabbinical Court to ask for a divorce and they may exert what pressure they can, possibly through the civil courts, to persuade the husband to co-operate, but there is no way such a woman can on her own obtain a civil divorce and re-marry. The problem lies in the fact that the husband has to give the *Get* himself, 'voluntarily' — so persuasion may be used to make him do so, sometimes even threats of punishment for not co-operating, but not force!

Cases exist where a husband has refused to co-operate unless he is paid, or retains the marital home and children, or has even chosen to go to jail rather than co-operate — and under the strict interpretation applying, there is nothing anyone can do to correct this manifest injustice.

According to *Halachah* a husband may even (under certain circumstances) re-marry without giving his former wife a *Get*. Such a marriage may not be fully valid — it is bigamous according to Israeli law for example — but it is acceptable by Jewish law, which is still based on concepts dating from a period when polygamy was allowed and any children born to him by his second wife are *halachically* acceptable. However, in contrast, any child born to his estranged former wife by a second husband would be classed as a '*Mamzer*', one ritually unfit to marry another Jew for generations to come…

To circumvent the manifest injustice of this situation, whereby a husband can threaten his ex-wife with keeping her indefinitely in the status of an '*Agunah*', 'One who is chained', not free to rebuild her life as an independent person, the Reform *Beit Din* may under certain specific circumstances — after attempting all reasonable means to encourage the recalcitrant husband to co-operate — issue its own *Get* document to free the former wife from a marriage that clearly exists in name only.

There has been much discussion in Orthodox and Reform Jewish circles concerning the amount of pressure that may legitimately be applied to such a husband without the *Get* being invalidated because it is no longer 'voluntarily' granted. In addition there have been moves to require parties contracting a marriage to sign a pre-nuptial contract agreeing to co-operate in the issuance — and acceptance — of a *Get* should the marriage fail. (See also in the chapter on *Kiddushin* the reference to the 'Lieberman *Get* Clause' in the *Ketubah*). The exact legal status of such contracts in the civil courts has been a major area of uncertainty, but the intention behind them is clear — to remove doubt and excuses and the misuse of one's position to extort concessions from the other party.

8. WAYS FORWARD

Divorce is never pleasant. It always implies some form of failure — of judgement or personality or relationship or trust. Yet — and this may seem obvious and was mentioned at the outset — every couple who divorce were married first! Presumably they would not have married had they expected from the outset that their marriage would end in divorce.

The inescapable conclusion is that greater education of couples is needed, before they marry, to ensure that they are as prepared as possible for at least some of the problems and pitfalls ahead. If they are more aware of what might go wrong and what strains may be placed upon them by ill-health, economic pressures, bereavements, family estrangements and so so, they would be at least better prepared for these problems when they occur and possibly better able to overcome them.

The divorce rate in many European countries is rising rapidly, yet we seem unable to cope with the effects on the individuals concerned, on their children or parents, or on society itself. There are even simple problems for teachers who have children in the class whose parents have a different surname! Too often the lawyers rub their hands at the prospect of lengthy and costly disputes over matters which in themselves are trivial ('Who gets the freezer?') but are seen as symbolic battlefields which have to be 'won' — whatever 'winning' means in this context.

Synagogues have great problems in organising such matters as subscriptions for divorced couples or individuals; or knowing whom to contact regarding education or youth events ('Which parent is Johnny with this weekend?'); the appropriate resolution of the needs of a Jewish child whose parents have re-married — but to someone non-Jewish; and so on. Statistically, in the majority of cases it is the mother who is left alone with the children after such a divorce, with almost no time for a private life of her own and with great financial and employment problems. When the father has visiting rights at weekends this eats into time for such things as synagogue services, Bar-*Mitzvah* preparation, youth outings or sleepovers and a whole range of other potential conflicts. What happens to the relationship between a former son- or daughter-in law and the former parents-in-law (who may of course also be the grandparents who do not wish to lose contact with their grandchildren)?

It has been suggested — not facetiously — that there ought to be some sort of synagogue ritual to mark the ending of a marriage; Some form of public statement that a person is now free and 'available' once more. In fact, as we have seen, the traditional *Get* procedure largely fulfilled this cathartic role, yet it is not seen as appropriate, or desirable, by the majority of those that have to use it. Perhaps a greater degree of 'Education for Divorce' may help?

CHAPTER 32

DEATH AND FUNERAL CUSTOMS

1. INTRODUCTION

Death comes to us all — and usually unexpectedly. Throughout history the mortality rate has remained steady at 100%. Despite the vast experience the human race has accumulated, surprisingly little is known about the process.

It is true that scientists can discuss concepts such as 'brain death' and analyse electrical impulses in the cortex or whatever, much in the way they can observe the processes of ovulation and conception.

But no one can really explain 'Life' itself and how it starts and in consequence no one can really explain the End of Life or what comes after it — commonly called Death. Yet — this universality of experience has led to every culture creating systems to handle the aftermath of a death and to come to terms with its consequences, for the dead and for the living. (Even some animals seem to have an awareness — for example, Elephants.) Of course we tend to see the world through the eyes of a specific species of mammals. 'Life' on our planet takes many forms, including insects, yeasts, fungi, viruses and bacteria, plants and trees, reptiles, birds, fish... yet when people sometimes ask whether animals have souls they are usually thinking of a specific pet dog or cat, not of all the other beings which somehow come into existence, their cells multiply in different ways, they exist for different spans of time and they often display some form of consciousness, or instinct, or awareness, or reaction to their surrounding physical environment. In Genesis Ch. 1 God is portrayed as the creator of all and everything, even though not all is named.

Judaism, having existed for many centuries, has developed different approaches during different periods to questions of life and death. Of course we are mainly concerned here with that of human beings.

When one hears of a death the correct response is '*Baruch Dayan HaEmet*' — 'Blessed is the true Judge.' God has decided — for whatever reason — that now is the time for a person to leave this world, and we have to accept this decision.

2. DYING

We shall all have to do it, sooner or later. Some will die young, some older, some quickly, some slowly, some by natural causes, some by accident, some by violence. For some it means leaving before they feel ready, for some it is a release from pain and discomfort. We say we believe in eternal life, but we purchase life insurance. It is always good advice to live as though one could die at any time without leaving too many loose ends behind, unresolved conflicts, things left unsaid or unwritten. It is good to have a Will, clear and fair — and there is a long tradition of Ethical Wills in which one bequeaths good advice and not just material goods.

Active assistance in dying is not permitted in Judaism but a subtle form of passive assistance comprises simply 'allowing a person to die' when their time has come — such a person, who may have been declining for some time, is called a 'Gossess' — they can no longer feed themselves or drink on their own, their eyes are sunken, there is clearly no hope of recovery. Let them go. The key text in this debate is *Ketubot* 104a where Rabbi Judah is dying; his colleagues declare a fast and pray around him and effectively make it impossible for the 'Malach haMavet', the Angel of Death to perform his duty. Eventually his maidservant, moved by his sufferings, throws a jar from the roof — the sound of it shattering interrupts the rabbis in their prayers momentarily and so Rabbi Judah can finally expire.

Both Moses (Deut. 34:5) and Aharon (Num. 20:28) died traditionally by a 'divine kiss' — God, who breathed life into them when they were born, sucked it out when it was time for them to die.

3. THE BODY

When someone dies a Body is (usually) left behind. (Those who die at sea or in a major explosion or aviation disaster present a different problem; in such cases the mourners have no physical remains to form a focus for their grief.)

What should one do with the Body? On the one hand it is the last tangible reminder of what a dead friend or relative looked like; on the other hand it is a lump of flesh that will soon start to decay and decompose, now that the internal systems for keeping it alive and constantly renewing have stopped.

In Jewish thought there is a place for everything and everything should be in its place. A Body has a place — under the earth. Living people walk on the earth, dead people lie in it. It's really quite simple. Rather than exposing the Body on a tree-top for the vultures, or floating it down-river in a burning long-boat, or eating it, as some other cultures do, Judaism takes the view that the Body should be buried. It is to be treated with respect for it was, for the duration of a person's life, the repository of that person's soul — but now it is only a corpse, the soul has left it and it needs to be prepared and buried. Traditionally the Body was to be left intact.

To avoid any indignity being inflicted upon the Body it will (in traditional circles) be 'watched' from the moment death is known until burial. Is this practice still necessary? It was, in all likelihood, a defence against corpse-mutilators, necrophiliacs, Body-stealers and all those likely to treat the corpse with disrespect. If there is still a risk of this, logic would demand that precautions be taken. Nowadays a locked morgue is assumed to be a 'safe' place of storage but even this cannot always be guaranteed and there are still occasional scandals.

In principle Judaism is against 'unnecessary' Post-Mortem examinations (often such are carried out merely for 'practice') but of course if civil authorities demand investigation, considering the cause of death to be suspicious, this has to be accepted. This will affect what *Taharah* is possible. (See below).

ORGAN DONATION

Though many are opposed to cutting into a Body to remove organs for donation and possible re-use, it is becoming increasingly common for Jews also to carry an 'Organ Donor Card' and the idea that one can 'save a life' for someone, even posthumously, is increasingly perceived as an important and worthwhile *Mitzvah* which may be fulfilled even at the cost of one's own Body being cut and left no longer intact.

4. THE SOUL

Where IS the Soul? This is a different topic, but anyone who has had contact with a corpse will know the feeling that the Person is no longer in the Body itself — which does not necessarily mean that they are not 'somewhere nearby'... There is no way that a brief paragraph can do justice to this topic, but the following non-scientific and personal perspective may be helpful.

A Human Being is composed of a Body (flesh, bone, blood, muscle, organs, nerves) and... Something Else. But what? There are several Hebrew terms which to some extent overlap.

This Something Else includes '*Ru'ach*' — 'Breath'; the act of breathing oxygen into the lungs where it can be transferred into the bloodstream is a vital process and as long as one can do this the chances are that one is alive (even if medical assistance is needed with pumping). Everything that is alive, even animals, fish and insects have to breathe — even plants, which follow a reverse chemical process. When it stops breathing — for longer than a very brief period — it is dead.

There is '*Nefesh*' — which is often translated as 'Life' or 'Soul' but can perhaps be translated as 'Life-Force' — this could be understood as the instincts that impel us to move, to seek food, light, to flee danger, to mate and create and care for offspring. Once again all living creatures possess this in some way — possibly even plants and other totally different life-forms.

And then there is '*Neshama*', which is the 'Soul', the 'Personality', the element that makes each person different, individual, what and who they are. Once the breathing stops and the life-force dims — this is the 'something else' which is considered (by many) to survive, to continue but in different dimensions. The Body is flesh and subject to the physical laws of entropy and decay — but the light behind the eyes, the memories, the feelings — these do not necessarily all disappear totally just because certain electrical impulses in the brain, or hormones in the bloodstream, cease to have effect. (However, there is a prayer which begins '*Nishmat kol-Chai*' — usually translated in *Siddurim* as 'The breath of all living creatures...')

Throughout human history there have been references in different literatures to 'dead people' appearing, speaking, appearing in dreams to advise or to warn, appearing suddenly to provide protection in times of danger... There are accounts of 'near-death experiences' where people describe being outside their own bodies, observing, aware. People who awake from a coma (a sort of intermediate state between life and death) sometimes recount experiences that cannot be explained rationally. Whilst a lot of all this may be fantasy or wishful thinking it is this awareness of 'something else' that underlies all religious approaches to the question of an Existence After Death, whether as a personal continuation or as a re-birth in a new Body or as a re-joining of the mass 'bundle of Life'. Different Religions differ in their opinions as to what extent experience or actions here during life will have an impact on what comes next, whether there is a punishment or a reward, whether a soul moves upwards or downwards on a putative scale, whether one can still contact them and how. But they all work on the basis that there IS 'Something' and this is what we call the 'Soul'.

There are different and contradictory concepts in Biblical and later texts, some referring to 'She'ol', a shadowy underworld.

In Genesis 4:9 God asks Cain 'Where is Abel your brother?' — to which Cain can only respond that he has no way of knowing, this being, after all, the first time that a death is mentioned in the biblical text. But God responds that '*Kol Damei Achicha tzo'akim eilai min-haAdamah*' — 'The voice of your brother's bloods call out to me from the ground.' Abel is dead, but somehow still protesting.

In Genesis 25:8 Abraham dies and is 'gathered to his people' — '*veyamat... vaye'assef el-Amav*' — an interesting phrase because it cannot be used in the physical or geographical sense, for his Body was buried in Machpelah in Hebron whereas in Gen. 12:1 he was told to leave his family in Haran, having already left his ancestral homeland in Ur in Mesopotamia. In Gen. 25.17 the same phrase is used of Ishmael, who had been sent away by his father Abraham!

In I Samuel Ch. 28 King Saul goes to a 'wise woman' of '*Eyn-Dor*' — either a place-name or signifying 'the Well of the Generations' — who is able to summon up the spirit of the prophet Samuel 'out of the earth' ('*min-HaAretz*'); In 28:15-19 the spirit shows irritation at being disturbed, a full awareness of the current political and military situation — and prophesies that by the next day Saul will have joined him!

These few examples merely illustrate that the idea of a person existing further in some form is very ancient.

5. THE BURIAL

The burial of someone who has died would normally take place as soon as possible. Many reasons are given for this — hygiene in hot countries being an obvious example — but the true reason is the one stated above — the Body is in the 'wrong place'. It is therefore 'unclean', '*Tamey*'. It is a sign of respect to put it in the right place at the first possible opportunity. It is therefore not uncommon for someone in Israel to be buried on the same day they died.

This is not always possible elsewhere. Modern bureaucracy demands registration, certification, perhaps a post-mortem examination; modern cemetery authorities need notice to prepare graves; public holidays can make the right steps difficult to pursue in a hurry. Sometimes a synagogue or a Jewish community will own its own cemetery and can side-step some of the delays caused when a local Council is in charge, but often in this country — and elsewhere — the due process of law has to be followed.

In Great Britain a corpse belongs technically to the Crown and the 'Coroner' (the Crown's Representative Officer) has the right to retain it for as long as is considered necessary before 'releasing' it to an authorised funeral director who can then release it to the family for burial. If there is any doubt about the cause of death, sufficient to delay the issuance of a certificate, then there is very little one can do but wait. Sometimes a synagogue authority will attempt to prevent a post-mortem examination and the authorities are often well-disposed to such requests — but they alone retain the right to decide. (See below for notes on Cremation — the law requires additional paperwork and often crematoria require to be booked some days in advance, adding to potential delays.)

6. THE CEMETERY

A Jewish cemetery does not have to be 'consecrated' though this is the term often used when a new piece of ground is dedicated. The ground itself does not, as in Christianity, become 'sacred'. However a cemetery ought to be well delineated and used solely for that purpose — i.e. 'dedicated'. It should be surrounded by a hedge, fence or wall, even a symbolic low one, marking it off if necessary even from another part of the same larger cemetery — and the graves should be marked. The purpose is not only to mark the spot where someone lies, it is also to prevent a person — especially a *Cohen* — from inadvertently coming into contact with a corpse. This may seem unlikely to us today, living in an ordered society, but not in a time when those who were found dead in the road were just buried in the ditch — as also occurs after natural catastrophes or wars.

Nowadays there are also Woodland Cemeteries which have a very different atmosphere; (There is also the issue of cremated ashes which may often be scattered elsewhere at some chosen spot or even at sea.)

One traditional name for the Cemetery was the euphemistic '*Beit Chayim*' — 'House of Life'. The occupants had, after all, gone on to Life — elsewhere.

The small funeral chapel often erected at the cemetery is usually known as the '*Ohel*' (literally the 'Tent'). They are often built with separate entrance and exit doors so that the coffin leaves by a different way than it came in.

In Judaism it is not the Cemetery but the Grave (*Kever*), (plural *Kevarot*), which is 'holy' and so Jews can be buried in any cemetery if necessary — this is relevant in cases of military cemeteries, or small communities which cannot afford their own and use a municipal cemetery, or for mixed-faith couples who wish to be buried together. (Some, but not all communities have sections in their cemeteries where non-Jewish relatives may be buried or such pairs may be buried together, or 'first-degree relatives' of community members — the usual rule being that no religious rites of another religion may be used and no symbols of another religion be on the gravestones.)

Many modern non-Jewish cemeteries only lease a grave plot — for reasons of population pressure — and one finds that a grave can be 'cleared' after twenty or twenty-five years — unless the family is prepared to pay for a further time extension. Although one believes that one 'buys' a grave, in fact one is purchasing only the right to use it for a specific period. Jewish cemeteries in contrast should be 'eternal', which makes purchase of land for a new Jewish cemetery sometimes difficult — one can never know when a plot of land might not be needed in a century or so for a new road, airport extension, pipeline, whatever... Whereas in ancient Israel bodies were often put in a stone tomb to decay and the bones then gathered together and placed in an Ossuary (hence possibly the term 'to be gathered to one's ancestors' understood in a physical sense) there is now a feeling that the Body should lie undisturbed, and exhumation is usually only permitted for the purpose of 'increasing the level of holiness' for a Body — for example, by moving it from a temporary battlefield site to a proper cemetery, or for moving it to Israel. In Israel there can be almost hysterical reactions when archaeologists or builders uncover some human bones. (Consider the feeling of respect for 'war graves', that one should not disturb a sunken ship or other wreck but let the dead lie there... whereas in contrast sometimes the remains of a re-discovered aeroplane crew will be moved and formally reburied with honours in a military cemetery.) At sites of mass murder there may be mass graves (marked or unmarked) or areas in which bodies or ashes were once anonymously dumped... places which are de facto cemeteries although not in a formal landscaped manner.

Many feelings concerned with Death are well beyond anything rational — which does not mean they are 'wrong', just hard to explain.

7. PREPARATION OF THE BODY

Under normal circumstances a Body is prepared for burial by washing it, dressing it and placing it in a coffin. Abnormal circumstances could include violent accidents, attack by wild animals, warfare, fire, explosions etc., or even occasions when a Body is not found until some time has passed, or where a post-mortem examination has been held; in short, any circumstance which means that the Body is so disfigured that little attempt can be made at cleaning it. In Jewish tradition, in such circumstance, one would encoffin everything that was bloodstained — Body, clothing etc. so that one was 'buried with one's blood.' This also explains why, after terrorist attacks in Israel, members of the 'Zak'a' organisation or others do their best to ensure that all body parts are gathered together.

(A). CHEVRA KADISHA

Nowadays much of this work is carried out by professional undertakers and their staff, but in small communities in earlier times the act of preparing one's fellow human being for burial was considered to be one of the highest of *Mitzvot* of 'Gemilut Chesed', of loving deeds dutifully done, for there was no way the recipient of your care could ever repay you or reciprocate. This came into the category of 'Kibbud HaMeyt', the principle of showing respect to the dead, from the moment of death to the act of burial. Most communities had a 'Holy Brotherhood' (known in Aramaic as the 'Chevra Kadisha', plural 'Chevrei Kadisha') whose task — voluntarily undertaken — was to handle all arrangements from a death to (and after) the burial. It was always considered best that only Jews should handle Jewish bodies; only men should handle men, and only women should handle woman and children, and that at least three persons should be present at all times. Whether these traditions are based on religious understanding or (more likely) unfortunate experiences and pragmatism is a matter for discussion. Several communities still maintain a voluntary *Chevra Kadisha* formed of members who can be called upon when necessary.

Traditionally a day for the *Chevra Kadisha* to meet or to fast was 7th. *Adar*, understood as both the birthday and the day of death of Moses — a memorial to the fact that God buried Moses. (*Megillah* 13b.)

(B). TAHARAH

The ritual preparation is called 'Taharah', making something 'Tahor' or 'clean' in a ritual sense. Essentially it consists of the following stages:
(i). Washing from the Body any actual dirt or blood. Cloths and sponges etc. may be used.
(ii). Washing the Body ritually, with running water, usually poured on in one continuous stream from several containers, and then drying it.
(iii). Dressing the Body in plain white shrouds ('Tachrichim').
(iv). Placing the Body in the coffin, with some soil from Israel if possible. For a person who had a *Tallit* it may also be added, draped round them but with a corner cut off so that it is technically 'possul', no longer having four corners.

Some communities will also cut finger- and toe-nails. The act of cleaning might involve also combing hair, cleaning finger-nails, removing any extraneous matter such as bandages, false teeth, cosmetics etc. The basic idea is that one enters the world without any 'extras' — make-up, artificial limbs, wigs — and one should leave it in the same way. In practice modern medical science makes it increasingly likely that a Body might be buried with some plastic tube, or a heart pace-maker, or an artificial hip still inside, or even a plaster cast on the outside. Here one needs to be pragmatic. Has something become 'a part of the Body'? If so, it can stay in. False teeth are a different matter — if they can be removed, they should be, but if *rigor mortis* has set in and it is impossible to open the jaw without using force they may have to be left where they are. Rings and other jewellery need to be removed (and kept safely for return to the family). A modern phenomenon is of course a variety of studs and rings in all sorts of public and private places on the Body — here some discretion is called for, in terms of what can be removed without damaging the Body and thus adding to indignity. The old concept was that one was to appear before the Heavenly Court looking as smart as possible! And if one chose during one's lifetime to wear a metal stud through the cheek or the tongue, or a ring through the nose, or anything else… well, that was your choice. Judaism frowns on any such 'abuse of the Body' as it would be perceived, but even people who have made such life-choices will eventually die…

The Body is usually laid on its back on a slab or metal table, if possible tilted slightly to enable water to drain off. Some communities have their own mortuary with all equipment, some use the facilities of a cemetery or a funeral director, some just use a pair of trestles and a plank. Important is only that one has the facility, some privacy and that one can work at a comfortable height. Those taking part often dress in protective clothing — plastic gloves, water-proof aprons or boots — as there will be a lot of splashing. Often a cloth or towel is kept over the genital area for reasons of modesty. Once the initial cleaning has been done the custom is to pour a specific amount of water — say, three buckets full, poured one after the other so that the stream is continuous — while reciting the words 'Tahor, Tahor, Tahor.' The Body is dried thoroughly and then dressed in the Tachrichim, then lifted into the coffin. The coffin is plain and usually contains nothing else except perhaps the (cut) Tallit — this is because one leaves the world with nothing and also discourages grave robbery.

It is also customary to stand for a moment at the end and formally ask the deceased for forgiveness should anything have been omitted or performed incorrectly. Indeed there is sometimes a 'feeling in the air' that the person is somehow present and it is not considered proper to speak disrespectfully of the deceased or to make jokes during the work.

The principle is: Just as a new-born baby needs cleaning and dressing in simple white clothing by those who care for it, so a dead person is treated in the same way. However, being heavier and helpless, unable to assist in any way by moving a limb or shifting their weight, it may well be necessary for two people to lift or turn a Body over so that a third can wash behind. It is vital to dry the Body properly afterwards, as otherwise it is almost impossible to pull the Tachrichim onto it.

The Tachrichim come usually in packages, sometimes prepared by groups in the community who sew them as a Mitzvah, often purchased from specialist suppliers. There are many variations on the basic theme but a typical set (usually on the basis of 'One Size Fits All' though there are also extra-large versions) comprises a set of trousers, a tunic blouse that goes over the head and with sleeves, a second over-tunic likewise, a bonnet that fits over the head and with straps to tie beneath the chin to keep the mouth closed, maybe baggy mittens for the hands and similar for the feet. As the old proverb says, it has no pockets… All is made from simple white cloth, roughly sewn together.

It is considered important not to tie firm knots but special knots which hold the clothing together but are releasable.

Nowadays many bodies come from hospitals or Care Homes where an initial 'laying out' will have been carried out by nurses or attendants. This means that the main dirt or blood has been removed but there may be sticking-plasters or bandages over open wounds and cotton-wool placed in various orifices to prevent leakage. It is usually advisable to leave these where they are, again on the basis that removal will do nothing to add dignity and probably the reverse.

If a person died from some infectious disease then usually *Taharah* is impossible — the Body will be wrapped and sealed in a plastic bag and that's all that can be done... Care for the welfare of the living members of the *Chevra Kadisha* takes priority.

Many communities will keep a container with a bit of earth or sand from Israel (maybe brought back in a jar from a holiday) and a small amount would then, when all is complete and the Body has been lifted into the coffin (also a difficult task — the term 'dead weight' takes on a new meaning) be scattered over the eyes, the mouth, the heart and, for men, the '*Makom Brit Kodesh*' — 'the place where they had entered the holy covenant' by being circumcised. This is just a tradition — the idea is that if one cannot go to be buried in the Land, a bit of the Land comes to you — and is not vital, but adds a nice touch.

As a matter of principle nothing of value should ever be buried with a person — this would only encourage later grave-robbery and the living can use the valuable object much more than the dead can! However, it sometimes happens that people wish to bury something very personal, such as a person's false teeth, or some flowers, or — in the case of a child — some favourite toy, and most liberal rabbis will permit this. It is also occasionally necessary for the synagogue to bury old *Siddurim* and other religious texts which have become unusable and when a grave is in any case being opened this is an opportunity to dispose of them properly. It is considered an honour when this is done.

(C). EMBALMING

Normally the aim of a Jewish funeral is that the Body should decay underground fairly quickly and not be 'preserved', mummified, displayed etc. For those occasions when a Body is to be transported to another country other measures need to be taken. Firstly, additional paperwork is required (even to remove a Body from Scotland to England!); secondly, if it to be transported by air, the airlines will often insist on the Body being embalmed first and then being placed in a sealed metal coffin.

Embalming involves, after initial washing, pumping into the artery embalming fluid (formaldehyde) which then pushes the blood out of the veins. A process well-known in the ancient Near East, it is not normally practised by Jews except under these special requirements. Joseph for example had his father Jacob embalmed and mummified in Egypt (Genesis 50:2) to enable the Body to be transported to the Land of Canaan and be buried there at Machpelah in Hebron (50:13); he himself was then embalmed in Gen. 50:26 and stored in a coffin for future transport to the 'homeland' — he was eventually taken (Exodus 13:19) and finally buried at Shechem (Joshua 24:32).

8. THE COFFIN

Coffins were not normally used in the ancient Middle East. Wood was far too scarce and expensive to 'waste' in this way. Bodies were — and in Israel usually still are — buried wrapped only in a winding sheet. However we know that Rabbi Jochanan ben Zakkai was taken from Jerusalem hidden in a coffin during the siege of 70 CE, so it is clear that some people were so buried — and of course stone sarcophagi were used by the wealthy.

A coffin ('*Aron*') should be plain and inexpensive. The modern American industry of elaborate lined opening 'caskets' in expensive woods and with fancy handles would be an anathema. Everyone enters the world equal — so all should leave it as equals, without undue ostentation. Further, the relatives should not be placed under emotional blackmail at a time of grief to 'show how much they loved the dear departed' by spending vast amounts of money unnecessarily. This is a basic principle laid out clearly and beautifully in the *Talmud* ('*Mo'ed Katan*' 27a-b):

'Our Rabbis taught:

Formerly they were wont to serve drinks in a house of mourning, the rich in white glass vessels and the poor in coloured glass, and the poor felt ashamed; they instituted therefore that all should serve drinks in coloured glasses, out of deference to the poor.

Formerly, they were wont to uncover the face of the rich and cover the face of the poor, because their faces turned livid in years of drought and the poor felt ashamed; they therefore instituted that everybody's face should be covered, out of deference to the poor.

Formerly, they were wont to bring out the rich for burial on a Dargesh [a sort of state bed, highly ornamented] and the poor on a plain bier, and the poor felt ashamed; they instituted therefore that all should be brought out on a plain bier, out of deference for the poor...

Formerly the expense of taking the dead out to his burial fell harder on his near-of-kin than his death, so that the dead man's near-of-kin abandoned him and fled. Until at last Rabban Gamliel came forward and, disregarding his own dignity, came out to his burial in flaxen garments, and thereafter the people followed his lead to come out to burial in flaxen garments. Said Rabbi Papa: 'And nowadays all the world follow the practice of coming out even in a paltry shroud that costs but a few *Zuz*.'

From this magnificent text we see how customs changed and why they changed; elaborate funerals simply cost too much, people were unable to take on the responsibilities or felt embarrassed that they could not match the ostentation practised by others — until the rabbis forced them to look at the whole matter differently by setting a good example.

9. THE FUNERAL

The Hebrew term for a funeral is a '*Levayah*', from '*Levayat HaMeyt*' which means the *Mitzvah* of 'accompanying the dead' on their final journey.

The Funeral is the simple act of burying the Body. No rabbi is necessary — a layman can officiate. Certain traditional prayers or poems (e.g. '*Tzidduk haDin*') are said, but none of them is indispensable. Since the *Kaddish* is one of these prayers and since this should normally be said with a *Minyan* it is normal to attempt to gather a *Minyan* together and in some communities even to hire one, to pay several elderly members to be present to form the quorum if necessary as '*Minyan* Men'! In Reform Judaism this is not stressed.

The grave is often dug in such a way that (in some communities) the head or (in other communities) the feet point towards Jerusalem. Theoretically this is so that, when the Messiah finally appears, the dead can either hear the trumpet blast better, or can sit up and start walking straightaway in the right direction!

The coffin should be covered with earth before final *Kaddish* or other prayers are said — it is then 'under the earth'. All those present may join in this positive physical action if they wish, either with a spade or with a symbolic small trowel. One is then involved in 'performing the *Mitzvah*' of burying someone rather than just observing while others do it.

As already mentioned it is traditional to place a small amount of soil from Israel in the coffin, if this is available. Some pious Jews used to carry a small bag of this soil with them at all times, in case! One hopes that it was the 'real stuff'. Nowadays a *Chevra Kadisha* will often keep an amount at the mortuary, 'topped up' by small amounts brought back from holidays in Israel.

10. CREMATION

Increasingly in modern times Cremation is being turned to by Jews — and their families — who find Burial distasteful or perhaps space-consuming, or who want the remains to be transported to another country. In Britain at present a rough estimate is that almost half of the ceremonies are cremations rather than burials — though in some cases the ashes are then buried later. Many feel they have no need for an expensive marked grave as there are none who will come to visit; some are concerned about the shortage of land; some may even wish to identify with relatives who, during the *Sho'ah*, were cremated. Orthodox Judaism frowns upon the practice, believing that the Body should be kept intact for future resurrection. Some even argue that a person who has been cremated will not be resurrected! At least the coccyx, the small bone at the tip of the spine, must remain intact. This is a bit hard on all those millions of victims of the Holocaust who were cremated involuntarily.

Reform or Liberal Judaism sees little need to keep the Body totally intact and therefore cremation becomes a valid alternative method of dealing with a Body, provided always that the preparation and the service are carried out with dignity and respect. (Undertakers need to be advised if the deceased had a pacemaker or some other internal 'fitting' that might affect the crematorium's facilities.)

Liturgically the service is identical; ritually the difference is that, rather than the coffin being lowered into a grave and the mourners assisting in the act of burial, the officiant indicates to the crematorium authorities an appropriate moment and the coffin either slides or rolls forwards or is moved downwards or a curtain closes — designs vary but this forms the moment when the coffin, as in a grave, disappears from sight, the formal farewell.

Ashes may be scattered or buried (depending on local laws). Few cemeteries allow ashes to be scattered indiscriminately — for other persons in the cemetery may have families who would object — but several Jewish cemeteries now have specific demarcated areas for ashes, maybe marked by a pattern of stones or a bush, or columbaria where urns may be placed in niches in a wall.

11. EULOGY

It is customary at a funeral (or cremation) to deliver a funeral oration or eulogy about the deceased. This is known in Hebrew as the '*Hesped*' and comes from the Hebrew word 'SaPaD' meaning 'to wail'. There are various traditions applied sometimes at Orthodox funerals that 'a *Hesped* should not be said at certain times' — e.g. at a funeral occurring shortly before *Shabbat*, during the month of *Adar*, on *Rosh Chodesh*, etc. This is probably derived from a misunderstanding; Whilst it may once in the past have been considered inappropriate to hire 'professional mourners' to wail and howl in the funeral procession on certain days which had been classed as 'joyful days', this is not the same as omitting all reference to a person and their life and deeds at their funeral. So we do not follow this restrictive custom.

The *Hesped* may be delivered by any person who feels they have something good to say and are in a position to speak without being hindered by excessive emotion. One always speaks well of the dead.

12. MOURNING

Once the dead have been buried, the living must still mourn. In the same way that the ritual from the time of death to the time of burial is designed to emphasise '*Kibbud HaMeyt*', from the point of burial onwards it is designed to support the mourners.

In Jewish tradition the Mourner (the '*Ahvel*') goes through several stages of mourning ('*Ahvelut*'), of coming to terms with a loss and bereavement.

The first, the most intense phase, is the '*Shivah*' (from the Hebrew for 'Seven'). During these first seven days of grief the mourner has no social duties or responsibilities — no duty to attend services, to wash, or shave, or look smart or offer hospitality to visitors — but should spend the time in reflection, tears and mourning. There is a duty of visiting a person in such a state, but one should bring and offer food rather than expect it and one should be prepared to sit in silence, offering comfort merely by one's supportive presence, rather than chatting and offering false and superficial consolations.

The second phase is the first thirty days (i.e. including the *Shivah*), known as the '*Sheloshim*' (Hebrew for 'Thirty'). The mourner begins to come to terms with the world again. Quite often memorial services for distinguished people are held to mark 'The end of the *Sheloshim*'.

This period is based on Deuteronomy 34:8 where, following his departure to die, the people mourn for Moses for thirty days.

The third phase ends at the anniversary of the death, marking a complete year. During this period a male mourner (in an Orthodox community) might attend synagogue regularly and say the *Kaddish* with a *Minyan*; he may cease shaving for this time. There is one (quaint) tradition that one mourns a whole year for a sinner; therefore, to show that the deceased was not a sinner, *Kaddish* is said for slightly less than a year! (See below §16 '*Kaddish*').

During the first year (allowing the earth to settle first) or after a year (in most communities) a tombstone ('*Matzevah*') is set over the grave, and this anniversary (according, usually, to the Jewish date) becomes the '*Yahrtzeit*'. (see below §16.) The 'Stone-Setting' or 'Unveiling' provides an opportunity for family and mourners to gather once again, without the time-pressure and stress and intense grief of the funeral itself. (See *Siddur* 8th. ed. p.433.) In a brief ceremony a cloth that has been previously placed over the *Matzevah* is removed, the inscription is read, *Kaddish* and maybe other prayers said.

The point of the mourning process in Jewish tradition, despite all its many variations, is that the mourner is allowed time and dignity to spend some while 'outside time' and without worrying about their dignity. All the pressures of keeping up with the daily schedule or maintaining a smart appearance are held back and one can allow the time and the emotional energy to mourn 'properly'. Those who have gone through the process often maintain afterwards that it was healthy and worthwhile, an important part of their coming-to-terms with their loss. Modern psychology describes different levels of mourning, with shock, anger, helplessness, guilt and more before a sense of acceptance can be reached. The community should just 'be there' to listen and provide the comfort that is needed, which is not necessarily what some people think is needed.

Modern society tends to frown upon public displays of mourning and people are told to 'pull themselves together' or 'keep a stiff upper lip'; 'Cheer up, I'll put the kettle on.' The last thing they often need is to be told to 'cheer up'... Instead, a chance to cry, to wail, to look over old photographs and to go over old memories, to talk about the departed and also to sit in silence — these are the natural and therapeutic processes one should encourage at such a time.

Nowadays, for all the above reasons, *Shivah* is often reduced to one or three days or even dispensed with altogether. Sometimes a person has spent a long time dying, or has been absent mentally for some time and relatives have already done a lot of their mourning whilst they were doing so.

Sometimes a funeral has to be held up for legal or procedural reasons — if, say, a Body is not released, or has to be transported from abroad — and the mourners are left 'in limbo' since, technically, mourning starts after the funeral. In these cases one should apply common-sense and commence the *Shivah* or at least some form of formal mourning even before the day of the funeral, if this is appropriate.

13. 'K'RIAH'

Literally 'Cutting'. Many cultures have public signs of mourning — armbands, black ties and gloves, etc. In Judaism one who was bereaved might 'tear his clothes' in a paroxysm of grief. Nowadays this has been ritualised to the cutting of an old item of clothing — a cardigan or a tie — and then ripping it slightly as an outward sign of inner turmoil. This custom is not universally practised or encouraged but is sometimes performed at funerals using a small pair of scissors.

14. SYMBOLIC FOODS

On the family's return from the funeral they are often served with a symbolic meal of eggs, herrings and/or bagels. These rounded foods and fish are thought to symbolise the continuity of Life (as they do, for example, in Christianity) and are therefore considered to be a comfort.

15. MIRRORS

In superstitious periods (i.e. including the present in some quarters!) it was considered necessary to cover all mirrors, screens and reflecting surfaces in a house of mourning. This would include open vessels filled with liquid. Some said it was to prevent the mourners seeing themselves looking so miserable with swollen, red eyes; others said it was to prevent the ghost of the deceased looking into the mirror and getting a shock at not seeing himself there!

Reform Judaism discourages this sort of approach, and mirrors do not need to be covered.

16. 'KADDISH'

The 'Kaddish' is an ancient Aramaic expression of the greatness of God. It originated in Talmudic times as a formal close, recited by a teacher to mark the end of a lesson. He would recite a formula looking forward to the messianic redemption and the students would respond with the line 'May His great Name be blessed for ever and ever!'

In the Minor Tractate 'Soferim' (dating from around the 8[th.] century) mention is made of the Kaddish being spoken, in the vernacular, to the whole assembly, at funerals — specifically at the funerals of scholars. This was in effect their final dismissal of their students. Later, because it was felt that a humiliating distinction was being made between those who were entitled to have the Kaddish said and those who were not, it was recited at all funerals.

There are several legends which link the behaviour of mourners on earth with the fate of the dead. In one ('Midrash Kalla Rabuta' Ch. 2 & 'Tanna D'vei Eliyahu Zuta' 17) Rabbi Akiva met a dead man walking around, who told him he could not rest from his torture in Gehenna because he had maltreated the poor during his life as a tax collector; the only way he could be released from this fate would be for him to have a son who could recite the Kaddish and the Bar'chu before a congregation, so that the congregation would respond by blessing the Divine Name. However, he had neglected his son's education. Rabbi Akiva therefore found the youth, taught him what to say, and so released the spirit of his father!

This fable from the Midrash is echoed by other statements in the Talmud, e.g. 'Rosh Hashanah' 17a, Mishnah 'Eduyot' 2:10 — that a son should recite Kaddish for twelve months after the death of his father, since it was considered (by some) that the punishment of sinners in Gehenna lasted this long. Later it was considered that to say Kaddish for the whole period would therefore imply that you thought your father to be a sinner and thus liable for Gehenna! As this would not be an honourable thought, the period of reciting the Kaddish was reduced to eleven months… ('Shulchan Aruch': 'Yoreh De'ah' 376:4, Isserles' gloss.)

Be that as it may, by the Ga'onic period (ca. 600-900 CE) the custom established itself of reciting the Kaddish as a mourner and an extended version was composed for this purpose, used in some liturgies. The *Kaddish* itself has no reference to Death or the Dead but is purely a doxology, that is, a hymn of praise to God. It can be seen as a reminder, even in difficult times of death and bereavement, that God is still there and is still great. Because the response should if possible be made by a congregation it is normally read (or recited) in the presence of a *Minyan*.

Nowadays the superstitious see the *Kaddish* as some sort of magic formula that must be said. People who know no Hebrew (or Aramaic) are concerned that it be said in an ancient language, if necessary by someone else or by reading the letters aloud from a transliterated, meaningless text. There are even Jews (and Yeshivot) not above imitating Roman Catholic institutions and, in the way that these will arrange to 'say a Mass for the dead' in return for a donation, offer to 'say *Kaddish* for the dead' for similar reward. Yet, despite the above ancient legends, *Kaddish* is not 'for' the dead, but is a glorification recited by and for the living.

Questions sometimes arise nowadays: Can one say a *Kaddish* for a non-Jewish family member? To which the answer is 'Of course — why not? It is not for Them but for You, to give you some comfort!'; and also: 'Can one say a *Kaddish* without a *Minyan*?' to which the answer is also 'Of course — why not?' There is much misunderstanding — just because a *Minyan* is missing does not mean that it is forbidden to pray, merely that it counts more as a private rather than a communal prayer. It is irritating that there are still Jews who try to prevent or prohibit other Jews from praying with such daft excuses.

17. 'YAHRTZEIT'

The anniversary of a death (usually calculated according to the Hebrew date where this is known) is known by this German/Yiddish word '*Yahrtzeit*' (also spelt 'Jahrzeit') which means literally 'Time of the Year'.

From around the 16th. century this name was used for the annual commemoration of the dead in a community, though prior to that it had been used by the Church in Germany during the Middle Ages. It appears therefore that this is yet another of the customs absorbed from Christianity. The custom of lighting a memorial candle in also probably derived from non-Jewish practice.

Prior to this time references in Jewish literature to the custom of honouring the dead on the anniversary of their death are few and refer only to the death of one's own father or teacher. In Talmudic times the anniversary was often a fast day. (For example, in '*Nedarim*' 12b, a quotation is given of a vow 'not to eat meat nor drink wine, as on the day that my father died.') Disciples would often gather to observe the anniversaries of their teachers' deaths.

The observance of *Yahrtzeit*, despite all the superstitions that surround it, is also for the living, not the dead. It is a chance to reflect and remember. Lists are sometimes prepared showing the equivalent Hebrew date for several years ahead. A candle is often lit on the evening, if possible a special one designed to burn for 24 hours or more, usually in a glass or tin container. (It is often referred to simply as a '*Yahrtzeit*' candle, in French as a 'Neshama' candle, i.e. referring to the soul; in Hebrew maybe as a '*Yizkor*' or simply 'Memorial' candle.) In some synagogues there is a memorial board with names and dates, possibly with an electric lamp for each, which may be lit for this day. Sometimes an exact date of death is not known — especially for victims of the *Sho'ah* — and an arbitrary date has to be calculated, based perhaps on what is known of deportation dates or the fate of a particular ghetto, or else a communal date is chosen. Sometimes a joint commemorative service is organised for the parents of babies who had died or been still-born. If one does not have the Hebrew date, the secular date can also work. The main thing is not to get further stressed about the details, but to find time for contemplation.

The prayers can be found in RSGB *Siddur* (pp.301-3; pp.430-431).

18. TOMBSTONES

It is necessary to mark every grave with a marker or '*Matzevah*'. In earlier times, before it became common to have especially set-aside cemeteries, bodies might have been buried in any convenient spot — under a tree, near the roadside — and a marker was a necessity (cf. Gen. 35:8, 35:19). It was also important as a warning to *Cohanim*, who had to keep clear from corpses so as to avoid ritual defilement.

The style of tombstones has varied throughout Jewish history. In most cases *Sephardi* custom was to have flat stones over the Body; however, many variations can be found to this and in Victorian England wealthier members of the Jewish community often erected vaults and memorials on a par with those being built in non-Jewish cemeteries. In modern cemeteries one has to take account of the presence of vandals and similar sick people who may try to knock stones over or break or deface them. This makes flat stones safer, and lettering that is inscribed is safer than metal letters fixed onto the stone that can be prised off.

We recommend simple, plain and above all not overly-expensive stones. In Death we are all alike, therefore it should not be necessary for some to have larger grave stones than others. Images are usually prohibited, apart from certain traditional symbols — see below.

Inscriptions can vary from the severely plain to the florid and verbose. Older stones are all in Hebrew, often using abbreviations or Biblical quotations and analogies, but as the community became more assimilated (or had to use the services of a non-Jewish stonemason) one can see how English became more common. However in most cases the stone will be headed with the Hebrew letters '*Peh*'-'*Nun*', the abbreviation for '*Poh Nistar*' ('Here lies' or 'Here is concealed') or '*Poh Nikbar*' ('Here is buried'). Then follows the name and the Hebrew name (if known), the date of death and the equivalent Hebrew date, any family references (e.g. 'husband of…'; 'widow of…'; 'missed by' etc.) and at the bottom the Hebrew letters '*Taf* ' *Nun* ' *Tzadi* ' *Bet* ' *Heh* ' — abbreviations for '*Tehi Nafshoh Tzaror Bitzror HaChayim*' (or the female equivalent '*Tehi Nafshah Tzarurah Bitzror HaChayim*') — 'May his/her soul be bound up in the Gathering of Life.'

Many cemeteries have rules regarding the layout of memorials. Some are 'lawn' cemeteries, permitting only a small stone laid flat in the grass so that grass-cutting equipment can reach all areas; others insist on the graves being laid in tight rows covered with stone chippings and a stone surround. There are Woodland Cemeteries where the graves are laid between trees or in glades, facing in different directions so as to use the space best. Sometimes a grave will be a 'double-decker', the first body being laid deeper to allow the grave to be opened and space for the second to be available without disturbing the first, and the same stone will be modified to include the second person. There may be rules regarding the maximum height of stones and regarding the wording, to encourage good taste — and in some there is a 'standard' headstone to indicate that all are equal. In Military cemeteries Jewish fallen are often marked with a '*Magen David*' on their stone, their fallen comrades having a cross, but the rest of the stone is standardised.

Jewish tombstones will not normally have any pictorial representation on them, with the exceptions of *Cohanim* whose stones may bear the image of two hands with fingers spread in the special priestly manner (thumb, two fingers and two fingers) and Levites whose stone may bear an image of a jug, as the Levites were servers in the Temple. Since Reform Judaism makes no distinction even for *Cohen* and *Levi*, even this is unnecessary. On the other hand, looking at older Jewish cemeteries one can find occasional exceptions — a merchant may have a ship engraved on his stone; someone who died young may be symbolised by a tree whose trunk has been cut down; etc.

19. REFERENCES TO THE DEAD

When a person has died the Body is often referred to as 'The *Meyt*' (from the Hebrew for 'Dead'). This is in contrast to modern euphemisms as 'The Deceased' or 'the Remains'.

On referring to someone who has died it is quite common to hear a person add the words '*Alav HaShalom*' after a man's name, and '*Aleha HaShalom*' after a woman's, meaning 'May peace be upon him/her.' Sometimes this is expressed in English: 'May he/she rest in peace.'

It is also common to hear, or see written, the words '*Zichrono LiVracha*' or '*Zichrona LiVracha*' — 'May his/her Memory be for a Blessing' or 'of blessed memory'. This is usually abbreviated in written form to the letters '*Zayin Lamed*' or 'z.l.' placed after the name.

20. NON-JEWISH FAMILY MEMBERS

If you convert to Judaism, you are by definition leaving your born family behind in some respects — although you are always permitted to show them respect and to attend family events even if these take place in churches or Christian cemeteries. However, if you wish to be buried with them in due course you need to be aware that, whilst Jews can be buried in non-Jewish cemeteries, most Jewish cemeteries do not permit the burial of non-Jews. A few do, usually in special sections and usually only the marriage-partners of members of the congregation or first-degree family members. Jewish cemeteries are usually 'private', owned or administered by a congregation, and the local community decides who may be allocated grave space there. Space is often limited, so non-members must expect to have to pay extra or to have to plead for a space. It may be a *Mitzvah* to bury the dead, but this does not mean they have to be buried, with all their family members, in a cemetery belonging to a community where they do not belong! As noted, burial can take place in other places too.

Even those Jewish cemeteries which permit the burial of non-Jewish spouses will insist that no Christian or other religious rituals are performed at the burial and that no such symbols appear on the tombstone.

You should mourn for your non-Jewish family members just as you do for Jewish ones.

21. SUICIDE

This is a taboo subject for all sorts of understandable reasons and is always a 'tragedy squared', loading surviving friends and families with additional feelings of guilt and anger (including anger turned inwards at having not reacted to a 'cry for help') to add to their mourning. Suicide often occurs when a person loses the ability to think long-term and perceives only the short-term problem — for example, a looming examination, a broken love affair, a personal financial crisis, a conflict at their place of work. They lose for a period the ability to see that there will be other opportunities to take an exam, that there are other potential partners if one allows time to find them, that money is not everything in Life, that there are other jobs… Sometimes people choose to die rather than continue with a long and debilitating and painful illness. In our history there were those who chose to die in their own home and at their own hand, rather than undergo deportation, torture and murder.

For the purpose of this book it must be sufficient to state that Judaism condemns the act of suicide except under three specific reasons for accepting the death of a martyr — but that when such a tragedy nevertheless occurs an assumption is made that the victim must have been (a) not thinking clearly but under great stress, i.e. mentally ill and (b) that they repented of the decision at the last second, even if unable at that point to prevent the fatal result — and therefore no objection is made to performing a full funeral within and not outside a cemetery. Things are bad enough without adding further to the distress of the mourners.

7

PART SEVEN:
SOME HISTORICAL AND OTHER THEMES

CHAPTER 33

APPROACHING THE 'HOLOCAUST' OR '*SHO'AH*'

This book cannot and will not attempt to cover all of Jewish History — there are plenty of other books for that. But at the same time there is no way we can get around the fact that, a mere generation or so ago — at the time of writing this book there are still a few living witnesses — an attempt was made to wipe Judaism out, not through theological argument or a 'Holy War' accompanied by attempts to convert or baptise the Jews to a different religion, but by physically destroying all communities and all individuals that came within the power of the racist fanatics who saw this as their duty — to 'free the world from a Jewish curse'. As far as they were concerned every Jew — and their definition included anyone with even a Jewish parent or grandparent, even people who had been born and brought up in Christian households — was somehow sub-human, an 'Untermensch', a different species, vermin, and did not deserve to live.

The definition was based on flawed concepts of 'Race' rather than Belief, Ideology, Behaviour or any other method of assessing a person. The victims comprised anyone whom they classed as 'unworthy', from infants to elderly, irrespective of nationality, class or culture. Depending on the political and military situations of the period — and there was during this period some confusion and contradiction within the ranks of the various National Socialist government departments, the military forces, their allies, the subordinate regimes in occupied countries — Jews were to be either humiliated and deported, exiled, or killed straight away under brutal circumstances, or in some cases kept alive just so long as their entire physical strength had been expended in slave labour. A few 'privileged' people or those with papers from certain countries were kept for a while as 'show objects' in the ghetto in Theresienstadt. Had the war lasted even a few months longer, even the last remnants would almost certainly have been exterminated — the obsessive efforts to wipe out the unwanted civilian populations, the prisoners, the slave workers, deserters and witnesses went on until the very last hours before liberation.

The theological problem with which all Jews (as well as others of course) are confronted is — that the fanatical anti-Semites essentially succeeded. That is to say, within a very few years — from the Nazi rise to power in the German Republic in 1933 to the final collapse of Europe in ashes and rubble in 1945 was a period of only twelve years; From the German invasion of the Soviet Union in 1941 till their expulsion by the Red Army in 1944-45 only four years — they actually carried out most of their programme. In this brief period the Jewish communities in many countries were effectively wiped out. Here and there some individuals survived, in hiding, each with a dreadful story to tell, and usually widowed, orphaned, bereft of all other family members. But the 'critical mass' had gone. Mere statistics and terms like 'the Six Million' may only numb us — there was an almost infinite range of individual fates. Some use the term 'Holocaust' to describe this period, from a Greek/Roman term for a 'burned sacrifice' whilst others prefer the Hebrew term '*Sho'ah*' which means 'Destruction'.

It is hard now to visualise what this means. Before the 1930s all Jews in Western Europe knew that in Eastern Europe there were fellow-Jews in quantity. They may have had different cultures and accents, but they were there, with their Yeshivot, publishing houses, their mere existence. In many places the Jews formed a half or even more of the population. (In 1939 Jews formed around 60% of the population of a small Polish provincial town called Oswiecim…) After the war — this was no longer the case. Throughout Western and Central Europe also, once the initial flows of Displaced Persons had found somewhere to go, the survivors could count the size of their communities in the dozens or the hundreds, but not the thousands. A situation still exists where all the rabbis of a particular country might know each other by name — whereas this cannot be said of all the Protestant or Catholic clergy. We have become an absolutely tiny minority. It is rare to find even a large European city with more than one synagogue, and there are entire regions without a single functioning congregation. Guide Books to Jewish life in Europe tend to concentrate on memorials, sites of specific massacres, and remains of old buildings. Here and there the local tourist industry has seized upon remnants of Jewish history to romanticize it. When Jews go on holiday or investigate family history they visit former synagogues and mass graves…

To put it into a single sentence — in this respect at least, Hitler won. Even if we spend much time and effort in trying to deny this or in fighting the consequences, working hard to create tiny new communities here and there (one Jewish theologian, Emil Fackenheim, described the effort to deny Hitler this posthumous victory the '614[th.] Commandment') the fact remains that there are very few Jewish families left in Europe and that almost every family lost members — sometimes many members — in the Holocaust.

This was not the first genocidal massacre in history nor, alas, the last. Earlier in the same bloody century the Armenians and the Assyrians, Russian farmers and the middle-class, various population groups in the Balkans or the Ottoman Empire, Spanish Anti-Fascists and others, many others had spilt their blood and lost their lives on the whims of political leaders or brutal soldiers. Many other groups also suffered dreadfully in this period in the 1940s — Sinti and Roma, Polish intellectuals, German Communists, Social Democrats, pious Christians, Homosexuals or resistance members, and of course the civilian populations everywhere who suddenly found their home towns and villages bombed or shelled, who were shot or died of hunger and cold as refugees, who lost all that they and their families had built up over previous generations. Men and women were called up to fight in various armed forces, were often shipped halfway across the world, endured great privations and fear and often wounds… Prisoners of War and civilians were arrested, mistreated, humiliated, tortured, executed, murdered in extremes of inhumanity.

None of this is new — even if there are still a few fools around who try to deny it ever happened, or who devote themselves merely to arguing about how to apportion the 'blame' — academic questions of 'Who Knew What?' or 'Who could have Done Something?' and so forth. This is material for historians (and unfortunately for journalists). For theologians, for those who are trying to deepen their religious faith or even adopt a new one, we are left with the problem — How could this happen?

We have no answer. Indeed, we classify as extremely dangerous and shallow those people who claim to have an answer.

Some have said that the near-destruction of European Jewry was a necessary precursor for the later establishment of the State of Israel. This is of course intellectual laziness. If it were so, what did the Lebanese, the Jordanians, Yemenis, Libyans, Egyptians, and others have to do in order to get their own nation-states established at around the same period — the 1940s-1960s — in Africa and Asia? There were indeed wars, rebellions, civil wars, suffering — but nothing really comparable with the *Sho'ah*. And a Jewish State was desperately needed in 1938, not 1948. It came ten years too late.

Elie Wiesel has written that 'not all the victims were Jews, but all the Jews were victims.' Dr. Esther Schulz-Goldstein of Berlin sees in Judaism a rebellion against the values of the Bronze Age and in the *Sho'ah* a deliberate attempt to return the world back to the values of the Bronze Age — which means that Jews were automatically classed as opponents of what was going on. Humanity was dragged backwards (and a large proportion went willingly) — several thousand years to a pre-Enlightenment, pre-Reformation, pre-civilised period of virtually tribal identity, to a time where human life was cheap and could be sacrificed, where prisoners had no rights, where 'the other' existed merely as prey to be robbed and raped and dispossessed. The concept of the 'Brotherhood of Man' was reduced to one specific race. Concern for women and children, the distinction between civilian and military, between healthy and sick, between strong and weak, all senses of mutual responsibility — all were deliberately removed.

Some have tried to blame the victims themselves, for having 'assimilated' or deviated from the true way, for having stayed too long in their home countries and not emigrated to then-Palestine, for having 'gone like sheep to the slaughter' rather than stealing guns and fighting back (albeit without any military organisation, training, supply mechanism, etc.). But none of this can explain the fate of a million children, or of those who had not assimilated, or of those who were killed whilst trying to do exactly what was recommended — such as the emigrants on the '*Struma*' in February 1942, all but one of whom were drowned in the Black Sea when their ship was sunk... those young emigrants trapped and murdered at Kladovo on the Danube. What about those who drowned in the last days of the war (3rd. May 1945) in the '*Kap Arkona*' through tragic misunderstandings or died on Death Marches or aimless 'death trains' like those from Bergen-Belsen to Tröbitz in April 1945 — or even those who died after liberation through sickness and hunger and weakness, or were even murdered when they went home... there are so many, many examples, depressing and frightening because of the way death so often came through random means, with no obvious link to any reason other than being 'in the wrong place at the wrong time'. One cannot build up a secure moral or spiritual system on the basis that life consists purely of trying to be 'in the right place at the right time'... that everything is a matter solely of random good fortune.

Those of us who have never experienced enemy aeroplanes suddenly flying overhead or tanks rolling into our village and setting everything on fire — with our neighbours still in their homes — or who have never been ordered to appear at a loading point on pain of being shot if we did not, or who have never been in the moral trap of knowing that an attempt to escape will lead to other people being killed, starting with our own families — those of us who have been fortunate to live lives of stability and relative security, with access to more information on political and military developments than was then the norm — should be VERY careful about apportioning any theological or moral blame on the Victims. There was no way a family in Croatia or Poland or White Russia or Holland or Greece or France in 1930 could possibly know what dreadful fate might await them and their entire towns some ten years later. Indeed it was precisely the fact that most people could not believe that such dreadful things could happen that allowed them to happen at all — many people reported voluntarily for their fates because they believed in the basic goodness of humanity, because they could not understand that a 20th.-century civilised and industrialised nation state would really want to eliminate whole swathes of the working population, would transport trainloads of healthy potential workers across the continent just to destroy them.

And we must not forget that although what is referred to as the Holocaust took place specifically in Western, Central and Eastern Europe, the USSR as far as the Ukraine, the Balkans and parts of North Africa — this is just historical fluke. A few minor changes in the military conduct of the war would have seen the British Isles, the rest of North Africa, Palestine itself under the same regime of terror, oppression and murder. The blame for the fate of some of the victims at least lies also with those nations which closed their borders and their harbours to the desperate refugees, which refused to issue visas, which demanded special markings for Jews in passports. There are many ways of killing a person and to deny them a chance to flee, to deny them hope, is one of them. Ironically one of the most successful techniques used by the Nazis was to offer their desperate victims Hope — until the very last seconds. People believed — because they wanted to believe — in 'Resettlement', in 'work details', in 'showers after a long journey'. They thought things could not get worse, only better... What do we believe?

Our problem is: How do we relate to God after such a catastrophe? What sort of characteristics does God display when such a genocide can happen and innocent people suffer? Is God 'punishing' or 'helpless to interfere' or 'absent'? How do we read prayers that say 'Blessed is God, who loves Israel'? How do we relate to texts that refer constantly to the time we were saved from Egypt, but ignore the time that we were not saved in Poland, Croatia, Norway, Tunisia? How do we balance the knowledge of the past with our belief and our needs in the present? The Book of Job and some of the Psalms show that we are not the first to have to cope with such questions; the Book of Lamentations ('Eycha') describes the anguish after the first Destruction and Exile 2,500 years ago; Many rabbinic discussions reflect approaches to the second Destruction in 70 CE; Many 'Kinot' (mournful songs) were written in Europe during the Crusades and other massacres.

Many Jews cope by the simple if remarkable method of not thinking much about it. Assuming that they have not totally and consciously 'dropped out' of Judaism, they live fulfilled Jewish lives concentrating on 'Simchas', on their children and grand-children. Others cope by devoting themselves almost fully to a secular culture of 'Remembering', which excludes any religious belief or observance. They go to Memorial Meetings rather than to synagogue services. Some of course devote themselves to the still-unfinished project of building a Jewish State in Israel. Some try to revive elements of the destroyed culture — especially Yiddish literature and music (especially so-called 'Klezmer' music). Some remain paranoid about every sign of unfriendliness towards Jews, seeing here the start of the next round of persecution. Some survivors threw themselves into rebuilding their lives and families, some remained deeply damaged, many stayed silent about their experiences but their children and grandchildren find that they cannot 'let go' of their interest in precisely the period which the family does not talk about... There is a well-defined 'Second Generation Syndrome' which affects those who have grown up in a family where there are missing grandparents or uncles and aunts, where silences and taboo subjects dominate so much of the family relationships. But the Third Generation does not remain unaffected either.

The point is that anyone who is seriously and consciously seeking a Jewish identity will be confronted with this question and cannot always escape in the way that other Jews have escaped from it. There are fears of repetitions in the future — not exact repetition, for that would be impossible, but nevertheless a physical threat to the existence of Jews and of synagogues in the world — attacks in Rome, Istanbul, in Djerba and in Buenos Aires and Paris, attacks on Jewish cemeteries all over the world show that this is no idle fear, even if it sometimes exaggerated into a form of paranoia. There really are people who hate Jews just because they are Jews — even if they have stopped being Jews! Even if they are dead Jews! And there are people who discover, often as a shock, that they have had a Jewish background all their lives but were unaware of it. There are synagogues and communities which organise major events for 'Yom HaSho'ah' and send their young people on organised visits to concentration camps, and others which seek to emphasize a positive or Zionist approach instead. But whichever way one tends, one cannot be wholly neutral. There are those who fear Zionism simply because, as they see it, so many Jews are concentrated into a small space and make a good target for a single cataclysmic attack… placing all the eggs in one basket.

And one must beware lest one's motivation for conversion at all is based upon 'making good the Holocaust' or 'replacing those who were lost' or 'atoning for the sins of the parents or grandparents'. These might be worthy motives for all sorts of good deeds, but not for conversion!

Very, very deliberately, we offer here no answers, no solutions. Jewish identity in the 21st. century means remembering and coping with the 20th. century — there is simply no way around it. And each person must find their own way.

CHAPTER 34

ISRAEL

1. WHAT DOES ISRAEL MEAN TO JEWS?

To be Jewish — or to become Jewish — means to have a relationship with Israel. One cannot remain totally neutral or uninvolved. The word '*Israel*' itself means 'The one who struggles with God' and is the name given to Jacob, the grandson of Abraham, after his struggle with a mysterious Being in the River Yabbok, in Genesis 32:28. From this time on the term was used to refer also to Jacob's descendants — the '*B'nei Yisrael*' — and Jews are also referred to and refer to themselves as 'Israelites'. In the book of Esther the term '*Yehudi*' is used for the first time — and is normally understood to mean a person from the Kingdom of Judah, the tribal area of Judea, who had been taken into exile, i.e. it has in this book an ethnic/geographic rather than a religious meaning. For better or worse, the Jews around the world are linked by both our friends and our enemies to the country or state of Israel. We would certainly encourage all those persons who wish to become Jewish, and who are physically capable of doing so, to visit the country, to get to know it, to tour it and to feel the atmosphere. Not all Jews will live in Israel — even many Zionists prefer to live outside the country — but all should know what it means to be there.

In modern times one has to distinguish between three separate terms:
The People of Israel,
The Land of Israel,
The State of Israel.

The People of Israel is defined as all those who are in the Jewish community and who wish to remain so. Traditionally this meant anyone who had a Jewish mother, or even a maternal grandmother. Of course, in reality this is no guarantee that someone may actually have received a Jewish education or lives Jewishly — hence the problems of applying such an '*Halachic* standard' uncritically. And often it is Anti-Semites who decide, according to their own standards, whom they wish to attack as 'Jews'. But in the State of Israel and in many Jewish communities this remains the basic starting-point for a definition. The queries then commence when a person or their parent or grandparent has deliberately chosen to leave Judaism — for whatever reason — and join another religion. There are also debates when someone chooses voluntarily to join the People of Israel, i.e. to 'Convert'. How is this to be achieved, what can be demanded?

The Land of Israel is defined roughly as that area of land at the eastern coastline of the Mediterranean Sea, north-west of Egypt and south of Lebanon and Syria, which was at one time the Land of Canaan and which was promised by God to the descendants of Abraham. The problem, of course, lies in knowing how to define the exact boundaries of this area in terms of modern geography and modern politics. It would appear that there are different definitions in different texts in the Bible, and a degree of compromise and flexibility is called for. But how much, and from whom? In Genesis 12:5 this is described as 'the land of Canaan' and already inhabited; in Gen. 13:7 there are Canaanites and Perizzites in the land. In Gen. 13:14 God promises Abram the land north, east, south and west of where he is currently situated, but without specifying boundaries. In Gen. 15:18 (compare with Deuteronomy 1:6-8) we read of the covenant in which God promises Abram the land 'from the river of Egypt to the mighty river Euphrates — the land of the Kenites, Kenissites, Kadmonites, Hittites, Perizzites, Rephaites, Emorites, Canaanites, Girgashites and Jebusites.' The 'river of Egypt' is understood to be the Wadi Arish at El Arish, and not the Nile! Naturally the current state is located in only a fraction of this area but when speaking later of 'Palestine' or 'Coelo-Syria' or various other names for the region during various eras and various rulers we see that essentially there is a strip of land linking the north-eastern tip of Africa to the western tip of Asia, with a coastal plain, a central mountain range, a deep Rift Valley, the mountains to the east of this, and then — empty desert. So taking the Sinai and Negev deserts to the south and south-west, the Arabia desert to the east, the Mediterranean Sea to the west, the big question is only how far the natural boundaries reach to the north and north-east along the 'Fertile Crescent' — where do the rivers flow, where were the trade routes?

The State of Israel is that legal entity which was formally called into existence in May 1948 as a sovereign state and as a member of the United Nations. It is a parliamentary democracy, having an elected Parliament ('*Knesset*') and an elected President, serving a fixed term — but no dynastic monarchy. There is a wide variety of political parties and a free Press. It has a self-imposed mission to provide a haven for oppressed Jews (or those classed as Jews and persecuted as such) from around the world, and therefore allows Jews certain privileges in immigration, but it is also open to others. Although the calendar is largely based on the Jewish one, there is religious freedom, and in Israel there are many denominations of churches, mosques, a Baha'i Temple, a Mormon university and other institutions. The Holy Places of all religions are respected. There are three official languages: Hebrew, English and Arabic. It should not be necessary to state all this, but in reality in many of these definitions Israel is unique amongst its neighbours.

It remains the only country in the entire world which is governed by and for Jews, although there are many which are ruled on Christian or Moslem or atheist lines.

2. A BRIEF MODERN HISTORY

The road which led to this situation was long and difficult. Until 1917 the entire region was controlled by the Ottoman Empire based in Constantinople (Istanbul). The First World War led in this region, as it did in Europe, to the break-up of empires and the growth of individual nationalisms based on ethnic or cultural or religious identity. This account can only scratch the surface of what is a very controversial period, but it is important that anyone becoming Jewish learns some of the facts from reputable sources.

Although the dream of a 'return to the Holy Land' had been kept alive in rituals and liturgy for centuries, the Zionist Movement was formally established in 1901 at a congress in Basel as a political movement dedicated to creating the conditions for Jews to return to this under-developed Turkish province. This included establishing institutions to raise funds to purchase land from the existing landowners and to establish settlements, farms (including the collective '*Kibbutzim*' and the co-operative '*Moshavim*', schools (such as the Gymnasium in the new town of Tel Aviv built on the sands adjacent to Jaffa) and more. Jews immigrated and established themselves and industries, political and cultural institutions.

During the First World War the Zionist movement moved its headquarters from Berlin first to neutral Copenhagen and then to London. Political lobbying led to the 'Balfour Declaration', an ambiguous statement that promised the British Government's support in establishing a 'Jewish national home' (whatever that was interpreted to mean — it falls short of a State but implies a degree of national autonomy). (It was written by Arthur Balfour, the British Foreign Secretary, to Walter Rothschild!) At the time it was issued, on 2nd November 1917 and published a week later, pleasing some but disappointing others, Britain did not yet actually control the land it was blithely promising…

> 'His Majesty's government view with favour the establishment in Palestine of a national home for the Jewish people, and will use their best endeavours to facilitate the achievement of this object, it being clearly understood that nothing shall be done which may prejudice the civil and religious rights of existing non-Jewish communities in Palestine, or the rights and political status enjoyed by Jews in any other country.'

Many of the Jewish inhabitants of the existing small settlement (the '*Yishuv*') sympathised with the Allies and were exiled by the Turks, who were part of the coalition of Germany and Austro-Hungary fighting Britain, France and Russia. (At this period the Ottoman forces were also busily massacring Armenian Christian inhabitants of the Empire.) In 1917 forces of the British Empire (including Arab irregular troops mobilised and under the guidance of officers from the British Secret Service, such as T. E. Lawrence) moving from Egypt across Sinai conquered this part of the Middle East and under the terms of a secret wartime Treaty with France (the 'Sykes-Picot

Treaty') divided the region into British and French spheres of interest. New countries were created out of the former Ottoman 'Sanjaks'. The countries known as Syria, Iraq, Saudi Arabia, Palestine and, from 1922, Transjordan all date from this period.

'Territory was divided along map meridians without regard for traditional frontiers (i.e. geographic logic and sustainability) or the ethnic composition of indigenous populations. The prevailing rationale behind these artificially created states was how they served the imperial and commercial needs of their colonial masters. Iraq and Jordan, for instance, were created as emirates to reward the noble Hashemite family from Saudi Arabia for its loyalty to the British against the Ottoman Turks during World War I, under the leadership of Lawrence of Arabia. Iraq was given to Faisal bin Hussein, son of the sheriff of Mecca, in 1918. To reward his younger brother Abdullah with an emirate, Britain cut away 77 percent of its mandate over Palestine earmarked for the Jews and gave it to Abdullah in 1922, creating the new country of Trans-Jordan or Jordan, as it was later named.'

(from: http://www.mythsandfacts.org/conflict/mandate_for_palestine/ mandate_for_palestine.htm)

The original scheme for 'Palestine' of 24[th.] April 1920 envisaged a total of 120,466 sq. km. — but then in 1922 the section east of the Jordan was detached, 92,300 sq. km. or 77%, leaving 28,166 sq. km. or 23% of the original area available for Jewish immigration. At this period a 'National Home' rather than an independent State was envisaged. Winston Churchill, then British Secretary of State for the Colonies, said in June 1922:

'When it is asked what is meant by the development of the Jewish National Home in Palestine, it may be answered that it is not the imposition of a Jewish nationality upon the inhabitants of Palestine as a whole, but the further development of the existing Jewish community, with the assistance of Jews in other parts of the world, in order that it may become a centre in which the Jewish people as a whole may take, on grounds of religion and race, an interest and a pride. But in order that this community should have the best prospect of free development and provide a full opportunity for the Jewish people to display its capacities, it is essential that it should know that it is in Palestine as of right and not on sufferance.'

The newly-formed League of Nations (founded in January 1920) with its fifty-one member states ratified this quasi-colonial division of the former Ottoman Empire between the victors by granting so-called 'Mandates', i.e. permission to rule in the name of the League — the ruling countries being required to submit regular reports as to how they were developing their territories for the benefit of the local population. Since there is widespread ignorance about this period, it is worth quoting here large sections of the original document:

'As finally approved by the Council of the League of Nations, Monday 24th. July 1922, and Accepted for Administration by His Britannic Majesty's Government.'

'The Council of the League of Nations:

Whereas the Principal Allied Powers have agreed, for the purpose of giving effect to the provisions of Article 22 of the Covenant of the League of Nations, to entrust to a Mandatory selected by the said Powers the administration of the territory of Palestine, which formerly belonged to the Turkish Empire, within such boundaries as may be fixed by them; and

Whereas the Principal Allied Powers have also agreed that the Mandatory should be responsible for putting into effect the declaration originally made on November 2, 1917, by the Government of His Britannic Majesty, and adopted by the said Powers, in favour of the establishment in Palestine of a national home for the Jewish people, it being clearly understood that nothing should be done which might prejudice the civil and religious rights of existing non-Jewish communities in Palestine, or the rights and political status enjoyed by Jews in any other country; and

Whereas recognition has thereby been given to the historical connection of the Jewish people with Palestine, and to the grounds for reconstituting their national home in that country; and

Whereas His Britannic Majesty has accepted the mandate in respect of Palestine and undertaken to exercise it on behalf of the League of Nations in conformity with the following provisions; and … Confirming the said mandate, defines its terms as follows:

Article 1.

The Mandatory shall have full powers of legislation and of administration, save as they may be limited by the terms of this mandate.

Article 2.

The Mandatory shall be responsible for placing the country under such political, administrative and economic conditions as will secure the establishment of the Jewish national home, as laid down in the preamble, and the development of self-governing institutions, and also for safeguarding the civil and religious rights of all the inhabitants of Palestine, irrespective of race and religion.

Article 3.

The Mandatory shall, so far as circumstances permit, encourage local autonomy.

Article 4.

An appropriate Jewish agency shall be recognised as a public body for the purpose of advising and cooperating with the Administration of Palestine in such
economic, social and other matters as may affect the establishment of the Jewish
national home and the interests of the Jewish population in Palestine, and, subject always to the control of the Administration, to assist and take part in the
development of the country.

The Zionist organisation, so long as its organisation and constitution are in the
opinion of the Mandatory appropriate, shall be recognised as such agency. It shall
take steps in consultation with His Britannic Majesty's Government to secure the
cooperation of all Jews who are willing to assist in the establishment of the Jewish
national home.

Article 5.

The Mandatory shall be responsible for seeing that no Palestine territory shall be
ceded or leased to, or in any way placed under the control of, the Government
of any other Power. [N.B. compare Art. 25 & see Note re. Transjordan at end.]

Article 6.

The Administration of Palestine, while ensuring that the rights and position of
other sections of the population are not prejudiced, shall facilitate Jewish immigration under suitable conditions and shall encourage, in cooperation with
the Jewish agency referred to in Article 4, close settlement by Jews on the land,
including State lands and waste lands not required for public purposes.

Article 7.

The Administration of Palestine shall be responsible for enacting a nationality
law. There shall be included in this law provisions framed so as to facilitate the
acquisition of Palestinian citizenship by Jews who take up their permanent residence in Palestine.

Article 9.

The Mandatory shall be responsible for seeing that the judicial system established in Palestine shall assure to foreigners, as well as to natives, a complete
guarantee of their rights…

Article 11.

The Administration of Palestine shall take all necessary measures to safeguard
the interests of the community in connection with the development of the country, and, subject to any international obligations accepted by the Mandatory, shall
have full power to provide for public ownership or control of any of the natural

resources of the country or of the public works, services and utilities established therein. It shall introduce a land system appropriate to the needs of the country, having regard, among other things, to the desirability of promoting the close settlement and intensive cultivation of the land.

The Administration may arrange with the Jewish agency mentioned in Article 4 to construct or operate, upon fair and equitable terms, any public works, services and utilities, and to develop any of the natural resources of the country, in so far as these matters are not directly undertaken by the Administration. ...

Article 12.

The Mandatory shall be entrusted with the control of the foreign relations of Palestine...

Article 13.

All responsibility in connection with the Holy Places and religious buildings or sites in Palestine, including that of preserving existing rights and of securing free access to the Holy Places, religious buildings and sites and the free exercise of worship, while ensuring the requirements of public order and decorum, is assumed by the Mandatory, who shall be responsible solely to the League of Nations in all matters connected herewith ... and provided also that nothing in this mandate shall be construed as conferring upon the Mandatory authority to interfere with the fabric or the management of purely Moslem shrines, the immunities of which are guaranteed.

Article 14.

A special Commission shall be appointed by the Mandatory to study, define and determine the rights and claims in connection with the Holy Places and the rights and claims relating to the different religious communities in Palestine. The method of nomination, the composition and the functions of this Commission shall be submitted to the Council of the League of Nations for its approval, and the Commission shall not be appointed or enter upon its functions without the approval of the Council.

Article 15.

The Mandatory shall see that complete freedom of conscience and the free exercise of all forms of worship, subject only to the maintenance of public order and morals, are ensured to all. No discrimination of any kind shall be made between the inhabitants of Palestine on the ground of race, religion or language. No person shall be excluded from Palestine on the sole ground of his religious belief.

The right of each community to maintain its own schools for the education of its own members in its own language, while conforming to such educational requirements of a general nature as the Administration may impose, shall not be denied or impaired.

Article 16.

The Mandatory shall be responsible for exercising such supervision over religious ... bodies of all faiths in Palestine as may be required for the maintenance of public order and good government. Subject to such supervision, no measures shall be taken in Palestine to obstruct or interfere with the enterprise of such bodies or to discriminate against any representative or member of them on the ground of his religion or nationality.

Article 17.

The Administration of Palestine may organise on a voluntary basis the forces necessary for the preservation of peace and order, and also for the defence of the country, subject, however, to the supervision of the Mandatory, but shall not use them for purposes other than those specified above save with the consent of the Mandatory. Except for such purposes, no military, naval or air forces shall be raised or maintained by the Administration in Palestine.

Nothing in this article shall preclude the Administration of Palestine from contributing to the cost of the maintenance of the forces of the Mandatory in Palestine.

Article 18.

The Mandatory shall see that there is no discrimination in Palestine against the nationals of any State Member of the League of Nations (including companies incorporated under its laws) as compared with those of the Mandatory or of any foreign State in matters concerning taxation, commerce or navigation, the exercise of industries or professions, or in the treatment of merchant vessels or civil aircraft. Similarly there shall be no discrimination in Palestine against goods originating in or destined for any of the said States, and there shall be freedom of transit under equitable conditions across the mandated area ...

Article 22.

English, Arabic and Hebrew shall be the official languages of Palestine. Any statement or inscription in Arabic on stamps or money in Palestine shall be repeated in Hebrew, and any statement or inscription in Hebrew shall be repeated in Arabic.

Article 23.

The Administration of Palestine shall recognise the holy days of the respective communities in Palestine as legal days of rest for the members of such communities.

Article 24.

The Mandatory shall make to the Council of the League of Nations an Annual report to the satisfaction of the Council as to the measures taken during the year to carry out the provisions of the mandate. Copies of all laws and regulations promulgated or issued during the year shall be communicated with the report.

Article 25.

In the territories lying between the Jordan and the eastern boundary of Palestine as ultimately determined [my emphasis. WLR.], the Mandatory shall be entitled, with the consent of the Council of the League of Nations, to postpone or withhold application of such provisions of this mandate as he may consider inapplicable to the existing local conditions, and to make such provision for the administration of the territories as he may consider suitable to those conditions, provided that no action shall be taken which is inconsistent with the provisions of Articles 15, 16 and 18.

Article 26.

The Mandatory agrees that, if any dispute whatever should arise between the Mandatory and another Member of the League of Nations relating to the interpretation or the application of the provisions of the mandate, such dispute, if it cannot be settled by negotiation, shall be submitted to the Permanent Court of International Justice provided for by Article 14 of the Covenant of the League of Nations.

Article 27.

The consent of the Council of the League of Nations is required for any modification of the terms of this mandate.

Article 28.

In the event of the termination of the mandate hereby conferred upon the Mandatory, the Council of the League of Nations shall make such arrangements as may be deemed necessary for safeguarding in perpetuity, under guarantee of the League, the rights secured by Articles 13 and 14, and shall use its influence for securing, under the guarantee of the League, that the Government of Palestine will fully honour the financial obligations incurred by the Administration of Palestine during the period of the mandate, including the rights of public servants to pensions or gratuities...

London, 24th. July, 1922.'

New colonial or quasi-independent governments were therefore installed in these newly-minted countries. In Palestine a Mandatory Administration was, as can be seen, obligated to encourage and assist Jewish immigration, the establishment of a 'Jewish National Home' and national organisations, and to use Hebrew as one of the main official languages. It is important to note this, since it is evidence that the original purpose of the British and League of Nations involvement was to enable Jews to come here and settle. It is often stated polemically that 'the Jews stole the land' or 'The Europeans set up Israel for the Jews because of their guilt over the Holocaust' — in fact Jewish immigration, the establishment of institutions and the creation of some autonomy was established and legitimated by international agreement long before the Holocaust, after the First and not after the Second World War. However, violent Moslem opposition to these measures and riots in 1922, 1930 and from 1936 onwards led to many changes in policy as the British tried to appease the Arab population. As noted, a large section of land was split off from the original '1920 Palestine' in 1922 to become the semi-autonomous 'Kingdom of Transjordan', and several attempts were made to divide the mandated territory in such a way that the Jews were in one part and the Moslems in another, with the capital and the holy places in some form of neutral separate area. In addition Jewish immigration was severely curtailed at precisely the time — the 1930s — that more and more Jews were seeking desperately to emigrate from Europe and most other countries were refusing to accept them.

During the Second World War, with the German and Axis forces heading across North Africa towards Egypt and also through the Ukraine towards Turkey and Syria, the Jews of Palestine took the side of the British Empire against the forces of Fascism. Once the War was over, and the full horror of what had happened to the Jews of Europe became known, and the surviving 'Displaced Persons' were still being refused admission to Palestine because of the pre-war immigration quotas, it transpired that British post-war policy still depended on appeasing oil-producing Arab States. In consequence Jewish resistance to British rule grew. In the meantime the separate state of Lebanon was formed (by dividing Syria into two parts) in 1946; Britain signed new treaties with Transjordan the same year; new arrangements were made with Egypt... but Palestine remained administered in the interests of the British imperial forces. (If anything, the withdrawal of British forces from bases in Egypt made those in Palestine even more important for regional policy.) Violence grew. Eventually the British Government, facing so many other urgent post-war issues at home and all over the world, handed the problem over to the newly-formed (April 1946) United Nations, the successor to the League of Nations, which sent in Commissions of Enquiry and decided in a vote on November 29th 1947 (Resolution 181) to partition Palestine after all into Jewish and Arab areas plus a neutral area around the 'holy sites'. The Jewish organisations accepted this split, though the shapes on the map indicated it would prove a difficult task to keep the country together; the Arab population, encouraged by neighbouring countries, refused to accept the decision.

A messy war broke out, in many respects a civil war between Jewish Palestinians and Arab Palestinians (after all, at this point they were ALL Palestinians!) but with military forces infiltrating from other Arab countries, and following the formal declaration of Statehood on May 15th. 1948 a full invasion was carried out by Egyptian, Syrian, Lebanese, Transjordan ('Arab Legion') and Iraqi armed forces.

When the fighting formally ended there were several temporary truces and armistices from February to July 1949 (with Egypt on 24th February, with Lebanon 23rd March, with Jordan 3rd April, with Syria 20th July, negotiated through the Mixed Armistice Commission). It was however the Rhodes Agreement and the Lausanne Conference of the United Nations Conciliation Commission for Palestine (UNC-CP) of April — September 1949 that formally ended this conflict — the cease-fire lines were deliberately described as being provisional and based only on the military boundaries; However, they eventually became effectively new borders and were not quite where the UN had intended. (Thanks to being drawn onto a map with a green pen these became the 'Green Line'.)

In addition several other Arab countries had invaded and occupied the land which the UN had originally allocated to the Moslem and Christian Palestinians — Egypt had occupied what became known as the 'Gaza Strip', the strip of coastal plain containing the towns of Rafah, Gaza and Khan Yunis; Transjordan had occupied the Jordan valley and the hill country to its west, including the Old City and East Jerusalem; Syria had occupied part of the Golan. This meant that no Arab country of 'Palestine' was established to partner the Jewish country of Palestine (which took the name 'Israel' only on becoming independent). But the Jews, at great cost in casualties, had succeeded in resisting the invading forces; in breaking the siege and retaining a part of Jerusalem and a land route to it; had kept the coastal plain from Nahariyya in the north to Ashkelon in the south; had kept the Negev with valuable access to Eilat and thus the Red Sea; and also parts of the Galilee.

The problem has been that this war has not been allowed to subside. Although there were many wars at this period — including a civil war in Greece, conflicts in Egypt, the violent separation of India and Pakistan, the establishment of independent countries in many parts of Africa and the Middle East, the emergence of the Cold War in Europe, conflicts in Indonesia and Korea, the Turkish invasion of Northern Cyprus, to name but a few — somehow this conflict over dividing the British Mandate Territory of Palestine and the sufferings of one particular group of refugees and one group who lost has been elevated to becoming the source of current hostility to Israel and Jews worldwide. It is an interesting question, why this should be the case? Many Jews were forced in the same period to flee their centuries-old communities in Moslem countries and to go to Israel — and their loss and suffering tend to be overlooked — whereas the fact that many Palestinian Arabs fled the conflict in Palestine and were only allowed to resettle as permanent 'Refugees' is something which is constantly cited as a major crime against humanity. There was a war, and wars are not pleasant, and people lose limbs, lives, family and homes in War — we do not wish to ignore or defend this — but merely to point out that there are other wars and other conflicts which for some reason get neglected. See the personal comments below on 'Criticism of Israel'. The suggestion is that there are often political and ideological, rather than ethical or humanitarian reasons for this interest.

Since 1948 Israel has remained in a perpetual state of conflict with all or most of its neighbours, many of which have refused to sign a full Peace agreement and several of which have at times encouraged or supported terrorist groups which sought and seek to infiltrate Israel across its land and sea borders and create fear and havoc. (e.g. in the period 1951-1956 ca. 400 Israelis were killed and 900 injured in 'Fedayeen' raids.) In 1956 Israel supported Britain and France in an attempt to re-open the Suez Canal to shipping by military force; in June 1967 it made a pre-emptive strike due to threats from Egypt and Syria and the closure of the Red Sea to Israeli shipping (the '6-Day War'); in 1973 it had to defend itself against concerted surprise attacks from all its neighbours (the '*Yom Kippur* War'); in 1982 it responded to rocket attacks from Lebanon by invading the southern part of that country and assisting the local Christian population against the Moslem extremists. In each case the initial advance was followed by a period of occupation and then in most cases a negotiated with-drawal — from the Sinai (including the new town of Yamit) in 1982, from Lebanon in 2000, and even from sections of the Gaza Strip and the northern and southern hill country. In 2005 Israel withdrew formally from the entire Gaza Strip, forcibly dismantling several villages that had been built for Israeli inhabitants.

The war has long ceased to be about 'Land'. Israel has made several concessions or withdrawals and allowed degrees of autonomy unheard of in other countries — one thinks of the Chinese involvement in Tibet, for instance! — and has instead become one of Ideology, in which peoples geographically distant from the conflict, in Iran or Indonesia or wherever, challenge Israel's very right to exist, or to exist in its current form. Against any ideological enemy concessions on the ground are point-less and Israeli society is split on the issue of how many compromises may or should be made, and what risks are attached to a physical withdrawal from certain areas.

3. WHAT ABOUT CRITICISM OF ISRAEL?

Is criticism of Israel permitted? Of course, but we demand that it should be informed criticism, constructive criticism and fair criticism. If it is not, then it is uninformed, destructive and unfair — and then we would oppose such criticism and question the motives of the one making it.

How to decide whether criticism is informed? It is important that the person criticising knows some of the history, the political background, the views of more than one side in the debate. They should not be responding merely to a shallow arti-cle or news item in the media or be reacting emotionally.

How to decide whether criticism is constructive? If a viable alternative policy is suggested, if advice is given which is realistic and which suits the needs of a situation.

How to decide if it is fair? The simple rule of thumb is: Is this criticism applied as appropriate to all parties in a conflict? Are the same standards demanded of all involved? Is only one side being criticised for doing what the other side is also doing? It is NOT fair for outsiders to demand higher standards from Israel or from Jews, for example, than they demand from Israel's enemies.

The simplest way to find out if any of the above standards is to perform a simple test. Reverse all the terms for, say, 'Israel' and 'Palestinians' or 'Jews' and 'Arabs'. Simply swap the words round. Would the person criticising then still criticise? If, say, in 1948 the Arab Palestinians had driven the Jewish Palestinians into exile — would the critic then be demanding the right of return for these Jews and their descendants? If, in 1967, the Arab countries had pushed the Israelis into a smaller enclave rather than Israel managing to occupy some of the high territory in Judea, Samaria and the Golan, and the Gaza Strip — would the critic be organising demonstrations, placards and slogans demanding that the Arabs give the Jews their half of Jerusalem back? If, in 1973, the Arab countries which attacked Israel on *Yom Kippur* that year had succeeded in beating back the Israeli Army — would the critic be showing the same concern about the exact location of cease-fire lines, borders and security barriers? Or the fate of Israeli refugees? If the answer is a sincere 'Yes, of course' — then the critic is an idealist whose criticisms deserve at least to be taken seriously. If however the answer is 'No' or 'I am not sure' — then the criticism is 'loaded' and is not sincere, but reflects bias and prejudice, and should not be taken seriously. In such cases we ask ourselves why otherwise-intelligent people are prepared to overlook so many other conflicts and injustices in the world and focus their entire anger and rage purely against Israel. And THEN we can define this form of criticism as 'Anti-Semitism', because it is directed against the Jewish State not because it is a State but simply because it is a Jewish State, not because it is so much worse or better than any other.

Of course, the unfortunate fact is that all Jews, everywhere, are singled out for attack by those who hate Israel, on the basis that we are all somehow linked — even if this is manifestly ludicrous. This is why it is impossible to stay totally 'neutral'. One must be informed, and aware. Every anti-Israel graffiti or article or programme or news broadcast or a call for a boycott is actually an attempt to undermine the right of a Jewish State to exist.

And at the same time, there IS of course much within Israeli society which is not perfect, and which deserves constructive criticism. The status of Liberal Judaism or the abuse of power by so-called 'religious' political parties or extremist fundamentalist groups are examples. We urge merely that those seeking to criticise do so in the correct forum and with the correct understanding, for Israel remains under siege from several of its regional neighbours, its very existence threatened by religious and political leaders, and this needs to be understood.

431

The history of Great Britain was also one of constant wars for centuries — English against Celts, against Scots, against Welsh, resistance against invasions by Normans or Vikings… People tend to forget that the Romans built two protective walls (Antonine and Hadrian) against the marauding Scots, the English in the 8[th.] century built Offa's Dyke as protection against the Welsh… There was a Partition of Ireland and a withdrawal in 1921 from most of it, which became the Irish Free State declared by a Treaty in December 1921 (acknowledged by Britain in December 1922 and which led to a civil war until 1923) which did not bring the peace hoped for as there remained Catholics in the six counties now under Protestant control. All over Europe borders changed after World War One with the collapse of the Habsburg Empire, the creation of Poland in 1918 (which had to fight against Russia for its existence in 1920) and the Baltic countries and Czechoslovakia and Yugoslavia, the loss of German territories; or when after World War Two ended with a new partition through the entire continent, expulsion of ethnic Germans, bloody conflicts between Poland and Ukraine… No map of France or Germany or Poland or Austria or Hungary or Italy or the Balkans shows the same borders as there were a few decades ago — and yet, on the whole and despite the rise of nationalistic groups, one has simply accepted these changes as a fact of life, the consequence of lost wars or ethnic self-determination. Why can the same people not simply accept the changes in the Middle East too — especially in a period when national boundaries are still a matter of dispute and conflict between Syrians and Turks and Iraqis and Kurds and supra-nationalist Islamists? Sometimes, after watching a polemical documentary or listening to a radio news broadcast filled with trivialities about Israel — the tragic death of one person, whilst hundreds are butchered not far away — one wishes that the rest of the world would simply shut up and stop interfering and let those living in the region get on with their lives and make their own pragmatic arrangements with their neighbours. In the end that will be the only way forward.

Current Arab Palestinians often refer to the events of 1948 as the 'Naqba' ('Catastrophe') — usually without any historical context as to why this became a catastrophe. Further, in 1975 the Iranian leader Ayatollah Khomeini called upon all Moslems worldwide to commemorate 'Al-Quds Day' (the Arabic for 'the Holy City', referring to Jerusalem) on the last Friday in the month of Ramadan and to cut off the hands of all Zionists and their supporters, to show solidarity for the Palestinians. Frequently demonstrations are held in European cities and Israel is publicly and loudly criticised and defamed or Israeli symbols destroyed.

The 'BDS' movement (Boycott, Disinvestment, Sanctions) seeks to isolate Israel politically, academically and economically. Israelis have been attacked by terrorists or humiliated while on holidays or business trips in many countries. It is such a shame that so much time and energy has to be devoted to opposing such hatred, countering propaganda, protecting students from attacks on campus, organising counter-demonstrations, monitoring anti-semitic comments on websites and social media, arranging security for synagogue worshippers, and more. Why should this have to be necessary? The fact is — it is. Denial does not help.

4. ISRAEL FOR DIASPORA JEWS TODAY

By definition a lot of Jews live in the '*Diaspora*' — the Dispersion. Some refer to this still as 'Exile' ('*Galut*') but, if the possibility exists to go to Israel, and one does not take it, staying voluntarily in another country, one cannot really claim to be in exile any more. There are still unfortunately some Jews whose circumstances do not allow them to move freely, and these are still 'captive' to some extent. There are also many Israelis who have left the country to seek their living and luck elsewhere. (Those who emigrate to Israel are described as 'making *Aliyah*' — 'going up to Israel' — in the same way as one 'goes up' to the capital city of a country — and are '*Olim*'; Those who leave long-term or permanently to live elsewhere are therefore sometimes described as 'making *Yeridah*' and are '*Yordim*' — 'those who go down'.)

Not all Jews are Zionists, and not all Zionists — those who believe that Israel is the homeland for all Jews — are Jewish. Some fundamentalist Christians share these values, often for theological reasons of their own!

Nevertheless, the majority of Jewish communities will mark or celebrate to some extent *Yom Ha'Atzma'ut* — Israel Independence Day — and some the *Yom HaZikaron* on the day before it — the day commemorating Israel's fallen soldiers and also the many civilian victims of violence against Israel and Israelis. Some mark *Yom Yerushalayim*, the day when the Old City of Jerusalem with the historic site of the Temple was recaptured in June 1967 and the city reunited. One will find Israeli flags in some synagogues, leaflets about Israeli projects, attempts to encourage purchase of Israeli products; Youth movements will encourage teenagers and students to spend some time in Israel, charities will seek support for projects in Israel, local Jewish newspapers will cover Israeli news more fully than the rest of the press, and Israeli government agencies will distribute material encouraging Jews to consider *Aliyah* — emigration to Israel.

In short, Israel plays a part in the calendar and in the programming of many Jewish organisations, and while it is not compulsory to support all these, it would be expected that one somehow fits into this scheme of things. There are of course many, many agencies, organisations and even governments that constantly attack and oppose and denigrate and even demonise Israel — Jewish students will find many well-funded and well-organised anti-Israel activities at universities, and some of the most virulent and pathologically anti-Israel speakers are themselves Jewish or Israelis — at least in name. The name 'Self-Hating Jew' is often used of such — this may be unfair, but one wonders why some academics and others cannot be content with being neutral 'Non-Zionist' and instead have to become actively 'Anti-Zionist' and share platforms with people who have a deep hatred for Jews and for Israel. There is even a bizarre phenomenon — the author knows personally of some cases — whereby some persons who have converted to Judaism then become anti-Israel and claim 'You must believe what I say; after all, I'm Jewish!'

On occasion it is necessary to become involved politically, when a certain invisible boundary of mutual tolerance is overstepped, when anti-Israel demonstrations or letters campaigns or boycott campaigns are organised. We should never forget that Zionism was, in essence, a response to the fact that many Jews felt threatened and unwanted in their home countries. The irony is that the mere existence of a Jewish State is now used by many to justify making the Jews in other countries feel threatened and unwanted! And so the cycle continues. Will it ever end?

And — very importantly — whenever a Jew wishes to grumble about the current state of Israel and its political system — one should never forget how wonderful it is to have a country to grumble about.

CHAPTER 35

MITZVOT

1. INTRODUCTION

To be Jewish — or to become Jewish — means to attempt to live according to certain basic standards. These standards are often termed '*Mitzvot*'. Technically this does not mean 'Good Deeds' but merely 'Commandments to be Fulfilled' or 'Obligations, Duties, Responsibilities' from the verb '*Tzavah*' — 'to command'. There are *Mitzvot* involved in the relationship with God (called '*beyn Adam v'Makom*' — here the word '*Makom*' meaning 'the Place' is a euphemism for God) and — very importantly — *Mitzvot* involved in the relationship with one's fellow human beings ('*beyn Adam l'Chavero*' — 'between a man and his fellow') an d even with animals — or we could extend the idea these days to the Environment. These are all aspects of belonging to a Community and helping to care for the weaker members of that community — the lonely, the sick, the bereaved, the depressed, the orphaned, the widowed. We may be the centre of our own personal universe, but this does not mean that we are the centre of the entire universe — a mistake that many people make.

Technically, in Judaism the fulfilment of an obligation is more important than a voluntary decision to do something positive. It is not that it is wrong to decide for oneself to donate something or to help someone or to pray — it is merely that this comes AFTER you have performed the legal requirements in any case. In other words, vague good-will is not a substitute for the fulfilment of your responsibilities to the world and its inhabitants (and its Creator).

The point is that we are given Free Will, the right and the ability to choose our actions. (In '*Niddah*' 16b — 'Everything is foreordained by the heavens except how we will choose to react' — or 'everything is in the hands of heaven except the fear of heaven'; likewise '*Pirke Avot*' 3:18 where Rabbi Akiva says that everything is foreseen by God and yet Mankind still has the choice.) There is no point in anything being 'commanded' unless we could realistically fulfil the command — or could deliberately decide not to do so. If we would do something automatically, instinctively anyway — such as breathe or sleep — there would be no need to command it; if we were incapable of doing something wrong — such as committing theft or murder — there would be no need to forbid it. Judaism sees the human being as being impelled by two 'urges' or 'inclinations', the 'Good Urge' ('*Yetzer Tov*') and the 'Evil Urge' —

'Yetzer haRah'. (According to 'Avot d'Rabbi Natan' we acquire the 'Yetzer Tov' only on attaining maturity and the ability to discern for ourselves, which is why from this age onward we are considered to be responsible for our actions; cf. Genesis 8:21 'A person's tendency is to do evil from his youth onwards' — which actually implies the opposite, that one is innocent as a child but can turn to evil from adolescence onwards.) Our task consists not of destroying or eliminating the 'evil' side of ourselves but in controlling it and channelling it. The term 'Evil Urge' must be carefully understood, for we need it to survive! In the *Talmud* '*Sanhedrin*' 64a is a remarkable story of the rabbis praying to be able to capture the Evil Temptation; Having imprisoned it (in the form of a fiery lion cub) for three days they then discover that there is not a single fresh egg in the whole country, normal life has come to a standstill, and so they decide they have to release it again! For the world to exist we need our desires for acquisition and our sexual urges — but they need to be kept controlled.

For Christianity the big sin in Genesis Chapter 3, using the metaphor of a juicy fruit from a tree, is somehow connected to the discovery of Sexuality; But in Judaism the story explains how mankind through eating this fruit of the Tree of Knowledge learned to distinguish between Good and Evil — which means we can no longer pretend we do not know the difference or use this as an excuse! In Christianity the man and woman see that they are naked; in Judaism they learn very quickly to make clothing!

In some respects the modern term 'Human Rights' occupies the space of '*Mitzvot*' in secular or political discourse.

Human rights can be defined as 'the rights of those who otherwise would have no rights', i.e. those without power or influence. Those who already have power and influence do not need 'Rights', for they have the power and the influence! But there are others who need protection from being exploited or attacked or driven out by those with the power and influence.

Judaism classically defined this group as 'the Widow, Orphan and Foreigner' ('*Almanah, Yatom veGer*'). To this could be added the Slave / Employee, the Prisoner of War and maybe even the chronically Ill, the Poor or Unemployed, the Handicapped, even the Dying, the Elderly and the Unborn.

Judaism is based on certain basic experiences, either universal or national, which influence the way we look at fellow human beings of whatever background or status.

One is the Creation. There is one God who created all humans and therefore at this basic global level we are all Created Beings with one Creator and are therefore similar.

A second is the Covenant with Abraham, later renewed at Sinai with the entire people. This means that this universal God has a relationship to what happens here in our world.

A third is the experience of Slavery in Egypt, then Liberation from Egypt, then life as homeless refugees in the desert. We should never forget any of these and in the *Torah* and liturgy — even in the first of the Ten Commandments — this is mentioned. God is defined as one who intervenes in history to help and rescue and lead Israel.

So, having known what it is like to be weak, we should care for the weak, those who need Protection. This is an obligation, *Mitzvah*.

Who protects a Woman? Normally in ancient times it was her Father and then in due course her Husband, to whose protection she was 'transferred' on marriage. But what happens when she is widowed? (Of course in some countries or cultures women have won much more independence than this — but not yet in all…)

Who protects a Child? Normally its Parents. But what about when the parents are unable to, or they have died and the child is alone? Or it is treated merely as cheap labour?

Who protects a Foreigner? There is no one who can save him from being abused, excluded (from jobs or accommodation), from being tricked and swindled due to inexperience of language and customs… so Society has to take over this role.

For the Employee or slave — there are rules, starting in the *Torah*, concerning free days, regular and punctual payment, respectful and not violent treatment, care to protect against accidents at work. Likewise for the person, male or female, captured in a war and taken prisoner. None of these are good situations to be in but the Jewish approach is much better than in most other societies, in Europe until recently or around in the Middle East even today… Although 'officially' prohibited, there are still thousands of sex-slaves in many European cities. In many countries workers labour long hours for low wages in appalling and dangerous conditions.

There are also concepts of Animal Rights — rules for the care of the donkey and the ox, which get their rest day, which must not be overburdened, which should not be harnessed together, or slaughtered painfully, etc.

In modern society one tends to speak much more of Rights than of Duties but of course it is a Duty to respect the Rights of others. What rights does one have to defend oneself against others who do not respect one's rights — such as cruel employers, brutal attackers, abusers? Where are the limits? In Judaism the Unborn have no rights, and the Dead have the right to be treated with respect but no rights any more to influence the lives of those left behind. e.g. Widows are freed to re-marry.

2. THE 'TARYA'G' MITZVOT

There are many books and guides to the various *Mitzvot* — the *Torah*, according to tradition, contains 613 commandments (hence the term 'Tarya'g Mitzvot' from the letters *Taf* for 400, *Resh* for 200, *Yud* for 10 and *Gimmel* for 3 = 400 + 200 + 10 + 3 = 613). However, there are some differences in the listing and many of these rules are in any case relevant only for priests, or in a sacrificial cultic ritual, or for farmers, or within the Land of Israel. The first mention is by Rabbi Simla in *Talmud 'Makkot'* 23b-24a, and they are understood to include 365 negative '*Mitzvot lo-Ta'aseh*' ('Thou shalt not!' — corresponding to the number of days in the solar year); and 248 positive ones ('*Mitzvot Aseh*' — 'Thou shalt!' — corresponding (apparently) to the number of bones in the human Body.

These are the '*Mitzvot D'Oraita*' — commands extracted from the *Torah*. To these should be added the '*Mitzvot deRabbanan*' — a whole range of ritual and liturgical and other commandments which are clearly not from the *Torah* but later. Nevertheless they are classed as obligations — e.g. to light the *Shabbat* candles or the Festival candles or to read the *Hallel* Psalms or the *Megillat Esther* — we still recite a *Berachah* which says '...*asher kidshahnu b'Mitzvotav, vetzivahnu l...*' — 'Who has made us holy by doing God's commands, and has commanded us to...' as though they were Biblical commands.

For some Jews Judaism became (and for some it still is) a slavish obedience to *Mitzvot*, especially ritual ones, and so it became the task of the Prophets to form an internal opposition to this attitude, warning the people of Israel that the ethical commands were just as or even more important.

3. SOME ETHICAL *MITZVOT*

Here we merely wish to indicate a few of these ethical *Mitzvot*, to encourage you to learn further. The basic principle behind all of them is the constant reminder in our tradition to remember that we were once landless refugees, escaped slaves, and that we are meant to be partners with God in improving our world so that all its inhabitants can enjoy their lives.

Judaism does not stress asceticism or vows of poverty or withdrawal from the world. Far from it — if we have one day of *Shabbat*, this means we also have six days on which we should be working and earning to support ourselves and those dependent on us! It is no sin to have possessions and to enjoy them, but if our possessions govern us, rather than the other way around, and if we find we have no time for helping others, then something important has gone wrong. These *Mitzvot* are guides and indicators of what needs to be done so that we can share the blessings we have ourselves received — the blessings of health and mobility, of security and food and friendship or companionship. Individually, one can never achieve a great deal — but that is not considered an excuse not to start, in the hope that if enough people take part a real change can be achieved. In *Mishnah* '*Pirke Avot*' 2:21 Rabbi Tarfon warns us that we are never going to finish the work, but that this is no excuse not to start at least and to stay involved!

(A). TZEDAKAH ('CREATING JUSTICE BY REDISTRIBUTING WEALTH')

Often translated as 'giving to charity' in fact the word '*Tzedakah*' means 'Creating Righteousness'. If one has money or material wealth, this comes with responsibilities. One is responsible for using this wealth sensibly, for not wasting it on trivialities and helping those who do not have enough. This redistribution of wealth increases righteousness in the world.

There are rules such as '*Pe'ah*' — which originally meant leaving the corners, the left-overs in the field, for the poor when harvesting (Leviticus 19:9). Few of us own fields or do our own harvesting, but the principle surely applies in terms of allowing a proportion, plus what would otherwise be lost or wasted or thrown away to be used by someone else whose need is greater than ours — through a Food Bank, Clothes Recycling, through donations of unwanted books and toys — the list of possibilities is endless and would make a useful group discussion.

Donations of Money — from small change to substantial amounts — are considered to do as much to transform the Giver as to help the one to whom it is given. After all, it is a reminder that we are born with nothing and we will leave this world with nothing — at least, nothing material — and so 'letting go' of property while we are still alive is a good training for the future. Many communities have a collecting box, a '*Tzedakah* Box', where donations can be given anonymously — one is, after all, not doing anything special, just performing one's duty.

There were collecting boxes in Temple times. *Tzedakah* boxes in synagogues are based on a custom of post-Talmudic origin and based on Proverbs 10:2 'Righteousness [*Tzedakah*] saves from death', or Proverbs 11:19 'Righteousness [*Tzedakah*] is a prop of life.'

Maimonides wrote:
'There are eight degrees in the giving of charity, one higher than the other:
- One who gives grudgingly, reluctantly or with regret.
- One who gives less than he should, but gives graciously.
- One who gives what he should, but only after he is asked.
- One who gives before he is asked.
- One who gives without knowing to whom he gives, although the recipient knows the identity of the donor.
- One who gives without making his identity known.
- One who gives without knowing to whom he gives, and the recipient not knowing from whom he receives.
- One who helps a fellow man support himself — by a gift, or a loan, or by finding employment for him, thus helping him to become self-supporting.'
We see that the manner in which one gives is as important as that one gives.

(B). GEMILUT CHASADIM ('ACTS OF KINDNESS TO OTHERS')

Generally translated as 'Acts of Lovingkindness' this is a vague term which encompasses a wide variety of social welfare projects, whereby the poor can be helped to live with dignity — maybe through loans of money, or loans of clothing and household equipment, special requirements for babies or small children, or for the sick and elderly, or the provision of subsidies for holidays or scholarships for study — the list of possibilities is almost endless.

(C). TALMUD TORAH ('LEARNING AND TEACHING')

'*Talmud Torah k'neged Kulam*' is an ancient comment from *Mishnah 'Pe'ah'* 1:1 — which indicates the value placed upon study. It can be translated as 'The Study of *Torah* is equivalent to everything else put together' or 'Study of *Torah* leads to everything else' or even 'Teaching *Torah* leads to everything.' It is hard to be a good Jew if one is ignorant. One has a duty — and it is classed as a duty, not as an option — to study and to learn what one's other obligations are and how to fulfil them. There is certainly no end to what one can learn. The largest place in the entire world is the human brain — one can put more and more into it, one's whole life long, and yet it is never full!

(D). BIKKUR CHOLIM ('VISITING THE SICK')

The Sick are often isolated from society — not necessarily due to the infectious nature of their sickness but simply due to their weakness. They cannot get out and about. They are therefore more-or-less immobile. The only way they will meet other people is if You go to Them, rather than expecting them to come to you! Moreover, they have practical needs — housework, shopping, messages to be delivered — and they will need encouragement and cheering-up at times when they are in pain or in great anxiety. None of us know how long we ourselves will remain healthy and independent, so visiting those who have temporarily or permanently lost these characteristics is also a way of reminding ourselves to be grateful for what we have.

(E). LASHON HARA ('A BAD TONGUE')

Speaking badly of someone is not the same as criticising them to their face, but speaking behind someone's back, spreading bad reports about them (even if true) is considered to be almost as bad as murder. Destroying someone's reputation (even by telling the truth!) can destroy their livelihood and their relationships. What has been said can never be totally taken back. It stays out there, in the world, and can be spread further by others...... (This is, incidentally, even more so in the digital world where comments effectively remain permanently 'on the web' and can be accessed years later.)

(F). HACHNASAT ORCHIM ('RECEIVING GUESTS')

The world comprises those who live where they are, and those who are on journeys, for whatever reason. In previous generations these would have comprised mainly pilgrims, wandering scholars, wandering pedlars and merchants — and refugees. Nowadays there are also tourists, people who travel for pleasure. In nomadic cultures no one lives in a particular place for long but even so there are those who have pitched their tents and those who are still 'on the road'.

Either way, it is considered an obligation to cater for the needs of visitors, strangers and travellers and to provide them with hospitality. There have been many times when we, as Jews, were 'on the road', often heading for a distant or unknown destination. Now it is good to invite those who need it, to be your guests.

In practical terms this can mean (amongst other things) inviting visitors to the synagogue for a meal, assisting when groups of visitors attend a congregation, involving oneself in welfare work for the homeless and the refugees. The act of providing a '*Kiddush*' in the synagogue was originally to ensure that all those who came got something to eat — it was not an excuse to spend large amounts on fancy table-decorations and then limit those who are invited to attend! (The writer knows one synagogue where only the members, not the visitors, are invited to the *Kiddush*, and visitors are not even informed where it is being held!) People might need overnight accommodation, or assistance in coping with strange languages and customs, or advice on finding medical help. We are, all of us, strangers in the world, on a journey — and we are always grateful when we get assistance along our way. So it is our duty to help others.

(G). LEVAYAT HAMET ('ESCORTING THE DEAD')

Bringing the Dead to their place of rest. The Dead can do nothing for themselves, so someone else has to do it for them — to prepare a grave, to wash the Body, to bring the Body where it belongs…… None of us knows where we might ourselves end up, the most we can hope for is that we might also have a known grave and be brought to it in dignity. This is classed as one of the highest *Mitzvot*, because the recipient is not in a position to reciprocate or thank you in any way.

(H). HACHNASAT KALLAH ('ESCORTING THE BRIDE')

Helping the Bride. It was especially important in most societies for a woman to be married, to come 'under the protection' of her husband. That might not sound very liberated — but since when have we been truly liberated? The problem was that, for an orphaned girl or one from a poor background, the chances of finding a suitable partner and of having an appropriate ceremony might be limited. Accordingly it was seen as a duty upon the local society to do what it could to find a life-partner for every unmarried girl and to ensure that she started married life with dignity and what she needed to start a household.

(I). TIKKUN OLAM ('REPAIRING THE WORLD')

It is a good question whether this is technically a '*Mitzvah*' but it is seen as an ethical imperative to do what we can to 'care for' and steward and where necessary 'repair' the world in which we live — this becomes an overall term then for all ecological initiatives, including recycling, opposing the loss of natural habitat and rain-forest, opposing the extinction of species, preventing or clearing pollution, etc. Linked to this is '*Bal Tashchit*' — 'Do not wastefully destroy'. There is a difference between using natural resources — which is allowed — and squandering or polluting or destroying them unnecessarily — which is not.

4. MODERN CONCERNS

The above categories — which are only a selection — describe an ideal situation, if it can ever be described as 'ideal' that some people have and others do not have. But of course, when one lives in a large city one's life is different than it was in a small village, one does not know all the other inhabitants and their needs and there is a certain anonymity and social 'distance' or isolation. Further, circumstances change when the State takes over certain responsibilities. (At the present time, though, many States are busily trying to divest themselves of certain responsibilities which they took on in the 20th century — such as health care, higher education, pensions for the elderly…)

The ethical commands of the *Torah* and of Jewish tradition are pretty clear — but they mostly originate in a very different society to ours. Villages and towns were small, communication was difficult, there was little concept of 'citizen' but of 'subject' or even 'serf'. Modern circumstances mean that constant redefinitions are necessary. Jewish tradition can sharpen our awareness and give us guidance — but we cannot always apply 5th- or 15th-century ideals to 21st-century political problems. The 'Golden Rule' of Leviticus 19:18, which has been expressed so often in different forms — 'Love other people in the same way you wish they would love and treat you' — or 'because they are like you' — with the same feelings and weaknesses and vulnerabilities — is a general discouragement against stealing or cheating or lying or slandering or abusing or insulting or humiliating or frightening or rejecting or hurting other people.

So we remain confronted — as always as Reform and Liberal Jews — with the task of trying to translate ancient good ideas into a workable modern context. Where does the Single Mother come into this? Or the lazy person who refuses to work, or the long-term Unemployed, or the Addict… Do we feel the same sense of obligation to help people who are in some way 'responsible' for their situation, their poverty, their obesity or their ill-health? Or do these obligations transcend any 'Blame Culture', any sense of judgement over the individual victim of circumstances? There is scope for discussion here. We are not going to give many answers, but instead raise questions — because a thinking Jewish person will constantly be confronted with difficult and complex moral questions and will have to make decisions based upon a variety of factors.

Our societies are confronting these questions on a daily basis. Politicians sometimes take positions when it comes to 'asylum seekers' or those who could/should be 'sent home' (wherever that may be) or denied citizenship, to the rights of those who 'misuse benefits' or turn down offers of work (whether appropriate or inappropriate work), to those who neglect to spare for their old age or knowingly do things which will affect their long-term health. Private insurance companies also draw distinctions between those who smoke or don't, or take part voluntarily in dangerous sports. Often the chronically sick or the physically handicapped will feel discriminated against. Many people who try, idealistically, to improve the lot of their fellow human beings get heavily discouraged when these fellow human beings then abuse their good will, show ingratitude, take more than they are entitled to, lie and trick and steal and worse. But then — people are not (yet) perfect. The concept of 'Mitzvah' sometimes needs fine-tuning, but the basic principle remains.

In a period when there was full employment, a person without a job could somehow be 'blamed' for being without work. But in a period where a large percentage of the population is always unemployed, and where it is impossible for most people over a certain age to find a new position — we cannot so easily apply a 'blame' culture. And yet — what rights and benefits and privileges should those members of society have, who are not contributing financially at present, or who never have, or who never will be able to?

Do 'Human Rights' include the right to die with dignity, at a time and in a manner of one's own choice?

To all this we will add one very important concept: that of Belonging to a Jewish Community, of paying one's membership subscription or dues and playing a part in communal life. 'Al tifrosh min-haTzibbur' ('Pirke Avot' 2:5) — One should not 'cut oneself off' from the community (however irritating it may sometimes be!) nor should one expect others to do everything that is necessary — the organisation of services, the catering, the children's programmes, the education, the security rota, the fundraising and more — without being prepared to help as far as circumstances permit. A community provides a support structure beyond the immediate family for those who need it. But it needs supporting itself, if it is to do this.

'Kol Yisrael arevim Zeh-laZeh' (Talmud 'Shevuot' 39a) is an old but important principle: all Jews are to some extent responsible for each other. We are bound by mutual rights and responsibilities. The actions of one Jew will reflect upon others, whether we like it or not. Our mutual fate is bound up with other people, other Jews, and their fate is bound up with how we also behave.

CHAPTER 36

THE MESSIAH

It sometimes seems as though human beings divide into two main groups: those who desire to lead, and those who desire to be led. They need someone to tell them what to do. There are some people who are happy only when they have a thick Book of Rules that regulates almost every aspect of their lives.

Of course this is too simple. People grow and change, and within hierarchies it is so that some people are partway up the structure, taking their orders from someone above and passing them on to others below. There are also differences between the domestic and the professional spheres. Nevertheless, within many traditional societies it was and is so that the husband decides and the wife follows — whether willingly or not — and often because she has never thought of any alternative to obedience. Within such societies the father — or the grandfather — decides and the children and grandchildren follow. Within the tribe there is a leader, a chieftain, a sheikh, a Godfather, a king or whoever who is the 'dominant' character — very occasionally this dominant person may be a female, but the principle is the same. We see good expression of this in the Biblical Book of Judges ('*Shoftim*') and until the Enlightenment, with its emphasis on the Individual, it was rare for this concept to be challenged. One belonged to a Group, whether large or small, whether linked by tribal or family or other factors, and the Group requires a Leader. The Leader got his authority partly through his personal qualities of strength or wisdom or knowledge or heroism or brutality or from his chronological seniority position in the family, but largely because it was simply assumed that there had to be a leader and the Holy Books or the cultic leaders gave divine blessing to the status quo.

And so we see that many people prefer to be led, rather than to take full responsibility for their own actions, and in many religions God is perceived as a sort of Father or Grandfather figure and usually referred to as 'Father' or 'King' — the religious and the human dimensions and vocabularies reflect each other for God is the King and the King is like God or appointed by God; God is the Father, and the Father is divinely placed there by God, and it is a *Mitzvah* to honour and respect the Father or the King as God's representatives on Earth.

What is one to do when things go wrong? What is one to do when the Father-Figure is a disappointment or dies or goes off and forsakes you? Or is abusive? What sort of hopes does one then have? There are two main possibilities: one is that one steps into the same role, one inherits the authority; the other, that one hopes for him to come back or for a successor to be appointed. One feels helpless when leaderless.

The 'Messianic' concept is largely a reflection of these social structures. The word itself is simply a Greek transcription of the Hebrew '*Mashiach*' — 'one who has been anointed' — one who has been singled out for authority, not by placing a crown on his head but by smearing him ceremonially with pure olive oil. This was one ancient form of marking a person — not by colouring or cutting their skin, not by a formal headdress or crown. Religious leaders — the priests — were so anointed, and civic or political leaders also. (The Prophets were not, for they usually operated outside and as opponents of the main Establishment system.)

When times are hard, when the present seems grim and the future even grimmer, then people look for Hope. They look for someone to help them, to protect them, to lead them out of this mess. Some turn to political figures, some to religious ones, some confuse the two and see in a human being a divine messenger, sent to cure their problems. Such a figure is often termed a 'Messiah'. He may (it is usually a mas-culine figure!) be charismatic, he may be described as a hero, a warrior, a pure priest, a saintly pacifist or a pathetic diseased beggar or anything in between — but the hope is that he will somehow — as a direct contrast to a Scapegoat figure — make everything better, either for everyone or at least just for a specific group of 'chosen ones'.

The tradition grew that the prophet Elijah would come as a messenger or pre-cursor of the *Mashiach*. (This is based on the idea that he went up to heaven on a fiery chariot but never actually died… and so still exists. II Kings 2:11) There are *Midrash*im in which Elijah is always waiting, prepared, just in case God decides the time is right to send the Chosen One…

There have been many such in our history. Whether or not Jeshua bar Miriam of Nazareth thought he was a Messiah remains a matter for scholars and theologians to argue about, but he was soon perceived as such by at least one group, which grew and became influential up to the present…

Rabbi Akiva in 132 CE thought that Shimon Bar Kochba was the saviour who would rescue the Jews by driving out the Roman occupiers. He was wrong, and paid for this mistake with his life.

There was Shabbetai Tzvi (1626-1676) from Smyrna (now Izmir in Turkey) who started a trend known as 'Sabbataeanism'. In 1648 he had a vision during the Bogdan Chmielnitski pogroms in the Ukraine, when maybe 100,000 Jews were murdered in brutal circumstances. Later he married, travelled extensively and in 1665 was de-clared the Messiah by Nathan of Gaza. This was the period of the Thirty Years War in Europe and all over Central and Eastern Europe and in Turkey and Egypt there were desperate times and a yearning for a saviour figure, so many believed in him and his (and Nathan's) teachings. Yet in September 1666 he was arrested and offered a choice of death or conversion to Islam — and chose the latter. Later he was accused of having deviated from Islam and was exiled to Albania, where he died. Yet those who believed in him continued to believe and were perceived as an underground threat within Jewish communities for centuries — many rabbis tried to ban the sect. Within Islam many formed the 'Donmeh' sect, maintaining some Jewish customs.

Jacob Lejbowitz, known as Jakob Frank (1726-1791) came into contact with Sabbatean groups in eastern Poland who were deliberately violating Jewish laws, maybe in an attempt to urge the Messiah to come. From 1755 he began to proclaim himself as the Chosen One, the reincarnation of Shabbetai Tzvi. He then preached that salvation would come by adopting 'the religion of Edom' i.e. Christianity, and thousands of Jews were baptised in Poland and elsewhere. However, the Church remained suspicious and later he was imprisoned for thirteen years, later went to Vienna and following problems there settled in Offenbach in Germany where he lived in luxury, supported by his disciples, who were known as 'Frankists', and was eventually succeeded by his daughter.

Menachem Mendel Schneerson (1902-1994) married the daughter of his cousin (though he remained childless) and moved to Berlin in 1928, then due to the National Socialists to Paris. He fled Paris at the last moment in 1940 and emigrated to America in 1941. In 1951 he succeeded his father-in-law as the seventh leader of the Lubavitch *Chasidic* movement based in Brooklyn, New York. The movement grew by leaps and bounds with an extensive outreach programme. In 1988 he was widowed, in 1992 he suffered a stroke making him unable to speak and in 1994 he died. Or did he? Though it remains a controversial issue there are many Lubavitch *Chasidim* who are still convinced he is merely 'sleeping' and will return when the time is right…

As far as is known, despite the claims of these and so many others, the world has not yet been saved and so we see no need to believe in any of them. Indeed Reform Judaism recommends avoiding any belief in a specific individual as a personal Messiah and instead placing our faith and hope in a Messianic Age — a time when humane values and religious ethics will at last become widespread, as indicated in the second paragraph of the '*Aleynu*' prayer.

CHAPTER 37

'SHALOM' AND ITS ALTERNATIVES

The word '*Shalom*' is used frequently as a greeting and as a concept, but it is often misunderstood or misused and it therefore makes sense to add some thoughts on this word here.

1. WAR

Judaism is not fundamentally a pacifist religion as such. It sees War as a necessary evil — that means, it is evil, but it can also be necessary. In the *Torah* we read of several conflicts. One of the first is in Exodus 17:8-16 when the Israelites, just emerged from their miraculous salvation through the Red or Reed Sea, are suddenly attacked by a nomadic tribe — the Amalekites. They defend themselves successfully, but the shock is great. As slaves in Egypt they were without rights, their babies could be murdered, but at least they had some commercial worth and were in that sense 'protected'. Outside in the big wide wilderness world they learn — the hard way — that they need to be able to protect themselves. Forty years later in Deuteronomy 25:17-19 Moses will remind them of this shock, of an 'unfair' attack, a cowardly attack on the rear, on the weak and the sick. 'Amalek' becomes the code word for any group that is prepared to carry out 'war crimes' as opposed to war itself.

By this time the Israelites have fought and massacred the Midianites — a very difficult passage for us to digest but it appears the leadership feared a form of spiritual annihilation from within (Num. 25:16-18 and then 31:1-54).

They also approach neighbouring kings to request a 'transit visa' through their territories, promising to pass straight through to their destination — and when this is denied them, they go through anyway, but this time in a state of war. It was Ephraim Kishon who wrote 'It is your enemy who decides whether you are at war, not you.'

In Numbers 20:14-21 they ask Edom, but Edom refuses, approaches fully-armed, and the Israelites turn away to make a detour. In Num. 21:1-3 the Canaanites attack, but this time the Israelites respond and the Canaanite forces are destroyed; in Num. 21:21 they ask Sihon, king of the Amorites for permission to transit; this is denied and the Amorites are destroyed up to the border with Ammon — which is strongly defended. But the Israelites carry out 'mopping-up' operations against other Amorites in 21:31-35. There is little sympathy for Sihon as he had himself earlier defeated and dispossessed the Moabites! (21:26). As noted above the Midianites with their five kings are conquered in Num. Ch. 31:1-12.

Then they come at last through Moab to the Land that had been promised to Abraham back in Genesis 15:18-21 and 17:8 — but even then it was not empty, there were Canaanites living in it. And so a 'War of Conquest' under the leadership of Joshua was necessary. (In Num. 34:1-12 the boundaries of the 'Land of Canaan' are described.) The war is described in the book of Joshua — the first key city is Jericho, by the ford over the Jordan and this forms the bridgehead for the further campaign. It is captured and destroyed after a week in 6:12-21. It is interesting that, although we mark every year the anniversary of the Exodus from Egypt, we totally ignore the date the Israelites entered the Land — see Joshua 3:14-17 and especially 4:19 (it was the tenth of *Nisan!* — in 5:10-12 we read how the Israelites celebrated the Passover in Gilgal four days later, at which point they eat for the first time of the produce of the land, and the regular supply of Manna suddenly ceases after forty years.)

Later books in the Bible are filled with various campaigns and alliances. It is clear that life in the region was just about as calm and peaceful as, say, Christian Europe in the 15th — 20th centuries! It is no coincidence that archaeologists busy themselves with Tels — the sites of towns that have been repeatedly destroyed — or get excited about finding an undestroyed bit of ancient fortification, a thick city wall or a defensible city gate. (In Deuteronomy Chaps. 2 and 3 Moses gives a brief history lesson, pointing out (2:4-7, 12 & 22) that Seir has been given by God to Esau and they should not be attacked, although they had themselves dispossessed the Horites; in 2:9-11, 18-21) that Ar and Moab have been given by God to the descendants of Lot and should not be attacked — though formerly the Emim were there and also the Rephaim who had been driven out (though in 3:11 King Og, the Amorite King of Bashan, corresponding roughly to the Golan region of Syria, is described as one of the last surviving Rephaim); In 2:23 'As for the Avvim, who lived in villages as far as Gaza, the Caphtorim, who came from Caphtor, destroyed them and settled in their stead...' In Numbers 21:26 Heshbon was 'the city of Sihon the king of the Amorites, who had fought against then former king of Moab and taken all his land... as far as the Arnon' — which then became (21:13) the new boundary between Moab and the Amorites... and so on and so on. The fact is that the Bible describes a long history of wars, population movements, invasions, expulsions, absorptions and there is no reality in nostalgic fantasies of an endless 'Peace' which was suddenly disrupted only when the Israelites came onto the scene.

2. LEGITIMATE WARS AND REACTIONS

Those wars carried out to defend the people against attack or to conquer the land in response to a divine command are known as a '*Milchemet Mitzvah*' (a war that is commanded) and the idea is simply that these wars were necessary in Biblical times. There later developed a concept of a '*Milchemet Reshut*' — a war that was 'authorised' by a *Sanhedrin* — whereby a King could only embark on an offensive or expansionist campaign if he had the equivalent of what would now be called the approval of Parliament or Congress. A personal ego or a feeling of spite against a neighbour for some assumed insult was Not considered enough. See *Talmud*, '*Sotah*' 44b.

This means that a defensive war is justified with no question. The debate over the role of the Israeli armed forces (named, let us note, 'Israel Defence Forces' — '*Tzava haHaganah LeYisrael*' or '*Tzahal*') is therefore to be understood in this context. While there may have been internal divisions concerning the legitimacy of attacking or invading Lebanon or Egypt, Israelis expect their government and their armed forces to defend them against attack — if necessary through a pre-emptive strike or if necessary through espionage, intelligence work, selective assassinations of terrorist leaders, diplomatic initiatives and so forth. Experts and Non-Experts (especially the latter, who form the vast majority!) may love to argue about what is an 'appropriate' precaution or response — a wall, a fence, a road block or check-post, an electronic security sweep, a jamming, a counter-attack, an 'elimination', an act of sabotage on the enemy's military installations, an attack on weapon supply routes, an air strike, a land incursion — and what is 'proportional' and what may be acceptable as (a horrible term) 'collateral damage'. There is often a tendency to see slingshots as 'boys' toys' and forget how David killed Goliath in I. Samuel Ch. 17 with such a deadly weapon. There is often a tendency to apply selective judgements when attackers dress as or use women and children to plant explosives, or commit suicide attacks — modern conflicts are mostly 'asymmetrical' and many combatants are not dressed as combatants and therefore the normal rules of war, the normal Geneva Convention regulations do not apply to them. (As an example: What can one do with a person whom one knows is planning to plant a car bomb but who has not yet done so? Should one wait until it is too late, or intervene before the crime has actually been committed? This is an example of where Western legal systems are currently confronted with new and difficult questions — but, where it can be a matter of life or death for scores of innocent people in a market or café or bus, there is little time for academic juristic debate.)

This brief account may not satisfy all readers but it is important to stress that from an Israeli perspective the State and its inhabitants — even when living abroad or on diplomatic missions abroad, even as sportsmen or as tourists — are frequently under attack and therefore any measures undertaken to reduce the risk is classed as 'defensive'.

In the *Talmud* '*Berachot*' 58a in the context of a rather bizarre and unpleasant story concerning an extra-judicial punishment the statement is made 'If anyone rises to kill you, kill him first' — this is derived from Exodus 22:1 where the killing of a burglar who has broken in at night-time when it is dark is classed as legitimate self-defence. 'If a thief be found breaking in, and be smitten so that he dies, there shall be no blood-guilt for him.' (The next verse limits this, should it be light enough to see the assailant.)

Christianity is influenced by texts such as Luke 6:27-29 —

> 'I say to you, Love your enemies, do good to those who hate you, bless those who curse you and oppress you. If someone strikes you on the cheek, turn the other to him, and if someone takes your coat, then give him your shirt too...'

and a slightly different equivalent in Matthew 5:38ff:

> 'You have heard that it is said 'An Eye for an Eye, and a Tooth for a Tooth'. But I tell you, do not resist anyone who comes to attack you, but should anyone strike you on the right cheek, then show him the other. And if anyone calls you before the court to demand your shirt, then let him have your coat too...'

This passive, non-violence approach has always struck me as rather unrealistic and even dangerously naive.

Firstly, there is no reason given why someone should attack you or wish to do so. Have you annoyed him, refused him, got in his way? Could it mean that he is in any way justified in hitting you and so you should just accept it? Or is he a madman who is running amok and striking out wildly at innocent people?

Secondly, what should you do if he strikes your second cheek too? Show him the other two, on which you normally sit? This could be interpreted as 'Provocation'. But what is the next move? What if he moves from a slap with the palm of his hand to the use of a fist or a stick or a weapon, if the situation escalates?

Thirdly, should you be equally passive if someone else is being attacked, next to you?

Fourthly, this implies accepting Injustice. But we are told to establish courts, appoint judges and pursue Justice! '*Tzedek, Tzedek Tirdof*!' (Deut. 16:18-20.)

'*Lex Talionis*': Like for Like

Jesus is quoted here as citing (and denying) a rule known as the '*Lex Talionis*' — Latin for 'an appropriate punishment', a punishment that fits the crime. This refers to a sentence that appears three times in the *Torah* — '*Ayin tachat Ayin*' — 'an eye instead of an eye.' They are:

> 'If two men are fighting and one hurt a pregnant woman so that she miscarries and loses the baby, though she herself remains healthy, then the assailant shall pay a fine as assessed by the husband and by the judges.

> But if she be harmed, then you shall give life for life, eye for eye, tooth for tooth, hand for hand, foot for foot, burn for burn, wound for wound, scar for scar.'

> ('*Nefesh tachat Nefesh; Ayin tachat Ayin; Shen tachat Shen; Yad tachat Yad; Regel tachat Regel; Keviah tachat Keviah; Petza tachat Petza; Chabora tachat Chabora.*')

> (Exodus 21:24f.)

'He that kills a man shall himself be put to death.

He that smites and kills a beast shall pay compensation.

And if a man maims someone, it shall be done to him likewise.

Fracture for fracture, eye for eye, tooth for tooth, just as he did to someone, so shall it be done to him.'

('*Shever tachat Shever, Ayin tachat Ayin, Shen tachat Shen; ka'asher yiteyn Mum ba'Adam, ken yinaten bo.*')

(Leviticus 24:17-21)

In the context of someone lying in court and thus placing an innocent man at risk of undeserved punishment, the false witness should be punished so that:

'those that remain shall hear, and fear, and shall henceforth commit no more any such evil; your eye should not pity — life for life, eye for eye, tooth for tooth, hand for hand, foot for foot.'

('*Nefesh b'Nefesh, Ayin B'Ayin, Shen b'Shen, Yad b'Yad, Regel b'Regel.*')

(Deuteronomy 19:20-21.)

Of course sentencing is always a controversial issue in all judicial systems. Is a fine, a custodial sentence, deportation or even execution appropriate? How high a fine, how long a sentence, what form of imprisonment, what form of execution? What is a minor civil matter and what a major criminal one? There are countries which have deported children to the other side of the world for stealing a loaf of bread; there are legal systems which allow for a thief to be maimed or an adulteress (but rarely an adulterer) to be executed. There are countries where simply criticising the government or making a joke or writing a blog can be brutally punished. There are legal systems which punish family members for crimes that they personally have not committed but for which they are held jointly responsible. Items which have been stolen and recovered can be forcibly returned, or recompensed financially, but how does one value Time lost through being kidnapped, or how does one put a price on Pain or Fear? When someone has been murdered their life cannot be simply restored; when someone has been wounded, who should pay their medical costs? If someone is rendered unfit to work through medical mistakes, how is the future earning capacity that has been lost to be measured? Or the costs of long-term care? May punishments be increased in times of national or military emergency? (e.g. for 'hoarding' food or 'spreading gossip'?) Before reacting or over-reacting it is sensible to take time to look at the contexts.

The Rabbis always understood these verses to have a limiting effect — one was entitled to take ONLY the value of an eye for the loss of an eye, no more, no unlimited damages, no judicial murder as an act of revenge. In the *Talmud 'Ketubot'* 22b and

'*Baba Kamma*' 82b-84a it is stated that the meaning is that the one responsible must pay financial compensation for the loss of an eye, a tooth, etc. '*Tachat*' is often used in the sense of 'replacing' or 'substituting' — e.g. in Genesis 44:33 Judah offers himself '*tachat*' his half-brother Benjamin as a prisoner. In I. Kings 1:30 David declares that his son Solomon will succeed him as King, '*tachti*'. In Joshua 2:14 the two spies offer Rahab in Jericho their lives '*tachat*' hers, should their agreement be broken.

Insurance companies and politicians love to argue about relative values; a scar on the face of a model or a slight injury to a professional athlete might be valued higher than on another person. How much is a kidney worth and is an operation on an elderly person, a pensioner rather than an income-tax payer, justifiable financially? There are no simple answers but, since this line is brought out with wearisome regularity to 'explain' why Jews or Israel reacts to attacks or injustices, it is important at least to have some source material for the inevitable 'discussion'.

3. RULES OF WAR

Although the descriptions of these wars seems very gruesome there are actually some very impressive Rules, rules which even nowadays are rarely applied. For example, in Deuteronomy Chapter 20 we find a summary of 'Rules of Engagement'. First, in 20:1-9 anyone who has recently got engaged or married, or built a house, or planted a vineyard, or who simply has no courage and does not want to take part — is exempted from the call-up! How humane this is, and in contrast how many young soldiers in all the Western armies in the 20th century were executed for 'cowardice' or 'desertion' or 'damaging morale'? How many were criminalised as 'Draft-Dodgers'?

Then in 20:10-11 an initial offer of surrender and submission must be made to any city — only if it refuses to submit may one attack it. (However, certain tribes are classed as 'elemental enemies' and come under a different category — it is a *Mitzvah* to fight them. Deut. 20:16-18).

Then in 20:19-20 the Israelites are commanded not to lay waste to a country when besieging a city, not to destroy the fruit trees or carry out a 'scorched-earth' policy. (The concept of '*Bal Tashchit*' — 'do not destroy' — is often employed nowadays to justify environmental action.)

In 21:10-14 strict rules are laid down for how to deal with a female prisoner captured in a war — the passage does not deny the tragedy of her situation but demands that she be given time to mourn and adjust to her new situation and that if later divorced she should have the same rights as a free woman and not be treated as a mere slave. A man may marry his prisoner but he may not rape her — from some women's perspective there may not appear to be too much difference, but alas, for anyone captured in 2015 by IS or Boko Haram or similar groups these ancient laws would appear revolutionary and vital.

4. PEACE

What is Peace? Peace is a situation whereby at least two partners are both satisfied with the situation. (The Greek word *'eireneh'* is something different and includes more an element of calm and quiet.) *Shalom* is satisfaction — both sides are satisfied because both have got either what they want or enough to satisfy themselves. Peace cannot be imposed from outside, though two parties in conflict can be encouraged to sit together and negotiate and find the best compromise for all. (The alternative is the 'peace of the grave' or at most a 'cease-fire'.) This is why all attempts by external politicians and well-meaning (and less-well-meaning, biased) interventionists to persuade Israel to 'make peace alone' through concessions and withdrawals are by definition doomed to failure, because both parties must be fully involved.

5. 'SHALOM'

The word 'Shalom' is often translated as 'Peace' but, as noted above, there are many nuances and it really means 'a state of being complete'. A period that is full is 'Shalem' — 'complete'. (It may derive from the name of a Canaanite 'God of Evening' — i.e. when a day was 'complete, finished'). In Deut. 25:15 this refers to a complete weight. In Gen. 14:18 Melchizedek is a priest and is 'King of Shalem' — this is often understood to be the original site of the city of Jerusalem. In Gen. 15:16 the sins of the Amorites are 'lo-shalem' — not yet full. In Gen. 28:21 Jacob makes a bargain with God, should he return to his homeland 'b'Shalom', unharmed. In Gen. 33:18 Jacob then arrives 'shalem' at the town of Shechem, i.e. with his possessions and family intact. Hamor the king of Shechem considers that Jacob and his family are 'shelemim' in 34:21 — peaceable, reliable, 'all right'. (It turns out he is wrong!)

A transaction between a vendor and a purchaser involves the purchaser paying for what the vendor sells him — both sides are then satisfied, for one has the goods, the other the payment — and the word for 'to pay' is 'leShalem' — to 'complete the deal'. Should the vendor refuse to sell, or the purchaser take the goods without paying, at least one party to the deal would have good reason to be dissatisfied and there would be no 'Shalom' between them. So BOTH sides have to feel happy.

A brief wander through biblical texts should serve to demonstrate how the word is sometimes used in not-very-pacifist contexts! You are encouraged to read the full texts.

Leviticus Chap. 26:

3. If you walk in my statutes, and keep my commandments, and do them;

4. Then I will give you rain in due season, and the land shall yield her produce, and the trees of the field shall yield their fruit.

5. And your threshing shall last to the time of vintage, and the vintage shall last

to the sowing time; and you shall eat your bread to the full, and dwell in your land safely.

6. And I will give peace in the land, and you shall lie down, and none shall make you afraid; and I will remove evil beasts from the land, nor shall the sword go through your land.

7. And you shall chase your enemies, and they shall fall before you by the sword.

8. And five of you shall chase a hundred, and a hundred of you shall put ten thousand to flight; and your enemies shall fall before you by the sword.

9. For I will turn myself to you, and make you fruitful, and multiply you, and establish my covenant with you.

Numbers Chap. 6: — the Birkat Cohanim.

A wish or hope for individual peace. v.26: May the Lord give you Peace.

Numbers Chap. 25: — Pinchas (who had just murdered two people!)

10. And the Lord spoke to Moses, saying,

11. Pinchas, the son of Eleazar, the son of Aaron the priest, has turned my anger away from the people of Israel, while he was zealous for my sake among them, that I consumed not the people of Israel in my jealousy.

12. Therefore say, Behold, I give to him my covenant of peace;

13. And he shall have it, and his seed after him, the covenant of an everlasting priesthood; because he was zealous for his God, and made an atonement for the people of Israel.

Deuteronomy Chap. 23:

4. An Ammonite or Moabite shall not enter into the congregation of the Lord; to their tenth generation shall they not enter into the congregation of the Lord forever;

5. Because they met you not with bread and with water in the way, when you came out of Egypt; and because they hired against you Balaam the son of Beor of Pethor of Mesopotamia, to curse you......

7. You shall not seek their peace nor their prosperity all your days for ever.

Joshua Chap. 9: Here the Hivites succeed in a diplomatic trick:

3. And when the inhabitants of Gibeon heard what Joshua had done to Jericho and to Ai,

4. They acted with cunning, and went and made as if they had been ambassadors, and took old sacks upon their asses, and wineskins, old, and torn, and bound up;

5. And old worn and patched shoes upon their feet, and old garments upon them, and all the bread of their provision was dry and mouldy.

6. And they went to Joshua to the camp at Gilgal, and said to him, and to the men of Israel, We come from a far country; now therefore make a covenant with us.

7. And the men of Israel said to the Hivites, Perhaps you live among us; and how shall we make a pact with you?

8. And they said to Joshua, We are your servants. And Joshua said to them, Who are you? and from where do you come?

9. And they said to him, From a very far country your servants have come because of the name of the Lord your God; for we have heard his fame, and all that he did in Egypt,

10. And all that he did to the two kings of the Amorites, who were beyond the Jordan, to Sihon king of Heshbon, and to Og king of Bashan, who was at Ashtaroth.

11. And our elders and all the inhabitants of our country spoke to us, saying, Take provisions with you for the journey, and go to meet them, and say to them, We are your servants; therefore now make a covenant with us.

12. This our bread we took hot for our provision from our houses on the day we came forth to go to you; but now, behold, it is dry, and it is mouldy;

13. And these wineskins, which we filled, were new; and, behold, they have split; and these our garments and our shoes have become old because of the very long journey.

14. And the men took of their provisions, and asked not counsel at the mouth of the Lord.

15. And Joshua made peace with them, and made a covenant with them, to let them live; and the princes of the congregation swore to them.

16. And it came to pass at the end of three days after they had made a covenant with them, that they heard that they were their neighbours, and that they lived among them.

17. And the people of Israel journeyed, and came to their cities on the third day. Now their cities were Gibeon, and Kephirah, and Beeroth, and Kiriath-Jearim.

18. And the people of Israel did not strike them, because the princes of the congregation had sworn to them by the Lord God of Israel. And all the congregation murmured against the princes.

19. But all the princes said to all the congregation, We have sworn to them by the Lord God of Israel; now therefore we may not touch them.

20. This we will do to them; we will let them live, lest anger be upon us, because of the oath which we swore to them.

21. And the princes said to them, Let them live; but let them be hewers of wood and drawers of water to all the congregation; as the princes had promised them.

22. And Joshua called for them, and he spoke to them, saying, Why have you deceived us, saying, We are very far from you; when you live among us?

23. Now therefore you are cursed, and there shall none of you be freed from being slaves, and hewers of wood and drawers of water for the house of my God.

24. And they answered Joshua, and said, Because it was certainly told your servants, how the Lord your God commanded his servant Moses to give you all the land, and to destroy all the inhabitants of the land from before you, therefore we were much afraid of our lives because of you, and have done this thing.

25. And now, behold, we are in your hand; as it seems good and right to you to do to us, do.

26. And so did he to them, and saved them from the hand of the people of Israel, that they slew them not.

27. And Joshua made them that day hewers of wood and drawers of water for the congregation, and for the altar of the Lord, even to this day, in the place which he should choose.

Joshua Chap. 11.

19. There was not a city that made peace with the people of Israel, save the Hivites the inhabitants of Gibeon; all others they took in battle.

20. For it was of the Lord to harden their hearts, that they should come against Israel in battle, that he might destroy them completely, and that they might have no favour, but that he might destroy them, as the Lord commanded Moses.

21. And at that time came Joshua, and cut off the Anakim from the mountains, from Hebron, from Debir, from Anab, and from all the mountains of Judah, and from all the mountains of Israel; Joshua destroyed them completely with their cities.

22. There was none of the Anakim left in the land of the people of Israel; only in Gaza, in Gath, and in Ashdod, there remained.

23. So Joshua took the whole land, according to all that the Lord said to Moses; and Joshua gave it for an inheritance to Israel according to their divisions by their tribes. And the land rested from war.

Judges Chap. 8.

7. And Gideon said, Therefore when the Lord has delivered Zebah and Zalmunna into my hand, then I will tear your flesh with the thorns of the wilderness and with briers.

8. And he went up from there to Penuel, and spoke to them likewise; and the men of Penuel answered him as the men of Succoth had answered him.

9. And he spoke also to the men of Penuel, saying, When I come back in peace, I will break down this tower.

II Samuel Chap. 10.

6. And Hadadezer sent, and brought out the Arameans who were beyond the river; and they came to Helam; and Shobach the captain of the army of Hadadezer went before them.

17. And when it was told David, he gathered all Israel together, and passed over the Jordan, and came to Helam. And the Arameans set themselves in array against David, and fought with him.

18. And the Arameans fled before Israel; and David slew the men of seven hundred chariots of the Arameans, and forty thousand horse soldiers, and struck Shobach the captain of their army, who died there.

19. And when all the kings who were servants to Hadadezer saw that they were defeated before Israel, they made peace with Israel, and served them. So the Arameans feared to help the Ammonites any more.

II Samuel Chap. 17.

1. And Ahithophel said to Absalom, Let me now choose out twelve thousand men, and I will arise and pursue after David this night;

2. And I will come upon him while he is tired and weak handed, and will make him afraid; and all the people who are with him shall flee; and I will strike the king only;

3. And I will bring back all the people to you; when all return, after the death of the man who you seek, all the people shall be in peace.

I Kings Chap. 3.

9. And it was told king Solomon that Joab had fled to the tabernacle of the Lord; and, behold, he is by the altar. Then Solomon sent Benaiah the son of Jehoiada, saying, Go, strike him down.

30. And Benaiah came to the tabernacle of the Lord, and said to him, Thus said

the king, Come out. And he said, No; but I will die here. And Benaiah brought word back to the king, saying, Thus said Joab, and thus he answered me.

31. And the king said to him, Do as he has said, and strike him down, and bury him; that you may take away the innocent blood, which Joab shed, from me, and from the house of my father.

32. And the Lord shall return his blood upon his own head, who fell upon two men more righteous and better than he, and killed them with the sword, my father David not knowing of it, Abner the son of Ner, captain of the army of Israel, and Amasa the son of Jether, captain of the army of Judah.

33. Their blood shall therefore return upon the head of Joab, and upon the head of his seed forever; but upon David, and upon his seed, and upon his house, and upon his throne, shall there be peace forever from the Lord.

34. And Benaiah the son of Jehoiada went up, and struck him down, and killed him; and he was buried in his own house in the wilderness.

35. And the king put Benaiah the son of Jehoiada in place of him over the army; and Zadok the priest the king put in place of Abiathar.

I Kings Chap. 5. (Peace through military might!)

1. And Solomon reigned over all the kingdoms from the river to the land of the Philistines, to the border of Egypt; they paid tribute, and served Solomon all the days of his life.

2. And Solomon's provision for one day was thirty measures of fine flour, and sixty measures of meal,

3. Ten fat oxen, and twenty oxen from the pastures, and a hundred sheep, apart from deer, and gazelles, and fallow deer, and geese.

4. For he had dominion over all the region on this side of the river, from Tiphsah to Azzah, (Gaza) over all the kings on this side of the river; and he had peace on all sides around him.

5. And Judah and Israel dwelt safely, every man under his vine and under his fig tree, from Dan to Beersheba, all the days of Solomon.

6. And Solomon had forty thousand stalls of horses for his chariots, and twelve thousand horsemen.

I Kings Chap. 20.

14. And Ahab said, By whom? And he said, Thus said the Lord, By the young men of the princes of the provinces. Then he said, Who shall open the battle? And he answered, You.

15. Then he counted the young men of the princes of the provinces, and they were two hundred and thirty two; and after them he counted all the people, all the people of Israel, being seven thousand.

16. And they went out at noon. But Ben-Hadad was drinking himself drunk in the pavilions, he and the kings, the thirty two kings who helped him.

17. And the young men of the princes of the provinces went out first; and Ben-Hadad sent out, and they told him, saying, There are men coming out from Samaria.

18. And he said, If they come out for peace, take them alive; and if they come out for war, take them alive.

I Kings Chap. 22.

42. Jehoshaphat was thirty five years old when he began to reign; and he reigned twenty five years in Jerusalem. And his mother's name was Azubah the daughter of Shilhi.

43. And he walked in all the ways of Asa his father; he turned not aside from it, doing that which was right in the eyes of the Lord; nevertheless the high places were not taken away;

44. For the people still offered and burned incense in the high places.

45. And Jehoshaphat made peace with the king of Israel.

Isaiah Chap. 9.

5. For to us a child is born, to us a son is given; and the government is upon his shoulder; and his name shall be called 'Wonderful counsellor of the mighty God, of the everlasting Father, of the Prince of peace'.

6. For the increase of the realm and for peace there without end, upon the throne of David, and upon his kingdom, to order it, and to establish it with judgement and with justice from now and forever. The zeal of the Lord of hosts performs this.

Isaiah Chap. 26.

> 11. Lord, when your hand is lifted up, they will not see; but they shall see with shame your zeal for the people, the fire which shall devour your enemies.

> 12. Lord, you will ordain peace for us; for you also have performed all our works for us.

> 13. O Lord our God, other masters beside you have had dominion over us; but by you only will we make mention of your name.

> 14. They are dead, they shall not live; they are shades, they shall not rise; therefore have you visited and destroyed them, and made all their memory to perish.

> 15. You have increased the nation, O Lord, you have increased the nation; you are glorified; you have enlarged all the borders of the land.

More positively — Isaiah 52:7 — '*raglei mevasser mashmi'ah Shalom.*' — 'the feet of the messenger announcing peace.'

or Ezekiel 37:26 — 'and I will make with Israel a covenant of peace for all eternity...'

It is rare however that God promises 'Peace' in the sense of having no enemies at all; more common is a promise that one will have some rest in spite of having enemies, using the terms '*Menuchah*' or '*Sheket*'. Here are some examples:

Deuteronomy 25:19, 'When God shall have given you rest from your enemies round about...'('*behaniach ...mikol-oyveicha misaviv*').

In Psalm 29:11, after describing how God's might and God's terrible voice strips the trees, causes enormous storms and earthquakes and terrifies animals, we read 'God will give strength to his people, God will bless his people with peace.' ('*Adonai Oz leAmo yiteyn, Adonai yevarech et-Amo vaShalom.*') There are those who point to the sequence as being significant — first one needs strength, only then does one have peace!

In Isaiah 14:3 'It shall come to pass in the day that the Lord shall give you rest from your troubles...' '*Vehayah baYom hani'ach Adonai lecha meyatzbecha...*'

In Joshua 11:23: 'So Joshua took the whole land... and the land had rest from war.' ('*veHaAretz shikta miMilchamah.*')

In Joshua 14:15: After Joshua has given Hebron to Caleb — 'and the land had rest from war.' ('*veHaAretz shikta miMilchamah.*')

In Judges 3:11: after Otniel has defeated the king of Aram: 'and the land had rest for forty years.' '*vatishkat haAretz arba'im shanah.*'

In II. Chronicles 14: 1, 4, 5, 6: 'And Asa did what was right in the eyes of God… and the kingdom was quiet before him. ('*Vayishkot haMamlacha lefanaiv.*')

'*Vayiven Ar metzurah biYehudah, ki-shakta haAretz veEyn imo Milchamah.*' 'And he built fortified cities in Judah, for the land had rest and he had no war in these years…'

'*nach lanu misaviv.*' '(God has) given us rest from all sides.'

6. THE WORD '*SHALOM*' AS A GREETING

The word is often used in the general context of saying 'Hello!' or 'Goodbye!' 'Hello' (or 'Hullo' or 'Hallo') apparently derives from the call to attract attention, being first known in the 19th century; 'Goodbye' is a corruption of 'God be with you.' (Even atheists say it!)

When Moses takes leave from his father-in-law Jitro in Ex. 4:18 Jitro says '*Lech l'Shalom*' — literally 'Go to Peace.' The *Talmud* ('*Berachot*' 64a) notes that Moses then went on to succeed in his mission, whereas David in II. Samuel 15:9 told his son Absalom 'Go in Peace' — '*Lech b'Shalom*' — yet Absalom was hanged. Therefore there is a feeling that '*L'Shalom*' can be used for the living and the dead, but '*b'Shalom*' is used for the dead. On *Shabbat* one says '*Shabbat Shalom!*' as a greeting.

PART EIGHT: CONVERSION

CHAPTER 38

CONVERSION TO JUDAISM

In the Introduction and Chapter 1 we have looked at issues of Jewish identity and how and whether one can 'acquire it'. In this section we look more closely at how Conversion to Judaism works today.

1. PROCEDURES

All conversions and other matters affecting personal Jewish status are regulated through a religious court known as a *Beit Din* (or Beth Din) — a 'House of Justice'.

Both the Movement for Reform Judaism (MRJ) and Liberal Judaism (LJ) have their rabbinic bodies and courts — see their websites for information.

The European *Beit Din* (E.B.D.) associated with the European Union for Progressive Judaism (E.U.P.J.) is currently based at: 80, East End Road, London N3 2SY, Great Britain. Tel. +44-208-349-2568. E-Mail through: administrator@eupj.org

There is a Convenor and a Secretariat. Courts are organised in different locations dependent on demand and the availability of suitably-qualified and acceptable Rabbis.

In Britain and Europe an individual rabbi who is a member of an acknowledged rabbinic conference is not able to perform a conversion by him- or herself. Instead they will act as the local representative of the *Beit Din* to which they belong and become the 'Sponsoring Rabbi', responsible for supervising an individual's candidate's case (or initially even deciding whether person can become a Candidate).

Different communities may have differing procedures for tuition and integration — there are for example small communities which cannot offer weekly services and regular tuition and others which are so large they impose specific attendance requirements upon serious candidates and structured classes.

There will be fees for registration, to cover administrative costs, and maybe costs for tuition, levied by the community or by an individual (recognised) teacher. In some communities you will be expected to become a member of the circle of 'Friends' or 'Associates', meaning that you are placed on the mailing distribution list and are welcomed to events but do not have Full Membership rights (e.g. a vote, or burial rights).

There are different sets of guidelines issued in different countries by the national associations, but the following can be taken as a minimum basis:

A candidate for conversion will be personally interviewed at least once by a Rabbi, the one responsible for the local community — who then becomes in effect the 'Sponsoring Rabbi', responsible for his or her case and who will need to maintain a file into which copies of relevant papers are collected. After attending services and other synagogue and other communal activities for an agreed period they will then be assigned to a period of tuition and integration into the community, culminating in preparations for appearance before a *Beit Din*. Males must be circumcised and this confirmed in a doctor's letter. All then appear in due course before an organised '*Beit Din*', a Court, almost always comprising three full Rabbis — who assess each candidate as to his or her knowledge, sincerity and commitment. If successful, the convert is then led to the *Mikveh* (ritual bath) for immersion and is given a certificate ('*Te'udat Giyur*') attesting to their conversion and including the Hebrew forename they have chosen. It can of course happen, if one or more of the officiating rabbis have doubts, that a candidate will be asked to return at a later time.

2. WHY ARE PEOPLE SOMETIMES TURNED DOWN?

Each individual case is different, but after several decades of experience the author of this book can assert that there are cases where a candidate makes an untrustworthy impression upon the Court, where they seem to be concealing important information or even denying their true origins or motivations. There may be practical reasons, such as when a person lives totally isolated geographically (or socially) from any Jewish community, or even in an area where becoming Jewish could mean personal danger. There may be issues of family dynamics — is it truly good for a marriage for one spouse to convert and not the other? Or some children but not all the siblings? The task of a *Beit Din* is, within practical boundaries, to investigate, to ask, to check — and then when appropriate to approve. The Sponsoring Rabbi's task is to ensure that the relevant information is made available — signed application forms, copies of personal identity papers, confirmation where appropriate of a circumcision, written approval where appropriate of another parent or partner, and more. There are cases where a person has had to acquire a new birth certificate or has changed their name, there are cases where the children in a family may have more than one biological father, or where children have been adopted — will the adoption agency permit a person to change the religion of the child placed in their care?

Making a mistake in reading Hebrew is not a major sin, nor is forgetting the answer to a question in your nervousness. But if a candidate has, for whatever reason, simply missed a significant part of the tuition, then there is no rush and the candidate should make up these deficiencies first... Or if it seems a person is denying or concealing something important — this will worry the rabbis who are acting here as *Dayanim*, Judges, and whose task it is to get to the real truth.

Sometimes people have simply not thought through the consequences of their actions properly. Say, for example, you work for a firm which regularly sends staff to a Moslem state — if you are Jewish you will not get a visa! So this affects your employment prospects too.

A candidate is often idealistic and a little naive; a rabbi has usually had much more experience in things that can go wrong or are well-intended but unhelpful. There are many possible reasons and motivations, but some are psychologically suspect. Very occasionally a candidate is seeking to take revenge on one part of their family by conversion to Judaism, maybe due to some lingering associated in-direct guilt for what relatives did in the 20$^{th.}$ century… A person who is interested in becoming Jewish because one grandparent was Jewish, is effectively rejecting the religion of the other three grandparents… — One (very) extreme example, but also a true story, is of a lady who wished to convert so that she could bear witness to Christianity inside the Jewish community!

It is for such reasons that one rabbi alone cannot and should not make such deep decisions which can affect a person's life and the lives of all around them and even into the next generations. With three independent colleagues who come 'fresh' to interview the candidate, and who are unlikely to be under any pressure from communal leaders or employers — and it has been known for community Board members to try to put a rabbi under pressure to convert their own partner or future daughter-in-law 'quickly and quietly' — then all involved are able to be open and honest with each other.

And let us be clear — when a person says they wish to live as a Jew and join the covenant with Abraham, then basically they need to convert themselves from with-in; all that any *Beit Din* can do is to check that the person concerned has learned enough, and is aware enough of the consequences, so as to be able to become a valu-able new member of the Jewish community and not (heaven forbid!) a neurotic, psy-chotic, obsessive, destructive factor in a congregation. Rabbis are not God and nor are Rabbis representatives of God (as the Priests in the Temple to some extent were) — we are just teachers and judges; our task is to teach — and to make judgements.

Being human, rabbis sometimes make mistakes; being academically trained, they try to learn from them. Some rabbis are more strict simply because they regret earlier decisions.

3. A WARNING...

There are no short cuts. You are wishing to be accepted as a full member of a community? And not just as a regular visitor, without voting rights? In that case you must do your best to become accepted within the local community. To turn up with a piece of paper acquired from the Internet or through the agency of a poorly-qualified rabbi (each Rabbinic Association has its membership rules involving length of training at specific recognised seminaries and institutions — not everyone who claims the title 'rabbi' is accepted by others!) will not help you at all.

The decision one is taking cannot be reversed. From a Jewish perspective, once you have converted you are Jewish, and once you are Jewish you remain Jewish, to death and beyond. If, after some years, you should decide to change your mind and become, say, Buddhist or Scientologist or Atheist, then from the Jewish perspective you are not a Buddhist etc. but a lapsed Jew. (You may be refused membership of a community, but you will still be classed as a Jew.) In such circumstances it is always better to take an extra year or two or more and to decide if this is really the way you wish to go through life. Remember — if you are still single, there is no guarantee that you will later find a partner who will be interested both in Judaism and in you; If you find one who is not interested in Judaism but is interested in you, then a whole new range of potential problems comes into play. You may even find a Jew who is wholly uninterested in their Judaism and is not supportive!

4. WHAT YOU NEED TO LEARN

For an initial period of up to several months candidates are expected to attend services, start reading and learning, and to become acclimatised to the realities of local Jewish life. (Many candidates commence with a romanticised or unrealistic vision, which can only lead to disappointment.) There will then commence a period of instruction lasting at the very least one full year, following all of the cycle of festivals, by the end of which they should be able to read from the prayer book in Hebrew and English, join in services, know the meanings and observances of the Sabbath and Festival rituals in the home and at synagogue, have some grasp of Jewish history and know how to run a Jewish home. Since Judaism is a communal religion it cannot be learned only from books or websites; it has to be lived and there has to be involvement in communal life, practice and worship.

You also need to learn how to react when people — possibly friends, colleagues, neighbours, even family members — make anti-Semitic jokes and remarks; when Israel is constantly criticised in the media and in your workplace; when you see unpleasant graffiti and suddenly realise they are referring to You! When (and these things have really happened in Berlin!) your landlord turns you out because he 'doesn't want to rent to Jews'; Or the tyres of your car are slashed because you have an Israeli sticker in the window...; Or a burglar, seeing Jewish ornaments in your home, adds painted swastikas on the walls to the other damage he causes...; When your children get insulted at school; when employers express amazement that you wish to take certain days free for religious festivals, when your pals grumble because you no longer eat the same things as they do...; Or when people make fun of your desire to take a different name... Most Jews in Britain and Europe have grown up with such 'background' phenomena and have adapted instinctively and often barely notice this 'low-level' atmosphere; but a person coming, filled with naive idealism and a love for Judaism, into this world needs to be aware and needs to acquire the necessary defence mechanisms and 'avoidance skills'.

5. HOW LONG DOES IT TAKE?

There is no simple answer to this question. One could say that it takes the whole of one's life! However, there are certain basic minimum requirements laid down in the procedures of the 'European *Beit Din*'.

You need first to allow yourself time to acclimatise to the idea, to try out synagogue services on a regular basis (maybe at more than one community if there is an opportunity), to read, to learn some Hebrew, to get to know the tunes of the hymns that are sung, and some aspects of the ritual and the essential parts of the community and the general outline of current events — by talking to people, reading newsletters and newspapers and websites and so forth.

This would require a minimum of at least six months.

You then need to allow time to Learn. We require that candidates, from the time they formally start, follow at least one cycle of the Jewish Year, experiencing the festivals and their special services and celebrations whilst they are candidates (even if they have experienced some before). There is no reason why this process should not take a great deal longer — there is no question of 'competition' or 'rush' in this; you are undergoing conversion to a new religion for your own sake, and you would not expect to master a new language or a new musical instrument in a rush — so why expect to master a completely new way of looking at Life, the Universe, God, your own Identity and destiny in just a few months?

Because there are many imponderables in this process and many reasons for possible delay it is recommended not to make any plans for things like weddings or a Bar-*Mitzvah* until the *Beit Din* has completed the process of acceptance into the community. If a couple are already living together and committed to each other as man and wife, then a civil marriage in a Register Office is advised. The conversion process is then no longer being followed for the sake of getting married but instead to enrich the existing marriage. That makes a difference. If a couple wish to start a family — there is no reason not to start trying, on the understanding that an infant can also be accepted into the community at the same time as the mother (and should a pregnant woman convert, her unborn child becomes 'Jewish' at the same time). Nothing is gained by waiting, nor by rushing, nor by applying pressure to the Rabbi or the *Beit Din*! Your conversion to Judaism is meant to be relevant to the rest of your life, and no one wishes to be rushed. If anything, such pressure tends to be counter-productive.

How long does it take? As long as it takes; as long as it needs; as long as you want; as long as you take.

6. ACCEPTANCE

For reasons which have as much to do with history and politics as with religion, not every conversion certificate is accepted as valid by every *Beit Din* or synagogue authority. For example, some Orthodox conversions from Israel have not been accepted in the UK! In terms of acceptance within the State of Israel there are 'turf wars' between government agencies and ministries and the 'Jewish Agency' ('*Sochnut*') and occasional alterations to laws. Most Orthodox communities will not accept Reform or Progressive conversions, but some 'unified communities' will. Progressive/Liberal communities will accept almost all conversions performed by recognised and respected *Batei Din* of whatever denomination, but not those performed over the Internet or through corrupt rabbis.

In Israel a Reform/Liberal convert will be accepted by the State for purposes of immigration but not necessarily by the Rabbinate for purposes of marriage. It is a very complex situation. In the '*Shema*' we remind Israel that God is One; but Israel itself, the people of Israel, is NOT 'One'.

Under normal circumstances it pays to get as much advice as you can before you start. If your main aim is to be able to marry a person in an Orthodox synagogue, then you may have to approach an Orthodox community and be prepared to lie about this motivation! If you plan *Aliyah*, (emigration to Israel) you need to check on the current requirements (these may include, for example, an attestation from your rabbi that you have diligently attended services for at least twelve months AFTER your *Beit Din* hearing — the aim here is to avoid cases where, for example, sportsmen are hurriedly 'converted' so that they can play for a specific team a few weeks later!

Unfortunately there ARE abuses of every system, there ARE cases of corruption and bribery and of forging papers; there are persons who offer conversion over the Internet (for a price). The author of this book has heard of cases where a person seeks conversion to Judaism simply so that he cannot be deported as an illegal immigrant! Such occasional scandals are unfortunate, but they do occur and this is why systems are set in place to ensure some degree of oversight and protection for all concerned — the rabbis, the congregations, the candidates and their families. There is no 'quickie' 'spur-of-the-moment' or spiritual kidnapping of vulnerable persons, there is no cult-like brainwashing and there should be no cases of financial or other impropriety...

7. CONVERSION OF CHILDREN

Infants and Children roughly up to the age of Bar- or Bat-*Mitzvah* can also be converted to Judaism — usually with the mother, though this is not absolutely always necessary. (But check with your rabbi for the specific exceptions that are allowed.)

The child is taught up to the level appropriate to their age and, whilst undergoing immersion and (when appropriate) circumcision, is not subjected to a test examination by the Court.

During and beyond Adolescence it is usually considered appropriate for a child to make his or her own personal approach to the *Beit Din*, as a Young Adult. When a child is adopted, conversion can usually be arranged whilst the child is still in infancy — but check that the adoption agency permits this.

8. CONFIRMATION OF JEWISH STATUS

If a person is *'halachically* Jewish' — that is, they were born to a Jewish mother and therefore by Jewish law (*Halachah*) are Jewish, even though they may have had no religious upbringing and are unable to bring any documentary evidence of their Jewish identity — the *Beit Din* can provide a document attesting to their Jewish status. It may be necessary to undergo a similar period of study as though they were converting, especially if they were not raised as active, knowledgeable and observant Jews, and of course it may be that circumcision was not carried out in infancy and needs to be done now, but essentially a person is confirming their Jewish status rather than acquiring it and so a different document is issued. The same restrictions may apply as in the paragraph on 'Acceptance' above.

9. THE *MIKVEH*

Following the interview with the *Beit Din*, and assuming that all has gone well, a candidate will be escorted to the *Mikveh*. Technically this is merely a bath filled with flowing water — i.e. it must not be a stagnant pool but a river or an artificial river created by a bath with water flowing simultaneously in and out. It is not for 'cleansing' but for 'purifying'. Of course a large number of rules have grown up concerning this essentially-simple principle and ownership or control of a communal *Mikveh* has become a political issue with some Orthodox communities refusing to let non-Orthodox Jews or rabbis use it or book it. Nowadays a *'kosher Mikveh'* will have water drawn in from tanks filled with rainwater — thus fulfilling the concept of it being 'natural' — and this will then be mixed with 'normal' tap water from the local plumbing system and reservoir; there are discussions about what sort of tiles are acceptable, how the water may be heated, exactly how many cubic feet of water are required, etc. None of this is relevant to the person now about to undergo *'Tevilah',* the act of entering the waters and symbolically washing away the past.

In most cases there will be a small suite of rooms with a cloakroom, a shower or bath, and then the *Mikveh* room itself. The person who has come to use the facilities will undress, remove any jewellery or make-up (and as far as possible any studs or any plaster bandages or other extraneous matter), maybe cut their nails or shave, wash or shower with soap or shampoo to remove any 'normal' dirt or sweat, and then walk down a set of steps into the *Mikveh* itself which is usually set low. An attendant (a *Balanit*) will remain within earshot or close by in case of any need, a collapse, a stumble... Rabbis may sometimes stand outside to act as witnesses whilst retaining some modesty and privacy — in other places they need to be inside — it depends on the layout.

One first enters the water until it can cover the head — usually this means crouching briefly — and care must be taken to ensure that the water can get Everywhere — including to the scalp, armpits and other areas of the Body. No air bubbles! Then rise again and recite the blessing.

'Baruch Atah Adonai, Eloheynu melech haOlam, asher Kidshahnu beMitzvotav, veTzivahnu al ha-Tevilah.' At which point one can plunge under the water again.

We now hit an interesting conundrum. One has said a Jewish blessing — but was one already Jewish at this point or does the split-second moment of transformation occur AFTER one has said it and immersed? Does it count? To be on the safe side, it is customary to repeat the blessing and the immersion! Then one is most certainly Jewish... and it is also appropriate to add the 'Shehechyanu' blessing of gratitude for having reached this point in one's life.

Children can enter the *Mikveh* with a parent to hold them. Babies can be quickly and symbolically 'ducked' (they may not like it — though some, brought slowly and calmly to the water, float and swim and enjoy the experience. Of course one should not use the *Mikveh* if one is menstruating or has an open wound. If someone has a phobia against immersion, some creative thinking and calm support is required.

The *Mikveh* can and should be used for other occasions once one has become Jewish — after menstruation for a woman, after a seminal emission by a man! (This often gets overlooked...) Before a wedding, and for some women it feels important to use it to mark *Rosh Chodesh*, or sometimes to mark life-cycle events such as a menopause — or sometimes even as part of a process of self-cleansing after abuse or rape. Of course in these cases there is no doubt concerning status and how often the *Berachah* needs to be said!

10. AFTER CONVERSION

There is usually a short ceremony of welcome into the Jewish community (*Siddur* pp.287f; **pp.363f. [*Lev Chadash p. 593*]**) performed either soon after the *Beit Din* hearing or at the first proper opportunity back at the home congregation — it may be considered appropriate to hold a Naming Service for any children who have converted, or to call a newly-converted person up to the reading of the *Torah* for the first time. If a couple are already married a *Chuppah* should be arranged as a religious rededication of their civil marriage.

As a full member of the Jewish community it is forbidden to embarrass a convert by reminding him or her of their method of entry into that community. It is hoped that the convert, the new Jew-by-Choice, will now become and remain fully involved, with the same rights, privileges and responsibilities as anyone born Jewish. Many people who have adopted Judaism in adult life have gone on to make major contributions to the life of the community.

11. WHAT DOES IT COST?

There is no simple answer because different synagogues and different countries have different procedures. What we can say is that you will have to acquire several books — prayer books, a Bible, cookery books, history books — and new household and ritual items — candle sticks, a *Chanukiah*, a *Mezuzah* or several *Mezuzot*, a *Kiddush* cup, items for *Havdalah* or *Pesach*, etc. Male candidates will require a circumcision operation; there may be a synagogue fee for tuition. There will be travel costs and a fee for the final Court appearance. But these are not so much 'costs' as 'investments' in your new Jewish life!

If you are going to have a holiday — it is recommended that you go to Israel and experience the country at first hand, even if only for a short while. Such a visit — especially if it is your first one — will be a meaningful experience. However, do take care not to book a holiday at such a time that you will miss major festival services in your own community! Israel would also be relevant for a honeymoon destination!

12. YOUR JEWISH IDENTITY

One of the greatest gifts a person can enjoy is to know Who They Are. Most Jews know they are Jews, because they have been told this all their lives — either positively or negatively. They may have grown up in a strong community with a Religion School and a youth club, celebrating Jewish festivals and life-cycle events, or they may only have been singled out for attacks in the school playground as a '*Yid*' — but they know what and who they are. Others might have been surprised to learn in later life who they are, after this has been hidden from them for years or decades.

But for people who convert voluntarily to Judaism there is often a great sense of insecurity. There is a perceived need to show the Jewish community what excellent, pious, knowledgeable and active Jews they are. There is a tendency to drift into extremes of observance. The community is rarely pleased with the results.

The best advice we can give is — Just Be Yourself. You do not have to be a scholar like Maimonides or a *Rebbe* from the 18th.-century *Shtetl* with the longest beard, most conspicuous *Tzitzit* and the shortest temper in the *shul*. You do not have to become a head-scarf-wearing, amulet-jangling, *Berachah*-mumbling Earth Mother medieval woman who can pluck a chicken in ten minutes and *kosher* its entrails while reciting sections of the '*Tzena'U'Rena*' in Yiddish and polishing her candlesticks. You do not have to be a *Tzaddik* or a Saint, a Professor or a Rabbi or a *Yenta* (or *Yentl*). You are not living in 19th-century Galicia. You do not have to '*davven*' with an assumed '*Oyshkenoysi*' accent. You simply have to fit in, and try to live the rest of your life in a reasonable way according to the values you have learned and to which you have committed yourself.

Of course you must develop, both as a Person and as a Jew. If someone thinks that they have been in some way 'born again' then logic dictates they must grow up again, must go through the growing pains and the adolescence to develop their new adult identity. They must mature. And often new converts display signs of Immaturity — just like adolescents who seek to shock or show off their limited store of knowledge and of life experience.

Sometimes someone who has converted through our *Beit Din* develops into a more observant approach, becoming dependent on rulings from Orthodox rabbis. In this case you gradually leave Liberal Judaism and enter Orthodox Judaism. This is your right. We wish you well on your personal spiritual journey. We ask only that you do not then display ingratitude at those who have helped you this far on your journey. It is hurtful for people to be told that they are no longer 'good enough'!

Sometimes one develops into a less observant approach, finding that the inner meanings of Judaism become more important to one than the outer rituals and symbols. This is also your right, though it is a pity if this means you cut your links to the congregation.

Sometimes a person becomes so excited at learning Jewish traditions that they want to go on and become a Rabbi straight away. No! Any reputable rabbinic training college will in any case insist that you have lived a certain number of years as a 'normal Jew' (if such a contradictory concept exists!) following your conversion, before you take up professional studies, and the non-reputable institutions (such as those that offer 'rabbinic training' over the Internet!) should be avoided in any case.

Conversion is not a one-off decision, a final diploma. It is a step along a personal spiritual journey. It is, as always, helpful if you can find someone to help you on your journey, to counsel and escort you (such as a rabbi or teacher, a fellow student, or someone who went through the same process a little earlier). But this is not always possible, and then you must face on your own the same pressures, towards assimilation or isolation, towards piety and superstition and dependence, towards anarchy and authoritarianism, which any other Jew has to face in determining the life they live and the community to which they belong — or not…

And we know how difficult this can be, for we can see how many born Jews find it impossible, for whatever reason, to continue…

BOOKLIST AND COURSEWORK

1 INTRODUCTION

It goes without saying that you cannot learn a religion just by reading about it. Nevertheless, within the terms and conditions of this course it is expected that you (and, where appropriate, your partner) will involve yourself in academic study to learn some basic history, theology, Biblical and other texts, Hebrew vocabulary, liturgy and so forth.

The actual practice of what you learn in this course or from this book will come through observance in the home and in the synagogue, through the part you play in the community's life, your attitudes to the world and to people around you. At times, people can learn together; At times, you must study and learn — and think and pray — on your own. At times we can teach each other or learn from each other or from observing. Each person studying this course comes to it with different strengths, different fears, different backgrounds, talents, even the amounts of time and energy available due to other commitments. The only consistency we can expect or demand is consistency of effort.

It is not possible to quote here all current books or current prices (or opportunities for on-line versions or on-line ordering) but we hope to give some initial guidance.

2. READING — PERIODICALS

Much of what you need to know consists of current developments in the Jewish world; These are often of more direct relevance than events in the Biblical period! There is a vast variety available either as paper or online. You should subscribe to and read as far as possible (amongst others) the 'Jewish Chronicle' (weekly), 'Jerusalem Post' (daily), 'Times of Israel' (daily), 'The Jerusalem Report' (fortnightly) — there are also excellent journals such as 'Jewish Quarterly' and the annual 'Jewish Travel Guide' and other guide books to Jewish sights , should you take a holiday elsewhere.

Even if you do not subscribe to all of these it is worth realising that there is more to the Jewish press than your local synagogue magazine.

3. READING — BOOKS
FORMING PART OF THE JEWISH HOME

Sooner or later you will need each of these at home:

A *Siddur*: e.g. '*Forms of Prayer* - Daily and Sabbath' or '*Lev Chadash*'.

A *Machzor*: e.g. '*Forms of Prayer* - Days of Awe' or '*Ruach Chadasha*'.

A *Chumash* — the Soncino or Hertz or Plaut editions have useful commentaries to the weekly portions.

A full *Tanakh*: Recommended is 'Holy Scriptures' (Jewish Publication Society) — a basic English text of the Hebrew Bible, translated by Jewish scholars, without irritating footnotes directing you to the New Testament.

A *Haggadah*: Especially useful is 'Feast of History' by Chaim Raphael. It is an interesting book about *Pesach* and contains an illustrated *Haggadah*. (Weidenfeld & Nicholsohn).

Haggadateinu. Our Haggadah. (MRJ 2013).

Haggadah B'Chol Dor Va-Dor. A Haggadah for all Generations. (LJ 2010).

4. READING — SOME REFERENCE BOOKS

You won't necessarily use these every day, especially when modern equivalents such as various Search Machines or Wikipedia or apps are available, but it will be handy to have them around:

The Jewish Catalogue. Siegel & Strassfeld. (Jewish Publication Society). In three separate parts.

Jewish History Atlas. Martin Gilbert. (Weidenfeld & Nicholson.).

Prayerbook Hebrew the Easy Way. Edited by Ethelyn Simon. (EKS Publishing, Berkeley, USA) Highly recommended, aids in both reading and understanding the prayer books.

5. READING — BASIC HISTORY

A History of Jewish Experience. Leo Trepp (Behrman House).
The Story of Judaism. Bernard Bamberger (Schocken Books).
Jewish People, Jewish Thought. Robert Selzer (MacMillan).
A Feast of History. Chaim Raphael.

6. READING — JEWISH FESTIVALS

The Jewish Holidays. Michael Strassfeld (Harper & Row.).
The Jewish Festivals. Hayyim Schauss (Schocken).
The Biblical and Historical Background of the Jewish Holy Days. Bloch (Ktav).

7. READING — NOVELS

You can learn a lot, quite easily (in terms of mental effort and concentration) by reading a good historical novel. Always remember, however, that they may be well researched but are essentially FICTION!!

Some examples (out of many in the genre):

The Séance
The Slave
The Spinoza of Market Street — all by Isaac Bashevis Singer.

The Chosen
The Promise
In the Beginning
The Book of Lights — all by Chaim Potok.

The Fixer
The Assistant — both by Bernard Malamud.

Exodus and
Mila 16 — both by Leon Uris.

The Source- by James A. Michener.

The Patriarch by Chaim Bermant.

As a separate category
Night
Dawn
The Testament
Souls on Fire
One Generation After
The Jews of Silence — all by Elie Wiesel, autobiographical and based on his experiences in the Holocaust. Not pure fiction, 'One Generation After' is for example described as a 'book of anecdotes, autobiographical fragments, conversations with victims, introspective analyses, dialogues of faith, and essays.'

8. READING — ABOUT JEWISH ATTITUDES OR CUSTOMS

This is My God. Herman Wouk (Fontana): Very popular American bestseller.
Basic Judaism. Milton Steinberg (Harvest).
I am a Jew. Moshe Davies (Mowbrays).

To Heaven with Scribes and Pharisees. Rabbi Lionel Blue (Darton, Longman & Todd).

The Lifetime of a Jew. Hayyim Schauss (UAHC).

The Jewish Family Book. ed. by Sharon Strassfeld and Kathy Green (Bantam Books) .

Running a Traditional Jewish Home. Blu Greenberg (J. Aronson).

A Guide to Jewish Belief, and

A Guide to Jewish Practice. Both by Rabbi Louis Jacobs.

and any good Jewish cook books.

9. READING — BOOKS ABOUT REFORM AND LIBERAL JUDAISM

Explaining Reform Judaism. Eugene Borowitz and Naomi Patz (Behrman).

Reform Judaism. Edited by Dow Marmur (RSGB). Historical essays about the Reform movement.

A Genuine Search. Edited by Dow Marmur. Sequel to the above.

Faith and Practice. Jonathan Romain (RSGB). An excellent book and first-rate companion volume to this material.

Reform Judaism and Modernity. SCM Reader, by Jonathan Romain (MRJ). A collection of Sources translated into English, sorted according to themes.

Liberal Judaism. The First Hundred Years, by Lawrence Rigal and Rosita Rosenberg. (LJ)

Liberal Judaism: A Judaism for the Twenty-First Century, by Pete Tobias (LJ). An explanation of Liberal Jewish Thought.

Additionally there are several pamphlets published by the MRJ and LJ.

All of the above are only recommended reading — you certainly should not have to do all of it but the more you read, the more things become understandable. Thanks to modern online facilities it is easy to find antiquarian copies of almost everything.

Learn also to be discriminating in your reading — there is a lot of attractive material around which presents a fundamentalist view, or sometimes even a Christian missionary one, or even rather nasty anti-Semitic material masquerading as a 'Guide to the *Talmud*' or similar — the Internet can be a strange and dangerous place.

APPENDIX II

A START TO LEARNING TO READ HEBREW

1. INTRODUCTION

(A). LEARNING TO READ HEBREW IS EASY!

Remember that and you won't get scared. There are only twenty-two letters in the alphabet, no nasty diphthongs, no worries about where to put a capital letter (since there aren't any!), none of the unpleasant complications of English. If you can read English and know how to pronounce 'tasty' or 'nasty', or 'potato' and 'tomato', or even 'cucumber', you will be able to cope with Hebrew.

(B). HEBREW SOUNDS AS IT READS

In Hebrew A is A and O is O.
In English A can by Ah or Ay or Uh! O can be O or Oh or Eeh!
Try this: He bound his bow tie and made a low bow; he bound a bandage round his wound.

> Do you know how to pronounce the word GHOTI?
> (This was a famous puzzle presented by G. B. Shaw.)
> It's actually pronounced 'FISH'. Dead easy, really —
> F as in 'Enough';
> I as in 'Women';
> SH as in 'Station'.
> = FISH!!

Why is 'GH' hard in Ghastly, soft in Enough and silent in Although? Why is Women pronounced differently from Woman?

And these are just a handful of examples of the problems that confront those trying to learn English!

In Hebrew you don't have to bother your head about these matters. The vowels will always be available to you in normal use from the Prayer Book or the Hebrew Bible. Without the vowels there are, it is true, other problems. You really need to know (or knead to no? Or node to knew?) what you are reading before trying to read it.

As an example, let us play a little game: Take two English letters — in this case 'P' and 'L'; although you can play this game with many other combinations. The Rules are — (i): these consonants must be the only ones used; (ii). they must remain in this sequence, but (iii). the 'P' could if necessary be softened to an 'F' sound ('Ph') and (iv). either or both consonants could be doubled.

Then add vowels to these consonants and see how many valid combinations you can make; e.g.

Pal; Opal; Pale; Peal; Peel; Polo; Pool; Feel; Fool; Fail; Foil; Folio; Appeal; Appal; Apple; Offal; Pill; Pile; Pall; Paul; Pail; Pole; Flea; 'Flu'; Full; Feel; Fill; Ply; Plea; even — by stretching a point about 'w' as a silent letter — 'Pillow'!

All of these — and maybe more — could have appeared in an 'un-pointed' (i.e. vowel-less) text simply as 'PL'.

'LST' could be Last, Lest, List, Lost, Lust...

There are no Hebrew capital letters, but some letters do have a different shape if they come at the End of a word, just as in English a capital letter would come at the Beginning of certain words — names and so on. These are called 'Nun Soffit' and 'Mem Soffit' and so forth.

(C). STRANGE SHAPES AND SQUIGGLES?

Do the strange shapes of the Hebrew letters put you off? There is no need for this. They are quite simple really. You have presumably already learned to read certain English letters or numerals in different forms, e.g.

A / a / *a* ; E / e / *e* ; F / f / *f* ; 4 / IV / *4*.

So you can cope already with different typefaces, with the swirling letters used in advertising or on neon signs. Another sign for 'N' or 'K' shouldn't faze you! If you can read '2nd' or 'Ltd.' aloud without choking, you can handle other combinations.

(D). ALL FOR WHAT PURPOSE?

All you need to be able to do initially is to read the Prayer Book during the services, read the Hebrew Bible or follow the readings, read blessings for use at home or be able to help a child with their Cheder homework. Perhaps you might need to read and decipher a name on a document or a tombstone. These are all quite basic skills.

If you go on holiday to Israel and try to read a Hebrew newspaper, well… that's rather more ambitious. But to read place-names and signs should be fairly easy.

For now, though, starting to learn to read some new letters aloud, all you have to do is remember the opening line of this section: LEARNING HEBREW IS EASY!

2. WHAT SHOULD YOU BE ABLE TO READ?

1. BASIC GOALS

The hope is that everyone who has followed this course will be fully at home with the prayers and the prayer books used in their community; able to join in the services; to lead some home observance without feelings of embarrassment and so forth.

We hope the time never comes when a parent who has graduated from a conversion course feels that his or her 8-year-old child at Cheder knows more than he or she does!

The following are, therefore, postulated as not more than minimum requirements:

(Note: The first page number refers to '*Forms of Prayer*' 7th ed. 1977; the second, in **Bold**, to '*Forms of Prayer*' 8th ed. 2008. [The number ins ***Bold Italics*** is from Lev Chadash.]

2. TO KNOW BY HEART

a). Blessing for Wine (p.270; **p.452**) *[p.564]*
b). Blessing for Bread (p.270; **p.453**) *[p.565]*
c). *Shema*: the first two lines and the first paragraph (p.34) *[p.137]*
d). Blessings over Candles for *Shabbat*; (p.312; **p.447**) *[p.69]* Yom Tov; Chanukah.
     (p.266; **p.375**). *[p.413: p.399]*

3. TO READ WITH FLUENCY

a). *Amidah*. First two paragraphs (p.36; **p.74**) *[p.140-141]*
b). *Kedushah* and responses (p.38; **p.76**) *[p.141-142]*
c). *Torah*: Blessings before and after the reading (pp.156/158; **p.90**) *[p.482]*
d). *Mah Tovu* (p.14; **p.32**) *[p.105]*
e). *Barchu* and response (p.32; **p.66**) *[p.135]*
f). *Kiddush* for *Erev Shabbat* (p.318; **p.452**) *[p.564-565]*
g). *Aleynu*, First paragraph (p.40; **p.310**) *[p.520]*
h). *Kaddish* (p.42; **p.316**) *[p.524]*
i). *Havdalah* (p.326; **p.458-9**) *[p.567]*
j). Grace After Meals — *Birchat HaMazon* — at least the first full paragraph
     (p.332; **p.466-7**) *[p.551]*

4. TO FIND YOUR WAY AROUND THE PRAYER BOOK

By being able to read, at least haltingly, almost any prayer at sight, on request. To know roughly the order of the service so that you can find what you are looking for; to know the Contents page well enough that if you need to find a specific prayer for a specific occasion you can find it.

NAMES

1. THE IMPORTANCE OF NAMES

Everything and everyone has a name. Indeed the worst that that Judaism can envisage is that someone's name should be removed, blotted out, eliminated, lost, forgotten utterly.

In the Bible we see the importance of names and their meanings. Names are even changed to mark a new identity or a new stage in someone's life. Avram becomes Avraham; Sarai becomes Sarah; Yaakov ('the Grasper') becomes Yisrael ('the one who has struggled with God').

2. YOUR CURRENT NAME

For someone who is adopting Judaism as his or her new identity there are several areas where the issue of Name could be important.

The first is the current forename (often called, typically, a 'Christian name'). In England and Europe many of the names given to children by their parents are names that have a Jewish origin or are at least from the Jewish Bible, e.g. 'Michael', 'Gabriel', 'Benjamin', 'Joseph', 'Samuel', 'Sarah', 'Rachel', 'Deborah', 'Miriam'. Others too are from other early cultures; some have specific religious overtones and from non-Jewish religions at that, whether Pagan or Christian! However, not every name appearing in the New Testament is necessarily laden this way — 'John', 'Mary', 'Elizabeth', 'Saul/Paul', 'Matthew'. Some have Greek origins but easy Jewish equivalents — 'Peter' is from the Greek 'Petros' for 'rock', which of itself doesn't sound religiously 'loaded'.

Other names used to have associations which are now largely lost — for example 'Natalie', which used to mean a person born around Jesus' Natal Day — i.e. Christmas.

Some, though, are clearly based on Christian messages and are not therefore appropriate for a Jew to bear. So — if a person happens to be named 'Christine', 'Christopher' or 'Christabel' or any other name which is so obviously linked to Christianity it would be appropriate for them to seek to change this name — by Deed Poll — or at the very least to change to the use of a second name.

It has been until now unusual for someone with a name like 'Mohammed' to seek conversion to Judaism. Technically this name honours a prophet whom the parents wished to commemorate.

3. ADOPTING A HEBREW NAME

Then there is the issue of adopting a new name for use in the synagogue — a Hebrew name.

There are a lot of misunderstandings about this. Until the time of Napoleon surnames were not universal. Aristocratic families had names of which they were proud, but many ordinary villagers bore names that were linked to their place of origin, their trade or professions, or some personal characteristic. Most European Jews retained the standard Hebraic style of name — 'So-and-so the son of So-and-so' — in some cases Jews had a Hebrew name which they used in their own circles and an English (or Latin) equivalent for use elsewhere. For example 'Baruch' (meaning 'Blessed') would be called 'Benedict' when trading with non-Jews. In Germany someone called 'Zvi' (a deer) might be called 'Hirsch' (German for the same animal).

The concept of using one's father's name as part of one's second name — a patronymic — is still common in Russia, Iceland etc. and of course in Arabic cultures.

As part of the rationalisation of society which accompanied the spread of ideas from the French Revolution — including such things as the metric system and house numbers — standardised surnames were often imposed — and on the Jewish population as well. Sometimes Jews were permitted to choose their new family surname, sometimes it depended on where they came from, sometimes local officials would give them deliberately rude or insulting names. However, within the synagogue context the use of Hebrew (or Yiddish) names and the patronymic was retained in practice.

So — every Jew and Jewess is entitled to have a name by which they are known when they are called up to the reading from the *Sefer Torah*, when they get married, or even to inscribe on their tombstone.

Someone adopting Judaism should adopt a Jewish name for such ritual purposes. The *Beit Din* will unless requested only place the forename(s) on the Conversion certificate. (It might be someone already has a Jewish father.)

Since there is no Jewish father in most cases, it is normal (but not compulsory) to become '*Ben-*' or '*Bat-Avraham*' — a 'Son or Daughter of Abraham', the first patriarch and hence 'father of us all', or if a convert does have a Jewish father or some other Jewish ancestor whose name is known, this could well be adopted as the patronym.

The custom is also being encouraged for both born Jews and Jews by Choice of adding one's mother's name — one is, after all, (usually!) a child of two parents. For a proselyte this might mean taking the name *Ben* (or *Bat*) *Avraham v'Sarah*. It may even be that you consider a foster-father or an adoptive mother to be so important to you that you wish to honour them in this way as though they were your biological parent. However, do note that we do not expect or require a proselyte to take a name which reveals to everyone, every time it is used, that they have converted to Judaism. What was originally intended as an honour — to have roots right back to the very first monotheist, who made a covenant with God! — is increasingly perceived as a stigma.

4. WHICH HEBREW NAME?

Which Hebrew name should you take?

There is no fixed rule. You might choose one that is equivalent in meaning to your present forename, or one that has the same initial letter, or one that sounds vaguely similar. You might choose one that reflects family history — the name of a deceased grandparent, perhaps, or even a deceased In-law if this is appropriate.

(The same process worked often in reverse when Jews took secular names — 'Moshe' became 'Morris', 'Ze'ev' became 'Wolf', 'Arieh' became 'Lionel' and so on. When pioneers made *Aliyah* to *Eretz Yisrael* they often took new names upon themselves — maybe adding a personal or political dimension. 'Ben-Chorin' means 'Son of Freedom'.)

If your given name already has a 'Jewish' association it makes sense to use it. You can take more than one forename if you wish but it seems unnecessary for a 'Benjamin' to take the Hebrew name Yosef... or a 'Sarah' to become Devorah...

You can take the name of a Biblical character with whom you wish to identify, or of some Jewish post-Biblical hero. Again, you can choose more than one if you actually like the sound of more than one.

This will become Your name — one you have taken yourself, not one given to you by your parents or by an official. It is the name by which you will be called when accepting the covenant, when entering your name on an official marriage document; it is the name by which you will be called at your funeral, on your memorial, at *Shivah* and *Yahrtzeit* ceremonies. Should you have children, they will become 'Ben' or 'Bat' whatever name you have chosen.

You should choose your name with care... It is the New You!

INTEGRATION

YOU AS A JEW: INTEGRATION INTO THE COMMUNITY

1. INTRODUCTION

There is Judaism — and there are Jews. The two are not identical. Judaism is an abstract religious system that has existed and developed in different countries and continents over thousands of years; Jews are people, normal, human, mortals with all the strengths and weaknesses of everyone else. (Someone once said 'Jews are like everybody else — only more so!') A Conversion course is not like an academic course leading to a certificate or a diploma.

What should be the intention behind conversion to Judaism? Every individual might have their own. What might be the results? From decades of experience in teaching adults, encouraging, mentoring, advising and warning, a few general results can be drawn.

2. REALISM

From the outset, you must be realistic. The Jewish community — wherever it may be, however large or small it may be — is not perfect. It can be parochial, inward-looking, divided upon itself in petty conflict. Some of its members can express quite alarming prejudices, many are (alas) terribly ignorant. Being Jewish does not automatically stop one having the 'normal' social problems — there are Jews who get divorced, Jewish alcoholics, Jewish wife-beaters, Jews in prison; there are Jewish beggars, Jews in long-stay mental hospitals, Jewish children who suffer in one way or another. Many of the books on Judaism that are available speak in glowing terms of the glories of Jewish family life and show pictures of a smiling Daddy, Mummy and Kiddies around the family dining table. Life CAN be like that (assuming you want it to be) but becoming Jewish is, in itself, no guarantee that it will be. If anything, it becomes your responsibility to help your fellow-Jews when they have problems (and ask) rather than to deny that they exist. Avoid romantic nostalgia or rose-tinted propaganda. Everything in the garden is NOT lovely.

Secondly, when you enter Judaism and voluntarily accept upon yourself the Covenant of Abraham and the 'Ol haMitzvot' — the obligation to follow Jewish life and rules — you are taking a decision which cannot be reversed. By Jewish law, once you become Jewish you stay Jewish — even if, in the future, you stop believing in it. You might then be classed as a 'Lapsed Jew', a 'Bad Jew', even a 'Baptised Jew' should you adopt Christianity — but you also stay Jewish as do, if you are a woman, your children. This is a long-term commitment, for the whole of your life and beyond. You enter the Covenant through all of Time and Space. The blessings and the curses of Jewish existence become your blessings, your curses. The curses include those of rejection by the non-Jewish world on occasion — and also rejection by the Jewish world too, since the Jewish world is constantly preoccupied in trying to define who is not Jewish as much as it is in trying to define who is, and those who convert into Judaism often find themselves the victims of ignorant prejudice from the very People whom they have joined. This is of course hurtful and wrong — but it happens. Be prepared.

3. YOUR JEWISH COMMUNITY

When you convert, you also enter the local Community — at the mundane, local, personal rather than the cosmic level. Sometimes the two might appear very different indeed! This Community, however, is for better or worse the local representative of that relationship between the Divine and the Human reflected in the thousands of years of Jewish thought and prayer.

It is vital that you become integrated into this community because Judaism is a communal religion and not (just) an individual one. From reading books or following a course of study you can learn some Hebrew, some History, some Home Rituals, some elements of Bible and Liturgy. From attending services in the synagogue you can learn some prayers, some melodies, some customs. At the end of this process, you might be able to demonstrate that you know about being Jewish in the home and the synagogue, but it doesn't mean that you feel Jewish where it counts, deep inside.

The best guarantee for this — nothing is ever 100% — is to be living as a part of a Jewish community, joining in its activities, becoming involved in its concerns, assisting in its needs, sharing its joys and sorrows, its hopes and fears. Without this the course of conversion remains just a course of study, not of inner change. As an individual you may feel deeply committed to Judaism, but unless you can also become a part of the group, experience shows the chances are that this feeling may fade, may drop away in time.

There are many non-Jews who are Judaic scholars, expert in Hebrew or Aramaic texts, able to discuss and teach elements of liturgy or practice — but they have never had a Jewish thought or prayed Jewishly. Learning Latin does not make you a Roman.

4. YOU AS A JEW

A parallel example might be the person who falls in love with someone else. The feeling of love, of devotion, of passion might be sincere enough — but what effect does it have if he or she is unable to express it? It just burns up inside. Then, if it is expressed — the difficult process begins of finding out whether this love is reciprocated, whether the person in reality is really as worth loving as they might seem from a distance or whether (close-to) their personal habits might be off-putting. There is the experiment to find out whether you can truly develop a long-term relationship with this other person, or whether it was just a passing infatuation. Then, assuming the two people concerned really are prepared to take upon themselves a long-term (even life-long?) commitment, there is still the problem of relating to the in-laws, the families, maybe even step-children from a previous relationship.

In the same way the person who comes to a Rabbi asking to be converted out of a deep love for Judaism may be totally sincere and committed in that love — but the Rabbi has a duty to guide the candidate gently through the pitfalls and problems and do their best to see if the candidate really understands what it is like 'close-up' to Judaism, whether they have the staying-power, whether the love is healthy and nourishing or instead destructive and possessive, whether they can get on with the rest of the 'Jewish family' or whether they might have some personal 'agenda' and motivation that could disrupt the community, whether they can accept the whole of Jewish history and variety — the baggage of past experience — or whether they are hooked on some naive, idealistic, abstract vision that bears no relationship to the realities of the present and the scars of the past. Sometimes one has to say, as a Rabbi, that Sincerity (while vital) is simply Not Enough.

Do you live many miles from the nearest synagogue, Jewish shop or community? Well — being Jewish won't be impossible — but it will be much more difficult than if you lived much closer by. Are you ready to accept that? Is your desire for conversion based partly at least on a relationship with somebody who is already Jewish? Well — this won't invalidate your sincerity, but could you really cope, would you really wish to continue with your Jewish identity, if that relationship were — for whatever reason — no longer there? Is your commitment based on some real experience of Jewish living in the present, or on a brief holiday in Israel or on a nightmare from the past, maybe even involving your own family? In such cases it could be that taking upon yourself all the religious duties of Judaism might not be the best way forward for you, even though you may well wish to support the Jewish world in other ways.

The key is to be involved in the Present of the Jewish People, not just in its Past or in vague dreams of its Future.

5. YOU AND YOUR FAMILY

What about your existing Family? It might be a shock to them to discover that their son or daughter, brother or sister, nephew or niece is leaving their religious community, leaving the community in which they grew up, or even adopting a religion — any religion — at all. Each individual and family is different so it is hard to generalise. However, it is important to be open with people, to make them feel free to come with you to a service or to meet with the Rabbi (who may also wish to interview them, to be assured that they understand what is proposed and entailed by the course of action you have chosen), to let them know that they can ask questions, that you are not being brainwashed into a cult or being forced to cut off all links with your family.

Remember — there may well be difficulties ahead and it is wise to discuss them with your Rabbi — and your family — in good time. If you are contemplating a marriage it might mean that your parents cannot play the same part at the wedding as they would if, say, you were marrying in their church; If there is a family bereavement it may be difficult for you to gain comfort from a funeral service which assumes that everyone present at least nominally believes in a Christian resurrection; If you suffer bereavement it could be difficult for your non-Jewish family members to know what to do at a Jewish funeral or a *Shivah*. How are grandparents going to cope with giving their grandchildren — your children — *Chanukah* rather than Christmas presents? Where will you fit into family gatherings in the future? Fear and embarrassment can be allayed — but only if you are prepared to be as open as possible. Dodging difficult subjects does not help in the long term.

What about your own children? Are you really able to make for them a choice that will affect their own lives to such an extent? This may depend on how old they are. There are additional complications if a member of your close family decides not to convert with you, or even opposes the idea of your doing so. In any such case, you must inform your Rabbi and obtain guidance. It would be wrong to (mis-) use a religion, any religion, as a tool, a weapon or a catalyst for damaging or destroying other elements of your personal life and that of others.

6. YOU AND GOD

If you become Jewish by Choice — you have no one else to blame should things appear to go wrong. If your faith is tested by setbacks or tragedies, if your security is threatened because of your new identity — these are the results of your own calm, considered, committed choice.

As a Jew you have direct access to God. There is no belief in any need to go through a priest or a prophet. No-one should be able to interfere. Prayer is direct, even if the answer is not always clear. Is Prayer a dialogue, or two monologues, or a one-sided dialogue? It is often hard to say. But nevertheless we address God personally, directly, even intimately — 'Blessed are YOU'.

Many people, born Jewish, try to throw off this identity. They perceive it as a burden, unnecessary, obstructing their desires, as socially or politically inconvenient and they blame 'historical accident' that they happened to be born as Jews. If you, not born as a Jew or not brought up as one, choose to learn and to make a commitment, this commitment must bind you thoroughly, or it is worth nothing.

No Rabbi or teacher can tell you what your reward (if any) might be, or your suffering. However, anyone who has accepted their Jewish identity, deepened it and who rejoices in it will assure you that Life, as a Jew, is what you make of it — it is never boring, but the blessings and the consolations are indeed there, for those who believe.

THE RELATION OF PROGRESSIVE JUDAISM TO OTHER MOVEMENTS WITHIN AND OUTSIDE JUDAISM

Reform, Liberal and Progressive Judaism (the labels vary but the content is largely similar) does not exist in a vacuum. Anyone trying to become or to be Jewish in Europe will at some point be confronted with various options, such as which congregation to join or which Rabbi to follow. The following list is not complete and comprises no more than 'thumbnail sketches' which are by no means neutral judgements — nor are they meant to be. But we have learned that there are limits to Tolerance and that people need guidance. Liberal Judaism, despite its emphasis on tolerance, openness and inclusivity, does not compel us to tolerate everything, especially movements which are hostile to Liberal Judaism or which seek to denigrate it or undermine it.

There are for example those who try to make a synthesis between Judaism and Buddhism, (often referred to as 'JuBu's') or Judaism and Hinduism, or who find many matters in common between Judaism and Islam. We will not explore these in detail, but merely comment that of course all religions have something in common for all are an attempt by human beings to relate to the Divine, to inner spirituality and to questions of Good and Evil, Life and Death and to define the correct relationships between people. But the following are groups which a reader in Britain or Europe may well encounter.

(a). MASORTI

The *Masorti* or Conservative Movement is based on the teachings of Zacharias Frankel (1801-1875) who attempted to create a combination of Tradition and Flexibility just as did the early founders of Reform Judaism — but with more emphasis on the Tradition and traditional observances. He established a training college for rabbis (the Jewish Theological Seminary) in Breslau, where he died. *Masorti* services will usually employ a more traditional format and more Hebrew than Reform ones and decisions are based upon a flexible but not radical approach to *Halachah*, but otherwise the differences between Conservative and Liberal Judaism are essentially quite slight and more political than religious. For example, women may also become Conservative Rabbis. *Masorti* rabbis are also trained at the Leo Baeck College in London.

(b). ORTHODOXY

The great irony is that the word 'Orthodox' is from the Greek and means 'the correct teaching'. The term has only been applied to a group within Judaism relatively recently, from the 19ᵗʰ· century, in an attempt to distinguish it from 'Progressive Judaism'. One finds a wide spectrum from 'Ultra-Orthodox' (who live their lives as far as possible in an enclosed society) to 'Neo-Orthodox' (who attempt to find a way to live according to traditional Jewish values but in an open society). Throughout Britain and Europe there are communities which claim to be 'Orthodox' but in practice hardly any of the members keep the commandments of *Kashrut* or *Shabbat* or *'Taharat Mishpachah'* or observe three daily services or any of the other things which one might legitimately assume defined an Orthodox Jew. The main distinguishing feature of all these groups is that they dislike each other but dislike Reform Judaism even more. One often hears the argument that if a community is run on Orthodox lines then Reform Jews can come too, whereas if it is run on Reform lines, then Orthodox Jews cannot come — and so, for the sake of unity, Reform should compromise whereas Orthodoxy need not. This argument is, frankly, rubbish. Let us not forget that Reform Judaism began precisely because so many people did not feel that they could worship any longer in the manner in which their contemporary communities were run!

(c). CHABAD-LUBAVITCH

The *Chasidic* (often written Hasidic) Movement began as a popular folk movement, very similar in some respects to the popular Protestant Christian non-conformist movements of the 18ᵗʰ· century. The founder is considered to be Rabbi Israel, the 'Ba'al Shem Tov' (abbreviated to 'Besht'), the 'Master of the Good Name'. Basic teachings include the importance of Joy over Learning and, as the concept developed, the *Rebbe* and the *Tzaddik* came to play prominent leadership rôles — the 'Rebbe' being the founder and leader of a *Chasidic* school (many of them led by dynasties, whereby the son, nephew or son-in-law of a *Rebbe* succeeds him) and the Tzaddik is a charismatic and 'holy' individual who can even intervene with God on behalf of an individual — as an intermediary — something totally alien to the rest of Judaism. Various schools of *Chasidim* grew around the teachings of specific rabbis and they are normally named after their place of origin — Ger, Satmar, Bratslav, Lubavitch etc. They encouraged a naive folk piety and although many *Chasidic* stories display great insight into human nature, others present a degree of superstition and anti-intellectual naivety distasteful both to Orthodox and Liberal Judaism. The major leaders of Judaism of the period fought against and resisted the growth of *Chasidism* — and become known as the *'Mitnagdim'*, 'Opponents'.

Lubavitch is named after the town not far from Smolensk in Belarus where the movement began. The term *'Chabad'* is an acronym from the initials for the Hebrew words *'Chochma, Binah, Da'at'* — 'Wisdom, Insight and Knowledge', a typically-modest self-description of their programme. Naturally the destruction of the centres of East European piety led also to the destruction of many *Chasidic* centres but some groups survived because they had established alternative centres or had moved before the *Sho'ah* to America or Palestine. Post-war the Chabad-Lubavitch movement began a programme of unprecedented expansion.

Schneur Zalman of Lyady (1745-1813) founded this branch of *Chasidism*. He was a pupil of Dov Baer the '*Maggid* of Mesritsch' and Menachem Mendel from Vitebsk. His son Dov Baer (1773-1827) moved from Lyady to Lubavitch in 1813.

It was the nephew and son-in-law of Dov Baer, Menachem Mendel (1789-1866) who continued the dynasty. In 1915 Shalom Baer (1866-1920) Menachem's grandson left the town of Lubavitch, but this name remains connected to the movement. They built centres in Poland, Latvia, Palestine and then in America — and hence they remained relatively 'intact' after the *Sho'ah*. They began a programme of Outreach, unlike the other *Chasidic* groups, which has made them well-known worldwide.

Under the leadership of Menacham Mendel Schneerson, known as 'The *Rebbe*' (1902-1994) emissaries were sent out to Jewish communities all over the world. In some places they were welcomed because they provided a service to fill the gaps in communal provision. In others they were perceived as a threat, taking over established communities from within like modern Sabbataeans and gradually spreading *Chasidic* ideology within the congregation. This includes a belief in the 'truth' of the *Midrash* and that Jews have a special 'spark' in their souls which non-Jews do not have — thus delegating non-Jews to the status of '*Beheymot*' or animals! This is a remarkably racist theory, reminiscent of the concept of 'Untermensch' which the Nazis used of the Jews!

Schneerson had a stroke and died some years later in 1994, having never designated a successor or had a son, but there are many *Chabad Hasidim* who still maintain that he is the Messiah (the '*Mashiach*' or '*Moshiach*') and is not actually dead but only awaiting the right time to return. This return can be accelerated (they maintain) by fervent observance of various rituals such as *Tefillin*, *Mezuzah* and the lighting of *Shabbat* candles. This is still pushed with a degree of fanaticism, coupled with a heavy use of the East-European *Ashkenazi* Hebrew accent (e.g. '*Schobbos*' for '*Shabbat*') and a sprinkling of Yiddish words that give the whole activity an aura of 'authenticity' which mesmerises, confuses and seduces many Jews. (This being accelerated by generous use of vodka). In fact, to assume that performing a *Mitzvah* has a specific impact on the decision of the Messiah to come, rather than on spiritual transformation of the person performing the *Mitzvah*, is more a matter of worshipping Magic.

One may admire the energy and self-sacrificing idealism of individual Chabad rabbis and their families, but it must also be stated that their teachings are inimical to Liberal Judaism and there is no reason to hide or deny this. They always claim to be 'there for everybody' but several times they were active in moves to make the State of Israel refuse to accept the validity of Reform conversions and where a Chabad rabbi has been appointed to lead a local community it soon becomes clear what 'Everybody' means. Liberal Judaism is tolerant, but there have to be boundaries to our tolerance. A sect which peddles superficial Kabbalistic teachings mixed with Messianism is neither attractive nor authentic, even if its practitioners wear beards, black hats and smile a lot while passing round the vodka bottle.

(d). 'MESSIANIC JUDAISM'

A further threat to religious belief is Syncretism — the attempt to mix two religions together. Usually carried out by well-meaning people, this is nevertheless a misguided attempt to join what cannot be joined by suppressing — sometimes violently — whichever factors refuse to be quietly absorbed into the new mixture.

In this case, Christian missionaries (or self-proclaimed 'Jews for Jesus') attempt to persuade Jews that they can believe in Jesus of Nazareth, whose life, career and teachings are partially represented in the books of the 'New Testament' as the Messiah and yet still remain Jewish. They can continue to pray in Hebrew, to sing Hebrew songs, to wear head-coverings and carry out various other external practices. Internally, however, in the moment that a person accepts Jesus of Nazareth as the '*Christos*', he is a Christian.

Judaism does NOT accept Jesus of Nazareth as a saviour, even if many of the teachings recorded in his name match those of other contemporary Jewish thinkers.

We do NOT believe that he was conceived through a 'Holy Spirit' within the womb of a Virgin.

We do NOT accept that his mother had any special function to fulfil, and so we do not worship her. We do NOT employ Baptism as a means of washing away sin and becoming 'saved'. (*Tevilah* is similar but different.)

We do NOT believe in 'Original Sin' and therefore we do not require the 'vicarious salvation' offered to cleanse us of it through the blood of the sacrificed 'Son of God'.

These are major and important differences in the way Jews and Christians view the world. For Christianity, Mankind is born in Sin and the individual must accept cleansing (through baptism or faith or good works) if they are to avoid Damnation; For Judaism we are born with a 'clean soul' (as stated in the prayer '*Elohai, Neshama sheNatata bi tehorah hi*') and we carry within us both the Good Urge ('*Yetzer Tov*') and the Evil Urge ('*Yetzer haRa*') and our spiritual task is to keep these in balance (interestingly, NOT to destroy or expel the 'evil' side — we need that too, to function fully as human beings! This is also a part of who we are and of how God created us, too.) We are responsible for our own actions and do not carry the blame for what our ancestors all the way back to Adam did (we may be affected by the consequences, but that is not the same as being responsible) and we must make Penitence for ourselves through '*Teshuvah*'.

We may respect Christians, many of whom have finally realised that they will never dominate the entire world and some of whom have become more aware of the Jewish roots of early Christianity and also of the violence carried out against Jews and Moslems in the name of Christian love; But we do not share all their beliefs and therefore any attempt to wash away the differences and pretend that one can be both Jewish and Christian at the same time is a dangerous, seductive mistake. These movements are however well-funded, sometimes by mainstream Christian churches, with the aim of 'saving the souls' of lost Jews by giving them the chance to be 'born again'. From our point of view, one can indeed choose to become a Christian — but only at the cost of ceasing to be a Jew.

(e). CHRISTIAN CHURCHES

In the 21st (Christian) century there are in many places friendly relationships with local Christian churches. The Churches have come to recognise their dependence on the Jewish origins of the earliest Christians and of their rituals. Some indeed show great interest in learning about Jewish festivals and rituals — though the motivation is sometimes a little misguided, for Judaism has changed substantially since 1st-century times as portrayed in the New Testament! Nevertheless, in contrast to earlier centuries where the relationship to Judaism was characterised by fear, hatred and an arrogant assumption that the Church had taken the place of Judaism by forging a new Covenant with God and that God therefore hated the Jews, this is remarkable progress.

In October 1965 following the Second Vatican Council the Roman Catholic Church promulgated the 'Declaration on the Relation of the Church with Non-Christian Religions' of the Second Vatican Council entitled 'Nostra Aetate' which redefined the relationship of the Church to all non-Christian religions; Part 2 covered Hindus and Buddhists, Part 3 Moslems, Part 5 speaks of the equal worth and rights of all people, and Part 4 says of the Jews:

> 'True, the Jewish authorities and those who followed their lead pressed for the death of Christ; still, what happened in His passion cannot be charged against all the Jews, without distinction, then alive, nor against the Jews of today. The Jews should not be presented as rejected or accursed by God, as if this followed from the Holy Scriptures. All should see to it, then, that in catechetical work or in the preaching of the word of God they do not teach anything that does not conform to the truth of the Gospel and the spirit of Christ. Furthermore, in her rejection of every persecution against any man, the Church, mindful of the patrimony she shares with the Jews and moved not by political reasons but by the Gospel's spiritual love, decries hatred, persecutions, displays of anti-Semitism, directed against Jews at any time and by anyone.' (Translation from Wikpedia).

Other, but not all Churches have also revised their attitudes and issued formal statements. We consider it important to acknowledge this positive relationship, whilst at the same time not forgetting that the two religions, Judaism and Christianity — in all their different forms — are still based on different and inherently incompatible beliefs on the nature of Man and God. We consider it important to work together with Christian communities where we can for social justice and to study together. Christianity has largely abandoned its earlier 'Triumphalism' and its desire to impose a monopoly on religious life and many Christians are interested in dialogue with other religions and cultures. We should take part in this process, but as knowledgeable Jews. It has been said that Christianity needs Judaism — for it bases its claims on Jewish texts — whereas Judaism does not need Christianity in the same way.

There are also unfortunately still a few 'throwbacks' to earlier ideas, organisations seeking to missionise and evangelise Jews, handing out missionary literature in synagogues, and with these people Dialogue is normally and sadly impossible.

(It should be noted that there are many people who have parents or grandparents who converted from Judaism to Christianity, but who are themselves interested in Judaism and even in becoming Jewish. Sometimes the term 'I have Jewish blood in me' is used. This is incorrect. The main people interested in the concept of 'Jewish blood' are those interested in spilling it. One does not inherit Judaism genetically, even though some research indicates that many Jewish communities have remained genetically enclosed, not mixing with surrounding populations. A person brought up within Christianity is a Christian, and if they wish to leave Christianity and join Judaism they are welcome to do so, but it is unlikely that their having had some distant ancestor who left Judaism will really help them in terms of knowledge. In such a case we would require that a person undergoes a full conversion procedure.)

(f). KABBALAH MOVEMENT

Not a specific organised 'Movement' as such, this phenomenon of a superficial interest in the mystic traditions of the *Kabbalah*, encouraged by persons totally unqualified to teach it or to learn it, has gained ground recently. Seminars and meetings are advertised widely. The idea is that, by attending such seminars, the sincere searcher will be granted the way to find happiness and fulfilment — as though the *Kabbalah* is a mystic cookbook from which one can take recipes. In fact traditional rabbinic Judaism is very wary indeed of Mysticism. It is something which is restricted to those who have years of life-experience and of training in basic Jewish texts and practices — it should never be treated as a substitute for these. It is dangerous, as it can potentially lead its practitioners out of the world in which we live and into mental instability. Liberal Judaism would urge people not to dabble in this area.

(g). A NOTE ON INTERFAITH AND MIXED CEREMONIES

Interfaith services and dialogue are important educational and symbolic activities — especially at a time when it is necessary to fight against prejudice, ignorance and intolerance. But they should never be a substitute for being Jewish as well! Unfortunately there are some people who are always willing to read a Jewish prayer in a church, but not in a synagogue! In order to take part effectively in such Dialogue you need to be well-rooted in your own community and to know your own liturgy and Bible texts well.

One will sometimes hear well-meaning people declare that Judaism and Christianity are 'almost identical' and 'we can say everything together'. Unfortunately this is not the case. The two religions are based upon diametrically-opposite assumptions about the nature of Man and of God. In Christianity, Man is born tainted with Original Sin and requires Salvation through a specific Messianic figure, a Son whom God sent specifically for this purpose and who should return; In Judaism, Man is born with a 'clean' soul, and the messianic salvation has not yet come. We approach the *Torah* and the prophetic messages from different directions — Christian theologians look for matters which they can claim have been 'fulfilled' through Jesus, whereas Jews read the texts embedded in their times as looking forwards — still.

Even a Psalm or another biblical text might be read very differently, with certain verses omitted, or with a christological ritual ending such as 'in the name of the Father and of the Son...' added at the end — words which are simply inappropriate for a Jew to say. It is possibly easier to say that 'we can often pray with each other but not together.'

Individual rabbis may be willing or unwilling to take part in joint religious services for Peace or Commemorations; it is usually much easier to meet on 'neutral' ground than in a church which is filled with religious symbols that are, quite simply, not Jewish. Out of respect for the dead it may be possible to co-officiate at a Funeral (and the early rabbis declared it a *Mitzvah* to bury even non-Jews 'out of respect and for the sake of peace' — '*mip'nei Darchei Shalom*' — '*Gittin*' 59a-61a). But most Liberal rabbis (at least in Europe and in Israel) would not normally take part in mixed Wedding ceremonies. The reasons are really simple — the Christian and Jewish concepts of a wedding ceremony are very different and even though both involve bringing a man and woman together in holiness they are not consistent with each other. In Catholic Christianity Marriage is a 'sacrament', in Judaism it is a Contract between two parties, 'according to the Law of Moses and Israel'. Such a contract can only be binding if both parties are theoretically subject to this legal code. See the chapter on '*Kiddushin*'.

493

EXAMPLE BEIT DIN QUESTIONS

(It should be clear that not all these questions apply to every individual candidate, nor is there a fixed set of questions 'always asked', but these are typical of the sort of questions the rabbis may possibly ask you...)

01. Describe the *Erev Shabbat* service.
02. Describe the *Shabbat* morning service.
03. What is *Kiddush*?
04. Can you recite and translate the blessing over Bread?
05. Can you recite and translate the blessing over Wine?
06. What happens when the *Sefer Torah* is brought out of the *Aron Kodesh* on *Shabbat* or Festival morning services?
07. What is the name of a portion of the *Torah* read on a *Shabbat* morning?
08. Into how many portions for public reading is the *Torah* divided?
09. What is the name of the morning service?
10. What is the name of the additional service on *Shabbat* and festival mornings?
11. What is the name of the Eve of *Yom Kippur* service?
12. What is the exact meaning of this name?
13. How would you describe this meaning to a non-sympathetic gentile?
14. What is the name for the final service on *Yom Kippur*?
15. Do you know what this name means?
16. What is the Hebrew name for a Ram's Horn?
17. When is it used in synagogues?
18. How many times would it be blown, in either an Orthodox or a Reform synagogue?
19. What is special about the *Kiddush* on *Rosh Hashanah*?
20. Describe the festival of *Purim* and translate the name.
21. Describe *Chanukah* and translate the name.
22. What is the name for the special *Menorah* used on *Chanukah*?
23. Recite and translate the blessing for lighting the candles before *Shabbat* and also before a festival.
24. How is a Leap Year coped with in Judaism?
25. How many times is there a leap year in the cycle and how many years are there in the cycle? What is the name of any additional month?
26. What is the term used for the start of a new month?
27. What is the meaning of the Hebrew word *Pesach*?
28. What is the name of the book used in the home on *Pesach* evening?
29. What is the ritual on the first eve of *Pesach* in the home called?
30. Describe this ritual in as much detail as you can.

31. Approximately how many Jews were killed by the Nazis and their helpers in the *Sho'ah*?
32. How many non-Jews were also killed by the Nazis in this period?
33. Knowing all this, are you still prepared to subject yourself and your children or future children to this danger?
34. What is the most important prayer — or statement — in Judaism?
35. Recite the first two lines of the *Shema* and translate them.
36. What is, or are, the meaning(s) of the word *Kallah*?
37. Name the canopy used at a Jewish wedding.
38. Do you know the significance of it?
39. What does your fiancé's (fiancée's) or husband's (wife's) family think of you converting?
40. What does your own family think of you converting?
41. In what way has your life been affected since you started attending the synagogue?
42. What do you admire about Judaism?
43. What don't you like about Judaism?
44. What have you least liked during your course of tuition?
45. How can you tell which animals, birds and fish can be eaten?
46. Name some animals birds and fish which should not be eaten.
47. How does one prepare meat and fowl (kashering) before cooking?
48. If we called at your home, how would we know we were in a Jewish home?
49. Which prayer do you like most?
50. What is the name for the Hebrew Bible and how is this name derived?
51. What is the *Talmud*?
52. What are the names of its two main constituent parts?
53. How many versions are there of the *Talmud* and what are their names?
54. Which harvest is celebrated on *Shavuot*?
55. What event happened at that time?
56. Which harvest is celebrated at *Pesach*?
57. What event happened at this time?
58. Which harvest is celebrated at *Sukkot*?
59. What special things do we make or use on *Sukkot*?
60. What is *Rosh Hashanah* leIlanot?
61. What is *Tu BiShvat*?
62. How many times do we recite *Kiddush* on *Shabbat*?
63. Do we recite the same words each time?
64. What is the Jewish method of slaughter of animals and fowl called?
65. What does it involve?
66. Why do we have to keep milk and meat foods separate?
67. How long should one wait before eating milk foods after having eaten meat foods?
68. What is the *Chumash*?
69. What is the *Siddur*?

70. Who prepared the first (known) *Siddur* and when?

71. Why do Jews no longer offer up sacrifices?

72. What is the name of the reading desk in the synagogue?

73. What is the Hebrew name for the Ark in the synagogue?

74. What do we call the wooden finials on a *Sefer Torah*?

75. What do we call the shield on a *Sefer Torah*?

76. What do we call the pointer on a *Sefer Torah* and why?

77. What will be the first thing you will do or say if the *Beit Din* agrees to accept you?

78. Why do we have two candles on *Shabbat*?

79. Why do we have two loaves of bread on *Shabbat*?

80. What are these loaves called and why?

81. Why do we cover these loaves with a cloth?

82. What is the name of the Israeli National Anthem and what does this name mean?

83. What are the Hebrew words for a bridegroom and bride?

84. What is the name of the Jewish marriage contract?

85. What is the Hebrew name for the Eternal Light in a synagogue?

86. What do we call food which is permitted?

87. What do we call food which is not permitted?

88. What does this word actually mean?

89. What is a *Machzor* and when do we use it?

90. What is a *Megillah*?

91. What is 'The *Megillah*'?

92. What are *Tefillin*? — and describe them.

93. What is a *Tallit*?

94. 1492 CE was an important year in Jewish history. Why?

95. What was important about the year 586 BCE?

96. In what year did the Romans destroy the Temple in Jerusalem?

97. Who were Ezra and Nechemiah and why are they important in Jewish history?

98. When were the Jews expelled from England?

99. With whom did a Dutch rabbi plead for the return of Jews to England and what was this rabbi's name?

100. What is a *Mitzvah*?

101. What is *Simchat Torah* and when do we celebrate it?

102. What does the word *Tzedakah* mean and why is it so important in Judaism?

103. By what Hebrew word do we call the Messiah?

104. What are the Ten Commandments and where can they be found?

105. What is the meaning of *Derech Eretz*?

106. Who wrote the *Shulchan Aruch*?

107. Who was Samuel?

108. Who was *Rambam*?

109. What is a *Minyan*?

110. What is a *Get*?

111. What is a *Yahrtzeit*?

112. What are the meanings of *Aliyah*?

113. When do we recite *Birchat HaMazon*?

114. What is meant by *Mikveh*?

115. Which festival is marked by staying up late and eating cheesecake?

116. Which festival is marked by spending the whole day in synagogue?

117. Which festival is marked by eating apple and honey?

118. Which festival is marked by cleaning out all the kitchen cupboards beforehand?

119. What blessings do you make on a Friday evening? In which order?

120. Define a *Challah*. What makes it different from (a) a *Kallah* and (b) a *Matzah*?

121. How does a *Chanukiyah* differ from a *Menorah*?

122. What is a *Haggadah*? Who wrote it? Whose name is not mentioned in it?

123. When do we say *Hallel* and what is it?

124. What is the *Aleynu* about?

125. Define the difference between *Kiddush*, *Kaddish* and *Kedushah*.

126. What starts at *Bar'chu*?

127. When is the *Al HaNissim* prayer said?

128. What do you know about the following people? Who were they, what did they do, roughly when did they live?
    - Maimonides
    - Chaim Weizmann
    - Manasseh ben Israel
    - Shabbetai Tzvi
    - Eliezer ben Yehudah.

129. What do you need to make *Havdalah*?

130. Who was *Rashi* and what did he do?

131. How many of the Ten Plagues that afflicted the Egyptians can you remember? List them if you can (the order doesn't matter…)

132. How do we recall the Plagues and when?

133. What do we do when reading the list?

134. Describe and define:
    - *Matzah*
    - *Maror*
    - *Karpas*
    - *Zero'ah*
    - *Mechirat Chametz*
    - *Haggadah*

135. Who are the Four Sons / Four Children at the *Seder*?

136. How long is the *Omer*?

137. What is *Pidyon HaBen*?

138. What do you know about the following terms:
    - *Kallah*
    - *Ketubah*
    - *Bedecken*
    - *Sheva Berachot*

    - *Chuppah*

    - *Get*

139. What is the traditional Jewish approach to mourning? How long does it take? What does one do? What can other people do to help?
140. Why do Jews use plain, simple coffins?
141. Describe a *Shofar*.
142. Who or what is *Akedah*?
143. What do you know about *Kol Nidrei*?
144. How did you celebrate *Purim* this year? *
145. What do 'BCE' and 'CE' stand for?
146. Do you know the blessing to be recited when called up to the *Torah*?
147. What is *Hagbahah*?
148. Why do you really want to be Jewish?
149. What other questions do you think we could ask you?

* Note, this is a trick question — the correct answer is 'I'm sorry, I cannot remember, I was totally drunk at the time!'

PART NINE: SOME USEFUL INFORMATION

LITURGICAL READINGS:
THE SIDROT & HAFTAROT
A BRIEF OVERVIEW

There are different versions of these listings. The 'Hertz' *Chumash* (London) gives when necessary both *Ashkenazi* and *Sephardi Haftarot*; The Hebrew-German 'Goldschmidt' Chumasch (Basel), which includes *Haftarot* in a sixth section at the back of the volume, lists in small print various rubrics such as:

- p.16 — (for '*Vayishlach*') — '*Kan matchilim HaAshkenazim Haftarat Vayishlach, aval b'K'K' F'F'd'M' veRov Ashkenaz maftirim beP' Vayishlach, 'Chazon Ovadiah*', dilkaman.'

'Here the *Ashkenazim* begin the *Haftarah* Vayishlach, but in the holy community of Frankfurt am Main the majority of *Ashkenazim* use as *Haftarah* on Parashat Vayishlach, 'The Vision of Obadiah' as follows.'

- p. 15 (for '*Vayetze*'), 'In the community of Frankfurt am Main the majority of *Ashkenazim* read as *Haftarah* for Parashat *Vayetze*, '*Vayivrach Ya'akov*' (from Hosea 12:13) and do not read '*Ve'ami T'luyim*' (Hosea 11:7) at all.'

- On p. 72, for '*Behar Sinai*', after Jeremiah 32:22, '*BeHarbeh Kehillot asseyamin kan*'— 'In many communities they stop here.'

- On p. 73, for '*Behukotai*', 'Whether the portions [*Behar* and *Behukotai*] are combined or kept separate, the Italians use this as *Haftarah* for Behar.'

We see therefore that there were different traditions between Eastern and Western *Ashkenazim* as much as between *Ashkenazim* and *Sephardim*. The Goldschmidt volume also uses terms such as 'nach portugiesischem Ritus' (p.25) and 'nach deutschem Ritus' (p.26), meaning of course '*Sephardi*' and '*Ashkenazi*'. There are issues of what to do when two portions are combined (but only one *Haftarah* will be read), and when a *Shabbat* falls on a 'special day' so that a 'special *Haftarah*' will be read instead. So there has always been scope for some flexibility.

SHABBAT	SIDRA	ASHKENAZI HAFTARAH	SEPHARDI HAFTARAH
Bereshit	Gen. 1:1 - 6:8	Isaiah 42:5 - 43.10	
Noach	Gen. 6:9 - 11:32	Isaiah 54:1 - 55:5	
Lech-Lecha	Gen. 12.1 - 17:27	Isaiah 40:27-41:16	
Va'era	Gen. 18:1 - 22:24	II Kings 4:1-37	
Chayyeh Sarah	Gen. 23:1 - 25:18	I Kings 1:1-31	
Toldot	Gen. 25:19 - 28:9	Malachi 1:1 - 2:7	
Vayetze	Gen. 28:10 - 32:2	Hosea 12:13 - 14:10*	Hosea 11:7-12:12*(1)
Vayishlach	Gen. 32:3 - 36:43	Hosea 11:7 - 12:12*	Obadiah 1-21(2)
Vayeshev	Gen. 37:1 - 40:23	Amos 2:6 - 3:8	
Mikketz	Gen. 41:1 - 44:17	I Kings 3:15 - 4:1	
Vayigash	Gen. 44:18 - 47:27	Ezekiel 37:15-28	
Vayechi	Gen. 47:28 - 50:26	I Kings 2:1-12	

Notes:

In the Book '*Bereshit*' there are 12 *Sidrot*.

(1) Goldschmidt *Chumash* gives only the *Sephardi* version. * The Verse-numbering is different in Christian Bibles. Hosea 12:12-14:9, and 11:7 - 12:11.

(2) Goldschmidt *Chumash* on p. 16 gives here the Vayetze *Haftarah* — (Hosea 12:13 - 14:10) and on p. 18 the Obadiah text with rubric 'According to the custom of the *Sephardim* and in Frankfurt/Main.'

SHABBAT	SIDRA	ASHKENAZI HAFTARAH	SEPHARDI HAFTARAH
Shemot	Ex. 1:1 - 6:1	Isaiah 27:6-28:13, 29:22-23.	Jeremiah 1:1 - 2:3
Vayera	Ex. 6:2 - 9:35	Ezekiel 28:25 - 29:21	
Bo	Ex. 10:1 - 13:16	Jeremiah 46:13-28	
Beshallach	Ex. 14:1 - 17:6	Judges 4:4 - 5:31	Judges 5:1-31
Yitro	Ex. 18:1 - 20:23	Isaiah 6:1 - 7:6; 9:5-6*(3)	
Mishpatim	Ex. 21:1 - 24:18	Jeremiah 34:8-22, 33:25-26	
Terumah	Ex. 25:1 - 27:19	I Kings 5:26-6:13*(4)	
Tetzaveh	Ex. 27:20 - 30:10	Ezekiel 43:10-27	
Ki Tissa	Ex. 30:11 - 34:35	I Kings 18:1-39	I Kings 18:20-39
Vayakhel	Ex. 35:01 - 38:20	I Kings 7:40-50	I Kings 7:13-26

SHABBAT	SIDRA	ASHKENAZI HAFTARAH	SEPHARDI HAFTARAH
Pekudey	Ex. 38:21 - 40:38	I Kings 7:51-8:21	I Kings 7:40-50

Notes:

In the Book '*Shemot*' there are 11 *Sidrot*.

(3). According to Goldschmidt p.37, *Sephardim* end at 6:13 and only *Ashkenazim* continue into Chapter 7.* Also, the Verse-numbering is different in Christian Bibles; Isaiah 9:5-6 is 9:6-7.

(4). In Christian Bibles, I Kings 5:26 is I Kings 5:12.

SHABBAT	SIDRA	ASHKENAZI HAFTARAH	SEPHARDI HAFTARAH
Vayikra	Lev. 1:1 - 5:26	Isaiah 43:21 - 44:23	
Tzav	Lev. 6:1 - 8:36	Jeremiah 7:21-8:3; 9:22-23.*(5)	
Shemini	Lev. 9:1 - 11:47	II Samuel 6:1 - 7:17	
Tazria	Lev. 12:1 - 13:59	II Kings 4:42 - 5:19	
Metzora	Lev. 14:1 - 15:33	II Kings 7:3-20	
Acharey Mot	Lev. 16:1 - 18:30	Ezekiel 22:1-19	
Kedoshim	Lev. 19:1 - 20:27	Amos 9:7-15	Ezekiel 20:1-20
Emor	Lev. 21:1 - 24:23	Ezekiel 44:15-31	
Behar Sinai	Lev. 25:1 - 25:55	Jeremiah 32:6-27	
Bechukotai	Lev. 26:1 - 27:34	Jeremiah 16:19-17:14	

Notes:

In the Book '*Vayikra*' there are 10 *Sidrot*.

(5). In Christian Bibles this is 9:23-24.

SHABBAT	SIDRA	ASHKENAZI HAFTARAH	SEPHARDI HAFTARAH
Bemidbar	Num. 1:1 - 4:20	Hosea 2:1-22*(6)	
Naso	Num. 4:21 - 7:89	Judges 13:2-25	
B'ha'alotecha	Num. 8:1 - 12:16	Zechariah 2:14-4:7*(7)	
Shelach-Lecha	Num. 13:1 - 15:41	Joshua 2:1-22	
Korach	Num. 16:1 - 18:32	I Samuel 11:14 - 12:22	
Chukkat	Num. 19:1 - 22:1	Judges 11:1-33	
Balak	Num. 22:2 - 25:09	Micah 5:6 - 6:8*(8)	
Pinchas	Num. 25:10 - 30:1	I Kings 18:46 - 19:21	

SHABBAT	SIDRA	ASHKENAZI HAFTARAH	SEPHARDI HAFTARAH
Mattot	Num. 30:2 - 32:42	Jeremiah 1:1-2:3	
Mass'ey	Num. 33:1 - 36:13	Jeremiah 2:4-28; 3:4; 4:1-2*(9)	

Notes:

In the Book '*Bemidbar*' there are 10 *Sidrot*.

(6). In Christian Bibles numbered Hosea 1:10 - 2:20.

(7). In Christian Bibles numbered Zechariah 2:10 - 4:7.

(8). In Christian Bibles numbered 5:7 - 6:8.

(9). According to Goldschmidt only *Sephardim* add the last section from Jeremiah Ch. 4.

SHABBAT	SIDRA	ASHKENAZI HAFTARAH	SEPHARDI HAFTARAH
Devarim	Deut. 1:1 - 3:22	Isaiah 1:1-27(10)	
Va'etchanan	Deut. 3.23 - 7:11	Isaiah 40:1-26(11)	
Ekev	Deut. 7.12 - 11:25	Isaiah 49:14 - 51:3	
Re'eh	Deut. 11:26 - 16:17	Isaiah 54:11 - 55:5	
Shoftim	Deut. 16:18 - 21:9	Isaiah 51:12 - 52:12	
Ki Tetze	Deut. 21:10 - 25:19	Isaiah 54:1-10	
Ki Tavo	Deut. 26:1 - 29:8	Isaiah 60:1-22	
Nitzavim	Deut. 29:9 - 30:20	Isaiah 61:10 - 63:9	
Vayelech	Deut. 31.1 - 31:30	Hosea 14:2-10; Micah 7:18-20; Joel 2:15-27*(12)	
Ha'azinu	Deut. 32.1 - 32:52	II Samuel 22(13)	
Vezot - haBracha	Deut. 33:1 - 34:12	Joshua 1:1-18	

Notes:

In the Book '*Devarim*' there are 11 *Sidrot*.

(10). '*Shabbat* Chazon'— The Sabbath of the Vision. (Before *Tisha B'Av*).

(11). '*Shabbat Nachamu*'— The Sabbath of Comfort. (After *Tisha B'Av*).

(12). '*Shabbat Shuvah*'. In Christian Bibles this is Hosea 14:1-10.

(13). Goldschmidt offers three options — p.111 'nach deutschem Ritus' Joel 2:15-27; p.112 'nach portugiesischem Ritus' II Samuel 22:1-51; p.115 'nach dem Ritus mancher Gemeinden' Ezekiel 17:22 - 18:32.

General Notes:

- In general we see that the *Haftarah* is always much shorter than the *Sidra*.
- Noticeable is how in Leviticus the Chapter breaks and the *Sidrot* coincide through-out. A total of 34 of the *Sidrot* start at a new chapter break (counting, of course, the five opening *Sidrot* in their respective books).
- We see that Isaiah 54 is used as *Haftarah* for both *Noach* and *Ki Tetze*.
- During the readings from Deuteronomy, simply because of the time of year in which this book is read, the *Haftarot* are almost exclusively occupied with warning before and comfort after *Tisha B'Av*, or with Repentance.
- *Bereshit* (12) + *Shemot* (11) + *Vayikra* (10) + *Bemidbar* (10) + *Devarim* (11) makes a total of 54 *Sidrot*. In practice it is common to combine some in pairs when necessary, these being:

Vayakhel-Pekudey;
Behar-Bechukotai;
Tazria-Metzora;
Acharey Mot - Kedoshim;
Mattot-Mass'ey;
Nitzavim-Vayelech;
and '*Vezot HaBracha*' is rarely read as a separate weekly *Sidra*.

LIST OF TERMS AND ABBREVIATIONS

Transliteration and Transcription into European Languages

Note that in all cases where a Hebrew word is transliterated there are potential problems for the simple reason that not every letter in the Hebrew alphabet has an exact equivalent in other languages. (Just as there are issues with a French *cedilla* or accent, or a German Umlaut…) There are two Hebrew letters which can be pronounced or transliterated as 'T' — '*Tet*' and '*Taf*' — but to make life complicated the *Taf* can under certain grammatical circumstances be softened to an 'S' in certain East European and Yiddish accents (e.g. '*Tallis*' instead of '*Tallit*', '*Shabbes*' instead of '*Shabbat*'). Then there are two letters for 'S' — '*Sin*' and '*Samech*' — and the '*Zayin*' is a soft 'z' as in 'Zoo'. The hard 'z' as in '*Matzah*' would be the '*Tzaddi*' and could be written 'z' or 'tz' or even 'ts'.

The letters '*Kaf*' and '*Kuf*' are both pronounced as a hard 'k' but are sometimes transliterated as 'q'.

The letters '*Chaf*' or '*Chet*' are both pronounced with a guttural deep-throat 'ch' — not a hard 'ch' as in the English 'church' but a softer one as in '*Bochum*' or '*Bach*', or the Dutch 'g' as in '*goed*'. But since there is no single English letter or even diphthong for this, this means that one has to decide whether to write it as an 'H', as an 'H' with a dot underneath to signify the change, as 'kh' or as 'ch'. Is it '*Chanukah*', or '*Hannukkah*'? Rabbi Yohanan or Yochanan?

There are letters which are normally silent but — well, the *Sephardim* pronounce the '*Ayin*' as 'ng'. There are letters which can be soft ('v') or hard ('b') depending on a dot which isn't actually there in written texts, only in printed ones… There is a letter ('*Vav*') which can be a consonant 'v' or a doubled-consonant 'vv' or a vowel 'o' (as in 'dot') or a vowel 'u' (as in 'oo')… The 'y' can be substituted by 'j' in some versions — 'Joshua' or 'Yehoshua'; And so on.

Hebrew is written without vowels, but often printed with markings which serve as vowels. But is a specific vowel in English pronounced as 'e' or 'ei' or 'ey' or 'ay'? One will find the words '*Beth*', '*Bet*' and '*Beit*' all to mean 'House. (Just think how the letter 'u' is pronounced differently in 'cucumber'!) Sometimes in the Hebrew a letter is doubled or combined or just drops out but is pronounced anyway — this also makes transliteration a challenge. '*Shabbat*' is '*Sha-bat*' and not '*Shab-bat*'. The '*sh'wa*' vowel is merely a glottal stop between two consonants, so '*Shema*' is pronounced '*Sh'mah*' and not '*Shee-mah*'.

Almost every language employs specific symbols for specific sounds — just look at the choice of fonts and languages accents on a keyboard, even one just using the 'Latin' alphabet letters, and not Arabic or Urdu or Tamil! — and then within each country there are regional accents and dialects as well. Hebrew the norm is to stress the penultimate syllable, whereas in Yiddish the norm is to stress the final syllable. So it is '*Ta-LEET*' or '*TAH-lis*'; '*Shab-BAT*' but '*SHAH-Bes*'.

In the end all this doesn't matter too much, except that we feel it necessary to advise you that if you do not find a word here under one entry, it may just possibly be spelt differently and be located elsewhere!

And of course — such a short explanation or definition can never be completely satisfactory.

GLOSSARY

A

Adon: 'Sir', 'Lord'. A word used for God is often either written or pronounced as 'Adonai' which is grammatically inexact but effectively means 'My God', 'My Lord'.

Adon Olam: Hymn. 'Lord of the Universe'.

Afikoman: A piece of *Matzah* used ritually at the *Seder*, eaten at the end.

***Agunah* (pl. *Agunot*)**: A married women whose husband has either vanished or refuses to divorce her; she is therefore considered as still 'chained' to her husband, until either his death can be proved, or he can be (gently and without force) persuaded of his own free will to 'release her'. (The alternative method, of his death being arranged and her status being altered to 'Widow', is not normally recommended.)

Ahvel (or ***Avel***): A Mourner. *Ahvelut* — The period of Mourning after a bereavement.

Akedah or ***Akedat Yitzhak***: The story of the Binding of Isaac, Genesis Chap. 22.

Al Chet: 'For the Sin'. Confessional and penitential prayer used on *Yom Kippur*.

Al HaNissim: lit. 'Concerning the miracles...' A prayer in two versions, one for *Purim*, one for *Chanukah*.

Aleynu: A prayer, formed of two paragraphs, normally recited towards the end of each service.

Aliyah: Literally 'Going Up'. 1. It is used to mean 'going up to Israel' or for emigration to Israel — one 'makes *Aliyah*' and is thereby an 'Oleh'. 2. It is also used as a noun in the synagogue, to mean the invitation to 'go up' to the *Bimah* and recite a blessing — one 'gets an *Aliyah*'.

Almemar: Platform or reading desk in a synagogue. (Another term for *Bimah*).

Am Yisrael: The People of Israel. Jews.

Amidah: lit. 'Standing' — the sequence of prayers incorporated into each of the statutory daily and other services.See '*Shemoneh Esreh*'.

Amorah: A teacher of the generations that produced the *Talmud*. (cf. Tanna — a teacher of the generations that produced the *Mishnah*).

Amud HaSchachar: The rising of the Dawn. Part of the sequence of Sunrise and Morning.

Aravot: Willow branches used on *Sukkot*.

Arba Minim: The Four Species of greenery carried and waved on *Sukkot*. (Palm, Myrtle, Willow and *Etrog*.)

Aron haKodesh: The 'Holy Cupboard' — or 'Ark' — the cupboard in a synagogue used for storing the *Sefer Torah* (or *Sifrei Torah*) and other ritual items. The term is derived from the case in which, according to the Book of Exodus, the original stone tablets of the *Mitzvot* were placed and which was then carried through the desert.

Arvit: Evening Service. (also '*Ma'ariv*')

Asseret haDibrot: Lit. 'The Ten Words'. Used for the Ten Commandments in Exodus Ch. 20 and Deuteronomy Ch. 5.

Asseret Yemei Teshuvah: Ten Days of Return or Penitence — between *Rosh Hashanah* and *Yom Kippur*.

Ashkenazim: Jews of Germanic or Eastern European tradition.

Atzei Chayyim: Lit. 'Trees of life' (sing. '*Etz Chayyim*') — the wooden rollers onto which the ends of scrolls are sewn.

Av: 'Father'. **Avinu**: 'Our Father.'

Avot: Lit. 'Fathers'. Name assigned to the first paragraph of the *Amidah*. Also a reference to '*Pirkei Avot*', ' Sayings of the Fathers' or 'Ethics of the Fathers' in the *Mishnah*.

Azazael: A mysterious name for a mysterious demonic entity — the Scapegoat in the old *Yom Kippur* ritual was sent 'to *Azazel*' and this is often used as an insult in terms of 'Go to the Devil!'

B

B.C.E.: Before the Common Era. Used to define a date. (Equivalent to 'B.C.' which means 'Before Christ' and is therefore avoided by Jews.)

Ba'al: Actually an ancient Near-Eastern word or name for a god or a Master. Now in Hebrew used in contexts such as '*Ba'al haBayit*' ('Head of a Household'), '*Ba'al Koreh*' — a Master of reading the Hebrew text; '*Ba'al Tefillah*' — one capable of leading the prayers; '*Ba'al Tekiah*' — one capable of blowing the *Shofar*.

Balanit: The (female) attendant at a *Mikveh*.

Bar-Mitzvah / Bat-Mitzvah:Aramaic — a Son/Daughter of the Commands; one who reaches the Age of Majority in religious terms — traditionally understood as 13 (+ 1 day) for a boy and 12 or 12½ (+ 1 day) for a girl. From this point they may take a full part in religious life — in Progressive communities this includes synagogue rituals for both genders — and are bound to obey *Mitzvot* — commands to pray, to fast etc. Often used incorrectly as in 'to have a *Bar-Mitzvah*' — i.e. to celebrate the event with a special service and party.

Bassar: Meat, Flesh. *Bassari* — Food derived from meat.

Bat- [name]: Daughter of [parent's name].

Bat Avraham: daughter of Abraham.

Bat-Mitzvah: 'Daughter of the Commandment'. See above, *Bar-Mitzvah*. Also used for the ceremony celebrating a girl's attainment of ritual maturity.

Bavli: The *Talmud Bavli* or Babylonian version of the *Talmud*.

Becher: (Yiddish): Special beaker or wine cup. As in '*Kiddush* Becher'.

Bedikat Chametz: Searching for the *Chametz* on the evening before *Pesach*.

Beit Chayyim: Cemetery. Lit. 'House of Life'.

Beit Mikdash: lit. 'House of Holiness'. The Temple (in Jerusalem).

Beit Din (plural *Batey Din*): A religious Court, either the organisation or a specific sitting of the Court. Normally formed of three rabbis acting as *Dayanim*.

Beit haKnesset: A House of Gathering; term used for a Jewish community centre; the Greek word for this is 'Synagogue'.

Beit haMikdash: The 'Holy House'; Term used for the former Temple in Jerusalem.

Beit Midrash: A House for Discussion and Explanation — i.e. A study house, an Academy.

Beit Olam: a 'House of Eternity' — term used for a Cemetery.

Beit Tefillah: Synagogue. Lit. 'House of Prayer'.

Ben [name]: Son of [parent's name].

Ben Avraham: Son of Abraham.

*Berachah (*or *Berachah) (*pl. *Berachot)*: Blessing(s).

Bikkur Cholim: Visiting the sick.

Bimah: Reading desk or reading platform / pulpit in a synagogue.

Birkat haMazon: Grace after Meals.

B'nei Mikra: The Karaite group.

Boker: General term for Morning. '*Boker Tov*' = 'Good Morning!'

Brit (and *Brit Milah*): The Covenant. (Covenant created through circumcision). (Yiddish: '*Bris`*)

C

C.E.: Common Era. Used to define a date (equivalent to the secular 'A.D.' which means 'Anno Domini' — 'Year of our Lord' and refers to the Christian calendar. See 'BCE')

Chag: Festival. '*Chag Same'ach!*' — greeting on a festival, 'May you have a happy festive day!'

Chalavi: Food derived from Milk or milk products. Yiddish: '*Milchig*'.

Chalitza: The ceremony whereby a childless widow is released from any further obligations to her deceased husband. (See *Yevama*).

*Challah (*pl. *Challot)*: Originally the small piece of dough offered as part of a sacrifice — as in '*Challah* has been taken' — it now refers to the special loaves of bread baked for *Shabbat* (twisted) and for certain festivals (rounded). Often covered in poppy-seed or other seeds.

Chamesh Megillot: The 'Five Scrolls' (of Esther, Ruth, Song of Songs, Ecclesiastes, Lamentations.)

Chametz: Leavened food, forbidden for *Pesach*.

Channukah: (or '***Hannukah***') 'Dedication'. An 8-day Festival in the winter month *Kislev* commemorating a victory in 164 B.C.E. by a relatively fundamentalist militia (the 'Maccabees', 'Hammerers') against assimilationist and conformist or collaborationist political forces in contemporary Judaism; the Temple in Jerusalem was captured and cleansed and re-dedicated. Festival of Lights.

Chanukat haBayit: Dedication of a new home.

Chanukiyah (pl. Chanukiyot): the nine-branched candle or oil lamp holder(s) specific to *Chanukah*. (Actually 8 + 1).

Charedim (or Haredim): lit. The 'Tremblers'. A term used for the fundamentalistic ultra-Orthodox groups in Israel.

Chasser: a 29-day 'short' month. 'Lacking'.

Chasid: orig. A pious person. pl. *Chasidim*.

Chasidism: A movement within Judaism (though some feel it belongs just outside it) dating from the early 18[th.] century in eastern Europe — originally an ecstatic and semi-mystic movement. *Chasidism* is divided into various forms based upon the teaching of various historical dynasties and is now a major political force. The best-known group is Lubavitch, which likes to refer to itself as 'Chabad' from the initial letters of *Chochma, Binah and Da'at* — 'Wisdom, Understanding and Knowledge'. (The word 'Modesty' is missing.)

Chatan: Bridegroom.

Chatunah — a Wedding ceremony.

Chatan Bereshit and ***Chatan Torah***: The 'Bridegroom of the Beginning' and 'of the *Torah*', a symbolic honour given to a congregant during the *Simchat Torah* services.

Chavurah: Lit. 'a group of friends' — ('*Chaver*', '*Chaverim*') — an informal gathering for purposes of prayer, study, eating… A '*Chavurah* meal' refers to a 'pot-luck dinner', with the food contributed by those who come and share what they have brought.

Chazan: Cantor, one who leads the synagogue service by chanting or singing the liturgy. The art of such singing is called **Chazanut**.

Chazer: The Hebrew for a Pig and therefore used for (forbidden!) pork and pork products.

Cheder: lit. 'A room', usually used to mean 'Classroom' or 'Religion School for children, at a synagogue'. (In a Kibbutz one will have a '*Cheder Ochel*' — 'Dining Room'.

Chevra: (Yiddish — from '*Chavurah*'). A club or society. e.g. '*Chevra Shass*' — a society for study of the *Talmud*.

Chevra Kadisha: The 'Holy Brotherhood'. The voluntary organisation that deals with matters surrounding death and burial — collecting and washing the Body and preparing it for burial and often also organising the *Shivah* services and other matters in connection. (Much of this work is currently carried out by professional firms but some communities have groups of men and women to carry out the ritual washing of the bodies.)

Chevruta: Aramaic for 'Study Friend' — students learn in pairs, 'with a *Chevruta*'. (cf. '*Chaver*').

Chiloni: Term used for 'secular' non-observant Israelis.

Chodesh: Month. '*Chodesh Tov!*' — a greeting at *Rosh Chodesh* / New Moon.

Chol: Ordinary, normal. e.g. a normal weekday. Not a 'holy' day.

Chol HaMo'ed: the ordinary, mundane days in the middle of the festival period of *Pesach* or *Sukkot*.

Choq: A category of law that 'just is' with no explanation.

Choshen: The (usually silver) decorative breastplate hung on the front of a *Sefer Torah*.

Chukkat HaGoy: Doing what Non-Jews do.

Chumash (pl. Chumaschim): A bound volume of the Five Books of Moses (i.e. the

Torah) laid out for use in the synagogue, i.e. Divided into or marked with the regular weekly readings, and usually containing also the *Haftarot* readings.

Chuppah: The canopy, representing a shared roof, under which a couple marry. (Originally it meant a tent to which they went to consummate the marriage — a sort of 'Honeymoon Suite'. It is referred to as such in Psalm 19:5) Also used colloquially to mean 'Wedding Day' as in 'they had a *Chuppah*'.

Churban: Hebrew term used generally for 'Catastrophe' and used specifically for the destruction of Jerusalem and the Temple in 70 C.E. '*Zichur laChurban*' — a symbolic 'Remembrance of the Catastrophe'.

Chutzpeh: More than mere rudeness, a form of self-assertiveness, ignoring any obstructions or etiquette, demanding one's rights.

Cohen (pl. **Cohanim)**: Priest; now used for someone who is (or claims to be) a descendant of the family of Aharon the brother of Moses. Often used in some form (also Kahn, Kochan, Cohn, Katz, etc.) as a surname.

D

Dayan: Judge. (Hebrew). Three *Dayanim* form a *Beit Din*.

Derech Eretz: lit. 'the way of the world'. Correct behaviour, etiquette, good manners.

Diaspora: The Dispersion. Jews were dispersed in many countries already before the Temple was destroyed. After that point it could be said that they were in '*Galut*' (Exile) because there was no homeland to return to even if they wanted to and hence one could also argue that since the State of Israel was re-established *Galut* has ended, but there are still many Jews living outside it — 'in the *Diaspora*' or 'as *Diaspora* Jews'.

Dreidl: (Yiddish) Spinning top, a toy often associated with *Chanukah*.

E

Eid: A Witness (to a document or in a court).

Eidot Mizrach: 'Eastern Communities' — The name given to Jews in or from Arabic-speaking countries.

'El Maleh Rachamim': 'God, full of Mercy'. A prayer used at funerals, memorial and *Shivah* services.

Elohim: God (or gods).

Emet: Truth.

Eretz Yisrael: The Land of Israel. (The boundaries have varied over the Millennia but this is the term for the geographical as opposed to the political entity.)

Erev: Evening. The initial period of a Hebrew day. Hence '*Erev Shabbat*', '*Erev Pesach*' etc.

Eruv: lit. A courtyard — an enclosed space which can be defined as an area where one may carry on a Sabbath. Often used for an artificial 'enclosure' formed by wires or cables to define an area within a town.

Eshet Chayil: A passage from Proverbs Ch. 31 praising the qualities of a good wife and read aloud by the husband on *Erev Shabbat*. Sometimes used to describe a strong woman — as in: 'She was an *Eshet Chayil*', 'A Woman of Valour'.

Etrog: The citrus fruit used as one of the *Arba Minim* at *Sukkot*.

Eyd: Witness. (pl. *Eydim*). Certain ceremonies or procedures require the presence and/or signatures of two witnesses who must be independent, Jewish, adult, mature, mentally fit, (male) and in short able to testify in a court if required that what was said or written really was so done.

F

Fleischig: Yiddish for '*Bassari*' — Related to Meat products.

Frumm: Yiddish: Especially pious and observant. (When carried to extremes referred to sardonically as '*meshuggeh frum*' — obsessively, neurotically pietistic.)

G

Gabbay: A warden or attendant in the synagogue.

Galut: Exile. Since Jews were driven from their land they were for many centuries in exile, powerless, defenceless and essentially homeless. (Yiddish: '*in Golus*')

Gehenna: Place of torment, hell. (Taken from the place name — '*HaGay B'nei Hinnom*' — 'the valley belonging to the sons of Hinnom' — where dreadful things took place.)

Gelilah: The rolling-together and re-dressing of a *Sefer Torah* after it has been read from. By the '*Golel*' (fem. '*Golelet*').

Gemara: Rabbinic discussion on the *Mishnah*; collated and forming the major part of the *Talmud*.

Gemilut Chasadim: Performing acts of kindness.

Ger (Female: ***Giyoret***; pl. ***Gerim***): A Stranger. A '*Ger Toshav*' is a stranger who lives amongst the Jewish community as a 'resident alien', a '*Ger Tzedek*' is one who has chosen to cease being a foreigner and to join the Jewish people — i.e. to convert. Despite this, one will (alas) often hear the term '*Ger*' being used dismissively and inaccurately, as in 'She/He is just a *Ger*'.

'Gesundheit!' : Yiddish 'Health!' — greeting used after someone sneezes.

Get: (also known as a *Shtarr Get*; Plural ***Gittin***) The document of divorce which allows a woman to be freed from any obligations to her husband and to remarry if she wishes. It can only be given with her consent.

Giyur: The term for Conversion to Judaism — ironically it could be interpreted as 'becoming a stranger' but in fact it is used to mean 'becoming one who is no longer a stranger'. See '*Ger*'.

Goy: Technically in Hebrew this just means 'a nation', a people' — the Israelites should also be, for God, a '*Goy Kadosh*', a holy people. In practice and in Yiddish the term is usually employed to mean 'the Other people' — non-Jews. It is often used in a derogatory sense — as in 'She married a *Goy*!' or inasmuch as someone makes a good impression on the non-Jewish world — 'That's *Goyim-naches*'.

Greggers: Yiddish: Rattles used at *Purim* to make a noise when Haman's name is read.

ℋ

Hachnasat Orchim: Bringing in, or welcoming Guests.

Hadassim: Myrtle-tree twigs used at *Sukkot*.

Hadlakat HaNerot: Lighting the Candles /Lamps.

Haftarah: Despite appearances in the transliteration the word has nothing to do with '*Torah*' as a different Hebrew letter 'T' is used. It refers to the reading from the Prophets (on very occasional cases from the Writings) following a *Torah* reading at a *Shabbat* or Festival morning service.

Hagbahah: The act of raising-up the *Sefer Torah* during a service to display it to the congregation (by the '*Magbi'a*').

Haggadah shel Pesach: 'Narration'; the book or booklet with prayers, stories, illustrations and songs used at the *Seder* evening at the *Pesach* festival. (Plural *Haggadot*)

Hakkafah: (pl. Hakkafot). Procession around the synagogue, holding the *Sefer Torah* (or, on some occasions, a *Lulav*).

Halachah: From the verb 'to walk' and therefore 'The way one should walk' or 'The entire corpus of Jewish Law.' One says 'That is according to the *Halachah*' — but of course any good lawyer can always find a different interpretation of the same comma.

Hallel: The Psalms of Praise (Psalms 113-118) recited on certain occasions.

HaMakom: 'The Place' — a term sometimes used for God.

Hamantaschen: (Yiddish — the Hebrew equivalent is '*Osnei Haman*') 'Haman's Pockets' or 'Haman's Ears'. Seed-filled pastries, a *Purim* delicacy, referring to the villain of the story.

HaMotzi: Lit. 'The one who brings out'. The blessing over Bread. ('*haMotzi Lechem min-HaAretz*').

HaOlam Haba: lit. The World to Come. A reference to life after death. (contrast: '*HaOlam haZeh*' — This World.)

HaShem: 'The Name' (of God). Often used as such colloquially as in '*Baruch HaShem*' — 'Blessed be God.'

Hashkivenu: Lit. 'Cause us to lie down'. An Evening prayer.

Haskalah: The Enlightenment — a period of growing intellectual freedom and awareness in the 18th. and 19th. centuries.

HaTefillah: The Prayer. i.e. The *Amidah, Shemoneh Esreh*.

Hatikvah: 'The Hope'. National Anthem of Israel.

Havdalah: 'Division' — The brief ceremony marking the division between the Sabbath and whatever comes next (usually a normal weekday — so one divides '*beyn Kodesh v'Chol*' — but sometimes a festival immediately follows the Sabbath, in which case one makes the formal division '*beyn kodesh v'kodesh*' — between the two different holy days).

Hechsher: A rabbinic certificate or stamp that something — a foodstuff or a catering establishment or some ritual item — is officially considered *kosher*.

Hesped: Eulogy about a deceased person.

ℵ

Kabbalah: 'What is Received' — the term used for the mystical texts reflecting esoteric interpretations of Jewish tradition.

Kabbalat Ol Ha-Mitzvot: The receiving of the 'burden' of *Mitzvot* — when the Israelites received the *Torah*; also used for a ceremony in synagogues when new converts are formally welcomed.

Kabbalat Shabbat: The receiving of the Sabbath.

Kaddish: A text, normally recited in Aramaic, praising God and used at 'difficult times' (i.e. when in mourning or at a funeral) and also in shorter form to mark the end of different sections of a service or the end of the service itself.

Kahal: Community (see *Kehillah*).

Kallah: Bride.

Kallat Bereshit: The 'Bride of the Opening Section' — a symbolic honour given to a female congregant (in Reform and Liberal synagogues) during the *Simchat Torah* services.

Kapparah: Custom relating to Atonement used specifically of a ritual of waving a chicken or money, later donated to charity. (Yiddish: '*Schlog Kappores*')

Karpas: Green vegetable used on *Seder* table at *Pesach*.

Kasher: Fit for use, fit for purpose, may be consumed. *Kashrut* — Fitness for use.

Kavvanah: A state of mind fit for praying, concentrating, meditating; the intention to do so.

Kedusha: 'Holiness'. The third section of the *Amidah*.

Kehillah: A community. *Kehillah Kedosha* — 'a Holy Community' i.e. one founded for religious purposes.

Ketubah: A document — specifically the Marriage Contract. Actually a Contract laying down the duties and responsibilities of both partners, witnessed and signed.

Kibbutz: A communal settlement with all property held in common.

Kiddush: The word comes from 'Holy' and refers directly to the blessing or sanctification recited over wine and bread, at home or in the synagogue after services. (Note: Not the wine and bread themselves are sanctified, but the One who made them!). It therefore indirectly refers to any buffet refreshments or light meal served in connection with a religious service or event — 'a *Kiddush*'.

Kiddush HaShem: 'Sanctifying God's Name'; a euphemism for Martyrdom.

Kiddushin: Marriage.

Kinah (pl. Kinot): A poetic lament.

Kippah (pl. Kippot): Symbolic head-covering, worn by some (men) only at religious services and ceremonies, by others also in daily life (See *Yarmulka*). In Progressive communities women may also wear a *Kippah*.

Kittel: White robe worn on High Holy Days; by the leader at the *Seder*; by a Bridegroom. Actually a Shroud.

Klaf: The piece of parchment on which the relevant texts are written for the *Torah* or for *Tefillin* or rolled and placed inside a *Mezuzah* casing. (The *Sefer Torah* is written with many *Klappot* sewn together.)

Klezmer: from 'K'ley Zemer' — musical instruments. A form of folk music that developed in Eastern Europe, often involving violin, bass, clarinet and Yiddish lyrics for songs.

Knesset: The Parliament (lit. 'Assembly') of the State of Israel.

'Kol HaKavod!': A form of congratulation, equivalent to 'Well done!'

Kollel: An 'advanced' Academy of Jewish studies — the level above a *Yeshivah*.

Kol Nidrei: *Yom Kippur* Evening service. Named after an opening text 'All the Vows'.

Kosher (Yiddish): Fit for use. See *Kasher*.

K'riah: Torn or cut clothing — a sign of Mourning.

Kvatter (Yiddish): A man who hands the baby to the *Mohel* at a circumcision — 'as the Father'.

Kvatterin: the female equivalent.

L

'*Labri'ut!*': Greeting in Hebrew when someone sneezes — 'Health!' — cf. 'Gesundheit!'

Lag BaOmer: 33ʳᵈ· Day of the *Omer* period.

L'Hitpallel: Hebrew for 'Prayer', lit. 'To work on oneself.'

Lailah: End of Evening; Night.

Lashon Kodesh: 'The holy tongue' — i.e. the Hebrew language.

Lashon haRa: Evil speech. Slander or insult.

'*L'Chaim!*': lit. 'To Life'. A toast.

Lecha Dodi: Poem welcoming *Shabbat*, sung on Friday evenings.

Lechem: Bread.

Levayah, Levayat HaMet: A funeral, the carrying or escorting of the dead Body to the place of burial.

Levi: Descendant of the tribe of *Levi*; in the *Torah* they were assistants to and porters for their relatives the *Cohanim*, the Priests who could officiate in the Sanctuary.

Luach (pl. *Luchot*): Calendar(s) or diary formatted to the Jewish year.

Lulav: A Palm branch, also used to refer to two other species (Myrtle — '*Hadas*' —

and Willow — '*Arava*') which, bound together and held with an *Etrog*, form the 'Four Species' ('*Arba Minim*') waved during the *Sukkot* festival. The term '*Lulav*' is often used to refer to all four together.

M

Ma'ariv: The Evening Service. From '*Erev*' — Evening.

Machzor: Literally 'cycle', the word is used to refer to a prayer book for the cycle of Jewish festivals i.e. a '*Siddur* for the Festivals', incorporating specific additional prayers not found in the 'Sabbath and Daily' liturgies. One could refer to a '*Machzor* for the *Shalosh Regalim*' (i.e. for the three festivals of *Pesach* / *Shavuot* / *Sukkot* & *Simchat Torah*) or a '*Machzor* for the *Yamim Nora'im*' (for the High Holy Days of *Rosh Hashanah* and *Yom Kippur*.)

Magen David: Shield or Star of David; a frequently used symbol (since the 19th. century — prior to this a *Menorah* was more often employed). It appears also on the Israeli flag.

Mah Tovu: lit. 'How good!' Passage from Numbers 24:5 used at start of service.

Maleh: lit. 'Full'. A 30-day month.

Mamzer: A child who should not have been conceived; the result of incest or adultery.

Ma'oz Tzur: *Chanukah* hymn.

Maror: The bitter herbs (often horseradish is used) on the *Seder* Table at *Pesach*, to remind us of the bitter taste of slavery and oppression.

Mashgiach: Supervisor of *Kashrut* at a factory, kitchen, catered event.

Mashiach: Messiah.

Mashlo'ach Manot: gifts of food at *Purim*.

Masorah: Tradition. Hence '*Masorti*' — a religious movement based on adherence to Traditions.

Matan Torah: The Giving of the *Torah*; i.e. the Revelation from God to Moses.

Matza or Matzah: The flat, hard, unleavened bread — normally sold in flat oblongs in packets, though they can be round. During *Pesach* one may not eat other forms of bread.

Matzevah: (pl. Matzevot): Tombstone.

'Mazal Tov!' — or (Yiddish) *'Mazzeltov'*: lit. 'a good star' — used as a greeting 'Congratulations!' or 'I wish you good luck!'

Mechatonim: Parents-in-Law; the parents of your marriage partner.

Mechirat Chametz: The sale of any *Chametz* left in one's home, so that it technically no longer belongs to you during the week of *Pesach*.

Mechitza: A divider between men and women in Orthodox synagogues. It could take the form of a curtain, a screen, a wall or even a balcony.

Medinat Yisrael: The State of Israel.

Megillah (pl. Megillot): A scroll. *Megillat Esther* — the Scroll of Esther read on *Purim*.

Melachot: 'Categories of Work' — there are 39 such — prohibited on *Shabbat*.

Menorah: Seven-branched candlestick or lamp, as used formerly in the Temple and also used now frequently as a symbol (e.g. outside the *Knesset* or on Israeli coins.)

Mesader Kiddushin: Literally 'The One responsible for organising the act of a Holy Union' — i.e. the rabbi responsible for ensuring that a wedding may take place, that the two partners are legitimately able to marry according to *Halachah*.

Meshuggeh: (Yiddish): Slightly mad.

Mezonot: Bread which is sweetened and classed as 'Cakes', as general food rather than as '*Lechem*'. *Mezoynos-rolls* (Yiddish)

Mezuzah (pl. Mezuzot): lit. 'Doorpost'; Used now for the casing and the *Torah* text placed inside a casing on the doorpost. (It is NOT just the casing alone!)

Mezuman: A group of at least three persons so that two can be invited by the third in joining in Grace After Meals.

Midrash (pl. Midrashim): The art of expounding on and explaining Biblical texts, filling in gaps or resolving contradictions. The term is used for an entire form of imaginative and analytical study or of volumes, as in 'The *Midrash* tells us...' or 'The *Midrash* says...'

Mikra'ot Gedolot: An edition of the Hebrew Bible incorporating several translations into Aramaic, plus commentaries by classic rabbinic authors and an academic apparatus — footnotes etc. giving references to other texts.

Mikveh (*pl. *Mikva'ot): lit. A 'Gathering' — in this case a gathering of water into one place — i.e. a bath; specifically used for a ritual bath, built according to specific norms involving materials and the way fresh water flows through, so one can step down into it for full immersion. Used for ritual cleansing.

Milah: Circumcision. The surgical removal of the foreskin on males.

Milchig: (Yiddish): connected to milk products.

Minchah: The Afternoon Service.

Minyan: Quorum of ten for a service or certain prayers.

Mishnah: from 'Repetition' — referring to the way that knowledge was transmitted orally, by the teacher and pupil repeating the material until it was memorised. Later used for the teachings which were written down and codified by Rabbi Jehudah *haNasi* as a compendium of Jewish law and forming the basis for the later *Talmud* (see also *Gemara*). Each paragraph is also called 'a *Mishnah*', pl. Mishnayot.

'Mishneh Torah': Book title, 'the Repetition of the *Torah*', by Maimonides, a systematic compendium.

Mitnagdim: Opponents of *Chasidism*. (from '*Neged*' 'against')

Mitzrayim: Egypt. (Technically this word is a 'dual' form meaning 'two' or 'a pair'; in this case it refers to Upper and Lower Egypt.)

Mitzvah (*pl. *Mitzvot): A Command. Used to mean a Divine Command, whether ethical or ritual or legislative — one refers to the '613 *Mitzvot*' in the *Torah*. 365 Negative Commands ('Thou shalt not...') and 248 Positive Commands ('Thou shalt...'); sometimes the word is also used to refer to taking a part in the ritual, being asked to read something, carry something, to open the ark or similar — one 'gets a *Mitzvah*'.

Mo'ed: A special period, used also as Festival.

'Mo'adim leSimchah!': 'May you have a happy festive time!' — Greeting said during *Chol HaMo'ed*, the intermediate days of *Pesach* and *Sukkot*.

Mohel (pl. *Mohalim*): Ritual circumciser(s), surgeon, who performs *Milah*.

Moshav, Moshavah: Co-operative settlement in Israel.

Mussaf: The 'Additional' Service added to the Morning Service on Sabbaths and Festivals, reflecting the manner in which in Temple times additional animals were sacrificed on certain occasions.

ℵ

Ne'ilah: The concluding service on *Yom Kippur*.

Ner (pl. *Nerot*): Light. This used normally to be an olive-oil lamp and later became associated with the Candle. Hence '*Ner Shabbat*' and '*Nerot shel Chanukah*'.

Ner Tamid: The light in a synagogue, usually kept lit continuously, as a reminder of the 'Eternal Lamp' in the Temple which was not allowed to go out.

Nes (pl. *Nissim*): Miracle. '*Nes Gadol Hayah Sham*' — a motto for the *Chanukah* festival — 'A great miracle happened there.' The initials of these words are written on the Dreidl.

Netilat Yadayim: The action of (and blessing for) washing hands ritually before eating.

Nevelah: An animal that is found dead — and can therefore not be eaten as *kosher* meat.

Niggun: a wordless chant — '*oy-oy-oy*' or 'la-la-la' often employed in *Chasidic* circles and intended to create an atmosphere through the melody alone.

O

Ohel: lit. Tent. Term often used for a Cemetery Chapel.

Ol HaMitzvot: The 'yoke' of the Commandments — the idea that accepting the duties and responsibilities of Judaism is like an ox which carries a yoke as a burden but also as a means to pull the plough or wagon. It isn't easy, but it is necessary…

Omer: The forty-nine day period between *Pesach* and *Shavuot*. Lit. 'A Sheaf'.

Oneg Shabbat: Sabbath pleasure, enjoyment. Party or concert on *Shabbat*.

P

*Parashah (*pl. ***Parshiyot)***: Weekly reading(s) from the *Torah.*

*Pareve (*or ***Parve)***: neutral. Food which is neither milk nor meat and can therefore be used with either.

Parochet: A curtain or hanging in front of the *Aron Kodesh.*

*Passul (*or Yiddish ***'Possul')***: Invalid, spoiled, unfit for use. Not *kosher.*

Perushim: The *Pharisees,* a group from the Temple period.

Pesach: (also referred to as Passover): The springtime festival, originally associated with the new lambs and the new grain, later applied to the celebration of Liberation from Egypt.

Pidyon haBen: Redemption of the First-Born Son. Ceremony to release him from any obligations to the priests.

Pumbeditha: Location of an academy in Talmudic times — in modern Iraq. (also Sura and Nehardea).

Purim: Festival in month of *Adar;* the Scroll of Esther ('*Megillat Esther*') is read with great hilarity and to celebrate that the genocidal plans of Haman in the then-Persian Empire were foiled at almost the last minute. There is much celebration, consumption of alcohol, dressing-up and production of parodies.

Purim Katan: A 'little *Purim*', a local festival of celebration for a rescue.

Purim-Spiele (Yiddish): Comic *Purim* plays and cabaret acts.

R

*Rabbi (*pl. ***Rabbanim)***: Rabbi(s). Persons ordained and qualified to teach and to make judgements on religious matters.

Rav: Teacher, rabbi.

Refuah Shelema: Greeting '(I wish you) a complete recovery!'

Ribbono shel Olam: 'The Great One of the Universe' — a title for God.

Rimmonim: lit. 'Pomegranates'. Decorations placed on top of the *Atzei Chayim*, the wooden rollers with which a *Sefer Torah* is held.

Rosh: 'Head'. Used for *Rosh Chodesh* — the 'head' of, i.e. the Beginning of a new Month; *Rosh Hashanah*: New Year; *Rosh Hashanah le'Ilanot*: New Year for Trees. (i.e. *Tu B'Shvat*).

S

Sandek: Person privileged to hold the baby boy for the *Mohel* at a circumcision ceremony.

Seder / Seder shel Pesach: The Order of Service — including an extensive meal of several courses! — to celebrate the evening of *Pesach*. The *Haggadah* is read.

Sefer: Book. (pl. *S'forim*.)

Sefer Torah (pl. *Sifrei Torah*): The Book of the *Torah* i.e. the five books of Moses. By 'Book' we usually mean a piece of writing — nowadays this can mean a hard-cover bound book, a paperback book, a spiral-bound book, an e-Book, a Download… but in former days it meant something written by hand in ink with a pen on parchment and onto different sections (*Klaf* / pl. *Klappim*) which were then sewn together and then the whole rolled together. Sometimes for ease of carrying and opening one or both ends would be attached to a wooden roller. The *Sefer Torah* comprises the Five Books of Moses, written in this manner in sequence and combined into one Scroll.

Selichah: Forgiveness. *Selichot*: Prayers and penitential service preceding the High Holy Days.

Semicha: Rabbinic ordination, through the 'laying-on of hands'.

Sephardim: Jews of 'Iberian' or Southern European tradition.

Sha'atnez: Rules for not mixing wool and linen in clothing.

Shabbat (pl. *Shabbatot*): The Sabbath, the seventh day, beginning on the evening of Friday and ending on the evening of Saturday.

Shabbat Hagadol: 'The Great *Shabbat*' — the *Shabbat* before *Pesach* on which a special *Haftarah* is read.

Shabbat Machar Chodesh: The Sabbath falling one day before the *Rosh Chodesh /* New Moon.

Shabbat Mevarchin HaChodesh: The Sabbath which precedes a New Moon. An additional prayer is said 'blessing the month', i.e. wishing for a good and healthy month.

Shabbat Menuchah: Sabbath rest.

'Shabbat Shalom!': Greeting — 'Sabbath Peace!'

Shabbat Shekalim: The Sabbath on which one reads the extra portion and *Haftarah* concerning the payment of a head tax (Exodus Ch. 30) and the supervision of donated funds.

Shabbat Shuvah: The Sabbath of Return or Repentance; between *Rosh Hashanah* and *Yom Kippur*.

Shabbat Zachor: The Sabbath of Remembrance; The *Shabbat* before *Purim*.

Shacharit: The (daily or Sabbath) Morning service.

Shadchan: One who arranges marriages (See *Shidduch*).

Shaliach: One who is sent, as an Emissary — usually used nowadays to refer to a representative of an Israeli organisation sent out to the *Diaspora* communities to assist them in organising Jewish or Zionist activities. But can be used in other contexts, e.g. as someone sent to represent one of the parties before a *Beit Din*.

Shaliach Tzibbur: The one who represents the community at prayer by leading the service.

Shalom: Used as a greeting for 'Peace' — actually it refers to 'Completeness', 'Wholeness' which is a pre-requisite for Peace. '*Shalom Aleychem*' — 'Greetings to You!' — the response is '*Aleychem haShalom*'.

Shalosh Regalim: The Three Pilgrimage Festivals — *Pesach*, *Shavuot* and *Sukkot* — in which, in the Temple period, it was expected that Jews should make a pilgrimage to the Temple in Jerusalem to take part in the rituals.

Shamash: (1). Servant (in a synagogue); (2): Servant candle, used to light the *Chanukah* candles.

Shanah: Year. '*Shanah Tovah!*' — Greeting — 'I wish you a Good Year!'

Shavuah: Week. The greeting after *Havdalah* is '*Shavuah Tov!*' — 'May you have a Good Week!'

'*Shavuah Tov!*': Greeting at the end of the *Shabbat* — 'I wish you a Good Week!'

Shavuot: The summer harvest festival — coming seven weeks after *Pesach* — hence known as 'The Festival of Weeks'. Now linked to a commemoration of the Revelation of the *Torah* on Mount Sinai.

'*She'assa Nissim laAvoteynu…*': From the '*Al HaNissim*' Blessing on *Purim* and on *Chanukah*.

Shechita: Ritual slaughter of animals for food.

She'elah (pl. *She'elot*): Question(s) or religious enquiry/ies. Sometimes referred to as a *Shaylah* or *Shailah*. (See also *Teshuvot*).

'*Sheko'ach!*': Greeting of congratulation (actually from '*Yashar Kochacha!*') after someone has done something worth being congratulated for. e.g. being called up for an *Aliyah* in the synagogue.

Sheloshim: 'Thirty' — the first thirty days of Mourning, (including the first intense seven days of the *Shiv'ah* period) following a death.

Shema: The declaration of God's Unity, taken from Deuteronomy Ch. 6. Recited twice daily, evenings and mornings, by some also on going to sleep.

Shemini Atzeret: Eighth Day of Solemn Assembly. The closing day / celebration of *Sukkot*.

Shemoneh Esreh: lit. 'Eighteen' — the 'Eighteen Benedictions'; another name for the *Amidah* prayer sequence.

Sheva Brachot: The Seven Blessings recited at and after a wedding ceremony (and at mealtimes in the following week).

Shevarim!: One of the *Shofar* calls — blown in staccato, 'broken' fashion.

Schicksa: (Yiddish) Actually a dreadful insult, it is used in a derogatory manner to refer to a non-Jewish woman but is derived from the word '*Sheketz*' which is something abominable and disgusting.

Shidduch: An arranged marriage; effecting an introduction between two potential partners (See *Shadchan*).

Shikker: (Yiddish). Drunk.

Shiv'ah: Seven — the Seven days of intense mourning following a death of a relative or friend.

Shnoddering: From the Hebrew '*she-nodeh*' — 'he who makes an offering'. The practice in some synagogues of asking those who are called up to the *Torah* (an *Aliyah*) or who receive some other honour in the synagogue service to make a public declaration of the sum of money they will donate (of course, after the Sabbath is over!). Or even of auctioning the honours, so that he who makes the best offer gets the *Aliyah*.

Shnorrer: (Yiddish) A Beggar, but a Beggar who insists upon his dignity and his rights.

Sho'ah: The Hebrew term for the mass destruction of Jewish communities and the dispossession and expulsion and murder of Jewish communities in Europe under the National Socialist ('Nazi') oppression 1933 — 1945. Many use the term 'Holocaust' which has Greek origins and refers to an offering to the gods by fire, others find that this implies a voluntary deed whereas the Jews were victims of atrocities and their burning was by no means voluntary and in no way connected to any form of worship.

Shochet: A ritual (licensed) slaughterer of animals for food. Performs *Shechita*.

Shofar: The horn, from a ram or a deer, used for blowing at the New Moon (*Rosh Chodesh*) and New Year (*Rosh Hashanah*).

Shomer: A supervisor of *kosher* food and food preparation.

Shtiebel (pl. Shtieblach): (Yiddish) lit. 'a little room', (German: '*kleine Stube*') used for a small prayer room by a small and not wealthy community meeting in a room rather than in an imposing purpose-built synagogue.

Shul: (Yiddish) lit. 'School' — a reminder that people came to the shtiebel to study the sacred texts together as well as to pray.

Shulchan Aruch: A Law Code originally written in *Eretz Yisrael* by Joseph Caro and then modified and annotated by Moshe Isserles of Poland for use in *Ashkena-*

zi communities. Originally laid out in simple systematic fashion for 'untrained and unscholarly people', it is now often cited as the ultimate authority and even scholars struggle with it.

Siddur (pl. **Siddurim**): from 'Order, Sequence'. The term for a Prayer Book, in which the various prayers for Daily and Sabbath use are printed in the right order for use on specific occasions.

Sidra (pl. **Sidrot**): The weekly reading(s) from the *Torah*. The name is then applied to the week so that one can say 'in the week ending with the *Sidra* so-and-so'.

Simcha: A celebration or party. (Yiddish: **Simche**)

Simchat Torah: Festival to mark the end of the *Sukkot* period. Introduced later to mark the end of the cycle of regular readings from the *Torah* — and thus the beginning of the next such cycle.

Sochnut: The Jewish Agency, the quasi-governmental organisation responsible for arranging *Aliyah* (emigration to Israel) and caring for new immigrants.

Sofer (pl. **Sofrim**): A scribe, qualified to write specific holy texts accurately — 'Sofer Stam' means one who can write a *Sefer Torah*, *Mezuzah* and *Tefillin* texts.

Sukkah: A small temporary hut built for the *Sukkot* festival.

Sukkot: The autumn Festival — the festival of the Booths and Huts, lasting seven days in Israel, eight days in *Diaspora*.

Sura: One of the locations for an academy in Talmudic times in what is now Iraq (see also Pumbeditha).

S'vivon: Hebrew for a spinning top, a child's toy connected in the popular mind with *Chanukah* (see also *Dreidl*.)

T

Tachrichim: Shrouds and grave clothes used to dress a corpse.

Taharah: Formal ritual cleansing and washing of a corpse before burial.

Tallit (pl. **Tallitot**) (Yiddish: **Tallis**, pl. **Talleisim**): A Prayer-Shawl, usually white or white-ish with blue (often very dark blue) stripes) — nowadays there are other more colourful and decorated versions.

Talmud: lit. 'Learning'. Used to refer to the 63 volumes (*Massechet* / pl. *Massechtot* — Tractates) of the rabbinic discussion on the *Tanakh* and the *Mishnah*. There are two versions — the '*Bavli*' and the '*Yerushalmi*'.

Tanach or **Tanakh**: An abbreviation from 'T' for '*Torah*', 'N' for '*Nevi'im*' and 'Kh' from '*Ketuvim*' — the 'Five Books of Moses', the 'Books of the Prophets' and the 'Other Books — Writings' — all combined to create the Hebrew Bible. (Christians refer to this as the 'Old Testament' to distinguish it from a later collection of books — four versions of biographies of Jesus, a memoir of missionary travels and activities, several Letters, etc. — which they call the 'New Testament'.)

Tanna: A teacher of the *Mishnaic* period (see also Amora).

Taryag Mitzvot: An acronym from the numerical value of the letters — the 613 Commandments.

Tashlich: A ceremony on *Rosh Hashanah*, symbolically throwing one's sins into flowing water to be carried away.

Tashmad: Destruction.

Tefillah: Prayer.

Tefillin: The boxes, fitted to leather straps, containing *Torah* texts, fitted to or worn on the forehead and the arm during Daily Morning services.

'Tekiah!' and **'Tekiah Gedolah!'**: Calls for the *Shofar* on *Rosh Hashanah*. A long tone or an even longer one.

Tekufah: The Spring or Autumn Equinox.

Terefah: (Yiddish '*Treyf*'): lit. 'torn' — an animal unfit for consumption, because not properly slaughtered. Used generally for anything not *Kosher*.

'Teru'ah!': One of the *Shofar* calls on *Rosh Hashanah*; a wailing tone.

Teshuvah: Repentance, penitence.
Also:
Teshuvah (pl. **Teshuvot**): A response to a question on religious matters. (See *She'ey-lah*).

Te'udah; Te'udat Giyur: An official identity document; a document/Certificate of Conversion.

Tevilah: Immersion in a *Mikveh*, a ritual bath.

Tikkun Leyl Shavuot: A late-night or all-night study session on *Shavuot*.

Tikkun Olam: Improving or Repairing the World.

Tisha B'Av: Ninth day of the month of *Av*; Commemoration of the destruction of the Temple(s).

Torah: In its widest sense 'Learning and Enlightenment', but usually used to refer to the Divine Revelation in either a narrower version — the Five Books of Moses — or a wider version — to include all the later rabbinic comments, explanations and discussions based upon this. (One refers to the '*Torah sh'Bich'tav*', the '*Torah* which was always Written-down' and the '*Torah sh'Be'al Peh*' — 'The *Torah* in the Mouth', or the 'Oral *Torah*', which was originally passed down in parallel to students. Later this was also written down, but the name retained to distinguish it from the 'authoritative' original text.) '*Matan Torah*' — the Giving of the *Torah* — the Revelation on Mount Sinai.

Tosefta: Additional texts to the *Mishnah*, dating from the same period.

Treyf, Terefa: Animals which have died a violent death and have been 'torn' — are forbidden for consumption. So the word comes to mean simply 'forbidden, not *kosher*'.

*Tzaddik (*pl. *Tzaddikim)*: A righteous person(s).

Tzahal: abbbreviation: the Israel Defence Forces (IDF). ('*Tzavah leHaganah le-Yisrael*').

Tzedakah: Righteousness, charity, a fair redistribution of wealth.

Tzet HaKochavim: The coming-out of the Stars — a stage in Evening.

*Tzitzit (*pl. *Tzitziyot)*: Fringe(s) of a prayer shawl (*Tallit*).

U

Unetanneh Tokef: Mystical prayer and meditation on destiny; in the *Rosh Hashanah* and *Yom Kippur Mussaf* services.

Ushpizin: The 'holy Guests' invited symbolically into the *Sukkah*.

ν

Vidui: 'Making known'; Confession. (Sequence of confessions during *Rosh Hashanah* and *Yom Kippur*.)

V'shamru…: Command (Ex. Ch. 31:16-17) to keep the *Shabbat*. A text sung in the service and at the *Shabbat* Morning *Kiddush*.

Υ

Yad: Hand. Normally used to refer to a wooden or silver 'pointer' shaped like a hand, used to aid in reading from a *Sefer Torah* so that one's own finger does not need to touch the parchment (and thus possibly dirty or damage it.)

Yahrtzeit (Yiddish): The anniversary of a death. (Usually according to the Hebrew calendar.)

Yarmulkah: A small round symbolic head-covering. (See *Kippah*).

Yayin Mevushal: Wine which has been heat-treated (lit. 'cooked') — pasteurised.

Yeridah: 'Coming Down'. Used as a dismissive term for those who leave the Land of Israel to live elsewhere — they are a *Yored*, (pl. *Yordim*.) Opposite of *Aliyah, Oleh* (pl. *Olim*).

Yeshivah: An academy for young men (usually!) where *Talmud* and other texts are studied.

Yetziat Mitzrayim: The Exodus from Egypt. The defining historical point in the creation of a nation and used as an example of God's ability to intervene in history. There are those who attempt to argue, based on Egyptology or archaeology, that this never occurred as an historical event; nevertheless Jewish biblical and liturgical and ethical literature is based heavily on the awareness that we were once strangers, we were once slaves, we were once liberated… and that this awareness should influence our own attitudes.

Yevamah: In Biblical times the responsibility of a wife was to bear a child (preferably a son) for her husband; If she became widowed, still childless, then she could fulfil this responsibility posthumously through the brother of her late husband! And he, as the '*Yibum*', had the responsibility to make his widowed sister-in-law pregnant in order to give his deceased brother an heir. But that was Then… (See '*Chalitza*')

Yichud: Period of solitude of a bridal couple after wedding ceremony. Lit. 'One-ness'. i.e. Together as one.

Yichus: (Yiddish) Family ancestry, links and ties. Usually something to be proud of.

Yigdal: Hymn based on Maimonides' 'Thirteen Principles of Faith'.

'Yishar Kochahah!' (or female: *'Yishar Kocheych!'):* Greeting of congratulation after someone has performed a function within the synagogue service or read something.

Yizkor: Memorial service.

Yom: Day *(pl. Yamim).* Hence '*Yom Tov*' — a Good day, a Festival; *Yom Shabbat* — the Sabbath Day; *Yom Holedet* — Day of Birth — i.e. Birthday; *Yom Kippur* — a day for Atonement; *Yom haShoah* — the day for commemorating the *Shoah; Yom haAtzma'ut* — the anniversary Day of Israel's Independence; etc. *Yamim Nora'im* — the Days of Awe, or High Holy Days.

Yom Tov: Festival, event. Lit. 'A good day'. Yiddish '*Yonteff*.

Z

Zachor!: Remember!

Zei Gesund! (Yiddish): exclamation after a sneeze; 'Be healthy!'

Zecher Yetziyat Mitzrayim: In memory of the Exodus from Egypt.

Zemer (pl. Zemirot): hymn(s) sung especially at the Sabbath table.

Zero'ah: Lamb bone, symbolic of the former sacrifice, used at *Seder* at *Pesach*.

Zichron le'Ma'asey: In memory of the deeds.

Z'man Simchatenu: The time of our Rejoicing. A festive day.

Zohar: A mediaeval Kabbalistic interpretation of the *Torah* in several volumes.

CONCLUSION

This book has no conclusion — it is open-ended. Every time I teach one of these subjects new ideas, new insights emerge. In discussion with students new perspectives and contributions constantly appear. And this is how it should be. Judaism lives on and every attempt until now to seal it within the covers of a book (or whatever equivalent there may be, from a scroll to a screen) has been superseded by some later author — which shows that it is still alive. You may not agree with all of the author's viewpoints but if so — don't worry, the author himself often doesn't, either! Rewriting a book first published twenty years previously is a good way of being reminded how much one has oneself changed, due to different life experiences, just getting older, seeing more of the world, gathering a few scars along the way. Maybe I may be allowed to rewrite it again in another twenty years — or maybe this will be someone else's task.

Keep breathing and keep learning and thinking — these are the main commands.

ON THE AUTHOR AND THE HISTORY OF THE BOOK

The best way to understand this Basic Judaism study course is to understand its history.

It has evolved over a period of years, indeed decades, in an attempt to provide some material which would help adults in a British Reform congregation learn the things they would need in order to be able to fit in as well as possible in a provincial Jewish community — and this was then extended in the light of experience to aid those learning about or converting to Judaism in a European context. It was written to supplement available books rather than to replace them, but of course there is a degree of overlap between this and several other books which aim to provide an Introduction to Judaism.

Nevertheless it was found that when one wished to teach a class of potential proselytes and their partners about Reform Judaism as practised in Great Britain in the 1980s and 1990s there were few adequate books available. Items on sale — this preceded of course the introduction of the Internet — reflected either American Reform experiences (with references to 'Temple' rather than 'Synagogue') or an idealised Orthodox viewpoint with descriptions of how 'traditional' families lived and pictures showing only men praying.

Further, there were a lot of books about Judaism but few that seemed to address the question 'How does one Become Jewish?' Accepting that one cannot become Jewish just by reading a book — or websites — there were still vast areas of Jewish life and experience that were not touched by these books — such as how a Synagogue worked, who ran it, who could take part in it, what happened behind the scenes, aspects of the Life Cycle events apart from the public rituals of weddings or funerals and of course some of the major differences of attitude and practice within Judaism.

Someone entering the Jewish community as an adult needs to acquire, and smartly, a smattering of jargon, the ability to read between the lines of a Jewish newspaper, to hold their own in a conversation in the local delicatessen (including knowing what some of the more obscure food references are and how to read a label), how to handle upsets at the local school when their child is attacked firstly for being Jewish, and then perhaps for not being 'Jewish enough' — all aspects of the reality of daily Jewish living that those already within the community tend to take for granted and which do not appear in books intended for general readerships.

A further question is the extent to which this course is aimed specifically at those converting within one specific denominational movement or within one specific country. Here all we can say is that some things are universal, some things are general and some things are specific. Different prayer books for example may have largely the same content, but each has separate additions and each has different page numbering. Each Jewish movement has a distinctive history and structure, often moulded by specific personalities or the general situation within a country or region. There are small but significant differences which ought to be mentioned if possible — but it is not always possible, without being clumsy or repetitive. It is the author's hope that any reader from any background will at least be able to find a substantial amount of useful information and insight. But it is a personal book, not one written by a committee from any rabbinic conference. The views represented are my own.

I have on occasion given references to specific sources; otherwise the material as it is has been developed by me and I take full responsibility for the contents. I should like to thank those colleagues and friends who have looked through the materials and have sometimes used it themselves to gain experience in its use with Adult Education classes.

The first edition was entitled 'Jewish by Choice' and appeared in Leeds in January 1994 and was made available as a series of photocopies by the *Beit Din* of what was then the Reform Synagogues of Great Britain (R.S.G.B.) in London and is now the Movement for Reform Judaism (M.R.J.). It was typed at that time by two friends, Gillian Bailey of Leeds and David Moss of Halifax, in those Dark Ages before everything became easily digitalised. Alas, this later made the text as inaccessible as though it were written in cuneiform on clay tablets. Later I left the community in Leeds and moved to work in Austria, then the Caribbean and then in Germany, and gradually additional notes and even chapters were prepared. Many of these were then incorporated in a much more extensive version in German — 'Der Honig und der Stachel', 'The Honey and the Sting' — translated and commented by Dr. Ulrike Offenberg — and this was published by the Gütersloher Verlag in 2009. Of course the state of Judaism in Germany — or Austria, or Switzerland, or the Netherlands — was very different to that in Great Britain, partly due to the pre-war experiences, then the horrors of the mid-20th. century, then the post-war and post-'Reunification' demographic and political changes. One needed new chapters to cope with new historical and political developments as well, especially within the State of Israel but also as the State of Israel became more and more isolated in the world.

In some respects, like any good book, there is an element of team-work, of inspiration from others that should never be denied. Any good teacher will admit how much he or she learns from their students, from informal comments, from facial gestures and body language, from communal developments and conflicts... In a sense no book like this will ever be finished, for as long as there are Jews, including those Jews who are seeking to learn or reclaim their heritage, and those who are seeking to become Jewish so as to form a relationship to God based upon the Jewish texts and concepts.

Rabbi Dr Walter Rothschild. Berlin. 2015.

Lightning Source UK Ltd.
Milton Keynes UK
UKHW05f1816220818
327653UK00007B/471/P